Scotland for Gardeners

Scotland for Gardeners

THE GUIDE TO SCOTTISH GARDENS, NURSERIES AND GARDEN CENTRES

Kenneth Cox
Photography by Ray Cox

BIRLINN

First published in 2009 by
Birlinn Limited
West Newington House
10 Newington Road
Edinburgh
EH9 1QS

www.birlinn.co.uk

ISBN: 978 1 84158 576 5

British Library Cataloguing-in-Publication Data
A catalogue record for this book is available
from the British Library

Designed and typeset by Mark Blackadder

Every effort has been made to ensure that
this book is as up-to-date as possible. Some
information, however, such as contact details
and opening times is liable to change. The
publishers cannot accept responsibility for any
consequences arising from the use of this book,
or for any material on third-party websites.

Title page illustration: Dawyck Botanic Garden

Printed and bound in China

Contents

Introduction

Hidden walled gardens of enormous size or strange shape, swaying semi-tropical plants on windy seasides, ferry journeys to secret plant paradises, packed woodlands of towering Himalayan treasures, sculptured stones carved with arcane riddles, vast expanses of aristocratic estates and small town gardens filled with tiny alpine treasures. These are just a few examples of the surprises and delights in store for those who take the time to explore the gardens of Scotland. My native land's extraordinary diversity of garden and plant riches is what inspired me to embark on this book. Though I've lived in Scotland most of my life, in common with most of us, I'd not seen the half of it. All I needed was a good excuse to go and see for myself all those places I'd heard or read about but never got around to visiting. It did not take long for word to get around, and with all the suggestions my gardens quest turned into a two-year marathon resulting in almost 600 entries. It has been a pleasure and a privilege to travel the country, meeting many of Scotland finest gardeners and nurserymen as they showed me their treasures.

This is a guidebook, certainly. It is also very much a celebration of Scottish horticulture, both contemporary and historical. Some of Scotland's gardens are well known internationally: Crarae; Royal Botanic Garden, Edinburgh; Inverewe; Crathes and many more. Needless to say, these gardens are included, as are all the gardens which open for significant periods through the months of spring and summer. The book also features over 200 private gardens, many of which open mainly under the banner of *Scotland's Gardens Scheme* perhaps once or twice a year, some only every second year. Many are happy to accept visitors outside official opening times, but only by appointment. The garden centres and most of the nurseries listed open to visitors; a few are principally mail-order businesses and do not encourage personal callers. Every garden and nursery listed has something to offer. Some are wonderful at any time, for others it pays to visit mainly when their star turns are at their peak, whether these are snowdrops, rhododendrons, roses or perennials. The book also covers a wealth of specialist societies, organic gardens, allotments, community gardens and gardens used for therapy, as well as some of the country's most outstanding woodlands and wildflower sites.

Gardens can and should be deemed part of Scotland's cultural and artistic wealth and heritage, in the same way our historic buildings are. Gardens are complex and dynamic entities which evolve over time, providing a great deal of pleasure both to those who create and those who admire them. As well as describing gardens and nurseries, I have tried to consider Scotland's garden heritage in the widest context, examining its contribution to culture, landscape, architecture, history, pleasure and leisure. I examine gardens' historical importance, plant collections, design and aesthetics, and monitor how actively each site is being gardened. My aim has been to evaluate what we have in Scotland, how good it is, how safe or at risk this heritage is, and how things may change in the future. From time to time I have suggested ways that gardens might be improved. I realise that some might find all this controversial or presumptuous, but I hope that with the inevitable time constraints most people have, readers will find the assessments useful so they can choose to go and visit gardens most suited to their tastes and enthusiasms. It goes without saying that assessing gardens is a subjective exercise and I don't expect readers to agree with everything I say. My aim is not to criticise, but to celebrate Scotland's magnificent horticultural tradition in its widest sense. Almost anyone can enjoy a good garden. Above all, I want to encourage everyone, whether resident in Scotland or just visiting, to step out and experience this country's horticultural wonders.

While I was working on this book, a group of garden designers and journalists under the banner ThinkinGardens held a symposium at RHS Wisley in 2007. Garden writer Stephen Anderson addressed some resonant themes:

> There is a need to make more acceptable the idea that gardens can be viewed by everybody and written about with an analytic, deconstructive eye. Too many people are frightened of the idea of gardens being approached this way, and the word 'criticism' is seen as inevitably pejorative. In fact constructive criticism is the greatest respect a garden can be paid; it may seek to argue the writer's opinions, of what is good and possibly bad about a garden, but more importantly it will show how a garden makes its effects, and give it a wider cultural context by comparing it to other gardens. It will show a garden's ambitions and the extent to which they are achieved.

To this I would add that unless we are prepared to judge or evaluate gardens properly, we cannot address the issues of whether gardens can and should be conserved and how conservation should be managed and funded. Which, in this era of financial instability and the knock-on effect on budget and incomes, must be done as a matter of urgency.

A Short History of Gardening in Scotland

Scots have been referred to as 'a nation of gardeners' but this is probably only in the last 250 years or so. Scots cannot boast the 1000–2000-year garden history of Italy or Japan. Scotland certainly had medicinal and monastic gardens during the Middle Ages, most of which were destroyed in the Reformation, but traveller accounts of Scotland up until the mid eighteenth century lead us to believe that the general Scots population had little or no interest in gardening or plant cultivation. In his *History of Greater Britain* of 1521 John Major wrote of the Scots: 'Neither do they plant trees or hedges for their orchards, nor do they dung the land.' In the seventeenth century Fynes Moryson wrote: 'in the northern parts of England they have small pleasantness, goodness, or abundance of Fruites and Flowers, so in Scotland they must have lesse or none at all.'

Dr Johnson, travelling later in the eighteenth century, was similarly unimpressed. Much of this may have been due to his general level of peevishness, but he was evidently disappointed in most of the gardens he saw, though ironically Johnson's biographer and travelling companion, James Boswell, had a fine family garden at Auchinleck in Ayrshire. My grandfather, Euan Cox, admits in his *History of Gardening in Scotland* that most travellers were so badly fed in Scotland in those days that they tended to assume that the extremely narrow diet, based on the tiny range of crops grown, must have been be due to ignorance or laziness. Even John Claudius Loudon, himself a Scot, writing in 1834, relates how Scottish gardeners have less skill than their southern counterparts (themselves often émigré Scots): 'Gardeners in Scotland have no idea of the care and expense taken and incurred in England to protect the blossoms of fruit trees.' He goes on to list all the errors such gardeners make and then concludes that 'Few country gentlemen in Scotland would go to the necessary expense to remedy these practices even if they were appraised of them'. Were these assessments fair?

There are reports of significant Scottish gardens from the seventeenth century and earlier. In his book *The Landscaping of Scotland,* garden historian Christopher Dingwall lists several significant seventeenth-century gardens and landscapes, of which little or no trace remains today. These include Pinkie, Saltoun House (four walled gardens), Lethington Castle (now known as Lennoxlove), all in East Lothian, Dalkeith Palace and Hatton House near Edinburgh, and Coltness House and Hamilton Palace, in Lanarkshire. Daniel Defoe in his account of his extensive tour of Scotland in the 1720s describes Drumlanrig near Dumfries as 'a palace so glorious, gardens so fine, and every thing so truly magnificent, and all in a wild, mountainous country'. In his account *Journey Through Scotland* (1732) John Macky is equally impressed. In contrast, Reverend William Gilpin in his 1776 account, waxes lyrical on other Scottish gardens but lambasts Drumlanrig: 'what contrivance hath been used to deform all this beauty . . . a vile waste of expense'. As Suki Urquhart concludes in *The Scottish Gardener* (2005), judgement on early Scottish gardens is mostly a matter of 'point of view'.

Though I explore the origins of Scotland's older gardens in the individual entries in the book, I'm not attempting to write a garden history. I'm not a garden historian and you'll find several excellent books in the bibliography written by far more learned and erudite authorities. The history of Scottish gardens is, of course, often fascinating and illuminating. The people who make and made them are/were often the movers and shakers of their age. Scotland's gardens tend to be owned by families whose ancestors fought with or against Robert the Bruce or for or against Bonnie Prince Charlie, or massacred their neighbours or were massacred by them, or were for a time the richest family in Scotland and then lost the lot. Though this book is filled with garden history, it is more about gardens now than gardens then.

My research covered a great deal of history and theory of landscape design, romantic back-to-nature treatises and so on, some of which have been illuminating and informative. There are many schools and movements, too many to describe in detail here: arcadian, romantic, picaresque, gardenesque and so on. Behind the florid language most garden design theory comes down to a single basic dialectic or series of opposing positions which can be summarised as formal versus informal, design versus freeform, straight lines verses curves, order versus freedom, man-made versus natural. Scotland's first gardening manual, John Reid's 1683 *The Scots Gardener* gives a sense of the requirement for order some garden designers feel: 'I take a survey of the work and when I find several regular and irregular things done on one side of the house, and nothing correspondent on the other, I mark the very same on the opposite side, and this I continue to do till two irregularities produce one uniformity.' The need to tame wild, savage, frightening nature into order, boundary and domestication seems to be the driving force here. On the other side are the Rousseau-inspired romantics who see gardens as an extension of nature itself and abhor the formality and artificiality imposed by man on the perfection of nature.

More often than not, fashions and tastes swing back and forth. Very often, those styles vilified for a decade or two are back in vogue again within a few years. In Scotland, probably for economic reasons, grand formal gardens were rarely the dominant style, and informal approaches have dominated. J.C. Loudon (1783–1843) wrote the influential *Encyclopaedia of Gardening* (1822), advocating a style which he called 'gardenesque'. This is close to what we now consider 'woodland gardening': filling woodland with exotic plants such as rhododendrons. Many Scottish gardens from the last 300 years have fairly closely followed Loudon's design precepts. The formal versus informal argument reached its peak in the late Victorian era with the natural/wild faction led by John Ruskin and William Robinson opposed by formalists such as John Dando and Reginald Blomfield, who called the Robinson style 'an absence of design'. Into this pie-throwing contest arrived the voice of reason, Gertrude Jekyll, who calmly entered the hitherto male-dominated world of garden design and was asked to take sides. She immediately saw what a lot of hot air and nonsense was being issued forth and swatted both sides down with a simple 'Both are right, both are wrong.'

Jekyll's solution was to have formality nearer the house with rectangular beds, terraces and straight lines, with wilder, more natural gardening further away which would eventually merge sympathetically into the surrounding countryside. If there is a Scottish gardening style, Jekyll's aesthetic seems to sum it up rather well.

The evolution of gardening styles over the ages has meant that many great older Scottish gardens have been so altered, sometimes several times over, that little or no trace of the original design remains. Unlike France and Italy, where many great sixteenth- and seventeenth-century gardens still survive, Scotland has virtually no pre-eighteenth-century larger gardens intact. Linlithgow Palace, Edinburgh Castle and Holyrood Palace had extensive, mostly formal gardens in the European style, but none have survived. The formal gardens at Drummond Castle in Perthshire and Pitmedden in Aberdeenshire are perhaps the closest we have today on the grand scale, but both are recreations and interpretations. Political events have had a profound effect on the creation/destruction and survival of gardens. The Reformation saw most of the monastic gardens destroyed, while Cromwell's troops laid waste many significant houses and gardens in the mid seventeenth century. The 1715 and 1745 Jacobite rebellions caused significant changes in ownership. Many of those who fought for the losing side – Catholic families in particular – forfeited titles, lands and funds. Those who lost out included the Seatons at Winton and the earls of Perth at Stobhall as well as many clan chiefs such as the MacGregors, McLarens and Stewarts. Some great Scottish dynasties managed to sail though these choppy waters unaffected, while others had sympathetic relatives hold lands till they were allowed to return. In contrast, those who backed the 'winning team' (the English) were rewarded with favourable land deals and influential positions by the 'Commissioners of the Forfeited Estates'. Those newly landed and ennobled went on to build and create some of Scotland's finest eighteenth-century houses and gardens, designed by William and Robert Adam and their followers.

The Victorian architects who followed the Georgians have a lot to answer for, Scottish ones in particular. Many of them were commissioned to cover the fine classical lines of the eighteenth-century houses with turrets, gargoyles, parapets and frippery. The ringleader of the Scottish branch of this movement was David Bryce. His best buildings are iconic examples of their age. The Bank of Scotland on Edinburgh's Mound, the French Gothic turrets of Fettes College in Edinburgh and Balfour Castle in Orkney are all examples of Bryce at his best. Unfortunately, his style caused an infectious rash of imitators; other Scots architects, many trained in Bryce's practice, were commissioned to 'improve' many a fine seventeenth- and eighteenth-century country house. Robert Lorimer, one of Scotland's finest architects and landscapers, commented shortly after the end of the Victorian age that 'so many Scottish houses were ruined by Bryce and others, fifty or sixty years ago'. The Lorimer family's restoration of Kellie Castle and its gardens was largely inspired by this dislike of the Victorian shells and embellishments. These Victorian 'Disneyesque' châteaux, some ugly, some ridiculous, do still tend to dominate a number of Scotland's significant gardens. Conservationists have listed most of them, so they could not be demolished or returned to their former grandeur, even if there were a will to do so.

The Industrial Revolution saw huge profits made by many of Scotland's business barons, landowners and entrepreneurs through investments in docks, coalmining, iron, railways, shipbuilding, jute and other industries. With their wealth they purchased or built country houses, and several great Scottish gardens came into being at this time: Wemyss Castle and Hill of Tarvit in Fife and Geilston near Glasgow are some examples. As the nineteenth century gave way to the twentieth and Manderston became the 'swansong of the great country house', the First World War saw greenhouse heating turned off, gardens grubbed up to produce food crops and gardeners sent off to fight in the trenches from where many never returned. A similar pattern was repeated during the Second World War, with 'dig for victory' gardens turned over to growing vegetables. It is astonishing how many gardens survived this double abandonment and were restored to their former glory. Gradually after the Second World War, it seemed that everyone wanted to garden, in suburbs, back gardens and allotments, while at the same time, many of the 'great' private gardens were donated to the National Trust and The National Trust for Scotland and were opened to all. In the 1970s gardening became popular on television, with Percy Thrower its first star, and garden centres sprang up on the outskirts of every town. Gardening was now Britain's most popular pastime.

So What Makes a Good Garden?

This is, of course, not an easy question to answer. It is, as has already been noted, largely a matter of 'point of view'. Taste is a fickle thing. And tastes seem to change faster than ever in our media-obsessed age. Gardening styles used to take fifty years to evolve; now they come and go in a decade or less, often with a degree of snobbery involved. I often hear and read that plants such as roses, rhododendrons and even grasses and prairie planting are no longer 'in fashion'. Clearly most Scottish gardeners just ignore the style mafia and continue to grow plants which do well and look good. The gardens which are consistently good over long periods are usually the ones which are beyond taste and the latest styles; these often set the trends of their era, though because their owners were not themselves led by fashion, they were not necessarily appreciated at the time.

Rather than try to relate gardens to current fashions, it seems to be more fruitful to communicate what the essence of each garden is, its strengths and sometimes its weaknesses. If it is a good example of its type, it deserves recognition. I have resisted any temptation to give gardens a 'star' rating, as I think this tends to be divisive. Everyone has his or her own likes and dislikes. There are few gardening styles that I can't appreciate, though I struggle to find much enthusiasm for dahlia borders, formal rose gardens of hybrid-teas, any garden with a variegated *Aucuba*, 1970s rockeries, solitary beds of hostas . . . but I'm on the lookout for the best examples of everything, even most of those listed above. Threave has a great dahlia border, Tollcross Park has fantastic hybrid tea roses. What became apparent as I journeyed the length and breadth of Scotland is just how good our gardens are. Very few were poor and almost every one was worth visiting; most gardens, large or small have something special or exceptional. Some gardens are probably really worth seeing for only a few weeks a year, others have longer seasons of interest. I have therefore tried advise on the best time of year to visit. Inevitably some gardens were in need of more TLC than their often rather elderly owners could manage. In one or two cases the next generation had taken over, inheriting an ancient gardener, often well beyond retirement age, gamely struggling to maintain control. Gardens with a fair few weeds or overgrown corners are often just as enjoyable as those which are manicured with nail scissors; a bit of wildness never hurt anyone, though I do tend to notice when things are becoming over-shaded by trees. There are some gardens which are, it has to be admitted, out of control, overgrown and at, or almost at, the point of no return. I have commented on this from time to time, purely in the hope that something might be done before it is too late.

It is useful to assess what gardens and nurseries have to offer in the widest sense: not just to gardeners and garden lovers, but to 'dragees' too. This made-up word which I heard being used at an American rhododendron conference, refers to a person who is dragged along to places or events, because of their spouse/partner/parent's interest, be it golf, vintage motorbikes, football or garden visiting. Garden and garden centre dragees are often children and many of Scotland's garden owners have tried hard to cater for their dragee visitors, offering them alternative entertainment such as shopping, cafes and playparks. My children Jamie and Finn often joined me as I inspected gardens and they assessed the play parks, animals, mazes, fountains and other distractions.

Gardens are fickle things. Out of season, on a rainy day, when you have a hangover, scratchy children, financial worries, sometimes you won't be in the mood to appreciate any garden, however good. Some gardens are like fireworks, a brief explosion of colour, and then nothing much for the rest of the year. Catch these on the right day and you are in paradise. Arrive out of season and you wonder what the fuss is about. Other gardens are more about setting and views, formal landscaping, buildings, things that don't change with the seasons so the timing of the visit is less important.

Gardens are also ephemeral. It takes only a few months of neglect before nature starts to reclaim them. Many of Scotland's best gardens are owned and cared for by elderly gardeners, some of whom have astonishing stamina and fitness for their age. One day they won't be able to prune and weed. And unless they are lucky enough to be able to pass their garden on to someone who will love it as they did, it may disappear. This pattern has always been the case, and though we may mourn, we know that round the corner someone else will decide to carve their own piece of paradise out of a new plot of land, a barren moorland, an ancient forest. And so it goes.

On my travels I noted two gardening extremes which I have classified as 'gardens as stamp collections' and 'gardens as theatre'. The 'stamp-collector' gardener has lots of rare plants, including all the latest ones on the market. The plants are all well labelled, and sometimes the labels are larger than the plants. The rarer it is, and often the more insignificant, the better. Such gardens are usually crammed full, with little planning, aesthetic or structure. The owner neither knows nor cares what is fashionable; what matters is that they have the one and only surviving form of this or that rarity. Their garden appeals to like-minded gardeners. Stamp-collector gardeners can often be obsessive, which hinders the pleasure they derive from their passion. They can inspire terror in their less knowledgeable visitors who are bombarded with endless Latin and lengthy expositions. Perhaps they have an NCCPG (National Council for the Conservation of Plants and Gardens) national collection of *Aucuba*, or *Pachysandra* or some other genus which no one else loves. I'm exaggerating of course, but most of us know someone who gardens like this.

The other extreme is the 'garden as theatre' style. Nikolaus Pevsner wrote in 1944 that gardens are 'Britain's greatest contribution to the visual arts'. Perhaps a concept which the vast majority of gardeners would run a mile from. There is no doubt that many gardens are extremely theatrical, where design and bold statements are key to major structural and planting decisions. Such gardens are often deliberately 'fashionable', often built at great expense, planned and sometimes planted by a garden designer and/or landscaper. You may find exotic lighting, fountains and follies, colour co-ordinated planting schemes in blue or inevitably white, minimalism, pleached trees, topiary. Plants are chosen for their form and colour and are never labelled, as labels are ugly. Such gardens are often divided into rooms with hedges and each path/allée has an object at the end: a building, statue, seat or focus planting. Design-obsessed gardeners often find it equally hard to take pleasure from their gardens, as there is always some carefully planned plant partnership or effect which did not work out or failed to wow the last people to see it. Don't get me wrong; there is definitely a place for theatrical gardens. Sir Roy Strong's garden at the Laskett in Herefordshire is a fine example, and as Strong describes himself as 'a frustrated stage designer', I don't think he would mind being accused as belonging to the 'gardens as theatre' movement.

Thankfully, few gardens are as clear-cut as either of the above extremes. In my opinion, what makes a really good garden is a balance between careful plant selection *and* excellent form and structure. There is nothing better than stumbling across a garden with exquisite design touches and plant combinations which you have seldom or never seen before. Most great gardens are 'great' because they have both elements and because they do one or two things really well: large or small, they have that certain magic which comes from a perfect vista or where the form, structure and colour combination just take your breath away; what Gertrude Jeykll calls creating 'garden pictures'.

Scotland is full of superb 'garden pictures'. Sadly not every day, or even every year; wet weather may be great for hydrangeas but many perennials just go leggy and mouldy. Rhododendrons and magnolias can be frosted overnight, leaving mushy grey destruction. There is often an element of luck to being at the right place at the right time. This is part of the pleasure of visiting gardens; unlike a historic house, a garden will always be different, however many times you visit. Even the greatest gardens can be miserable in wind and rain; though I did visit plenty of them in downpours in the summers of 2007 and 2008 and still managed to enjoy them. The gardens which most excite me are not always the obvious ones; those untouchable classics that everyone has heard of. Their fame precedes them, and at times the weight of expectation just cannot deliver that 'wow' factor that you were perhaps expecting. In contrast, I walked into some of the gardens in this book knowing little or nothing about them and came away delighted. I realise that by waxing lyrical about them, I'm raising your expectations, but I hope that when you discover them, you'll be purring with pleasure as I was. Many private gardens are a particular pleasure to visit because you can meet and be guided by the owners and creators. Their enthusiasm makes the visit doubly interesting and informative. You can't do that at museum gardens whose creators are long dead and which are now steered by committee.

Peter King, author/editor of *The Good Gardens Guide*, wrote a fine essay on the difficulties of judging gardens, and much of what he says is very pertinent: 'I would . . . suggest that all good gardens have 'style': a style individually formulated by its creator, or successive creators, and given a shape under his or her direction. It is a process which in other people's eyes may succeed or fail, but never mind; if they have consulted the genius of the place, then the style they aim for will show through.'

Author of *The Authentic Garden*, American Claire E. Sawyers, confirms the importance of a sense of place: 'to discover and preserve what is special about your site, its *genius loci*. This means working with what you've been given, not struggling against it'. She goes on to explain how good gardens should 'involve the visitor' and decries what she calls 'garden porn' or gardens designed to shock or provoke.

Many gardeners struggle to comprehend how *avant garde* garden design and landscape architecture can be deemed gardening at all when plants are obviously such a secondary consideration and sometimes barely feature at all. The festival of garden design a few years ago at Westonbirt in Gloucestershire featured gardens which were attention-grabbing, often provocative, but were really nothing more than gallery installations which happened to have been created outside.

Some strands of contemporary garden design raise a furious response. Author and garden designer Noel Kingsbury expresses his frustration at what he views are contemporary gardening trends: 'I think I speak for a lot of people who are fed up with modernism and minimalism. We want ornamentation, detail, complexity, and BEAUTY!' (writing in response to the ThinkinGardens website).

This brings home the polarised views which exist when trying to evaluate good gardens and gardening. I hope I'm receptive to all styles and eras of gardening, and I'm often very stimulated by daring and contemporary garden design. I am advocating a very broad-minded view of what gardening can be. In Scotland we have been lucky enough to have two iconic and ground-breaking twentieth-century garden designers in the late Ian Hamilton Finlay and Charles Jencks – both artists/architects-turned gardeners who have pushed the boundaries of what gardens and gardening might be capable of into hitherto largely uncharted territory. Their creations are considered amongst the world's most important gardens of the last 100 years. Whether these two pathfinders turn out to be the leaders of the future direction of gardening or an interesting sideshow, only time will tell. But we should be proud that they are part of Scotland's gardening heritage.

Scottish Gardening 'Style' and What Makes a 'Scottish Garden'

I don't think there is a very strong argument for the existence of a school or style of Scottish gardening as such, but Scottish history, landscape and climate have all contributed to moulding the gardens we have. The one factor which makes Scottish gardens unique is the striking landscape in which many of them are set. Scottish gardens are seldom flat, and many have stunning coastal or mountain backdrops. Garden historian Christopher Dingwall draws attention to this in his forthcoming book, *Landscaping of Scotland:* 'While their English counterparts were struggling to create picturesque and sublime landscapes with the help of artificial rocks and cascades, many Scots gardeners and landowners simply took advantage of the natural features to be found in the landscape which surrounded them.' The natural settings of Culzean, Inverewe, Arduaine, Floors Castle and many other Scottish gardens are as fine as anywhere in the world. In the following pages I attempt to summarise some of the other key ingredients, features and motifs which have come to define what makes a Scottish garden.

Trees

We take it for granted these days that Scotland is well covered with trees, but this was far from the case 500 years ago. The Middle Ages saw most of Scotland deforested for firewood and building, with virtually no replanting. Successive monarchs and their governments passed legislation to protect trees and encourage replanting, but this was never enforced. Virtually all the native forest disappeared and contemporary travellers commented on the desolate treeless landscape. Yet in 1828 Sir Henry Steuart was able to describe Scotland as a 'Planting Nation' or to speak with more correctness, a 'Nation of Planters'.

The reversal of fortune began in the seventeenth century, when a new law was passed which this time was successful in forcing landowners and tenants to plant trees. John Evelyn, author of one of the first books on forestry, published in 1678, inspired his friend the earl of Tweeddale to plant trees on a large scale at his estates at Yester, near Haddington. Architect William Bruce used trees in his designs for Hopetoun House and Kinross House in the late seventeenth and early eighteenth centuries, and Daniel Defoe commented on the scale of tree-planting he encountered on his grand tour of Scotland between 1724 and 1727. By now it was fashionable for great houses to have wooded parkland, and competitiveness between owners led to planting on an ever larger scale. The dukes of Argyll and Atholl were the pioneers of grand-scale planting and one extraordinary incident in 1685 saw the Murrays celebrate their victory over the Campbells by the looting of 34,000 trees, ripped up from Inveraray Castle and replanted at Blair Atholl over 100 miles away.

The eighteenth century was the age of parkland landscaping and the heyday of 'Capability' Brown and Humphry Repton. By then, tree-planting and the creation of woods and parkland on the grand scale was common all over the UK. The dukes of Atholl planted trees on a hitherto unmatched scale; it has been calculated that the second, third and fourth dukes planted over 21 million trees on 15,000 acres of ground. Other estates with substantial tree-planting during this period include Drumlanrig, Monymusk, Duff House, Tyninghame, Drummond Castle, Inveraray and Glamis. Many of these woodlands still exist, with particularly fine beech, oaks, lime, sycamore and larch. The elms, sadly, have mostly gone due to Dutch Elm disease, though Aberdeenshire has managed to hold onto a good many, at least till recently. As this book was going to press, an exciting proposal for a National Arboretum of Scotland, perhaps combining several sites, was put forward. This would be an excellent way of raising awareness of Scotland's extraordinary arboreal heritage.

Plant Hunters in North America, Conifers and the Pinetum

It was not surprising that the already enthusiastic tree-planting Scottish land-owning classes fell over themselves to grow the latest conifer introductions from North America brought back by Scottish plant hunters such as Archibald Menzies (*Araucaria*, the monkey puzzle), David Douglas (sitka spruce, Douglas fir, noble fir, grand fir) William Murray, William Drummond and John Jeffries (western red cedar, lawson's cypress etc). These fast-growing conifers changed the Scottish landscape for good. Several Scottish landowners clubbed together in 1849 to finance expeditions to bring back further seed from the Americas. The 1854 and subsequent introductions of giant redwoods from California account for the number of these huge trees found all over Scotland from Castle Kennedy and Benmore in the south and west to the Tay valley in the east. Pinetums were established to show off these collections of giants on a grand scale at gardens in Perthshire and Angus such as Glamis, Scone Palace, Blair Castle, the Hermitage and Murthly Castle as well as at Balmoral on Deeside, Ardkinglas in Argyll and Dawyck in the Borders. Many of Scotland's now tallest trees were planted at this time and form the present-day backdrop to many of the finest gardens and plant collections.

Plant Hunters in Asia and the Scottish Woodland Gardens

The period from the 1840s onwards saw plant hunters turn towards the east, particularly to China and the Himalayas, now accessible to outsiders for the first time. Scotsman Robert Fortune arrived in China as a plant collector in 1843, returning in 1851 when he famously broke the Chinese monopoly on tea by taking thousands of *Camellia* plants to India. Joseph Hooker was funded through his father at Glasgow Botanic Garden to explore Sikkim and other parts of northern India in the 1850s. He brought back large quantities of seed, particularly rhododendrons, and the seedlings raised were planted in many Scottish gardens such as Castle Kennedy, Kilmory and Stonefield, where some of them can still be seen. Equally significant were the hundreds of hybrids bred from the newly introduced rhododendron species which, planted with their parents, began to form part of the William Robinson-inspired woodland gardens from the late Victorian era onwards. George Forrest, trained at the Royal Botanic Garden, Edinburgh was sent on his first collecting foray to China in 1904, the first of seven collecting expeditions to Yunnan, on which he amassed over 31,000 herbarium specimens and introduced several hundred significant garden plants via copious quantities of seed. Not only numerous rhododendrons were introduced, but also *Primula, Meconopsis, Magnolia, Pieris,* maples, *Sorbus, Berberis* and many other common garden plants which we now take for granted. Forest's last expedition between 1930 and 1932 had several Scottish sponsors, including K. McDougal from Logan, J. Horlick from Gigha, D. MacEwen from Corsock, E.H.M. Cox from Glendoick, the Rentons from Branklyn, F. Balfour from Dawyck and J. Stirling Maxwell from Pollok – a veritable roll-call of great Scottish rhododendron gardens. These sponsors received more seed than they could grow themselves, so in turn they sent some of it to their friends and relatives: to the MacKenzies at Inverewe, the Duchess of Montrose at Brodick, the Campbells at Crarae, Inveraray and Arduaine, to the Christies at Blackhills and Sir John Noble at Ardkinglas. In this way almost all of the great Scottish woodland gardens had access to wild-origin material, and most of them had acres of space to plant the resultant seedlings in.

There were numerous other important collectors who enriched Scottish gardens: Ernest Wilson, Reginald Farrer and Euan Cox, Frank Kingdon Ward, Joseph Rock and Frank Ludlow and George Sherriff all contributed to the steady stream of new introductions of rhododendron and other plant species from all over the China-Himalayan region. Scot George Sherriff shared his wild collected seeds with many Scottish gardeners, particularly those keen on alpines such as the Rentons at Branklyn, nurserymen Jack Drake and Alec Duguid, Bobby Masterton at Cluny, the Knox Findlays at Keillour and Euan Cox at Glendoick, as well as planting his own fine garden at Ascreavie. Of all the plants brought back, none had more impact on Scotland's landscape than the hundreds of species of rhododendron, which in many ways became the defining plant of Scottish gardens. The Coxes founded the Glendoick nursery in 1953, and in subsequent years was the main source of rhododendrons for Scottish gardens, taking the place of the seed supplies from Asia, which was largely closed to plant hunters till the 1980s. Vita Sackville-West may have despised rhododendrons: 'they are like fat stockbrokers who we do not want to dinner', but Scotland was not Sissinghurst and clearly few Scots agreed with her. The list of significant rhododendron-dominated Scottish woodland gardens is long. Some of the best include Blackhills, Arduaine, Crarae, Benmore, Glenarn, Inverewe, Glendoick and Corsock.

In recent years there have been a significant number of contemporary Scottish plant hunters, from the Royal Botanic Garden, Edinburgh, the Scottish Rock Garden Club as well as owners of nurseries such as Ron McBeath, the Rankins from Kevock, Ian Christie, Michael Wickenden, myself and my father Peter Cox (with Peter Hutchison), all of whom have scoured the globe for new plants, many of which are proving to be fine garden subjects.

Alpines

The same plant hunters who brought back so many rhododendrons also introduced quantities of alpine plants from high mountain areas of Asia. Scotland's own mountains and cliffs contain a fine range of alpine plants. Some of these are suitable as garden plants; others, such as *Loiseleuria procumbens*, are challenging to cultivate at low altitudes. Alpines from other countries are often more adaptable to lowland Scotland, where our cool summers suit their needs. The nineteenth- and twentieth-century collectors, already mentioned, were also responsible for the introduction of huge numbers of alpine plants from Asia to add to those coming in from Greece, Turkey, South Africa and South America. Plant hunter and writer Reginald Farrer's pioneering *The English Rock Garden*, published just after the First World War, inspired several significant Scottish rock gardens. Some of the many notable collectors of alpine plants assembled in the period either side of the Second World War included the Sherriffs at Ascreavie, the Knox Findlays at Keillour, the Rentons at Branklyn, Jack Drake at Inshriach, Alec Duguid at Edrom, Bobby Masterton at Cluny and the Leith-Hays at Leith Hall. Their gardens boasted dwarf rhododendrons, primulas, meconopsis, lilies, *Nomocharis*, saxifrage, *Daphne* and many other genera. The largest rock garden of all, at the Royal Botanic Garden, Edinburgh, was constructed in 1908 and rebuilt in 1914 after Farrer criticised it for its artificiality. The growing popularity of alpine plants lead to the formation of the Scottish Rock Garden Club in 1933. Scotland has long boasted a significant number of excellent alpine specialist nurseries including Edrom Nurseries, Jack Drake, Ian Christie, Kevock Garden Plants, Lamberton and Ardfearn.

Walled Gardens

What is it that makes walled gardens so fascinating and irresistible? Perhaps it's the mystery of what lies behind those high walls . . . if only we can find the way in. Or perhaps it's the shelter and 'apartness' to be found inside, away from noise of traffic, wind, other people . . . An enormous number of Scotland's finest gardens are to be found within high walls. Enclosed gardens are described by Sir Robert Lorimer as 'a sort of sanctuary' a 'chamber roofed by heaven'. They find their origins in castle gardens – Edzell for example – and monastery gardens enclosed by a courtyard or cloisters. The variety in the shape, topography and size of Scotland's walled gardens is fascinating. It does not take much imagination to work out why walled gardens are so important to Scotland. The simple answer is the climate. We tend to forget these days just how cold winters were in the eighteenth and nineteenth centuries. Without the protection of walls, often heated by coal fires and boilers, it would not have been possible to grow such a wide range of ornamental and food plants. Walled gardens were built primarily to allow great houses to have a high degree of self-sufficiency. Great skills in cultivation were developed and important breakthroughs in plant-breeding were made in them. They provide protection from wind, particularly important for seaside gardens such as those at Inverewe and Dunbeath. The walls and gates keep out rabbits and deer and undoubtedly also prevented appropriation of the produce by locals. The microclimates provided by the walls allowed trained fruit to be grown successfully and the south-facing wall was usually the site of one or more lean-to greenhouses or conservatories, used to protect tender plants in winter, raise exotic fruit and flowers and to force plants into flower for the house for winter and early spring decoration.

Many of Scotland's walled gardens were built on a prodigious scale. Some of the largest I found on my travels were Hopetoun (over 20 acres), Brechin Castle (13 acres), Blair Castle Hercules Garden (9 acres), Amisfield (7 acres) and Wemyss Castle (6 acres). In contrast, some of the finest walled gardens are small: Elizabeth MacGregor's at Ellenbank and Ann Fraser's at Shepherd House are bijou perfection. Some, like Mertoun and Knockdolian, are built on top of a hill, while others such as Blairquhan have a hollow in the middle, sloping up at both ends, which allows for spectacular vistas. Cambo's walled garden has a burn running through it, while Hercules' garden at Blair Castle boasts large ponds. Most are square or rectangular; exceptions include Netherbyres (elliptical), Carolside (oval), Kinlochlaich House (hexagonal), Inverewe (curved) and Brechin (irregular). Several, such as Wemyss and Novar, are double or even triple gardens. Many walled gardens have only three walls, with the lowest point left open to allow frost to drain out. Glendoick's is an example of this.

Most Scottish walled gardens are sited some distance from the house they belong to and several present-day owners have told me how much they regret this, as they can't just nip out to get some herbs or do a bit of weeding. The separation of house and garden was something that particularly aggrieved Sir Walter Scott, quoted in the *Quarterly Review*, vol. 37: 'The garden . . . has by a strange and sweeping sentence of exile . . . sequestered in some distant corner where it may be best concealed from the eye to which it has been rendered a nuisance, the modern garden resembles nothing so much as a convict in his gaol apparel, banished, by his every appearance, from all decent society.'

So why were walled gardens constructed far from the house? There are several theories. The use of 'night soil' (human waste) to grow vegetables and fruit made some kitchen gardens smell unpleasant. Gardeners were often housed in cottages and bothies in the garden walls and it was considered desirable to have labourers' accommodation some distance from the house. And the walled garden's cutting and flower beds were ideally though to be 'a short stroll distant', a suitable destination for the ladies to take a turn to after lunch.

As well as Walter Scott's own three-part walled garden at Abbotsford, built to demonstrate how he thought it should be done, there are many fine examples of walled gardens right next to the dwelling they belong to, often with the house or castle forming one of the walls or boundaries. Some of the best examples include Earlshall Castle and Kellie in Fife (both Lorimer designs), Pitmuies, Crathes and Cawdor. At Cally, Netherbyres, Tyninghame and Carnell, the present owners have built new homes or extended old bothies and apple stores so they can live in or alongside their walled gardens. Such gardens afford unforgettable views from the upper windows of their castles and houses. Most walled gardens suffered greatly during both world wars, when most of the ornamentals were ripped up and replaced with food crops as part of 'dig for victory'. Needless to say, many gardeners never returned home; the First World War saw many gardens lose all their staff in the futility of the Western Front. Post-1945, many gardens were returned to their former glory, but others were abandoned, grassed over, used for market gardens or perhaps worst of all, used for growing Christmas trees. Thankfully, walled gardens seem to be enjoying a renaissance and many old gardens are finding new uses. Some of the best recent restorations include Drum's rose garden on Deeside, Dunbeath's complex series of garden rooms and the garden architecture at Wormistoun in Fife. Floors Castle's contains a garden centre as well as excellent herbaceous borders, fruit and vegetables. Woodside Walled Garden, Smeaton and Quercus Garden plants use walled gardens as nurseries while Redhall in Edinburgh is used to help those recovering from mental illness. There are few things more depressing than abandoned walled gardens. There is almost always some potential good use for any unloved walled garden and I'm tempted to propose that the Scottish Executive should consider defining a new crime of 'owning a walled garden without due stewardship'. I can't help thinking that some of the other abandoned ones could and should be used for allotments (there is always a huge demand for these). The buildings in and around walled gardens are equally varied and often fascinating: greenhouses in all shapes and sizes, often with the remains of their elaborate heating systems, pavilions, summerhouses, doocots, apple stores (the one at Earlshall has Lorimer stone monkeys on top), and the *pièce de résistance,* the Pineapple at Dunmore.

Scottish Plant Breeding

Scotland has a long history of significant plant breeding which probably dates back to the selection of apple varieties and other fruit in monastic gardens in the Middle Ages. Roses were bred by Dickson and Brown in the eighteenth and nineteenth centuries and James Cocker and Sons in the twentieth. Despite their North American origins, the world centre of *Penstemon* breeding from 1870 till 1968 was at the firm of John Forbes of Hawick in the Borders, while rhododendrons were hybridised by Cunningham's nursery in Victorian times and by my family at Glendoick, more recently. Breeders of alpine plants include James Grieve (of apple fame) William Buchanan, Jack Drake and more recently Ian Christie and Ian MacNaughton. The Scottish Crop Research Institute, Invergowrie is world-renowned for the breeding and selection of many varieties of raspberry, blackcurrant as well as the tayberry. An important contemporary player is Orkney farmer Alan Bremner, who has been breeding hardy geraniums for the last 20 years.

Scottish Wild Flowers and Plants

Due to Britain's island geography and intense glaciation during the last ice age, Scotland has a relatively impoverished native flora and very few endemic plants (those which are found *only* in Scotland). Scotland's climate during the last ice age is thought to have been comparable to that of Greenland today, with only true arctic vegetation surviving. As the climate warmed up again, trees and conifers such as birch and juniper were able to move north and arctic plants such as *Saxifraga oppositifolia*, *Gentiana nivalis* and *Loiseleuria procumbens* became confined to mountain tops such as Ben Lawers and the peaks of the Angus Glens, where sharp-eyed walkers can still enjoy them. Scotland does have a fine range of wild flowers, and several spectacular plants, not all of them native, dominate the landscape at certain times of year. While some such as gorse, broom and heather are indigenous to Scottish, many now wild plants such as *Rhododendron ponticum* were introduced from elsewhere. Scotland's relatively short list of native trees includes Scots pine, yew, rowan, willow, alder, hazel and oak. The Romans probably introduced beech and chestnut to the UK, while the last three centuries have seen the introduction of many other trees now very much part of the landscape.

Snowdrops (*Galanthus*) are certainly one of Scotland's most conspicuous wildflowers, very much at home in Scotland, multiplying happily without any human intervention, and yet most authorities agree that they are not British natives. Late February and early March is the peak of snowdrop flowering. (see p. 458 for the pick of snowdrop gardens). As winter turns to spring, **primroses** (*Primula vulgaris*) start to flower all over Scotland in March, April and May, with their pale yellow flowers, historically associated with Easter. Some of the best displays I have seen lie along the A816 from Oban to Lochgilphead and on Skye. May brings on one the finest wild-flower sights in Scotland when the **bluebell** woods come into flower. The third week of May is usually the peak, but an early spring can make them earlier and they run into June in the far north. There are great examples all over Scotland. Some of the best include Castramon Wood, near Gatehouse of Fleet, Yellowcraig Wood near Stirling, Glen Nant, Argyll, Craigvinean Forest near Dunkeld and Darroch Wood, Blairgowrie, as well as many of the oak woods on Loch Lomondside. **Wild garlic** (*Allium ursinum*), pungent as you walk through it, produces its white flowers at the same time as the bluebells and they often grow together. The woods around Jura House contain what may be Scotland's most impressive wild garlic carpets. The warming of the climate over recent years means that **gorse** (*Ulex europaeus*) can open some of its bright yellow flowers almost all winter, but the peak is in spring, usually in mid May, when dry hillsides turn bright yellow. Some of the best places to see it include along the A90 from the Forth Bridge to Perth, along the East Lothian coast, in parts of Dumfries and Galloway and around Oban in Argyll. Broom joins in a little later in May. *Rhododendron ponticum* flowers from late May to late June and it occurs in quantity where rainfall is highest, on the west side of the country. Some of the finest displays include those in Mull, around Loch Fyne, Loch Awe and further north in Wester Ross around Kishorn. It was introduced from Spain and Portugal in the eighteenth century and was widely planted for shelter and game cover. In high rainfall areas (so not generally in eastern Scotland) it is able to seed and spread with suckers to form a dense carpet where few other plants can thrive. Foresters curse it and the Scottish Executive are in the process of banning its planting, a bit late in the day, if you ask me, as the plant is seldom grown commercially anymore. It is important to stress that of all the 900 species of rhododendron and azalea, *R. ponticum* is the only one to be invasive in this way. The others stay where they are put. Fossil records indicate that *R. ponticum* grew in Britain before the last ice age. **Heather** is perhaps Scotland's most famous wild flower, the finest moorlands tend to be on the drier east coast slopes of the Angus glens and Grampians. These carpets of purple in late summer are ling – *Calluna vulgaris* – often accompanied by delicious blaeberries (*Vaccinium myrtillus*). The other wild heather species, *Erica cinerea* and *E. tetralix*, are found on cliffs and boggy ground respectively.

Many of the richest wildflower habitats in Scotland are coastal. Clifftops are often particularly rich and reserves around the coast, famous for their seas birds, are also rich in a wide range of wildflowers. St Abbs Head near Berwick and Handa Island in Sutherland are two good examples, as is the limestone-dominated island of Lismore north of Oban. **Machair** is a particular west coast habitat where a lime-rich sand is covered with grass, sometimes fertilised with seaweed for grazing. This sharp-draining sand is a perfect habitat for many wild flowers including vetch, trefoil and ox-eye daisy, providing a spectacular summer display. Calgary Bay on Mull, and the islands of Coll, Tiree and Islay, as well as parts of the peninsula of Ardnamurchan, have good examples of machair.

The Existential Gardener or, What Makes a Gardener Garden?

What makes people devote so much hard work and money to the cause of a beautiful garden? Many gardeners tend their acres well into old age; and when I enquire if there is anyone else to take on the burden, the answer is often 'no'. Their children have perhaps long seen the absurdity of their parents' gardening obsessions and determined not to be caught in the same trap. In many cases, the garden will no longer exist after they have gone. The motivation for gardening often seems to me to be the process or task itself, which brings to mind Albert Camus' definition of existentialism in *Le Mythe de Sisyphe* ('The Myth of Sisyphus') in which he describes Sisyphus' endless task of pushing a heavy rock up a hill only to see it roll back down again as soon as he nears the top. 'The struggle itself is enough to fill a man's heart.' And Camus considers that this may indeed be a form of 'true happiness'.

Many people love to work in the outdoors, they love the contact with the soil, the pleasure of looking out onto a beautiful garden. But even with all these other motivations, I'm convinced there is an existential side, for almost all gardeners. Building a house or restoring a car, or walking from Lands End to John o' Groats are long and laborious tasks. But all these have a beginning and end, and then you can relax. Gardening is not like this: as all gardeners know, as soon as you have 'finished', your plants grow and crowd one another, pests and diseases strike, greenfly, blackspot, mildew, rain, storms, drought, you mow the grass, the grass gets longer again, weeds grow where you've just weeded . . . and gardeners just push that stone up that hill, over and over again. The best we can do is have the occasional rest, while admirers come to praise the shape of our rock, the pose in which we push it and the perfectly balanced route or rut we have worn down the hillside. It is simultaneously glorious and futile.

When does the gardening bug strike? It often appears to relate to 'nurture'. Caring for something to make it grow. Usually but not always, a hitherto mild affection for the garden increases when children reach a certain stage. For some, it might be when they go off to primary school, and don't need constant attention. For others it might be when they pack off their offspring to boarding school, university or work, leaving a hole in a parent's life for something else which needs to be nurtured. This time they can choose something which does not answer back, grow distant or turn into a teenager. Gardeners forgive plants which do not perform, assuming that either they did something wrong or the climate and soil are to blame. It's not the same trauma we go through wondering if we are doing a good job as parents. When children stop draining our income and start to earn some of their own . . . we decide to spend some of the money that this frees up on plants and gardening.

Is it possible to say what makes a great gardener? Is this really not the same question that I've just been trying to answer when evaluating a good garden? I'm not sure that it is. Most great gardeners are enlightened dictators with huge amounts of energy and a single-minded vision, often ignoring advice from others. Sometimes they fail; the clever ones take stock, remove the failures and move on. It is the daring, risk-taking attitude and the vision to see what something will look like in years to come that makes a great gardener. This is why I am wary of gardening by committee. When committees run gardens, everyone has a say. 'You can't do this, that tree was planted by the earl of somewhere . . . you can't do that, we have always had rose beds there . . .' This resulting lack of decisiveness all too often causes committee-run gardens to fall into a gradual but terminal decline through lack of innovation. No one is prepared to get out the chainsaw and make the bold decisions. You can't pickle a garden in vinegar and preserve it; a garden is a process not an object, a dynamic entity which can grow and deteriorate at equal speed. All good gardens thrive on evolution and change. A great expert on this subject, and one of Britain's greatest ever gardeners, Graham Stewart Thomas, wrote at length about this issue; he found it reared its head again and again in his work as gardens director of the (English) National Trust: 'We have learnt that committees are unsatisfactory for running gardens; all great gardens have been made by an individual or a succession of individuals. The mere fact that a committee is formed so that there shall be majority agreement, carries with it obvious dangers.' (Graham Stewart Thomas, *Gardens of the National Trust*)

Every great garden evolves, decade on decade; momentous decisions have to be made from time to time: to cut down woods or overgrown avenues of trees, to knock down walls, to get rid of tired old sections, to fill in or dig ponds, to give up growing roses. Great gardeners take risks. Committees are risk-averse. It can't be helped. Which brings us on to the subject issue of garden conservation.

The Conservation and Preservation of Scotland's Gardens

Some of Scotland's gardens and planned landscapes have been tended by members of the same family for hundreds of years. Generations have kept adding, changing, reviving and improving them.. But most great gardens are at risk of disappearing when their creator moves on. The National Trust for Scotland has conserved and preserved many great gardens of course, but it cannot save them all. Other gardens are cut adrift from their funders: Dundee, St Andrews and Cruickshank botanic gardens are no longer required by their universities for research or teaching so their lack of financial security is an ongoing concern. When significant gardens are sold, it is pure chance whether the new owners will have the interest or means to maintain or improve a garden, so more often than not they slip quietly off the radar and disappear. A woodland garden may be able to fend for itself for a few years, but a formal or walled garden is almost defenceless: nature will reclaim these in a matter of months. However even after years of neglect, old gardens can be brought back to life when there is a will, as many were after the world wars.

Scotland's gardening history is intrinsically bound up with landownership and social class. Gardens for pleasure rather than for growing food were until relatively recently almost entirely the preserve of the aristocracy and landowning classes. Such pleasure gardens were large-scale, high-maintenance and labour intensive. Most of Scotland's major landowners have or had significant gardens. Scotland is a country where the concentration of ownership of land in so few hands has long been controversial. Andy Wightman's illuminating book *Who Owns Scotland* details the feudal background to Scotland's land tenure and also illustrates how the landed families have managed to hang onto their lands through a combination of strategic marriages and complex, often secretive financial arrangements. Much of Scotland's land is held by around 1,500 estates varying in size from 5,000 to 260,000 acres. Many have been held by families for generations, while the ownership of some estates is hidden behind trusts which take a bit of work to unravel. One or two asked me not to reveal the name of the garden/estate owners, which I have respected with some reluctance. As I was, however, able to find out who owned all of them with a quick Google search, such secrecy seemed out of date and pointless. Indeed, it has persuaded me that transparency of land ownership in Scotland should be made a legal requirement on public record and freely available on the internet, as it is in almost all other European countries.

It is impossible to research a book such as this without noticing Scotland's powerhouse landowning dynasties: the dukes of Atholl, Argyll, Sutherland, Buccleuch and the marquises of Bute are some of the most significant examples. These estates alone account for almost 600,000 acres of Scotland (whose total land area is 19 million acres) and the wealth these families have accumulated has allowed them to garden on a huge scale. By comparison, the National Trust for Scotland owns 175,000 acres (1995). These families (mostly via trusts) still maintain some of Scotland's finest castles, gardens and landscapes on a significant and impressive scale. It must be borne in mind that the stewardship of many of the great gardens of Scotland for generation after generation is carried on for motives which are seldom for financial gain, and we should acknowledge the efforts and foresight of some of Scotland's major landowners. There are, however, persuasive arguments for further land reform in Scotland as there are many legal and feudal anachronisms which have no place in a democracy in the twenty-first century. It is heartening to watch the progress of recent community buyouts of Eigg, Gigha and Assynt, all of which suffered previously under the ownership of sometimes absent, careless, incompetent, or bankrupt owners.

Some of Scotland's best gardens are owned and looked after by people who inherited or bought them, often unaware what they were letting themselves in for. I have met many such slightly shell-shocked owners embarking on a steep learning curve, particularly those who had sometimes unwittingly managed to 'marry' a great garden when they walked up the aisle. Some rise to the challenge while others don't, usually due to financial constraints or lack of interest. Many once great Scottish gardens have been lost in this way or are in terminal decline or no longer open to the public. It has been relatively easy to assess the loss of gardens by comparing the garden entries in this book with those of its predecessor, *Gardens of Scotland*, edited by Allan Little and published in 1981. As an example, over 60 per cent of the gardens listed in the South-East Scotland section of *Gardens of Scotland* are not in this one 25 years later. I wonder what remains of Belhaven House (Sir George Taylor's garden), Addistoun, Biel, Bridgelands, Chiefswood, Clechhead, Craling Hall, Eden House, Elvingston, Glenburn House, Hawthornden Castle, The Holmes, Houndwood House . . . I'm sure that some of these are still good gardens, no longer open or accessible by the public. Some might be in such a condition that they could be rescued and brought back to life, should a new owner wish to do so. But many will have gone for good.

In assessing the extent of Scotland's garden heritage we now have a valuable resource available to us in Historic Scotland's Inventory of Gardens and Designed Landscapes. This is a detailed survey, now available at *www.historic-scotland.gov.uk*. This survey may lead to legislation for greater statutory protection of listed landscapes from inappropriate development, but there seems little chance that significant funds will be made available to preserve the gardens themselves.

Gardens are not frozen in time but evolve constantly. There is a tendency to assume that garden restoration is a good idea, but this is a complex and often contentious issue. Who decides whether an original garden design is really worth recreating? There are sometimes good reasons that gardens have disappeared, whether for financial or aesthetic considerations. If we decide to restore a garden, then how do we decide to which period? A historic garden is a process, not a snapshot, and this often presents interesting challenges. Falkland Palace is a particularly knotty example. This NTS Fife property is a Victorian restoration of a sixteenth-century palace which had been abandoned for almost 200 years and had no remaining gardens. Falkland Palace now has a mixture of Victorian-style shrubbery, a Percy Cane post-war design and some National Trust committee gardening. Many agree this garden is not very satisfactory but it is almost impossible to reach a consensus on what type of garden should be restored or created here. Personally, I think the Cane design should go, but many others feel equally strongly that it should be preserved.

I leave the last word on this subject to one Britain's most erudite gardeners, Sir Roy Strong, who I heard speak in 2008 on the subject of garden conservation and his own garden at the Lasket, ending his talk with a rallying-cry: 'My mandate is: if it is boring, old fashioned, overgrown, demolish it, rip it out, start again. Because that is what gardening is about . . . it is about starting again and it is about change and it is about embracing change. It is not about making static shrines.'

The National Trust for Scotland

The National Trust and National Trust for Scotland have saved many of Britain's greatest gardens from certain decline and probable destruction. But donating a garden in this way is not without its trials, particularly if you give it away while you are still alive and sentient. Creator of Sissinghurst, Vita Sackville-West put it bluntly: 'Never. Never, never. Not that hard metal plaque at my door. Nigel can do what he likes after I am dead, but as long as I live, no Nat Trust or any other foreign body shall have my darling.' Sissinghurst was eventually given to the National Trust in 1967.

It is impossible to over-estimate how important the two trust organisations have been to the conservation of British gardens. Gardens in private hands seldom last for more than two or three generations and this is particularly true of the grandest gardens, on a vast scale, unsustainably expensive to maintain. Some such gardens have required serious renovation work when the Trust bodies have take over, while others have needed to be restored almost from scratch.

Sad though it is to see gardens lost, not all of them can or should be saved. As was made clear by the announcement of proposed property closures in March 2009, The National Trust for Scotland cannot afford to look after the many gardens it has, and there is little chance of them taking on any more. Indeed several listed in this book are under threat of closure unless public outcry and government intervention can save them. So what alternatives are there? Private garden trusts seldom work in the long term without a generous benefactor. There is simply not enough income and the trustees who run them are rarely able to take the daring decisions needed to move the gardens on. Decline is usually inevitable. Every year another great garden slips off the radar, usually away from public view. Though the Historic Scotland Gardens and Planned Landscapes Inventory lists many of them, it has no power to intervene. Likewise the Garden History Society can write reports and recommendations but has no power to act further. At best planning or development restrictions might be invoked, but current legislation cannot save gardens.

I'm not easily persuaded that state handouts can be used to save gardens. It should always be borne in mind that most of these large gardens were created as self-conscious extravagance. Part of the point of their existence was to demonstrate how rich the owners were, what 'good taste' their money could buy and how many gardeners they could afford. These gardens were never meant to be affordable or sustainable. Pitmedden in Aberdeenshire is a good example of the resources required to maintain a large-scale formal garden: 3 miles of box hedging clipped at least twice a year and 30,000 annuals to plant out is extremely labour intensive. With the exception of the great botanic gardens, almost all of Britain's 'great' gardens have been made by rich individuals.

The setting-up of the National Trust and the National Trust for Scotland has led to public access to many of Britain's 'great' houses and gardens. Few of these gardens were created with any plans for the general public to enjoy them. They were built by the exclusive few for the exclusive few to enjoy. Popping in for a look in those days would have been risking being peppered with shot by one of the gamekeepers. Now that the gardens are publicly owned or in the Trust, the playthings of the rich have in effect been 'nationalised' for us all to enjoy.

Conservation of Private Gardens

Could Keillour, Ascreavie, Belhaven House, Balbithan and some of Scotland's other fine private gardens have been saved for the nation? Those who remember the Knox Findlays, Sir George Taylor, George and Betty Sherriff and Mary MacMurtrie will of course mourn the passing of their gardens as much as of their owners. However, I doubt that many of them could or should have been 'saved', particularly these intensely personal plantsman's gardens, so intrinsically linked with the character and history of their creators. Without their input and energy, is there anything lasting which can be preserved?

As some gardens die new gardens are born every year, which makes things exciting for visitors and garden writers alike. There are also heart-warming stories of gardens which are rescued from oblivion and given a new lease of life. Examples include Mike and Sue Thornley's on-going stewardship and improvement of the woodland garden at Glenarn, near Helensburgh and the restoration of Ascog Fernery on Bute by Wallace and Katherine Fyfe. The National Trust for Scotland has taken on Arduaine and Crarae in recent years, two of the west coast's finest woodland gardens, though sadly the latter may be threatened with closure in NTS budget cuts.

This book is definitely not solely about the so-called 'great' gardens that most people have heard of. There are many exceptional little known private gardens, on a manageable and modest scale, that I celebrate in this book. Each year Scotland's Garden's Scheme seems to have more great smaller gardens opening to the public, often several opening together in one street or village; many are excellent. The NCCPG, or National Collections, have allowed many keen hobby gardeners recognition for their work in collecting and conserving sometimes unfashionable plants to prevent them from being lost. And all over Scotland there are thriving community gardens. Britain's range of commercially available plant species and cultivars is wider than ever, which can be witnessed in the ever increasing girth of the *RHS Plantfinder*, now listing over 70,000 plants. In this area at least, we have never had it so good.

The Scottish Tourist Industry

Scotland has between 15 and 16 million tourists per year (2006–07 figures) and the tourism industry contributes around £4 billion to the Scottish economy. Surveys conducted by VisitScotland suggest that gardens are one of Scotland's top five draws for tourists. You would therefore imagine that VisitScotland, the organisation responsible for Scotland's Tourism industry, would give marketing gardens a high priority. But you would be wrong.

The organisation charged with promoting tourism in Scotland, VisitScotland is an organisation with many talented people working for it, particularly at the local level. The ones I have met are dedicated, hard-working and efficient. However, they are let down by poor leadership and often naïve political meddling. One of the most disruptive aspects is the almost constant and expensive restructuring which has gone on in recent years, which demoralises staff and destroys continuity. I have failed to elicit anything other than placatory marketing speak in response to my enquiries to VisitScotland.

Do these restructurings bring an improved service or better initiatives? I have failed to see much evidence. Most garden owners and accommodation owners feel that VisitScotland demand ever higher fees for service which is lower value for money. One example is the dismantling of the popular and well respected food and restaurant marketing initiative 'Taste of Scotland' with its guidebook and rating system. This was replaced with a new and as far as I can see, inferior 'EatScotland' initiative which has not enhanced Scotland's tourist offering. Another frequent complaint raised by gardens and visitor attractions is that local Tourist Information Centres (TICs) are closed down, merged or have vastly reduced opening hours. The latest initiative has been to demand that local attractions pay a monthly fee to ensure that their leaflets are displayed in TIC leaflet racks. So out go the leaflets of the small gardens with little income and marketing budget and in comes the muscle of the mega-attractions (many of which are outside the local area), so that everyone loses: the visitor and local attraction owner alike.

It is becoming increasingly unclear whether the purpose of VisitScotland, and particularly its website VisitScotland.com, is to attract and inform visitors or simply to make money. These two parts of its remit are clearly in danger of a serious conflict of interest. Public/private partnerships such as the one running the website seem to have maximising revenue as their driving force, leaving the information side floundering. The Rampant Scotland website is far more informative to the visitor, not just because of the excellent content, but also because it is not primarily trying to sell you something (*www.rampantscotland.com*). I'm hopeful that at last the politicians have woken up to this issue, as the Scottish goverment's Economy, Energy and Tourism Committee Report of 10 July 2008 stated: 'With respect to VisitScotland.com, we believe that the current business model is patently flawed and obsolete. We recommend that this is rethought, focusing on information provision and a comprehensive, free listing service and does not attempt to provide accommodation availability and booking services directly to users but refers them on.'

Gardens are one of Scotland's most significant attractions and many of them are attached to historic houses and castles. They are cheap to visit, seldom subsidised by the taxpayer and bring pleasure to millions. I want to persuade our politicians and civil servants in Westminster and Holyrood, and VisitScotland in particular, to take this extraordinary and unique resource seriously. If we are to believe in VisitScotland's avowed ambition to 'boost Scottish tourism revenue by 50 per cent during the next decade', then effective marketing gardens is clearly one of the principal ways that they might achieve it. Garden and nursery tourism of course has a beneficial knock-on effect on hotels, catering, transportation and other parts of the economy. I want to make visiting gardens easier by providing a single informative resource so that people can find out what is open and what is worth seeing in any part of Scotland in any given month. I hope this book will be part of this resource as well as the website which we hope to develop alongside: *scotlandforgardeners.com*.

Marketing and Promoting Scottish Gardens

In common with some other visitor attractions, visitor numbers for some Scottish gardens have been static or declining in the last couple of years, though Scotland's Gardens Scheme seems to have bucked this trend. There are several possible reasons. The weather is sometimes to blame; wet weekends are a garden-visiting disaster. Other factors may include budget airlines making trips to the sun more accessible, a strong pound, midges, poor marketing and alternative visitor attractions. We may well have rather too many fine gardens for the number of people who live here. Few Scottish gardens receive more than 10,000 visitors a year and therefore entry fees can rarely make gardens self-sustaining, however good they are.

There is a perception amongst some Scots that garden visiting is simply posh people visiting other posh peoples' gardens. Scotland's Gardens Scheme 'Yellow Book' gardens and their owners tend to confirm the impression that garden visiting is a middle-aged, white, middle- and upper-class activity. Contrast this with gardening itself, which is enjoyed by a huge range of Scotland's population, of every demographic. The reality is that anyone, of almost any age or background, can enjoy a good garden. I'd like to inspire more people to get out and around their country on short breaks to see what we have to offer. What better thing to do on a crisp February weekend when few other visitor attractions are open, than go for a walk through carpets of snowdrops? Why not spend a weekend in the woodland gardens of Argyll in April or May when the rhododendrons are at their peak, or in Perthshire and Fife with lots of fine gardens close enough to visit several in one day? Why not go island hopping to Gigha, Jura, Arran or Bute, all of which have excellent gardens, or tour the south-west's perennials nurseries and woodland and walled gardens? For house and garden combination, you can't do better than Aberdeenshire's castle trail. With this book in hand or the Scotland's Gardens Scheme (SGS) 'Yellow Book', you can spend Sunday afternoons in some of Scotland's other hidden garden jewels. You'll be amazed at what there is. I noted on my travels that it is often the gardeners who claim they don't have time to visit other gardens in other parts of the country. This year, why not put down your spade, leave the weeds to grow for a few days and get out and about and meet people just like you, who can't wait to show off their gardens? Wherever you come from and whatever your age, some of Scotland's gardens should certainly delight you and might inspire you to create your own piece of paradise . . . ready for inclusion in the next edition of this book.

Problems and Issues Facing Scottish Gardens and Horticulture

In many ways we are enjoying a golden era of Scottish gardens and nurseries. However, I'm not complacent enough to think that all is rosy in the world of Scottish horticulture. The National Trust for Scotland announced in spring 2009 that many of its properties were unsustainable. Some of those covered in this book are threatened with closure or severely reduced access and/or maintenance. Britain has a major shortage of skilled and trained gardeners and horticulturalists. This is a traditionally low-paid profession and many gardeners used to be trained on the job as apprentices; however, vocational gardeners have often found the need to seek higher-paid jobs (due to the inexorable rise of house prices, for example), with the consequence that fewer stay within the profession. Increasingly, horticultural colleges are shrinking or closing down. It might have seemed like a good idea in the 1980s to open up education to the free market, but the result is that there are now too many mediocre courses and a shortage of experienced lecturers. Scotland needs a small number of well-funded centres of horticultural excellence with first class tuition. The Royal Botanic Garden, Edinburgh, Threave and Auchincruive have traditionally trained Scotland's most talented gardeners and horticulturalists. Without such centres of excellence, the quality of teaching and therefore of graduating student, is not high enough. The National Trust for Scotland's new initiative, the 'Centre of Excellence in Heritage Horticulture', using some of its gardens to create an educational resource, is an important new development which I hope proves to be a success.

Much of the horticultural industry in Scotland is in decline due to cheap imported plants and the rise of DIY and garden centre chains which demand uneconomic margins of their suppliers. Take with a pinch of salt any supermarket/garden centre chains which claim they buy locally. I have spoken to most of the Scottish wholesale nurseries and they have told me what payment terms, discounts and rebates the big chains demand and that their habit of frequent cancelling of booked stock means that the nurseries cannot afford to do business with them. Most Scottish producers are too small to absorb such treatment and are forced to walk away. The result is that more and more plants sold in Scotland come from Holland and Italy, grown in over-small pots with misleading labels. Scottish gardens are much better off with Scottish-grown plants which have travelled fewer miles, are better acclimatised and probably selected because they grow well in Scotland. (See *Garden Plants for Scotland* for further details on this.)

Pests and diseases have long been something gardeners have battled with, whether using chemicals or cultivation practices. Almost all the effective chemicals still licensed for use in gardens are now under threat from the EU, which up till now has banned only the most toxic or dangerous. The latest list under review includes sodium chlorate (banned from 2009), glyphosate (Roundup), myclobutanil (used for rose mildew and rust) and many others. I guarantee that if all this comes into law Scotland's farmers and gardeners are in serious trouble, whatever the badly informed MEPs and the green lobby may claim.

A major concern, as I was writing this book, was the advent and spread of the disease *Phytophthora ramorum*, which seems to have originated in America and is now spreading through parts of the UK, including western Scotland. This fungal pathogen attacks *Rhododendron, Camellia, Magnolia, Viburnum, Drimys* and many other plants, particularly in shady woodland gardens, and has caused serious damage in some of the famous Cornish woodland gardens. There are attempts to eradicate it, but I suspect that this will likely be in vain and we will just have to live with this disease as we already live with so many others. The most worrying thing is that it spreads readily in the wild *Rhododendron ponticum*, often causing dieback, not necessarily fatally, and then this infection can spread to other trees and shrubs. As a result, Scotland's great woodland gardens may be under threat from this disease. Time will tell how serious it turns out to be. Climate change is, of course, another concern; the change in rainfall patterns, leading to flooding and increased fungal diseases, seems to be one consequence which is already taking place. Other changes are almost certain to follow.

Ten ways of Improving Scotland's Gardens and Horticultural Industry

1. The National Trust for Scotland has the responsibility of conserving and maintaining much of Scotland's most significant garden heritage. It must not be allowed to close down some of its most significant gardens, Arduaine for example and the magnificent house and garden combination of Kellie Castle, both of which are threatened by budget cuts by the Trust.

2. Gardening needs to be more widely recognised as a major force for social good. Community gardens all over Scotland foster inclusion, pride, fitness and healthy eating. Gardens have a role to play in education and the physical and mental health of the nation, typified by places such as Redhall in Edinburgh.

3. Scottish gardens and planned landscapes need to be recognised at government level as being of national and international importance. Gardens are part of the heritage and culture of Scotland and great gardens are no less culturally significant than paintings, buildings or music? Who decides that Little Sparta is less worthy of subsidy than Scottish Opera, for example?

4. The Historic Scotland Planned Landscape Inventory has limited value unless it

leads to protection of the landscape of sites listed. With protection must come assistance to owners with upkeep and repairs, in the forms of grants, labour, favourable tax and inheritance breaks. A recent UNESCO report condemned the failings of UK planners to protect the integrity of landscapes such as New Town Edinburgh, Skara Brae and the Tower of London.

5. VAT rates for significant landscape and garden restoration should be similar to that for listed building repairs: i.e. zero rated.

6. Private gardens open to the public should be able and encouraged to apply for match funding for tree surgery and major repairs to significant structures such as walled gardens, greenhouses etc. An endowment fund could be set up for this which gardens could apply to.

7. There seems to be little government interest in or support for the future of the Scottish horticultural industry. There is considerable scope to market Scottish plants for Scottish gardens. The issue of 'plant miles' needs to be brought to the fore, and the country of origin of plants should be compulsory on plant labels.

8. VisitScotland and other organisations (NTS, SGS, RBGE and so on) which market Scotland's visitor attractions need to work *together* to market Scotland's gardens in a professional, accessible manner.

9. The VisitScotland website *must* have a properly designed gardens section easily accessible from the VisitScotland home page, fully comprehensive and updated regularly. If they can't or won't provide it, it should be outsourced.

10. Scotland needs a small number of properly funded training in horticulture in centres of excellence. As well as lecturers, Scottish horticultural experts such as nurserymen, designers and garden centre owners should be encouraged and funded to lecture or teach the next generation. Students need guidance from those working in the trade.

Criteria for Entry in Scotland for Gardeners

This book's core consists of entries describing Scotland's gardens, nurseries, garden centres and horticultural organisations. I have included limited coverage of some of Scotland's best wildflower and forest/woodland sites; for further details on Scotland's wild places, consult the excellent guides listed in the Bibliography. I have listed details of some environmental and conservation bodies too.

Gardens

I have tried to include almost all gardens in Scotland open to the public regularly or by appointment. There are some gardens which only open for Scotland's Garden Scheme one day a year and I have even slipped in one or two which are not really open at all but are so good that you will need to write a persuasive letter to let you in. Be aware that gardens change their opening and closing times at short notice, so make use of the 'Yellow Book', the Scotland's Gardens Scheme and Glendoick/*scotlandfor-gardeners.com* websites to check the latest information. Many of Scotland's best gardens are owned by people who don't want constant visitors but don't mind a few from time to time. Your tact and good behaviour will let you in and probably the next people who ask.

Nurseries and Garden Centres

Scotland is blessed with a huge variety of specialist retail nurseries and excellent independent garden centres. Most of these are automatically included if they grow their own plants. I have not included nurseries and cash and carries which are trade/wholesale only. For garden centres I asked myself two questions. Does it have a speciality? And is this a place a non-local would be interested in visiting? This is true whether the garden centre sells a huge range of seed potatoes, rhubarb, azaleas, ferns, pots, grows its own bedding, has a huge range of Koi carp or a great restaurant. All are equally deserving of inclusion. If the answer is no to both questions I have generally not included them.

As Tesco takes over Dobbies, Scotland's successful garden centre chain, the non-specialist centres had better beware and up their game or be forced out of business. There are plans for 200 Dobbies in the UK. Every time Tesco, Asda and the like open a store, they squeeze the life out of independent retailers. They drive greengrocers, butchers, chemists, bakers and hardware stores out of business and I have no doubt the same fate awaits garden centres and nurseries. One of Scotland's best garden centres, Sandyholm, was sold to Tesco/Dobbies as I was writing this book. It certainly won't make it a better garden centre, and many of the independent nurseries who used to supply Sandyholm will now longer be able to do so, as they are not national Dobbies suppliers. Cockers new garden centre site in Aberdeen was sold to Dobbies several months later. On and on it goes. The big chains demand ridiculous terms and rebates from their suppliers, many of whom are small family-owned nurseries who cannot afford to cut their margins. They get driven out of business too, which means that in future you may struggle to buy Scottish-grown plants at all. As gardeners, you currently have the choice to support your local and independent businesses; enjoy it while you can.

Scotland's Horticultural Societies

This book lists many specialist horticultural societies, which cover a wide spectrum of interests from vegetables to flower arranging, sweet peas to rhododendrons (see p. 451). In addition, Scotland has an astonishing number of national and local horticultural societies. These vary greatly in size and some come and go from year to year so there is never a definitive list. Some have websites and this is usually the best way to get in touch with them, as the society office bearers tend to change from year to year. Most offer a similar range of activities: lectures and workshops, journals and newsletters, garden visits and shows.

I had toyed with the idea of including all Scotland's local horticultural clubs and societies in this book until I learned that there may be as many as 400. Thankfully, the Scottish Gardeners Forum (see p. 456) has a database of nearly all of them. All you need to do is contact SGF and they'll put you in touch with your nearest one.

Shows

Though shows have seen somewhat of a decline over the last 50 years, there are still plenty of good ones around the country, some large and some small. The Scottish Rock Garden Club runs shows in several Scottish towns and cities in spring. Many other societies have annual shows: the Scottish Rhododendron Society and the Royal Caledonian Horticultural Society for example. Some shows are covered in the entries under the societies themselves and forthcoming dates can be found on their websites. 'Gardening Scotland' at Ingliston is Scotland's largest show. Abandoned by the RHS almost before it had got going, it was taken on by Rural Projects and has been well run by Jim Jermyn and his team in recent years. This show has actually become a better and more relaxed event without the RHS and attracts thousands to Ingliston the first weekend in June. The indoor displays are usually impressive and you are certainly in retail heaven if you like sourcing interesting plants from specialist nurseries. The main disappointment is the generally relatively low standard of outdoor gardens, partly due to the weather and the lack of available sponsorship. Late summer sees the Ayr and Dundee flower shows, somewhat swamped by the selling of tat and clobber, but with astonishing displays of carrots, parsnips, Kelsae onions, leeks, fuchsias, dahlias and chrysanthemums.

Note on Excluded Gardens and Nurseries

The following gardens and nurseries asked not to have an entry in this book. Most of the gardens below have been open under SGS in recent years; one or two remain open but most are retiring from opening their gardens and/or are passing them to the next generation: J. Tweedie Fruit Trees; Cairness; Cluniemore; Coilte; Conaglen; Cowhill Tower; Dunecht House; Easter Weens; Glenearn House; House of Aigas; House of Aldie; Knockdolian; Machany; Raesmill.

Getting Around Scotland

It is possible to visit many of the gardens in this book by public transport if you have plenty of time, but there is no doubt that a car is almost essential for garden visiting in many rural areas. Car hire can be relatively cheap in the UK, but petrol is expensive and narrow roads in the west are best navigated in small cars. Trains cover much of the country and some gardens can be reached by the rail network with a bit of walking or use of taxis. Rail rover tickets valid for several days are good value for touring the country. The Highland Rover includes trains, buses and some CalMac ferries in the Highland region, while the Freedom of Scotland passes cover the whole country. Some of these tickets are for non-UK tourists only, and must be purchased before you arrive in the UK. Scotland has a good network of buses and local buses will generally let you off as near gardens as they can, on their route. In remote areas post buses are used but beware, as they only follow the route once a day. You can try hitching, but this seems to be a declining way of getting around. Several operators offer minibus tours of gardens which are good value for small groups. Scheduled garden tours are offered by Brightwater Holidays based in Fife (see p. 453). Islands usually require the use of CalMac ferries (0990 650000. *www.calmac.co.uk*). It is not necessary to take your car to Torosay (Mull), Achamore (Gigha), Colonsay, Brodick (Arran) or Bute as public transport to the major gardens is good.

How to Use This Book

I have divided Scotland up into regions. The boundaries, particularly in the centre, can be rather arbitrary. I have taken distance into account so each region could be used as a day or two-day trip to visit several gardens in one go. Many villages and towns open collections of gardens under SGS every year, or alternate years and these group garden openings are mentioned within the regional introductions rather than among the main entries, as the gardens tend to change from year to year.

I've tried to make the entries as up to date as possible but unfortunately it is inevitable that one or two of the gardens and nurseries close each year. To that end I will be setting up a website which you can access via *gardensofscotland.com* and *www.glendoick.com*, which will be a source of the most up-to-date information on garden openings. Do let me know via the website if you find that any gardens in this book are closed or no longer worth a look. And even more important, let me know of anything I have missed, which can be included in any further editions.

The opening times and other details of gardens are believed to be correct at time of writing but be aware that times can change at short notice. Make use of websites to ascertain latest opening status of gardens. Many gardens listed open for Scotland's Gardens Scheme on one or more days per year and many also accept visits by appointment. If you really want to see a garden which is not open at a convenient time, write a decent, old-fashioned, well-informed letter saying why you want to visit. 'I have heard about your amazing new peony border and as I have the national collection . . .'

I cannot over-emphasise how important it is to 'behave' when visiting gardens. Don't kid yourself that your 'wee bit of pocket-stuffing' does not matter. Taking seed heads and cuttings is stealing. And if you do steal things, you are likely to cause garden owners to shut their gates. People are always telling me how their mum 'nicks a few plants or cuttings', as if this were OK. It is particularly depressing when many of the rare treasures dug up in full flower are almost certain to die. No one wins. Most gardeners are happy to share with those who ask.

Most gardeners welcome children, but don't let them run riot. My own children, Jamie and Finn, have test-driven many of the children's attractions on offer and I have included information on these where available. Dogs are welcome at some properties but many insist that dogs are not allowed. Almost without exception, dogs must be kept on a lead at all times. If a garden has no dog symbol, you can assume that dogs are not allowed. Ballindalloch (see p. 62) gets my unofficial award for Scotland's most dog-friendly garden. It even has a dog maze!

I have included disability access information where available. I have, however, noted that many SGS gardens claim good disabled access when frankly the terrain, steps and gravel paths mean that you would need a strong helper to get a wheelchair round. The wheelchair symbol enclosed in brackets means that the garden is partly or theoretically accessible.

Apart from walking in the countryside, garden visiting is just about the cheapest activity available. Gardens are astonishing good value and few of them charge more than £5. Many are free. You usually pay as much for the latte and scone at the end as you do for an hour or two visiting the garden.

Key to Entries

Opening Times and Prices

Gardens tend change opening times and prices from year to year, so I have endeavoured to give general details about likely opening times for the foreseeable future. Many NTS and larger gardens open at Easter or 1 April, whichever is earlier, and close in September or October. Prices are given in bands:

£: up to £3   ££: £3–£5.99   £££: £6+   £*/££*/£££*

* The price band with an asterisk indicates that gardens are free to those with an appropriate membership or season ticket for organisations such as National Trust for Scotland, National Trust, Historic Scotland or Perthshire Gardens Collection. Some gardens have free entry to Royal Horticultural Society members, though sometimes on off-peak days only. These gardens are listed in the RHS handbook and its magazine, *The Garden.*

Contacting Gardens

Where possible I have given several methods of getting in touch with garden owners with address, phone, fax, email and website details. Some owners do not want phone/email details published and you may have to write to apply to visit. Email is excellent for those who use it regularly but beware: some email addresses are clearly rarely used. If phoning/faxing from abroad the UK code is 44 and you need to remove the 'o', so for example 01738 860205 becomes 441738 860205. Many garden owners have expressed frustration that occasionally people make appointments to visit and then do not turn up. It is only polite to make contact and cancel if you can't make it.

Dogs

Only those gardens which are marked with the dog symbols allow dogs, on a lead. Assume that you can't take your dog, if there is no symbol. Those with the ⊡ symbol allow dogs in the woodland and/or policies but not in the gardens themselves. It goes without saying that you should take away anything which your dog leaves in any part of a cultivated garden.

Catering

Most gardens open under Scotland's Gardens Scheme offer teas at the garden or nearby on open days, so I have not included this as a symbol. The catering mentioned under the entries ⊡ is for cafés and restaurants only.

Plants for Sale

Likewise many gardens offer surplus plants for sale on SGS open days but only those gardens with a nursery/garden shop or general production of plants are listed with the ⊡ symbol.

Symbols

ID   Self-catering accommodation for rent

B&B   Bed and breakfast

   Catering (café/restaurant, etc)

   Disabled

   Partly accessible, or accessible with help

   Dogs allowed, all dogs MUST be on a lead. If the dog symbol does not appear, assume that dogs are not allowed

   Dogs allowed in part of property, usually policies only but not in the gardens

   Gift shop

H   Hotel with meals

[H]   Exclusive use hotel: you need to book the whole building, so only possible for groups

   House or castle can be visited

   Mail order nursery

   Plant sales

WC   Toilets

Scotland for Gardeners

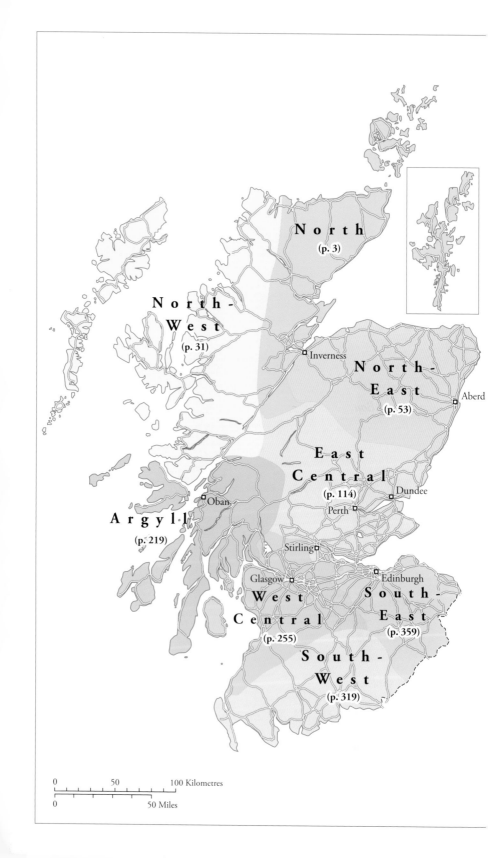

North
(p. 3)

North-
West
(p. 31)

□Inverness

North-
East
(p. 53)

□Aberd

East
Central
(p. 114)

□Dundee

□Oban

Perth□

Argyll
(p. 219)

Stirling□

Glasgow□

□Edinburgh

West
Central
(p. 255)

South-
East
(p. 359)

South-
West
(p. 319)

0   50   100 Kilometres

0   50 Miles

North (including Orkney and Shetland):
Black Isle, Caithness and East Sutherland

The north of mainland Scotland contains some important gardens, often quite widely spaced apart, but the routes between them are mostly spectacular. Most gardens are not far from the sea, which means that a loop around the coastal roads takes in most of them, with a detour across the Black Isle. Some of the best gardens include the castles of Dunrobin and Dunbeath on the east coast and House of Tongue on the north coast. Significant nurseries on Loch Ness, the Black Isle and Beauly Firth include: Abriachan, Ardfearn, Highland Liliums and Poyntzfield Herbs. Other gardens occasionally open in this region, not included in the listing which follows, include: Ardvar Lodge, Brackla Wood, Croc na Boull, Duirinish Lodge, Drumbeg, Sutherland. Dunnet Gardens and Thurso seaside gardens.

Dunrobin Castle

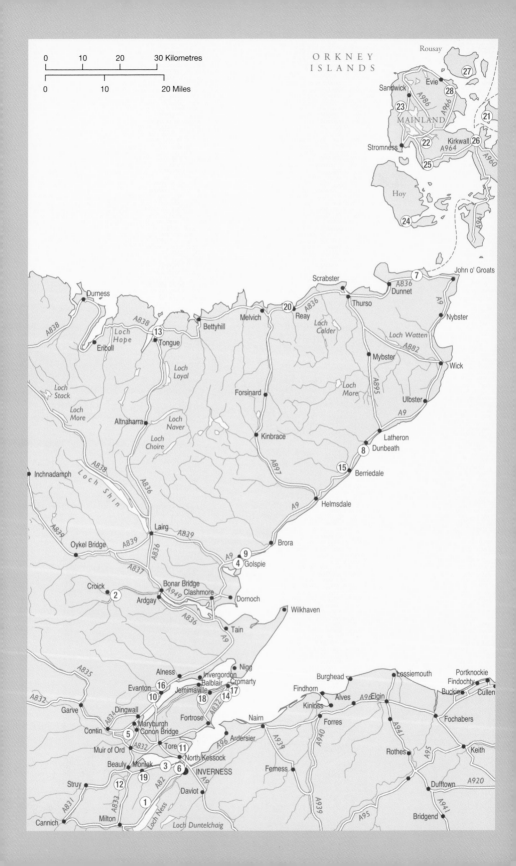

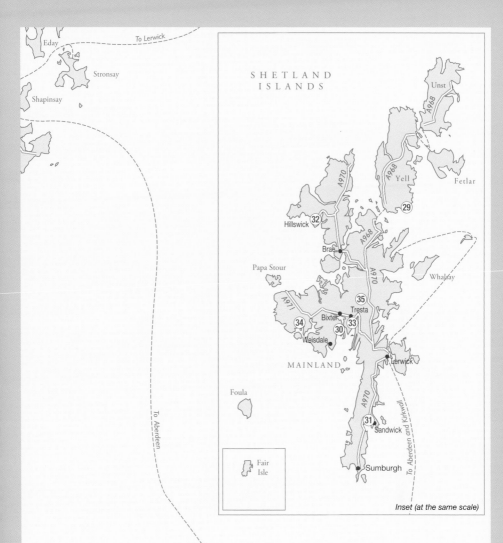

To Lerwick

Eday

Stronsay

Shapinsay

SHETLAND
ISLANDS

Unst

A968

A970

Yell

Fetlar

A968

29

Hillswick 32

A968

Brae

Papa Stour

Whalsay

A970

35

Tresta

A971

34 Bixter 33

30

Weisdale

MAINLAND

Lerwick

Foula

A970

To Aberdeen

To Aberdeen and Kirkwall

31

Sandwick

Fair
Isle

Sumburgh

Inset (at the same scale)

Portsoy
Banff Macduff
A98
Cornhill A97
A95
Aberchirder
Turriff
Huntly
A96 A947
A920

Mainland Scotland
1 Abriachan Garden Nursery
2 Amat
3 Ardfearn Nursery
4 Biblical Garden, Golspie
5 Brahan
6 Bught Floral Halls
7 Castle and Gardens of Mey
8 Dunbeath Castle
9 Dunrobin Castle
10 Foulis Castle
11 Gardens Scotland and Craigiewood B&B
12 Highland Liliums Garden Centre and Nursery
13 House of Tongue and Eddie's Garden
14 Hugh Miller Museum and Birthplace
15 Langwell Lodge
16 Novar
17 Old Orchard (The)
18 Poyntzfield Herb Nursery
19 Reelig Glen
20 Sandside

Orkney Islands
21 Balfour Castle Gardens
22 Happy Valley
23 Kierfiold House
24 Melsetter House
25 Schoolquoy
26 Tankerness House Gardens/Orkney Museum
27 Trumland House Gardens
28 Woodwick House

Shetland Islands
29 Burravoe Haa
30 Da Gairdins
31 Garden and Ecological Trail, Shetland (Gaets)
32 Hillswick Health Centre Gardens
33 Lea Gardens
34 Voe House
35 Weisdale Kirk

Abriachan Garden Nursery
Lochness-side,
Inverness, IV3 8LA
(*map, pp. 4–5*)

Mr and Mrs D. Davidson
February–November:
daily 9am–7pm or dusk if earlier;
gardens £, nursery free
A82 Inverness–Drumnadrochit
road. Right on the roadside,
do NOT follow signs to
Abriachan village
T: 01463 861 232
E: info@lochnessgarden.com
www.lochnessgarden.com/
Coffee machine

Abriachan Garden Nursery

Carved out of a steep, south-facing hillside overlooking Loch Ness, this is a wonderful terraced woodland garden which seems to be in perfect harmony with its surroundings. This small nursery specialises in *Auricula*, *Helianthemum* (a national collection), hardy geraniums and has all sorts of choice and common plants, especially herbaceous and grasses. I admired a New Zealand grass *Chionochloa conspicua* near the car park. The Davidsons are an excellent team, a contrast in styles in the way they impart their extensive plant knowledge: she talks non-stop, he listens and interjects briefer pearls of wisdom and they both know their onions. If you need to know what to grow in this area and how to grow it, this is the place to come. They seem to be able to grow almost anything here: steep slopes provide good frost drainage to the loch below, and there is free-draining soil. And the views from the top of the garden over Loch Ness are wonderful. As they say on their website: 'On one level it is a garden of infinite detail; on another the eye follows sweeps of colour leading into the surrounding magnificence of loch and mountain. The garden is full of plants from the countries where we have previously lived and gardened . . . olearias, pittosporums and flaxes from New Zealand; tea berries and diddle-dee from the Falkland Islands.'

Amat

Amat House is a Ross clan chieftain's hunting lodge in typical Victorian style with castellations and a small square tower. The remote setting boasts one of the best bits of relict Caledonian pine forest. The house stands on the River Carron, famous for its salmon fishing, and is surrounded by fine trees underplanted with rhododendrons. There are woodland walks along the river bank and you may be lucky enough to spot foxes, stoats, pine martens and otters and who knows, perhaps escaped animals from Paul Lister's fenced animal park estate next door: moose, wolves, wild boar.

Amat
Ardgay, Sutherland,
IV24 3BS
(*map, pp. 4–5*)

Jonny and Sara Shaw
1 weekend SGS
or by appointment; ££
Off A837, take road from
Ardgay to Croick 9 miles
T: 01863 755320
F: 01863 755320
E: Saraamat@btinternet.com
www.amatsalmon.com

Ardfearn Nursery

Ardfearn Nursery was established in 1987 on the south shore of the Beauly Firth, 4 miles from Inverness, in an old farm; cattle byres and milking sheds were converted to plant sales and production. The nursery was founded by Jim Sutherland and is now headed by his son, Alasdair. The nursery has long been well known for its range of alpines, but they now also grow a huge range of perennials and shrubs as well as bare-rooted hedging and trees in winter. They grow 95% of what they sell on-site and I can't think of anywhere else with this huge range of home-grown stock in this part of Scotland. Alpines are demonstrated in a range of display beds and alpine troughs. Ardfearn also run a gift shop which is eastern and alternative in its range of products. The nursery's mail order is currently suspended, pending broadband connection locally.

Ardfearn Nursery
Bunchrew, by Inverness,
Highland, IV3 8RH
(*map, pp. 4–5*)

Jim and Alasdair Sutherland
Daily: 9am–5pm; free
A862 between Inverness and
Beauly, approximately 4 miles
from Inverness
T: 01463 243250 or
01463 223607.
www.ardfearn-nursery.co.uk/

Biblical Garden, Golspie
Seaforth House, Golspie,
Sutherland, KW10 6RH
(map, pp. 4–5)

Ground owned by
Highland Council
Always open; free
On the main A9 road in Golspie
town centre, opposite the
Orcadian Stone Geology Centre

Biblical Garden, Golspie

One of two biblical gardens in Scotland, this is the better one, a
millennium project created by members of St Andrews Church in
Golspie in the grounds of Seaforth House, an old people's home. The
garden contains biblical references, an open tomb with a large boulder
for example, and has contemporary design touches. It is well
maintained by volunteers co-ordinated by Anne Barclay. Thankfully
the biblical plant connections have been loosely interpreted, as most
of the desert plants of Israel and Egypt don't much care for Scotland's
climate. Jacob's Ladder gets in due to the name, for example, as do
obvious candidates such as *Cercis* (the Judas Tree) and myrtle. When
we visited in June, this was a blaze of colour, with lavender, lupins,
delphiniums, valerian, poppies etc. A stone cross and coloured mosaic
added structure. Designed with good access for wheelchairs along
gravel paths, this is one of the best community-run gardens in
Scotland, definitely well worth a short stop on the A9 or in combination with Dunrobin Castle nearby. The main path provides good
wheelchair access, though the side gravel paths may need assistance.

Brahan
Near Dingwall, IV7 8EE
(map, pp. 4–5)

Mr and Mrs A. Matheson
Dell open year round,
SGS 1 day some years;
Dell free, gardens ££
A835 west from Maryburgh
roundabout, 2 miles,
well-signposted
E: info@brahan.com
www.brahan.com

Brahan

Brahan is a 4,000-acre estate not far from Inverness. The original
house was demolished in the 1950s. It is not a garden as such, but
more a rather wild and overgrown arboretum (the dell) planted along
the driveways, with a collection of fine mature trees, including some
UK champions. Most of the best are conifers: wellingtonia, spruce,
hemlock, *Thuja*, pines etc, and most are labelled. There are also a few
species rhododendrons as well as abundant wildlife/bird life in the
lochs, swamps and alongside the River Conon which runs down to
the Cromarty Firth. The trees would benefit from a bit of work to
remove dead and hanging limbs and there is little sign of recent
planting. Brahan was the home of Scotland's own version of
Nostradamus, Kenneth Mackenzie, known as the Brahan Seer. He
was executed in the seventeenth century for his prophecies and
predictions, many of which have apparently come true. There are
several holiday properties for rent on the estate.

Bridges for Gardens

I can't do better than quote the website for this Inverness business. 'In our 12 years of making bridges we have supplied them to golf courses, fishing lakes, borough councils, Millennium committees, schools and hotels but mainly to private gardens . . . They have been sited over ponds, rivers, streams, ditches, gullies, culverts and flower beds as well as from balconies and patio doors. We have hauled bridges up cliffs, lowered them down cliffs, lifted them over fences and taken them through houses (even via a window). We have been stung (wasps), bitten (Jack Russell and Doberman), immersed (over-enthusiastic helper), sunburnt and frozen but it is still the best job in the world!' The website gives comprehensive information.

Bridges for Gardens
Achnacloich, Kiltarlity,
Inverness-shire, IV4 7JQ

Alan Gough
Visitors to workshop
welcome by appointment
T: 01463 741085 (24 hours)
M: 07787 517 586
E: info@bridgesforgardens.com
www.bridgesforgardens.com

Bught Floral Halls

This park and greenhouse complex opened in 1993, next door to the former Inverness Council nursery. Outdoors there are numerous beds of shrubs, alpines and bedding, raised beds and an impressive wildflower meadow. A training programme for people with learning difficulties is run in the gardens. The most popular attractions are the two linked greenhouses, one, with a sunken walkway, is filled with a fine collection of cacti and related plants, the other, with a more tropical feel, boasts houseplants, bromeliads, a waterfall and ponds filled with Koi carp. Bught is a popular place, with thousands of visitors each year.

Bught Floral Halls
Floral Hall and Training Centre,
Bught Lane, Inverness, IV3 5SS
(*map, pp. 4–5*)

Highland Council
Daily: April–October 10am–5pm,
Nov–March 10am–4pm; £
Follow signs to Fort William/Fort
Augustus from centre of Inverness
on A82 road to the western edge
of town. Turn left just before the
bridge over the Caledonian Canal
T: 01463 713553
www.invernessfloralhall.com
Coffee shop; open April–October
10am–4.30pm; tel. 01463 229778
for groups

Castle and Gardens of Mey
Thurso, Caithness, KW14 8XH
(*map, pp. 4–5*)

The Queen Elizabeth
Castle of Mey Trust
Daily: May–end September
10.30am–4pm, closed first
2 weeks August. SGS open days
several times a year; ££
(castle extra)
Well signposted between
Thurso and John O' Groats
T: 01847 851473
F: 01847 851475
www.castleofmey.org.uk

Castle and Gardens of Mey

The Queen Mother bought this castle on the windswept north coast of Scotland in the early 1950s as a dilapidated ruin. The garden is phased for August and September, when she used to holiday in Caithness. The walled garden, right next to the castle, has a 12ft seaward wall to cut down salt spray and is divided into compartments, with hedges and attractive corner turrets. It is rather a jumble of plants, rhododendrons, roses in island beds, buddlejas, herbaceous, mixed borders and lots of fruit on the walls. There are also fine glasshouses. Outside the walled area in the East Garden are planting of *Fuchsia, Potentilla,* masses of *Astilbe,* impressive drifts of *Primula florindae* and a bed of rugosa roses, with gnarled sycamores providing some wind shelter. The castle is much more of a home than the various royal palaces and the many guides in the rooms will tell you the Queen Mother's story as you go round.

Dunbeath Castle

Dunbeath is one of north Scotland's most exciting recent garden projects and it is being improved and expanded each year. The site is stunning, with the fine gleaming white castle perched on the cliff top, with views out to sea and North Sea oil platforms in the far distance. The tree-lined drive frames the castle from afar as you approach, in a deliberately designed piece of drama by nineteenth-century architect David Bryce, who made alterations to a much older (fourteenth-century) castle. Given Dunbeath's situation, wind is obviously an

issue; the Threiplands report 100-mile-an-hour winds that can blow a human over, so most of the plantings are in the shelter of the 1860 walled garden. A complete design for this was drawn up in 1998 by Chelsea Gold Medallist Xa Tollemache, whose garden at Helmingham in Norfolk had greatly impressed the Threiplands. The plan has been gradually implemented since, though Claire Threipland has been free to add her own touches as the garden has evolved. The garden is reached via an arch which leads to the main axis, consisting of long mirror-planted herbaceous borders running the whole length of the garden. Off this is a series of six garden rooms or compartments on each side, most divided into four squares, each one a contrast to the next, setting up a sense of theatre and surprise. The planting choices are bold and innovative, you won't often see an artichoke and allium combination for example, and some of the colour combinations will take your breath away. Two compartments are filled with vegetables. The various sections are divided by hedges, *Fuchsia magellanica* and others plants, or wrought iron pillars and pergolas. Julie Edmonstone, Scotland inspector for *The Good Gardens Guide*, considers Dunbeath the best designed walled garden in Scotland. The long greenhouse contains houseplants, peaches, figs and apricots. A vantage point to look down on the whole garden is provided by the turret, which also provides a great view of the castle. Gardeners Neil Milman and Kathleen Gunn enjoy talking to visitors and you may even be offered a cup of tea in the potting shed. There are also extensive oriental-style water gardens under construction in the second walled garden, and a wildflower meadow. This looks like 'his' project with an amazing cascade, but it needs a little more design and planning, not to mention planting, to match the other walled garden in effect. This far north, summer is the best time to visit. Open by appointment only.

Dunbeath Castle
Dunbeath Estate Office,
Dunbeath, Caithness, KW6 6ED
(*map, pp. 4–5*)

Mr and Mrs S.W. Murray
Threipland
By appointment only ££
Coming north on A9 the castle entrance is on the right, south of Dunbeath village, just before the bridge
T: 01593 731308
F: 01593 731241
E: enquiries@dunbeathestate.com
www.dunbeath.co.uk

Dunrobin Castle
Golspie, Sutherland,
KW10 6SF
(*map, pp. 4–5*)

Lord Strathnaver
Mid March to mid October:
Monday–Saturday 10.30am–
4.30pm, Sunday 12–4.30pm; £££
castle and gardens
Clearly signed just north of
Golspie on the A9 Inverness–Wick
road, 50 miles north of Inverness
T: 01408 633177
F: 01408 634081
E: info@dunrobincastle.net
www.dunrobincastle.co.uk
Café in the castle

Dunrobin Castle

Dunrobin has probably the most extensive gardens in the north of Scotland, combining formal lines best seen from the castle high above it, and good planting, best appreciated close up. The nineteenth-century castle, over the top by any standards, was remodelled from an older building and designed for the duke of Sutherland by Sir Charles Barry, designer with Pugin of the Houses of Parliament. Inspired by French chateaux, with a Victorian Gothic twist, a hint of Disney and a great deal of profligate extravagance, with 189 rooms (only a few of which are open on the tours), Dunrobin is easily the largest house in northern Scotland. The dukedom once covered 1.3 million acres, from which crofters were evicted in the Highland Clearances in the early nineteenth century and replaced with more lucrative sheep; presumably the proceeds were spent on the house. The instigator of the Clearances, the first duke of Sutherland, managed to have a statue erected to himself with an inscription which was surely written with bitter sarcasm by the 'grateful tenantry', bearing in mind that 15,000 crofters were evicted from his lands. The views from the hills where the monument stands are fine. Barry also designed the formal gardens, which were apparently influenced by those at Versailles and Trentham, near Stoke.

The castle is perched high on the rocks, in front of which a series of steep terraces leads down to the flat lawns and the sea beyond the walls at the bottom. The steep bank covered with scrubby shrubs is a somewhat neglected opportunity. The garden below is divided into two parterres, each laid out around circular fountains, surrounded by mature trees. The parterres are well planted with a succession of colour through the seasons; tulips give way to wallflowers, to summer bedding and fuchsias and in autumn, penstemons and dahlias. Rooms are formed by hedges of *Sorbus* and beech. Step-over

trained apples are used to line some of the parterres, while height is given by wooden wigwams, which echo the turrets and minarets of the castle above, onto which climb roses, clematis and sweet peas. Beneath these are bold borders of *Nepeta, Geranium*, tulips, Asiatic lilies and other perennials and bedding plants, while *Aralia elata* is used as a feature plant. This is an old landscape which is being gardened by Ian Crisp and his team in a contemporary manner. Important, courageous strategic decisions are being made to cut down overgrown parts and replant, which is to be applauded. As Patrick Taylor notes, the parterre looks great from the castle and the castle from the parterre. There are fine snowdrops, daffodils and bluebells in spring. A spectacular castle, good café, odd museum in the summerhouse and falconry displays make Dunrobin a good day out for all the family. The entry price includes the castle, museum and grounds.

Foulis Castle

Foulis Castle, seat of the clan Munro, was built in the eighteenth century when the previous one was burnt down after the 1745 uprising. The policies have spectacular snowdrops, daffodils, some rhododendrons and azaleas and a young arboretum. The main attraction is the two-part courtyard garden on two levels behind the main house. The lower section by the house is paved, and is dominated by shrub roses; the upper section is gravelled with a peony border, perennials and shrubs including some more usually associated with the west coast, such as *Abutilon, Carpenteria, Leptospermum scoparium* and *Olearia* 'Henry Travers'.

Foulis Castle
Evanton, Ross-shire, IV16 9UX
(*map, pp. 4–5*)

Mrs E. Munro of Foulis
By appointment in writing only, and please well in advance.
Just off the A9 south-west of Evanton
T: 01349 830212
F: 01349 830212
www.clanmunro.org.uk/castle.htm

Gardens Scotland and Craigiewood B&B

At their bed and breakfast, Gavin and Araminta Dalmayer are excellent hosts for garden lovers who want somewhere to stay in the north of Scotland. Gavin is a garden designer and keen plantsman who can organise tours to the gardens of northern Scotland or advise you where to go. Araminta is a travel consultant and a cookery demonstrator with Claire Macdonald. Craigiewood can accommodate up to six guests and is situated just north of Inverness, on the Black Isle, within an easy day's driving distance of gardens such as Inverewe, Cawdor and Dunrobin. Tours can be for half or full days or for several days and nights. Gavin can suggest accommodation, arrange and make bookings and pick you up at the place you are staying. The B&B website is *www.craigiewood.co.uk* and *www.gardens-scotland.co.uk* is the garden website.

B&B

Highland Liliums Garden Centre and Nursery

This is both a wholesale nursery and a small garden centre. It no longer specialises in lilies, but rather in a wide range of perennials and alpines which are produced in their own nursery. The garden centre also stocks a fine range of roses, shrubs and trees. It is a bit of a challenge to find it, as it lies down a series of winding single-track lanes, but there are road signs. This is an old-style nursery with a great range of plants and Neil MacRitchie and his staff under Dougie Paterson and Sue Mullins really know what grows well in this part of Scotland. A new shop was built in 2006, making this more like a garden centre.

House of Tongue and Eddie's Garden

One of Scotland's most northerly and isolated gardens, House of Tongue was built by the Mackays in 1678 and 1750 and is the home of the Countess of Sutherland. The key to its success is the walled garden, which provides shelter in an exposed, windy site and it is a pleasant surprise to find this oasis of horticulture on the north coast of Scotland. Gardener Richard Rowe looks after a fine collection of shrub roses and deep herbaceous borders filled with spectacular lupins, peonies, *Geranium, Thalictrum* and bedded-out dahlias. By late June the colour is really getting going and the cool northerly location helps things last well, wind and rain permitting. There is also an orchard, a glasshouse with pelargoniums and a terrace. Another

House of Tongue

surprise awaits at the end of the drive: Sinclair Cottage is the home of Eddie Mackie, a retired bus driver who rescued the derelict small walled garden by the stable block in the early 1990s and turned it into a charming labour of love, full of herbaceous, annuals, a small pond and a homemade greenhouse, almost overwhelmed with cascades of colour. Eddie does not open as such but he has said that visitors to House of Tongue are welcome to come by and have a look.

Hugh Miller Museum and Birthplace

One of eastern Scotland's most attractive villages with many beautifully restored houses, Cromarty was formerly a thriving trading port, specialising in salted fish. Hugh Miller was a Scottish Victorian stonemason, amateur geologist and fundamentalist Christian, whose writings aggressively rejected Darwin's theories of evolution and who was one of the founders of the breakaway Free Presbyterian Church of Scotland. Lionised by some and condemned by others, he remains a controversial if fascinating figure; he took his own life in 1856. He was born in Cromarty and his thatched cottage birthplace and three-storey Georgian house next door are now a museum run by the National Trust for Scotland which contains a large collection of Hugh's fossils and other artefacts. The Friends of Hugh Miller, founded in 2006, helped raise the funds for the tiny contemporary courtyard/garden next to the museum known as 'Miller's Yard' which features stone carvings and ferns and is designed to be used as an

Hugh Miller Museum and Birthplace
Hugh Miller Museum and Birthplace Cottage, Church Street, Cromarty, Inverness, IV11 8XA
(*map, pp. 4–5*)

NTS
21 March–30 September: 1–5pm; 1–31 October: 1–5pm; ££*
Signposted in Cromarty
T: 0844 4932158
E: mgostwick@nts.org.uk
www.nts.org.uk and
www.hughmiller.org

outdoor classroom. The garden of the cottage next door is designated a wildlife garden of native plants. It was a flattened mess of weeds when I visited in July. For further information on Hugh Miller, look at the website *www.hughmiller.org*.

Langwell Lodge
Berriedale, Caithness,
KW7 6HD
(*map, pp. 4–5*)

The Lady Anne Bentinck
SGS 2 days in August and
by appointment; ££
Turn off the A9 just south of
Berriedale, signed to Aultbea
and Wag
T: 01593 751278

Langwell Lodge

One of northern Scotland's outstanding gardens, Langwell is planned to peak from late July to September for the shooting season. Gardener Francis Higgins, on the verge of retiring after 25 years, has done an excellent job here. The garden is reached along a very long single-track drive and lies in a sheltered valley and is far enough from the coast to suffer from spring frosts which can singe the *Rodgersia*, hostas and other soft growth. The walled garden is crammed full of plants spilling out onto the paths with abandon. There are trained fruit trees on the walls and box-edged rose beds. Garden rooms are divided by yew hedging, with *Tropaeolum* growing through it, leading to a formal pond at the bottom end. Recent developments include a fine herb garden and there is a collection of cacti and succulents in the greenhouse. There are some uncommon plants such as *Paradisea* and *Bulbinella* for the enthusiast to enjoy. It is well worth making a detour to see this in late summer, but phone first to make an appointment.

Novar

Novar house is an imposing 1760 mansion above the Cromarty Firth. The huge (5-acre) walled garden, with a gardener's cottage set into the wall, is divided into two, with three impressive arches under one of which a long border of *Aruncus, Hosta* and *Alchemilla* runs the width of the garden. The eastern half has an oval pool filled with Koi carp, and a large lawn used for weddings, while the western part contains vegetables, trees and a croquet lawn. The extensive water gardens to the west of the house were created by the present owner's father, who loved hydraulic engineering and was said to be able to make 'water flow uphill'. A series of natural ponds are linked with waterfalls and steps, now somewhat over-shaded, but with impressive *Gunnera, Rodgersia*, rhododendrons, maples and two follies. There is also a lochan in the parkland. The Fyrish Monument, a folly with several arches on the hill behind Evanton, was built by Hector Munro in 1792 to commemorate one of his military victories in India. It is quite a climb though pine woods to reach it.

Langwell Lodge

Novar
Evanton, Ross-shire,
IV16 9XL
(*map, pp. 4–5*)

Mr and Mrs Ronald
Munro Ferguson
SGS 1 day in June.
Groups by appointment; ££
A9, passing Storehouse of Foulis,
then turn left on B817 to Evanton.
Continue through the village
T: 01349 831062
F: 01349 830880
E: enquiries@novarestate.co.uk
www.novarestate.co.uk

Old Orchard (The)
Miller Road, Cromarty, Black Isle,
IV11 8XJ
(*map, pp. 4–5*)

Ken and Kristina Dupar
Open to small groups by
appointment
Cromarty High Street eastwards,
turn right, continue to the end of
Shore Street, left to Miller Road,
right onto the Causeway. Park in
lay-by or car park above bowling
green on left
E: kdupar@ecosse.net
www.spanglefish.com/OldOrchard

Old Orchard (The)

The 'Old Orchard' surrounds Cromarty's oldest inhabited dwelling house, part of which dates back to c. 1690. The vast walled garden originally belonged to Cromarty House, which lies to the south. The old orchard is formed from the eastern section of the old garden and forms a handsome enclosure around the beautifully restored house. When the Dupars bought the property, the garden was a grassy meadow with a few old apple trees. They found metal apple labels on the walls which had belonged to long dead trees and they decided to attempt to replant the historical apple collection. The spoil from constructing a pond and patio was used to create a series of undulating mounds and former Moray Parks boss Donald McBean advised the Dupars on the initial plantings. The garden is a fine mix of tasteful contemporary work such as the summer house and ponds and more traditional plantings of conifers and heathers. An outstanding area is the dry stone wall terrace and raised bed herb garden on the slope between the house and the garages. The Dupars have created an idyll here and have clearly enjoyed the whole process, taking great pleasure in showing us round. They welcome groups of visitors by appointment.

Poyntzfield Herb Nursery

This is a long-established nusery, founded by Duncan Ross over 30 years ago, long before the current vogue for herb growing. Duncan is primarily concerned with the healing properties of the plants, the ornamental properties are an added bonus. The catalogue lists up to 450 herbs, grown under organic and biodynamic principles. The range includes British natives and others from further afield, including India, Nepal and Sikkim and more recently from Japan (Kanpo tradition). Some of the very toxic plants such as *Aconitum* are used for homeopathic remedies, and herbal medicine workshops are held at the nursery. Duncan Ross has produced three booklets: *Growers' Guide to Herb Gardening* is a useful guide to herbs and their use, *Herbs of the Highlands and Islands of Scotland* details traditional uses for native plants, many of which are on sale. The latest is *Herbs of the Himalaya and India* and follows Duncan's work collecting herbs in Asia. Mail order operates all year round and they sell both small plants and seeds. The walled garden of the imposing pink Poyntzfield House is divided into sections by yew hedges and contains impressive long beds containing the stock plants of the herbs sold by the nursery. This is the key place of pilgrimage in Scotland for anyone interested in herbs.

Poyntzfield Herb Nursery
Near Balblair, Black Isle, Dingwall,
Ross and Cromarty, IV7 8LX
(*map, pp. 4–5*)

Duncan Ross
1 March to 30 September:
Monday–Saturday 1–5pm;
May–August also Sunday 1–5pm
B9163 to Cromarty, turn right after
junction with the B9160 just
before Jemimaville
T: 01381 610352
E: info@poyntzfieldherbs.co.uk
www.poyntzfieldherbs.co.uk

Reelig Glen
Moniack, Beauly,
Inverness IV5 7PQ
(*map, pp. 4–5*)

Forestry Commission
Free
1 mile off the A862 Inverness–
Beauly road, c. 8 miles west
of Inverness. Leave the A862,
signposted Moniack and Clunes.
Bus service to the Old North
Inn on A862

Reelig Glen

Known as the 'tall trees walk', this woodland contains Dughall Mor, a
64-metre Douglas fir, the tallest tree in Britain (and possibly the tallest
in Europe) which is one of a group of trees over 55m tall. Other fine
trees include the beech glade planted in 1870, known as the
'Cathedral'. There are great views from the viewpoint off the higher
path. The Moniack winery is nearby.

Sandside

This garden demonstrates what a walled garden and a good shelter
belt of trees will allow to be grown, even on the north coast of
Scotland, where 100-mile-an-hour winds are not uncommon. The
Minters moved here in 1994 and created the garden out of a field,
constructing a low-walled sunken garden (to keep it out of the wind),
well designed around two circular lawns, with small beds in the
centre. Around these are wide herbaceous borders, with further beds
against the walls. Bedding is used to fill in and create bold drifts of
colour. The ground rises outside the garden, allowing good vantage
points to appreciate the design. From the house there are views out
towards Orkney. Escallonia is used here as an ornamental and
effective windbreak.

Sandside
Reay, Sutherland KW14 7DF
(*map, pp. 4–5*)

Mr and Mrs Geoffrey Minter
By Appointment.
Along the A836, c. 10 miles
west of Thurso, just west of
the Dounreay Nuclear Power
Station
T: 01847 811 540

Orkney

Though Orkney does not have any famous must-see gardens, some of them are charming, Elaine Bullard MBE has probably had the most influence on Orkney gardens in her work on native plants, her journalism and in providing invaluable advice on gardening in Orkney's wet and windy climate. She famously conducted her research into Orkney's flora in her three-wheeler Reliant Robin.

Balfour Castle, Shapinsay

Balfour Castle Gardens
Isle of Shapinsay,
Orkney, KW17 2DY
(*map, pp. 4–5*)

Mrs Zawadzki, Patricia Lidderdale
May–September: Sunday tour
from Kirkwall 2.15–5.30pm, hotel
guests can visit anytime. Castle on
market 2008–09 so arrangements
may change. Ferry, tour and tea
£20 (£10 children).
Take the Shapinsay ferry from
Kirkwall Harbour, Mainland,
Orkney, (25 minutes)
The castle is a one-minute drive
from Shapinsay Pier
T: 01856 711282
F: 01856 711283
E: balfourcastle@btinternet.com
www.balfourcastle.co.uk
Restaurant; home-baked Orcadian
tea part of tour.

Balfour Castle Gardens

This is the largest garden and most extensive policies in Orkney. The impressive castle, built in 1847–48 by David Bryce, is clearly visible from the ferry crossing to Shapinsay and even from Kirkwall itself. The castle, now a hotel, is set in Orkney's largest mixed woodland of 30 acres, planted in c. 1800 with sycamore, horse chestnut, alder, larch, rowan, whitebeam, willow and elm with a few beech. There are carpets of bluebells in spring. A tree-lined path, with herbaceous at the base, leads to the two large walled squares, one to the north of the other with some greenhouses in various states of order, sheds and old cottages as well as an impressive corner bed of candelabra primulas and poppies in June. The Victorian kitchen garden provides fruit and vegetables for the hotel and has impressive espaliered apples on the walls. The garden and buildings could clearly do with some renovation. The castle has a fine conservatory planted with honey-suckle, jasmine and pelargoniums. This is a great base for bird watching and exploring the sea caves. On Sundays there is a return trip to Balfour from Kirkwall at 2.15pm, including afternoon tea, tour and entry to the gardens. As we went to press the castle was to be put up for sale, so future arrangements may change.

Happy Valley
Happy Valley, Orkney
Stenness, Orkney
(*map, pp. 4–5*)

Orkney Islands Council
Open access; free
No signs, no directions but ask
any locals and they'll probably
guide you to the entrance

Happy Valley

The story of Orkney's secret garden is a modern-day Victorian fairytale. Gunner and electrical engineer Edwin Harrold took up residence in an old stone cottage with a heather roof at Bankburn in 1948 on an 'unofficial basis'. The cottage had no power or running water; later Edwin managed to rig up a car battery to run some headlights to illuminate the cottage, which he warmed by burning peat. He set to work transforming the barren hill and burnside into a secluded, wooded glen. Not content with planting trees, including

Araucaria, oak, lime, *Nothofagus*, hazel, juniper, flowers and carpets of bluebells, he also set to building bridges, grottoes and paths, sometimes blasting with dynamite to achieve his aims. No one gave him permission and nobody stopped his work. Locals of all ages came to love the place and Edwin's fame grew. Christopher Lloyd came to see him in the 1970s. Before he died, aged 97 in 2005, he made clear his wish that his 'Happy Valley' be preserved for locals to enjoy. It turned out that the land was part of Ibster Estates, and Professor William Ibster agreed to donate the land with additional fields to the council. An unofficial Friends group has planted a further 800 trees. Edwin's house is now completely derelict, with trees growing out of it. Locals Jenny Taylor and Christine Skene and the garden's 'Friends' seem determined to ensure that Edwin Harrold's amazing landscape is preserved. Time will tell how they get on.

Happy Valley

Kierfiold House

It's a very pleasant surprise to stumble across this fine garden surrounded by magnificent but somewhat bleak Orcadian moorland. Behind the stone walls and the low hedges of rose and sycamore is a Victorian garden absolutely crammed with old trees, shrub roses, fuchsias, grasses, poppies, *Kniphofia, Meconopsis,* with lovely low dry stone walls spilling over with treasures such as *Celmisia*. The garden is overlooked by a Victorian house which offers bed and breakfast, and enjoys panoramic views over the Loch of Harray and to the rounded hills beyond. A field known as 'the paddock' next to the house provides an impressive display of daffodils, primroses, cowslips and wild orchids. While southerners might not appreciate the garden, it is outstanding for this part of the world, with Orkney's wind and cool summers to contend with. Skara Brae is nearby and you may catch a glimpse of rare Scottish native *Primula scotica* on the seashore.

Kierfiold House
Sandwick, Orkney, KW16 3JE
(*map, pp. 4–5*)

Euan and Fiona Smith
Daily: 9am–5pm; £
Leaving Stromness turn left onto the A967/A966 signposted to Sandwick. Continue for 3 miles and when you arrive at the junction, go straight ahead on B9056 to Skara Brae. At the edge of the loch take the 2nd right onto B9057 to Dounby. Go up the hill and Kierfiold House is on your left
T: 01856 841583
E: euan@kierfiold-house.co.uk

Melsetter House

Melsetter House
Hoy, Orkney
(map, pp. 4–5)

Elsie Seater
March–October: Thursday and
Sunday strictly by appointment,
the house, chapel and gardens.
On south side of Hoy, reached
by B9047 from the ferry
which docks at Lyness
T: 01856 791352

This is one of Orkney's most significant houses, built in 1898 on the island of Hoy with the profits from the manufacture (in Birmingham) of bicycle seats. The Middlemores, who built Melsetter, were disciples of William Morris and commissioned architect William Lethaby to build the house around a paved courtyard in Arts and Crafts style. The Seater family, who now own Melsetter, have been restoring the house, chapel and gardens, which are open by appointment in summer. Landscape components include a kitchen garden, rose garden and walled garden as well as woodlands. The high walls keep out the wind, so the conditions are ideal for growing a wide range of plants. Melsetter can be combined with a visit to The Old Man of Hoy; follow the path from the village of Rackwick in the north of the island.

Schoolquoy

Schoolquoy
Scorradale Road, Orphir,
Orkney, KW17 2RF
(map, pp. 4–5)

Alan and Brenda Clouston
Early June to end August:
Thursday–Monday 12–5pm
(closed Tuesday/Wednesday)
or by appointment; £
Off A964, on the south side of
Scorrabrae hill in Orphir
T: 01856 811293

This garden, at the back of an old school, overlooking spectacular Scapa Flow, was started 20 years ago on a windswept site by first creating a shelterbelt of *Fuchsia* and terracing the steep slopes with stone walling, creating beds planted with annuals and a rock garden packed with alpines, which are positioned around a circular lawn. Pots, statues and benches are placed round the garden and there is also a rectangular pond. The garden was first opened in 2007 and was popular with visitors so the openings seem set to continue, with plants offered for sale to visitors.

Tankerness House Gardens, Orkney Museum

You'll find this popular small garden/park behind the Orkney Museum in Kirkwall, accessible via the museum itself. Essentially it's a large courtyard with a lawn in the centre and a range of trees, shrubs (lots of spiky things in particular) and herbaceous beds planted mainly around the edges. It is a popular spot for lunchtime sandwich eating. It is dominated by Gow's Folly, also known as the 'Groatie House' because of the shells which decorate it, a tall narrow pyramidal structure which looks like a lopped-off church steeple and was built out of ships' ballast of volcanic rock. It was moved here from another site in Kirkwall in 2005. The pile of rocks in one corner look as though they are in search of a rock garden. I understand that they may have been left over from building St Magnus Cathedral. The greenhouses are used by the local authority.

Tankerness House Gardens, Orkney Museum
Broad Street, Kirkwall, Orkney. KW15 1DH
(*map, pp. 4–5*)

Orkney Islands Council
Museum: May–September
10.30am–5pm, October–April
closed 12–1pm. Gardens: daylight hours; free
In the centre of Kirkwall opposite St Magnus Cathedral
T: 01856 873535
F: 01856 871560
E: museum@orkney.gov.uk
www.orkney.gov.uk

Trumland House Gardens

The tall, imposing 1876 Trumland House, clearly visible from the ferry to Rousay, was built by General Sir Frederick William Traill Burroughs, quite probably the most hated landlord in Orkney history due to his attempts to 'clear' the island of crofters in the 1880s. In the end the government intervened on behalf of the crofters. Trumland House was purchased, more or less as a burnt-out ruin, by the Greggs in 2001 and both house and garden are under much-needed restoration. The garden falls into two parts. The woodland garden has a birdcage-like white gazebo from which there are good views up the burn. A castellated arch and some fine new gates here lead into the walled garden, made from attractive pale local stone. Structure is provided by wigwams to support climbers and trellis sections, and

Trumland House Gardens
Trumland House, Rousay, Orkney KW17 2PU
(*map, pp. 4–5*)

Brian and Elaine Gregg
May–October: Monday–Friday
10am–5pm, other times by appointment; £
Island of Rousay. Ferry from Tingwall on West Mainland.
House is a 10 minute walk up from the Rousay ferry terminal
T: 01856 821322
F: 01856 821322

25

though the planting is young, the garden is maturing well. Trumland Farm Hostel, Cottage and Camp Site are a few minutes away. Rousay has many ancient brochs and cairns (160 sites in all), as well as excellent bird watching.

Woodwick House
Evie, Orkney, KW17 2PQ
(*map, pp. 4–5*)

James Bryan (manager)
Open to residents or by
appointment; free
From Kirkwall or Stromness,
A965 to Finstown; take A966
north towards Evie. After 7 miles
take next right after Tingwall ferry
turning, then first left all the way
down the track to the house
amongst trees.
T: 01856 751330
F: 01856 751383
E: mail@woodwickhouse.co.uk
www.woodwickhouse.co.uk
Restaurant

Woodwick House

This popular Orkney hotel is famous for the 12 acres of sycamore woodland and bluebells, unique on these windswept islands, through which passes an attractive burn rushing down to the sea over stepped waterfalls. There are stone benches and some giant fuchsias which flower all summer. The rocky shore is an ideal location for bird and seal watching. Next to the house is a perennial and shrub garden dominated by a round raised, white-walled pond which is not really a thing of beauty. The wedding chapel, converted from a doocot, is wonderful, complete with ivy which has invaded from the walls outside and hangs inside like a leafy veil.

Shetland

Despite the challenges of the climate: lack of summer heat, almost constant wind and very acidic soil, there are some fine gardens on Shetland: Lea Gardens and Da Gairdins are probably the most significant but there are several others well worth popping into if you are touring the islands.

Da Gairdins, Sand, Bixter

Burravoe Haa

Overlooking the sheltered harbour on the Shetland island of Yell, the striking whitewashed Old Haa of Brough, built in 1672, is now a museum. The garden alongside was planted and tended until recently by Mary Ellen Odie, whose late brother was the well-known Shetland naturalist Bobby Tulloch. As well as a good selection of plants such as hardy geraniums, lilies and poppies, there are some curious artefacts including a propeller rescued from a crashed aircraft. Yell is said to be the best place in Britain for spotting otters.

Da Gairdins

Despite Shetland's challenging gardening climate, Alan and Ruby Inkster have embarked on an ambitious project on their site, a 7-acre garden and woodland with fine views out to the neighbouring islands. The key to gardening here is wind shelter and a woodland of Sitka spruce has been augmented with other trees including poplars and willows, which has created enough of a wind barrier to plant rhododendrons and other woodland plants, many of which are now doing well. A series of ponds is designed to attract wildlife and are surrounded by a number of New Zealand native plants such as *Olearia* which the Inksters grew from their own seed collections. Sensibly, they have concentrated on genera which thrive in the conditions here: *Phormium tenax* (huge towering clumps), Pampas grass and a large collection of *Hebe* are all settling in very well. *Aronia*, with its flaming autumn colour, is another rarely seen shrub which seems to love Shetland. The key here will be whether the drainage is good enough to avoid prolonged waterlogging, which is fatal to so many plants in this challenging climate. The almost constant wind, very acid soggy soil and a lack of summer heat combine to cause many otherwise hardy plants to fail in Shetland. This garden will hopefully inspire other Shetlanders to give more ambitious gardening a go. If you can establish shelter, it is amazing what can be achieved. Note that there are unfenced ponds here, so please supervise all young children.

Garden and Ecological Trail, Shetland (Gaets)

A developing school and community garden with links into a network of footpaths leading to other areas of interest in this part of Shetland. Links with RSPB and SNH; planting has involved local residents, Sandwick Primary School, the local girl guides and the football club.

Hillswick Health Centre Gardens

This award-winning community garden on the side of Ura Firth was instigated in 1988 by Dr Susan Bowie, whose husband Tom Morton has a daily show on Radio Scotland, broadcast from Shetland. It incorporates traditional flowers, medicinal herbs and dry stone dykes. A few years later, another garden area was added when the Shetland Conservation Volunteers planted trees and flowers.

Hillswick Health Centre Gardens
West Ayre, Hillswick,
Shetland, ZE2 9RW
(*map, pp. 4–5*)

A970 to Hillswick from Brae

Lea Gardens

Rosa Steppanova is well known in Shetland for her forthright gardening columns in the *Shetland Times* and her book *The Impossible Garden*, which describes the triumphs and tribulations of gardening in one of Britain's more challenging climates. She and her husband Jamie McKenzie, the tree warden of Shetland, have created Lea Gardens, which may be accorded the status of the UK's most northerly Botanic Garden, around their croft near Tresta, not far from Lerwick airport. They have spent the last 20 or more years rewriting the rule-book on what exactly hardiness means in a climate like this, with cool summers, almost constant wind and salt spray, as they are only 200m from the sea. Robert McNeil from the *Scotsman* writes: 'Here, gardening is more battle than hobby. Here, you need optimism, energy and a determination not to get downhearted. Rosa Steppanova has these qualities by the barrowload.' And that is certainly true: the number of plants which have been killed over the years is enough to have put most gardeners off years ago. Scores of so-called 'hardy' plants were soon added to the compost and lots of 'that will never grow here' plants are thriving. Rosa has persevered, and she has proved without doubt that providing wind shelter and sharp drainage are the most important factors. Lea Gardens is particularly suited to plants from southern New Zealand islands, Tasmania and southern Chile where the cool, windy climate is comparable. Extremely rare New Zealand megaherb *Bulbinella rossii* is successful here and Rosa plans to use her garden as a conservation centre for

Lea Gardens
Tresta, Shetland ZE2 9LT
(*map, pp. 4–5*)

Rosa Steppanova
and Jamie McKenzie
March–October: 6 days a week,
closed Thursday; ££
At Tresta, north-west of Lerwick
on the A971, 5 miles from
Shetland airport
T: 01595 810454

these hard-to-please, little known plants. Apart from the 1,500 species of plants, the garden contains Rosa's sculptures, often made from things washed up on the beach such as fishing nets. The 'ship' at the garden entrance is a spectacular example. You will doubtless also meet the collection of dogs and cats. Rosa corresponded with many gardening gurus such as Derek Jarman and Christopher Lloyd, and probably no one knows more about what to grow and how to grow it in Shetland. Surplus plants are offered for sale.

Voe House

Voe House
Walls, West Mainland, Shetland
(map, pp. 4–5)

1 April–30th September
(or by arrangement)
Off the A971 Tresta to Sandness
road signed to Walls
T: 01595 693434
E: info@visitshetland.com

Overlooking the picturesque village of Walls, Voe House is a restored 'Böd' or bothy formerly used to house fishermen and their gear during the fishing season. It has been restored using recycled building materials. You can stay in it but need to bring your own bedding and cooking equipment (contact VisitShetland, Market Cross, Lerwick, ZE1 0LU). The garden, planted and looked after by the Shetland Amenity Trust, is built around a cobbled circle, sheltered by ruined walls, and contains a good selection of Shetland good-doer plants, a laburnum walk, Alaskan-origin trees, herbs, vegetables and soft fruit.

Right. Voe House

Weisdale Kirk

Weisdale Kirk
Weisdale, Mainland,
Shetland, ZE2 9LW
(map, pp. 4–5)

On the A9075, just off the A971

Weisdale Kirk, formerly 'The Free Kirk', was built in 1863 and in recent years the gentle slopes at one end of the church have been made into a community garden with meandering gravel paths. With help and advice from Rosa Steppanova, the terraced garden has a good range of native plants, grasses, alpines, bulbs, and *Darmera* by the stream. The garden is looked after by local volunteers. Nearby, the head of Weisdale Voe is an excellent bird-watching site, while 1855 Weisdale Mill contains a fine arts and crafts gallery and a café.

North-West:
West Sutherland, Skye and Outer Hebrides

Gardens on the mainland are few and far between in this part of Scotland but there are some fine gardens here: Attadale, Inverewe, House of Gruinard, Dundonnell House and Kerrachar form a chain through some of Britain's finest scenery. Gardens not covered in separate entries in this book, which open some years under SGS include Ben View, Lochyside; Bluebell Croft, Strontian; Camusdarach, Arisaig; and Spean Bridge gardens.

Inverewe Gardens, Poolewe

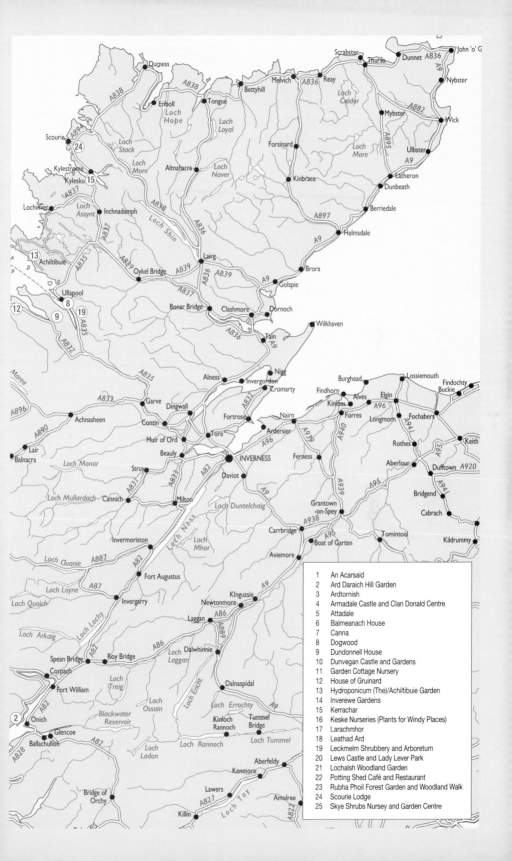

1   An Acarsaid
2   Ard Daraich Hill Garden
3   Ardtornish
4   Armadale Castle and Clan Donald Centre
5   Attadale
6   Balmeanach House
7   Canna
8   Dogwood
9   Dundonnell House
10 Dunvegan Castle and Gardens
11 Garden Cottage Nursery
12 House of Gruinard
13 Hydroponicum (The)/Achiltibuie Garden
14 Inverewe Gardens
15 Kerrachar
16 Keske Nurseries (Plants for Windy Places)
17 Larachmhor
18 Leathad Ard
19 Leckmelm Shrubbery and Arboretum
20 Lews Castle and Lady Lever Park
21 Lochalsh Woodland Garden
22 Potting Shed Café and Restaurant
23 Rubha Phoil Forest Garden and Woodland Walk
24 Scourie Lodge
25 Skye Shrubs Nursery and Garden Centre

An Acarsaid
Ord, Sleat, Isle of Skye,
IV44 8RN
(*map, pp. 32–33*)

Mrs Eileen MacInnes
April–October: 10am–5.30pm;
donations (SGS)
Take A851 from Broadford or
Armadale. Ord is signposted
5 miles from Armadale

An Acarsaid

This quirky garden lies a few miles down a single-track road off the Kyle–Armadale road. My wife Jane nicknamed it 'a garden for trolls or pixies' due to the extraordinary cobbled paths, steps and walls which lead around the garden, built by the late Mr MacInnes. The 2-acre garden is perched on cliffs above the shore of Loch Eishort, and if you are lucky with the weather you'll get stunning views to the Cuillins. This is a mixed garden with perennials and grasses around the house and shrubs and trees around the viewpoint. Don't miss the skeleton by the entrance, which according to the label was a cousin of the Loch Ness Monster.

Ard Daraich Hill Garden
Ardgour, Fort William,
Inverness-shire, PH33 7AB
(*map, pp. 32–33*)

Norrie and Anna Maclaren
££
On the A861 north of Corran
ferry. Unless coming from the
north-west, you will likely arrive
from the Corran ferry, which
is reached from the A82
T: 01855 841 384
E: annaraven@btinternet.com
www.arddaraich.co.uk

Ard Daraich Hill Garden

Ard Daraich was the holiday home of food guru Constance Spry before becoming the home of David Maclaren and Lady Edith. It is now the home of their son Norrie and his wife Anna. The 8–9-acre woodland/hillside garden, with steep paths and steps, contains a good collection of rhododendrons, trees and shrubs including *Acer, Styrax, Davidia, Liquidamber* and *Stachyurus* and large collections of *Camellia* and *Sorbus*. The garden is still being expanded up the rocky hillside. There are some plants for sale and a range of home produce from the Constance Spry 'bible'.

B&B WC

Ardtornish

This remote garden on the Ardtornish estate on the Morvern peninsula has been owned by the Smith/Raven family since the 1930s and is created from 28 acres of rocky hillside. Most reach it by taking the short hop over via the Corran ferry from the A82. The garden can also be reached from the Mull ferry from Fishnish to Lochaline. The season begins in March with drifts of daffodils and early rhododendrons. The extensive collection of species and hybrid rhododendrons reaches a peak in May, with azaleas, *Embothrium* and candelabra primulas in early June. Late summer highlights include a group of *Eucryphia* 'Nymansay' and a fine *Hoheria lyallii* as well as scented white *Rhododendron* 'Polar Bear'. Skunk cabbage (*Lysichiton*) runs riot here in boggy areas and stream sides. The well-loved Ardtornish walled garden nursery run by Ian and Helen Lamb is now closed down as they have retired. Faith Raven lives at Ardtornish and has overseen the garden's development for many years. Her son Andrew Raven was an important figure in Scottish land reform and conservation/stewardship before his death from cancer at the age of 46. Andrew's sister is the well-known garden writer and broadcaster Sarah Raven, while another sister, Anna Raven/Maclaren gardens nearby at Ard Daraich. The Victorian castellated Ardtornish house is now divided into flats. There are fine views along Loch Aline.

Ardtornish
Lochaline, Morvern,
by Oban, Argyll, PA34 5UZ
(*map, pp. 32–33*)

Mrs John Raven
Daily: 1 March–30 November:
8am–8pm; ££
From A82 via Corran ferry to
A861, turning left before Strontian
onto A884, signposted Lochaline.
Entrance to estate two miles
before Lochaline village. Entrance
to garden from Estate Yard
T: 01967 421288
F: 01967 421211
E: tourism@ardtornish.co.uk
www.ardtornishgardens.co.uk
Whitehouse Restaurant in
Lochaline nearby.

Armadale Castle and Clan Donald Centre

The extensive gardens and grounds at Armadale belong to a house which is now little more than a shell, burnt out in a fire in 1855, partly replaced by David Bryce and then abandoned again in the 1920s. The ruined house is a strange and depressing place, with staircases going nowhere and weeds all over the ground floor. Katie Campbell comments that Armadale is 'not so much a garden as the corporate headquarters of the Clan Donald'. The grounds hold the Museum of

**Armadale Castle and
Clan Donald Centre**
Armadale, Sleat,
Isle of Skye, IV45 8RS
(*map, pp. 32–33*)

Clan Donald Lands Trust
April–October:
daily 9.30am–5.30pm; ££
Via the Skye Bridge at Kyle of
Lochalsh, 14 miles south of
Broadford, along A851 at
south end of Skye. Ferry
to/from Mallaig nearby
T: 01471 844305
F: 01471 844275
E: office@clandonald.com
www.clandonald.com
80-seat restaurant

Armadale Castle

the Isles, opened in 2002, which details Skye's history, including much mismanagement and cruelty (runrig agriculture, clearances etc) by its wealthy landowners, including the lairds of Armadale. The 20,000-acre Armadale Estate was put up for sale in 1971 and was purchased by the wealthy MacDonald diaspora, forming the Clan Donald Trust. The 40 acres of woodland garden are based around a nineteenth-century collection of exotic trees and much of the garden has been restored. New features include the fine ponds, rockery, herbaceous borders and terrace walk with shapely urns planted with *Aeonium* succulents. There are 4 miles of nature trails and good views across to Mallaig and Knoydart. The prairie-style plantings of billowing grasses and black-purple *Phormium* around the museum are striking.

   WC

Attadale
Strathcarron, Wester Ross,
Ross-shire, IV54 8YX
(*map, pp. 32–33*)

Nicky MacPherson, Geoff
Stephenson (gardener)
April–October: Monday–
Saturday; ££
On the A890 between
Strathcarron and South Strome
T: 01520 722603
F: 01520 722603
E: geoffattgdns@yahoo.co.uk
www.attadale.com
DIY tea, coffee, reading room;
restaurant 1 mile away

Attadale

This is an excellent west coast garden with the usual woodland and rhododendrons of course, but lots more besides. Attadale has been gardened over 300 years and has passed through the hands of several families including that of Hamburg banker Baron Henry Schroeder, who planted trees and rhododendrons, some of which are now towering specimens. The severe storms of the early 1980s, which felled many of the mature trees, were the catalyst for much of the garden's more recent development, with advice from Michael Innes (then at the National Trust for Scotland) and Professor Douglas Henderson from the Royal Botanic Garden in Edinburgh, and Inverewe. Attadale is now a 'woodland' garden, largely without the woodland overhead,

and all the better for it. The increased light allows perennials, wild flowers, bulbs and weed-smothering ground cover to thrive under the rhododendrons, trees and shrubs. The linear water garden which starts near the entrance is well planted with several species of *Gunnera* and the usual waterside favourites: *Astilbe, Iris, Rodgersia, Primula,* backed by rhododendrons and maples, connected by several curved bridges. Through the rhododendron walk the path leads to a viewpoint with vistas over Attadale house west via Loch Carron to Skye. Behind the house in a bothy there is a self-service coffee machine, picnic tables and lots of useful information on the garden's history. Beyond this lies the vegetable garden with raised beds and one of the many sculptures to be found here, a slate urn by Joe Smith from Dumfries who also made the obelisk by the sunken garden. From here you can't miss the geodesic dome which houses some tender tree ferns which were donated by Peter Hainsworth. Passing some giant rhododendrons, the path leads round to the Japanese garden with statues, azaleas and conifers. I really liked the stone paving and gravel patterning. Returning in front of the house, the path reaches the sunken garden with summer colour from perennials and roses. Attadale is a fine garden, full of singular ideas and surprises and good planting, created by the team of owner Nicky MacPherson and skilled head gardener Geoff Stephenson. Plenty of helpful labelling and carefully planned planting for year-round interest makes this one of the west coast's best private gardens. Attadale is a model of how good interpretation (guidebook, wall displays and labelling) can greatly add to the value and enjoyment of a garden.

Balmeanach House
Struan, Dunvegan,
Isle of Skye, IV56 8FH
(*map, pp. 32–33*)

Mrs Arlene MacPhie
end April–mid October:
Wednesday and Saturday
11am–4.30pm; ££ (SGS)
Off the A863 between Dunvegan
and Struan (5 miles from each),
sign for B&B, a mile up the
rough road on left
T: 01470 572320
E: info@skye-holiday.com
www.skye-holiday.com

Balmeanach House

At first sight, this small croft garden does not seem to amount to much. It is a series of small enclosures with hedges of *Olearia* and *Fuchsia* with perennials, bulbs and shrubs and some small ponds. It takes skill to establish anything up here on heather moorland: shelter belts and improved drainage are essential before most plants will survive at all. This is a good garden to visit if you are struggling to establish plants in similar conditions: many of Skye's croft houses with their sea views have similar problems with wind and salt spray. It is probably worth talking to Mrs MacPhie who also sells 'Plants 'n Stuff' at the Atholl Service Station, Main Road, Dunvegan, which is open 8am–8pm Monday–Saturday and 10am–5pm on Sundays.

Canna
Isle of Canna,
West-Coast Islands, PH44
(*map, pp. 32–33*)

NTS
Open all year, daily
Year-round sailings on CALMAC
ferry services from Mallaig,
6 days per week
T: 0844 4932242
www.nts.org.uk
Harbour View Tearoom
and Craft Shop

Canna

The Isle of Canna, 4½ miles long and 1 mile wide, is one of the Small Isles (Eigg, Rhum, Canna, Muck and Heisgeir), lying south of Skye and west of Mallaig, north-west of Rhum. In 1981 John Lorne Campbell and his wife Margaret Fay Shaw gifted the Isle of Canna to the National Trust for Scotland. The John Lorne Campbell Archive of island and Gaelic culture will be housed in Canna House, built by Donald McNeil in the 1860s, which lies in the centre of the existing 2-acre walled garden. The garden, divided into sections with hedges of *Fuchsia, Escallonia* and *Olearia,* was in a pretty bad state when Neil Baker took over in 2008. He has recently been appointed gardener, funded for two years by a donation from an American benefactor. He spent 2008 recovering the structure of the garden from the undergrowth, including the rope-edged paths, and has begun to produce fruit and vegetables for the community. There are 40 fruit trees in various states of health and features revealed include an *Escallonia* arch with views down the bay to Rhum. Canna has a population of around 20 people and it remains to be seen how sustainable the island will prove to be. Cruise ships are now visiting in significant numbers. Elsewhere on the island, the machair (sandy grassland by the beach) has fine displays of wild flowers in spring and summer and the cliffs boast large colonies of seabirds, including shags, puffins, razorbills and black guillemots. Canna is now rat-free, following a programme of extermination, which should help boost seabird numbers.

Dogwood

Tony Schilling was curator of Wakehurt Place, Sussex for many years, and his wife Vicky ran the Tree Register of the British Isles with Alan Mitchell. They retired to the north and have planted a garden, around 1 acre in size, on an exposed site in the hills to the east of Ullapool with fine views over Loch Broom. The garden is stuffed with treasures in a rock garden and dry stone wall terraces, wildflower meadow and shrub and tree borders. The Schillings are enthusiastic, amusing and sometimes irreverent guides.

Dogwood
Dogwood Braes,
Ullapool, IV26 2SZ
(*map, pp. 32–33*)

Tony and Vicky Schilling
By appointment, with a
few days warning please.
Donations
On the eastern outskirts
of Ullapool
T: 01854 613238

Dundonnell House
Little Loch Broom,
Ross-shire, IV23 2QW
(*map, pp. 32–33*)

The Lady Rice/Dundonnell Estates
SGS up to 3 days per year or
by appointment; ££
A832 between Braemore and
Gairloch take Badrealloch turn
for ½ mile, c. 40 mins from
Ullapool
T: 01854 633 335
Tea on June SGS open day only.
Summer: Maggie's tearoom
at Camusnagaul for lunches,
teas, snacks

Dundonnell House

Lady Rice has been energetically restoring this garden in the last few years and it is well worth a visit en route to or from Inverewe. The partly walled garden, which adjoins the house, is dominated by a truly magnificent ancient yew tree and a couple of very old hollies. The garden is divided into a series of themed sections divided by box-lined gravel paths, punctuated with well-placed urns and statues. Some of these include fruit and vegetables, a potager, perennial borders, a pond surrounded by pear trees, a bamboo and fern garden and a rather unusual restored Victorian glasshouse in the shape of a tunnel house. A variety of surfaces has been used around the garden: a pebble mosaic celtic cross, a gravel path with diamond paving and a cobbled circle, and we liked the hedge with a scalloped or undulating top dividing one section off from the rest. Further afield along the woodland walks are *Eucalyptus*, spring displays of camellias, magnolias, rhododendrons and bulbs. Gardener Will Soos, formerly at Inverewe, is clearly enjoying the challenge of this garden, with lots of new developments including introducing a range of Chilean and South African plants to join some already monster *Eucryphia*. On SGS open days you can enjoy teas in the ballroom at the house where previous owner Alan Rogers, a bonsai collector, held his famous soirees. At the end of the road is the track which leads to Scoraig, one of Scotland's remotest mainland communities, only accessible on foot or by boat.

Dunvegan Castle and Gardens

I mentioned in the introduction to this book that getting to Scottish gardens was part of the pleasure of visiting them. Dunvegan is perhaps the best example: reaching it is undoubtedly one of Britain's finest journeys. Quite apart from the mainland route to Kyle of Lochalsh (which can be done by car, bus or train), on Skye itself the one-hour and sometimes as much as two-hour drive from the bridge skirts round the majestic but brooding Cuillins, often shrouded in cloud, and up the stunning coastline with endless bays, extraordinary flat-topped hills and clusters of white crofting houses. Dunvegan is one of Skye's most popular tourist attractions. Situated on a rocky outcrop by the sea, the grey castle clan-stronghold has an 800-year history. The gardens are more recent; the walled garden and woodland were built and planted in the 1830s, then abandoned, with another burst of planting in the 1920s, abandoned again, and then more planting from the early 1980s onwards, with much of it done by head gardener David McLean in two different stints at the garden. Devastating storms do considerable damage from time to time, uprooting trees in the shallow soils, but such storms can often lead to planting opportunities and often better plant performance when more light is let in. The walk in from the car park leads through thickets of ubiquitous purple *Rhododendron ponticum* which has to be hacked back over much of the garden to allow anything else to grow. There are lots of fine rhododendrons and azaleas all over the garden with extensive recent plantings, often with hydrangeas alongside to extend the season into summer and autumn. The restored walled garden is quirky and well designed: two unusual features are a raised pool and a mini Mayan temple. The garden is divided into several rooms with yew hedging, with vistas along paths to doors and seats. The garden features roses, old fruit trees on the walls, and quite a number of tender southern hemisphere plants which enjoy the mild climate. Outside the walled garden it is worth walking up the small hill to the viewpoint over the semi-formal round garden with the castle in the distance. From here, meander down through recent plantings to the

Dunvegan Castle and Gardens
Dunvegan, Isle of Skye, IV55 8WF
(*map, pp. 32–33*)

Chiefs of the Clan Macleod
Easter/April–mid October: daily
10am–5.30pm. Last admission
5pm. November–March by
appointment; ££ gardens; £££
gardens and castle
North-west corner of Skye. Kyle
of Lochalsh to Dunvegan 45 miles
via Skye Bridge (toll) and A863
T: 01470 521206
E: info@dunvegancastle.com
www.dunvegancastle.com
Café: soups and snacks

excellent water garden. Waterfalls at the top end lead to a series of pools down the slope towards the castle, with dwarf rhododendrons such as the rare *R. dendrocharis, R. parmulatum, R. recurvoides* on the rocks, and the usual water garden favourites: *Gunnera, Ligularia, Primula, Rheum,* skunk cabbage and much more. This looked good even in late summer and is one of the best waterside plantings in Scotland. In spring there are massed displays of bulbs and summer sees the Chilean favourites *Embothrium, Crinodendron, Desfontainea, Drimys* and myrtles come into their own. The trouble with Dunvegan is that despite being one of Skye's flagship visitor attractions, it has slipped behind the times. Years of under-investment means that it simply does not reach the standard of great Scottish private house visitor attractions such as Glamis, Blair Castle and Scone; this one is stuck in a time warp, particularly the prefab café. The castle seems to be harled in grey pebble dash, in the same shade as 1970s council houses, and I have it on good authority that journalist Derek Cooper aptly described Dunvegan Castle as 'looking like someone threw porridge at it'. The late clan chief, who lived mainly in Chelsea, attempted to 'sell' the Cuillins to pay for a new Dunvegan roof. The gardens are definitely worth visiting, but the castle is disappointing inside. Dunvegan could be so much better with some investment and an injection of hands-on energy and imagination.

Garden Cottage Nursery
Tournaig, Poolewe, Achnasheen,
Wester Ross IV22 2LH
(*map, pp. 32–33*)

Ron, Lesley and Ben Rushbrook
Mid March to mid October:
Monday–Saturday 10:30am–6pm
7½ miles north of Gairloch along
the A832 (the main road) village of
Tournaig, signed gate on the east
side of the road
T: 01445 781777
F: 01445 781777
E: info@gcnursery.co.uk
www.gcnursery.co.uk

Garden Cottage Nursery

Founded in 1979, this is a family-run retail and mail order nursery which specialises in plants for coastal gardens. Specialities include *Brachyglottis, Cassinia, Hebe, Ozothamnus* and Britain's largest range of *Olearia.* They also have a large range of Asiatic primulas, particularly the candelabra types, as well as bulbs, alpines, grasses, heathers, trees and shrubs. There are good display beds around the nursery, so you can get an idea of how things will look at maturity. This nursery is only a mile from Inverewe so can easily be combined with a visit to that garden. Ben Rushbrook is a mine of useful information on west coast gardening and his wisdom appears on the excellent nursery website. I would particularly recommend looking at the page on Gondwana, a pre-historic super-continent which gradually broke up to form Australia, New Zealand, South America and Africa. The web pages trace the floral connections between these continents. Other useful information includes pages on rabbits, windbreaks and coastal gardening. Ben's father Ron, who founded the nursery, has started up a small second-hand bookshop in the nursery 'to give customers somewhere to shelter from the rain and for bored husbands to occupy themselves while wives examine the plants'. And hopefully vice versa too.

Olearia, a speciality of Garden Cottage Nursery

House of Gruinard

Most of the people on the tour buses heading for Inverewe 12 miles to the south hurtle past this fine west coast garden without even knowing of its existence. When gardener Fiona Clark arrived here 30 years ago, the existing gardens were overgrown and largely abandoned. The gardens have been transformed using a framework of New Zealand shrubs such as olearias to provide shelter from the fearsome winds. This garden has some of the best displays of candelabra primulas in wonderful drifts in late May and June, when the garden is usually open under SGS. There are bold plantings of many other perennials later on in summer. The garden paths lead down to the beach, where there is a ruined croft and views out into Gruinard Bay.

House of Gruinard
Laide, By Achnasheen,
Ross-shire, IV22 2NQ
(*map, pp. 32–33*)

Hon. Mrs A.G. Maclay,
Fiona Clark, gardener
SGS open days (often on
Wednesdays), individuals and
groups (max. 20 persons) by
appointment (apply in writing); ££
On A832 12 miles north of
Inverewe, 5 miles north of Laide
T: 01445 731235 or 01445
731391 (Gardener)
F: 01445 731558

**Hydroponicum (The)/
Achiltibuie Garden**
103 Achiltibuie, Ullapool,
Highland, IV26 2YG
(*map, pp. 32–33*)

Achiltibuie Garden Ltd
Closed at time of writing. See
website for up to date details; ££
Off the A835 north from Ullapool
for 10 miles, then left on to single
track road. New site to be
constructed
T: 01854 622202
F: 01854 622201
E: info@thehydroponicum.com
www.thehydroponicum.com

Hydroponicum (The)/ Achiltibuie Garden

This experimental visitor attraction in windswept coastal Sutherland, with fine views out to the Summer Isles, was set up in the 1980s by Viscount Gough in a series of greenhouses, to provide fresh produce for the nearby Summer Isles Hotel (Scottish Hotel of the Year 2006), famous for its restaurant. Hydroponics uses mineral nutrient solutions instead of soil to grow crops without pesticides. It is claimed this method of production requires only 5 per cent of the water used by traditional farming to produce the same weight of food for areas with water shortages and dwindling rainfall. Ironically, shortage of rain is not a problem in Sutherland, where it falls out of the sky most of the time. Unfortunately visitor figures were not able to sustain the enterprise commercially and closure seemed certain until it was sold in 2006 to three former employees who are determined to resurrect the business. The old site is to be demolished and the whole enterprise moved to a new location with new buildings and not before time; the old Hydroponicum was an eyesore. I'm not alone in finding the tatty collection of plastic buildings unappealing. Anna Pavord writes: 'Nobody, not even Viscount Gough, could call the hydroponicum a beautiful building.' To truly inspire, this enterprise should be a holistic building/business which is either hidden in the landscape, by being underground for example, or should try to reflect the vernacular architecture. The very people drawn to such enterprises tend to be sensitive to the way humans interact with the environment and the fact that it looked like a chicken farm rather than something more organic and in tune with its surroundings may have been partly responsible for its financial position. The new owners are clearly sensitive to this and have promised a much more pleasing building, which is due to be built in 2009–10.

Inverewe Gardens

Inverewe Gardens
Poolewe, Ross-shire, IV22 2LG
(*map, pp. 32–33*)

NTS
Daily: 1 April–31 October
9.30am–6pm or sunset if earlier,
November–March 9.30am–4pm;
Shop: April–September only; £££
On A832, by Poolewe, 6 miles
north-east of Gairloch
T: 01445 781200
F: 01445 781497
E: inverewe@nts.org.uk
www.nts.org.uk

Inverewe is one of Scotland's most famous and most visited gardens and always seems to have several coaches parked outside: amazing considering how remote a garden it is. Its establishment by Osgood MacKenzie from the 1860s onwards is the stuff of legend: apparently there was only a single 3ft tree standing on the windswept moorland on the Am Ploc Ard peninsula. Over a 15-year period MacKenzie planted three species of pine and *Rhododendron ponticum*, followed by alder, birch and rowans in order to establish a windbreak. The shelter was growing well by the time plant-hunters George Forrest and Frank Kingdon Ward began to send back rhododendron seeds and many specimens raised from their seed collections were planted at Inverewe, together with bamboos and other new finds. MacKenzie particularly loved the 'big-leaved' rhododendron species such as *Rhododendron falconeri* and *R. hodgsonii*. After his death in 1925 his daughter Mairi carried on planting, donating the garden to the NTS on her death in 1953. Despite the northerly situation, 'north of Moscow . . . on a latitude with southern Alaska', the gulf stream gives the garden a very favourable climate; visitors are astonished at the tree ferns, palms and other exotics. Nearest to the visitor centre is an unusual walled garden which follows the curve of the beach that runs along the garden's south side, with perennials and vegetables growing right by the sea. Don't miss the *Watsonia, Dierama* and *Tritonia* from South Africa. Beyond is the large woodland garden is famous for its large collection of rhododendrons and azaleas, underplanted with *Meconopsis* and *Erythronium*, with *Astilbe, Rodgersia* and *Ligularia* in the damper areas. There are many meandering paths through the woodland; follow signs to the viewpoint for a panorama of the bay, the Isle of Ewe and the garden itself. There is good autumn colour from leaves and berries and the mild climate allows late-flowering perennials to thrive. The National Trust for Scotland is establishing collections of

many other plants here to extend the season, including many which
are only hardy outdoors in the mildest coastal locations such as this.
Asian trees and shrubs such as *Daphniphyllum*, South African bulbous
plants, Chilean plants such as *Gevuina* and *Ourisia*, Australasian
plants, including national collections of *Brachyglottis* and *Olearia*, and
Cistus are all doing well in various parts of the garden. *Drimys* and
Hoheria self-seed to the extent of being weeds. The magnolias and
species rhododendrons early in the year (March and April) can be
stunning if you time it right and the weather is kind. The garden has
free guided walks at 1.30, Monday–Friday, mid-May to early
September. I am aware that some visitors to Inverewe are disappointed – perhaps expectations for it are too high? – and it has not
been well managed in recent years, but things are looking up under
new gardener Kevin Ball. The windbreaks have been suffering in
recent storms and much replacing will be needed. The woodland
garden is not as exciting as Argyll gardens such as Crarae and
Arduaine, partly due to the topography (there is no gorge and burn
for example) and partly due to a lack of design in some of the older
plantings. The blocks of mature rhododendrons are rather monot-
onous, for example. Other gardens and nurseries worth calling into
nearby include House of Gruinard (by appointment only) and
Garden Cottage Nursery, and there are plenty of other excellent
gardens to combine with routes to the north: Dundonell (by
appointment), Leckmelm, Kerracher and to the south via Attadale,
through the most magnificent Scottish coastal scenery.

Kerrachar

One of Scotland's remotest and most isolated gardens, getting there is
certainly part of the pleasure, passing the majestic Sutherland
mountains of Suilven and Stac Pollaidh, over the futuristic bridge at

Kylesku, to the 30-minute boat trip along Loch a Chairn Bhain to Kerrachar. The boat trip normally allows about an hour in the gardens. It docks at a small pier and the garden is theatrically revealed through a tunnel of shrubs and a high fence. It consists of two main sections on either side of the house and a smaller section in front. The place is absolutely crammed with plants; there must be thousands of varieties jostling for space, protected by seaside shrubs such as *Hebe*, *Ozothamnus*, *Olearia* and *Pittosporum*. *Lilum canadense* was particularly impressive on a visit in July, while in September the range of *Crocosmia* in shades of yellow, orange and red, caught Ray's attention. A rock/gravel section is constructed with dry stone wall terraces. David Austin roses were doing surprisingly well. A new development, the Darwin garden, is to feature Chilean plants, and they have also planted a bed of *Protea*. Plants, propagated and grown at the gardens, are available for sale along with postcards and light refreshments. It is clear what the Kohns have achieved here when you see what surrounds the garden: nothing but bracken, heather and birch scrub, from which the garden was carved. Kerrachar is situated on land which forms part of the Assynt Crofters' Trust; the 21,000-acre estate was purchased by the trust from the hands of bankrupt property speculators in 1992. It is now debt-free and has allowed the people who live here to control their land, free from the whims of absent and careless landlords (*www.assyntcrofters.co.uk*). Visiting Kerrachar is dependent on the boat, so it is best to contact the boat owners to confirm sailings and book places.

Kerrachar
Kylesku, Sutherland,
IV27 4HW
(*map, pp. 32–33*)

Peter and Trisha Kohn
The Statesman sails to Kerrachar
Gardens from the Old Ferry Pier
in Kylesku at 1pm May–mid
September, Tuesday, Thursday,
Sunday (check for updates as
arrangements may change); £££,
includes boat trip. Parking in
Kylesku just off the A894
T: 01571 833288
Boat: 01971 502345
F: 01571 833288.
E: info@kerrachar.co.uk
www.kerrachar.co.uk
Light refreshments at the garden,
meals at the Kylesku Hotel

Keske Nurseries (Plants For Windy Places)

I have Peter Irvine to thank for this one, as he featured it in *Scotland the Best*. I have to admit I have not been to North Uist to check it out, though I did once spend a week there proving that I can't fish and can't see the point of fishing either . . . I digress . . . This is an excellent small nursery, established in 1993 with a carefully chosen range of shrubs, herbs, vegetables and bedding plants mostly raised on-site. They cleverly advertise their range as 'Plants for Windy Places', which is exactly what these islands need. Owner Laura Donkers explains: 'The decision to grow-on all our plants outside has proven to be the secret of our success. This, together with the minimal use of fertiliser so that the foliage will not get too lush, and therefore more prone to wind damage, has also allowed a greater certainty that plants will establish well into Uist gardens.' The nursery holds an annual fundraising garden open day on the third Saturday in June. Laura also let me know about an annual tour round the local gardens run by charity Ros Craobh. There is no doubt that Keske is *the* place to go for plants and information on gardening in Benbecula and the Uists.

**Keske Nurseries
(Plants For Windy Places)**
Clachan, Locheport,
Isle of North Uist,
Outer Hebrides, HS6 5HD
(*map, pp. 32–33*)

Laura Donkers
April–August: Monday–Saturday
10am–5pm
South of Lochmadddy on the
Benbecula road, turn off near
Clachan Stores
T: 01876 580333
F: 01876 580333
E: keske.nurseries@
btopenworld.com

Larachmhor
Arisaig, Argyll,
PH39 4NH
(map, pp. 32–33)

Arisaig Estate
Dawn–dusk (no formal
arrangements)
On the outskirts of Arisaig,
park and walk back along the
road towards Fort William.
Go 200 yards, through an
unmarked gate and down
a track

Larachmhor

John Holmes, businessman, art collector and fanatical rhododendron collector, planted gardens at Formakin outside Glasgow and at Larach Mhor (Larachmhor) outside Arisaig. Sir Robert Lorimer designed the house at Formakin and its gardens were soon filled with Holmes' extensive rhododendron collection. Holmes soon ran out of space, so to cope with the overspill he acquired the lease of 28 acres of the Arisaig estate in 1927. He determined to obtain every available species from nurseries and private collectors throughout Britain, having plants delivered by rail to Arisaig. Unfortunately Holmes lived well beyond his means and eventually creditors and bailiffs came calling. Many of Larachmhor's rhododendrons were sold off, but some were too big to move. Gardener John Brennan remained at Larachmhor until his death in 1959, living in a small wooden bothy without electricity or water. Staff from the Royal Botanic Garden, Edinburgh, formed the Larachmhor Consortium in the 1960s and over the years many RBG staff members have come on weekend work parties to manage the woodland, making use of the bothy till it burnt down in 2007. Alan Bennell and Ian Sinclair have been the mainstays in recent years and have instigated new planting. It is well worth popping in for a wander round, particularly in spring.

Leathad Ard
Upper Carloway,
Isle of Lewis, HS2 9AQ
(map, pp. 32–33)

Rowena and Stuart Oakley
Mid June–late August: Tuesday,
Thursday, Saturday, 2–6pm; ££
SGS, or donation for local charities
A858 from Shawbost to Carloway,
first right in the village, opposite
football pitch
T: 01851 643204
E: oakley1a@clara.co.uk

Leathad Ard

The only garden in Harris and Lewis in the SGS 'Yellow Book', Leathad Ard is Gaelic for 'steep hill'. The sloping garden has fine hilltop views towards East Loch Roag. The Oakleys initially had to contend with the high winds and shallow peaty soil. The very necessary shelter hedges divide the garden into separate areas with a bog garden, daffodil meadow, herbaceous borders, cutting borders, patio, vegetables and raised beds. Terraces have been built in front of the house, using large stones from the previous building on the site.

Leckmelm Shrubbery and Arboretum

This arboretum was first planted in the 1870s with many of the newly introduced trees from the Himalaya and North America: wellingtonias, *Araucaria* and cedars, some of which are now of record-breaking size. The gardens were restored and replanted by the Troughton family from 1985 onwards and the gardens contain species rhododendrons, azaleas and shrubs. Warmed by the gulf stream this tranquil woodland setting has an alpine garden and paths to the sea. It is worth a detour if you are visiting Inverewe. Though there are fine trees, they are being spoiled by overcrowding, and seedling trees not being removed. It does need some urgent attention from an experienced forester to save it. Another place nearby worth a visit for tree lovers is Lael Forest Garden, on the A835 south near the head of Loch Broom. There are several champion trees here in the woodland, which is now managed by the Forestry Commission.

Leckmelm Shrubbery and Arboretum
Leckmelm Arboretum
by Ullapool, Highland,
IV23 2RH
(*map, pp. 32–33*)

Mr and Mrs Peter Troughton
1 April–31 October 10am–6pm;
££
On A835 3 miles south of Ullapool. No parking for buses or large vehicles

Lews Castle and Lady Lever Park

Overlooking Stornoway, this is an important planned landscape, the only one on the Historic Scotland Register in the Western Isles. Designed by Charles Wilson in 1848–60, Lews Castle is a castellated mansion, funded with profits from the opium trade by Hong Kong-based Jardine Matheson. Many of the outbuildings such as the lodges and walls share the castellated style. It was briefly owned by Lord Leverhulme, founder of Lever Brothers, (now Unilever PLC). Lady Lever Park is now a golf course with groups of mature trees, and the surrounding extensive mixed woodlands are much appreciated by the people of Stornoway. The woodland garden holds an impressive collection of trees including cedar, *Araucaria*, chestnuts, *Thuja plicata* and *Thujopsis dolabrata* as well as masses of *Gunnera*. The grounds are currently in a rather sad state and the battle to keep the *Rhododendron ponticum* and salmonberry under control is currently being lost. The castle grounds host the annual Hebrides Celtic Festival in July. There are plans for the castle, formerly used as a college but currently vacant, to be turned into a hotel and museum, subject to funding.

Lews Castle and Lady Lever Park
Stornoway, Isle of Lewis
(*map, pp. 32–33*)

Daylight hours; free
North-west side of Stornoway harbour overlooking the town
T: 01851 770000
E: aofficele@lews.uhi.ac.uk

Lochalsh Woodland Garden
Balmacara, Kyle,
Ross-shire, IV40 8DN
(*map, pp. 32–33*)

NTS
Daily: 9am–sunset
(woodland garden); ££*
3 miles east of Kyle of
Lochalsh on the A87
T: 0844 4932233
F: 01599 566359
E: balmacara@nts.org.uk
www.nts.org.uk

Lochalsh Woodland Garden

Not far from Kyle of Lochalsh, this is a pleasant woodland stroll alongside the shores of Loch Alsh, with views across to Skye and the hills above Glenelg. The garden has been created in a woodland of mature Scots pine, oaks and beeches, planned largely by Euan and Peter Cox who supplied many of the rhododendrons in the 1950s and '60s. These have been added to more recently with extensive collections of ferns, bamboo, fuchsias and particularly good hydrangeas, mainly planted around Lochalsh House. The car park is a 700m walk through the woodland to reach the garden, which is explored on narrow and quite steep paths. Do go down to the shore-side lookout, you might be lucky enough to see an otter fishing as we did. The garden forms part of a 5,000-acre crofting estate owned by the National Trust for Scotland which extends as far as Plockton to the north. The NTS have downgraded the maintenance regime on this garden and I can't believe this won't have the effect of seeing it gradually decline.

**Potting Shed Café
and Restaurant**
Applecross, Wester Ross,
IV54 8LR
(*map, pp. 32–33*)

John Glover
Signed in Applecross village,
reached via B road from the A896
near Kishorn
T: 01520 744440
www.eatinthewalledgarden.co.uk

Potting Shed Café and Restaurant

The Potting Shed Café and Restaurant, which opened in 2003, can be found in the walled garden of Applecross House, reached by one of Scotland's most spectacular switchback roads via the 2,053ft pass Bealach na Ba with its spectacular views of the Cuillins of Skye. The derelict walled garden has been restored and grows fruit and vegetables used in the restaurant. Seafood is landed at Applecross, so it can't be much fresher, and venison and lamb are sourced from farms and hills around. For accommodation, there is the highly recommended Applecross Inn, with its seven rooms, and famous restaurant. It needs to be booked well in advance for most of the high season (tel. 01520 744262). There is also a café 'The Flower Tunnel' at the Applecross campsite, open from June to August. This out of the way corner is one of Scotland's best destinations for food lovers.

Rubha Phoil Forest Garden

Rubha Phoil Forest Garden, which now has crofting status, is a 15-acre wooded site on a small peninsula right next to the Skye–Armadale ferry car park. Sandy Masson bought the abandoned woodland in 1983 and began the woodland garden in 1990 working alongside friend Samuel Bennett with help from students from Larenstein Agricultural College in the Netherlands. The mixed woodland is used as a demonstration of permaculture with a range of vegetables, herbs and soft fruit, interspaced with top fruit grown in the woodland, adapted from Robert Hart's forest garden model (see his book *The Forest Garden* for details). A polytunnel and cloche/cold frame system have been built which are to be heated using power produced on-site from simple renewable energy sources. The whole garden is cultivated organically. Permaculture is a method of growing a range of plants together so that they shelter and protect each other from pests and diseases. The leaf-fall from the trees and shrubs is left to rot down providing a natural, slow release fertilising system similar to that on a forest floor, and worms and seaweed are also used for replenishing nutrients. Native species of plants and wild foods are encouraged due to their climatic suitability. Permaculture studies have produced a list of over 5,000 edible plants which can be grown in Great Britain. Successes in Skye have included mashua (tubers similar to potatoes) and quinoa. Rubha Phoil have also participated in trials run by the HDRA (Henry Doubleday Research Association) and grow herbs and forest trees for sale. It is an interesting place to go for a wander, with informative signage and leaflets available at the entrance in English, French, German, Japanese, Chinese and Gaelic. Down by the shore you might be lucky enough to spot seals, otters, herons, Arctic terns and sea eagles. Sandy is now retired and is hoping to secure the long-term future for the project, which is somewhat a victim of its own success as so many people visit and wear out the paths. She is now involved in composting projects on Skye and the mainland and the new glass-fronted compost bins are getting lots of comment. There is definitely useful work going on here, even if some of the locals we met neither understand nor approve of it. It can be muddy, so take boots.

Rubha Phoil Forest Garden
Rubha Phoil,
Armadale Pier Road,
Ardvasar, Sleat,
Isle of Skye, IV45 8RS
(*map, pp. 32–33*)

Sandy Masson
Entry by donation
By the old pier at Armadale,
Skye, take the A851 and follow
signs to the Mallaig ferry
T: 01471 833458
E: gnowersark-
sandy@yahoo.co.uk
www.skye-permaculture.org.uk

Scourie Lodge
Scourie, Sutherland,
IV27 4TE
(*map, pp. 32–33*)

Mr and Mrs Gerald Klein
March to October, open to
guests and on request.
A894 in Scourie, take
road opposite the hotel
T: 01971 502248
www.scourielodge.co.uk

Scourie Lodge

Scourie Lodge was built in 1835 by the Duke of Sutherland on the spectacular Sutherland coast and was later lived in by his factor, an infamous man who played a key role in the Highland Clearances. The Lodge is now a guest house with a walled garden with mixed plantings of shrubs, perennials and grasses, lines of apple trees and a greenhouse, surrounded by hillsides of gorse outside.

B&B

**Skye Shrubs Nursery
and Garden Centre**
Skye Shrubs, Viewfield Road,
Portree, Isle of Skye, IV51 9HT
(*map, pp. 32–33*)

Fran Gooch
Spring–autumn: 10am–5pm
(closed Sunday, Monday),
shorter hours in winter.
On the main road going into
Portree from the south, opposite
the BP filling station, 35 miles
from the Skye Bridge
T: 01478 613132
E: online@skyeshrubs.co.uk
www.skyeshrubs.co.uk

Skye Shrubs Nursery and Garden Centre

This garden centre, on the outskirts of Portree, run by Fran Gooch, is probably the best source of plants on Skye. Most importantly, much of the plant material sold at the garden centre is grown at Skye Shrubs' own nursery and certainly if you are looking for information as to what does well in these windswept islands, this is the place to come. The garden centre is 'old-style'; i.e. they sell plants, composts, seeds and bulbs with no frilly add-ons. A small native plant demonstration garden for the education of local school children was planted in 2008 behind the garden centre by the drive up to Viewfield House.

North-East:

*Aberdeenshire, Don and Dee valleys north to
Moray Firth and across to A9*

*This corner of Scotland has a range of fine and varied gardens which
could take a week or more to visit. There are unmissable National Trust
for Scotland house/castle/garden combinations such as Crathes and
Drum, as well as large private gardens such as Cawdor and
Kildrummy. A loop along the Don and Dee valleys gives a good daytrip,
as does the set of castles and gardens north of Aberdeen which includes
Cragievar, Castle Fraser, Fyvie and Pitmidden. The Speyside whisky
trail can be combined with visits to Leith Hall and Ballindalloch,
Logie and the strange topiary of Tormore Distillery. Outstanding
smaller private gardens worth seeing on open days include Carestown
Steading and Daluaine. Aberdeen probably has Scotland's finest
collection of parks and its public plantings are excellent: don't miss the
roses at roundabouts (said to be 2½ million bushes); there are a lot of
roundabouts.*

*Gardens occasionally open under SGS, not included in the main
entries include: daffodil woods at Auchmacoy, Ellon; Woodlands,
Nairn; Muir of Balnagowan House, by Ardersier.*

Cawdor Castle

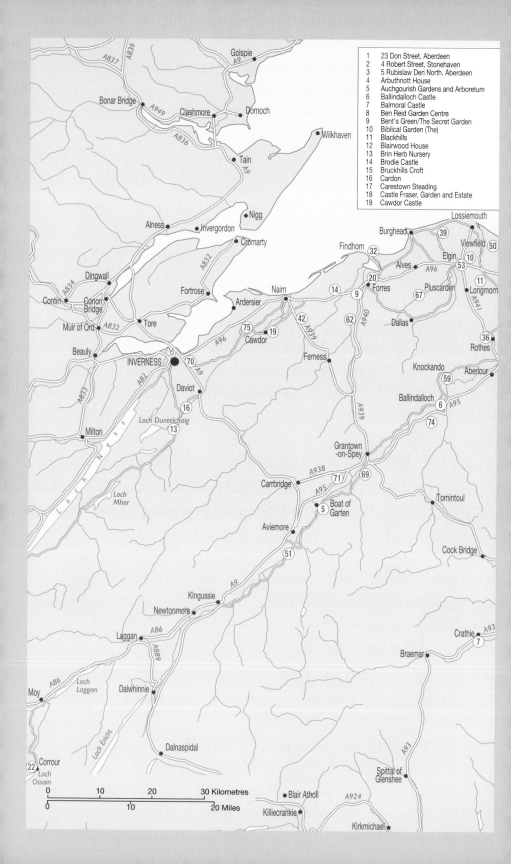

1	23 Don Street, Aberdeen
2	4 Robert Street, Stonehaven
3	5 Rubislaw Den North, Aberdeen
4	Arbuthnott House
5	Auchgourish Gardens and Arboretum
6	Ballindalloch Castle
7	Balmoral Castle
8	Ben Reid Garden Centre
9	Bent's Green/The Secret Garden
10	Biblical Garden (The)
11	Blackhills
12	Blairwood House
13	Brin Herb Nursery
14	Brodie Castle
15	Bruckhills Croft
16	Cardon
17	Carestown Steading
18	Castle Fraser, Garden and Estate
19	Cawdor Castle

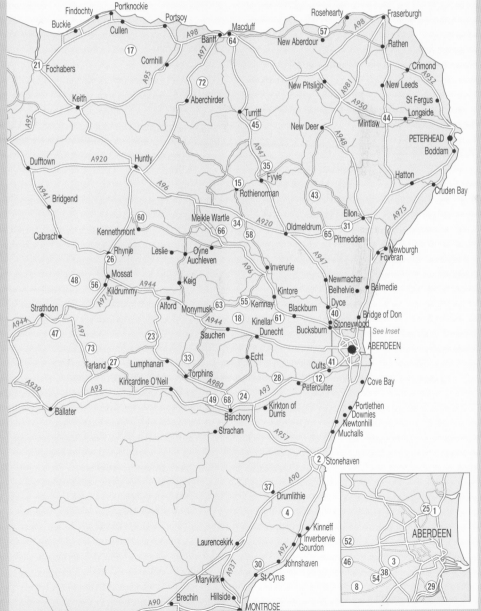

23 Don Street, Aberdeen
23 Don Street,
Aberdeen AB24 1UH
(*map, pp. 54–55*)

Muriel MacKechnie
SGS or by arrangement; ££
North off A978 St Machar Drive,
between Tillydrone Avenue and
King St. On open days park at
St Machar Cathedral
T: 01224 487269

23 Don Street, Aberdeen

This atmospheric small walled garden was derelict when Muriel
MacKechnie bought it from the University of Aberdeen. Don Street
in Old Aberdeen is one of the most attractive in the city, but the
house front gives no clue to the fine garden behind. The garden walls
are covered with honeysuckle and climbing roses and the gravel and
paved paths meander through informally planted beds with plants
spilling out in cottage garden style with urns, bird baths and statues
cleverly placed to provide framing and vistas. A huge range of bulbs
including *Narcissi, Crocus, Allium, Camassia* and lilies compete for
space with the reds, purples, pinks and whites of *Knautia, Geranium,
Campanula, Salvia* and *Penstemon* which carpet the ground beneath
the scented roses. The grey stone sets the planting off well and this
garden is a perfect example of a small, enclosed, peaceful town
garden.

4 Robert Street, Stonehaven

This small walled garden with a bungalow in the middle was formerly an orchard. On a steep slope, it provides quite a challenging site. Rather than remove the gnarled and frankly unproductive apples, the Reids instead saw them as an opportunity for growing rambling roses and clematis, which provide a spectacular display in July. Roses include 'Rambling Rector', *R. mulliganii*, 'Betty Sherriff''s rose, originally from Ascreavie, and the ever popular 'Paul's Himalayan Musk'. The garden has a small flat area with a greenhouse and vegetable patch and some paved terrace with pots, but the rest is on slopes which provide lots of planting opportunities. The Reids bought this house in 1998, and created what is their fifth garden (their previous one in Dunnecht was also open under the SGS). Michael Reid pointed out some of his more interesting plants including *Holodiscus*, a spiraea-like Chinese shrub, and two plants of the large-leaved *Rubus odorata*, which produce floppy-felty pink flowers all summer. At the back of the house is a shady bed of ferns. This garden demonstrates how to pack large numbers of plants into a small garden by going up as well as out, into any available support. Most of this garden is definitely not suitable for wheelchairs.

4 Robert Street, Stonehaven
4 Robert Street,
Stonehaven, AB39 2DN
(*map, pp. 54–55*)

Sue and Michael Reid
1-31 July: by arrangement; ££
Take first Stonehaven exit from south; off Evan Street from Stonehaven Market Square. Left at traffic lights in square, second right after square behind block of flats. Bungalow in walled garden
T: 01569 763877
E: reid60@tiscali.co.uk
Tea and cakes can be arranged for visitors

5 Rubislaw Den North, Aberdeen
5 Rubislaw Den North,
Aberdeen, AB15 4AL
(*map, pp. 54–55*)

Dr Tom Smith
SGS some years and by
appointment; ££
Leave the A90 east onto Queen's
Road, left at the next roundabout
and second left. Ignore 5a
and 5b and go to number 5
T. 01224 317345

5 Rubislaw Den North, Aberdeen

Retired professor of Physics, Tom Smith, has had a sideline in
designing gardens all his life. Tom has developed his own 1-acre
garden in Aberdeen over many years. The tall mature trees in neighbouring gardens form a 'borrowed' backdrop to his plantings, so that
the garden appears as tall as it is wide. Lining the wall of the house is
a box parterre in three sections which divides the house from the
semicircular lawn. Around this, a long curved double border of mixed
perennials is backed by the side walls, shrubs, conifers and trees. A
clump of *Tricyrtis latifolia* with leopard-skin yellow and brown flowers
caught my eye. Beyond this is the shaded woodland area which seems
much larger than it is with the many paths which run through it. The
woodland centres round a clearing bordered by a bamboo grove, with
a rill, bronze grasses and a rustic chair. The garden is so densely
planted and well planned that it takes some time to wander the series
of narrow paths, hidden corners, dead ends, delightful surprises and
eye-catching design features. On each visit I kept discovering more
and more, and unravelling it is pure pleasure. It is a plantsman's
garden, filled with carefully chosen treasures, and everything is meticulously recorded. Tom showed me the card index detailing all the
plants which have gone in throughout its existence. Not all have
survived of course, but some have proven surprisingly durable: Tom
pointed out *Lyonothamnus floribundus* ssp. *aspleniifolius* from a
Californian island. I had only ever seen this before at Arduaine in
mild Argyll, it would normally be considered too tender for
Aberdeen, as would living TV aerial *Pseudopanax ferox*, now 15ft high
on the wall of the house, with *Clematis viticella* clambering through

it. The garden never stands still; the latest addition is a border which maps out the evolution of primitive plants from ancient mare's tail (*Equisetum*), via ferns, conifers to grasses with the early flowering plants (*Magnoliales*), represented. Tom Smith has a singular and at times challenging vision of gardening in all its facets. You'll find echoes of Charles Jencks and Ian Hamilton Finlay here in the references to physics and stones carved with formulae and epigrams, but Tom Smith places more emphasis on plants and pleasure than these two. For Tom, gardening is 'a process of interrogation of your deepest feelings and ideas; that is how you know what is right'. This garden reminds me of Borges' *Labyrinths*: compact and succinct but also a garden about all potential gardens woven from different narratives and metaphors, the garden is a poem of allusions to creation, astronomy, experience and consciousness. It may sound pretentious, but it is not. A circle of narrow fastigiate poplars frames the sky, cathedral-like, but maybe closer to Stonehenge, which Tom calls a 'sky telescope'. A hedge of box awakes and unwinds from a 'pool' of black *Ophiopogon* and sets off snake-like through the undergrowth demanding to be followed as it slithers through the ferns, under the trees and peeling-barked rhododendrons. A Japanese-style 'cloud tree' turns out to be *Chamaecyparis* 'Boulevard'. In common with many physicists, Tom's research has revealed beauty and wonder, and a certain spirituality and he considers this is something to celebrate and explore. Science and spirituality can co-exist, simply requiring intellectual maturity and openness. This duality allows Tom to derive a complex pleasure from the process of gardening: a love of plants, art and design and enquiry; he bounds around with as much enthusiasm and energy as someone half his age and he looks after the garden with minimum help. To be guided around by him is a privilege; it might be transformative, especially if you are looking for inspiration in garden design. Tom Smith is a man of wisdom and experience, a twenty-first-century sage, whose ideas are sometimes clear and sometimes more metaphysical and harder to grasp. He proves that gardeners can and should reach for the stars.

♿

Arbuthnott House
Laurencekirk,
Kincardineshire, AB30 1PA
(*map, pp. 54–55*)

Viscount of Arbuthnott
Daily 9am–5pm; £
3 miles west of Inverbervie on
B967 between A90 and A92. Turn
off A90 between Laurencekirk
and Inverbervie
T: 01561 320417
E: keith@arbuthnott.co.uk
www.arbuthnott.co.uk
Café at Grassic Gibbon
Centre nearby

Arbuthnott House

This is an ancient garden, first laid out in 1685. Unsurprisingly, it has since had centuries of additions and improvements, as has the house itself, which is a mixture of styles and finishes. The garden, walled on two sides, lies on a steep slope and, running horizontally across the contour, three main walks which are connected by a series of diagonal paths, some of which are lined with yew and other hedges, including an effective formal clipped hedge of *Rhododendron ponticum*. The top of the garden contains several wide herbaceous borders, punctuated by box balls, packed with *Astilbe, Crocosmia, Filipendula* and other summer favourites. The tall walls are lined with sections of soft fruit and vegetables. The mature trees in the centre have mostly suffered wind damage, though the cedar is fine. The central parts on the steeper slopes contain shrub rose borders while the west wall is lined with a long lupin border which runs down the hill. The bottom of the garden is flat and sometimes waterlogged. The fine bridge to the north of the castle is crying out for a woodland walk and wild garden underneath. Reached by a long rhododendron-lined drive, the house is open c. 12 days per year for guided tours, while the gardens can be visited any time.

Auchgourish Gardens and Arboretum

Retired forester and tree obsessive Ian Brodie purchased a forestry plantation near Boat of Garten at the foot of the Cairngorms which he opened as 'Scotland's Millennium Botanic Garden'. Planted with trees, shrubs and perennials, mostly of wild origin and mostly grown from seed by Ian himself, the garden is a series of beds under Scots pine, arranged into areas corresponding to the bio-geographic regions of the world from where the plants come: a Japanese section with raked gravel, and another for the Sino-Himalaya for example. The plants are mostly very well labelled. This is gardening in an extreme climate, high up and inland; the year we visited, Ian had suffered frosts on 25 June and 1 July. The growing season is very short, and many plants struggle to survive. *Acer palmatum* was one example, In contrast, genera doing well include *Alnus, Arisaema, Betula, Clematis, Iris, Lilium, Malus, Paeonia, Primula, Prunus, Pyrus, Rosa, Rubus, Salix* and *Sorbus*. Ian is an evangelist, single-minded and determined, but this enterprise is a Sisyphean combination of heroism and madness. Despite a debilitating back condition, Ian works 10–12 hours a day on his own, carving something out of wilderness which in reality is only of interest to serious plantsmen. Many people, expecting something more ornamental, probably feel short-changed as there is not much to 'see', most plants are small and he has no cultivars or hybrids, so often little flower and no great displays. Ian has a tunnel house of plants for sale round the back which are also available mail order.

Auchgourish Gardens and Arboretum
Street of Kincardine,
by Boat of Garten,
Strath Spey,
Inverness-shire,PH24 3BP
(*map, pp. 54–55*)

Ian Brodie
Daily: Easter–October
10am–5pm; ££
B970 which runs parallel
to the River Spey between
Coylumbridge and
Boat of Garten
T: 01479 831464;
M: 07737 914292
F: 01479 831672
E: auchgourishgardens@
falsyde.sol.co.uk
www.auchgourishgardens.org

Ballindalloch Castle
Ballindalloch,
Banffshire, AB37 9AX
(*map, pp. 54–55*)

Mrs Oliver
Macpherson-Grant Russell
14 April–30 September:
10.30am–5pm (not Saturdays);
£££ castle and grounds
££ grounds
Turn off the A9 at Aviemore.
Ballindalloch is 29 miles north-
east of Aviemore and 14 miles
north-east of Grantown-on-Spey
on the A95 on the road to Keith
T: 01807 500205
E: enquiries@ballindalloch
castle.co.uk
www.ballindallochcastle.co.uk
Tearoom.

Ballindalloch Castle

The formidable Clare Macpherson-Grant Russell, 'the lady-laird of
Ballindalloch' as she describes herself in her bestselling cookbook, has
developed this family estate (in the family since 1546, should you ask)
into a fine Speyside visitor attraction. The castle is open to visitors, as
are the extensive grounds. Clare explained that this inland river valley
was so cold and damp that many supposedly hardy plants could not
tolerate the conditions; she therefore chooses to garden with plants
which are tough and reliable. This is a quirky and personal garden,
with some unusual features, particularly those for children. In April,
the 2 miles of daffodils are one of the finest and most extensive
displays in Scotland. You could visit Ballindalloch and Brodie Castle,
not far away, in one day and see enough daffs to last you for a year.
The second week of April is normally the peak. In May the rock
garden with rhododendrons and the bluebells come to the fore, with
the fine curved laburnum arch blooming in early June when the *Iris*
and *Celmisia* join in. There is a long informal pond-side planting of
iris and other waterside favourites. The 1.5-acre walled garden was
redesigned with help from Suki Urquhart, with a fountain in the

centre, and extensive plantings of shrub and climbing roses, underplanted with *Viola cornuta*. The most notable feature is the series of
pollarded cherries around the edge of the garden which support roses
and clematis. Clare gives credit to her long-serving gardener Bill
Taylor for the upkeep of the extensive gardens. There are plans afoot
for a new water feature and doubtless it will be spectacular. This is a
dynamic place, with plenty to do, and you'll more than likely meet
one of the family on your visit. The garden has also won an award for
its dog-friendliness: there is a grass maze for dog walking and a shaded
dog-parking area. Please note that dogs are not allowed in some of the
garden areas.

Balmoral Castle

Balmoral Castle
Ballater, Aberdeenshire,
AB35 5TB
(*map, pp. 54–55*)

HM The Queen
Daily: 1 April–end July
10am–5pm, last admissions 4pm;
£££ castle and grounds
6 miles west of Ballater on A93,
at Crathie
T: 012297 42534 (estates office)
E: info@balmoralcastle.com
www.balmoralcastle.com
Restaurant and café

Queen Victoria fell in love with Scotland, inspiring her husband
Prince Albert to buy the Balmoral Estate for her in 1852 and build the
castle. Albert sadly died shortly afterwards, leaving Victoria to mourn,
clearly heart-broken, largely at Balmoral. The story is told in the film
Mrs Brown starring Judie Dench and Billy Connolly, though it was
actually filmed at Osborne House on the Isle of Wight. Apparently
generations of British prime ministers have lived in dread of being
invited by kings and queens to Balmoral and Cherie Blair relates
another story which I won't repeat here. The Dee Valley near Braemar
is one of the coldest places in Scotland, suffering late frosts into June
and as early as late August or early September. The formal gardens,
covering some three acres, also contain a range of glasshouses and a
conservatory. Queen Mary added the sunken rose garden in 1932 and
the water garden was created in 1979. Trees and stone cairns commemorate members of the Royal Family and visiting dignitaries. Forester
and author Alistair Scott drew my attention to the well-labelled and
well-spaced collection of North American conifers on either side of
the Balmoral drive, some of which were planted by Prince Albert.
Balmoral is designed to be in full flower between August and
October, when the Royal Family is in residence, so the gardens are
not really at their peak when public access is allowed from April to
the end of July. For some reason, visitors get to see very little of the
castle indoors, only the ballroom, and frankly I'm not convinced that
the whole experience offers value for money. Prince Charles' property,
Birkhall, at the edge of the Balmoral Estate, previously owned by the
Queen Mother, is very occasionally opened to interested groups, who
must apply in writing well in advance. Birkhall's setting is very fine
and the gardens consist of terraces, a walled garden and a stumpery.
Prince Charles seems to be running a single-handed campaign for the
revival of this Victorian fashion; he also has one at Highgrove.

Beechgrove Garden
PO Box 10137,
Aberdeen, AB11 6WA

Tern Television
Not open
Advice Line 01224 252314
E: beechgrovegarden@terntv.com
www.beechgrove.co.uk

Beechgrove Garden

It is somewhat ironic that Scotland's best-known garden, where Jim McColl and the other presenters create their magic, is not actually open to the public. The Beechgrove Garden started life on a small plot outside the old BBC TV studios in Aberdeen. This used to be a popular visitor attraction on annual open days. Since the garden was moved out to a site in the country west of Aberdeen, public access has been restricted. I once visited it to appear on the programme and I'm sure many people would like to see it for themselves. You can visit it on your computer via a 360-degree virtual tour on the Beechgrove website, which also offers fact sheets from the various programmes.

Ben Reid Garden Centre
Countesswells Road,
Aberdeen, AB15 7AL
(*map, pp. 54–55*)

Monday–Saturday 9am–5pm,
Sunday 10am–5pm; free
Turn off the A90 at the North
Deeside road and and bear right
into Countesswells Road. The
nursery is on the outskirts
of the city
T: 01224 318744
www.ben-reid.co.uk

Ben Reid Garden Centre

This is an old-style nursery and garden centre on the outskirts of Aberdeen whose website boasts: 'Supplying gardeners in Aberdeen and North-East of Scotland for over 250 years'. It stubbornly looks exactly like all garden centres did in the 1970s, with a greenhouse added onto a nursery. There is no café, no gift shop, no food hall. Just plants and things that plants need: compost, pots, fertilisers . . . And lots of the plants are grown right there on-site, so they should be tough. When I visited in August 2007, the plant area was tired and rather disorderly and I would have struggled to find what I wanted. But if you want a real nursery and to buy plants from people who know what grows around Aberdeen, this is a good place to shop.

Bent's Green/The Secret Garden
10 Pilmuir Road West, Forres,
Moray, IV36 2HL
(*map, pp. 54–55*)

Mrs Lorraine Dingwall
SGS 1–2 days in summer
and by appointment; ££
From centre of Forres take Nairn
Road, turn left at BP garage into
Ramflat Road; at end turn right
into Pilmuir Road then sharp
left into Pilmuir Road West
T: 01309 674634
E: fixandig@aol.com
www.simplesite.com/hosta

Bent's Green/
The Secret Garden

This is a small garden of less than half an acre, lovingly crammed with plants by plant enthusiast Lorraine Dingwall, who moved to Moray from the Lake District with her locally born husband. Her aim is to have the longest possible season of interest starting with snowdrops, crocus and other bulbs in spring, a wide range of hostas, perennials, *Geranium, Crocosmia* in summer, and finishing the year with coloured stems and berries. The back garden features an attractive rectangular raised pond, while the smaller front garden has a *Physocarpus* 'Diabolo' hedge and some pollarded *Eucalyptus*. Lorraine operates a small mail order nursery (Secret Garden) specialising in *Hosta* and she's always open to exchanging material, as long as you have something she wants!

Biblical Garden (The), Elgin

Oddly, there are two Biblical gardens in north and north-east Scotland, the other (which I prefer) is in Golspie, further north. This one, situated next to Elgin Cathedral, is a 3-acre walled site which apparently contains all 110 plants mentioned in the Bible. I can't help thinking that plants from Israel, Jordan and Egypt might feel a little homesick grown in Elgin and I looked in vain for an olive grove. I thought the various sculptures depicting the parables, figures of Samson, John the Baptist and Jesus were hideous-beyond-kitsch but I daresay some will disagree. There is also a desert area depicting Mount Sinai and a central walkway of paving slabs in the shape of a Celtic cross. As well as a structure of shrubs, there is lots of colourful bedding in summer. When I visited in July, the garden was full of visitors, and the ruined cathedral precinct next door is impressive. The garden is maintained by volunteers (Friends of the Biblical Garden) and students from Moray College.

Biblical Garden (The), Elgin
King Street, Elgin,
Moray, IV30 1HU
(map, pp. 54–55)

The Moray Council
May–September: 10am–7pm;
Donation
King Street, Elgin, just around
the corner from the entrance to
the cathedral
T: 01343 557053
E: landsandparks@moray.gov.uk
biblicalgardenelgin.com/

Blackhills
Blackhills Estate,
By Elgin, Moray, IV30 3QU
(*map, pp. 54–55*)

John Christie
SGS: 1–2 Sundays in May
and by appointment; ££
Turn off the A96 east of Elgin
onto the B9103 and turn right
signposted to Blackhills
T: 01343 842223
F: 01343 842223
E: info@blackhills.org.uk
www.blackhills.co.uk

Blackhills

This wild woodland garden of c. 60 acres is planted in two steep-sided glacial valleys. Blackhills has a very fine collection of rhododendron species, including many not normally considered hardy in this area, planted by three generations of the Christie family. Because the emphasis is on rhododendron species rather than hybrids the display is not as showy as many Scottish rhododendron gardens, but it has one of the UK's best collections of wild origin species with collector's numbers. There are also fine specimen trees including Cedar, *Davidia, Cryptomeria* and *Picea breweriana*. Probably the best feature of the garden are the two lochs/ponds which, on a still spring day, reflect the woodland backdrop and rhododendron flowers.

Blairwood House
South Deeside Road,
Blairs, AB12 5YQ
(*map, pp. 54–55*)

Ilse Elders
Mid June to beginning of October,
by appointment only; ££
On the B9077 South Deeside
road, 5 minutes' drive from
Bridge of Dee, towards Maryculter,
Aberdeen, the turning in is
opposite Blairs museum,
before Copland Motors
T: 01224 868301

Blairwood House

This is a half-acre country garden overlooking fields along the River Dee. Ilse Elders has ambitious plans for the garden and is still evolving its style, but some fine design features are already in place. There is an impressive, tightly packed collection of herbs behind the house and a small sunken patio. There are plans to extend into the field in front of the house as a wild or wildflower meadow. This is one to watch.

Brin Herb Nursery

This nursery, well off the beaten track at an altitude of 700ft in the hills south of Loch Ness, lists up to 300 varieties of herbs and wild flowers. It has a small café, and food for sale including Spoff oatmeal, which was developed here. There is a small, rather rough-and-ready display garden of herbs, perennials and alpines.

      WC

Brodie Castle

The Brodie family has a long history in this part of Scotland as they probably gained lands as early as 1160 from King Malcolm IV. The handsome sixteenth-century castle was added to in the seventeenth century and with rare restraint in the nineteenth century. It contains fine French furniture; English, continental and Chinese porcelain, and a major collection of paintings. From the castle there is a fine vista down the avenue of beech and lime trees to the recently dredged and restored loch, surrounded by bird hides for observing the wildfowl. Brodie is more a parkland landscape than a garden and it is particularly known for its daffodils, many of which were bred here by the 24th Brodie of Brodie. There are drifts of daffodils under the trees along the great avenue. Gardener David Wheeler and the NTS have been endeavouring to collect as many of the 440 named Brodie daffodils as are still available; this task has been quite a challenge as none of the Brodie varieties proved a great commercial success. The Brodie daffodil collection is lined out and labelled in the nineteenth-century walled garden, which lies to the east of the castle. Some of the Brodie *Narcissus* are available to buy in late summer and by mail order.

Brin Herb Nursery
Flichity, Farr,
Inverness-shire, IV2 6XD
(*map, pp. 54–55*)

Margaret Mackenzie
Garden and plant sales daylight hours year round. Shop and café Friday–Monday, summer only 11am–5.30pm; free
7 miles from the A9 west along the B851 (Daviot to Fort Augustus) in Strathnairn
T: 01808 521288
F: 01808 521464
E: enquiries@brinherb nursery.co.uk
www.brinherbnursery.co.uk

Brodie Castle
Brodie, Forres,
Moray, IV36 2TE
(*map, pp. 54–55*)

NTS
Grounds: 9.30am–sunset, year round. Castle: Easter–end October; Grounds free, castle £££*
Off the A96 4–5 miles east of Nairn, 5 miles west of Forres, 24 miles from Inverness
T: 0844 4932156
F: 0844 4932157
E: brodiecastle@nts.org.uk
www.nts.org.uk
Tearoom and shop 11am–5pm

Bruckhills Croft
Rothienorman,
Inverurie, AB51 8YB
(*map, pp.* 54–55)

Mrs Helen Rushton
SGS: 1 Sunday, July; ££
From Rothienorman take the
B9001 north, just after Badenscoth
Nursing Home (approx 2½ miles)
turn left, Croft is after 1 mile
T: 01651 821596
E: helenrushton1@aol.com

Bruckhills Croft

This is a slate-built croft with an informal country cottage garden with an orchard, fruit and vegetables, a butterfly-attracting planting of heathers and shrubs, and borders of perennials and annuals. A recently developed large pond attracts ducks and other birds and is usually not accessible to visitors in order to protect nesting birds. Unusual features at the front of the house include a standing stone with a glass eye, several box topiary peacocks and a line of raised stone troughs.

Cardon
Balnfoich, Farr,
Inverness, IV2 6XG
(*map, pp.* 54–55)

Caroline Smith
SGS; ££
Turn off A9 for Daviot 3½ miles
on B851 on right-hand side
towards Farr
T: 01808 521389
E: scsmith@kitchens01.fsnet.co.uk

Cardon

This is a recently planted garden with a somewhat challenging climate. Set in c. 5 acres of woodland with paths through it, there are several sections which include lawns, a pond area, rock garden and cottage garden-style perennial plantings. Caroline Smith admits that she is learning how to garden here as she goes along and the garden is starting to mature well.

Carestown Steading
Deskford,
Buckie, AB56 5TR
(*map, pp.* 54–55)

Rora Paglieri
SGS and by appointment; ££
East off B9018 Cullen–Keith
road, 3 miles from Cullen.
F: 01542 840963

Carestown Steading

Italian Rora Paglieri was on holiday from her home in Kenya with a friend in north-east Scotland when she was shown this ruined steading up for sale, in the hills inland from Buckie. Rora bought it and later moved to Scotland and set to work transforming this collection of old farm buildings into one of Scotland's most delightful and impressive private gardens. Carestown Steading is built around a courtyard which forms the garden's centre piece, overlooked by most of the rooms in the stylish house. The courtyard's structure is provided by a box parterre on a gentle slope. All sorts of plants enjoy this sheltered site: *Dianthus* spreading over the paving, echiums, tree

ferns, and spirals of topiary. I loved it. On the north side of the house is a *coup de théâtre*, a long lavender 'Hidcote' hedge in front of a 7ft drop, which is the front wall of the hidden swimming pool which lies under the terrace. What is the secret of some of the best lavender I have seen in Scotland? Rora shared her skills: ensure perfect drainage, in a site with plenty of wind to keep the foliage dry, pruned twice a year, a foliage trim in the spring and flowers pruned off in autumn. To the west of the house is one of the oldest parts of the garden, a tree-lined path follows the perimeter with a pond in the centre. Below the swimming pool are beds of David Austin roses, beyond this are several rooms or sections: a formal area of clipped privet hedge, with a

bubbling water feature in the middle, a new area planted with trees, a wisteria pergola and seating, and an extensive vegetable patch; I was jealous of the perfect rows of artichokes and asparagus. On the east side, by the drive are banks of *Sedum* and saxifrage, showing how well these can cover large areas, with flowers all summer and good autumn colour. Here too are excellent hebes and a maze of yew based on the shape of the skull of a cow which was discovered by archaeologists nearby. The next project is a Japanese garden. Not surprisingly, Rora assured me it would be 'done her way', which makes it all the better. Bypassing most local advice about what can be grown around here and with careful selection of the most sheltered sites and good drainage, Rora somehow succeeds with apricots and figs out of doors. This is one of Scotland's most surprising, exuberant and inspiring private gardens, a meld of daring design, adventurous planting and familiar elements tweaked and transformed into something else entirely.

Castle Fraser, Garden and Estate

Castle Fraser boasts one of Scotland's more colourful histories and is well worth a tour. Don't miss the 'Laird's Lug' or secret room from which guests could be overheard. At least two of the lairds were executed for being on the wrong side, one supporting William

Castle Fraser, Garden and Estate
Sauchen, Inverurie,
Aberdeenshire, AB51 7LD
(*map, pp. 54–55*)

NTS
Gardens and estate: open all year round; castle: 1 April–30 June and 1–30 September: Friday–Tuesday 12–5.30pm, 1 July–31 August: daily 11am–5.30pm; £££*
Off A944, 4 miles north of Dunecht and 16 miles west of Aberdeen
T: 01330 833463
E: castlefraser@nts.org.uk
www.nts.org.uk
Tea room (opening times same as castle)

Wallace and the other Bonnie Prince Charlie. The gardens, unsurprisingly, are more recent, with a Capability Brown-style parkland landscape laid out in the last years of the eighteenth century. Next to the car park is a newly designed children's play area with a new woodland planting of trees and rhododendrons underplanted with spring bulbs, which is intended to lead visitors round to the castle via the wide herbaceous borders on the south-facing walled garden walls, originally planned by Jim Russell and now netted to keep out voracious rabbits. Head gardener Damon Powell has completely redesigned the fine walled garden, and explained that the excellent drainage allows a huge range of plants to be grown, including some not normally considered hardy enough for inland Aberdeenshire. The central borders are designed with plants which remain low enough to see over. Taller perennials are planted along the walls. The garden is divided by two copper beech hedges. Behind one is the extensive vegetable garden boasting a huge range of both common and unusual vegetables. The other copper beech hedge is lined by a border of white Japanese anemones and white peonies in an experiment to see if they can co-exist. The anemones look the more vigorous so far.

Cawdor Castle

Cawdor Castle, with its Macbeth associations, is one of the major visitor attractions in this part of Scotland. The castle dates back to the fourteenth century, while the earliest records of a garden here date from the seventeenth century, when the walled garden was built. This was once filled with vegetables which were unofficially taken advantage of by the locals, but now contains a fine holly maze surrounded by a laburnum archway. The maze is sometimes closed due to the effect of excessive soil compaction of thousands of feet on the hedges. Beyond the maze, Angelika Cawdor has built a symbolic garden in three sections representing the fall, purgatory (with a selection of thistles . . . is this a comment about Scotland?) and paradise, the inner sanctum, which is entered through a narrow gap and contains a bronze pillar, surrounded by camomile and white flowers such as *Philadelphus*. On the opposite side of the castle is a more traditional formally designed eighteenth-century walled garden with a mixture of rhododendrons, perennial beds, roses and shrubs, with a long season of interest well into September. This looks particularly fine from the upper floors of the castle. On the steep banks between the castle and river is a wild woodland garden with mature rhododendrons and shrubs. Extensive walks radiate from the castle, through the 'big wood' with five waymarked nature trails, varying in length from ¾ of a mile to 5 miles. Forester and writer Alistair Scott remarked that 'the handling of the trees of Cawdor is close to

Cawdor Castle
Nairn, Moray, IV12 5RD
(*map, pp. 54–55*)

Cawdor Estates, The Dowager Countess Cawdor
Daily: 1 May–2nd Sunday in October 10am–5.30pm, last admission to castle 5pm; £££ (castle and grounds); ££ grounds only.
On the B9090 3 miles south of Nairn. Well-signposted
T: 01667 404401
01667 404674
E: info@cawdorcastle.com
www.cawdorcastle.com
Café-restaurant in the castle courtyard

exemplary', which is high praise indeed. One path leads towards the
dower house at Auchendoune, whose garden is also open to visitors
(Tuesdays and Thursdays, May–September), which has a good
collection of rhododendrons and other Himalayan plants, and a fine
vegetable garden. Jack, the fifth Earl of Cawdor, joined plant hunter
Frank Kingdon Ward in 1924–25 on his greatest expedition to the
Tsangpo Gorges in Tibet and a collection of plants found on this
expedition has been reassembled at Cawdor in recent years. I was
allowed to look at Jack's diaries of the expedition when I was
researching the new edition of *Riddle of the Tsangpo Gorges*, Ward's
account of the expedition, which I edited a few years ago. Jack
Cawdor had a tough time, not always seeing eye to eye with Ward,
and he never went plant hunting again.

Christie Elite Nurseries Ltd

Established in 1925, this is Scotland's largest forest tree nursery. Their trees are grown from Scottish seed where possible and if you need to plant a few acres of Scots Pine forest, or a hedgerow, this is the place to get the young plants. Christies now own Tillhill and Ben Reid forestry nurseries too.

Christie Elite Nurseries Ltd
Forres, Moray, IV36 3TW
(map, pp. 54–55)

T: 01309 672 633
F: 01309 676 846
sales@christie-elite.co.uk
www.christie-elite.co.uk

Christies of Fochabers Garden Centre

This popular garden centre on the outskirts of Fochabers, owned by the fifth generation of the Christie family in the horticulture business, stocks a good range of plants. It is also a popular tourist and visitor attraction with some unusual 'add-ons': an aviary with birds of prey, a floral clock and famous collection of teapots on display. The popular café has recently been extended and upgraded and there is a good children's play area.

 WC

Christies of Fochabers
Garden Centre
Fochabers,
Moray IV32 7PF
(map, pp. 54–55)

R. Christie
On the A98 on the eastern
outskirts of Fochabers
T: 01343 820362;
tree nursery: 01542 835632
Recently extended café
www.christiesoffochabers.com

Corrour

Corrour is one of Scotland's remotest mainland gardens, situated at 1,300ft on the north side of Loch Ossian next to Rannoch Moor. You can get there either by train on the Fort William line and walk down the road, or you can take the 12-mile-long forestry road off the A86, along which I once met some Jehovah's Witnesses on foot looking for customers. I was unable to persuade them that the stalkers who lived there might be not be all that receptive . . . You need to know the code in order to get through the roadside barrier, so you will need to make an appointment if you wish to see the woodland gardens. The extensive rhododendron collection was planted on a steep hillside by John Stirling Maxwell and added to by Donald Maxwell MacDonald in the 1980s. The garden is surrounded by several Munros, including Beinn na Lap, Sgor Gaibhre, Carn Dearg, Chno Dearg and Stob Coire Sgriodain. The estate was sold in 1996 and in 2003 the new owners constructed the spectacular modernist extravaganza Corrour New Lodge, designed by architect Moshe Safdie, with imported Portuguese granite and towers which look like inverted ice cream cones. London designer Jinny Blom was called in to advise on the gardens around the new house.

 B&B

Corrour
Corrour Trust,
Corrour Estate, by Fort William,
Inverness-shire, PH30 4AA
(map, pp. 54–55)

The Corrour Trust
By appointment
Take A86 from Dalwhinnie to
Spean Bridge to end of Loch
Laggan just before Moy.
Track of 12 miles to Corrour.
Or get off the train at Corrour
station and walk along
Loch Ossian
T: 01397 732200
E: mainoffice@corrour.co.uk
www.corrour.co.uk
B&B, Youth hostel and
restaurant at Corrour Station.
Tel. 01397 732236
(closed Wednesday)

Craigievar Castle
Alford, Aberdeenshire, AB33
8JF(*map, pp. 54–55*)

NTS
April–end June: Friday–Tuesday
(closed Wednesday and
Thursday), 12am–5.30pm; July
and August, daily 12–5.30pm.
Castle closed till late 2009; £££*
(castle); £ grounds
On A980, 6 miles south of Alford,
15 miles north of Banchory and
26 miles west of Aberdeen
www.nts.org.uk
Small shop, picnic area

Craigievar Castle

This striking creamy-pink harled Scottish tower house was remodelled by William Forbes in the mid seventeenth century. The designed landscape contains fine trees along the drivesides including beech, a wide *Araucaria* and a line of Douglas fir. The small fenced kitchen garden has been extensively restored with a series of small raised beds of vegetables, a fruit cage and cutting borders. The policies have extensive walks with primroses, bluebells and anemones. The castle's extensive renovations should be completed in late 2009, when it will reopen. Until then, only the grounds and garden are open.

Crathes Castle, Garden and Estate

One of the National Trust for Scotland's flagship gardens, Crathes Castle is a magnificent sixteenth-century tower house, now free of the Victorian extension which was burnt down in 1966, standing in an estate granted to the Burnett family in 1323 by King Robert the Bruce. Bruce presented them with the ancient Horn of Leys, which you can see today in the Great Hall and which was added to the family coat-of-arms. There are large policy woodlands and lawns at Crathes but the main attraction is the series of garden rooms in the extensive walled garden at the side of the castle descending via a series of terraces. The ancient yew hedges have recently been hard pruned in a rolling programme of regeneration, which, though initially shocking,

has encouraged masses of fresh young growth. Gertrude Jekyll visited Crathes in the 1890s and described it in her book *Some English Gardens* (sic). The garden was partly abandoned for a time and was rescued and redeveloped in the 1920s by Sir James and Sybil Burnett. As well as Jekyll's writings, Hidcote provided inspiration with the creation of eight garden rooms and several colour-themed borders radiating out from the giant mushroom-domed Portuguese laurel in the centre of the lower part of the garden. Crathes has some of Scotland's most exuberant and striking planting schemes. Perhaps most famous is the white border, with scented *Philadelphus*, giant *Buddleja* and *Hydrangea*, and pure white *Phlox*, backed with red-purple-leaved *Prunus*. The grass path has been reinstated, which shows off the whites better than the old paved one. Crathes' white plantings predate those of the famous Sissinghurst white garden. The June border runs towards the corner doocot along a diagonal path leading west, which in turn leads through the red garden and back via the yellow garden with conifers and shrubs and perennials (giant *Inula* for example). If you sit there for long as we did once to feed our hungry children, the sulphur-lime-lemon acidity can start to make you feel queasy. Heading east from the giant Portuguese laurel along the multi-coloured double late summer borders brings you to the beautifully restored Mackenzie & Moncur greenhouse complex, stuffed with tender plants, and a collection of Malmaison carnations. Next door, as well as an enormous *Davidia* with its white handker-chiefs in June, is a path lined with a collection of *Enkianthus campan-ulatus*, now venerable plants with pink and white bells in spring and fiery autumn colour. The terraces shelter some surprisingly tender shrubs which long-time head gardener Calum Pirnie pointed out to

Crathes Castle, Garden and Estate
Banchory, Aberdeenshire, AB31 5QJ
(*map, pp. 54–55*)

NTS
1 April–end September: daily 10.30am–5.30pm, October daily, closing at 4.30pm, November–March, Wednesday–Sunday (closed Monday and Tuesday) 10.30am–3.45pm; £££*
A93 2 miles east of Banchory
T: 0844 4932166
E: crathes@nts.org.uk
www.nts.org.uk
Café, picnic area.

me; who would have thought that *Polylepis australis* could survive
here? The two best-known sections of the upper garden are Lady
Burnett's perennial-surrounded pool garden below the castle walls and
the fountain garden with its parterre filled with August-flowering blue
and purple annuals, with a background of smaller mushrooms of
Portuguese laurel. Calum Pirnie has taken many plaudits for the way
Crathes looks, though he is quick to pass much of the credit to
Douglas MacDonald, his mentor, who was in charge of the gardens
from 1951–92. As Calum explained, Crathes is unusual in that gardens
from many different eras have been created, one on top of the other,
with elements of all of them surviving to the present. To best appreciate the layout, head for the top of the castle to the room known as
'the gallery', from which two windows give birds'-eye views over the
garden; the topiary in particular stands out from up here. After
exploring the walled garden, do take the time to wander further
afield. Woodlands to the west contain impressive *Nothofagus*,
Taiwania and a giant *Eucryphia x* 'Nymansay' while to the north is a
new arboretum in which Calum Pirnie has assembled a significant
collection of conifers, many from wild origin seed. There are
numerous trails on the estate and you may be lucky to see some of
the bird and animal population which includes otters, red squirrels
and woodpeckers. There is lots to do for children, including a good
playpark and a popular café.

Cruickshank Botanic Garden

Cruickshank Botanic Garden
St Machar Drive, Aberdeen,
Grampian, AB24 3UU
(*map, pp. 54–55*)

Aberdeen University
and Cruickshank Botanic
Garden Trust
Monday–Friday 9am–4.30pm year
round, Saturday and Sunday
2–5pm (May–September only); ££
(on SGS days), otherwise free
www.abdn.ac.uk/biologicalsci

Founded in 1898 with land and a bequest from Anne Cruickshank, this garden always had a dual purpose as a botanic collection and a pleasure space for the people of Aberdeen. Further purchases of land have now made an 11-acre site of rather curious shape. The garden is surrounded by Aberdeen University buildings including the Department of Plant and Soil Sciences and their greenhouses and frames. The southern part of the garden consists of a lawn surrounded by mature trees: some of the highlights are a collection of Aria section *Sorbus*, a fine pair of top-grafted weeping Camperdown Elms, a huge *Quercus frainetto* and a fine multistemmed *Acer griseum*. To the west, designed around a central sunken rectangle, is a collection of old roses: albas, bourbons etc reflecting Aberdeen's important role in rose breeding. There is an impressive long herbaceous border and the rock garden and pond area contain dwarf rhododendrons and a huge range of spring bulbs such as *Trillium* and *Erythronium*. The garden boasts a favourable microclimate, being around a mile from the sea, where plants not thought to be hardy in north-east Scotland are doing well: *Buddleja colvilei*, for example. Other fine plants to look out for include two *Hoheria lyalii*, a collection of regional whitebeam microspecies such as the rare *S. arranensis*, a large *Paeonia ludlowii* and one of the largest *Arbutus unedo* in eastern Scotland. The arboretum

at the northern end of the garden is attached to the rest of the site by a narrow, rather gloomy path. The arboretum is the poorest part of the garden, simply a mixed collection of overcrowded mature trees. The Cruickshank is worth a visit from early spring into autumn. The labelling is good and the fine collection of plants, well looked-after considering the minimal staffing. Like many such city botanical gardens, the Cruickshank has an uncertain future. No longer required for scientific study, should the garden inform and/or entertain, and if so, how? Upkeep is expensive and some trees and shrubs are overgrown. Despite campaigning and hard work by the trustees and Friends of the Cruickshank over the years, there does seem to be a certain gloom about the future prospects, particularly if the university ceases to part fund it.

Daluaine
Rhynie, Aberdeenshire,
AB54 4GG
(*map, pp. 54–55*)

Mary Ann Crichton-Maitland
By appointment, occasional
open days, tours; ££
In Rhynie follow sign saying
Manse Road, Rhynie cemetery.
Drive is cattle grid, stone
pillars (last road on left in
village if coming from north)
T: 01464 861638

Daluaine

Mary Ann Crichton-Maitland and her husband David have gardened at Daluaine for two periods, interrupted by a move down to Renfrewshire in between. This old manse in the Aberdeenshire hills on the outskirts of Rhynie has been transformed into an ambitious and expanding garden in recent years. Along the drive is a collection of slightly over-shaded rhododendrons. Above the house is a small, densely planted walled garden which we hit at its peak in summer 2006. It is packed with roses, including many rarely seen in Scotland, underplanted with a wide range of perennials. This garden would be rather a lot for most retired couples to look after but not Mary, who gets up each day in summer at 6am and does two hours' work in the garden before breakfast. Purchases of land along the River Bogie

below the house, on the far side of the church road, have allowed a large expansion of the garden to be made, and it is now 10 acres in extent. Most of this new section is filled with an extensive collection of trees (*Acer, Sorbus, Prunus,* conifers and many more) with a burn and pond-side planted with waterside favourites; candelabra primulas doing particularly well. The woodland boasts carpets of spring bulbs and there are a number of animal sculptures dotted around. Daluaine is a single-minded and on-going adventure which is an amazing achievement. There are few signs of slowing down, despite the fact that David is in his 80s.

Douneside House

Lying in 15 acres of gardens and grounds, with fine views over the Howe of Cromar to the Grampians, Douneside is used as a holiday country house for serving or retired commissioned officers of the armed forces and their families. The trust which owns the garden was established by Lady Rachel MacRobert in memory of her three sons, who were all killed as aviators in WWII. The gardens have been re-covered and replanted in recent years, from a very overgrown state. There are plantings of roses and perennials on a series of terraces in front of and next to the house, and a walled garden with vegetables and flowers for cutting as well as restored glasshouses. I thought that the best features were the rock and water gardens which line the banks of a burn with several waterfalls and bridges. These have been cleared of invasive bamboo and huge conifers and head gardener Steve McCullum is replanting with all manner of waterside plants. This is a garden on the up.

Douneside House
Tarland, Aberdeenshire, AB34 4UL
(*map, pp. 54–55*)

MacRobert Trust
SGS 1 day 2008 and by appointment with the gardener; ££
On the outskirts of Tarland B9119 towards Aberdeen, follow signs to MacRobert Trust
T: 07775 967776
F: 013398 81255
E: douneside@irl.co.uk
www.dounesidehouse.co.uk

Drum Castle and Gardens,
Drumoak, Banchory,
Aberdeenshire, AB31 5EY
(*map, pp. 54–55*)

NTS
Gardens open daily all year.
Castle: July–August, daily
11am–5pm, Easter–end October
12.30–5pm, closed on Tuesday
and Friday, ££* (gardens);
£££* (castle)
A93 between Peterculter
and Banchory
T: 0844 493 2161
F: 0844 4932162
E: drum@nts.org.uk
www.nts.org.uk

Drum Castle, Garden and Estate

On a wet weekend in June, before the main rose season had started, I visited this garden for the first time. From the car park a meandering path leads past some fine deep-coloured *Rhododendron* 'Purple Splendour' and a large pond, to the beautifully restored walled garden which contains the Garden of Historic Roses, opened in 1991, designed by Eric Robson, now mature and one of the best rose gardens in the UK. I returned in August to see the roses in full flower. Rose gardens can be tedious: serried ranks of gaunt hybrid tea roses with black spot don't do much for me. But this is different. As these are species roses, shrub roses, with climbers and ramblers, they make fine and handsome well-clothed bushes, with climbers on the walls and pergolas, others in formal beds. Underneath them are carpets of perennials: geraniums, *Santolina, Nepeta* and bedding plants. All rose gardens should do this, it cuts down on weeds and looks so much more pleasing. The labelling is good too, so you can follow the history of the rose as you walk round the garden. There are four quadrants, divided by distinctive shaggy hemlock (*Tsuga*) hedges with arches over the paths, each section representing one century of rose-breeding/development. Here you'll find the gallicas, damasks, scotch roses and rugosas which are the breeding lines for many of the modern roses and which in many cases make better, more disease-resistant garden plants. In one corner is a small 'room of the rose' with details of the layout of the garden. The walls are not only covered with well-pruned climbing roses but also *Clematis*, hops, ivies, jasmines and many other climbing shrubs. The garden's central axis leads from the entrance gate, via a wooden gazebo based on one at Tyninghame House, to a Lorimer bench based on one at Kellie. The pink rose 'Constance Spry' growing through it was an exquisite combination in June. Long-time head gardener Diana Robertson is key to this garden's success: she has battled with the soil and climate here, neither of which is ideally suited to roses, to create an excellent garden with new innovations each year, the latest of which is a multi-coloured *Achillea*-dominated herbaceous border in one corner which was spectacular when we visited in August. From early June to early autumn this garden is a blaze of colour and perfume. A perfect compliment to Crathes next door, these are two of north-east Scotland's best summer gardens. The Irvine family has a 21-generation 650-year-old history at Drum Castle, having been granted lands here by Robert the Bruce. You can climb out onto the battlements of the castle for great views. Recent archaeological work has revealed the existence of a seventeenth-century formal garden under the lawn to the west of the castle. The Old Wood of Drum, with its ancient oaks, has a series of waymarked paths and an arboretum and you may spot squirrels and woodpeckers. Dogs are allowed in the woodlands but not in the walled garden.

Duthie Park and David Welsh Winter Garden

This park and its greenhouses are an amazingly popular attraction, claiming up to 350,000 people per year, making them Scotland's third most visited garden. Duthie Park's 43 acres were donated to the city of Aberdeen by Lady Elizabeth Duthie and were laid out in 1883. The magnificent 1899 palm house is sadly no longer, damaged in 1960s' gales. The replacement winter gardens were largely inspired by the enthusiasm of Aberdeen Parks director, later director of the Royal Parks, David Welsh, and the gardens were named in his honour after the remaining old greenhouses were restored, enlarged and completely replanted. The complex claims to hold the largest indoor horticultural collection of its type in Europe and consists of a series of linked greenhouses each with a different theme: bromeliads, ferns, perfumed plants, tropical plants and so on, with good labelling and interpretation. Some of the houses are underplanted with somewhat incongruous carpet bedding. Best is the arid house, containing a major collection of cacti and succulents, and a perfect contrast to the heat and humidity of the bromeliad house next door. The potted pelargoniums and geraniums on staging were another spectacular display when I visited in June. A popular children's attraction is the McPuddock frog which pops up from time to time out of the pool in the fern house. The floral courtyard next to the greenhouses is a blaze of colour in summer with bedding, perennials and grasses planted in rectangular white granite block beds which look rather bleak in winter, but which work much better when the plants spill out of them in peak season. The Japanese garden is overgrown and needs to be replanted or replaced. Outdoors in the main park, the most popular feature is the 'Rose Mountain', a gaudy massed display of bright modern roses on a mound flowering in July and August, which

Duthie Park and David Welsh Winter Garden
Polmuir Road, Aberdeen,
AB11 7TH
(*map, pp. 54–55*)

Aberdeen City Council
Gardens open daily from
9.30am–4.30pm every day except
25 December and 1 January; free.
On Riverside Drive. Coming north
on A90 turn right (east) at
roundabout on north side of River
Dee. Bus No. 17 from city centre
T: 01224 585310
F: 01224 210532
E: wintergardens@
aberdeencity.gov.uk
www.aberdeencity.gov.uk
Café

is covered with crocus in early spring. The west side of the park contains a long herbaceous border and more of the silly rhododendron 'bedding' which is also a theme in Aberdeen's Johnston Park; clearly they got a cheap job lot a few years back. Duthie Park's ponds, currently dry, are awaiting restoration as part of a lottery bid. Aberdeen has a good claim to have the best maintained set of public parks in the UK and has won *Britain in Bloom* competitions more often than any other city. Certainly Aberdonians know about the David Welsh Winter Gardens but I am not sure that they have the profile they deserve in the wider world.

    [WC]

Ecclesgreig Castle
St Cyrus, Kincardineshire, DD10 0DP
(*map, pp. 54–55*)

Farquhar Estates Ltd.
SGS Snowdrops; ££
Head inland on the minor road from St Cyrus
T: 01674 850 100
F: 01674 850 150
E: enquiries@ecclesgreig.com
www.ecclesgreig.com

Ecclesgreig Castle

It is no surprise when you clap eyes on this place that the castle is supposedly partly the inspiration for *Dracula* when Bram Stoker stayed here. The castle is a whimsical Hammer Horror fantasy of turrets, portcullis and crow-stepped gables but was in a very sorry state when Gavin Farquhar bought it. Half a mile inland from the village of St. Cyrus on a hilltop, it offers spectacular views over the North Sea. It still needs a huge amount of work, just to stop it falling down. A substantial amount of garden restoration has been done, reshaping the topiary in the Italian garden, replacing stolen statues, replanting herbaceous borders and adorning the woodland paths with massed snowdrops. Gavin reckons that they may have planted a million bulbs and they are already putting on an impressive show which should improve from year to year.

Ecclesgreig Castle

Esslemont

Esslemont is a Victorian house set in a much older enclosed garden. The double yew hedging dates back to the seventeenth and eighteenth centuries. The central axis consists of domes of box and a centre bed of Pampas. A sunken paved area with rather utilitarian 3 × 2 concrete slabs is planted with lavender, grasses, ferns *Achillea* and many other plants.

Esslemont
Ellon, Aberdeenshire, AB41 8PA
(*map, pp. 54–55*)

Mr and Mrs Wolrige-Gordon
of Esslemont
SGS 1 day; ££
A920 from Ellon. On
Pitmedden/Oldmeldrum Road.
T: 01358 720234

**Findhorn Community Garden
and Cullerne Gardens**
The Park, Findhorn, Forres,
Moray, IV36 3TZ
(*map, pp. 54–55*)

Findhorn Foundation
Guided tours in summer 2pm,
see website for days. Self-guided
(guidebook) or guided tours; ££
Findhorn Park A96 roundabout
turn onto B9011. Turn left at the
first lights in Kinloss following the
signs for Findhorn. The entrance
to the Park is about 1 mile on the
right. Local bus from Forres
T: 01309 690311
F: 01309 691301
E: enquiries@findhorn.org
www.findhorn.org
Blue Angel café and very good
shop for picnic provisions.

Findhorn Community Garden and Cullerne Gardens

The Findhorn Community is still going strong, celebrating its 45th anniversary in 2007. Founded in 1962 by Eileen and Peter Caddy and Dorothy MacLean, Findhorn has had a considerable influence worldwide and was featured in a fascinating Channel 4 documentary. It has grown from a small cluster of caravans to a small township incorporating many different businesses and initiatives, an education centre, and an eco-village of 29 buildings. Even if you are sceptical at claims that Findhorn founder Dorothy could intuitively contact the spirits of plants – devas – who gave her instructions on how to garden at Findhorn, there is much to admire in the organic techniques developed here long before such things became fashionable. When I first visited, the site was a rather ugly mess of ramshackle buildings but the whole place (with the exception of the caravan park) is now much more attractive with lush greenery everywhere, more like a forest with buildings in it. Virtually the whole site is 'gardened' to some extent and judging by the plantings around the houses, most of the community members are keen on both edible and ornamental plants. The 'Original Garden' can still be found next to the 'Original Caravan', where organic vegetables were first grown. The 'Living Machine' is a filter bed system which treats Findhorn's waste water through huge tubs full of plants. It is open to visitors on Tuesday and Thursday afternoons. Findhorn runs a variety of guest programmes and courses, many of which give people the opportunity to work in the gardens. In 1994 an organic and biodynamic agriculture scheme,

EarthShare, was established to increase use of local produce and the scheme has expanded from 5 to 15 acres, spread over 3 sites. Currently it provides more than 70 per cent of the community's fresh food requirements and supplies 200 individual households, running what is Scotland's largest organic box scheme. The four wind turbines provide all the power that the community needs and the surplus is sold to the grid. Findhorn visitors can take self-guided tours (with the map/guide) or guided ones in summer (see website for times). The Phoenix Shop opposite the visitor centre stocks a bewildering range of organic, eco and fair-trade products, including produce from the Findhorn farms and other locally sourced goods. The newly opened Moray Arts Centre holds exhibitions; I caught the opening show, a retrospective of local artist and writer John Byrne. I really like Findhorn: you can hardly fail to be charmed by the friendly atmos-phere and laid-back pace. People always seem to have time to stop and chat and yet this is a focused and tightly run community with outreach in NGOs, via Cifal Findhorn, for training and sharing infor-mation internationally. The organic vegetable production (which you can see part of at Cullerne Gardens) is impressive and was years ahead of its time. Anyone interested in sustainable, or energy efficient/eco-housing would be advised to have a look at what has been achieved here. Most of the houses look Scandinavian in design and examples of innovation include straw bale house, homes made out of giant recycled whisky barrels, use of breathing walls, living roofs, heat pumps and solar panels, and the treatment of sewage using plants. There are several B&Bs at Findhorn if you wish to stay for short periods. If you enrol on courses, accommodation can be arranged.

Findrack

Redesigned over the last 15 years, set in fine wooded countryside at around 700ft, the garden at Findrack consists of several sections around the house. The partially walled garden behind the house is laid out with a central circular lawn with a centrepiece pergola covered with the rose 'Albertine', off which are four further circular lawns each surrounded by herbaceous borders, backed by shrubs. There are stone pavilions, summerhouses or pergolas in the corners and the gardens were planned with input from designer Michael Balston. Next to the house is a terraced courtyard with a raised octagonal pond from which a path leads along the back of the house where gardener Brian Sinclair has planted an unusual double screen with a base of *Prunus lusitanica* with pleached *Prunus serrula* (*thibetica*) above. A wide expanse of lawn leads to the impressive bogside/streamside water garden. This was a mass of multi-coloured *Primula florindae* in early August when I visited and in early summer is a mass of blue and monocarpic *Meconopsis*, both of which sow

Findrack
Torphins, Aberdeenshire,
AB31 4LJ
(*map, pp. 54–55*)

Mr and Mrs Andrew Salvesen
SGS 1 day per year; ££
Leave Torphins on A980 to
Lumphanan. After ½ mile turn off,
signed Tornaveen. Stone gateway,
1 mile up on left

85

themselves freely around. Beyond the walled garden is a narrow hedged cutting and vegetable garden, while further afield is a newly planted woodland garden, with island beds and a small arboretum.

**Fordmouth Croft
Ornamental Grass Nursery**
Fordmouth Croft,
Meikle Wartle, Inverurie,
Aberdeenshire, AB51 5BE
(*map, pp. 54–55*)

Ann-Marie Grant
By appointment
Meikle Wartle, some 8 miles
north-west of Inverurie
T: 01467 671519
E: ann-marie@
fmcornamentalgrasses.co.uk
www.fmcornamentalgrasses.co.uk

Fordmouth Croft Ornamental Grass Nursery

This specialist grass nursery in rural Aberdeenshire lists an impressive range and the catalogue is full of detail. It includes many grasses and grass-like plants, the usual suspects: 30 varieties of *Carex* and 10 of *Festuca*, for example. But there are also strange and wonderful things: you may well not have heard of *Ammophila arenaria, Ampelodesmos mauritanica, Andropogon gerardii, Andropogon virginicus, Anemanthele lessoniana* . . . Grasses have been very much in vogue in recent years, though Scotland has perhaps been slower than further south to embrace them. Not all grow well up here, with many of them tending to rot in winter wet, so it is important to choose the right varieties: some are better in heavy wet soil while others need sharp drainage. The nursery offers mail order year round and the catalogue is available on the nursery website. There are impressive beds of grasses behind the house but this is mainly a mail order business, with customers welcome by appointment only.

Fyvie Castle, Garden and Estate

In 800 years, Fyvie Castle has been owned by some of north-east Scotland's major landed families: the Prestons, Meldrums, Setons, Gordons and Forbes-Leiths. The handsome ochre-coloured stone Scottish Baronial castle dates back to the thirteenth century and has been much altered and added to ever since. Inside it is mainly Edwardian in style and contains an important collection of paintings, Raeburns in particular. Much of the parkland landscaping dates to the early nineteenth century and the long, narrow Loch Fyvie alongside the drive is a fine feature, currently under-utilised. Part of the 6-acre eighteenth-century walled garden has recently been redeveloped as a garden of Scottish fruits and vegetables, laid out as a large parterre, the pattern for which was a ceiling in the castle. I'm not convinced of the wisdom of this garden design; the absence of a vantage point makes the layout hard to appreciate and when I visited in mid summer the fruit and vegetables on their own tended to look gaunt and sparse, with many empty sections of bed. Perhaps more significant is the wide area of empty space, covered in red gravel, punctuated by a few white wooden containers. These blank areas have the effect of making the garden seem half empty. A denser potager of mixed flowers, herbs and fruit is probably more suited to this type of layout. The garden walls are lined with trained fruit; as well as apples and pears there are more unusual cordon and fan-trained currants. Outside the walled garden, the so-called American garden is a path which leads to the castle, lined with rhododendrons and perennials, with fine Acers and other trees overhead. One potential future development at Fyvie is the establishment of a college for traditional crafts such as dry stone walling, in some of the extensive out-buildings next to the walled garden.

Fyvie Castle, Garden and Estate
Fyvie, Turriff, Aberdeenshire, AB53 8JS
(*map, pp. 54–55*)

NTS
Grounds: Daily, year-round 9.30am–sunset; castle: April–end October Saturday–Wednesday, 12–5pm, open daily July and August; ££
Just off the A947 between Turriff and Oldmeldrum
T: 01651 891266
F: 01651 891107
www.nts.org.uk

Glen Grant Distillery Garden
Glen Grant Garden, Rothes,
Aberlour, Banffshire, AB38 7BS
(map, pp. 54–55)

Glen Grant Distillery Co Ltd
Mid January–mid December
Monday–Saturday: 9.30am–5pm
(last distillery tour 4pm), Sunday
12–5pm (last tour 4pm); ££
North end of Rothes,
c. 10 miles south of Elgin
on the A941 Grantown-on-Spey
road. Bus stop very near
T: 01542 783318
F: 01340 832104
E: mail visitorcentre@
glengrant.com
www.glengrant.com
Tea room

Glen Grant Distillery Garden

Described by Katie Campbell as 'a glorious piece of nineteenth-century kitsch', this garden was mainly the creation of James 'The Major' Grant, a businessman and playboy who slaughtered plenty of Scottish and African wildlife, even bringing back a servant boy from Africa as part of his booty. The garden, which lies up the valley from the distillery and visitor centre, follows a swift-flowing peaty burn. The whole garden has been restored in recent years by Karen Ellington and her team, who have recreated the woodland walks, lily pond, bridges and the Major's famous 'dram hut'. I remember being called in to advise on the restoration/replanting of the garden and I was curious to see what had been achieved since. The work on the infrastructure has been impressive and the long rustic walkways which run up the ravine are quite a feat of woodwork though I suspect there were once better vistas, now obscured by undergrowth. The flatter part of the garden lower down consists of lawns, planted with apples and other trees with a waterside planting of *Iris, Ligularia, Lysmachia* and *Gunnera*. The dominant ornamentals are rhododendrons and azaleas, in two large blocks, so the best time to see the garden is late May and early June. When I visited in July, there was not much colour apart from masses of purple and yellow candelabra primulas and some wild roses. This is not a garden I'm very fond of, it seems to be very much of its era, like a gloomy Victorian public park, without the carpet bedding to liven it up. As most visitors come in July and August, I think the summer interest should be improved, which would be quite easily achieved. The garden can be visited on its own or in combination with a tour of the distillery. Children under eight are not allowed in the distillery but are welcome in the garden.

Glenbervie House
Drumlithie, Stonehaven,
Kincardineshire, AB39 3YA
(map, pp. 54–55)

Mr and Mrs A. MacPhie
SGS and by appointment; ££
8 miles north-east of Laurencekirk,
6 miles from Stonehaven off
A90 on minor road, 3 miles
west of Drumlithie
T: 01569 740226

Glenbervie House

Not to be confused with the hotel of the same name near Stirling, this is a fine woodland and walled garden near Stonehaven, with enviable topography. The handsome, recently repainted gleaming white house, dates back to the thirteenth century in parts, and perches above the Bervie river. The steep bank down to the river was a mass of yellow daisies in June when I visited, while a noble monkey puzzle stood sentinel over an assortment of deciduous azaleas. The wooded drive runs alongside the Pilkerty burn and is planted with rhododendrons, primulas and *Meconopsis* and naturalised daffodils. The south-sloping, free-draining walled garden, in continuous cultivation for 300 years, is divided into quadrants, separated by pole-and-rope rose borders, underplanted with nepeta. The centrepiece is a pair of yews and a Gothic Victorian folly draped with climbers. Glenbervie has long been a fine perennial garden, famous for its *Fuchsia* hedge, *Phlox*

border, *Dianthus* border, dense plantings of day lilies, a fine display of delphiniums as well as less common subjects such as *Veratrum* and *Kirengeshoma palmata.* The handsome greenhouses, originally built by Moncrieff in the 1860s, still in fine condition, are stuffed with passionflowers, bougainvilleas and vines and kept warm with waste heat from the family-owned food factory next door. Nearby is the graveyard where many of Robert Burns' family are buried. Knowledgeable head gardener Kevin Whyte is clearly on top of things here and somehow has time also to look after his own fine garden by the cottage behind the walled garden. Generations of green-fingered Nicholsons and MacPhies have created and maintained Glenbervie and it appears to have a secure future.

Gordon Highlanders Museum

The striking black and white museum stands in the nineteenth-century garden which formerly belonged to painter Sir George Reid. The walled garden consists of three small sections, one with trees and terraced herbaceous beds, a garden of contemplation and a secret garden. Shrubs and trees are labelled with dedications to individual soldiers. The design and plant choice were made by Dr Tom Smith, whose wonderful Aberdeen garden is nearby. The museum itself has interactive displays covering the history of the Gordon Highlanders from the Napoleonic wars to the present, including the 19 Victoria Crosses earned by members of the regiment. Johnston Gardens are just round the corner and are also worth a visit.

Gordon Highlanders Museum
St Luke's, Viewfield Road,
Aberdeen, AB15 7XH
(*map, pp. 54–55*)

April–October: Tuesday–Saturday
10.30am–4.30pm, Sunday
1.30–4.30pm; ££ (museum and
garden). See website for winter
hours
Turn off the A90 at the Queens
Road roundabout and head west
along the B9119. Turn second left,
signed
T: 01224 311200
E: museum@gordon
highlanders.com
www.gordonhighlanders.com
Popular café overlooking the
gardens

Gordonstoun School
Gordonstoun, Elgin,
Moray IV30 5RF
(*map, pp. 54–55*)

SGS 1 day and by appointment,
but not in term time; ££
Entrance off B9012, 4 miles
north of Elgin, signposted in
Duffus Village
T: 01343 837837
F: 01343 837838
E: lambies@gordonstoun.org.uk
www.gordonstoun.org.uk/

Gordonstoun School

This private school, founded by Kurt Hahn, lies in the planned landscape of Gordonstoun House, an imposingly handsome Georgian building of 1775/6 incorporating an earlier seventeenth-century house built for the first marquis of Huntly. Most unusual is the building known as the 'Round Square' built around a circular courtyard. The parkland was laid out in the eighteenth and nineteenth centuries. The central north–south axis runs through the house. On the north side is an avenue of yew, buried behind some beech trees which would be better removed. On the south side, a wide lawn is edged on the east side by a long herbaceous border, beyond which is a wide chestnut-lined avenue and canal which leads to the southern boundary of the former park. From halfway down the canal the 'silent walk', planted with daffodils, leads east to Michael Kirk. The cricket pitch on the north side of the house has a very fine oak which lies inside the boundary. If you hit the tree, it is four runs. From here, the rather brutal St Christopher's Chapel is visible through the trees. There is also a beehive doocot. The extensive planned landscape is well maintained and heavily wooded and peace is only spoiled by the jets from Kinloss and Lossiemouth; they don't fly on Sundays, so open days should be quiet.

Grandhome
Grandhome Estate, Danestone
near Aberdeen, AB22 8AR
(*map, pp. 54–55*)

Mr and Mrs D.R. Paton
By appointment; ££
From north end of Anderson's
Drive, A90 over Persley Bridge,
turn left at roundabout,
2 miles on left
T: 01224 722 202

Grandhome

Grandhome, which lies on the banks of the Don north of Aberdeen, is a handsome eighteenth-century house with terraces on the slopes facing the river, the walls of which are planted with a fine collection of plums and gages. The main attraction here are the trees, which include mature *Tsuga*, limes, chestnuts, pines and a recently planted collection of beech cultivars, underplanted with bulbs and azaleas. I liked the pet monument, a curious sculpture with all the family pets' names: the dogs, the fish, the cats . . . The eighteenth-century walled garden, built in an 'L' shape, is forlorn and neglected.

Greenridge

This is the garden equivalent of the popular television series *Life on Mars*. I drove in one wet Saturday morning and thought I'd woken up in the 1970s. As if in a time capsule, this is exactly the sort of garden I remember Percy Thrower wandering around in, and it was a pleasant surprise to see a garden preserved like this. The house is used by its owners, BP, as a conference centre and the terrace is a bedding-plant extravaganza. A short distance away is the small walled garden, which you can look down on from above. It is laid out with a series of island beds planted with heather and conifers in Adrian Bloom style, with neat rows of bedding planted around the terraces, borders and an oval rose bed, in multi-coloured swirly patterns. It is obviously lovingly maintained and long may it last.

Greenridge
Craigton Road, Cults, AB15 9PS
(*map, pp. 54–55*)

BP Exploration
By appointment, July and August
Turn off North Deeside A93 road
in Cults, north onto Baird's Brae
and 2nd right is Craigton Road.
Coming from Aberdeen road
splits into A93 and Craigton
Road (right fork)
T: 01224 860200
F: 01224 860210

Green's Nurseries

This nursery grows grasses and perennials wholesale and these are offered for retail sale, alongside a good range of trees, shrubs, alpines and bedding in a small garden centre in the countryside south of Nairn.

Green's Nurseries
New Fleenas Farm, Nairn,
IV12 5QN
(*map, pp. 54–55*)

A939 Nairn–Grantown road,
c. 4 miles south of Nairn
T: 01540 651 287
F: 01540 651 656

Haddo House and Garden

Home to the Gordon family for hundreds of years, Haddo is a fine example of an eighteenth-century house and landscape on a grand scale. Like Kinross House, it is designed with a long vista both back and front, with the eye being drawn through avenues of trees to distant monuments. Haddo's magnificent lime avenue is now rather too thick, partly concealing the vista beyond, and the trees should be thinned or pruned. The Classical eighteenth-century house is fronted by a series of terraces and geometric beds filled with bedding, with a fine stone fountain in the centre. Below the terrace on either side are long herbaceous borders with bold plantings of *Macleaya* and other summer favourites. I think the site deserves a more ambitious garden

Haddo House and Garden
Ellon, Aberdeenshire, AB41 7EQ
(*map, pp. 54–55*)

NTS
Garden: all year, daily 9–sunset.
House open Friday–Monday
Easter–October, daily July and
August; £££* (house and gardens)
Off the B9170 south of Methlick,
a few miles north of Pitmedden
T: 01651 851440
F: 01651 851888
E: haddo@nts.org.uk
www.nts.org.uk

than it currently has. Next door is Haddo Country Park with monuments, lochs and woodland trails for children to run around. There is a good children's play area, a pond to feed the ducks and an obstacle course to wear out your dog (and children at the same time I dare say).

Happy Plant Garden Centre

Happy Plant Garden Centre
North Street, Mintlaw,
Peterhead, AB42 5HH
(*map, pp. 54–55*)

Garden Centre: Monday–Saturday
9am–5pm, Sunday 10am–5pm;
coffee shop closes 4.30.
On the A 952 on the northern
outskirts of Mintlaw
T: 01771 623344 store
F: 01771 624066
E: office@happyplant.co.uk
happyplantgardencentre.
rws-flexiweb.co.uk
Coffee shop

Happy Plants is a well-known and popular garden centre, the largest in this corner of Scotland, with a florist service and a very popular café/coffee shop as well as a large, well-stocked plant area and a good range of pet products. The website even advertises gluten-free dog food. Whatever next?

Hatton Castle

The grounds of Hatton seem to be a pheasant factory and the birds are inclined to run under your car. Mrs Duff led me from the castle up the sloping lawns past the beds of deciduous azaleas, through the bluebell woods to the fine 2-acre walled garden which (in common with many such owners) she wished was a bit nearer the house. This garden has one or two unusual features: instead of the usual box edging, much of the garden is lined with *Astilbe*, mostly white, but with some sections of pink and red. The edging is surprisingly effective and quite easy to look after, though the 2006 drought did burn them a bit. I'm surprised this has not been tried elsewhere. The main structural features are the very attractive curved pleached hornbeam allées (or stilt hedges) which divide the garden in two, with curved herbaceous and rose borders beneath them which can be viewed from either side under the trees. In the centre is a huge domed yew. The impressive and extensive vegetable garden lies to the lower end of the garden while a small herb parterre has been made at the top end. The garden falls away on one side, through a grass meadow down to a stream, lined with bog plants. This is a well looked after garden with some interesting design features.

Hatton Castle
Turriff, Aberdeenshire,
AB53 8ED
(*map, pp. 54–55*)

Mr and Mrs James Duff
SGS by appointment; ££
A947 2 miles south of Turriff,
signed to Hatton estate
E: jjdgardens@btinternet.com

Hazlehead Park

Aberdeen boasts many of the best public parks in Scotland. Hazlehead's substantial tract of land – 180 hectares – was apparently granted to the city of Aberdeen by Robert the Bruce in 1319 and can be considered Aberdeen's lungs. Apart from sports fields, extensive woodlands and golf and pitch and putt courses, these are mostly well-maintained gardens, with two of the most impressive plant displays in

Hazlehead Park
Groats Road at Hazlehead Avenue,
Aberdeen,
AB15 8BE
(*map, pp. 54–55*)

Aberdeen City Council
Daylight hours; free
Queen's Road to Skene Road.
Turn right into Groats Road.
Buses from city centre
T: 01224 814773
www.aberdeencity.gov.uk
Café in summer

93

Scotland. The first, reaching a peak in the last week of May, are several acres of Mollis (and some Exbury and species), azaleas, mainly in reds, oranges and yellows. This is by far Scotland's largest such display and rivals Exbury on the south coast of England in its scale. The azaleas are planted with large blue-leaved hostas (I'm not sure this is a particularly pleasing combination), complemented by a range of stone and metal sculpture, some rescued from demolition and development in other parts of the city. Impressive though the azaleas are, the narrow range of varieties and seemingly random planting is a missed opportunity. There are far too many identical Mollis seedlings and I would have preferred to see more colour-coordinated plantings and a wider range of azalea varieties used; the spectacle is Keukenhof-like in its repetitive garish clashing of colours. But boisterous it undoubtedly is. The azalea garden leads into the two-part giant formal rose garden, which looks very well maintained; every rose I saw had been meticulously pruned and mulched. The garden consists of two large rectangles: the Queen Mother Gardens to the west and the North Sea Memorial Gardens to the east, in memory of the 1988 Piper Alpha disaster in which 167 people lost their lives. The roses reach their peak of flower in July and August and in reasonably dry summers the displays are amazing, though disease sometimes takes its toll. The heather and conifer garden to the east has had considerable refurbishment, but it won't amount to much unless someone has the courage to take out some of the trees and conifers which are now overshading the area. Heathers need full sun, as anyone who has seen them grow on moorland can attest. The notoriously difficult-to-escape-from privet maze (it even has an emergency exit) was planted in 1935. I could not find out why it appeared to be closed when I visited in 2008. Voted Britain's best park in 2004 I would certainly consider it one of Scotland's most impressive public parks, with its pet area, playground and terrace café to keep the whole family occupied.

Hillockhead
Glendeskry, Strathdon,
Aberdeenshire, AB36 8XL
(*map, pp. 54–55*)

Stephen Campbell
and Sue Macintosh
SGS; ££
From Deeside, head north on
A97 for 9 miles, turn sharp left
at crossroads shortly after
Boultinstone. After ½ mile take
first left SP 'Ardgeith Fishings'.
Hillockhead is 2 miles along
road on right
T: 01975 651458

Hillockhead

One of Scotland's highest and more remote mainland gardens, at 1,300ft, this is an interesting addition to the SGS 'Yellow Book'. Hillockhead has outstanding views of Morvern, wildflower areas, herbaceous borders and organic fruit and vegetables, punctuated by 'sit-ooteries' and quiet corners enclosed with dry stone walls.

Howemill

This is a maturing and rather wild, informal garden with a wide range of unusual alpines, shrubs and herbaceous plants and climbers engulfing the house. Owner David Atkinson is a landscaper and the garden is maintained with help from a botanist neighbour. There is a megalithic site nearby.

Inchmarlo House Garden

This is a good example of how a change of use for a large property can result in the saving of a garden which might otherwise have disappeared. This estate on the outskirts of Banchory has an impressive collection of mature trees which provide the shelter for a woodland garden originally planted by Colonel and Mrs Bowhill,

Howemill
Criagievar, Aberdeen, AB33 8TD
(*map, pp. 54–55*)

Mr D. Atkinson
SGS 1 day in June, and
by appointment; ££
From Alford, turn off the A980
Alford–Lumphanan road.
South-east of Rinmore
T: 01975 581278
E: davidmatkinson@tiscali.co.uk

Inchmarlo House Garden
Inchmarlo House, Inchmarlo,
Banchory, AB31 4AL
(*map, pp. 54–55*)

Skene Enterprises (Aberdeen) Ltd
1 day in May SGS and by
appointment; ££ (SGS) or
donation
Inchmarlo is approximately 1½
miles to the west of Banchory on
A93. Ignore turning for Inchmarlo
golf course. Entrance to Inchmarlo
is c. ½ mile after this on right
T: 01330 824981
F: 01330 825828
E: info@inchmarlo-
retirement.co.uk
www.inchmarlo-retirement.co.uk

with guidance from E.H.M. Cox in the post-World War II period.
These plantings are now mature and very fine, with drifts of azaleas
and giant rhododendron species and hybrids, underplanted with
spring bulbs and wild flowers, with primulas and other plants
alongside the ponds. North of the woodland garden is an open area
with a putting green with three long herbaceous borders; lupins were
the dominant plant in flower when I visited in June, though I gather
these are being replaced. There are fine specimen trees on the lawns
between this and the woodland. The estate is now a retirement village
with flats and houses, and the grounds, gardens and trees are well
maintained. The rhododendron displays are some of the best in the
north-east and there is an interesting oriental garden, with a dry river
bed, designed by Peter Rogers, next to one of the housing complexes.
There are plans to further improve the gardens and extend the
flowering season.

Innes House Gardens
Innes House, Elgin,
Moray, IV30 8NG
(*map, pp. 54–55*)

Mr and Mrs Mark Tennant
Open to parties of 20 or more
by appointment; ££
Turn off the A96 near Lhanbryde,
go through Urquhart and entrance
is just outside village of Viewfield
T: 01343 842410
F: 01343 842148
E: enquiries@inneshouse.co.uk
www.inneshouse.co.uk

Innes House Gardens

Innes House is a striking white seventeenth-century Scottish Baronial
tower with Edwardian additions. It is set in walled gardens which are
divided into sections and allées bordered with clipped yew hedging.
The garden contains a centrepiece sundial, herbaceous borders and a
sunken garden with a rectangular pool, restored in recent years by
Mark and Hermione Tennant. The rose garden in a separate hedged
compartment features flagstone paths and box-edged beds filled with
popular floribunda 'Iceberg'. The house is surrounded by parkland
with a good collection of mature trees, many planted by owner Mark
Tennant's mother Emma, including *Davidia, Parrotia, Acer griseum*
and *Eucryphia*. The garden is used as a wedding venue in summer,
with a marquee in the courtyard garden on the east side of the house.

Jack Drake's Alpine Nursery, Inshriach

This famous name was founded by Jack Drake and John Lawson in 1949, and was the first of several great Scottish alpine nurseries. John Lawson carried on the nursery after Jack Drake retired but by the time he sold it in 1999 the whole nursery was rather run down. The Borrowmans have kept the propagation of alpines going, though no longer selling plants mail order, and are extending the display garden plantings of alpines, perennials and other plants around the nursery. They are becoming more and more famous for their cake shop, where homemade, very fattening and delicious cakes and coffee are on offer. Out of the café windows the bird feeders attract huge numbers of birds and red squirrels. My children loved it. Not a bad combination: a small nursery with something to amuse the kids. Definitely no dogs allowed for obvious reasons.

Jack Drake's Alpine Nursery, Inshriach
Aviemore, Inverness-shire, Highland, PH22 1QS
(*map, pp. 54–55*)

John and Gunnbjørg Borrowman
March–end October: 10am–5pm, closed Wednesday
4 miles south of Aviemore on B970. Brown signs at Inverdruie and Kingussie (A9)
T: 01540 651287
F: 01540 651656
E: info@drakesalpines.com
www.drakesalpines.com
Fantastic café specialising in coffee and Norwegian cakes
Groups by arrangement

James Cocker and Sons

One of Scotland's greatest nursery dynasties, Cockers nursery was founded in 1840 after James Cocker, then a gardener at Castle Fraser, refused to work on the Sabbath and resigned to start his own nursery, now run by his great-great-grandson Alec. Once the nursery moved to Whitemyres farm in the 1960s rose-growing and breeding became the nursery's speciality. Alec Cocker Senior bred an enormous number of internationally important roses including: 'Silver Jubilee', 'Alec's Red', 'Glenfiddich', 'Remember Me' and 'Gordon's College'. Cocker's Garden Centre was opened in 1986 and is well known for its rose trial beds, which are a blaze of colour in July and August. Much of the rose-growing land has been sold for development, and planning permission had been granted to relocate the business to a new site on the western outskirts of Aberdeen in the near future, but this site was then sold to Dobbies. Apparently the rose mail order will continue and there are plans for a new trials garden.

James Cocker and Sons
Whitemyres, Lang Stracht, Aberdeen AB15 6XH
(moving shortly)
(*map, pp. 54–55*)

Alec Cocker
Daily: 9am–5.30pm
T: 01224 313261
F: 01224 312531
E: sales@roses.uk.com
www.roses.uk.com

James Cocker and Sons
(*Rosa gallica Versicolor*)

**Johnstons of Elgin Cashmere
Heritage Centre**
Johnstons, Newmill, Elgin,
Morayshire, IV30 4AF
(*map, pp. 54–55*)

Monday–Saturday 9am–5.30pm,
Sunday 11am–5pm
Just off the A96 in the centre
of Elgin
T: 01343 554099
E: shop@johnstonscashmere.com
www.johnstonscashmere.com
Café

Johnstons of Elgin Cashmere Heritage Centre

Johnstons of Elgin is now the only cashmere company in the UK
which produces the whole product from fibre to finished article in
their own mill and factory. You can take a free guided tour of the mill
and buy their scarves and jumpers at their shopping complex in
Elgin. This consists of two buildings side by side, the older with the
clothes shop, food hall and café and the newer, opened in 2008,
around a courtyard, beautifully converted, with gifts, books and
kitchenware and a spectacular display on cashmere production.
Outside is a small garden centre, which can only be described as 'chi
chi', which I mean as a compliment. The garden beyond is under
development.

Johnston Gardens

Aberdeen has several of Scotland's finest parks and this small one is well worth a visit. The gardens, which lie in a ravine with a stream and a series of linked ponds running through it, used to belong to Johnston house, now demolished. One of the best features is the painted railings and bridges, which show up well in winter and summer. The largest bridge is a startling pale blue, while the remainder of railings and bridges are black. The garden is Japanese in feel, with conifers, a fine selection of green and red maples, azaleas and rhododendrons, underplanted with ferns, astilbes, *Hemerocallis*, lilies, hostas and other plants. Probably at its best in spring and early summer but good year round. It would not take much work to turn this little gem into a great garden; it is crying out for some courageous swashbuckling with a chainsaw to open it up. There are far too many trees, too many over-large rhododendrons and some idiotic recently planted carpet bedding with young rhododendrons, with ill-chosen varieties such as the mildew-magnet 'Virginia Richards' planted in dense shade where there is no chance of a good display. The centre-piece blue bridge is partly buried behind some tired old hybrid rhododendrons. All this could be sorted out in a few weeks one winter. There were three gardeners working when I visited, so labour is clearly available.

Johnston Gardens
Viewfield Road,
Aberdeen AB15 7XE
(*map, pp. 54–55*)

Aberdeen City Council
Dawn till dusk; free.
Turn off the A90 at the Queens Road roundabout and head west along the B9119. Turn second left, past the Gordon Highlanders museum and turn right. Car park on the left, entrance on right
T: 01224 522734

Kemnay Quarry Observation Point

**Kemnay Quarry
Observation Point**
Kemnay, Aberdeenshire,
AB51
(*map, pp. 54–55*)

All year; free
Turn off the A96 north-west of
Aberdeen, signed to Kemnay.
Don't try to get in by the quarry
entrance, instead use the car park
on Fyfe Park, which can be
reached either via Fraser Place or
off the B994. You may need to ask
directions as there are no signs

I'm a fan of land art, so I was keen to check this out. Kemnay quarry
has supplied high-quality granite for over 160 years, for the floor of
part of the new Scottish Parliament, for example. In 1996, to celebrate
the hundred and fiftieth year of the quarry, 'The Place of Origin
Project' was conceived by artists John Maine RA, from Salisbury,
Glen Onwin from Edinburgh and Brad Goldberg from Texas.
Apparently they moved 100,000 tons of granite and other stone to
make the mound or hill. While I can see that the Dutch or the Danes
might have found artificial hill-building a worthwhile exercise,
Scotland is surely blessed with enough of them not to have to build
one more. At best, I daresay it looks a bit like a white hill fort, and
the views into Kemnay quarry itself are quite dramatic, though the
barbed wire and fence rather spoil the effect. As from almost everywhere in the area, there are fine views of Aberdeenshire's landmark
peak of Bennachie. Next to some of the paths there are arrangements
of granite blocks. The hill is being reclaimed by willow herb and other
weeds and the community woodland planting does not look very well
maintained. I suspect that the whole place is now mainly used for dog
walking and as a mountain bike track for local teenagers. As an
example of land art, it is mediocre: it hardly has the magic of
Callanish standing stones, Robert Smithson's Spiral Jetty or one of
Charles Jencks' constructions. I can't find much to recommend it; it
all looks half-hearted and apologetic. If you or your dog want a brisk
walk, it might be worth a look. The trouble is that you'd probably
never find it. There are no signposts and nothing apart from a sign by
the car park to tell you it is there. The whole enterprise seems to be
slinking guiltily into the undergrowth, to be buried for some confused
future archaeologist to find.

Kildrummy Castle Gardens

What a setting this garden has, every gardener dreams of such riches, created in a ravine, widened through quarrying, and crossed by a replica of one of Aberdeen's old bridges. This enormous structure gives both a fantastic vantage point to look down on the gardens below, and provides the perfect frame through which both halves of the garden can be seen. This is one of Scotland's finest water gardens, apparently planned by Japanese designers for the owner, soap manufacturer James Ogston, in the early years of the twentieth century. On the south side of the ravine lie the ruins of thirteenth-century Kildrummy Castle which, amongst other things, was where the 1715 rebellion was plotted by the Earl of Mar. Now managed by Historic Scotland, it had to be restored to 'acceptable Victorian ruin standards' in 1898, as much of the stone had been appropriated to build Kildrummy House next door, (now a hotel). Kildrummy's water gardens are fed by a constant flow of water, over several waterfalls and through pools, surrounded by primulas and skunk cabbage. On the banks, on each side, are swathes of mature rhododendrons, *Ribes*, and other spring-flowering shrubs. There can be few finer sights in Scotland than the lower pond framed by the bridge arch in May. The lawns are surrounded by mature plantings of *Acer, Embothrium, Eucryphia* and other trees and shrubs. There are several stone installations and a quirky museum in a small hut in the midst of the garden. In a tiny tea room you can buy prints by local botanical artist Mary

Kildrummy Castle Gardens
Kildrummy, by Alford,
AB33 8RA
(*map, pp. 54–55*)

Kildrummy Castle Gardens Trust
April–October 10am–5pm; ££
2 miles south-west of Mossat,
10 miles from Alford. Take A944
from Alford and turn onto A97
T: 01975 571203
E: information@
kildrummy-castle-gardens.co.uk
www.kildrummy-castle-gardens.co.uk

McMurtrie, who was still painting at 100 years of age. Why this garden is not one of Scotland's most famous is a mystery: the setting and planting are first class; perhaps it is just too far off the beaten track. Much of the success is down to gardener A.J. Laing, who does a spectacular job holding it all together, and has been there for 30 years. What really needs to happen is for the hotel, gardens and old castle ruins to be integrated into a single attraction, rather than the unsatisfactory muddle that currently exists. It would surely make for one of the north-east's finest days out. This garden is very special and must be preserved; recent revelations that the bridge is badly in need of repair further threatens the survival of this great garden.

Kiln Den
Bankhead, New Aberdour,
Fraserburgh, AB43 6HS
(*map, pp. 54–55*)

Mrs A. Michie
By arrangement mid to end July;
££
Signposted from village of
New Aberdour
T: 01346 561217

Kiln Den

This farmhouse garden has outstanding views overlooking the Moray Firth coast and its beaches. The views are maintained by keeping the hedges low, but still sufficient to provide enough shelter to protect perennials and shrubs from the worst of the east winds. The garden contains alpines, roses, shrubs and collections of hostas and pelargoniums as well as a separate walled garden with fruit bushes and trees, vegetables and perennial borders.

Kirkdale Nursery

Kirkdale Nursery
Daviot, Inverurie,
Aberdeenshire, AB51 0JL
(*map, pp. 54–55*)

Alistair Scott
Kirkdale Nursery is situated
4 miles north of Inverurie
on the B9001
T: 01467 671264
F: 01467 671282
E: info@kirkdalenursery.co.uk
www.kirkdalenursery.co.uk

This nursery was founded in 1989 by Alistair Scott and stocks a fine range of trees and conifers. The website boasts over 4,000 different plant varieties through the year. Trees are containerised on-site, and some they propagate themselves. A small shed has stocks of peat, composts etc. Jeff Frogdale is a mine of information on what trees and other plants will do well in north-east Scotland. The range of stock, including hedging shrubs and perennials, takes in many items you don't see elsewhere in Scotland. Some of the trees were a little neglected when I visited, so choose carefully. The website is worth a look, though it is not always up to date. Call before you come to make sure they have what you want. Mail order also offered, in winter. I don't advise relying on their email or website as they don't always respond. Best to phone up.

Knocknagore

Knocknagore
Knockando, Moray,
AB38 7SG
(*map, pp. 54–55*)

Dr and Mrs Eckersall
SGS Sunday in April and July
or by appointment (contact
by fax); ££
Entrance from cottage road
which connects the B9102
Archiestown to Knockando road
with Knockando–Dallas road
F: 01340 810554

This quirky garden takes a bit of finding but is worth the effort. The first thing you notice are the stunning views from this moorland site, high in the hills north of the Spey, even the wind farm on the horizon can't spoil the vista of the distant Cairngorms. This garden consists of three main areas. Around the house is a mixture of shrubs and perennials, the highlight in late June was the amazing bank of red poppies. Behind the house is a wild garden with two peaty lochans, complete with plastic ducks and native plants. And behind the outbuildings is a small courtyard, known as the 'sit-ooterie', sheltered by the walls, with a roofed but open-at-the sides greenhouse/conservatory. This garden is obviously a labour of love for its owners.

Leith Hall Garden and Estate
Huntly, Aberdeenshire,
AB54 4NQ
(*map, pp. 54–55*)

NTS
Gardens: year round,
9am–sunset; house weekends
only May, June, September,
7 days July and August; ££*
Off the B9002. 1 mile west of
Kennethmont and 34 miles
north-west of Aberdeen
T: 0844 4932175
www.nts.org.uk

Leith Hall Garden and Estate

James Leith built Leith Hall in 1650 and the gardens were well established by the mid 1750s; there have been extensive additions and alterations made to both the hall and the gardens through the ages.
Charles and Henrietta Leith-Hay were responsible for much of the
modern layout of the steeply sloping garden from 1900 onwards,
including the well-known moon gate in the north wall with
descending steps clothed in *Alchemilla*. This moon gate has always
been oddly under-utilised as a feature; it would normally be expected
to have a vista on both sides of it, to be framed by the gate. The high
point of the garden enjoys views over the walls and hedges over the
house to the rolling hills beyond. The Leith-Hays donated Leith Hall
to the National Trust for Scotland in 1945, the second property it
received after Culzean. Sadly, the way the trust looked after the
garden in the early days left something to be desired and much of the
character of the garden was lost. I don't think that the Trust really
appreciated the value of the garden and they misguidedly demolished
both the rock garden and the Mackenzie & Moncur greenhouses
which formed the garden's focal point. The rock garden was one of
the finest in the UK and what remains, a small section, planted up by
Scottish Rock Garden Club, is a poor alternative. The remaining
rocks are piled up below the garden and the NTS has the long-term
aim of returning at least part of it to its former glory. The garden is
probably best known for its zigzag herbaceous border running up the
steep hill, featuring *Filipendula, Campanula, Echinops* and other
vigorous favourites, and opposite, along the garden wall, the two
signature beds of catmint *Nepeta* 'Six Hills Giant'. Both sides were

being replanted in 2008–09. At right angles to this bed, running east, towards the rock garden, is the early summer shrub and perennial border with roses, *Deutsia* and *Philadelphus*. The walled garden contains fruit, perennials and a rose garden with mostly shrub roses, underplanted with *Aquilegia* and violas. If you are visiting in summer, don't miss the various sections of differential mowing, with a spiral surrounded by rocks and the saltire pattern uphill from the castle. Other parts of the garden contain fine mature trees and there are spring bulbs along the woodland walks. Leith Hall is now under the wing of a talented young gardener, Toby Loveday, who is determined to wrestle this much-loved place back into the very fine garden that it undoubtedly should be.

Lochan House

This is a fairly new 1½-acre garden featuring a shelterbelt planting designed to encourage wildlife, ponds and a waterfowl collection, herbaceous and grass plantings, a formal courtyard and views of Bennachie.

Lochan House
Blackchambers, near Blackburn,
Aberdeenshire, AB32 7BU
(*map, pp. 54–55*)

Mrs M. Jones
By appointment; ££
A96, 2 miles south of
Kinellar roundabout, follow
signs for Millbuie
T: 01224 791753

Logie House Walled Garden

Logie House has belonged to the Grant family since the 1920s. The family's fortunes came from the invention of the digestive biscuit; Alexander Grant worked for McVities, first as a delivery boy, gradually working his way up, eventually becoming chairman of the company. The imposing white Logie House stands on a slope above the River Findhorn. The fine walled garden below the house is now looked after by the third generation of the family at Logie, Alasdair and Panny Laing who have also developed the Logie Steading complex next to the garden into a café, book shop, garden and plant

Logie House Walled Garden
Logie Steading, Forres,
Moray, IV36 2QN
(*map, pp. 54–55*)

Panny and Alasdair Laing
Daily: April–Christmas
10am–5pm; ££
6 miles south of Forres, on the
B9007, sign-posted off the
A940, close to the well-known
'Randolph's Leap' on the
River Findhorn
T: 01309 611278
E: panny@logie.co.uk
www.logie.co.uk
Café

shop with several workshops. The walled garden is divided into hedged sections, two of which are dedicated to vegetables, a fine fruit cage of raspberries and currants, tree fruit and cutting borders. The main planting schemes are mixed borders of shrubs and perennials with some striking and unusual combinations. Though not on the coast, the garden seems to boast a benign Moray Firth climate judging by the range of plants I noted: *Clethra barbinervis, Paulonia, Hoheria lyallii, Buddleja colvilei, Carpenteria californica* and *Leptospermum* are some examples. The latest development is a bog garden planted along a recently unearthed burn which was previously piped underground. There are also fine walks to be enjoyed along the Findhorn river.

Monymusk Walled Garden
Home Farm,
Monymusk, AB51 7HL
(*map, pp. 54–55*)

Mr R. McGregor
Summer: Tuesday–Sunday
10am – 5pm, winter:
Wednesday–Sunday 10am–4pm.
Closed Mondays (and
Tuesdays in winter).
A993 Kemnay–Tillyfournie
road
T: 01467 651543
www.monymusk.com
Coffee shop

Monymusk Walled Garden

This walled garden was the eighteenth-century kitchen garden of Monymusk House, seat of the Grant family, providing the house with fresh fruit, herbs, flowers and vegetables as well as young trees for the estate woodlands. Monymusk has an attractive eighteenth-century village square, with exhibitions in the Arts Centre. The walled garden is now run as an organic nursery with an endearingly rustic appearance: wooden signs, gnarled apple trees and a feeling that things are a little out of control. The daffodil displays are pretty good. As well as plants and gardening items, there is a selection of crafts made by local artists. It was described to me by one of their neighbours as 'a bit hippie'. And if you like that sort of thing, you'll love it here.

Pitmedden Garden
Ellon, Aberdeenshire,
AB41 7PD
(*map, pp. 54–55*)

NTS
1 May–end September: daily
10am–5.30pm; ££*
Approximately 1 mile west of
Pitmedden on the A920,
14 miles north of Aberdeen
(Ellon road)
T: 01651 842352
F: 01651 843188
www.nts.org.uk
A small gift shop and café serving
good value soup, sandwiches,
cakes, tea and coffee

Pitmedden Garden

One of the best loved NTS properties in north-east Scotland, Pitmedden is an elaborate formal garden of terraces, pavilions and parterres. On the site of an ancient garden, the current layout was created in the 1950s by the National Trust using various seventeenth-century designs, principally from Holyrood Palace, whose gardens are now lost, though details of the garden are visible on the contemporary engraving 'Birds'-Eye View of Edinburgh' by Gordon of Rothiemay. Pitmedden's terraces and one of the two pavilions allow good views of the complex designs of the lower garden with four bedding-filled parterres, designed to peak in August–September. Dividing the middle axis of the parterres are lines of tall pyramids of box while around the lower terrace edges, multicoloured, broad herbaceous borders are backed by fan and espaliered fruit trees on the walls. I could not work out from a distance what the tall purple haze was in

August along one wall. Closer inspection revealed a very effective and imaginative border of artichokes and *Verbena bonariensis*. The two parterres with herbs and gravel on the upper level are less successful, partly through choice of plants used, which don't seem to like the climate/drainage. In any case, as there is no vantage point from which to look down on them, they are rather pointless. These are a recent addition and I suspect they will be removed in due course. The whole garden, with its hedges and buttresses of yew and several avenues of pleached limes and other trees, is labour-intensive; there are said to be 3 miles of box which have to be clipped, and 30,000–40,000 annuals. The garden was immaculate when I visited in mid August. After Drummond Castle, which wins out with its high vantage point, this is the best garden of its type in Scotland, and the structure is so good that even if you don't like bedding, you can enjoy the design. This is horticultural excellence under head gardener Susan Burgess, coura-geously set in motion by the National Trust for Scotland in the 1950s. There has been criticism from some garden historians due to 'lack of authenticity' in the use of bedding plants and perennials, not in seventeenth-century style. Pitmedden also boasts a rather delightful museum of farming life with cottages filled with tableaux, traditional farm implements and furniture.

Ploughman's Hall
Old Rayne,
Aberdeenshire, AB52 6SD
(*map, pp. 54–55*)

Tony and Jean Gardner
By appointment, SGS 1 day
June/July; ££
Off A96, 9 miles north of
Inverurie. Turn off for Old
Rayne and first left
T: 01464 851253
E: tony@ploughmanshall.co.uk

Ploughman's Hall

This hilltop garden has been created by the Gardners, who bought the almost derelict 1820s farm building in 1990 and created a delightful house and garden combination. The views of Bennachie and the surrounding countryside are impressive, but wind was a major problem and it took some time to get their beech hedges, grown from their own locally sourced seed, to establish sufficiently to provide shelter for the rest of the 1-acre garden. Jean is the daughter of local botanic artist and gardener Mary McMurtrie, whose garden at Balbithan was much loved around this part of Aberdeenshire. Ploughman's Hall is packed with rare and interesting plants, including seven different varieties of *Celmisia* from New Zealand, some spiky *Dierama* and a small plant of *Sorbus megalocarpa* which was grown from seed from one at Leith Hall, not far away. This is a garden of self-sufficiency, with much of the stock in the garden grown from seed, including some from expeditions to Nepal and elsewhere. There are impressive espaliered and step-over apples and a wonderful vegetable and herb garden, attractively lined with lavender hedges. Jean makes soft toys, dried flower bouquets and other crafts while her husband Tony has created a database of all the plants in the garden, complete with pictures. Both are charming and very welcoming to visitors.

  [WC]

Pluscarden Abbey

This medieval abbey, founded in 1230, was restored and donated to the Benedictine order by the owner, the fourth marquis of Bute and reopened as a community in 1948. As well as wooded grounds with rhododendrons, there is a productive kitchen garden alongside the walls of the abbey, surrounded with hedges, containing a selection of apples. This is the ideal place to visit for insomniacs as it opens at 4.30am for the first service of the day.

Pluscarden Abbey
Elgin, Morayshire, IV30 8UA
(map, pp. 54–55)

Benedictine order
Daily: 4:30am–8:30pm;
donation
6 miles west of Elgin
T: 01343 890258
www.pluscardenabbey.org

Raemoir Garden Centre

This popular garden centre, founded by Banchory GP Dr Frank Mair, is run by several members of the Mair family. It is one of the best and most popular garden centres in the north-east. You can't miss the roadside walls planted up with exuberant summer colour and your children will spot the excellent play area, suitable for various ages. The shop is entered via the well-planned gift area, which leads into the garden centre itself, no enormous shed, but moderately sized with well-chosen stock and an impressive pet supplies department. The plant area crams in a huge range of stock. The famous restaurant, one of the best in any garden centre, is so popular you may well have to wait for a table. All in all this is a great package, much appreciated by the residents of Banchory, who are so far spared the big garden centre chains. Plans are afoot for a food hall and other developments.

Raemoir Garden Centre
Raemoir Road, Banchory,
AB31 4EJ
(map, pp. 54–55)

Dr and Mrs F. Mair, Elliot Mair
Daily: 9am–5.30pm
Signposted off the A93 in
Banchory, on the A980
T: 01330 825059
F: 01330 825058
E: info@raemoirgarden
centre.co.uk
www.raemoirgardencentre.co.uk

Revack Estate
Granton-on-Spey, PH26 3NH
(*map, pp. 54–55*)

Edinmore Properties Ltd
Daily: 10am–5pm except
Christmas and New Year.
Coaches by appointment.
Signposted on the A95, just
south of Granton-on-Spey
T: 01479 872 234
F: 01479 872 722
E: revack.estate@lineone.net
Restaurant

Revack Estate

This is a 15,000-acre estate, purchased in 1999 from the Ogilvie-Grant Nicholson family who had owned it for 900 years, by the property arm of the Cayzer family, who own several estates in Perthshire and Angus. Revack boasts 10 miles of walks and trails, good opportunities for wildlife-spotting (with some of the tamest red squirrels I have ever seen), and some woodland plantings of rhododendrons, particularly along the side of the meandering drive. There is a steeply sloping walled garden, several ornamental lochans and ponds, a small wooded adventure playground, gift shop and restaurant. There used to be a garden centre here, now closed.

**Simpsons Garden Centre
and Coffee Shop**
3A Inshes Holdings,
Inverness, IV2 5BA
(*map, pp. 54–55*)

Off the B9006 (Westhill road),
just off the A9 just south of
Inverness
T: 01463 250200;
florist: 01463 250 777
www.flowersbysimpsons.co.uk
Coffee shop

Simpsons Garden Centre and Coffee Shop

This popular and long-established garden centre near the A9 is embarking on an ambitious expansion programme at time of going to press with a new shop and restaurant. This is the largest of the independents in Inverness now that Howdens has been taken over by Klondyke. They have a popular floristry business which has online and telephone ordering.

Speyside Heather Centre

This is a small garden centre, a Scottish gift shop, an antique centre and a popular restaurant, famous for its 20 variations on the clootie dumpling – a heavy, steamed sweet or savoury pudding. A well-presented, multilingual heather exhibition is informative and the selection of heathers to buy is extensive. Anything heather-related you can think of, and many things you'd never guess, are also on sale, not all in the best of taste . . . The display gardens of heathers are somewhat disappointing. It is evidently a popular tourist attraction, particularly with coaches.

   WC

Speyside Heather Centre
Skye of Curr, Dulnain Bridge, Inverness-shire, PH26 3PA
(*map, pp. 54–55*)

David Lambie
Daily: March to end October
Monday–Saturday 9am–5.30pm, Sunday 10am–5pm. Slightly reduced opening times during the winter (see website).
Clearly signposted on the A95, halfway between Grantown-on-Spey and Boat of Garten.
Turn off the A9 at Aviemore
T: 01479 851 359
F: 01479 851 369
E: enquiries@heathercentre.com
www.heathercentre.com
Café/restaurant.

Thistle Mill Nursery

Unusually, this enterprising family-run garden centre, nursery and floristry business takes its wares out on the road to local farmers' markets in Huntly, Elgin, Banff and Inverurie. The wide-ranging website includes a blog, some far-fetched theories about the effects of the moon's phases on gardening, and is being developed to link local people interested in flower arranging. The nursery grows much of what is sold in four tunnel houses, using stock plants from the display gardens, which are at their best in early summer. They also make candles with flowers on them on-site. You can order online for local delivery.

   WC

Thistle Mill Nursery
Thistle Mill, Kebholes, Banff, Aberdeenshire, AB45 3XT
(*map, pp. 54–55*)

Michael and Alison Bolger
All year for floristry
Monday–Saturday 10am–6pm, Sunday 10am–4pm. Nursery open March–October.
Off B9025, near Aberchirder. Turn off north between Cranna and Boghead
T: 01466 780708
E: mail@thistlemillnursery.com
www.thistlemillnursery.com

Tillypronie

Tillypronie is a good illustration of how a cold, inland, high-altitude garden can grow a remarkable range of plants thanks to sharp drainage on the southern slopes, which also allow good frost drainage down the hillside. A huge clump of *Agapanthus* had evidently been here for years, and in full sun with perfect drainage it was quite at home. The house, built in 1860–70, lies at 1,000ft with commanding views south across the Dee Valley. The terracing around the house was constructed by Sir Thomas Royden, who then sold the estate to Mr Gavin Astor, whose wife Lady Irene Haig's family home was Bemersyde in the Borders. They were responsible for much of the planting at Tillypronie, which is being continued by their son Philip and gardening team of Mike Rattray and his daughter. The terraces are well planned with a wide range of climbers, shrubs and perennials and below this is an impressive rock and scree garden with some recent grass borders next door. Drifts of deciduous azaleas and *Rosa rugosa* provide structure and wind shelter. Heather gardens are not something I particularly like, but the one at Tillypronie is one of the

Tillypronie
Tarland, Aboyne, AB34 4XX
(*map, pp. 54–55*)

Trustees of Tillypronie Trust/ The Hon. Philip Astor
SGS 2 days, spring and late summer, and by appointment; ££
4½ miles west of Tarland via A97
T: 01339 881238

best I have seen; naturalistic, with curved sweeping beds of *Calluna, Erica* and *Daboecia* sloping away to the lawns in front of the house. The secrets of success are the altitude, the full exposure and the strimming every couple of years after flowering, keeping them dense and compact. This way they have lasted for over 30 years without being replanted. Below the lawns and mature conifers are a burn and ponds with bold waterside plantings of *Astilbe, Ligularia* and other favourites. To the east is a collection of fine trees, some of which are doing surprisingly well for such a cold inland garden. Notable broadleaves include a 12-metre *Cercidiphyllum* and a *Betula medwedewii*, while conifers include a number of redwoods (some planted by former prime minister Harold MacMillan), *Juniperus recurva, Picea breweriana*, and a *Chamaecyparis nootkatensis* and more surprisingly, *Athrotaxis cupressoides* and *Podocarpus salignis*. Along the eastern garden boundary is the yellow garden, planted for the Queen's Golden Jubilee, which I found a little acidic and strident, but it was softened by the wildflower meadow around it. Tillypronie is a fine landscape, with good plants, well maintained and with considerable recent plantings.

Tormore Distillery
Grantown-on-Spey,
Moray, PH26 3LR
(*map, pp. 54–55*)

Pernod Ricard
Distillery tours: September–June,
Monday–Thursday 1.30pm-4pm.
The gardens are free; distillery
tours are paid for.
On the A95, north-east
of Grantown-on-Spey,
near Ballindalloch
T: 01807 510244

Tormore Distillery

I stumbled across this garden and photogenic distillery and housing complex at Tormore as I drove along the A95 between Ballindalloch and Grantown-on-Spey. It was designed by Sir Albert Richardson and completed in 1960. What caught my eye were the three sections of topiary. At the west end is a line of golden topiary bells with green conifers behind. The main entrance to the imposing distillery building, with a blue pool in front and two whisky stills of clipped yew, has an eclectic mix of topiary shapes on either side of the door. The main event, up the burnside, is a wacky assortment of cake

stands, spirals and candelabras, which look as if they were designed by someone fired up by the effects of a few drams. The whole garden is well maintained and does not take itself too seriously. The distillery clock apparently plays several Scottish tunes, which must be pretty annoying for those who live there. It did not go off while I was wandering round.

West Lodge, Kilravock

West Lodge, Kilravock
Kilravock, Croy,
Inverness, IV2 5PG
(*map, pp. 54–55*)

Mr and Mrs C. Buss
1 June–30th September: by appointment; no children; ££
B9006 towards Culloden/Cawdor, turn left into Croy village, second right up hill past shop, last cottage on right, opposite war memorial/village hall
T: 01667 493736
E: scrumpyjack9@yahoo.co.uk

This is a small, wooden-fenced, cottage-style garden built since 2005 using recycled materials to form planted islands/raised beds, some with dry stone walling, separated by gravel paths. The garden features a large collection of day lilies (130+ varieties), shrubs, trees, perennials, alpines and bulbs and the prairie-style plantings of grasses and perennials are maturing well. The Busses run this garden as a team: Colin is responsible for the construction side while the plant input comes from Mitch, who has worked in horticulture for many years and is a keen plantswoman.

East Central:
Angus, Perthshire, Fife

East Central Scotland can easily provide a week of garden and tree visiting at almost any time of year. **Perth and Kinross** has a varied range of gardens, from the formal landscapes of Kinross House and Drummond Castle to the rhododendrons and woodland plants of Glendoick, Bolfracks, Cluny and Branklyn and the impressive herbaceous borders at Blair Castle. Perthshire is also 'Big Tree Country', with some of Britain's most impressive trees (see the entry for more details). Perthshire gardens open some years under SGS, but which do not have individual entries include: Cluniemore, Pitlochry; Boreland, Killin; Carig Dhubh, Bonskeid; Inchyra House, by Perth; Stobhall, Perth; Ardnashiel, Delvine.

    Fife contains some of Scotland's most outstanding gardens and the compact size of the county means that you can visit several in one day without having to drive too far. Try to avoid going through Glenrothes if you can, as unless you are a local you'll probably get lost on the roundabouts. Only a few of Fife's best gardens are open to visitors for long periods of the year. These include Kellie Castle and Cambo. Many

Cambo perennials

of the others such as Balcarres, The Murrel, Earlshall Castle, Wormistoune and Wemyss Castle are open occasionally under SGS and otherwise by appointment. Fife has many village garden openings, many open every second year, and they include some which are not in the SGS scheme: St Monans village gardens, Crail gardens, Ceres gardens, Blebo Craigs gardens, Falkland small gardens, Lathrisk gardens, Strathkinnes gardens, Bella Ramsay's Cottage and sometimes other gardens in Kilconquhar, near Elie. Several small St Andrews gardens open annually for the St Andrews Preservation Trust, under the banner of Hidden Gardens of St Andrews.

Few **Angus** gardens are open more than occasionally. (House of) Pitmuies is probably the finest of all and the bluebells and walled garden at Dunninald are impressive, as are the rhododendrons and trees at Brechin Castle and Cortachy. A fine, newer but maturing garden is Ethie Castle near Arbroath. Gardens open from time to time which don't have their own entries include Melgam House, Edzell village gardens.

Kellie Castle

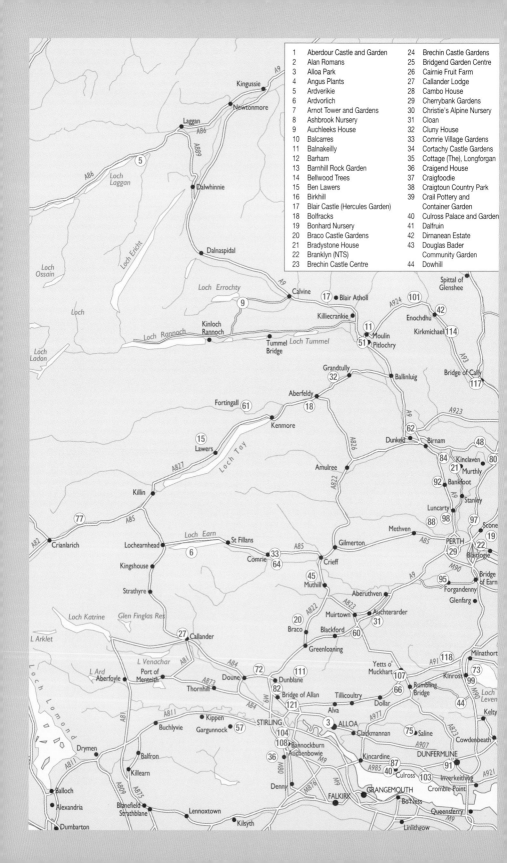

1	Aberdour Castle and Garden	24	Brechin Castle Gardens
2	Alan Romans	25	Bridgend Garden Centre
3	Alloa Park	26	Cairnie Fruit Farm
4	Angus Plants	27	Callander Lodge
5	Ardverikie	28	Cambo House
6	Ardvorlich	29	Cherrybank Gardens
7	Arnot Tower and Gardens	30	Christie's Alpine Nursery
8	Ashbrook Nursery	31	Cloan
9	Auchleeks House	32	Cluny House
10	Balcarres	33	Comrie Village Gardens
11	Balnakeilly	34	Cortachy Castle Gardens
12	Barham	35	Cottage (The), Longforgan
13	Barnhill Rock Garden	36	Craigend House
14	Bellwood Trees	37	Craigfoodie
15	Ben Lawers	38	Craigtoun Country Park
16	Birkhill	39	Crail Pottery and
17	Blair Castle (Hercules Garden)		Container Garden
18	Bolfracks	40	Culross Palace and Garden
19	Bonhard Nursery	41	Dalfruin
20	Braco Castle Gardens	42	Dirnanean Estate
21	Bradystone House	43	Douglas Bader
22	Branklyn (NTS)		Community Garden
23	Brechin Castle Centre	44	Dowhill

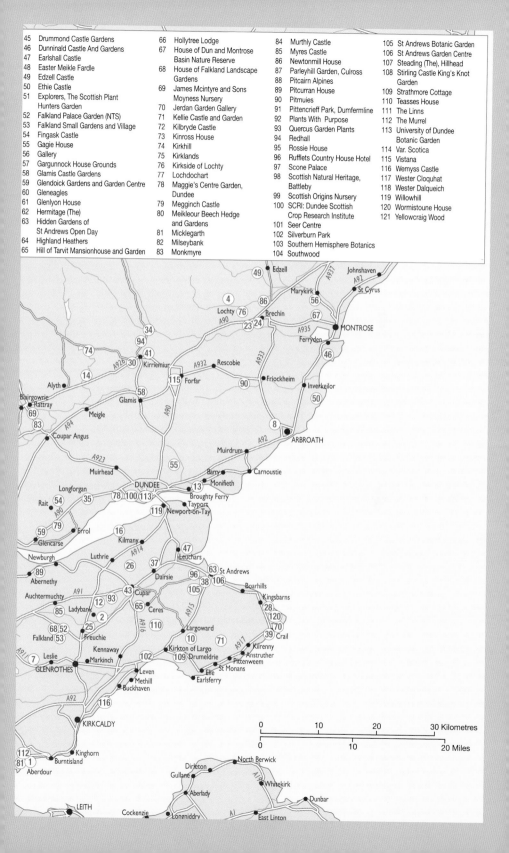

45 Drummond Castle Gardens
46 Dunninald Castle And Gardens
47 Earlshall Castle
48 Easter Meikle Fardle
49 Edzell Castle
50 Ethie Castle
51 Explorers, The Scottish Plant Hunters Garden
52 Falkland Palace Garden (NTS)
53 Falkland Small Gardens and Village
54 Fingask Castle
55 Gagie House
56 Gallery
57 Gargunnock House Grounds
58 Glamis Castle Gardens
59 Glendoick Gardens and Garden Centre
60 Gleneagles
61 Glenlyon House
62 Hermitage (The)
63 Hidden Gardens of St Andrews Open Day
64 Highland Heathers
65 Hill of Tarvit Mansionhouse and Garden

66 Hollytree Lodge
67 House of Dun and Montrose Basin Nature Reserve
68 House of Falkland Landscape Gardens
69 James Mcintyre and Sons Moyness Nursery
70 Jerdan Garden Gallery
71 Kellie Castle and Garden
72 Kilbryde Castle
73 Kinross House
74 Kirkhill
75 Kirklands
76 Kirkside of Lochty
77 Lochdochart
78 Maggie's Centre Garden, Dundee
79 Megginch Castle
80 Meikleour Beech Hedge and Gardens
81 Micklegarth
82 Milseybank
83 Monkmyre

84 Murthly Castle
85 Myres Castle
86 Newtonmill House
87 Parleyhill Garden, Culross
88 Pitcairn Alpines
89 Pitcurran House
90 Pitmuies
91 Pittencrieff Park, Dumfermline
92 Plants With Purpose
93 Quercus Garden Plants
94 Redhall
95 Rossie House
96 Rufflets Country House Hotel
97 Scone Palace
98 Scottish Natural Heritage, Battleby
99 Scottish Origins Nursery
100 SCRI: Dundee Scottish Crop Research Institute
101 Seer Centre
102 Silverburn Park
103 Southern Hemisphere Botanics
104 Southwood

105 St Andrews Botanic Garden
106 St Andrews Garden Centre
107 Steading (The), Hillhead
108 Stirling Castle King's Knot Garden
109 Strathmore Cottage
110 Teasses House
111 The Linns
112 The Murrel
113 University of Dundee Botanic Garden
114 Var. Scotica
115 Vistana
116 Wemyss Castle
117 Wester Cloquhat
118 Wester Dalqueich
119 Willowhill
120 Wormistoune House
121 Yellowcraig Wood

Aberdour Castle and Garden
Aberdour, Fife, KY3 0SL
(*map, pp. 116–117*)

Historic Scotland
Daily: April–October
9.30am–6.30pm. Winter times:
October–March 9.30–4.30pm; ££*
At the east end of Aberdour
High Street
T: 01383 860519
www.historic-scotland.gov.uk
Tiny but nice café

Aberdour Castle and Garden

Aberdour Castle was first built in the thirteenth century and was extended in the fifteenth, sixteenth and seventeenth centuries by members of the Douglas family, who owned the castle from 1342. Only part of the building still has a roof and floors, the rest was burnt in a fire in the seventeenth century. Recently a painted roof with animals and flowers was uncovered under plasterwork in one of the towers. The present-day gardens mainly lie in a square walled garden with recently replanted herbaceous and shrub borders around the walls with a lawn in the middle featuring a complex sundial. This garden is spoiled by a hideous concrete building (the vestry for the church next door) in one corner which should, at the very least, be disguised. On the sea side of the castle is a mostly recently planted apple orchard with a good collection of Scottish and English apples, well mapped and labelled. The impressive series of walls and terraces, which may date back as far as the 1570s, clearly formed a substantial garden in the sixteenth and seventeenth centuries. The terraces were destroyed in the early twentieth century and restored in the 1970s. There is a very fine beehive doocot at the south end. I was shown some ambitious plans to restore the terraces to create a sixteenth-century garden, based on a plant list which was supplied to Aberdour in 1687 from the Edinburgh Physic Garden. Whether it will be completed remains to be seen.

Alan Romans

This family business is run by Scotland's leading potato expert. He supplies seed potatoes and flower, herb and vegetable seed by mail order. The seed potato list includes 100+ varieties, including many extraordinary heritage names such as Highland Burgundy Red, Shetland Black and Salad Blue. Alan Romans is author of *The Potato Book*, now in its fourth edition, as well as the *Guide to Seed Potatoes*. Alan can usually be found at Gardening Scotland, Dundee Flower show and he also sells Eden Greenhouses through Bridgend Garden Centre, Freuchie (see p. 135).

Alan Romans
72 North Street, Kettlebridge, Cupar, KY15 7QJ
(*map, pp. 116–117*)

Alan Romans
T: 01337 831060
E: admin@alanromans.com
www.alanromans.co.uk

Alloa Park

This would probably have become the largest garden/planned landscape in Scotland, created by the Earl of Mar from 1706 to 1714. It included avenues of trees, canals, parterres and wilderness. Daniel Defoe saw it at its prime and said it was Scotland's finest garden, and it was also admired by John Macky on his *Journey through Scotland*, published in 1723:

Alloa Park
Alloa, Clackmannanshire
(*map, pp. 116–117*)

Built by the Earl of Mar;
Alloa Tower NTS
Brown signs to Alloa Tower
in Alloa

> It far exceeds either Hampton Court or Kensington, the gardens consisting of two and forty acres, and the wood, with vistos [*sic*] cut through it, of one hundred and fifty acres. To the south of the house is the parterre. From this runs a fine terras or avenue, from whence and from the parterre you have thirty two different vistos, each ending on some remarkable seat or mountain at some miles distance.

The Earl of Mar was the leader of the 1715 rebellion and was forced to flee into exile as the garden was almost completed. Shortly afterwards it was more or less abandoned and the town of Alloa was built on the site. Almost no trace of the landscape remains apart from Alloa Tower (NTS) which formed the centrepiece of the original design.

Angus Plants
3 Balfour Cottages, Menmuir,
by Brechin, Angus, DD9 7RN
(*map, pp. 116–117*)

Dr Alison Goldie, Mark Hutson
Nursery daily 10am–6pm by
appointment only (please phone);
SGS 1 day per year.
Turn off A90 to Lochty just south
of Brechin exit. Or can be reached
from Brechin. SGS days ££
T: 07972 026109
E: Alison@angusplants.co.uk
www.angusplants.co.uk

Angus Plants

This is a recently-established mail order nursery specialising in auriculas. The nursery is a small narrow cottage back garden, stuffed with plants, ranging from bamboos and thymes to *Meconopsis, Fuchsia, Trillium* and *Hosta.* Behind this are two houses full of *Primula auricula* cultivars in pots. Here, for the first time, I was able to appreciate (to a degree) what auricula fanciers get so excited about. Single and double varieties in every imaginable shade with over 250 different kinds. Though they can be grown out of doors in a well-drained site with some protection, they are best indoors where the rain can be kept off them. Dr Alison Goldie also designs and plants gardens locally.

Ardverikie
Kinlochlaggan, Newtonmore,
Invernesshire, PH20 1BX
(*map, pp. 116–117*)

Ardverikie estate
SGS 1 day a year and by
appointment; ££
Spean Bridge–Newtonmore road
at the east end of Loch Laggan
through the imposing gatelodge,
3-mile drive in
T: 01528 544300
E: Ardverikie@ardverikie.com
www.ardverikie.com

Ardverikie

The house at Ardverikie starred in the BBC drama, *Monarch of the Glen* so the great views will be familiar to television viewers. Built in the Scottish Baronial style in 1870 on a promontory overlooking King Fergus's Island on Loch Laggan with its ancient ruins, a 3-mile private drive winds past the largest inland beach in the country and round the south side of Loch Laggan. Ardverikie played host to Queen Victoria and Prince Albert for a month in 1847 before they bought Balmoral. The estate was purchased by Sir John Ramsden in 1871 and he planted over 10,000 acres with some 34 million trees, particularly noble fir and grand fir, introduced by David Douglas. The gardens, sheltered by mature woodland from the south, lie at an altitude of 1,000ft in cold central Scotland, consisting of a walled garden with good displays of *Fuchsia* and *Astilbe* and a rock garden. There are particularly fine trees, including several large Japanese maples which,

with *Enkianthus* and others, provide impressive autumn colour. Aberarder on the opposite side of the loch, part of the same estate, is usually open with Ardverikie under SGS.

Ardvorlich

It will keep you fit, this wild woodland garden which lies on either side of a burn-filled ravine which runs up the steep slopes on the south side of Loch Earn, with views across the loch to Ben Chonzie. You can also climb the Munro Ben Vorlich from here. Ardvorlich is predominantly a wild rhododendron and azalea garden with both species and hybrids planted in a wood of oak, beech and rowan. The steep paths can be muddy and boots are advisable.

Ardvorlich
Lochearnhead, Perthshire, FK19 8QE
(*map, pp. 116–117*)

Mr and Mrs Sandy Stewart
Early May–early June: dawn–dusk; ££
3 miles from Lochearnhead, 4½ miles from St Fillans along the south Loch Earn road which is signed off the A84 and A85 at either end
T: 01567 830218 or 01567 830335

Arnot Tower and Gardens
Leslie, Fife, KY6 3JQ
(*map, pp. 116–117*)

Benjamen and Helen Gray
Tuesdays in summer; ££
A911 between Scotlandwell and
Auchmuirbridge. Leave A90
at Milnathort exit
T: 01592 840115
M: 07740 182 140
E: events@arnottower.co.uk
www.arnottower.co.uk

Ashbrook Nursery
Forfar Road, Arbroath,
Fife, DD11 3RB
(*map, pp. 116–117*)

Francis, Joe and Anne Webster
Daily: 10am–5:30pm
On northern outskirts of Arbroath,
on A933 Forfar–Brechin road,
opposite the RM *Condor*
marine base
T: 01241 873408
F: 01241 873408
E: ashbrooknursery@
hotmail.co.uk
www.ashbrooknursery.co.uk

Arnot Tower and Gardens

The picturesque ruins of fifteenth-century Arnot Tower lie beside a modern, rather strident house which rather dominates the garden. Terraced on two sides, the main axis leads down steps to the water garden, a series of rectangular ponds with impressive fountains, bordered by contrasting combinations of perennials which Christopher Lloyd would have approved of: deep blue iris next to huge red poppies for example. Around the ruined castle are softer plantings of herbaceous and climbers and there are plans to restore the old quarry pond nearby, while towards the entrance road are mature rhododendrons. The whole garden can be lit up at night, the effect of which can be seen on the garden's website. 2008 saw the start of the restoration of the half-acre Victorian kitchen garden which will grow vegetables, fruit and cut flowers. This is a garden to watch: its enthusiastic owners have ambitious plans for it and the 10-acre site certainly has considerable further potential.

Ashbrook Nursery

This is a family-run nursery which moved to its new garden centre site in 1990 but still looks like a 'proper' old-fashioned nursery. The Websters grow most of their alpines, herbaceous, bedding plants, herbs and vegetable plants on-site. Trees and shrubs are sourced where possible from Scottish growers. I noted particularly good ranges of grasses, *Delphinium*, wallflowers, *Lychnis, Heuchera* and *Cyclamen*, but the overall selection is impressive too.

  [WC]

Auchleeks House

This classical Georgian house between Calvine and Loch Rannoch is set amongst fine scenery. The house is garlanded with climbing roses and a small parterre in front has a stone sphere centrepiece and is planted with coloured stem dogwoods for winter interest and cosmos and lilies for the summer. The terrace is lined with a row of 12 topped dark green fastigiate yews and looks over the substantial sloping walled garden which divides into two along the central axis, a wide double herbaceous border with shrub roses at the south end. The terrace wall is planted with climbing roses. Auchleeks was formerly owned by Rear Admiral and Mrs John Mackenzie, now at East Meikle Fardle, who opened it regularly, and the current owners, the MacDonalds, with their enthusiastic and clearly dedicated gardener Bill Brown, have retained much of the structure and charm of the older garden, while gradually evolving it. An underground burn splashes under a flight of stone steps via two sunken ponds at the east end, while the border along the south wall is a planting of some of the lushest hosta clumps I have seen, with thriving *Meconopsis* at one end. This is a charming garden, in a peaceful and remote valley, which you can hardly fail to enjoy.

Auchleeks House
Calvine, Perthshire, PH18 5UF
(*map, pp. 116–117*)

Mr and Mrs Angus MacDonald
SGS 1 day; ££
North of Blair Atholl, turn off A9
at Calvine, B847 towards Kinloch
Rannoch, 5 miles on right
T: 01796 483263
E: amacdonald@
efinancialnews.com

Balcarres
Balcarres (Estate Office),
Colinsburgh, Leven,
Fife, KY9 1HJ
(*map, pp. 116–117*)

Earl and Countess of Crawford
and Balcarres
SGS 1 day or by appointment; ££
Off the B941 between
Largoward and Colinsburgh

Balcarres

Fife undoubtedly has several of the best gardens in Scotland and Balcarres is one of several gems which open only for a day or two a year. There are two long drives into the estate, through mature parkland, which eventually reach the large house, improved and extended by William Burn and David Bryce in the nineteenth century. Lady Crawford is to be seen most days in her golf buggy, tending to her beloved perennials and discussing her latest planting ideas with Donald Lamb, her gardener for over 30 years. Together they have created one of Scotland's finest perennial displays. The Lindsay family/earls of Crawford have lived at Balcarres almost continuously since the sixteenth century. The old walled garden was abandoned to livestock many years ago, and the perennial borders have been constructed on the lawns around the house. In front of the main house is the rose garden, a series of beds, underplanted with *Geranium* and *Stachys*, which softens the gaunt lines of the hybrid teas and floribundas. Toward the west end of the house lies a newer garden, which Lady Crawford has created with well-drained gravel beds full of *Salvia* and other sun-lovers and an outrageous colour clash of perennials inspired by her friend the late Christopher Lloyd, who used to come and stay. A fine balustraded terrace looks down onto a formal garden, part of a nineteenth-century layout, now partly grassed over, with clipped yews and box parterres, and gives fine views down to the Forth estuary with the Bass Rock on the horizon. The largest block of herbaceous lies to the south-east of the house and is formed by four large, colour coordinated beds: white, orange-peach, yellow and purple, forming a large rectangle. I was particularly taken by the collection of *Knifophia* in shades of orange, salmon, yellow and bronze. To the north is a long border dominated by the ancient clipped box balls 2m × 2m+ which are held in by wires to prevent snow damage. To the east is a fine blue/purple border of *Nepeta*, *Lythrum*, *Sedum* and a long border of *Agapanthus* under fruit trees. Further east and across the drive is a more informal woodland garden.

This starts with bulbs and rhododendrons in spring and clumps of vigorous summer-flowering perennials: *Astilbe, Veronicastrum, Macleya* and shrubs such as *Deutzia setchuenensis* in summer. Further still is a hilltop seventeenth-century chapel and fine mature yews, a pond garden and policies of mature trees. Designer James Russell lived here during his retirement and influenced the gardens, so Lady Crawford has had some of the best gardening advice available. She also admires Margery Fish, Beth Chatto and Piet Oudolf but the whole approach at Balcarres is singular and not like anything else in Scotland. The labelling is excellent and Lady Crawford keeps meticulous records of plants and planting combinations.

Balnakeilly

This is a spring, burn-side garden in highland Perthshire with daffodils, rhododendrons and azaleas, perennial borders and some large *Abies procera*, with good views around Moulin into the hills behind.

Balnakeilly
Pitlochry, PH16 5JJ
(*map, pp. 116–117*)

Col and Mrs Stewart Wilson
SGS 1 day; ££
From Pitlochry take Kirkmichael Road through Moulin, 400 yards on left past Moulin Hotel

Barham

Between the house and the roadside is a small woodland garden with spring bulbs, snowdrops, rhododendrons and azaleas, ferns, helle-bores, *Dicentra* and a particularly good display of *Trillium*. On the far side of the house is a small but well planted summer garden around the front lawn. The walls are covered with impressive *Wisteria* and rambling roses. Lady Spencer-Nairn propagates significant numbers of plants for sale, with all proceeds going to medical research charities.

Barham
Bow of Fife, Fife, KY15 5RG
(*map, pp. 116–117*)

Sir Robert and Lady Spencer-Nairn
15 February–30 September by appointment, some years SGS open day; ££
A91, 4 miles west of Cupar, ½ mile west of the Scottish deer centre on left. From west, 2nd right entrance after the round-about
T: 01337 810227

Barnhill Rock Garden
The Esplanade, Barnhill,
By Broughty Ferry, Dundee
(*map, pp. 116–117*)

Dundee Council
The garden is always open.
Glasshouse open Monday to
Friday 9am–4pm; free
On the shore road, signposted
off the A930 between Monifieth
and Broughty Ferry

Barnhill Rock Garden

This garden, run by Dundee Council, lies right on the seafront between Monifieth and Broughty Ferry, outside Dundee. The garden was begun in 1955 by clearing an area of volcanic rock which was once the old shore line of the Tay and extending out over former sand dunes. The rock garden was constructed with rock from Carmylie Quarry while one of several ponds is filled from a natural spring. The garden is a mixture of woodland, under pines, Eucalyptus and other trees, and more open areas along the seashore road with island beds of perennials, grasses and alpines. There is plenty of colour from early spring (snowdrops) onwards and the mild climate and good drainage allow a wide range of plants to be grown, despite the sometime fierce salt-laden winds. When I visited in June, I particularly noted the fine *Iris*, white *Libertia*, pale lavender *Abutilon* and bright yellow lupins. The small Geddes Greenhouse contains information on the gardens and its plants. The garden is supported by a 'Friends' group. You may spot seals off the shore and even dolphins which live in the Tay estuary.

Bellwood Trees
Brigton of Ruthven, Meigle,
Perthshire, PH12 8RQ
(*map, pp. 116–117*)

Craig Wemyss, Managing
Director; Andrea Grey,
Sales Manager
Visits by appointment
T: 01828 640219
F: 01828 640623
T: info@bellwoodtrees.com
www.bellwoodtrees.com

Bellwood Trees

Bellwood Trees is Scotland's largest nursery, covering 320 acres. They specialise in mature trees and supply huge landscaping projects such as Wembley Stadium and the Scottish Parliament as well as private clients. They are essentially a trade nursery not normally open to the public except by appointment, They offer a consultancy service for their clients to ensure that the right trees go to the right site. They have up to 100,000 trees on-site in their nurseries, which are scattered around the Alyth and Meigle areas, and they list 250 varieties. Mature hedging is a new addition to their range.

Ben Lawers

Ben Lawers, at 1,214m (almost 4,000ft), is the highest point of a long ridge formed by six peaks, five of which are Munros, sited about as far away from the sea as it is possible to get in Scotland. The terrain is moorland and grass with some rocky outcrops; more unusual are the slopes between the south and west ridges, which contain steep crumbling mica-schist limestone cliffs on which grow some of Britain's rarest arctic alpine plants. These include *Saxifraga oppositifolia, S. aizoides, Silene acaulis* (moss campion), *Myosotis alpestris* (alpine forget-me-not), *Gentiana nivalis*, the fern *Woodsia alpina* and *Loiseleuria procumbens* the so called 'trailing azalea'. I recall trying to climb Ben Lawers on a school trip in early June and being beaten back by blizzards and a complete white-out, so no matter what time of year you go, do take precautions: suitable clothes, food, water, compass and a map. The National Trust for Scotland runs the visitor centre (threatened with closure at time of writing), which lies at 1,000ft, so you have 'done' the first quarter of the climb before you start. The minor road from Amulee up Glen Quaich to Kenmore gives magnificent views of Ben Lawers and Loch Tay on a clear day.

Ben Lawers
Taymouth, Perthshire
(*map, pp. 116–117*)

NTS/SNH
Site: all year, daily; information centre and shop: 30 March–30 September, daily 10am–5pm (closed between 1pm and 2pm). Site free, visitor centre ££ Signpost off A827 Taymouth–Killin road on north side of Loch Tay. Mountain visitor centre and car park 2 miles up hill road
T: 0844 4932136
www.nts.org.uk

Ben Lawers
(*Saxifraga oppositifolia*)

Birkhill

Birkhill
Birkhill, Cupar, Fife, KY15 4QP
(map, pp. 116–117)

Earl and Countess of Dundee
SGS some years, by appointment
and occasional openings for
charity; ££
Turn off the A92
Dundee–Glenrothes road and
head for Hazelton Walls.
Unmarked stone gates just
before some blue farm buildings.
Coming from Newburgh,
take the A913
T: 01382 330 200
F: 01382 330 230
E: info@birkhillcastle.org.uk
www.birkhillcastle.org.uk

This 10-acre woodland garden is planted on either side of a burn which runs down to the south bank of the River Tay. Mossy paths run along the valley sides and bottom. Highlights include huge magnolias and a *Hydrangea petiolaris* which climbs over 30ft up into a tree, as well as a fine display of rhododendrons and azaleas underplanted with daffodils and *Erythronium*. There is also a 2½-acre Victorian walled garden with old yews, vegetables, fruit and huge greenhouses with grapes, figs, white peaches, nectarines and apricots. Birkhill can be hired for weddings and corporate events and the castle has been run as an upmarket B&B by the irrepressible Siobhan Dundee.

B&B

Blair Castle (Hercules Garden)

Blair Castle (Hercules Garden)
Blair Atholl, Perthshire, PH18 5TL
(map, pp. 116–117)

Blair Charitable Trust
1 April–end October: daily,
9.30am–4.30pm; ££* (castle £££)
Blair Castle and the village of
Blair Atholl are just off the main
Perth–Inverness road (A9), 35
miles north of Perth, 8 miles
north of Pitlochry
T: 01796 481207
F: 01796 481487
E: bookings@blair-castle.co.uk
www.blair-castle.co.uk
Self-service restaurant.

The 'planting' dukes of Atholl were responsible for much of the spectacular tree planting on either side of the A9 from Dunkeld north as well as much of the 2,500-acre designed landscape around Blair Castle, one of Scotland's most important tourist attractions. 'Atholl Estates' is one of Scotland's largest, covering a large part of north Perthshire. The imposing drive of lime trees leads to the castle and car park from where several rides radiate out, part of the eighteenth-century landscaping at Blair. The policies contain some of Scotland's champion trees including a group of Douglas fir, the tallest of which is over 50m in height. You should catch site of the arches of the 'whim' folly from the drive or car park, an example of a landscape feature known as an 'eyecatcher'. Paths through the policies lead to

the folly, other parts of the woodland and to the ruins of St Brides Kirk, last resting place of Bonnie Dundee, killed at the Battle of Killiekrankie nearby.

From the car park by the gleaming white castle, a tree-lined path leads east to the walled garden known as Hercules Garden after the statue which overlooks it. This 9-acre giant slopes down to a lake in the centre with a round 'island' and a causeway and a bridge over the narrowest part. The gardens had become badly overgrown and neglected, full of unwanted Christmas trees. Research by garden historian Christopher Dingwall and the detailed castle archives of invoices from nurseries allowed the gardens to be restored in the 1990s. The many statutes have been cleaned up and placed throughout the garden. Very long herbaceous borders lie along two walls, backed by trained fruit. The long mixed border at the highest point of the garden sits on top of a low wall and has excellent drainage, allowing many Mediterranean plants to be grown. This bed is a little too narrow to be as effective as it might be. On the top side of the path, a wider border is planted with shrubs and perennials with yew buttresses. An extensive tree fruit collection is planted in the centre of the garden and there is also an impressive vegetable section. It is commendable that such a huge restoration project has been undertaken after significant research. The garden is so vast, it still does rather dwarf what is planted in it, but the place is dramatic and unusual and well worth a visit. The apple store museum and summer pavilion have pictures and information on the gardens in former times. Don't be put off by the coachloads and hoards at the castle, most of them have no idea that the garden exists, so you'll find it a peaceful place.

Bolfracks
Bolfracks, by Aberfeldy,
Perthshire, PH15 2EX
(map, pp. 116–117)

Athel and Ann Price
Early April–October: 10–6pm; ££
2 miles west of Aberfeldy on the
A827 towards Loch Tay/Kenmore
T: 01887 820344
F: 01887 829522
E: info@bolfracks.fsnet.co.uk
www.bolfracks.com
Tea available for groups
by appointment

Bolfracks

Bolfracks house was converted in Victorian times, by major Aberfeldy landowners the Menzies family, from an eighteenth-century farmhouse to a castellated house. The garden was mainly created by the late Douglas Hutchison from the 1960s onwards, his family having acquired Bolfracks in the 1920s. This is a hillside garden with wonderful views north over the Tay valley to the hills beyond. The woodland water garden constructed around the fast-flowing stream which runs up the west side, is surrounded by extensive and impressive plantings of dwarf rhododendrons most of which came from Glendoick. The steep paths lead up to the high point of the garden from where the best views can be had. Walking along the top of the garden, the first section is the eighteenth-century burial ground and mausoleum, which contains some mature trees and is under-planted with spring bulbs. The southern face is covered with heathers. Past the early herbaceous border, the top path is lined with fruit trees which are garlanded with clematis and sweet peas and forms the boundary of the sundial and rose gardens (mainly shrub roses), which are surrounded by a dramatic closely clipped copper beech hedge. When I visited, the ends of the various lateral vistas along the paths were rather spoiled by compost heaps and other obstructions. Below this are two further long borders across the contour, the upper one herbaceous and the lower one lined on one side by a long border of rugosa roses in several colours, which leads back to the entrance past several fine mature trees including an impressive *Prunus serrula* with flaking bark. This is a well laid-out garden, in a fine setting, with a surprising mix of formality and woodland. It has been planned to give plenty of colour from spring to autumn (*Gentian, Colchicum* etc) and there is considerable planting and renovation going on. The garden is on a steep slope so it is not suitable for those lacking in mobility. There is also a series of footpaths through pinewood on Kenmore Hill, part of Bolfracks estate, details in the garden entrance hut.

Bonhard Nursery

This charming small nursery and garden shop (it would be rude to call it a garden centre) in an old walled garden in the hills above Scone, near Perth, is a secret gem for the locals who pop up regularly to buy plants and eat cakes in the tiny café. The Hickman family know their plants and grow some of them in plots in the walled garden. Plants spill from tables onto the ground around the front door and the old greenhouses are stuffed with plants. The small tea room serves great homemade cakes and scones. This is what visiting a nursery used to be like. Long may it continue.

    [WC]

Bonhard Nursery
Murrayshall Road, Scone,
Perth, PH2 7PQ
(*map, pp. 116–117*)

Charlie and Amanda Hickman
Daily: 9am–5pm (spring–autumn)
or 9am–dusk (winter); free
A94 Perth–Coupar Angus road,
turn off southern outskirts of
Scone, signposted Bonhard
T: 01738 552791
F: 01738 552791
Tea room

Braco Castle Gardens

Not far from Drummond Castle, along an equally long, if somewhat bumpier drive, lies Braco Castle, the oldest part dating to the sixteenth century when it was a stronghold of the Graham family, much added to in subsequent centuries. Around the house are extensive plantings of snowdrops, erythroniums and swathes of daffodils under recently planted trees. West of the house is a mature woodland with rhododendrons and azaleas, daffodils, with bluebells in May, along paths leading to the partly walled garden, open at the front, with a terrace-edge pond. This is a curious mix of ancient and modern hedging, providing compartments with herbaceous and other

Braco Castle Gardens
Braco, Perthshire, FK15 9LA
(*map, pp. 116–117*)

Mr and Mrs van Ballegooijen
Daily: 1 March–31 October,
10am–5pm or by appointment; ££
2 driveways lead from Braco
village, (signposted Braco castle
farms) off the A822, turn off the
A9 at Greenloaning, signposted
for Crieff. Park in front of castle
T: 01786 880437

plantings. A large atmospheric ruined lean-to greenhouse lies at the back of the garden. Everywhere are signs of new plantings: rhododendrons, trees, perennials and bulbs and a wildflower meadow. Owner Teuna van Ballegooijen and gardener Jodi Simpson seem to be an excellent team and this garden should go from strength to strength.

Bradystone House

Bradystone House
Murthly, Perthshire, PH1 4EW
(*map, pp. 116–117*)

SGS and Mr and Mrs James Lumsden
By appointment; ££
Between Stanley and Caputh on the B9099. At Murthly crossroads turn right opposite the road to Kinclaven; if coming north from A9 via Stanley, signed to Brandystone, then left
T: 01738 710 308
F: 01738 710 308
E: plumsden@amserve.com
Teas on opens days and may be available for groups

Carved out of a set of old farm buildings next to a farm house, on a windy site outside Murthly, the Lumsdens began planting shelter little more than 10 years ago and have then created a fine contemporary cottage garden. The property boundary is ringed by trees and a beech hedge, with a busy duck pond by the main gate whose inhabitants seem to think they own the garden. The three-sided courtyard garden, open to the south, has a square of planted low walls surrounding a terrace and fountain in the centre. The courtyard walls are clothed with *Clematis*, roses, *Wisteria* and other climbers. Gravel paths separate the beds and the planting is bold and exuberant, with three colours of *Centranthus* (valerian) spilling over along one section, with *Iris, Dianthus, Geranium* and other plants providing cascades of colour. A delightful small garden.

Bradystone House

Branklyn

Created from old orchard fields by John and Dorothy Renton with the help of seed collections from plant hunters such as Ludlow and Sherriff, in the 1940s and '50s, this was a garden filled with the rarest alpine gems, which attracted admiring visitors to see the rock and scree garden and peat beds. Graham Stuart Thomas, one of Britain's greatest gardeners, was entranced by it. Inevitably, much of the collection of rare and tricky plants was lost during the Rentons' declining years and the subsequent handover of the garden to the National Trust for Scotland. The garden is now enjoying a renaissance under gardener Steve McNamara, who has gradually augmented the fine collection of rhododendrons, (particularly those in subsection Taliensia) alpines and herbaceous, assembled national collections of *Cassiope* and *Lilium* (Mylnefield) and replaced many of the overgrown older plants. There are fine mature trees including a double *Eucryphia glutinosa, Embothrium, Hoheria*, the famous groups of *Acer palmatum* and *Betula albosinensis* var. *septentrionalis* and a huge fastigiate

Branklyn
116 Dundee Road,
Perth, PH2 7BB
(*map, pp. 116–117*)

NTS
Daily: late March/early
April–October, 10am–5pm; ££*
On the outskirts of Perth on
the Dundee road, at the 30mph
sign, clearly signposted. The
car park is west of the
garden further up the hill
T: 01738 625535
E: smcnamara@nts.org.uk
www.branklyngarden.org.uk
Small shop, plant sales

hornbeam. Under the trees and shrubs are *Erythronium, Meconopsis, Primula, Anemone* and other woodland perennials. The winding paths and undulating beds packed with plants have inspired many Scottish gardeners and Branklyn always seems larger than it is. It was one of the first gardens to use peat walls to create terraces for acid-loving plants and these have recently been restored, using peat blocks from sustainable sources in Sweden. At its best in spring but plenty to see in summer and into autumn too. There is a small selection of plants for sale and a tiny gift shop.

Brechin Castle Centre

Brechin Castle Centre
Haughmuir, Brechin,
Angus, DD9 6RL
(*map, pp. 116–117*)

Dalhousie Estates
Daily: 9am–6pm (5pm in winter),
opens 10am Sundays;
££ (country park)
Signposted off A90
Dundee–Aberdeen road,
take Brechin turn-off
T: 01356 626813
F: 01356 626814
E: enquiries@brechincastle
centre.co.uk
www.brechincastlecentre.co.uk
Large restaurant

The Brechin Castle Centre is a gift shop, popular restaurant and garden centre by the side of the A90. There are good children's activities in the country park (separate admission), including a play area, lake with a model boat racing club, a miniature railway in summer, nature trails and farm animals. The Pictavia audiovisual exhibition is also on-site. The 250-seat restaurant, with good views of the park, is usually busy and the plant area has been extended and is now largely covered.

Brechin Castle Gardens

Brechin Castle Gardens
Dalhousie Estates, Dalhousie
Estates Office, Brechin,
Angus, DD9 6SG
(*map, pp. 116–117*)

Lord Dalhousie
Gardens SGS in May, house and
garden tours in early summer, see
website for details. Groups house
and gardens by appointment; ££
Leave A90 onto A933/935 to
Brechin
T: 01356 624566 (Fay Clark)
F: 01356 623725
E: fay@dalhousieestates.co.uk
www.dalhousieestates.co.uk
Café at Brechin Castle Centre,
1 mile away

Brechin Castle's extensive parkland and policies are magnificently planted with mature trees, many of which date back to the eighteenth and nineteenth centuries. Substantial areas in the policy woods are carpeted by acres of snowdrops, some of which were presented to the earl of Dalhousie, Governor General of India during the Indian Mutiny. Between the walled garden and the castle are spectacular informal plantings of rhododendrons with particularly fine deciduous azaleas, providing one of Scotland's finest displays. The potentially fine views down the steep slopes to the River South Esk and the castle beyond are rather obscured by scrub. The beautifully constructed walled garden, which lies around half a mile from the castle, is one of Scotland's largest, covering slightly over 13 acres. The layout is unusual in the marriage of geometrical paths and vistas along the axes of the garden, softened by more meandering informal woodland garden paths and some substantial trees. This is achieved partly by the size and odd shape of the gardens and also by the steeply sloping terrain. The original formal design was completed by Alexander Edward for the fourth earl of Panmure in 1708. Successive earls have taken a strong interest in gardening, which has led to continuous plantings on a large scale right up until the present day. Tender *Rhododendron dalhousiae*, named by Joseph Hooker after the then India Governor

General can be seen in one of the greenhouses. Formally clipped yews, terraces, ponds and vistas are lined by fine trees and shrubs including a copse of seven of my favourite flowering cherry 'Tai Haku', a grouping of three *Cercidiphyllum japonicum* and a huge *Acer griseum*. One of the best features of the garden is the beautiful long, curved peach house which lies in the kitchen garden annex to the north of the main walled garden. It looks like the inspiration for Nicholas Grimshaw's Waterloo Eurostar terminal. Alongside this is a fine collection of trained apples, pears, plums and cherries on the walls. I really enjoyed these gardens; somehow maintained by one, seemingly super-human gardener. The best time to visit is probably in late May when the deciduous azaleas are at their peak.

Bridgend Garden Centre

This small Fife garden centre, owned by George MacKinlay, probably has the largest range of seed potatoes available in Scotland, up to 100 varieties, including many obscure and heritage varieties. Potatoes are sold from Christmas onwards from open sacks, as many or as few of each variety as you like, so you can plant a potato patch with small amounts of a range of varieties. 'Arran Victory, Argos, Ambo, Belle de Fontaney . . . ' the list is impressive. Potato expert Alan Romans also runs his greenhouse franchise from this garden centre. Two other specialities of the garden centre are 50 different types of gravel and a huge range of ceramic pots. This garden centre is an excellent model of how independent garden centre operators can find niche markets which makes them unique, drawing people from afar.

Bridgend Garden Centre
Ladybank Road, Freuchie,
Cupar, Fife, KY15 7HY
(*map, pp. 116–117*)

George MacKinlay
Summer: Monday–Saturday
9am–6pm Sunday 10am–6pm;
Winter (October–March):
Monday-Saturday 9am–5pm,
Sunday 10am–5pm
Just off the A92 north of
Freuchie
T: 01337 858293
E: enquiries@bridgendgc.co.uk
www.bridgendgc.co.uk
Café

Cairnie Fruit Farm
Cairnie, Cupar, Fife, KY15 4QD
(*map, pp. 116–117*)

Maze: 17 July–end October
10am–6pm. Farm shop:
May–August, closed Mondays
in October, November; ££ (maze)
Signposted off A92, turn off at
Rathillet Village coming from
Perth. Or from A91 from Cupar
go past hospital and continue
on this minor road
T: 01334 655610
E: info@cairniefruitfarm.co.uk
www.cairniefruitfarm.co.uk

Cairnie Fruit Farm

This is a Fife fruit farm with great pick-your-own (or ready-picked) strawberries, raspberries, currants, gooseberries, tayberries, brambles and cherries. In addition, the fiendishly hard maize maze is grown each summer specifically so you can lose your children for long periods while you enjoy the popular tea room and farm shop.

Callander Lodge
Leny Fues, Callander, FK17 8AS
(*map, pp. 116–117*)

Miss Caroline Penney
1 April–31 August by
arrangement; ££
On the western edge of Callander
on A84, turn right at sign for Leny
Feus. Garden at end on the left.
Go through gate marked with
house name
T: 01877 330 136

Callander Lodge

This Victorian garden on the outskirts of Callander was first laid out in 1863. It consists of four acres of mature trees with extensive plantings of rhododendrons and azaleas, shrubs, herbaceous and rose borders. At the bottom is a shady bog garden and fern grotto. Due to steps and hills, the garden is not suitable for wheelchairs.

Cambo House

This garden on the Fife coast near Crail is best known for its snowdrops in February and March. Catherine Erskine realised that the Cambo snowdrop woods were something special and over the years, as more and more visitors have come to see them, Peter and Catherine Erskine developed this into a Snowdrop Festival which is now run in gardens all over Scotland. The 70 acres of woodland carpeted in snowdrops, snowflakes and aconites follow the burn down to the sea and visitors will notice that, unusually, most of the snowdrops here are doubles. Much of the woodland was becoming choked with ivy so Catherine enlisted the help of Helen and Emma, two now famous pigs who root up the ivy but leave the snowdrops. Catherine has collected over 200 varieties of specialist snowdrops, which is now recognised as a National Collection. The snowdrop experience at Cambo is much more than the walk around the woods; a café is set up in the old stables and there is a snowdrop gift shop, art displays, children's painting competition and other activities and you can buy snowdrops in the green or have them sent mail order. Other early spring colour is provided by hellebores, and masses of other spring bulbs. Cambo's other outstanding attraction is its walled garden, bisected by a burn crossed by wooden bridges; this garden has gradually been transformed to have some of Scotland's best contemporary herbaceous displays. It formerly contained 'marching rows of dahlias' according to the website. The different areas and beds have nine different themes, the most prevalent being long or short grass prairie or steppe planting with the use of bold drifts of perennials and grasses in a style originally devised by Dutchman Piet Oudolf and now much imitated, though not so often in Scotland. Other parts of the garden are designed for cut flowers, early flowering perennials, moisture-loving plants and so on. The low rainfall and well-drained soil of this part of Fife are obviously a key factor in the success of this style, but so too are the irresistible planting combinations which head gardener Elliot Forsyth has created. By the entrance, the long deep double border stresses the bronzes and creams of the grass heads with flowers in purples and deep pinks, in a restful combination. Just behind this is the more outrageous annual potager garden with irregular-shaped beds and plants spilling over onto meandering paths. This is perhaps my favourite part of Cambo and I think one of Scotland's best bits of gardening: blue cabbage, Swiss chard, fennel, the fluffy sideways heads of barley (*Hordeum jubatum*) and furry *Pennisetum* share a stage with bright red *Coreopsis*, shocking yellow

Cambo House
Cambo House, Kingsbarns, St Andrews, Fife, KY16 8QD
(*map, pp. 116–117*)

Catherine Erskine
Daily: 10am–5pm,
1 day per year SGS; ££
Between Kingsbarns and Crail on A917 south of St Andrews
T: 01333 450054
F: 01333 450987
E: catherine@camboestate.com
www.camboestate.com
Tearoom and giftshop at snowdrop time and during the week at other times

Rudbeckia and *Achillea*; almost every combination of foliage and flower demands attention, truly inspirational planting, which evolves from year to year. In 2008 larger blocks of plants were used; one eyecatcher was lollo rosso lettuce surrounded by fluffy *Stipa tenuissima*. Beyond the potager is a dry garden with Mediterranean plants: *Verbena, Verbascum, Salvia*. The eastern side contains extensive fruit and vegetable plots while the western side has box-lined sections filled with grasses, annuals and perennials. On an early June visit I enjoyed the lilac walk with 26 varieties of *Syringa*, the 'Kiftsgate' rose smothering an old apple tree, the *Iris Sibirica* and the *Rodgersia*, but this is just a prelude to the main event in later summer. The perennials and grasses in the walled garden have a very long season, from late June well into autumn when the grass flowering is at its peak; indeed, the seed heads of perennials and grasses are left until spring and they still look effective in February at snowdrop time. Though the garden has little in the way of labelling, as it is considered to detract from the effect, there is useful explanatory material available in the potting shed, highlighting the most significant plant displays season by season. Catherine Erskine has a singular grasp of how to make a great garden into a visitor attraction, 'an all season's plantsman's paradise', with energy and imagination. She deservedly won the 2007 Thistle Award for tourism for her work in promoting snowdrops and if you want inspiration on how to market your garden to visitors, Cambo is the model. This is undoubtedly one of Scotland's garden jewels and a demonstration of how a significant garden can be maintained and marketed with limited resources. There are various work schemes for students and 'woofing' (Willing Workers on Organic Farms). Apply via the excellent website. There are always surplus plants available for sale.

Cherrybank Gardens

Cherrybank Gardens,
Necessity Brae, Perth, PH2 0PF
(*map, pp. 116–117*)

A9 Broxburn roundabout, on
western side of Perth, follow signs
to Perth. At the 3rd mini roundabout turn right (brown tourist
sign for Cherrybank Gardens)
Daily, opening times unavailable
at time of writing; free

I think we all assumed that this garden was lost when the lottery bid for the Calyx, a national garden for Scotland, was turned down in 2007 and the garden was closed. Just before this book went to press it was announced that the garden would be gifted to Perth and Kinross Council and is due to re-open in 2009. Though replanting will need to take place. The national collection of *Erica* and *Calluna* and a wide range of their relatives means that Cherrybank is the most extensive heather collection you'll see anywhere in Britain. The 6-acre garden, originally created by the whisky firm of Bells, has a rich mix of colour throughout most of the year and the great thing about the heather family is that they do their thing at times of year when little else is in flower. There are apparently 50,000 plants and over 900 varieties of heather planted on a north-facing landscaped slope with artworks and sculptures, water features including an acoustic pool and trout stream. Labelling is good for the heathers, but unfortunately non-existent for everything else, which visitors may find frustrating.

Christie's Alpine Nursery

Christie's Alpine Nursery
Downfield, Main Road, Westmuir,
Kirriemuir, Angus, DD8 5LP
(*map, pp. 116–117*)

Ian and Ann Christie
A926 from Kirriemuir to Alyth road
Group visits, specialist societies
and interested individuals by
appointment
E: sales@alpine-plants.co.uk
www.christiealpines.co.uk/

Alpine enthusiast and plant hunter Ian Christie is a well-known figure in Scottish gardening circles and his nursery outside Kirriemuir has long been a mecca for gentian, *Trillium*, orchids, snowdrop and alpine enthusiasts. Ian and his wife Ann have begun to scale down operations for their retirement but they are still operating the nursery and supplying mail-order plants. The website lists selected snowdrops, *Corydalis, Gentiana, Meconopsis, Primulas* and fine ranges of other alpines, bulbs and ericaceous plants. The gardens around the house can be visited by groups by appointment. The *Meconopsis* and autumn gentians are particularly fine.

Cloan
by Auchterarder,
Perth, PH3 1PP
(*map, pp. 116–117*)

Mr and Mrs Richard Haldane
SGS some years, groups by
appointment; ££
South out of Auchterarder (Abbey
Road) over A9, right at T-junction
and up the hill (left fork), under
railway bridge to castle-like
house on hillside
T: 01764 622936/622299
F: 01764 644 199
E: rwh@cloanden.co.uk

Cloan

This very striking tall Victorian house, visible from some distance away, perches on the side of the Cloan or Dalry burn and gorge, surveying the Earn valley and Auchterarder below. Cloan was designed in the 1850s by Andrew Heiton, who ran his architectural practice in Perth and Dundee, building churches, stations and many large country houses in the area including Pitlochry landmark, the Atholl Palace Hotel. The Haldane family has included eminent politicians and scientists, and four generations of the family have lived at Cloan. This garden was one of those which opened at the foundation of the Scotland's Gardens Scheme in 1931. There are some fine trees around the house and up the glen walk behind, probably planted at the same time the house was built, including an impressive *Sequoia sempervirens*, not nearly as commonly planted as its relative the 'Wellingtonia'. Mature rhododendrons and azaleas and maples surround the house and lead to the walled garden, replanted in recent years with perennials and gardened on organic principles. The steps leading up the centre are lined with sphinx statues. Beyond this is a small rectangular garden with castellated hedging and some interesting topiary which leads on to a wild garden/meadow with ponds and statues. The walk up the glen leads to a reservoir which is planted with a good range of trees.

[♿] [WC]

Cluny House

This woodland garden overlooking the scenic Strathtay valley, was planted and developed from 1950 by Bobby and Betty Masterton, who received seeds from Ludlow and Sherriff and other plant hunters. Cluny was inherited by the Mastertons' daughter Wendy and her husband John Mattingley, who have risen perfectly to the challenge of

keeping this amazing garden and its plant collections going. The garden begins on the terraced lawn around the house and pitches steeply down the wooded hillside via a series of narrow meandering paths. Beneath the extensive collection of mature trees, is a canopy of rhododendrons, acers, rowans and birches, beneath which are lilies, *Meconopsis, Arisaema, Erythronium*, skunk cabbage and one of the best collections of Asiatic primulas in Europe (a former national collection). Spectacular cardiocrinums flower in mid summer. On one April visit I noted a large number of *Clematis macropetala* and *C. alpina* clambering up the rhododendrons, which looked most effective. This is a garden well worth visiting as early as March to see the Petiolaris section, primula species and snowdrops. You'll also find a champion *Sequoiadendron giganteum* which has been measured as the widest conifer in Britain (11m girth). No chemicals are used in the garden and weeding is carried out by hand, allowing the numerous self-sown seedlings to establish. A viewing platform has recently been constructed and all the steps replaced. Patrick Taylor comments that 'as naturalistic gardens go, few give the appearance of so little human intervention as Cluny. This is of course an illusion'. Cluny does indeed look 'wild' and undesigned which is a large part of its charm. It is also a good place to see wildlife, particularly red squirrels and many birds including fieldfares and siskins. You need to be fit to get around the garden, and have stout shoes. The tree cover is becoming a little dense for some of the plants and is also starting to obscure many of the best views of the surrounding countryside. Many of the perennials in the garden are offered for sale; this is a great place to look for *Lilium*, Primulas and *Trillium*, for example. Why not combine a visit with Bolfracks on the other side of the Tay valley and drop into the wonderful Watermill bookshop in Aberfeldy, which also has great coffee?

Cluny House
Aberfeldy, Perthshire, PH15 2JT
(*map, pp. 116–117*)

John and Wendy Mattingley
March–October: daily 10am–6pm,
groups of 10+ by arrangement;
££*
From A9, turn off at Ballinluig
onto A827. At Grandtully cross
bridge to north side of Tay (follow
brown signs) left and left again
towards Weem. Turn right after
3 miles
T: 01887 820795
E: wmattingley@btinternet.com
www.clunyhousegardens.com

Comrie Village Gardens
Contact Patricia Onions,
Allium Cottage, 21 Tay Avenue,
Comrie, PH6 2PF
(*map, pp. 116–117*)

Various
SGS 2–3 Sundays per year,
4–5 gardens; ££
From A85 turn into Bridle Street
(between RBS and White Church),
follow road past fire station, first
left. Tickets and map from Pat
Onions, 21 Tay Avenue
T: 01764 671121 (Mrs Onions)

Comrie Village Gardens

Comrie is an award-winning Britain in Bloom village on the River
Earn, with fine views to the surrounding hills. Several gardens open
most years under SGS, usually 2–3 times per year, organised by Mrs
Onions from Allium Cottage. During Comrie Fortnight, there are
several other gardens which also open for the local church. Mrs
Onions' garden and that of Sandy and Evelyn Grey can be open by
appointment in the summer.

Cortachy Castle Gardens
Cortachy, Kirriemuir,
DD8 4LY
(*map, pp. 116–117*)

Earl and Countess of Airlie
SGS 1 Sunday in early June; ££
B955, 5 miles north of Kirriemuir,
which is signposted off the A90
Dundee–Aberdeen road
T: 01575 570108
F: 01575 540400
www.airlieestates.com
Tea in castle on June
Sunday open day only

Cortachy Castle Gardens

The Ogilvy family acquired Cortachy in 1625. The magnificent
planned landscape around the castle mainly dates back to the early
1800s with broad vistas from the castle over the River South Esk and
north towards the church. The arboretum or 'American garden'
contains fine specimen trees planted by family members and visiting
royalty over 150 years. There are several UK champion conifers
amongst them. Most of the trees have a slightly kitsch white heart-
shaped planting plaque. Next to the church is a curved laburnum
arch, underplanted with scented *Rhododendron luteum*, in flower in
late May and early June. This was planted for Lord and Lady Airlie's
golden wedding in 2002 and is a cousin of the one at Airlie Castle,
nearby. In the opposite direction, a rhododendron and azalea-lined
path leads away from the imposing cream-coloured castle towards the

main garden. After 400m it opens into a partially walled garden with formal yew hedging and two main borders. The 'ladies' border', backed by some large, leaning, clipped yews is planted around a structure of *Potentilla* (better than it sounds). The 'walled border', backed with high wall-covered climbers, has a centrepiece of a blue and white border with beaded iris, backed by the shocking yellow of golden hop. The remainder of this large walled garden is largely grassed over now, with sections bordered by yew hedges with some fruit and vegetables. Beyond this through a yew tunnel is a complete contrast, with an informal woodland–water garden combination. The large pond is surrounded by extensive rhododendron, azalea and *Meconopsis* and primula plantings with *Gunnera, Rheum, Rodgersia* and the usual waterside favourites. I was lucky to visit on a still day with the azaleas reflected in the pond water, creating a magical effect. A blue-green pagoda was constructed to mark the millennium and this acts as a fine focal point for views across the water. Cortachy's vast undulating parkland and gardens are well maintained and a pleasure to wander around. On SGS open days you can have tea in the castle itself, overlooked by portraits of Ogilvy ancestors. In addition, a series of network footpaths has been created in and around the policies and visitors can follow the waymarked routes. The climb up to the Airlie Monument is worth making for the fine views of the Angus countryside and hills.

Cottage (The), Longforgan
36 Main Street,
Longforgan,
Dundee, DD2 5ET
(*map, pp. 116–117*)

Dr Andrew and Margo Reid
SGS most years; ££
Turn off A90 at Longforgan sign
between Perth (15 miles) and
Dundee (5 miles). Halfway along
Longforgan Main Street. Street
parking
T: 01382 360247

Cottage (The), Longforgan

The Reids have gardened here in the attractive Carse of Gowrie
village of Longforgan for 30 years and this is one of the finest smaller
gardens in the area, immaculately maintained, packed with plants,
designed to have a long season of interest. The rectangular garden lies
behind the attractive house, somewhat larger than most people's
concept of a cottage, gradually sloping away towards the River Tay
and Fife hills which can be seen in the distance. The garden is fringed
with trees, shrubs and wide borders while the lawn itself contains
several island beds, one of which contains a pond and bridge. The
year starts with rhododendrons, azaleas and spring bulbs which are
mainly to be found along the western side of the garden. At the south
end, furthest from the house, a carefully selected collection of trees of
various ages can be found. These include a *Metasequoia*, *Acer griseum*,
gleaming white-barked *Betula utilis* var. *jacquemontii* and *Stewartia*.
When I visited in late June an 'L'-shaped perennial bed near the house
was in full flower, overflowing with peonies, *Delphinium*, *Lysmachia*,
Penstemon and *Geranium*. The patio which runs along the house
features a line of five standard small-leaved Korean lilacs, clipped into
balls, which flower in late May and June. Below this a rose border
features many of the Reids' favourite varieties: yellow 'Korresia', white
'Pascali', blush 'Rennaissance' and in a bed nearby, a planting of
several pure white 'Margaret Merril', 'Rosamundi' and the truly outrageous red and white striped 'Ferdinand Pritchard'. Clearly a great deal
of love and a deal more hard work goes into maintaining the garden
to this level.

Craigend House

This handsome black and white house is on the site of another, formerly much larger, the walls and foundations of which form part of the terrace garden at the back. The garden behind the house is partially walled, with rhododendrons and azaleas on the wooded side, while the walled side is filled with roses and shrubs and a good range of perennials. At the front of the house, the Auchenbowie burn feeds a series of three ponds which were originally used for pioneering experimental fish farming but are now home to trout and iris.

Craigfoodie

One of the newest of Fife's many excellent private gardens, this is an interesting project, both for its design and the range of plants. The original house, more than 300 years old, was remodelled in handsome Georgian style and is gleaming white. Next to it is a series of terraces, the lowest of which leads out from the kitchen. Above the top terrace is a rather striking ruined doocot, the sloping roof has gone, revealing the nesting boxes. The terrace's south-facing, sheltered aspect and the perfect drainage mean that all sorts of tender exotics are thriving up here: New Zealand's reptile-like *Pseudopanax ferox* and a vigorous *Musa* (banana) are two examples. From these terraces there are fine views of St Andrews' golf links in the distance and of course this is an excellent vantage point to appreciate the formal layout of the garden below with its box-lined beds. All that remains of the old garden are two rows of box hedging, a few trees and shrubs including a corkscrew hazel and some mature yews. The garden is now split into

Craigend House
Auchenbowie, Stirling, FK7 9QW
(*map, pp. 116–117*)

Philip and Lynette Penfold
SGS; ££
J9 of M9 take A872 to Denny, after approx. 1 mile first right to Auchenbowie Caravan Park – signposted at this stage. At T-junction immediately past the caravan park, turn left and follow the road for ½ mile. Craigend House is first on the right, parking next right at Craigend Farm on open days
T: 01786 811070
www.craigendhouse.co.uk

Craigfoodie
Dairsie, Balmullo, KY15 4RU
(*map, pp. 116–117*)

James and Lindsay Murray
SGS 1 day per year; ££
Off the A91 at Dairsie, between Guardbridge and Cupar. Turn left at Dairsie school
T: 01334 870291
E: jamescmurray@btinternet.com

several sections: below the house on the west side is a series of parterre beds with lavender edging in-filled with herbaceous geraniums with bay tree balls in the centre. Along the central box-lined path are shrub roses with a long herbaceous border on the east side on the far side of a lawn. A pleached hedge divides the section nearest the house from the vegetables, trained fruit trees and narrow hedged walk beyond. Through a narrow door is a so-far-unplanted but attractive triangular lawn which in turn leads across the drive to the small section of woodland garden with some rare and unusual rhododendrons, trees and shrubs. The McMurrays are obviously enjoying creating this garden and there are further plans, with a new sculpture being built for 2008–09 and the introduction of water. Definitely one to watch and word is spreading, as they had 500 people on their last SGS open day.

Craigtoun Country Park

Craigtoun Country Park
St Andrews, Fife, KY16 8NX
(*map, pp. 116–117*)

St Andrews Parks
All year, facilities May–August, weekends only April and September; £–££
T: 01334 473666
F: 01334 473666

This large, popular park is a wonderfully nostalgic place to visit for all those who recall a childhood spent in the great city parks of yesteryear with boating ponds and bedding schemes. The trip down memory lane is on a grand scale, with both fine landscaping and plantings and lots for children to do. The park is part of a large Victorian planned landscape for Craigtoun House, formerly a hospital and now boarded up and unloved. Many of the old landscape components are now incomplete or rather forlorn, particularly an artificial mound which once had a temple on it, now overgrown. If it were cleared of undergrowth it would make a fine viewpoint. A sunken garden filled with funereal hostas looks like part of a necropolis; a bit of colour would not go amiss. Elsewhere, the new plantings and modern landscaping are much more effective with a water garden along the stream side, fine displays of rhododendrons, perennials and an extensive bedding scheme in front of the greenhouses. It would help the aesthetic if St Andrews' youth might be dissuaded from writing their names on the glasshouse painted shading. This is debouncing-kids-heaven with a

well-maintained play area, a miniature train which runs round much of the park, and an extraordinary boating pond, with extensive buildings designed by architect Paul Waterhouse in most unexpected Franco-German picturesque style. It looks rather as if Portmeirion has come to Scotland. Craigtoun has lots of fine trees, huge expanses of lawn and ample space for most of the population of St Andrews to enjoy themselves. And needless to say, there are golf opportunities nearby.

Crail Pottery and Container Garden

Crail pottery was founded in 1965 and the yard out the back is crammed full of decorative pots, some for sale, others filled with plants, under some gnarled old fruit trees. All pots are hand-thrown and made on-site. Various members of the family make different styles of pottery including stoneware, earthenware and raku for kitchen, ornamental and outdoor use.

Crail Pottery and Container Garden
75 Nethergate, Crail, Fife, KY10 3TX
(*map, pp. 116–117*)

Stephen, Carol, Sarah and Ben Grieve
Daily: Monday–Friday 9am–5pm, Saturday and Sunday 10am–5pm; free.
Off Castle Street/ Rose Wynd, which lead off the High Street
T: 01333 451212
www.crailpottery.com
Coffee and tea

Culross Palace and Garden
Culross, Fife,
KY12 8JH
(map, pp. 116–117)

NTS
Open April–October, daily; £££*
Off the A985, 7 miles (11.3km)
west of Dunfermline, easily
reached from the A90 or
the Kinkardine Bridge
T: 0844 4932189
F: 0844 4932190
www.nts.org.uk
Charming café

Culross Palace and Garden

Culross is pronounced 'coo-ross' and is one of Scotland's most beautiful villages; the steep, twisting wynds (streets), white-washed walls and cobbles make it seem like Mediterranean-on-Forth on a sunny summer's day, which is the ideal time to visit the palace and its gardens. Unfortunately the potentially fine views across the Forth are to Grangemouth, Scotland's major petrochemical complex, which itself can be a thing of beauty lit up at night, but in daytime is rather less fetching, and next door the menacing chimney of Longannet power station is not much better. Much of the village has been very well restored by the National Trust for Scotland but is still very much lived-in and avoids being twee or precious. There are little cafés and galleries and it is well worth walking up to the abbey high on the hill above the village for the fine views over the village. You'll also find Parleyhill Garden up here (see p. 190). To see the gardens at Culross you need a ticket for the palace too, as the entrance and exit are through it. The 'palace' is not royal as such but rather was a rich merchant's house (fortune made in coal and salt pans), now painted a striking yellow-brown, with a tiled roof. It looks as if it might have been transplanted from Tuscany or Andalucia. When I visited in 2007, there was an excellent exhibition on medicinal plants in one of the rooms, created by one of the palace volunteers, which deserved to be made permanent. The palace garden, looked after for many years by Mark Jeffery, is a re-creation of a seventeenth-century garden on a steep terraced slope, now run on organic principles. There were no

records of the original garden, but the range of plant material used comes from lists from similar contemporary gardens. Most of the plants have culinary or medicinal uses and on a sunny day I noticed how aromatic this garden was: the geometric beds are edged with sage, lavender, rosemary, curry plant and others. Around the walls are fruit trees and vines, including mulberry and a medlar. For the best view walk up to the terraces at the back and enjoy the vista of the garden, the palace, the village and the Forth beyond. The lower part is planted with masses of pink and red hollyhocks The top terrace, with its roses and other plants, and structure of wooden pergola, seats and fencing, is known as the Mary Luke Garden and was opened in 2008. The main garden's paths are covered with crushed white shells from the beach and the walls are lined with willow hurdle. For some reason I missed the 'Old Scots Dumpy' hens, a tough old breed, which provide eggs to the café. In late summer the garden can look a bit scruffy, as herbs often do, but if you use all your senses, you'll find this a rather special place.

Dalfruin

Keen members of the Scottish Rock Garden Club, James and Ellen Welsh have packed an unbelievable number of plants into their small garden of around a third of an acre with a handsome church as a

Dalfruin
Kirktonhill Road,
Kirriemuir, DD8 4HU
(*map, pp. 116–117*)

James and Ellen Welsh
1 day SGS May or early June and groups by appointment (in writing please); ££
From centre of Kirriemuir turn left up Roods; Kirktonhill Road is on left near top of hill just before the school 20mph zone. Please park on Roods or at St Mary's Church

backdrop. Visitors are often envious of their connoisseur plants such as *Dactylorhiza* orchids, *Hepatica, Codonopsis*, tree peonies, *Meconopsis*, and over 20 varieties of *Trillium*. Some of the trees and shrubs come from Ludlow and Sherriff collections which were originally grown at Ascreavie. Two ponds connected by a small stream were added in 2000 and I like the very narrow dwarf conifer bed which runs down the side of the house. On trees and pergolas overhead are several vigorous rambling roses including 'Kiftsgate' and 'Paul's Himalayan Musk'. The owners are justified in their claim that there is not much room for weeds as it is so tightly packed.

Dirnanean Estate
Enochdhu, Blairgowrie,
Perthshire, PH10 7PD
(*map, pp. 116–117*)

Mr John Manning
First weekend June–last weekend August: daily 11am–5.30pm and for advertised events at other times; ££
10 miles east of Pitlochry, on A924 just before Enochdhu. From Blairgowrie follow the A93 to Bridge of Cally and left on the A924 (towards Pitlochry), 2 miles after Kirkmichael
T: 01250 881400
E: jm@johnmanningarchitect.co.uk
Picnic spots in the garden. Several pubs in Kirkmichael nearby

Dirnanean Estate

This is a curious and rather eccentric, rough-and-ready garden in highland Perthshire, at 1,000ft above sea level. A walled garden has some wind-battered fruit trees, roses and some shrubs, while the lawn and burnside walks boast some mature, gnarled rhododendrons, a squat fat giant redwood and some rare trees and shrubs such as *Abies mariesii, Tsuga chinensis, Betula alleghanensis* and *Stewartia monadelpha*. Don't miss the shed full of old tools, a menagerie of ducks, geese and hens and best of all, a walk up the burn through the Fox Den to a spectacular waterfall.

Douglas Bader Community Garden
Duffus Park, Cupar,
Fife, KY15 5AS
(*map, pp. 116–117*)

Fife Council
In Duffus Park, Cupar
T: 01334 650881
E: info@dbcg.org.uk
www.dbcg.org.uk

Douglas Bader Community Garden

There are ambitious plans afoot to restore and extend this small garden in Duffus Park, Cupar. At the moment the garden is derelict and restoration depends on winning £2 million of funding. The original garden was designed for use principally by the disabled and it was opened by Douglas Bader and his wife, Lady Joan, in 1982.

Dowhill

Dowhill
Kelty, Kinross, KY4 0HZ
(*map, pp. 116–117*)

Colin and Pippa Maitland-Dougal
May: Tuesdays and Thursdays 10am–4pm; ££
Junction 5 on M90, near Kinross, west on B9097 towards Yett's o' Muckhart, 1 mile on the left
T: 01577 850207
E: dowhill@onetel.com

When the Maitland-Dougals arrived in the mid 1980s Dowhill was overgrown and forlorn, but they fell in love with the 1710 house and the site as a potential garden. They found that broken drains were flooding part of the property and killing trees, so they constructed a series of linked ponds to take the excess water away. The nine ponds are planted with shrubs and herbaceous and are popular with wildfowl. There was a fine *Embothrium* in flower when I visited in June and carpets of blue poppies and candelabra primulas. There is lots of interest over a long season with perennials, shrubs, climbers and many fine trees. Behind the house is a large woodland area with extensive plantings of rhododendrons and mature trees which leads up a meandering track to the ruins of Dowhill Castle, from which

there are good views over Loch Leven. Below the garden are two newer, larger ponds with an attractive bridge and bold plantings of iris and other vigorous pond-side plants. The garden makes much use of the landscape in which it is set and is one of the best in this part of Scotland. *Good Gardens Guide* says: 'This is an exceptional garden, perhaps best described as a "proper" country garden.'

Drummond Castle Gardens

There is nothing in Scotland to match the panorama of Scotland's finest formal gardens, viewed from the vantage point of the upper terraces between the keep of old Drummond Castle and the more modern mansion. It is worth watching visitors' faces break into a smile of pleasure as they take in the incredible spectacle. This is the nearest thing Scotland has to the gardens of the great French chateaux and it is almost incongruous amongst the rolling hills of Perthshire. The drive is special too, with a mile-long avenue of beech trees. Apparently John Drummond, fourth Earl of Perth, had intended for the avenue to lead all the way to the city of Perth 20 miles away. This amazing garden has been made, abandoned and re-laid several times in its history. The first formal garden was laid out in French style in 1630 but Cromwell's vandals destroyed it and it was later overgrown by trees. John Reid, Scotland's first horticultural author, worked at Drummond in the late seventeenth century. The Drummonds backed the Jacobite cause and were forced into exile till 1785 and the formal

Drummond Castle Gardens
Drummond Castle, Muthill,
Crieff, PH7 4HZ
(*map, pp. 116–117*)

Grimmsthorpe and Drummond
Castle Trust Ltd
Easter weekend (four days) then
May–31 October: daily 1–6 pm;
££*
Off the A823 Crieff to Gleneagles
road just north of Muthill
T: 01764 681433
F: 01764 681642
E: thegardens@drummond
castle.sol.co.uk
www.drummondcastle
gardens.co.uk

gardens were not re-established till the nineteenth century, when they were designed by Lewis Kennedy, who had previously worked for the Empress Josephine at Malmaison in France. He used the saltire as the main design element and created the main axis vista down the elaborate staircase, between the parterres out beyond the garden through the woods on the hillside opposite the terraces. The 12-acre rectangular formal garden is bisected by 2 diagonal lines, forming the St Andrew's Cross with 5 parallel paths from north to south, and 2 large ponds at either end. The Victorian gardens were widely proclaimed as the best of their type and *Country Life* declared it the finest Edwardian garden in Britain. Two world wars were the cause of another period of decline and abandonment and it was Phyllis Astor, wife of the earl of Ancaster, who restored the gardens once again during the 1950s. The ancient yew and beech hedges and some topiary remain from Victorian days, with the fine red Japanese maples a clever addition which not only provides fiery autumn colour but, with *Prunus pissardii*, a startling contrast with the yellow fastigiate yew throughout the summer. The box parterres are filled with *Anaphalis triplinervis*, lavender and roses and there are rounded hedges surrounding Italianate statues and urns. There are two narrow terraces at the top, a steep grassed slope to a further terrace wall and then steps down to the garden itself. The choice of planting makes this formal garden attractive all year long, even in winter, as the structure is strong. What makes it so magnificent is the height of the vantage point. Of Scotland's other formal gardens on this scale, Dunrobin shares the clifftop vista; it is a pity Pitmedden can't boast a similar vantage point. Do walk right down to the far side of the garden, where there is an impressive kitchen garden with greenhouses and some fine mature copper beech apparently planted by Queen

Victoria. It has to be admitted that walking though the gardens, though worthwhile, is somehow a bit of a let-down after the magnificence of the view from above. There is no doubt that this is one of Scotland's must-visit gardens.

Dunninald Castle and Gardens

This James Gillespie Graham-designed 1824 castle and garden, half a mile from the cliffs which line the Angus coast, has an astonishing display of bluebells through acres of woodland. Apparently this display started as a small patch under the mature beech trees, and spread over the last 30–40 years to provide one of Scotland's most breathtaking sights. Mostly they are blue, but in some places the whites and resulting lavender hybrids have been allowed to establish. Under a mature canopy of limes, beech, oaks and other trees, underplanted with rhododendrons and other shrubs, the ground is a carpet of colour, set off beautifully by the pale green shades of the young growth emerging all around. This is a garden worth travelling a long way to see at its peak, usually the second and third weeks in May. There is also a compact, well-maintained eighteenth-century walled garden with curved walls and a complex wrought iron gate commemorating the union of England, Scotland and Ireland. The garden contains tulips, herbaceous borders, old roses, vegetables and a collection of espaliered apple trees.

Dunninald Castle and Gardens
Montrose, DD10 9TD
(*map, pp. 116–117*)

Stansfeld family
SGS May and by appointment.
House and garden open daily in
July except Mondays; ££
2 miles south of Montrose on
A92 off Lunan–Montrose road
T: 01674 674842
www.dunninald.com

Earlshall Castle
Leuchars, Fife, KY16 ODP
(*map, pp. 116–117*)

Paul Veenhuijzen, Paula Josine
SGS 1–2 days per year, house and
gardens by prior arrangement; ££
Off A919, turn of onto Earlshall
Road, ¾ mile east off Leuchars
T: 01334 839 205
E: veenhuijzen@btinternet.com

Earlshall Castle

Earlshall was architect Robert Lorimer's first professional commission at the age of 26. Lorimer took a partially derelict castle which dated back to 1546 and restored it for Robert MacKenzie in the 1890s. Lorimer lamented the 'Victorianisation' of old houses and determined to restore Earlshall, as he had his family's own castle at Kellie, by retaining the original structure and character. Like fellow Scot Charles Rennie Macintosh, whose career took off at around the same time, Lorimer focused on detail as well as the grand design; Earlshall Castle and garden are full of brilliant touches: look out for the iron-work grilles on the ground floor, and the small stained-glass panels in the smaller windows, the group of stone monkeys which sit on the corner tool-house/cottage roof as well as the carvings and inscriptions around the garden walls. Dutchman Paul Veenhuijzen almost purchased Earlshall in 1996 from the self-proclaimed Baron of Earlshall, Robert Baxter (see the castle brochure for wax-worklike photographic evidence), but was put off by the screaming Tornado jets of Leuchars, whose runway lies just outside the garden walls. But when the castle was back on the market two years later, Paul could not resist. He has carried out meticulous research into Lorimer, built an archive of material on Earlshall and is restoring the castle and garden as much as possible to the original plans. Suki Urquhart sums up Lorimer's achievement very well as 'a one-man version of the English Gertrude Jekyll and Sir Edwin Lutyens partnership – combining the skills of both architecture and horticulture into a homogeneous whole'. Both Kellie and Earlshall are ample evidence of Lorimer's genius. Earlshall has the finest topiary in Scotland, though it is hard to appreciate the scale and layout without a vantage point from the castle's upper floors. My brother Ray and I spent some time on the castle roof, where the best views are to be had. When my wife Jane saw the pictures from the top of the tower, her first comment was that someone had spilled a packet of green liquorice allsorts on the lawn, while I find it has a certain *Alice in Wonderland* quality. From the garden itself the sensation is different, more like being surrounded by a collection of giant green Henry Moore sculptures. But don't be deceived; there is nothing random in the layout. This garden is exquisitely designed; every axis leads to a focal point, a bench, a sundial, a door, through yew arches and allées; I can't recall a more complex series of criss-crossing vistas in one garden; one of the best of these leads to a flaming *Embothrium*, framed by a topiary arch. Topiary dominates the central section, but there are also herbaceous borders, a double *Rosa rugosa* border, a double *Weigela* border, a formal rose section, a fine vegetable garden, lots of trained fruit, a sunken garden which is surrounded by dense herbaceous plantings, a new box and yew garden which was on Lorimer's plans, and an orchard. It is only the massed bedding-out of hybrid rhododendrons along some of the walled garden walls which is not in keeping and might be better removed. The outbuildings, the gatehouse, the garden

walls themselves, as well as the patterned cobbles and paved paths in the garden, are all part of the master plan, as is the double avenue of pollarded limes from the gatehouse past the castle to the south. The excellence of the garden over the years was largely due to gardener Henry Collier, who retired a few years ago well into his 80s having worked at Earlshall for 68 years. His successor, Nicky Macintyre is carrying on the tradition and the garden is beautifully maintained. Earlshall is a masterpiece of architecture and garden combined and it is all the more heartening to see the love its owner and gardener put into it. Earlshall is without doubt one of Scotland's horticultural highlights as well as being one of Lorimer's masterpieces.

Easter Meikle Fardle

The Mackenzies have travelled a great deal through the Rear Admiral's naval career and this is not the first garden they have made. Auchleeks House, near Calvine, now open under SGS once more, was created by Ursula Mackenzie, which she reluctantly left in the 1990s. Easter Meikle Fardle is a young but surprisingly mature garden created around a fine barn-conversion house. Annual flooding from the Tay nearby makes gardening here a challenge, but the high water table makes trees grow at an impressive rate. The garden is packed with plants and well designed, with several sections. To the south of the house is an enclosed space packed with perennials and fine alliums. Between this and the house, the gravel car-parking area is surrounded by climbers, shrubs and perennials. On the north side of

Easter Meikle Fardle
Meiklour, by Perth, PH2 6EF
(*map, pp. 116–117*)

Rear Admiral and Mrs
John Mackenzie
May–mid-August
(by appointment, please); ££
Take A984 Dunkeld to Coupar
Angus 1½ miles, from Spittalfield
towards Meikleour, third house
on left after turning to Lethendy
T: 01738 710330
Light meals/afternoon tea
can be arranged

the house a conservatory, enclosed pergola, lawns and further beds of shrubs and perennials lead to the top of the bank with a 'reading area' bower enveloped by golden hop. From here a wall holds back the flood waters which can fill the bog garden and ponds below. The whole garden is stuffed with a huge range of plants and I was particularly struck by the range of bulbs: daffodils give way to *Camassia* and tulips of every colour and shape. This is a well-designed garden with lots of great plant combinations and structural ideas.

Edzell Castle
Edzell, Angus, DD9 7UE
(*map, pp. 116–117*)

Historic Scotland
April–September: daily
9.30am–6.30pm, October–March,
Saturday–Wednesday 9am–4pm;
££*
6 miles north of Brechin,
A90 to B966
T: 01356 648631
www.historic-scotland.gov.uk

Edzell Castle

What you make of Edzell Castle's small enclosed garden rather depends on your expectations. Garden historians consider it of major importance but while I was exploring it, I overheard several people asking one another 'was that really all there was?'. The garden dates to 1604, one of the oldest 'pleasure gardens' in Scotland, and was restored in the 1930s. It is a simple design in a small, high-walled courtyard with a tower/pavilion banqueting hall in the corner. There are symbolic allusions in the layout and carvings. The garden's creator David Lindsay had themes of family heraldry, astrology and numerology encoded into the designs carved into the walls. Katie Campbell compares these to the stone carvings of Little Sparta, almost 400 years later. The small box parterre is planted with roses (not a great choice) and late summer bedding, and a series of niches in the walls are planted with lobelia. Patrick Taylor describes it as 'sketchily planted', while garden historian Christopher Dingwall calls it 'austere and rather anachronistic'. Though there are no records of

what the garden contained, I think the present planting could be improved with a little imagination. The parterre can be viewed from high above, from both the fine castle ruins and the banqueting hall.

Ethie Castle

Ethie is a restored red sandstone castle, part of which dates back to the fourteenth century, long owned by the earls of Northesk. The gardens were almost buried under sycamore and conifers when the de Morgans bought it, and they have spent the last several years removing trees, restoring greenhouses and expanding and planting the gardens, which are now becoming impressive. The main formal garden, surrounded by mature yews, north of the house, was designed by Michael Innes and planted in 2006. It consists of a box-lined parterre, with gravel paths, pool and fountain and shrub/perennial borders with a long season of flower, and by late summer 2008 it was looking remarkably mature. The views of the garden from the upper floors of the castle are stunning, particularly in late summer. Don't miss the extraordinary folly made of granite blocks, lined with pebbles, built in 1907, which lies on the seaward side of the garden. Adrian de Morgan showed me the large walled garden, entered via some imposing iron gates, made in Vietnam about five years ago by craftsmen taught there by the French. A central axis is planted with yew hedging, and in the middle of the garden are vegetables in extensive beds next to the beautifully renovated eighteenth-century greenhouse filled with vines which produce good crops of grapes. There are plans to plant a large orchard of fruit trees, including a

Ethie Castle
Inverkeilor, by Arbroath,
Angus, DD11 5SP
(*map, pp. 116–117*)

Adrian and Kirstin de Morgan
SGS 1 Sunday per year, open to
guests and by appointment; ££
Take A92 north from Arbroath,
turn right after Shell petrol station,
at T-junction turn left. Continue
for approx. 3 miles and you will
come to a glass BT telephone
box on the left-hand side. Gates
are straight ahead, signed
'Ethie Barns/Private'
T: 01241 830434
F: 01241 830432
E: kmydemorgan@aol.com
www.ethiecastle.com

collection of cherries. In front of the house, across a field, is a loch, the surrounds of which are being planted with azaleas and vigorous perennials. Ethie operates as an up-market bed and breakfast, one of the Wolsey Lodges, recommended by Alistair Sawday, and is also available as a venue for corporate hire. The impressive website has lots of pictures of the garden. This is obviously a labour of love and the garden is being improved all the time. This is certainly one to watch for the future.

B&B ♿

Explorers, The Scottish Plant Hunters Garden
Pitlochry Festival Theatre, Pitlochry, Perthshire, PH16 5DR
(*map, pp. 116–117*)

Pitlochry Festival Theatre, Julia Cordon
April–end October: 10am–5pm; ££
Turn off the A9 to Pitlochry and follow signs to the Festival Theatre. The garden is next to the car park
T: 01796 484600
www.pitlochry.org.uk/garden.php
www.explorersgarden.com
Café, bar and restaurant in the theatre next door

Explorers, The Scottish Plant Hunters Garden

No other country can boast Scotland's rich history of plant hunters: Fortune, Douglas, Menzies, Forrest, Sherriff and many more. Tough Scotsmen (and they were mostly men) were sent by botanical institutions or rich patrons, or they financed their own expeditions, to all parts of the globe to bring back plant material which might be of use in gardens or of economic use in some part of the empire. Setting up a garden to celebrate the Scottish plant hunters was an excellent idea, with both plants and history/biography creating a living museum. Unfortunately, this project was naively managed at the outset, so that the garden opened with a fanfare of publicity with only the paths and buildings in place. The garden was under-staffed, largely unplanted and full of weeds and word soon got around. Thankfully things have now improved considerably. Gardener Julia Cordon, who arrived just at the point when rescue was needed, has worked tirelessly to plant and maintain the garden, despite being short-staffed. The setting is fine, on a steep wooded slope above the Pitlochry Festival Theatre with views to Ben Vrackie. The hard landscaping is first class, with interesting architecture, sculpture and dry stone walling. As with all young gardens, many of the plants are still small, but the *Primula, Meconopsis* and other perennials are now starting to put on a good display in May and June. A crevice garden designed by Peter Korn was planted in 2008 and features *Phlox* and *Lewisia*. There are guided walks and various activities through the spring and summer and the garden has also been used for multimedia performances. The site is challenging, with little soil and too much competition from the mature oak and beech trees around the site: there simply are not enough suitable open spaces to plant a garden of this type and many plants are suffering in too much shade. In order to do justice to the amazing stories of the Scottish plant hunters, interpretation and plant labelling needs to be improved. At the very least, a film show or video in one of the under-utilised buildings would put it all in some perspective. This is an interesting project and its establishment here was a courageous move. The website is excellent, with lots of information and history. There was a good selection of unusual perennials and alpines on sale at the entrance when I visited in late summer. The theatre building at the garden's entrance offers gifts, food and drink and beyond this is the famous salmon ladder. Maddeningly, the garden closes at 5pm, missing a golden opportunity for theatre attendees to walk round the garden before dinner or a performance. The Festival Theatre has had recent funding cuts, which may impact on the garden in future.

Falkland Palace Garden
Falkland, Cupar, Fife, KY15 7BU
(*map, pp. 116–117*)

Crown Estates, NTS
1 March–31 October:
Monday–Saturday 10am–5pm;
£££* (palace and gardens)
Well-signposted in Falkland and
off A90 A91, A913. Buses from
Perth, Glenrothes, Cupar
T: 01337 857397;
shop: 01337 857918
F: 01337 857980
www.nts.org.uk

Falkland Palace Garden

One of central Scotland's most attractive villages, Falkland is well worth a visit, huddled under the impressive Lomond hills, full of attractive houses and pretty gardens, some of which open together under the SGS. You can also walk around the grounds of Falkland House. Pillars of Hercules Organic Farm, just north of the village, is also well worth calling into. Falkland Palace used by Mary Queen of Scots and James V, was a royal hunting lodge. It was set on fire, apparently by accident, by Cromwell's troops, and was later abandoned. Walter Scott admired it as a ruin and wanted it left alone, but the third marquis of Bute (1847–1900), who was later responsible for the extravagant Mount Stuart on Bute, determined to restore it, at great expense, as a building 'once more fit for kings'. He had not finished it when he died, but a large proportion was completed and there is plenty to see inside, with fine tapestries and paintings. The National Trust for Scotland faces the dilemma of what exactly it is conserving, in both house and garden. There are records of gardening here as early as 1456, so this is one of Scotland's oldest horticultural sites. Today, the gardens are a hodgepodge of styles and influences. The best bits are the walls around Britain's oldest functioning real tennis court (now home to a number of pigeons), planted with *Ceanothus*, a huge *Wisteria*, roses, clematis and some *Vitis* coiled around two giant urns, in a classical combination. The rectangular raised lily ponds have some upright conifers leaning in different directions around them; the effect is comical, I imagine not intentionally. Leading back towards the palace is a wide 180m-long colourful herbaceous border along the wall on the east side. On the west side, down the hill, is a 10-acre orchard with a collection of Scottish apples; I struggled to find labels on the ones I examined. The trees and shrub-

beries were planted by the Marquis of Bute as part of his restoration but much of the garden was ripped up and used for potato growing during the two world wars. Society garden designer Percy Cane was commissioned to redesign the garden in 1947. And herein lies the nub of the conservation dilemma: Cane is said to have used a 1693 painting of the palace for inspiration. There are terraces which lead nowhere, ugly conifers along one side, and various beds of shrub roses, shrubs and perennials, none of them exceptional. We are urged to conserve Cane's work by garden historians such as Katie Campbell, but I'm not convinced that what remains here is good enough. Cane's design has already been substantially tinkered with and I can't see much justification for keeping it. The popular *Delphinium* border was removed in 2002–03 as it was not part of Cane's plan, to considerable outcry, and I'd put it back in. This is a Victorian restoration of a Renaissance royal palace and the garden belongs to neither period. I feared I was the only one who disliked it, but it is comforting that Patrick Taylor calls Falkland 'one of the oddest ensembles in Britain' and Cane's garden 'a risky gamble'. This is a garden which cries out for enlightened dictatorship to make some really bold decisions. Fife has some of Scotland's most glorious gardens, and I'm afraid that as it stands, Falkland Palace's garden is not in the major league.

Falkland Small Gardens and Village
Falkland, Fife
(*map, pp. 116–117*)

SGS every 2nd year; ££
Leave M90 at junction 7 or 8, follow A91 and then turn right onto A912, or turn off A92 north of Glenrothes

Falkland Small Gardens and Village

Falkland is one of Fife's most delightful villages and has one of the best village garden openings, usually every second year, when up to 15 gardens open together. One of the gardens usually open is Betty and

Tom Hamilton's walled cottage garden at Weaving House which is only 12 × 14m in size and packed with goodies, including at least 70 varieties of snowdrop, lots of *Erythronium, Trillium, Pulmonaria* and other plants, grown in dappled shade. It is also worth visiting Falkland Palace, Falkland House parkland, Pillars of Hercules and Loch Leven's Larder (on the way to Milnathort). There is also a great pizza restaurant, Luigino's, with a proper Italian wood-burning pizza oven.

Fingask Castle

Fingask Castle
Fingask Castle, Rait,
Perth, Perthshire, PH2 7SA
(*map, pp. 116–117*)

Andrew Murray Threipland
Open under SGS for snowdrops,
alternate years in May and by
appointment; ££
A90 Errol/Rait flyover, signed
to Rait, turn right at crossroads:
signs to Fingask and car park
T: 01821 670777
E: events@fingaskcastle.com
www.fingaskcastle.com

I can't do much better than quote Tim Longville, who described Fingask in *Country Life* as an 'engaging oddity'. He goes on to comment: 'Throughout the centuries, little attention has been paid here to the fashion of the day. Fingask has always done its own thing, sometimes behind the times, sometimes in advance of them, mostly ignoring them completely.' Which is largely a good thing in my book. The Threiplands have bought and lost (for supporting the Jacobites) and bought back and sold this castle several times in their history but it is firmly back with Andrew Murray Threipland, the current laird. The castle itself is in Baronial style, mostly rebuilt in the 1920s, though it looks older, with *Clematis armandii* on the walls and *Osteospermum* at the base. The castle and garden lie at the edge of a narrow valley surrounded by mature trees, with a wide ravine at the bottom with a stream running through it, now dammed into three ponds. While I'd turn this valley into a sumptuous woodland garden, were it mine to play with, Andrew intends to leave it more as a wild wooded valley and he has constructed several quirky buildings to go into it. What Fingask is really known for is its statuary and topiary. The rather kitsch granite statues commemorate scenes from the works of Burns and are thought to date from the 1840s. The topiary consists

of a series of lopsided swirls of yew, layered goblets, like piles of badly stacked plates, and knobs of holly, which Tim Longville aptly describes as 'drunken . . . surrealism', seemingly plonked at random on the front lawn. The backdrop of hybrid rhododendrons in May set them off very well. The overall effect of Fingask is surprisingly contemporary: the topiary would probably win medals at the Chelsea show. The huge white wedding marquee on the lawn is what Prince Charles would call a 'carbuncle' but as Andrew says, there are great views of the garden from it. Fingask is not a plantsman's garden and is better considered an eccentric theatre set. But it is well worth a visit, if nothing else, to prove that Scottish gardens have a sense of humour.

Gagie House

Gagie was once part of the large Guthrie family estates which covered a large part of Angus. The gardens at Gagie consist of a semi-wild pond garden which leads to a woodland walk and a walled garden (which is not open to the public). The 1-mile circular springtime woodland walk lies in a secluded den along both sides of the Sweet burn and its artesian ponds. There are extensive drifts of naturalised snowdrops which have been increased by further plantings in recent years, followed by daffodils, bluebells, primroses and candelabra primulas amongst the rhododendrons and azaleas. The fields to the south of the garden are lined with impressive rows of poplars. Snowdrops for sale.

Gagie House
Gagie House, Duntrune, near Dundee, DD4 0PR
(*map, pp. 116–117*)

France and Clare Smoor
1 February–31 May: 10am–5pm; ££
From A90, c. 2 miles north of Dundee, east signposted 'Murroes'; 2 miles, wood on left, sharp right bend ahead; turn in to left signed 'Gagie', through stone gateposts at end (marked private road), car park signposted on right
T: 01382 380207
E: smoor@gagie.com
www.gagie.com
DIY picnic bothy

Gallery
Logie Pert, Montrose, DD10 9LA
(*map, pp. 116–117*)

John Simpson
SGS first Sunday in summer,
and sometimes groups by
appointment; ££
From A90 take road to Hillside,
then follow signs to Gallery and
Marykirk. White 3-storey house;
you can't miss it
T: 01674 840 550

Gallery

The gardens at Gallery were created out of a historic formal garden which was much neglected. When they bought the house, the Simpsons had no particular gardening skills but they admired the garden rooms at Crathes and wanted to create something with a similar feel at Gallery. They enlisted garden designer Veronica Adams, an art college friend of the late Mrs Simpson, who drew up elaborate plans for the garden which have gradually been brought to fruition. Gardener Ron Steven turned out to be the perfect man to realise the dream: not only planting and maintaining the garden, but also doing the hard landscaping, including dry stone walls. The results are fine. Almost like a maze, with occasional dead ends, the garden is planned with a new vista and a pleasant surprise round every corner. This is a garden of theatre: each path leads to a focal point: an urn, seat, fountain or plant, and there are quirky features to make you smile. The hosta borders are interspaced with stone mushrooms. One garden room features pink and purple shades, in another yellow dominated with conifers and laburnum. The pièce de résistance, last to be completed, is the white garden, built around a fountain and pond, and which should be visited last as a grand finale, as it was when John Simpson took me round. Here accompanied by the sound of water, are delphiniums, peonies, roses, *Dicentra, Aruncus* and other favourites. This garden was skilfully planned and is well planted and maintained.

Gargunnock House Grounds

Gargunnock House is an extended sixteenth-century tower house with a Georgian south front. It is now divided up into several holiday rental units, bookable through the Landmark Trust. There is also a

Gargunnock House Grounds
Gargunnock, Stirling, FK8 3AZ
(*map, pp. 116–117*)

Gargunnock Charitable Trust:
Willie Campbell
SGS open days + Sundays and
Wednesdays, February–March
(snowdrops), Wednesday 2–5pm;
£–££
Off A811 near Kippen, signed
on open days
T: 01786 860392
E: williamcampbell@
btinternet.com

castellated octagonal doocot. Behind it lies a small formal garden with
one of Scotland's largest clumps of *Kalmia latifolia*, a fine *Stewartia*
and some new plantings of rhododendrons and perennials. The
woodland behind contains a collection of mature rhododendrons.
Willie Campbell, who gardens the estate, has been considerably
extending the plantings of rhododendrons in the partially thinned,
but still rather overshaded woodland. The garden is also noted for its
spring bulbs and autumn colour, particularly good along the drive
side, with *Acer palmatum, Liquidamber, Fothergilla* and *Euonymus
alatus*. A largely empty walled garden may be replanted in the future.
Willie Campbell is happy to give guided tours for groups, booked in
advance.

Glamis Castle Gardens

Glamis is one of Scotland's great houses, home to the earls of
Strathmore. It was one of the fiefdoms of Shakespeare's Macbeth;
more recently it was a childhood home of Elizabeth, the late Queen
Mother. The castle is approached by one of the most impressive long
straight driveways you'll ever see, lined with oaks and limes underplanted with daffodils. The huge parkland, filled with mature trees, is
used for a variety of events in summer. The Italian garden is a 2-acre
hedged enclosure with interesting topiary and structures, planted with
all the usual herbaceous favourites. The dominant features are two
pleached beech allées which Antoinette Galbraith likens to 'tents on
stilts'. I thought they looked more like flying beds, upturned boats or
coffins. Either way you'll remember them once you've seen them, but
they are not truly a thing of beauty. From the Italian garden you can
exit, past a rather tacky memorial to Princess Margaret, to the

Glamis Castle Gardens
Glamis, Angus, DD8 1RJ
(*map, pp. 116–117*)

Earl and Countess of Strathmore
Daily: mid March–end December
except Christmas Day; ££,
castle extra
Signposted from A90 Dundee–
Aberdeen road, near Forfar and
from the A94 Forfar Coupar
Angus road
T: 01307 840393
F: 01307 840733
E: enquiries@glamis-castle.co.uk
www.glamis-castle.co.uk
Café/restaurant (famous for the
Forfar Bridie) and food hall

Pinetum, a well-labelled collection of giant, mainly North American conifers, underplanted with bulbs. This path leads over a bridge to a really fine walled garden, currently more or less empty, save for a couple of greenhouses and some young trained fruit. Apparently it will be restored if someone will sponsor it, which seems rather a fanciful wish. The plans are on display just inside the gates. Another path leads back to the castle, past a large number of nannying blue no-entry signs. The sunken or 'Dutch' gardens with a series of parterres now planted with herbaceous, are not open to the public. The castle itself is a very popular attraction with guided tours and you can easily spend several hours at Glamis as the whole designed landscape extends to 1,000 acres. Tree lovers should seek out the enormous (4m in girth) lopsided sweet chestnut on the lawns. The gardens at Glamis have a great deal more potential than are currently realised.

Glendoick Gardens

It's quite hard writing the entry for your own garden . . . Glendoick House, built in 1747–48 is a stylish Georgian mansion purchased by Dundee jute baron Alfred Cox in 1899. By 1930 the jute industry was in terminal decline, to the relief of my grandfather Euan Cox, who was much more interested in plants than making cloth and ropes. Euan managed to avoid the jute business for a time by accompanying plant hunter Reginald Farrer on his last expedition to Burma in 1919 and on his return he realised that Glendoick, with its valley and burn, could be turned into a Himalayan woodland garden. He began planting it in the 1920s and it has been much extended and improved by my father Peter and myself ever since. Next to Glendoick House is one of the world's largest collections of dwarf rhododendrons, including several NCCPG national collections. The woodland garden

or 'den' lies on south-facing slopes on either side of the Glendoick burn and contains a huge collection of rhododendron species and hybrids, as well as many other plants such as *Meconopsis, Sorbus, Clethra, Clematis, Magnolia* and *Hydrangea*. The walled garden is now largely given over to plant production, and visitors can enjoy the new hybrid trial beds where future named varieties are selected and tested. Glendoick also includes an important collection of trees, including the largest *Tetradium danielii* (*Euodia hupehensis*) in Europe, with its elephant's foot-like trunk. The E.H.M. Cox arboretum boasts a particularly fine selection of *Sorbus*. Recent plantings include a collection of newer magnolias and a selection of the best hydrangeas for Scotland. Peter Cox began hybridising dwarf rhododendrons in the 1950s and there are now over 25 named 'birds' such as 'Curlew', 'Razorbill' and 'Ptarmigan' as well as evergreen azaleas bred for the Scottish climate named after mammals such as 'Panda' and 'Wombat', some of which were bred by myself, Kenneth Cox. The new red-leaved rhododendrons such as Everred [85/1C] are the latest release from the breeding programme. Peter Cox has made over 20 expeditions in search of plants, mainly to the China-Himalaya region but also to South America, while I have concentrated on the Tibet/northeast India border region. Many Cox-collected plants can be found throughout the gardens at Glendoick. The three generations of Coxes have written many books on rhododendrons and Glendoick is considered a mecca for rhododendron collectors worldwide. The mail order nursery grows mostly open-ground rhododendrons and azaleas and other acid-loving plants, which are sent all over the world during the winter months. The nursery is open by appointment and all bare-rooted plants need to be pre-booked; they cannot be lifted while customers wait. Containerised stock is available year round at the garden centre. The website with the online catalogue is very informative and includes links to the Scottish Garden Plant Award and to this book.

Glendoick Gardens
Glencarse, Perth, PH2 7NS
(*map, pp. 116–117*)

Peter, Patricia, Kenneth and Jane Cox
Mid April–mid June: Monday–Friday, 10am-4pm also Saturday and Sunday afternoons in May or by appointment; ££*
On the A90 between Perth (8 miles) and Dundee (14 miles), clearly signposted with brown signs
T: 01738 806205 (nursery)
F: 01738 860 630 (nursery)
E: orders@glendoick.com, (nursery)
www.glendoick.com
Popular café and foodhall at garden centre

Glendoick Garden Centre and Restaurant
Glencarse, Perth, PH2 7NS
map, pp. 116–117)

Peter, Patricia, Kenneth
and Jane Cox
Daily: March–October,
9am–5.30pm; Winter, 9am
(10am Sundays)–5pm
A90 Perth–Dundee road,
Glencarse, Perth PH2 7NS
T: 01738 860260 (garden centre),
01738 860265 (restaurant)
F: 01738 860735
E: gardencentre@glendoick.com
www.glendoick.com

Glendoick Garden Centre and Restaurant

Peter Cox's wife Patricia was instrumental in opening Glendoick Garden Centre in 1973. This popular place sells Scotland's largest range of rhododendrons and hydrangeas, as well as a huge range of trees, shrubs, perennials and other plants, plus all the other garden-related things you would expect to find. There is a display garden here too, designed by Patricia Cox. Jane Cox oversees the very popular café and food hall, the 'Food Library'. The turn off the A90 is now much improved and safer, with a new flyover. The garden centre and nursery are run separately and the nursery is only available to visit by appointment outside the main garden opening season.

Gleneagles
By Auchterarder, Perth PH3 1PJ
(*map, pp. 116–117*)

Martin and Petronella Haldane
Occasionally open under SGS,
and by appointment only; ££
On A 823 Crieff–Dunfermline
road, just south of A9
T: 01764 682 388
E: petronella@gleneagles.org

Gleneagles

Not to be confused with the famous hotel on the other side of the A9, eighteenth-century Gleneagles House, and the ruined laird's tower next door have been around a lot longer than its namesake and have been home to the Haldane family since the twelfth century. The house is approached down a magnificent lime avenue, planted to commemorate the 1797 Battle of Camperdown, a naval victory over the Dutch. The main garden east of the house consists of informal beds of trees, shrubs and roses which lead to a two-part loch surrounded by flag iris, red hot pokers and *Persicaria*. By the house is a wildflower maze and beyond this, a meadow of lupins which were in full flower when I visited in June. Petronella Haldane likes quirky sculpture: the Helen Denerley sheep has an old radiator as a body, and a plump wooden figure can be found in the trees near the lupins.

Glenlyon House

The attractive village of Glenlyon, in a dramatic setting in the wilds of north Perthshire, is built in Arts and Crafts style with thatched roofs. Glenlyon House's walled garden, has a backdrop of attractive white buildings. Also striking is the vista along the border of pears, underplanted with *Nepeta*, to the hills behind. There are colourful herbaceous borders and annuals. The deep-cultivated, raised vegetable beds were inspired by the late Geoff Hamilton and the produce is used at the Fortingall Hotel in the village, nearby. The gardener at Glenlyon House also looks after the hotel garden. The famous Fortingall Yew, in the village churchyard, is well over 3,000 years old, some have estimated as much as 5,000 years. It is the oldest living organism in Britain and at one time it was 56 feet across, though it is in decline these days, not helped by souvenir hunters who have chopped bits off it.

  [H] [WC]

Glenlyon House
Fortingall, Perthshire, PH15 2LN
(*map, pp. 116–117*)

Mr and Mrs Iain Wotherspoon
SGS some years 1 day and by
appointment; ££ (donation to
Fortingall church)
Take A827 Aberfeldy, B846
Coshievillle then turn off for
Fortingall and Glen Lyon
T: 01887 830233
E: thewotherspoons@ednet.co.uk

Grampian Growers

This is a co-operative of 18 Scottish bulb growers who supply wholesale daffodil bulbs and cut flowers. The fields of daffodils in the farmland around Forfar, Stonehaven and Montrose, flowering in March and April, are an amazing sight. In 2005–06 the growers sold 5–7 million bunches of daffodil flowers and 4,000–5,000 tonnes of daffodil bulbs.

Grampian Growers
Head office: Logie,
Montrose, DD10 9LD

Various
Just enjoy them as you drive past.
T: 01674 830555
E: info@grampiangrowers.co.uk
www.grampiangrowers.co.uk

Hermitage (The)
Dunkeld, Perthshire, PH8 0HX
(*map, pp. 116–117*)

NTS
Daily: daylight hours; £ parking,
entry free
1 mile north of Dunkeld off A9
T: 0844 4932192
E: hermitage@nts.org.uk
www.nts.org.uk

Hermitage (The)

The Hermitage is not a garden as such; in the eighteenth century, when it was first created, it was more of one, with a walled garden with ponds, fruit trees and underplanted with bedding. What we have today forms part of Scotland's most historically important eighteenth-century picturesque landscape, created by the fourth duke of Atholl in 1783 as part of the extraordinarily foresighted burst of mixed tree planting by the dukes of Atholl over several generations. (see pp. 128, 191). The Hermitage is an attractive woodland walk alongside the River Braan past a series of spectacular waterfalls, the largest of which is the Black Linn, overlooked by Ossian's Hall, which has a viewing platform and was once filled with mirrors. William and Dorothy Wordsworth visited in 1803 and described flowers then planted amongst the rocks. Further up the river is Ossian's cave. Ossian was the hero of a supposedly ancient Scottish legend, which became a bestseller in the 1820s but turned out later to have been largely made up by author James MacPherson. The conifers here are spectacular, including a record-breaking group of Douglas fir. You may see salmon leaping in autumn, you have a good chance of spotting a red squirrel and 270 species of *Fungi* have been recorded here. After winter rains, the waterfalls are raging torrents and in freezing weather the spray can form stunning ice crystals on logs and rocks. The bluebells are spectacular in May. There are several paths and you can walk for half an hour or longer; there are maps and interpretive boards in the car park.

Hidden Gardens of St Andrews Open Day

**Hidden Gardens
of St Andrews Open Day**
St Andrews, Fife
(*map, pp. 116–117*)

Various
First Sunday in June–July:
11am–5pm, up to 11 gardens
opening together; ££
The Preservation Trust museum
has details of the gardens
T: 01334 477152
E: trust@standrewspreservation
trust.org.uk

This is an annual garden visit day organised by the St Andrews Preservation Trust in June, normally from 11am–5pm, and it seems to be a popular event: all the gardens had lots of visitors when I went round and there were plants for sale as well as home-baking. The mostly small and/or narrow town gardens are dotted around town and it's as much fun looking at those which are not open, over the fence, as the ones which are. If you don't know St Andrews well, you'll be amazed at the narrow lanes, closes and back gardens reached by zigzagging paths. It is clearly quite a challenge to create gardens in such conditions. Those opening seem to vary from year to year. The largest and best of those that I have seen is June Baxter's garden at 46 South St, which was designed initially by Michael Innes. I can't recall ever seeing a narrower garden than this one, it goes on and on and on, filling two rigs, one behind the other. By the house is a terrace with a planted wall full of *Astilbe*, surrounded by white and pale pinks from *Carpenteria, Philadelphus* and *Kolwitzia*. Beyond this is an orchard under which grass is left to grow long, encouraging ox-eye daisies. The next section is more formal, a geometrical scheme of shrub roses and paths, framed by one of Scotland's outstanding garden buildings, the castellated doocot. This delightful building has been converted into a summerhouse, complete with log fire, and I'd hazard a guess that almost anyone who sees it probably wishes they could move it stone by stone to their own garden. The high wall on either side of the doocot looks like the bottom of the garden, but through a door, is a further very well-planted cottage garden-themed section of roses, *Cistus, Astrantia* and shrubs. Another St Andrews garden which sometimes opens under SGS is Ladies Lake, a small saucer-shaped space next to St Andrews Castle with two terraces crammed with bedding plants.

46 South Street, St Andrews

Highland Heathers
Muirend, South Crieff Road,
Comrie, Perthshire, PH6 2JA
(map, pp. 116–117)

John and Elaine Davidson
From Comrie take the B827,
signed to Braco and turn left onto
South Crieff Road, brown signs
T: 01764 670440
F: 01764 670 655
E: enquiries@highland
heathers.co.uk
www.highlandheathers.co.uk

Highland Heathers

This small nursery and plant centre lies on the Crieff–Comrie road on the south side of the River Earn. They propagate up to 140 varieties of heather but the core range listed on their website is around 30 varieties. There is a small heather garden next to the nursery tunnel houses. They also sell composts, pots, trees and shrubs and offer garden design. An enormous *Hydrangea petiolaris* covers the wall of one of the farm buildings. The website now seems to be given over to their accommodation business.

Hill of Tarvit
Mansionhouse and Garden
Cupar, Fife, KY15 5PB
(map, pp. 116–117)

NTS
April–end May and September:
Thursday–Monday 1–5pm;
1 Jun–31 August: daily 1–5pm ;
£££* (house and garden)
Off A916, 2 miles south of
Cupar, brown signs. Trains
and buses to Cupar (2 miles)
T: 0844 4932185
E: hilloftarvit@nts.org.uk
www.nts.org.uk
Tearoom and shop
(open from 12pm)

Hill of Tarvit Mansionhouse and Garden

Hill of Tarvit mansion house was created in 1906 by a substantial remodelling of the seventeenth-century Wemyss Hall, by local Scottish architect Sir Robert Lorimer for one of the Dundee jute barons, Frederick Sharp. The house was designed to display Sharp's fine collection of French and Chippendale-style furniture, porcelain, tapestries and paintings, and visitors can also see the extensive 'below stairs' quarters where the servants worked. Don't miss Lorimer's decorative features from the ceilings down to the smallest doorknobs as well as the bowls of stone fruit out on the terraces. The impressive formal garden at the front of the house was also designed by Lorimer and consists of clipped yews on either side of a fine stone staircase leading down to a lower terrace with low hedges, so that views of the rolling Fife hills can be enjoyed from the house. At the south-east end of the house is a small formal sunken rose garden with extensive and effective lavender and hebe underplanting. The west end has a small

enclosed semi-formal garden with an unusual planting scheme of hellebores, *Oxalis* with a border of *Anaphalis* round the outside. The more extensive main garden lies behind the house; this is partially walled, with gently sloping lawns, and has some very fine shrubs and trees, including some of the best *Eucryphia* in eastern Scotland. There are specimens of *E. glutinosa* which are good, but it is the two forms of *E. x nymanensis* which are the finest of all, towers of creamy white in late August and early September. Indeed, this is an excellent time to visit, as this garden has lots of late summer colour in the main perennial border which runs along the back: *Rudbeckia, Helenium, Hydrangea* and a pale-grey/pale-pink-coloured *Buddleja x weyeriana* (which is more attractive than it sounds) as well as a catalpa (which was in flower when I visited, rare in Scotland). A particularly fine giant *Hoheria* is on the east side, in an area known as the shrubbery which also contains a small summerhouse, some impressive old rhododendrons, Japanese maples and a small heather garden. The gardens are well planted and have been looked after for over 20 years by head gardener Peter Christopher, who has plans for further restoration. This garden and its policies are run as a wildlife resource, attracting and sustaining an impressive range of birds, butterflies and red squirrels. Dogs are not allowed in the main gardens but via the fine iron gates are various woodland paths which seem to be popular with local dog-walkers, as is the Hill of Tarvit itself, a 1-mile walk through conifers and scrub. The monument at the top commemorates Queen Victoria's diamond jubilee and the views over Fife and beyond are impressive. At time of going to press, the NTS was considering closing the house to visitors, which would, in my opinion, make the garden unsustainable and probably see its gradual decline and loss.

Hollytree Lodge
Pool of Muckhart,
Clackmannanshire, FK14 7JW
(*map, pp. 116–117*)

David and Maureen Miller
SGS 1 Sunday in summer
some years; ££
A91 Pool of Muckhart, opposite
entrance to pub go down lane,
dogleg to right, white house at
end
T: 01259 781315

Hollytree Lodge

The garden was designed and planted by Ronnie Cann and Robert Bradford, who gardened it for 18 years till 2005 as 'Holestone Lodge' before moving on to a new garden project at Waterside Lodge near Moffat. Hollytree Lodge is about two thirds of an acre but the clever design makes it feel much larger. Beech hedges are used to create some garden rooms but other boundaries are made with shrubs and trees. The attractive white house, well-clothed in climbers, has a terrace along the front planted with wide shrub borders while the steps are lined with pots filled with phormiums and other statuesque plants. From here several borders run down towards the back of the garden, many of which are strikingly planted with grasses. The centre of the garden is planted with several impressive clumps of *Phyllostachys nigra* and other bamboos surrounding a circle of contemporary standing stones. Behind this is a yellow garden with golden conifers and yellow perennials such as *Verbascum* and *Inula*. A raised bed in the middle of this contains alpines and smaller grasses. The bottom of the garden is a more shaded area for rhododendrons and other spring colour, as well as ferns and a couple of small ponds. To the west of the house there is a parterre of herbs and a small knot garden with a lavender border running up the side of the house, and I enjoyed the contrasting barks of the *Eucalyptus* and *Acer griseum* along the boundary. Appropriately the eastern end of the house has an eastern theme, with a border of Japanese maples below the terrace and beside the house a dry Japanese river bed.

House of Dun and
Montrose Basin Nature Reserve

This is a fine Georgian house which overlooks the Montrose Basin
Nature Reserve, internationally important for its migratory wading
birds and wildfowl. The house, designed by William Adam, was
completed in 1730 for David Erskine, the thirteenth laird of Dun.
The last handloom weavers in Scotland have their workshop in the
courtyard. A series of formal terraces, punctuated by urns on plinths
at the front of the house, is planted with a semi-circular box parterre
and borders planted with lavender. There are rare Scottish apples and
pears trained on the walls. The row of laurels along the ha-ha in front
of the house has recently been hard-pruned. There are good displays
of spring bulbs and a long border of Nerines in autumn. A small,
rather charming walled garden at the east side, at its best in summer,
is planted with roses and perennials. Behind the house is an
impressive line of redwoods (*Sequoiadendron giganteum*) planted in
the mid nineteenth century. Lady Augusta's Walk, through the
woodland to the west, is being planted/restored in the Den of Dun,
and there is a fine bridge over the mill burn. The NTS has fishing
rights for part of the River South Esk. Contact the property for
details.

**House of Dun and Montrose
Basin Nature Reserve**
Brechin Road, Montrose,
DD10 9LQ
(*map, pp. 116–117*)

NTS
April–end June and September:
Wednesday–Sunday 12.30–
5.30pm; 1 July–31 August: daily;
11.30am–5.30pm
£ (grounds); £££* (house)
On A395, halfway between
Montrose and Brechin
T: 01674 810 264
F: 01674 810 722
www.nts.org.uk
Café/restaurant open with
the house

**House of Falkland
Landscape Gardens**
The Stables, Falkland Estate,
Falkland, KY15 7AF
(*map, pp. 116–117*)

All year, daylight hours; free
Signed in Falkland village. Buses
from Perth, Glenrothes, Cupar
T: 01337 858838
www.centreforstewardship.org.uk

House of Falkland Landscape Gardens

Not really a garden, this is a Victorian picturesque landscape
consisting of a network of pathways, rock features, bridges, waterfalls,
woodlands and tunnel. The overgrown thickets of sycamore seedlings
and scrub have been removed in recent years and it is now an
excellent place for walking. House of Falkland, designed by William
Burn in 1839–44, is in the English-Jacobean style. West of the house, a
tunnel leads into the Maspie Den and the path leads underneath the
Yad waterfall. Another path on the north side of the burn runs up to
the Tyndall Bruce Monument on Black Hill which is about a 1½-mile
walk. Ninian Crichton Stuart has set up the Falkland Centre for
Stewardship which is a holistic approach to responsible, long-term
land and property management. They run 'Big Tent', Scotland's
Festival of Stewardship, and training courses.

**James McIntyre and Sons
Moyness Nursery**
Coupar Angus Road, Blairgowrie,
Perthshire, PH10 6UT
(*map, pp. 116–117*)

The McIntyre family
A94 about half a mile out
of the centre of Blairgowrie
T: 01250 873135
F: 01250 875014
E: info@james-mcintyre.co.uk
james-mcintyre.co.uk

James McIntyre and Sons Moyness Nursery

The firm was founded in 1946 as a fruit producer, and James
McIntyre diversified in the 1960s into vegetable and raspberry cane
production. The garden centre was opened in 1973 and a landscaping
and floristry business are now also run from the site, with several
family members involved in the business. The nursery/32-acre farm
supplies fruit bushes to garden centres and to private customers' mail
order in winter months. As well as dozens of strawberries, raspberries,
currants, blueberries and other well-known fruit you'll find
jostaberries, tayberries and other less common items.

Jerdan Garden Gallery

This gallery in the East Neuk of Fife specialises in contemporary Scottish paintings, sculpture, ceramics, glass, woodwork, jewellery and nineteenth/twentieth-century art. The garden at the rear of the gallery is used to display sculpture.

Kellie Castle and Garden

What the Lorimer family achieved at Kellie, converting a roofless ruin into a stunning house and garden, is a remarkable achievement and this is without doubt one of the jewels of the National Trust for Scotland. Kellie Castle, completed around 1606, was originally home to the earls of Kellie. The fifth earl is said to have hidden in the garden for an entire summer in a burnt-out tree stump after the Battle of Culloden. The castle was abandoned in the nineteenth century but was rescued in 1877 by Professor James Lorimer, who rented it as a roofless ruin and gradually restored it with the help of his son, Robert, one of Scotland's finest architects. The castle has an intimacy and 'lived-in' feel, with a nursery full of children's toys, and rooms with furniture and linen collected by the Lorimer family. A Phoebe Anne Traquair mural, which Hew and Mary Lorimer had carefully covered up as they did not like it, has recently been uncovered in the drawing room. The most ornate room in the castle is the vine room on the top floor with intricate plasterwork and a round ceiling painting. The child prodigy Robert was only 16 when he helped his father design the layout for the walled garden. Robert Lorimer believed that a garden should be a place of repose and sanctuary and he particularly liked enclosed gardens. After the death of painter John

Jerdan Garden Gallery
Marketgate South,
Crail, Fife, KY10 3TL
(*map, pp. 116–117*)

David and Sue Jerdan
10.30am–5pm (closed Tuesdays)
Turn east off the St Andrews road
at the sharp right-hand bend
T: 01333 450797
E: david@thejerdangallery.com
www.thejerdangallery.com

Kellie Castle and Garden
Pittenweem, Fife, KY10 2RF
(*map, pp. 116–117*)

NTS
Castle: April–31 October,
daily 1–5pm; Garden: all year,
daily 9.30am–5.30pm; £££*
(house and garden)
Off the B9171 east of Colinsburgh,
signposted off the A917
Elie–Crail road
T: 0844 4932184
www.nts.org.uk
Tea room and gift shop
(open from 12pm)

Henry Lorimer, James' second son, Kellie's contents were sold off. Robert's son, Arts and Crafts sculptor Hew Lorimer and his wife Mary, took over the lease in 1937, and finally managed to buy the castle in 1948, selling it to the National Trust for Scotland in 1970. Kellie's garden was restored, with guidance from contemporary paintings by John Henry Lorimer, Gertrude Jekyll's accounts of Kellie in her book *Some English Gardens* and a 1906 *Country Life* article. The old stables house Hew Lorimer's sculpture studio and an exhibition on his life. The delightful walled garden adjoins the north wall of the castle. The outer, south garden wall is covered with a mass of entwined vines, peaches and nectarines, fig, kiwi, *Solanum, Clematis* and other climbers, with a bed of Japanese anemones below. Don't miss the clever cupboard-greenhouse for ripening peaches. There are views across the Forth to the Bass Rock and beyond, which can also be enjoyed from the castle windows. The walled garden, run on organic principles, is a perfect mix of productive, mainly around the walls, and ornamental. The walls are covered with trained apples and pears and the borders beneath are full of important historical collections of fruit and vegetables, providing seed for the Henry Doubleday seed library: 24 varieties of rhubarb, and a large range of strawberries, gooseberries-up-poles, leeks and other food crops. Surplus fruit and vegetables can often be found for sale in the Robert Lorimer-designed summerhouse. Opposite the garden entrance is the famous blue-green Hew Lorimer-designed seat forming the focal point of the path lined with yellow and purple borders. The paths and borders are lined with box, the shrub rose 'Rosamundi' and ramblers cover several arches over the paths. An armillary sphere forms the centre-piece of the blue and white borders which in late summer display the unusual but effective combination of *Galtonia* and *Nepeta*. The parallel lines of *Nepeta* look particularly good from the castle windows. There are two small hedged spaces, Robin's Garden and the Yew Enclosure. Kellie hosts potato and apple days in autumn, Halloween haunted tours and a Christmas Fair. Robert Lorimer called Kellie 'a little pleasaunce of the soul', while Katie Campbell considers Kellie 'one of the most romantic gardens in the whole of Scotland'. Though not as fêted as Crathes and Culzean, many rate Kellie as their favourite National Trust for Scotland house and garden combination and you can hardly fail to be captivated by it. I was absolutely dismayed to hear that the NTS was considering closing the house to visitors due to funding. It would be a tragedy. Combined with an afternoon in the East Neuk fishing villages nearby, this is as good a summer day out as eastern Scotland has to offer.

Kilbryde Castle

Kilbryde Castle
Dunblane, Perthshire,
FK15 9NF
(*map, pp. 116–117*)

Sir James and Lady Campbell
SGS (1 day May, 1 day June)
and by appointment; ££
Off A820 between Dunblane and
Doune (3 miles each), follow
sign to Kilbryde 300m from A9
E: kilbryde1@aol.com
www.kilbrydecastle.com

This is a magnificently sited garden on a hill surrounded on three sides by the River Ardoch, dominated by the castle, which was rebuilt in the 1870s. The house has been in the Campbell family since 1659. The gardens were created by the late Sir Colin and Lady Campbell in the 1970s and is now owned by their son James and his wife Carola. The woodland gardens, filled with rhododendrons, line a valley running down to the river. Along the river bank runs a charming path through the steep-sided gorge with its wild garlic and wild flowers. Several paths zigzag back up to the main garden, which is walled at one end, with a terrace from the castle enclosing another side. This contains extensive planting of herbaceous and shrub roses and other plants in numerous island beds, cleverly planted with vigorous ground cover such as *Hosta* and *Geranium* which help keep weeds at bay. I

noted a good peony border and a particularly fine bed of *Iris chryso-graphes* black. Two reconstructed archways salvaged from Dunblane Cathedral and a newly planted *Carpinus* walk, which is to be pleached, add a touch of formality. I liked this garden: showy but not fussy, with a lived-in feel, signs of children playing, tree houses and bicycles showing that this is a family home, which is worth visiting in spring for the large collection of rhododendrons and azaleas and in summer for roses and perennials. Catering can be arranged for group visits.

Kinross House
Kinross,
Perth and Kinross, KY13 8ET
(*map, pp. 116–117*)

Jamie and Lizzie Montgomery
Daily: April–September
10am–7pm; ££
Junction 6 M90, into Kinross,
turn right at the T-junction with
mini roundabout. Then take
the first left (signposted)
T: 01577 862900
E: jm@kinrosshouse.com
www.kinrosshouse.com
Very close to town of Kinross,
which has several options for
refreshments

Kinross House

It is quite a surprise to turn off Kinross High Street, through the gates and into such an imposing designed landscape, one of the best preserved of its type in Scotland. Through an avenue of trees the way leads to an expanse of lawn, used by the local cricket team, across which a huge house looms. Built in the 1690s by William Bruce, it was Daniel Defoe's favourite Scottish house and its scale, design and layout herald the Georgian era to come. Unusually, the landscape was planned first and the house placed in it rather than the other way round. Probably best appreciated from a plane, the axis of the design runs from the main entrance gates down the drive, through the front door of the house, out the garden side onto the terrace, down the slope via the 'fish gate' to the castle on Loch Leven where Mary, Queen of Scots was imprisoned. You would never guess that the house and gardens were abandoned from 1820–1902 and were rescued by Sir Basil Montgomery, whose descendents are the current owners. The entry to the garden is to the left of the house. The central axis from the front steps to Loch Leven castle is stunning. The steps from the upper to the lower terrace are flanked by a rather outré yellow low

hedge of golden box. The design of the garden is a series of allées, compartments and rooms, many on a grand scale, bordered with yew topiary and hedges. There are roses on the top tier in formal beds and on the lower tier a very fine long herbaceous border, at its best in July and August, backed by a perfectly clipped copper beech hedge. Round the perimeter are themed borders: to the north is an early herbaceous border peaking in June and a small enclosed area to the side of the house with a white garden. The rhododendron and azaleas are formally planted, one or two varieties to a bed, flanking the rose beds. There are large expanses of lawns dotted with specimen trees and statuary. To the south is another smaller enclosed garden with fine rose arches and a large white *Abutilon* next to the house. Outside the walls, fine mature trees provide wind shelter. The garden is at its peak in July and August with roses and herbaceous, but also good in spring and early summer with rhododendrons and azaleas. The structure provides a wonderful effect in winter hoar frosts. The best views of the garden are from the house, especially on the second floor, unfortunately not open to the public. This is a garden that was designed to impress by its formality, scale and amount of work required to maintain it. And impress it does. The website is very informative.

Kirkhill

This is a charming ¾-acre garden developed over the past 12 years, with rhododendrons and azaleas underplanted with *Primula, Meconopsis, Astrantia* and other herbaceous and bulbous plants. There is also a small herbaceous border and vegetable garden.

Kirkhill
Lintrathen, Kirriemuir,
Angus, DD8 5JH
(*map, pp. 116–117*)

Colonel and Mrs
Andrew Houstoun
1 April–31 July:
by arrangement; ££
Beside Lintrathen Church,
7 miles west of Kirriemuir and
signed off B951. From south, 6
miles north of Alyth on B954, 2
miles past Peel Farm Coffee Shop
T: 01575 560228
E: abhoustoun@btinternet.com
Home-baked teas for groups
of up to 12 people

Kirklands
Saline, by Dunfermline,
KY12 9TS
(*map, pp. 116–117*)

Peter and Gill Hart
April–September: Friday–Sunday
2–5pm, SGS 1–2 days per year
and by arrangement; ££
Directions: M90 J4. B914 to Saline
and Dollar. In Saline turn right into
North Road (by post office) and
immediately right again into
Bridge Street. 100 yards along
Bridge Street, turn right into the
drive between two high walls
next to the old graveyard gates
T: 01383 852 737
E: stay@kirklandshouse
andgarden.co.uk
www.kirklandshouseand
garden.co.uk
Tea on open days and can be
arranged for larger groups

Kirklands

The charming village of Saline in Fife has a long gardening tradition
and several gardens sometimes open together under the SGS.
Kirklands is a 2-acre garden set in a 20-acre woodland with a river
running through the ravine in between. Spring is heralded with
bulbs, rhododendrons and bluebells. By the house are a rock garden
and perennial borders. The small sloping walled garden has an interesting parterre at the top: box filled with nepeta and hardy
geraniums. Below are new terraces with asparagus beds. The many
perennials are divided and those not required are offered for sale.
Definitely a good choice for bed and breakfast for garden-lovers.
Don't miss the two pot-bellied pigs. There are plans to run garden
courses in 2009.

Kirkside of Lochty

This plantsman's garden, created by botanical artist Irene Mackie, is
absolutely packed with rare and unusual bulbs, perennials and ferns.
Irene designed the garden, with echoes of Hidcote, round the centrepiece of a rounded stone trough from which paths and vistas lead, via
arches, into several compartments. The range of over 80 ferns really
impressed me, as did some rare woodland perennials such as the
unusual *Polygonatum* species, *Podophyllum pleianthum* and an amazing
Podophyllum (Dysosma) delavayi with mottled red leaves. There are

Kirkside of Lochty
Menmuir, by Brechin DD9 6RY
(*map, pp. 116–117*)

James and Irene Mackie
By arrangement ; ££
Leave the A90 2 miles south of
Brechin and take the road to
Menmuir. After a further 2 miles
pass a wood on the left and a long
beech hedge in front of the house
T: 01356 660431
E: jjasmackie@btinternet.com
Tea and coffee available by
arrangement

eye-catching plant combinations at every turn, providing lots of great photographic opportunities and there is also a wildflower meadow. This garden, one of the best in Angus, is an exceptional combination of good design and choice plants and I highly recommend it. It is only a few minutes off the A90 Dundee–Aberdeen road. Irene Mackie's previous garden at Bent, near Laurencekirk, also used to open under SGS.

The Linns, see p. 210

Lochdochart

Lochdochart
Crianlarich, FK20 8QS
(*map, pp. 116–117*)

John and Seona Christie
1 Sunday SGS May–June; ££
4 miles east of Crianlarich–
Lochearnhead road A85, turn
off by Portnellan
T: 01838 300 315;
Estate office: 01838 300274
E: christielochdochart@
btinternet.com
www.lochdochart.co.uk

If this were anywhere else, you probably would not give it a second glance. Near Crianlarich, this is truly the cold, wet heart of Scotland and as hard a place to establish a garden as anywhere. The Christie family bought Lochdochart in 1906 and have made some attempt to garden in this soggy, windy site ever since. Even the *R. ponticum* had had its leaves stripped off by the wind when I visited in April 2008. The small walled garden has well trained apples, pears and plums on the walls and dedicated and enthusiastic gardener Alan McClellan raises sweet peas and other plants in the greenhouses. Some plants thrive here: *Lysmachia*, blue poppies and candelabra primulas. The front of the house has some old and young plantings of rhododendrons and azaleas, some of which managed to cope with the wind. The best thing is the setting, with Loch Lhubhair and brooding Ben More. Visitors can picnic on the beach of the loch and wander the paths and tracks.

**Maggie's Centre Garden,
Dundee**
Ninewells Hospital,
Dundee, DD2 1NH
(*map, pp. 116–117*)

Freely accessible but used as
part of Maggie's Centre; free
Follow signs to Ninewells
hospital A&E from Dundee
T: 01382 632999
E: dundee@maggiescentres.org
www.maggiescentres.org

Maggie's Centre Garden, Dundee

This is the only garden in the book which was partially constructed
and yet-to-be planted at time of writing, but it should be in place by
spring 2009. I did get a very good preview of it, on-site with its
designer Arabella Lennox-Boyd. At the back is a landform of grass
and stone. At the front, the garden is planned to have plantings of
white and pale pink rhododendrons, bold drifts of grasses and blocks
of vibrant blue *Geranium* 'Rozanne'. Trees are already planted on-site,
supplied by Bellwood trees in Meigle. The garden surrounds the
iconic 2003 Frank Gehry-designed Maggie's Centre next to Ninewells
Hospital in Dundee. The Maggie's Centres for cancer were founded
by Maggie Keswick, who envisaged designs by the world's top
architects. Maggie Keswick's own Garden of Cosmic Speculation was
created with her husband Charles Jencks at Portrack in Dumfries.

Megginch Castle
By Errol, Perth, PH2 7SW
(*map, pp. 116–117*)

H. Drummond, Giles
and Catherine Herdman
SGS 1 Sunday in April, or by
appointment; ££
Approach from Dundee side only,
directly off A90, on south side of
carriageway ½ mile on left after
Errol/Rait flyover. 10 miles
from Perth, 10 from Dundee
T: 01821 642 222
E: catherine.herdman@gmail.com

Megginch Castle

Megginch is an impressive fifteenth-century castle, altered by Robert
Adam in 1790, with a beautiful cobbled gothic courtyard and pagoda
doocot nearby. The garden, rather overgrown and neglected, is now
being restored. It is famous for its daffodils, clipped hollies and 1,000-
year-old yews with bulbs and *Alchemilla* planted beneath in the
gardens next to the castle. The huge walled garden is under
restoration. Cherry Drummond (Lady Strange) planted the astro-
logical garden in the smaller section of the walled garden.

Meikleour Beech Hedge and Gardens

The *Guinness Book of Records*, lists Meikleour's as the world's highest hedge and is one of Scotland's most impressive horticultural sights. The living wall of beech trees (*Fagus sylvatica*), 30m high and 530m long is believed to have been planted in 1745 by Jean Mercer of Meikleour and it was just let grow upwards, rather than being trimmed as usual, possibly because her husband Robert Murray Nairne was killed at the Battle of Culloden. The hedge is pruned every few years, which is around six weeks' work with a tall cherry-picker. Nearby are the impressive gardens of Meikleour House, which only open to the public on SGS days and by appointment. The wild garden runs along the north bank of the Tay in mixed woodland and is planted with rhododendrons, massed deciduous azaleas and maples, *Sorbus* and other shrubs. Several terraces and lawns by the house give fine views of the gardens, trees and River Tay. The current generation doesn't, as yet, share the previous generation's passion for gardening, so time will tell how this important landscape and plant collection face the future.

Meikleour Beech Hedge and Gardens
Meikleour, Blairgrowrie, Perthshire, PH2 6EA
(map, pp. 116–117)

Meikleour Trust, Mercer Nairne family
SGS: hedge free, gardens ££
On the A93 approximately 12 miles north of Perth, 4 miles south of Blairgowrie and 10 miles east of Dunkeld
T: 01250 883 424
F: 01250 883 309
E: office@meikleour.com
www.meikleour.com

Micklegarth
72a High St, Aberdour, near
Burntisland, Fife, KY3 0SW
(map, pp. 116–117)

Mr and Mrs Gordon Maxwell
SGS and groups by appointment;
££
Aberdour High St, up the
lane beside the Woodside Hotel
(east side) on the right. Name
is on the gate
T: 01383 860796
E: kathleen@micklegarth.co.uk
www.micklegarth.co.uk
Catering available at Woodside
Hotel next door

Micklegarth

This small garden, hidden away behind Aberdour High Street, is a labour of love for Mr and Mrs Maxwell who bought the plot, built their house on it, and have gardened it intensively for 30 years. There is barely an inch spare, it is packed with plants they have collected, in beds linked by winding paths. The mature trees include a blue cedar, several *Genista aetnensis* which smother themselves in yellow in summer, a large *Corylus avellana* 'Contorta', an unusually flat-topped *Parrotia* as well as a curious scarecrow. Beneath the trees are lots of shrub roses, rhododendrons, ferns, daphnes, and perennials of every kind, all jostling for space. Keen plantspeople could spend a long time chatting to the owners about their treasures, who do admit to arguing about what should go where.

Milseybank
Lecropt, Bridge of Allan, FK9 4NB
(map, pp. 116–117)

Murray and Sheila Airth
SGS 1 Sunday in April and by
arrangement; ££
Situated on the A9, 1 mile from
junction 11, M9 and ¼ mile from
Bridge of Allan. Milseybank is at
the top of the lane at Lecropt
Nursery and 250 yards from
Bridge of Allan train station. Open
day parking at Lecropt Church.
T: 01786 833866

Milseybank

There are two things you won't forget once you have visited this garden. One is the terraced steep slope with great views over Bridge of Allan. The other is the sets of pencils! The section of garden below the house is landscaped with stone terraces, built by the Airths, planted with a huge range of shrubs, bulbs and perennials and to recall that this was formerly a girls' school, embedded in the ground are at least four sets of giant pencils in different colours. The section beyond the house, equally steep is a wilder woodland area with magnolias, camellias, rhododendrons and an undercarpet of bluebells. The garden is probably too steep for any but the able-bodied.

Monkmyre

Monkmyre
Myreriggs Road, Coupar Angus,
Blairgowrie, PH13 9HS
(*map, pp. 116–117*)

Bobby and Jennifer Sommerville
By appointment after telephone
call to arrange time; ££ (all money
goes to PADS, Perth Abandoned
Dogs Society)
Off A923 Coupar Angus–
Blairgowrie road. Myreriggs road
T: 01828 627131
E: rsommerville120@
btinernet.com
www.monkmyre.net

Former alpine nurseryman Bobby Sommerville and his wife Jennifer bought this house with a 2-acre field in 1995 and have transformed it into a packed plantsman's garden. Hedgerow shelter was planted round the edge of the garden with a structure of trees such as *Acer* and *Sorbus*. Wide grass paths meander through the curved beds planted with all manner of shrubs and perennials. The pond is surrounded by *Rodgersia, Iris, Ligularia* and other waterside favourites and the vegetable garden is tucked away behind a *Rosa rugosa* hedge. There is also a herb garden. The owners have an express compost-making system (from the USA) which apparently allows compost to be made in 10 days from start to finish. They also have a colour Monkmyre garden calendar available each year which you can see and order on their website.

The Murrel, see p. 211

Murthly Castle

When Scone-born David Douglas walked through the conifer forests in Washington and Oregon in the 1820s and 1830s, he was amazed at the size and grandeur of the Douglas fir, redwoods and other trees. Short of travelling to the north-west corner of the USA, the best way to get an idea of what these forests feel like is to walk around the grounds of Murthly Castle. Dating back to the fifteenth century, the

Murthly Castle
Murthly and Strathbraan Estates,
Murthly, Perth, PH1 4HP
(*map, pp. 116–117*)

Thomas Steuart Fothringham
SGS every 3 years; group tours
(including castle) by prior
arrangement only; ££
Near Murthly village, near
Dunkeld. Directions will be
provided to visitors
T: 01738 630 666;
Estate office: 01738 710303
E: info@murthly-estate.com
www.murthly-estate.com

castle lies on the banks of the Tay, near Dunkeld, and has been owned by the Steuarts and Steuart Fothringhams since 1615. The 2-mile-long drive from Murthly village is stunning, with a long avenue of *Abies grandis* and *Sequoiadendron giganteum* and another of limes alternating with yew which leads to the gates of the walled garden. Further afield are avenues of cedar, oak and beech. Sir William Steuart, seventh baronet, explored parts of the American west himself, bringing back seed and seedling conifers to Murthly in the 1840s, as well as a herd of buffalo, which grazed the parkland. Having seen the magnificent North American forests, he knew how to space the trees to achieve the best long-term effect, with the result that 150 years later, the plantings are still in fine condition. Murthly has benefited greatly from continuity of interest in trees through three to four generations of the Steuart family, so planting has continued and overgrown avenues have been replaced, providing a succession of trees of different ages. Murthly is one of the sites of the International Conifer Conservation Programme and groves of Tasmanian and Chilean species have been planted as part of the ongoing ex-situ conservation project based at RBG, Edinburgh. The fine, planned landscapes at Murthly include the edge of Birnam Wood, famous from Shakespeare's *Macbeth*, and extend down to the Tay, with some of its finest salmon beats. North of the castle is a series of parallel rides and avenues. A gravel path lined with ancient yews leads to the chapel, while parallel to this is a sunken double rhododendron and azalea border which reaches a crescendo in late May and which in turn is bordered by an extensive group of Hemlock, noble fir and Douglas fir, giving the feel of native North American forest. Tree guru Alan Mitchell recorded several significant and champion trees at Murthly including *Abies alba* and *Abies grandis, Picea glehnii, Picea omorika, Pseudotsuga menziesii, Tsuga heterophylla, Tsuga mertensiana* and an avenue of *Thuja plicata* over 30m high. The formerly rather overgrown walled garden has been brought back under control. The castle walls are covered with climbers on a terrace which looks over the lawns and clipped yews. The seventeenth-century pavilion in one corner of the walled garden has been much imitated by architects including Sir Robert Lorimer and there are numerous fine urns and statues both inside and outside the garden. The grounds can be rented as a wedding venue and the gardens can be visited by appointment by groups, particularly those interested in trees.

Myres Castle

Myres Castle, outside Auchtermuchty in Fife, is one of Scotland's most exclusive hotels. The small walled 'Vatican' garden, is so named because its designer J.O. David had been a Papal Chamberlain, and took the layout from one of the Vatican's private formal gardens. On the outside of the garden is a walk of shrub roses leading from the helipad (yes it's that kind of hotel) to the castle itself. The walled garden's most striking feature is the four beds of grasses created by gardener Matthew Dixon, with a fountain in the middle, which look spectacular from midsummer till as late as February, when they are cut back. The bed is underplanted with *Heuchera* and *Ligularia* to add foliage texture, and the combination is both unusual and effective. Right up the middle of the garden on either side of the main axis is a startling double border of blue iris in flower in late May and early June. There are borders of roses and peonies and in one corner, a small sunken section which contains a giant chess set, behind which are a couple of tiled wall sections. Beyond the clipped yew hedge are two further sections of garden, on the left a yew maze which is suffering from waterlogging and on the right a small football pitch. I would have thought these two areas could be better integrated as part of the gardens. The garden is open under SGS most years and may be possible to visit outside these dates, guests permitting. Contact the hotel for information.

Myres Castle
Auchtermuchty, Fife,
KY14 7EW
(*map, pp. 116–117*)

Mr and Mrs Jonathan White
SGS or occasionally by
appointment (not when guests
are staying); ££
Station Road, south of
Auchtermuchty. Turn off A91,
signs for Dunshalt, Falkland
T: 01337 828350
F. 01337 827531
E: cosy@myrescastle.com
www.myrescastle.com

Newtonmill House
By Edzell, Angus, DD9 7PZ
(*map, pp. 116–117*)

Stephen and Rose Rickman
SGS every 2nd year, open to
guests and sometimes by
appointment; ££
From the Aberdeen–Dundee
A90 take the B966 signed Edzell,
1 mile on right. From Edzell,
take B966 towards Brechin,
2 miles on right
T: 01356 622533
E: rrickman@srickman.co.uk
www.newtonmillhouse.co.uk

Newtonmill House

This strikingly attractive eighteenth-century country house and garden is a very pleasant place to stay; Newtonmill is on the Alastair Sawday and Wolsey Lodge recommended lists. The walled garden has clearly been cultivated for a long time, in the 1950s and early '60s it was the home of very keen gardener Elizabeth Elphinstone, whose legacy includes some of the garden's structural elements and some now very large tree peonies. The Rickmans bought the house in 1985 and have evolved the garden ever since. The garden's most memorable feature is the double perennial border, peaking in June and July, backed with *Prunus pissardii*. It is best appreciated from the bottom of the garden looking back towards the house via a striking wheel-design gate. Off the main axis are paths, mostly box-lined, featuring shrubs, peonies, roses and *Iris* beds. At the bottom of the garden is an eighteenth-century doocot with a pond next door. The west side is a large vegetable garden with 27 types of carefully labelled potatoes including many rarely seen varieties. Next to the house is a rose-pergola patio. The policies and woodland total 25 acres in all and I noted the handsome eighteenth-century coach house on the western side.

[B&B] [♿]

Parleyhill Garden, Culross

This is an excellent small garden high up next to Culross Abbey with great views out over the Forth. Culross is an enjoyable place to wander around with several historic buildings as well as Culross Palace

to visit. Parleyhill is packed with plants, but also with plenty of great design elements, the best of which was the only *Hippophae rhamnoides* (sea buckthorn) I have ever seen trained like a Japanese cloud tree. This garden makes good use of grasses too and formally shaped yews both as low hedges and clipped to form flat-topped columns. Plants with weeping and pendulous growth: *Juniperus recurva* and *Dierama* are planted together with great effect. I loved the bucket and black standpipe surrounded by a sea of bronze grasses. The perfect drainage on the south-facing slope allows a great range of plants to thrive, including some which are on the tender side: *Agapanthus*, black-purple *Pittosporum, Lobelia, Tamarix, Abutilon, Hibiscus* and *Clematis heracleifolia*.

Parleyhill Garden, Culross
Kirk Street, Culross, KY12 8JD
(*map, pp. 116–117*)

Ron and Elizabeth MacDonald
SGS 1 Sunday; ££
Just below Culross Abbey, follow signs up the hill. Park at abbey or palace
Tea on SGS days at the manse garden. Several places to eat in Culross

Perthshire Big Tree Country

Perthshire Big Tree Country is the marketing umbrella dreamed up to celebrate the amazing range of trees in this part of Scotland. These include what is claimed to be Europe's oldest tree, the Fortingall Yew, the world's highest hedge at Meikleour and the sole survivor from Shakespeare's 'Birnam Wood'. The valley from Perth to Blair Atholl (the A9 corridor) is a demonstration of tree-planting at its best. The 'Planting' dukes of Atholl (the second, third and fourth dukes) were to plant over 21 million trees on some 15,000 acres of ground from 1700 to 1830. Larch was the most popular tree but they used Scots pine, oaks, beech, birch and other species. Some of the sites which come under the Big Tree Country banner have their own entries in this book: Blair Castle, Cluny, the Hermitage, Scone Palace etc. The Enchanted Forest is a *son et lumière* show in woodland between Pitlochry and Dunkeld each November and December which has

Perthshire Big Tree Country
Various, Perth: Dunkeld, Aberfeldy, Pitlochry;
see also individual garden entries

Free/variable depending on site/garden.
Most sites to the north and west of Perth off the A9 and A86.
E: enquiries@perthshire bigtreecountry.co.uk
www.perthshirebigtree country.co.uk

Kinnoul Hill, Perth

proven very popular with adults and children. To help make tree-visiting easier, the website groups sites of interest into six main cluster areas: Aberfeldy and Kenmore, Blair Atholl, Crieff and Strathearn, Dunkeld and Birnam, Perth and Blairgowrie, Pitlochry and the Road to the Isles. Each of these contains several tree sites which can be visited in a single day/afternoon.

Pitcairn Alpines

Pitcairn Alpines
Pitcairn Alpines, Scotts Park,
Pitcairngreen, Perth, PH1 3LT
(*map, pp. 116–117*)

Susan Band
Open day last Sunday in May
Pitcairngreen is signposted
off the A85 Perth–Crieff road
T: 01738 583213
E: susan@pitcairnalpines.co.uk
www.pitcairnalpines.co.uk

Susan Band sells a fine selection of woodland bulbs: *Anemone, Corydalis, Erythronium, Fritillaria, Galanthus, Trillium* etc. Bulbs can be ordered online or by post and are dispatched mail order bareroot in August and September only. There is a good website with pictures and secure ordering.

Pitcurran House

Pitcurran House
Abernethy, Perthshire, PH2 9LH
(*map, pp. 116–117*)

Mr and Mrs Noel-Paton
SGS; ££
On the eastern outskirts of
Abernethy on the road to
Newburgh
T: 01738 850933
E: patricianp@pitcurren.com

The Noel-Patons previously gardened at Dunbarny near Bridge of Earn, which was open under the Scotland's Gardens Scheme. They moved here in 2005 and are developing a new garden, due to open under SGS in 2009 or 2010. They brought some of their favourites from their former garden and have collected a huge range of unusual plant material. They have several *Sophora* and two mature *Robinia*, trees which normally need more heat, but they all flower in Abernethy. Other tender plants which are thriving include *Echium* and *Melianthus major*. Behind the house is a series of brick terraces topped with a hedge of low rose 'The Fairy'. Beyond this a rose arch walk is covered with a series of ramblers including 'Blush Noisette', 'Felicite Perpetue' and 'Paul's Himalayan Musk'. To the west is a series of beds, with a mixture of shrubs and perennials: the first is dominated by Hydrangeas, underplanted with Geranium 'Orion', others have white foxgloves and white willowherb, ferns, hosta and *Rodgersia*.

Pitmuies (House of Pitmuies)

Pitmuies
Guthrie, by Forfar,
Angus, DD8 2SN
(*map, pp. 116–117*)

Margaret Ogilvie
1 April–31 October:
10am–5pm; ££
7 miles east of Forfar by A932,
1½ miles from Friockheim
T: 01241 828 245
E: ogilvie@pitmuies.com
www.pitmuies.com

Quite rightly considered by many to be one of Scotland's finest private gardens, most of Pitmuies was designed by Margaret Ogilvie, who has gardening in her blood as she was brought up at one of Ireland's finest gardens, Castlewellan. She moved to Angus when she married Farquhar Ogilvie. Pitmuies, a seventeenth- and eighteenth-century house, was already an impressive designed landscape of some 40 acres, with an eccentric collection of buildings including a laundry which looks like a chapel and a castellated doocot. The fine parkland with mature trees has many impressive specimens of Spanish chestnuts, hornbeams and a particularly fine beech grove at the end of the woodland garden which leads to the black loch beyond, surrounded by trees and rhododendrons. The heart of the garden is the double-walled

garden on two sides of the house. Visitors first enter the kitchen garden with a border of roses and tender shrubs round the edge before passing through a further door into the larger walled section at the front of the house. Down the centre runs the famous double summer borders, backed with red-leaved *Prunus* 'Pissardii', on either side of an unusually narrow path with a small sundial in the middle. In June and July this is a tapestry of pink and white and is regarded as one of the best perennial plantings in Scotland. To the left is an area of lawn with a circular raised bed of *Acanthus, Galtonia* and *Eremurus*, with a small yellow-leaved elm centre-piece. Below this along the boundary of the garden are the eight *Prunus serrula* with their fat trunks of shining darkest crimson, through which can be seen a wall topped with rose and honeysuckle trellising. This garden is packed with exquisite design flourishes: each path leads to items of usually specially designed white furniture: a bower, a bench, a chair; and there are ornaments, statues and urns strategically placed for maximum effect. On the west side of the double border are the famous *Delphinium* beds, a jaw-dropping wall of deep blue and purple propagated from the same stock in the garden since the 1920s. This forms the border to the rose garden with a series of formal beds, and a central fountain with waterlilies. At the west end beyond a rose trellis are the double purple/blue and yellow borders, at their peak in midsummer. Do venture further afield, through the bulb and wildflower meadows, along the Vinny Water and loch and into the woodland garden where there are fine rhododendron species and spring bulbs. This garden has everything: an excellent collection of plants, superb design elements and daring planting combinations. You need to come several times during the season to see all it has to offer. As early as April and as late as September there is plenty of colour, but it is probably best known for its summer displays. Margaret's son Ruaraidh and daughter-in-law Jeanette are keen gardeners so Pitmuies appears to be a garden with a secure future.

Pittencrieff Park, Dunfermline
Dunfermline, KY12 7SH
(*map, pp. 116–117*)

Fife Council
Dawn to dusk; £ (car park):
entry free
Follow the brown signs towards
the town centre. There are car
parks at the east and west
end of the park
Lots of cafés nearby

Pittencrieff Park, Dunfermline

Don't be put off by Dunfermline's rather grim outskirts, plastic shopping malls and endless new housing; the old centre of the town is very fine and it was once Scotland's capital. Robert the Bruce is buried in Dunfermline Abbey (the abbey church is wonderful) which lies right next door to Dunfermline's enormous and impressive Pittencrieff Park. It was donated to the city with a legacy to maintain it by its most famous and richest son, Andrew Carnegie, who left Dunfermline aged 13 and via steel-making became the world's richest man. He also gave the town its library and swimming pool and you'll see his name everywhere in the city. The park covers 76 acres and is built around a deep ravine known as 'the glen' with The Tower and

Lyne Burn running through it. The tower is the remains of one of Macbeth's castles, so legend has it. This steep-sided and deep ravine was once well-landscaped and is a perfect setting for a fine woodland garden. That it has been allowed to fill up with weed trees and scrub is a great shame and this whole area should be restored before all the trees are spoiled. The rest of the park is much better maintained. One section, known as 'the laird's garden', contains a formal garden of roses, perennials and bedding in front of a series of glass houses with cacti and other collections. Beyond this are extensive lawns and mature trees. On the north side of the park is a good children's play area (there are two more elsewhere in the park) and an avenue of trees leads from Carnegie's statue to the main gates. The park offers fine views over the old town and abbey.

Plants With Purpose

This small organic mail order nursery a few miles north of Perth, just off the A9, grows what the owner Margaret Lear calls 'purposeful plants' which are defined as those which have uses beyond ornamental. She writes on her website: 'I shun plants that just sit there looking colourful but provide neither food for the table, remedies for ailments nor nectar for butterflies. I mean, what is the POINT of *Begonia semperflorens?*' Margaret also runs a garden design and consultancy service aimed at making gardens and horticulture more sustainable. Her shop stocks information booklets, herbal soaps, beeswax candles, dried herbs, bookmarks, plant greetings cards and a range of essential oils and runs workshops on organic gardening, herbs, cooking with herbs and wild plants, foraging for wild food and wildlife gardening. I'd definitely give the variegated ground elder she sells a wide birth. You can get all the properties advertised for this by using the wild stuff which you probably have anyway (see also Heart of Scotland Herb Society: *http://www.hshs.org.uk/*).

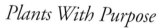

Plants With Purpose
Middlebank Cottage, Smith's Brae, Bankfoot, Perthshire, PH1 4AH
(map, pp. 116–117)

Margaret Lear
April–end of September, by appointment, or when the sign is out. Annual open days.
Turn off A9 (signed Bankfoot). Smith's Brae is a lane off the High Street in the centre, sign on pavement when open, park in High Street
T: 01738 787 278;
M: 07871 451579
E: mail@plantswithpurpose.co.uk
www.plantswithpurpose.co.uk

Quercus Garden Plants
Rankeillour Walled Gardens,
Rankeillour Estate, by
Springfield, Fife, KY15 5RE
(map, pp. 116–117)

Colin McBeath
1 weekend April–mid October:
Thursday–Sunday, 10am–5pm;
March: Saturday only 10am–5pm,
other times by appointment.
Rankeillour Estate, entered by the
East Lodge through stone pillars
(sign on pillar) from the minor
road to Springfield that connects
the A91 to the A914
T: 01337 810444
E: colin@quercus.uk.net

Quercus Garden Plants

Garden designer Colin McBeath started this nursery in Fife to supply 'easy and unusual plants for contemporary Scottish gardens'. The nursery is in the old walled garden of Rankeillour estate, west of Cupar. In the old greenhouses and new tunnels all sorts of plants are produced, and laid out on the nursery in categories according to their use: for wet or dry soils for example. I found a good selection of more unusual grasses, perennials and trees and shrubs when I visited. Colin is usually available at the nursery on Saturdays to advise customers. Word of mouth is spreading this nursery's reputation and it is well worth a visit. The 30-page catalogue is informative and the website should be up and running soon.

Redhall
Redhall, Kirriemuir,
Angus, DD8 4PZ
(map, pp. 116–117)

Mr and Mrs Bolt
Small groups by appointment; ££
Take the B955/Dykehead Road
from Kirriemuir, left just before
Prossen Bridge, left and left again,
or download a map from website
E: phb@redhall.org.uk
www.redhall.org.uk

Redhall (Angus)

This is a recently planted informal, 1-acre country garden around a Scandinavian-looking wooden house, surrounded by a collection of *Viburnum, Euonymus, Acer, Salix* and other shrubs, a good range of ferns and a particularly good collection of *Sorbus* which will be at their best with berries in autumn. There is a deck-surrounded wildlife pond, and you'll probably meet the quantity of peafowl and Scots Dumpy hens. The informative website has a fun 'cultivar' name game on it.

Rossie House

Rossie House lies just outside the village of Forgandenny about 7 miles south-west of Perth. The house, which has its origins in the seventeenth century, has been much altered and has a spectacular central staircase and cupola and a tall central arched loggia which can be seen clearly from the garden. When Judy and David Nichol bought Rossie, it already had a fine collection of trees and some mature rhododendrons as well as a substantial walled garden, planted by previous owner Sir James Hutchison and his family. Judy has tamed the undergrowth and created a fine display of plants in a woodland setting around a large lawn. Snowdrops and aconites dominate in early spring, giving way to bluebells and wild garlic carpets in May, when the rhododendrons reach their peak. The various paths lead to a water garden, with ponds, bridges and streams lined with purple candelabra primulas, *Rodgersia, Trillium* and *Meconopsis*. Notable plants include a giant old cedar, a *Davidia involucrata*, rare *Dipelta floribunda* with peeling bark, and a mature *Magnolia obovata (hypoleuca)*. A highlight in May was the mixed planting of purple *Allium* and white tulips along the outside of the walled garden wall. Late summer colour is provided by the herbaceous and roses planting in the walled garden, which is shared with a small herd of Castlemilk Moorit and Herdwick sheep, while the woodland area boasts *Stewartia, Hydrangea, Eucryphia* and *Sorbus*. Next to the house is a well-sheltered enclosed area, with a fine *Cornus kousa, Wisteria* and *Solanum crispum*. This is a charming garden, well-planned, planted and maintained, at its best in May and June, but worth a visit at almost any time of year. The Nichols offer bed and breakfast in the house, which would be a fine way to enjoy the garden. Guided tours and tea and coffee can be provided for groups.

Rossie House
Forgandenny, Perthshire,
PH2 9EH
(*map, pp. 116–117*)

Judy and David Nichol
SGS some years, 1 March–31
October by appointment; ££
Leave M90 at Bridge of Earn onto
A912 towards Perth. Turn left onto
A935 to Forgandenny. Entrance
on right just after Forgandenny
T: 01738 812265
E: judynichol@rossiehouse.co.uk
www.rossiehouse.co.uk

B&B   WC

Rufflets Country House Hotel
Strathkinness Low Road,
St Andrews, Fife, KY16 9TX
(*map, pp. 116–117*)

Mrs Murray Smith
SGS 1 day and to parties on
request. Rufflets open to
guests and visitors all year; ££
Follow yellow signs from SGS
days, park at Hepburn Gardens
or Argyll Street car park. Rufflets
is on B939 St Andrews–
Strathkinness road
T: 01334 472594
E: reservations@rufflets.co.uk
www.rufflets.co.uk
Bar meals and restaurant

Rufflets Country House Hotel

Rufflets is a 1924 house, built for a Dundee jute baron, which is now
a popular country house hotel on the outskirts of St Andrews. The 10
acres of gardens have been looked after by gardener Andy Duncan for
30 years. The south side of the house looks out onto a sheltered
terrace containing a formal topiary garden of yew and box, both green
and yellow shapes. The lawn on the west side has herbaceous and
shrub borders and one of the largest tulip trees in eastern Scotland.
The terrace steps lead down to a more informal woodland area and an
orchard with some fine mature trees including a blue cedar, with
Aruncus and other perennials along the sides of the two burns.
Rufflets gardens are open to residents and guests as well as on one
annual SGS open day.

Scone Palace

First things first for non-Scots. 'Scone' rhymes with 'moon' while the
edible 'scone' rhymes with 'on'. Neither rhymes with 'moan'. Home of
the earls of Mansfield, Scone was the once capital of the Pictish
kingdom and later the crowning place of Scottish kings was on Moot
Hill opposite the front door of the palace. One of Scotland's most
popular tourist attractions, there is enough to do at Scone in its 100
acres for a good few hours. The palace, much added to over the years,
is a huge but rather lumpen building with plenty to see inside,
including selected pots of orchids which are part of the largest private
collection in Britain, grown in the earl of Mansfield's greenhouses
(which unfortunately are not open to visitors). Scottish plant hunter

David Douglas, explorer of the American west and introducer of many fine plants (and some noxious weeds such as *Rubus spectabilis*) was born at Scone and the palace's pinetum, started in 1848, contains some giant conifers grown from Douglas seed. Many outstanding trees are here including a giant *Cunninghamia,* and fine *Picea breweriana,* one of the most handsome of all conifers, as well as the UK champion *Pinus jeffreyi.* Impressive snowdrops are followed by massed daffodils and primroses and beds of rhododendrons and azaleas in the grounds and gardens, with *Philadelphus,* roses, perennials and a butterfly garden to follow in the summer. Don't miss the beech maze designed by maze master Adrian Fisher. Scone's grounds were 'improved' by J.C. Loudon, the influential nineteenth-century Scottish author and garden designer with opinions on everything, who insisted on moving the village of Scone to create the entrance avenue. Scone's grounds are more a parkland than a unified garden, where you'll probably be joined by the peacocks, and are certainly well worth wandering round. Lady Stormont is gradually upgrading and replanting, including a new pinetum to replace some of the elderly and infirm gentlemen in the old one, but the scale of the site is dauntingly large and the scale of planting needs to be bolder than it is currently to make much impact. Many events take place at Scone during the year, including the Scottish Game Fair.

Scone Palace
Scone, By Perth, PH2 6BD
(*map, pp. 116–117*)

Rt Hon. Earl of Mansfield
and Mansfield
Daily: Easter/1 April–end October
9.30am–5.30pm (Saturdays palace closes at 4.30pm); ££ (grounds)
£££ (palace and garden)
2 miles north of Perth on A93
Perth–Blairgowrie road, clearly
signposted
T: 01738 552300
F: 01738 552588
E: visits@scone-palace.co.uk
www.scone-palace.co.uk
Old Servants' Hall Coffee Shop.
Picnic areas

Scotia Seeds,
Wildflowers of Scotland
Mavisbank, Farnell,
Brechin, Angus, DD9 6TR

Giles Laverack
Mail order only. Occasional
groups by appointment.
Mavisbank is off the A933,
3 miles south of Brechin
T: 01356 626425
F: 01356 629183
E: scotiaseeds@btconnect.com
www.scotiaseeds.co.uk

Scotia Seeds, Wildflowers of Scotland

This company specialises in Scottish wildflower seeds and seed mixes. All wildflower seed is produced from plants that have been grown on from native Scottish seed collections with the belief that locally sourced wildflowers should be better adapted to Scottish conditions than those from further south or the continent. As well as packets of wildflowers such as poppies, cornflower, cranesbill, primrose and other favourites, Scotia sells a huge range of wildflower mixes for different soil types and situations. Some of these include wet meadow mix, pond edge mix, cornfield annual mix, hedgerow mix, coastal mix and bee, bird and butterfly mix. This is a mail order nursery and does not deal directly with the public on-site, but it can offer occasional workshops and tours for groups interested in biodiversity and all aspects of wildflower management.

Scottish Natural Heritage,
Battleby
Battleby, Redgorton,
Perth, PH1 3EW
(*map, pp. 116–117*)

Scottish National Heritage,
contact Jim Carruthers
Open all the time. SGS open day
some years. Groups by
appointment; free, SGS days ££
Just off the A9,1 junction north
of Perth. Signed from A9
T: 01738 444177
F: 01738 458611
E: Jim.Carruthers@snh.gov.uk
www.snh.org.uk/

Scottish Natural Heritage, Battleby

The woodlands around Battleby House north of Perth were planted up with a fine collection of trees and shrubs by Sir Alexander Cross in the period 1947–63. The Battleby Centre was constructed for the Countryside Commission in the 1970s (now Scottish Natural Heritage). The grounds at Battleby have been maintained and added to over many years by gardener Jim Carruthers and include a wide range of trees, shrubs, bulbs and perennials which can be appreciated on a well-made circular route which runs right around the house. The range of rhododendron and azalea species and hybrids is impressive, so May is a good time to visit. The wildflower meadow in mid to late summer is good, as is the autumn colour in October–November.

Scottish Origins Nursery

This is a land and ecology management consultancy which covers nature conservation, landscape design, woodland management and tree surveys. They also have a wildflower nursery, with all plants grown from Scottish origin seed. Plants are supplied in plugs and larger pot sizes and are available retail and wholesale. Mail order is offered for deliveries of over 100 plants.

Scottish Origins Nursery
3 Brewery Lane,
Kinross, KY13 8EL
(*map, pp. 116–117*)

Erika Luukas and Stuart Grant
T: 01577 861437
F: 01577 861437
E: erikaluukas@scotorigins.co.uk
www.scotorigins.co.uk

SCRI Dundee: Scottish Crop Research Institute

How many people realise that Invergowrie is home to the world's centre of berry breeding: over 50 per cent of the world's blackcurrant production and 90 per cent of the UK production is from varieties named after Scottish mountains (Ben Sarek, Ben Lomond etc) bred at this crop institute, not far from the Tay in Invergowrie, west of Dundee. They have also bred an important series of raspberries, named after Scottish Glens (Glen Clova, Glen Prosen etc), reflecting the traditional importance of the Carse of Gowrie and surrounding areas as a major raspberry growing area. SCRI used to have the UK's major collection of heritage apples (over 900 varieties), which were short-sightedly grubbed out in the 1970s; thankfully wood was first sent to the national collection at Brogdale for propagation. SCRI hosts the Commonwealth Potato Collection, a major gene bank containing 86 different species, and is conducting important research into potato blight. Other areas of research include breeding of barley, crop pests and diseases, climate change, nutrition and genetics. It runs an extensive educational programme, producing material for schools and hosting students and school children. Every few years an open weekend is held, usually in June, with one day for school classes and one for families. These are very well run and my children really

SCRI Dundee
Invergowrie, Dundee, DD2 5DA
(*map, pp. 116–117*)

SCRI
Public open days every few years
(Friday and Saturday in June).
Events held through the year.
Groups and interested parties
by appointment; free
Turn off A85 Riverside drive into
Invergowrie. Follow Main Street
past the shops and Post Office,
turn next left into Errol Road,
signposted for SCRI. Follow the
road round a sharp right-hand
bend. The entrance to SCRI is at
the foot of the drive on your right
T: 01382 562731
F: 01382 562426
E: info@scri.ac.uk
www.scri.ac.uk

enjoyed the activities on offer, with almost surreal numbers of SCRI staff letting them try things: face-painting, dressing as scientists, making bugs, answering quizzes and so on. The SCRI is a Scottish success story with well-focused research and a sound commercial arm, bringing in royalties from the varieties bred there.

Seer Centre
Ceanghline, Straloch Farm,
Enochdhu, Blairgowrie, PH10 7PJ
(*map, pp. 116–117*)

Cameron and Moira Thomson
1 June–31 October: 10am–6pm,
visits by appointment for
individuals or groups; £–££
On the A924 Pitlochry–
Kirkmichael road at Straloch,
west of Enochdu. Car park
is signposted
T: 01250 870789
F: 01250 881789
E: moira@seercentre.org.uk
www.seercentre.org.uk

Seer Centre

The Seer Centre, a farm and garden, is situated at around 1,000ft on one of Perthshire's most scenic roads which climbs up from Pitlochry via Kirkmichael towards Blairgowrie and Braemar. It is a 6-acre site, with 4 acres of non-mechanised-access terraced gardens, paths and lawns. Its vegetable and fruit production is very impressive for such an exposed inland garden at altitude. The secret of the garden's success is, according to the Thomsons, their pioneering use of Rockdust®, crushed rock from a Perthshire quarry, which they claim is an excellent organic way to replenish soils which have been impoverished by overcropping and use of chemicals. They call this 'remineralisation' and amongst other things, they claim that soil treated in this way absorbs more carbon dioxide. I checked some scientific papers on this subject and was left unconvinced. But on the other hand . . . Moira showed me apple trees which have never been fed apart from their initial dose of rockdust, which were doing surprisingly well in such an unpromising environment. Whether you believe some of the more far-fetched claims for rockdust or not, the garden is certainly worth visiting; it is in a stunning setting and the terraces are planted with a huge array of flowers and vegetables. In early September the *Achillea* in shades of pink and white were particularly impressive. A tunnel house is filled with fan-trained fruit. You can of course buy rockdust to take home with you. The next stage depends on sourcing funding so that they can build a visitor centre and develop the education side,

which will start with rockdust and remineralisation courses in 2008–09. Vegetables from the garden are usually offered for sale.

Silverburn Park

Silverburn Park
Silverburn Estate, Largo Road, Leven, KY8 5PU
(*map, pp. 116–117*)

Fife Council
Dawn–dusk, daily; free
A915 between Largo and Leven

Silverburn Park lies midway between the towns of Leven and Largo and was gifted by the Russell family to Fife Council in the 1970s. It contains extensive mixed woodland, including specimens of *Taxodium* (swamp cypress) and *Ginkgo*, woodland walks and a large walled garden which is being restored, as is the retting pond (formerly used to soak flax before it was processed). There is a children's play house on stilts in one part of the garden. Silverburn used to contain a very popular mini-farm, now closed. Fife Council does not seem to have come up with a viable present-day use for the house and park, both of which have been allowed to deteriorate.

Southern Hemisphere Botanics
Gardener's Cottage, Shore Road,
Crombie Point, Fife, KY12 8LH
(*map, pp. 116–117*)

Ursula McHardy
Easter–October:
Sunday–Tuesday 10am–4pm;
donation (½ to charity)
Park in Torryburn off the A985
and it is a 15-minute walk along
the foot and cycle path of Shore
Road. You may be able to park
nearer by appointment only if
you have mobility problems
T: 07786 404198 (Lorna McHardy)
E: gardeners.cottage@virgin.net

Southern Hemisphere Botanics

Not long before the cut-off point for inclusion for gardens for this book a little brochure came through the letterbox inviting me to a garden opening . . . and it looked intriguing. Ursula McHardy and her daughter Lorna had set up what they call 'A Fifish Garden' or 'Southern Hemisphere Botanics' in a medium-sized walled garden on the banks of the Forth. I simply had to go and investigate, and I was amazed at what I found. This was formerly a walled garden for Craigflower House, latterly a prep school, used to grow vegetables and fruit. The McHardys have gardened here for three years and already this is a remarkable place. My heart sank slightly when I heard that the plants were laid out geographically, as I feared a stamp collection. I need not have worried; this is an artfully designed garden by an expert plantswoman who studied botany in her youth and has an almost frightening level of knowledge of southern hemisphere plants, which she and her husband fell in love with on numerous trips to South Africa, New Zealand and Tasmania. A series of round ponds, built by Doug Cann from Landmarkers, are linked by tumbling waterfalls as the gently sloping terrain is divided into sections, with paths and curving gravel paths. The River Forth provides a relatively benign climate, allowing tender plants to do well, though the south-westerly winds are fierce. Plants include *Eucalyptus*, tree ferns, parahebes and other Tasmanian and South Australian plants, then there are Chatham Island forget-me-nots from New Zealand and *Dierama* and bulbs from South Africa's Fynbos, Drakensberg and Table Mountain regions, with *Lapageria*, southern beech and monkey puzzles from Chile. On the outside of the walled garden, Ursula's daughter Lorna has designed a fine narrow sloping section with ponds, insectivorous plants and a wildlife hedge. There are plans for a woodland garden on the tree-clad slopes behind. A lot has been achieved in a few years and this is definitely one to watch.

Southwood

This town garden was redesigned in 1987 and is divided into four narrow sections, one is mainly grass, one has a double herbaceous border, one is mainly trees and shrubs including a Camperdown Elm, *Davidia, Embothrium* and cutleaf beech, rhododendrons and azaleas, and the last is mainly fruit and vegetables.

St Andrews Botanic Garden

Hidden away, not far from the centre of St Andrews, this is a fine garden, now owned and run by the council with help from the garden's Friends. In common with other botanic gardens, this one has been cut adrift from its university, which no longer needs it for teaching purposes. The planting is now mature, over-mature in some cases, with shrubs and trees jostling for light, but there have been extensive renovations and replanting in recent years. The garden was founded in 1889 but moved to the present 7-hectare site in 1960. Spring is an excellent time to visit as there are extensive plantings of rhododendrons, primulas, *Meconopsis* and other associated plants and a large rock garden and bog/pond garden around a series of ponds and cascades. There are significant collections of *Berberis, Cotoneaster* and *Sorbus*, including UK micro-species (local variants of native species) such as *S. pseudofenica* from Arran. The east end of the garden contains extensive perennial plantings at their best in July and August and a well-planned and maintained glasshouse complex, a

Southwood
Southfield Crescent,
Stirling, FK8 2JQ
(*map, pp. 116–117*)

John and Lesley Stein
SGS 1 day per year; ££
On open days signed from Carlton
Bingo (city centre). From south,
signed from St Ninian's Road.
From west and north, signed
from Drummond Place
T: 01786 475735 and 450737
F: 01786 450251
E: lesley@john-stein.co.uk

St Andrews Botanic Garden
Canongate, St Andrews,
Fife, KY16 8RT
(*map, pp. 116–117*)

St Andrews Council
Daily: April–September
10am–7pm, October–March
10am–4pm; £
From St Andrews town centre
(Westport) turn left down Bridge
Street, take the 2nd right into
Canongate (well-signposted).
T: 01334 476452
F: 01334 476452
E: botanic@standbg.plus.com
www.st-andrews-botanic.org
Tea Hut with vending
machine/new facilities soon

peat house with rhododendrons, tropical house, dry house, bromeliad and orchid house, cacti and succulents and an alpine house, in a linked series of small structures. Along the sides of many of the glasshouse walls are tender shrubs which benefit from the heat of the glasshouses in winter. Near the entrance is a small garden commemorating 50 years of the United Nations. There are still some traditional order beds which are used for teaching plant families. This is a little-known garden, only £2 to visit, worth a stroll at almost any time of year with a wide and varied collection both inside and out. The maples and sumacs provide fiery autumn colours to complement the berries of the *Sorbus* and *Cotoneaster*. A few plants are offered for sale. The garden's Friends offer an impressive lecture programme, plant sales and garden visits and there are wide-ranging schools and education projects run on-site, mainly in the 'glass class' greenhouse.

St Andrews Garden Centre
199a South Street,
St Andrews, Fife, KY16 9EE
(map, pp. 116–117)

Brian Rogers
Monday–Saturday: 9am–5.15pm.
Sunday: 10am–5pm
A small opening near the west end of South St, St Andrews
T: 01334 473342
F: 01334 477060
E: brian.clara@btinternet.com
www.standrewsgarden
centre.co.uk

St Andrews Garden Centre

This small garden centre and florists' opened in 1982, on the site of an old bakery garden which had been overgrown with rhubarb and apple trees. You'd never know it was there as you step into a narrow alley off St Andrews' South St into the close behind to find it open out into numerous rooms as well as an outdoor plant area. The landscape side of the business was sold in 2007 and the garden centre is also up for sale as Mr Rogers would like to retire. The floristry shop looked impressive when I popped my head in.

Steading (The), Hillhead

Fiona Chapman has been developing this 2½-acre garden, created out of a field, since 1992. Behind the converted farm steading, the sloping garden has a vegetable plot at the top and the planting is in a series of beds, some terraced, which end at the bottom of the slope with two ponds and a spiral-pruned conifer. This is a really well-planted garden, packed with interesting plants; the rock/gravel beds and terraces are outstanding. Structure and shelter are provided by the wide selection of shrubs, trees and conifers including a fine monkey puzzle. This garden is definitely one to look out for in future. Fiona clearly has gardening in her genes as her sister has created the fine garden at Aiket Castle in Ayrshire.

Steading (The), Hillhead
Hillhead, Yetts O' Muckhart,
FK14 7JT
(*map, pp. 116–117*)

David and Fiona Chapman
SGS 1 day per year, groups
welcome by appointment; ££
At the fork on the A91/A823 on
south east side of the road at
Yetts O' Muckhart, turn off M90
at Kinross or Dumfermline
T: 01259 781559
E: david.fiona.chapman@
gmail.com

Stirling Castle King's Knot Garden

Not so much a garden, but more of the 'ghost' of one, the King's Knot was one of the first formal gardens of its type in Scotland, which Jenny Uglow dates to 1502 and 1540, latterly for James V and his French wife Mary of Guise. It is interesting that the garden had already largely disappeared by 1724–25 when Daniel Defoe was on his Scottish tour. He wrote of it:

> In the park, adjoining to the castle, were formerly large gardens, how fine they were I cannot say; the figure of the walks and grass-plats [*sic*] remains plain to be seen, they are very old fashioned; but I suppose the gardens might be thought fine, as gardens were then; particularly they had not then the usage of adorning their gardens with ever-greens, trimmed and shaped; trees espaliered into hedges and such-like, as now. They had, indeed, statues and busts, vases, and fountains, flowers and fruit; but we make gardens fine now

**Stirling Castle King's
Knot Garden**
Stirling, FK8 1EJ
(*map, pp. 116–117*)

Historic Scotland
Visible from road and
Stirling Castle; free
Best views from Stirling Castle

many ways, which those ages had no genius for; as by scrouls, embroidery, pavilions, terrasses and slopes, pyramids and high espaliers, and a thousand ornaments, which they had no notion of.

All that remains today are the earthworks which you can spot below the castle cliffs next to the link to the A811. Locals call it 'the cup and saucer'. Visitors to Stirling Castle can get the best view of it from the nineteenth-century Queen Anne Garden and the Bowling Green Walk, planted with roses, perennials and annuals next to the walls of the castle.

Strathmore Cottage

This is the garden of fruit expert and well-known gardening personality Willie Duncan and his partner Barbara Whitelaw, who have collected an astonishing range of fruit trees in their garden including apples, cherries, pears and plums. Willie is a fruit evangelist and if you are lucky enough to visit the garden at apple time, you are likely to have to try a large number of apples. The garden is much larger than you'd expect for a cottage of this size and goes on for ever along winding paths. There are views across the Forth and to the Pentland hills beyond.

Strathmore Cottage
Drumeldrie, by Upper Largo,
Fife KY8 6JD
(*map, pp. 116–117*)

Willie Duncan and
Barbara Whitelaw
Limited number of groups
by appointment.
Directions supplied when
arranging visit
T: 01333 360283

Teasses House

Teasses is situated on one the highest points in eastern Fife and the panoramic views all around the garden are extraordinary, south over the Forth to Arthur's Seat and the Pentlands beyond and north to Ben Lawers and Schiehallion on the horizon. It is windy up here so the 50 acres of parkland and gardens are surrounded by conifer and sycamore woods, with some mature beech and oak which give some shelter to the plantings within. The partially walled garden has a long green-

Teasses House
Estate Office, Teasses Estate,
By Ceres, Leven, Fife, KY8 5PG
(map, pp. 116–117)

Sir Fraser and Lady Morrison
SGS, also to groups by
appointment with guided tours
by gardeners; ££
Between Ceres and Largo,
signpost on the road. Turn off
A916 onto B road to New Gilston
and Woodside. Left at T-junction,
through first crossroads,
entrance by 2nd crossroads.
Sign Teasses Estate, follow
tarmac road to estate office
T: 01334 828048
E: joanie@teasses.com;
bilsonrobert@hotmail.com

house at the top with a freely fruiting vine in one section. This garden
is largely used for the production of cut flowers for the house and
there are borders of peonies, phlox and anemones and banks of pink
and white *Echinacea* as well as a wide range of hydrangeas and some
beautifully trained apples and pears which are the work of gardener
Bob Bilson. The woodland garden follows a ridge behind the house
and is filled with rhododendrons and azaleas and several small feature
gardens, dedicated to Sir Fraser's daughters. Removal of the mass of
sycamore would improve the woodland considerably and encourage
better flowering and plant growth. The main drive is bounded by
lawns planted with cut-leaved beech, leading back to the front of the
Victorian Baronial turreted house where Sir Fraser used his
construction machinery to build his 'ravine garden', designed by
David Redmore. This is impressive and unusual planting, a series of
narrow curved blocks of plants, like feathers on a wing, with purple
and blue perennials: *Nepeta, Salvia, Perovskia,* backed with white roses
and tall grasses: a bold, almost futuristic statement, a bit Hollywood
for sure, on a grand scale. A swimming-pool building is surrounded
by a series of ponds and behind this, in a tree-surrounded hollow,
once a Victorian midden, is Sir Fraser's Garden, a peaceful space lined
with rhododendrons, *Hydrangea, Geranium, Gunnera* and several
Parrotia, another unexpected but pleasing planting combination.
Teasses is gardening on the grand scale and gardens and policies cover
50 acres; one of eastern Scotland's most ambitious recent garden
creations; it is well-designed and is a significant collection of plants.
Tours for groups can be arranged. Allow around two hours to see
everything.

The Linns
Sheriffmuir, Dunblane,
Stirling, FK15 0LP
(map, pp. 116–117)

Evelyn and Lewis Stevens
By appointment to groups
and individuals; ££
At main roundabout in centre of
Dunblane, up Glen Road (signed
Sheriffmuir), 3rd turn on left, 2
miles, track on right (signed
'The Linns'). House is out of sight
in a wood 1/3 mile from the road.
If you reach Sheriffmuir Inn
you have gone 1 mile too far.
T: 01786 822295
E: evelyn@thelinns.org.uk
www.meconopsis.org

The Linns

Evelyn Stevens is well known all over Scotland as the champion of
blue *Meconopsis*. Several years back she determined to sort out the
confusion of forms and names of the blue poppy species and hybrids.
To that end, the Meconopsis Group (website listed in contact details)
was founded. The Linns lies at high altitude in the windswept hills
above Dunblane and is a testing place for growing any plants. Built in
1985, the house is now surrounded by trees, without which gardening
would be well-nigh impossible. The grassy paths lead between island
beds with trees such as cherry and laburnum, underplanted with
hellebores, hostas, peonies and of course huge drifts of up to 100
Meconopsis selections which are stunning in early June when they
reach their crescendo. As well as the NCCPG National Collection of
Meconopsis (large perennial species and cultivars) there is also a
collection of over 100 snowdrops. A tunnel house and courtyard are
filled with divisions of some of the best forms, which are offered for
sale to visitors.

The Murrel

Though little-known, this is a historically important garden and is a combination of striking architecture and good planting. The house was designed by architect Frank Deas c. 1908 as his weekend retreat, and looks like a tiled Tuscan farmhouse. A friend of Robert Lorimer, Deas was evidently much influenced by the Lutyens–Jekyll garden/house combinations. Jekyll repaid the compliment by including The Murrel in her book *Gardens for Small Country Houses*. Deas designed the whole as a seamless piece with two buttressed terraces, a courtyard, walled gardens and greenhouses. The gardens have since been extended and much of the current planting was done in the 1970s and 1980s by then owner David Nicholl. The Murrel is fortunate in having had a succession of owners who have maintained and improved the gardens. Current owners Alistair and Trisha Bowen and their gardener are very much part of this tradition, renovating and changing with skill. The upper terrace provides a sheltered site for tender plants while the lower terrace contains a recently planted peony border and a herbaceous border backed by climbing roses, *Ceanothus* and other wall shrubs. Below this is a large *Cornus kousa*, an orchard and wildflower meadow. The west of the house has a fine recently replanted sloping rock garden with mixed alpines and some ornamental dwarf conifers. The walled garden is divided into 'rooms' with box hedges and there is also an inner courtyard which adjoins the old servants' quarters, also well planted. The walls are lined with climbers and there are areas for fruit and vegetables and the main axis is an impressive white border featuring a collection of *Cistus*. Below

The Murrel
Aberdour, Burntisland,
KY3 0RN
(*map, pp. 116–117*)

Alistair and Trisha Bowen
By arrangement early May–early
June, Wednesday 2–5pm; £££
1½km (1 mile) north of Aberdour
just south of Cullaloe Reservoir,
A987
T: 01383 860156

this is a sunken formal rose garden leading to the burn which runs west, lined with primulas and other waterside favourites, first through a rock garden of dwarf rhododendrons, now rather over-shaded, via a pond to a paddock with undulating sides, which is being planted up with spring bulbs and as a woodland garden with rhododendrons which have outgrown their space in the walled garden. Murrel Cottage, at the end of the drive, is likely to be open under Scotland's Garden Scheme in the future.

University of Dundee Botanic Garden
Riverside Drive, Dundee, DD2 1QH
(*map, pp. 116–117*)

Alasdair Hood (curator)
Daily: March–October 10am–4.30 pm, November–February 10am–3.30pm; ££
Off Riverside Drive beside the River Tay, which runs past Dundee airport towards Invergowrie. Turn up the hill at roundabout, signed.
T: 01382 381190
F: 01382 640574
E: botanicgardens@dundee.ac.uk
www.dundeebotanicgardens.co.uk
Coffee shop: Sunday–Wednesday 9am–8pm, Monday and Tuesday 9am–4.30pm; plant sales

University of Dundee Botanic Garden

Dundee Botanic Garden is a 9½-hectare garden founded in 1971, perched on the hillside above the airport overlooking the Tay, containing a collection of plants from all over the world. The structure of the garden was put in place by first curator Eddie Kemp. Long and narrow in shape, full of now maturing trees, it is a popular place for Dundee's citizens and the car park was full on a Sunday morning in late October, which shows what a draw the garden is even outside peak times of year. The main collections include Australasian plants: fine groves of *Eucalyptus*, a large collection of *Olearia* and related southern hemisphere daisies, a notable collection of conifers, and perhaps most important, a selection of native plant communities on a considerable scale, from montane to coastal and including beechwood, pine, birch forest, planted by former curator Les Bisset. The far end of the garden has a collection of Asian plants including rhododendrons and magnolias. The garden's showcase and outstanding feature is the Garden of Evolution, a new project designed by curator Alasdair Hood which will demonstrate land plant

evolution from green algae, via mosses, ferns and conifers to flowering plants. The slate dry stone walling and sculpture was completed in 2008–09 by the garden staff who became more and more confident as they went along, creating memorable patterns and swirls in the undulating sections of walls. As long as the planting matches the ambition of the structure, this looks an excellent new development. The glasshouses contain a collection of tropical and warm-temperate plants. There is also a small café, gift shop and plant sales area. For a botanic garden, the labelling is erratic and this really should be addressed as a matter of urgency. The garden's principal function was to supply plant material for teaching and research within the University of Dundee but as this role is no longer required, the funding of the garden is under threat and the long-term future of the garden hangs in the balance.

  [WC]

Var. Scotica

This company supplies Scottish native wildflower, native tree and shrub seed and also offers a range of forestry and arboricultural services. They have harvested seed from threatened native plants such as montane willow *Salix lapponum* from some of the few remaining high-level sites. Dave MacIntyre practises low-intervention tree care techniques developed in the US, which work with the tree's biology.

Var. Scotica
Lower Balnakilly, Kirkmichael,
Perthshire, PH10 7NB
(*map, pp. 116–117*)

Dave MacIntyre
T: 01250 881336
F: 01250 881336
www.varscotica.com

Vistana
'Vistana', Dundee Road, Forfar
(*map, pp. 116–117*)

Mr A. G. Webster
Not officially open
From south turn off A90 at
first Forfar exit. Garden on
right-hand side not long
after entering the town

Vistana

I stumbled upon this surprising garden on my way to Pitmuies, not far away. It is not open to the public but can be enjoyed from the roadside on the Dundee road into Forfar. The whole garden consists of hundreds of clipped conifers with shrubs in between and the occasional clump of pampas grass around immaculate lawns. There is not a weed in sight, with bare earth under the conifers. It is obviously a labour of love, it seems to be from another era and it is not my cup of tea, but striking and memorable it certainly is. The garden design was a happy accident. Owner Mr Webster asked a landscaper to 'do something' with the garden and this was the result. The clipping must take days every year.

Wemyss Castle
East Wemyss,
Fife, KY1 4TE
(*map, pp. 116–117*)

Michael and Charlotte Wemyss
SGS 1 day for bulbs, or by
appointment, Monday–Friday; ££
Off A955 between Dysart and
Buckhaven/Leven entrance in
Coaltown of Wemyss. From A915
1 mile east of Kirkcaldy turn
south onto unclassified road to
Coaltown of Wemyss, after 1 mile
at T-junction turn left into village,
after c. 500 yards opposite
bowling green turn right into
castle driveway, half mile down
drive take left-hand fork and
follow signs
T: 01592 652181
E: gardens@wemyss-em.com
www.wemysscastlegardens.com

Wemyss Castle

One of the many great things about this garden is the complementary enthusiasms of its owners: Michael is a tree fan, studied forestry and has planted hundreds of thousands of trees on the estate as well as collecting and planting rare and interesting trees in the garden. Charlotte is into roses, clematis and perennials. They have been restoring and replanting their 6-acre walled garden since 1993. It is filled with plants laid out with exuberance and on a grand scale, which you have to do if your garden is this large. He gardens the upper part and she the larger lower part. You get a completely different tour of the gardens depending on which of the two is your guide. Both are excellent and knowledgeable company but won't answer questions about the other's patch and there is evidently a low-level guerrilla war between the two on certain garden decisions. The high garden walls, once heated by furnaces in order to produce fresh fruit almost 12 months of the year, were fuelled by coal from the family coal mines nearby. Apparently one year in the nineteenth century, over 100 tons of coal were used to produce some of the

world's most expensive fruit; the gardener who authorised this was sacked for his extravagance! Those same walls are now covered with one of best-maintained collections of climbing roses in the country. Gardener George Dryburgh prunes and ties them in every year, ensuring that they are well clothed to the base. On the walls and clambering through many of the roses are a *de facto* national collection of *Clematis montana*, which really shows how good these can be with almost unlimited space; most people spend half their lives hacking them into some sort of control. The walled garden is divided by hedges and walls into several sections. Dividing two parts is the remains of a classical orangery which lost its roof to a Second World War exploding mine on the beach below. The walls now support a range of rambler roses with a slightly bizarre box parterre 'indoors' below. Another axis is a path lined with pleached hornbeams which leads downhill to a pond with a fountain in the centre. This part of the garden is filled with colour-coordinated perennial beds. Charlotte described her passion to Antoinette Galbraith in *Scotland on Sunday*: 'I didn't have any grand intentions. I simply wanted to create a garden that was peaceful, serene and romantic, heaving with good smells.' The imposing castle, the oldest parts of which date back to the thirteenth century, has woods on its three landward sides (the fourth side is a steep cliff down to the Forth estuary below) which are filled with spring bulbs: including snowdrops, aconites, *Scilla, Chionadoxa, Narcissus,* bluebells and, most strikingly, carpets of *Erythronium revolutum* on a grand scale, planted in the 1970s by Michael Wemyss' grandfather but which spread dramatically when the woods were thinned. To encourage further patches, Charlotte scatters the seed around in autumn. This garden is worth several visits: for the bulbs in April, for the *Clematis montana* in early June and the roses and perennials later in the summer. The opening arrangements are somewhat ad hoc but if you look on the website or email Wemyss, they will let you know what the latest arrangements are.

  WC

Wester Cloquhat
Wester Cloquhat, Bridge of Cally,
Blairgowrie, PH10 7JP
(*map, pp. 116–117*)

Brigadier and Mrs Christopher
Dunphie
SGS 1 day every 2nd year; ££
Turn off A93 just north of
Bridge of Cally and follow
signs for ½ mile
T: 01250 886320
www.cloquhat.co.uk/gardens
Teas on SGS open days

Wester Cloquhat

This garden boasts a fine situation with views down to the raging
River Ericht and the hills around Bridge of Cally. 1947 saw the first
plantings of trees, rhododendrons and azaleas by Colonel and Mrs
Dunphie. Their son Christopher has continued planting, adding
alpines and perennials, building a terrace and more recently an
enlarged water garden.

Wester Dalqueich

The Roulstons moved from Northern Ireland in the 1960s and have
been at Wester Dalqueich for 30 years. At 600ft in the Ochils, this is a
challenging climate, wetter (15 inches in January 2008), windier and
colder than most surrounding areas but with good drainage, so once
the shelter belts had been created, the Roulstons were able to grow a
huge range of plants. The garden is a series of interconnected areas
around the house, 3½ acres in total. On the far side of the house from
the entrance a bed is filled with dwarf rhododendrons and envy-
inspiring clumps of red and white *Trillium*. From here a circular path
leads back through informal woodland filled with rhododendrons and
azaleas, underplanted with *Hosta*, ferns and other perennials. This
slopes down to the burn, where a clearing features trees such as a
weeping beech. The path leads back on the other side of the house
into a perennial gravel section featuring three armillaries. Back across
the drive in front of the house are two sections of garden. In the
foreground are raised and gravel beds filled with *Celmisia* and other
choice alpines, backed with conifers and a bold clipped ball of golden
box. Here as elsewhere in the garden are sculptures, both wood and
stone-carved animals, totem pole-like wood carvings and some
contemporary metalwork. This section is dominated by a multi-
stemmed *Acer griseum* and a central planting of three handsome
white-barked birch under which graze three sculpted goats. The final
section is a paddock arboretum with an unusual dense hedgerow of
bamboo, *Rosa rugosa* and laurels which shelters a collection of trees
and conifers. This is an exceptional garden, packed with choice
material, well planted, full of excellent design elements and humour.
It has an extremely long season of interest and would be well worth
seeing anytime from spring to autumn. I was really impressed and
want to go back.

Wester Dalqueich
Carnbo, Kinross,
Fife, KY13 0NU
(*map, pp. 116–117*)

Mr and Mrs D. S. Roulston
1 June–31 August by
appointment; ££
Off A91, near Carnbo, leave M90
at J7, follow signs to Yetts O'
Muckhart. Leave A91 at Carnbo
Village Hall, west of Milnathort and
travel north for ½ mile
T: 01577 840229

Willowhill

This is a fine young garden, started in 2000 and covering 3 acres with a wide collection of plants and some winning colour combinations. Around the house a series of sections divided by walls and fences contains mixed borders of bulbs, shrubs, alpines on a stepped terrace and herbaceous perennials as well as a vegetable plot with raised beds of asparagus and other delights. To the north of the garden is a grassland area with wildlife pond and trees. It sometimes opens with the old parkland landscape of Tayfield House, nearby.

Willowhill
Forgan, Newport-on-Tay, DD6 8HA
(*map, pp. 116–117*)

Eric Wright and Sally Lorimore
SGS; ££
1½ miles south of Tay Road
Bridge. Take the B995 to Newport
off the Forgan roundabout.
Willowhill is the first house on the
LHS next to the Forgan Arts
Centre

Wormistoune House

Wormistoune or Wormistone is a seventeenth-century castle and walled garden which has been lavishly restored and extended in recent years. The white baronial castle is approached over a car-wrecking hump-backed bridge. To the south is a maturing water/pond garden and to the north of the castle a large mosaic Celtic cross has been built into the lawn. But it is the walled garden, adjoining the castle which is the main event here, entered through a beautiful wrought iron gate made by local metalworker Miles Auchenleck, who made other fixtures round the garden. The walled garden is divided into several 'rooms'. The main axis leads along an impressive yew-backed double herbaceous border, with an attractive path of pebbles inset in concrete and paving, to an arch with a wooden gate forming a striking moon window. Both from the outside looking in and from the garden out to the wider world outside, this is an excellent design feature which is on the cover of this book. On either side of the moon window are two moorish-style rectangular ponds joined by a rill, and in each corner, newly constructed pavilions, based on those at Melville House, which were awarded the Georgian Group architectural award in 2005. There is a fine box and lavender parterre next to some buildings on the outside of the walled garden walls. The whole garden is a masterclass of hard-landscaping effects: walls and buildings, paving, cobbles, coloured gravel, often in contrasting combinations. On one side of the walled

Wormistoune House
Crail, Fife, KY10 3XH
(*map, pp. 116–117*)

James and Gemma McCallum
1 day SGS or by appointment; ££
Off A917 Crail–St Andrews
road south of Carnbo, just north
of Crail
T: 01333 450356
E: info@wormistoune.com
www.wormistoune.com
Teas on SGS days

garden are four huge *Griselinia* underneath which are ferns and other shade-lovers. Next to the castle a contemporary swirling box and white gravel parterre is designed to be appreciated from the upper floors of the castle. Wormistoune is a fine combination of restoration, imaginative hard-landscaping and planting, and is simultaneously a traditional and a contemporary garden.

Yellowcraig Wood
near Causewayhead, Stirling
(*map, pp. 116–117*)

Mrs Rosemary Leckie
SGS 1 Sunday in May; ££
Take the B998 past the Wallace
Monument on your right.
Turn left just before the next
roundabout and go straight along
this road. Park at Logie Kirk
T: 07906 838205
E: rleckie@tiscali.co.uk

Yellowcraig Wood

Rosmary Leckie purchased the 70 acres of ancient woodland with a mixture of trees including oak, ash, birch, beech, gean, rowan, Scots pines and larches in the late 1980s. The wood is famous for its carpets of bluebells and the fine views from Witches Crag and Yellow Crag. The plantings have been augmented with trees, shrubs and naturalised daffodils. The lower part of the wood is on a very steep hill so take stout boots. It is worth combining this walk with a visit to the Wallace Monument nearby.

Argyll

This large western Scottish county consists of a number of peninsulas divided by numerous sea lochs and is Scotland's centre of woodland gardening; arguably the world's finest collection of such gardens, perhaps only Cornwall can compete. Rhododendrons and azaleas dominate, so most of the gardens are at their best in spring. Often as early as February there is colour to be seen from early rhododendrons and snowdrops and many have fine displays of bulbs too, later in the season. The flowering in most woodland gardens lasts well into June and thankfully the vicious Argyll midge tends not to be out in force till after the main flowering season. Many Argyll gardens have fine collections of trees too, examples include Ardkinglas, Benmore and Crarae, so it is well worth visiting for autumn colour. Many of the gardens are members of the Glorious Gardens of Argyll and Bute group who have a good website (www.gardens-of-argyll.co.uk), but no season ticket scheme. One of the pleasures of this area is the numerous fine island gardens; getting to them on scenic ferry journeys is part of the attraction. Amongst the best are Jura House (Jura), Achamore (Gigha), Torosay (Mull) and Colonsay House (Colonsay). Gardens on Bute are covered in the West Central section as they are usually accessed from Wemyss Bay, though there is also a ferry from Colintraive on the Cowal peninsula. Good bases for exploration in Argyll include Dunoon, Tarbert, Lochgilphead, Inveraray, Oban or Port Appin, all of which have a good range of hotels, B&Bs and eateries. For summer visitors some of the best gardens to visit include An Cala, Ardchattan Priory, Arduaine, Strachur and Jura House.

Argyll gardens occasionally open under SGS, not listed separately, include Knock Cottage, Lochgair; Ardno, Cairndow, Colintraive gardens, Crinan House, Shore Villages by Dunoon.

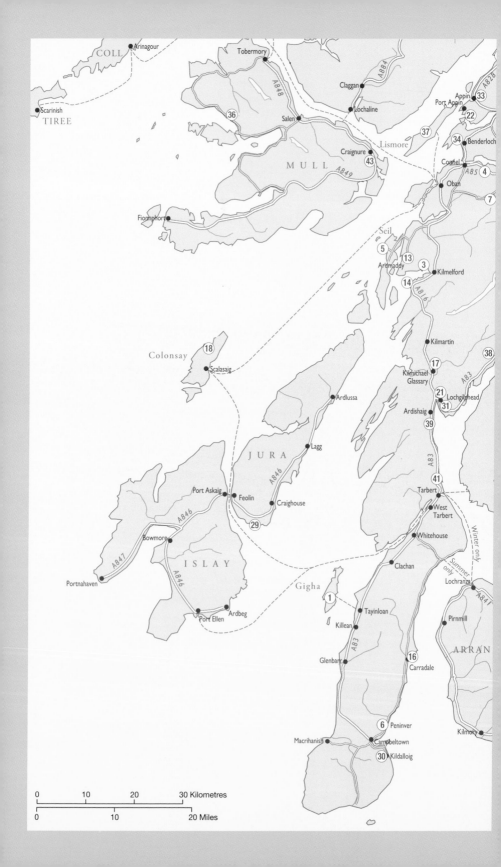

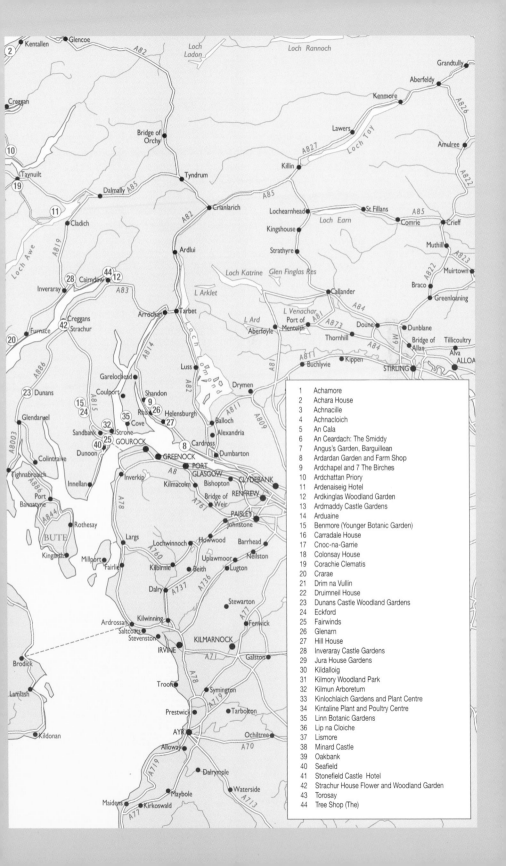

1 Achamore
2 Achara House
3 Achnacille
4 Achnacloich
5 An Cala
6 An Ceardach: The Smiddy
7 Angus's Garden, Barguillean
8 Ardardan Garden and Farm Shop
9 Ardchapel and 7 The Birches
10 Ardchattan Priory
11 Ardenaiseig Hotel
12 Ardkinglas Woodland Garden
13 Ardmaddy Castle Gardens
14 Arduaine
15 Benmore (Younger Botanic Garden)
16 Carradale House
17 Cnoc-na-Garrie
18 Colonsay House
19 Corachie Clematis
20 Crarae
21 Drim na Vullin
22 Druimneil House
23 Dunans Castle Woodland Gardens
24 Eckford
25 Fairwinds
26 Glenarn
27 Hill House
28 Inveraray Castle Gardens
29 Jura House Gardens
30 Kildalloig
31 Kilmory Woodland Park
32 Kilmun Arboretum
33 Kinlochlaich Gardens and Plant Centre
34 Kintaline Plant and Poultry Centre
35 Linn Botanic Gardens
36 Lip na Cloiche
37 Lismore
38 Minard Castle
39 Oakbank
40 Seafield
41 Stonefield Castle Hotel
42 Strachur House Flower and Woodland Garden
43 Torosay
44 Tree Shop (The)

Achamore
Island of Gigha, Kintyre,
Argyll, PA41 7AD
(map, pp. 220–21)

Isle of Gigha Heritage Trust/NTS
All year round, dawn until dusk;
££ + boat
Follow A83 south of Tarbert,
down Kintyre to Tayinloan.
Signposted 1½ miles from ferry
terminal. Ferry takes 20 mins.
On Gigha follow signs to the
gardens. 1 mile
T: 01583 505275
F: 01583 505244
E: gardens@gigha.org.uk
www.gigha.org.uk
T: 01583 505254 (Gigha hotel)
Lunch and dinner at Gigha hotel

Achamore

This is one of Scotland's more accessible island gardens, only a short boat ride from the mainland. James Horlick, whose company made the famous hot drink, bought the 6 × 1½-mile island of Gigha in 1944 principally in order to create a garden on it around Achamore House. With advice from James Russell, then at Sunningdale, James Horlick set about planting the shelter and rhododendrons. Achamore Gardens, though rather windswept, are virtually frost free and they are full of rhododendrons, azaleas, camellias and other exotic plants and trees, particularly from the southern hemisphere, such as *Metrosideros* (Rata), *Clianthus* and *Telopea*. The plantings extend to approximately 50 acres of sycamore woodlands and there are winding paths through them which connect a series of clearings or 'glades'. The large walled garden is divided in two: the southern end contains herbaceous borders, a pond garden and a large Mexican pine, the northern section contains some fine conifers. Children will enjoy the bamboo tunnel. Try to get a copy of the garden map to help you navigate to the small hill south of the walled garden, which has the best views, both of Gigha itself, and out towards Islay and Jura. When Sir James died in 1970, his rather unusual bequest left some of the plant collections, but not the garden itself, to the National Trust for Scotland. The NTS have probably had some misgivings accepting this as they have had to organise looking after the plants on land which was not theirs. Some of the plants were taken to Brodick, others remain on Gigha. Thankfully, continuity in the gardens was maintained by talented and dedicated head gardener Malcolm MacNeill, who looked after the place for more than 45 years before retiring in 2006. Micky Little, formerly at Castle Drogo, is now in charge and he intends to

restore some of the wonderful views to surrounding islands now blocked by overgrown plantings. The island of Gigha passed through a series of sometimes irresponsible owners, causing considerable hardship to those who lived on the island. On 15 March 2002, the island was purchased in a historic buy-out by its inhabitants and is now owned and managed by the Isle of Gigha Heritage Trust. Check out their website to look at the various island initiatives now taking place, including wind-power generation. The garden can be visited on a daytrip from Tayinloan, with up to 7 ferries per day making the 20-minute trip. Alternatively stay the night and enjoy the hospitality of the islanders. It is a romantic place. For ferry details, tel. Calmac 0800 066 5000, *www.calmac.co.uk.*

Achara House

This very handsome white baronial house, attributed to Robert Lorimer, is surrounded by an impressive and extensive collection of rhododendrons, azaleas and other woodland plants. These are planted in several sections: in front of the house, surrounding a pond behind the house and in an informal hillside garden, where they are doing surprisingly well without much shelter. There are fine views over Loch Linnhe to the brooding hills of Morvern and Ardnamurchan peninsula from up here. Both the lodge house and Achara House itself (which sleeps 10) are available for weekly rent and Achara would make a good base for exploring the area.

Achara House
Duror of Appin, Argyll,
PA38 4BW
(*map, pp. 220–21*)

Mr and Mrs Alastair
Macpherson of Pitmain
By appointment; £
A828 1 mile south of Duror,
7 miles south of Ballachulish
Bridge, 5 miles north of Appin
T: 07831 423059
E: mafmacpherson@aol.com

Achnacille
Kilmelford, by Oban, Argyll,
PA34 4XD
(*map, pp. 220–21*)

Mr and Mrs Robin Asbury
SGS 1 weekend and by
appointment; £
1½ miles from Kilmelford (A816)
on road signposted 'Degnish'
T: 01852 200377
E: robin.asbury@btopenworld.com

Achnacille

Not far from Arduaine, at the head of Loch Melfort, this 1-acre
garden, right on the seashore, was created by keen gardener Elizabeth
Asbury and her husband – and garden project manager – Robin, out
of a bare rocky hillside a few years ago. There are fine views of the
yachts anchored in the bay, and down the loch. A series of rock
terraces and island beds are planted with all manner of trees, shrubs,
grasses and herbaceous and there is a pond and streamside planting in
front of the house. Despite the very exposed site which saw *Escallonia*
hedges defoliated with salt spray in 2008, this garden has a lushly
planted display of perennials in summer, in various colour-planned
island beds. Eye-catching features included the *Akebia* arch and a
chain of linked weeping cherries along the drive side.

Achnacloich

This garden, sited on a promontory on Loch Etive, near Oban is a fine example of the 'Argyll garden', with several impressive walled viewpoints looking out over the loch with the hills behind. The extensive woodlands are filled with rhododendrons, magnolias, hydrangeas and other shrubs, underplanted with spring bulbs. The garden boasts a series of ponds, veteran Japanese maples and in late summer some fine *Eucryphia*, The yew terraces on the south side of the Victorian Baronial house are planted with roses, clematis and *Ceanothus*. The small walled garden is used for fruit and vegetables.

Achnacloich
Connel, Oban, Argyll, PA37 1PR
(*map, pp. 220–21*)

Mrs T.E. Nelson
March–October: 10am–6pm; £
Off A85 between Taynuilt and
Connel
T: 01631 710796

An Cala

Don't be concerned that you need a boat to reach the Isle of Seil. Unlikely as it may sound, there is a small bridge over the Atlantic Ocean to get there. An Cala was designed by Thomas Mawson in the early 1930s, using 30,000 tons of topsoil brought from Ayrshire as ballast for the boats coming to collect slate from quarries nearby. By the time Thomas and Sheila Downie bought the garden in the 1980s it was very run-down and they have transformed it into one of the best privately owned west coast gardens. You can hardly fail to fall for the attractive white and pale blue An Cala house, the backdrop to many of the best vistas in the garden. The garden is constructed on a series of slate terraces leading up the hillside. From the higher points

An Cala
Ellenabeich, Isle of Seil,
Argyll, PA34 4RF
(*map, pp. 220–21*)

Mrs Sheila Downie
Daily: 1 April–31 October,
10am–6pm; ££
Signed to Easdale on the B844
single track road, 16 miles
south of Oban off the A816,
Lochgilphead road
T: 01852 300237
F: 01852 300237
www.gardens-of-argyll.co.uk
Catering in the village nearby

of the site there are great views over Easdale and neighbouring islands. A terrace, planted with 'Mt Fuji' white cherries, has a rectangular pool and fir-cone-decorated summer house at the far end. An Cala's rhododendrons are mostly dwarf species, hybrids and evergreen azaleas planted on the rock garden. The *Good Gardens Guide* says: 'This is how rhododendrons and azaleas should be planted, enhancing rather than dominating the picture'. This is a garden with a long season with large numbers of perennials, clematis and Poulson roses to provide colour in summer and autumn. A series of wire grazing sheep will raise a smile. This is a must-visit garden, full of great design, with masses of interesting plants packed into a relatively small space. The word 'charming' was coined with An Cala in mind, and many people have told me that this is their favourite Argyll garden.

Don't miss Easdale island a few hundred yards off-shore, reached by a little boat which runs back and forth most of the day. This charming former slate-mining island has a pub with good food, a great little museum and some lovely cottage gardens too, including one right on the beach with extremely challenging growing conditions, as waves can break over the house. *Rosa rugosa* and grasses rule. Easdale is one of my favourite places in Scotland and I once came second in the World Stone Skimming championships held there in September each year.

An Ceardach: The Smiddy
Peninver, Campbeltown,
PA28 6QP
(*map, pp. 220–21*)

Christine and Livingston Russell
April–September: by appointment
On the B842 just south of
Peninver, 3 miles north of
Campbeltown
T. 01586 551762
E: christine.russell@virgin.net

An Ceardach: The Smiddy

Situated by the sea near Peninver on the east Kintyre coast just north of Campbeltown, it is surprising how well the trees and shelter have established, on what is essentially a raised beach sloping down to the sea, with a huge range of bulbs, rhododendrons and perennials beneath. The garden is full of fine landscaping using dry stonewalling and other materials, stone and glass sculpture and a spherical glass

water feature. A burn falls down a series of stone-built waterfalls. Worth visiting at any time of year but probably best in spring for its rhododendrons and bulbs. There are good beaches below the garden. The garden is not suitable for wheelchairs as it is very steep with many steps. The B842, which runs up the east side of Kintyre, is a switchback road with fine views across to Arran.

Angus's Garden, Barguillean

Angus's Garden is set in naturalised woodlands around the shores of a loch in Glen Lonan and covers 9 acres. The garden is planted in memory of Angus Macdonald, who was killed in Cyprus in 1956 by EOKA terrorists. Plantings include many varieties of rhododendrons and azaleas, and other flowering shrubs and trees. There are three colour-coded walks with approximate walking times. At its best in April, May and early June when the numerous rhododendrons are in full flower, though at any time of year it's a peaceful place to walk, with fine views of Loch Etive and Ben Cruachan to the east.

Angus's Garden, Barguillean
Taynuilt, Argyll, PH35 1HY
(*map, pp. 220–21*)

Sean Honeyman
Daily: 9am–dusk; £
2 miles along Glen Lonan Road,
turn off A85 at Taynuilt,
Tyndrum–Oban road
T: 01866 822335/822333
E: info@barguillean.co.uk
www.barguillean.co.uk

Ardardan Garden and Farm Shop
Ardardan Estate, Cardross,
Argyll, G82 5HD
(*map, pp. 220–21*)

Montgomery family
Tuesday–Sunday: 10am–5pm
A814 between Cardross and
Helensburgh
T : 01389 849188
E: enquiries@ardardan.co.uk
www.ardardan.co.uk
Tearoom
10am (11am Sunday)–4pm

Ardardan Garden and Farm Shop

This is a small Clydeside garden centre, walled garden and farm shop with good plants, a walled display garden and snowdrop walk, well-presented local/Scottish produce and a very popular tea room/café. May, Grant and Susan Montgomery seem to know most of their customers by name; it's a well-run, friendly place run by farmers with years of experience in the egg business. Geilston is more or less opposite the entrance to Ardardan and Glenarn is nearby.

Ardchapel and 7 The Birches
Shandon, Helensburgh,
Argyll and Bute, G84 8NP
(*map, pp. 220–21*)

Mr and Mrs J.S. Lang
SGS 1 day per year with
7 The Birches (nearby); ££
4 miles north of Helensburgh on
A814. Parking on service road
below houses

Ardchapel and 7 The Birches

Ardchapel is a well-established 3½-acre garden overlooking the Gare Loch, with mature trees such as a huge wellingtonia, a woodland burn, planted with rhododendrons, azaleas and camellias, a flower and vegetable garden and perennial borders. It sometimes opens with 7 The Birches next door.

Ardchattan Priory

The priory at Ardchattan was built in 1230 for the Valliscaulian monks, a strict order who largely cut themselves off from the outside world. This may be one of Scotland's oldest horticultural sites, as there is evidence of medieval monastic gardens. The priory became a private house after the Reformation and has been much altered and added to since, with the ruins of the original buildings still clearly visible next to the house. Plantings date from the Victorian era onwards, including trees, magnolias and rhododendrons, with a good display of perennials in front of the house and a wildflower meadow. The garden is at its best in summer. What I most enjoyed here was the small greenhouse absolutely crammed with Ardchattan gardener George Macnab's cactus collection. I'm not usually much of a fan, but this extraordinary display, lovingly maintained, is really worth a look. Access to the ruined chapel up the hill behind the car park is included in the admission price.

Ardchattan Priory
Bonawe, by Oban,
Argyll, PA37 1RQ
(*map, pp. 220–21*)

Mrs Sarah Troughton
Daily, April–end October:
9am–5pm ££, free to Historic
Houses Association members
10 miles north-east of Oban.
Cross Connel Bridge on the A828
north. First turning on the right,
(Bonawe) well-signed
T: 01796 481355
F: 01796 481211
E: sh.troughton@virgin.net
www.gardens-of-argyll.co.uk

Ardanaiseig Hotel

This William Burn-designed Scottish Baronial pile on the shores of Loch Awe was built by one of the Campbell clan and is now an up-market hotel. The extensive woodland garden is now rather a jungle of enormous rhododendrons and undergoing a long-term process of restoration. The views from the lawns over Loch Awe and its islands to Ben Lui are very fine and guests can arrange to arrive by boat. There are lots of impressive conifers: *Abies, Taxodium, Cryptomeria, Calocedrus,* under which are species and hybrid rhododendrons and azaleas. It does all look somewhat untameable, but no less spectacular for that; it is fun getting lost in amongst and under the American and Himalayan giants, with a carpet of bluebells and primroses beneath. The walled garden with curved walls contains a Judas tree (*Cercis*),

Ardanaiseig Hotel
Kilchrenan by Taynuilt,
Argyll, PA35 1HE
(*map, pp. 220–21*)

Benny Grey
Easter–end October; £
A85 to junction with B845,
follow to Kilchrenan Inn,
left to Ardanaiseig
T: 01866 833 333
F: 01866 833 222
E: info@ardanaiseig.com
www.ardanaiseig.com
Fine restaurant

229

greenhouses under restoration and beds of fruit and vegetables, used by the hotel. The latest planned development is for five turf-roofed rooms, buried deep in the hillside overlooking the loch. The 'hook and cook' courses for fishing and kitchen skills seem like a good idea and there are various activities in the Ardanaiseig Open Air Theatre in summer, weather and midges permitting.

Ardkinglas Woodland Garden
Ardkinglas Estate,
Cairndow, Argyll, PA26 8BH
map, pp. 220–21)

Ardkinglas Estate
Daylight hours, all year round
(Ardkinglas House and its private
gardens open by appointment); ££
In the village of Cairndow off
the A83 Loch Lomond to
Inveraray road
T: 01499 600261
F: 01499 600241
E: info@ardkinglas.com
www.ardkinglas.com
Loch Fyne Oyster Bar and
Argyll tree nursery nearby

Ardkinglas Woodland Garden

I think of Ardkinglas, not far from the shores of Loch Fyne, as the Gothic cathedral of west coast woodland gardens with its architectural structure of conifer trunks providing a high canopy. Under this, rhododendrons and other shrubs are planted on a steep hillside. While other woodland gardens reveal themselves via twisting paths through undergrowth, this one is open and uncluttered, with a great feeling of space and fine vistas from most of the paths. The conifers were planted in the nineteenth century by the Callender family who sold the estate to the Nobles in 1905. Sir John Noble and his son Michael planted the now mature rhododendrons. Highlights include five of Britain's tallest or largest conifers including a 200+ft *Abies grandis* (suffering from dieback and forming a new leader, it may have temporarily surrendered its champion's crown) and the gnarled mighty silver fir *Abies alba* with five separate trunks branching off it.

Nearby are some stunning huge pink and white *Rhododendron* 'Loderi' which perfume the bluebell-carpeted valley in May. For colour in the latter part of the year there is an extensive *Sorbus* glade which contains plantings of both native and Asian species and a considerable number of *Hydrangea*. There are lots of recent plantings by talented gardener Glynn Toplis who also manages the tree nursery, and the garden's labelling is pretty good. There are walks to the tree house built in an old ash tree and to a viewpoint which looks over Loch Fyne. Ardkinglas is a good place to spot red squirrels. The very fine Robert Lorimer-designed Ardkinglas House is open for guided tours (booking advisable), March–October, Friday only, at 2.30pm. The eighteenth-century 'house garden' is open on selected days or by prior arrangement and includes the 'Caspian' ornamental lake, a large D-shaped wall garden and the smaller Ladies' Garden with a good collection of deciduous azaleas. A fine garden loop in this area is Ardkinglas, Strachur and Benmore, which would be a good day's work. See also entry for 'Tree Shop' (see p. 254).

     [WC]

Ardmaddy Castle Gardens

Behind the Victorian castle, perched on a rock, lies the narrow walled garden at Ardmaddy. Straight lines of formal box hold back the rhododendron borders, the walls are covered with climbers including a fine, free-flowering *Wisteria,* and there are fine vegetable and fruit plantings. Behind this, following the stream, is a small planting of waterside plants and beyond this an extensive woodland with bluebells and mature species and hybrid rhododendrons. Some highlights when I visited in spring were the views from the driveside, the sheets of flower on *Rhododendron yunnanense* and the huge expanses of wild garlic. There are also great views out into the bay and the island of Torosay, in front of the castle. Owner Minette Struthers has spent the last 30 years restoring and redeveloping the garden with only minimal help and it is an impressive achievement.

   [WC]

Ardmaddy Castle Gardens
Balvicar, Oban, Argyll,
PA34 4QY
(*map, pp. 220–21*)

Minette Struthers
Gardens open all year round
dawn till dusk; ££
8 miles south of Oban A816, turn
right B844 sign Easdale. 4 miles
on turn left sign Ardmaddy,
1½ miles
T: 01852 300353
E: c.m.struthers@lineone.net
www.gardens-of-argyll.co.uk
Tigh an Truish Pub at
'Atlantic Bridge' 2 miles

Arduaine
Kilmelford, Oban,
Argyll, PA34 4XQ
(*map, pp. 220–21*)

NTS
9.30am to sunset, all year,
reception manned April–
September 9.30am–4.30pm; ££*,
free to Scottish Rhododendron
Society members
Just off the A816, midway
between Oban and Lochgilphead
(30 mins from each). The garden
shares an entrance with the
Loch Melfort Hotel
T: 01852 200366
F: 01852 200366
E: mwilkins@nts.org.uk
www.arduaine-garden.org.uk
and www.nts.org.uk
Bar and restaurant at Loch Melfort
Hotel by the carpark

Arduaine

Arduaine (pronounced 'Are-doo-knee'), one of the finest of the west coast's many woodland gardens, was established from 1903 onwards by tea planter James Campbell. Though the climate here is very mild, the windswept promontory required shelter, which was established with a mixed planting of conifers, cordylines and the dreaded *Rhododendron ponticum*. The garden was very much in decline when nurserymen brothers Edmund and Harry Wright bought Arduaine in 1971. They redesigned the lower garden, adding ponds and herbaceous plantings and considerably increased the rhododendron collection. The Wrights donated the garden to the National Trust for Scotland in 1992. As King Lear found out, if you give your kingdom away, you also give away your power. Sadly, the Wright brothers stayed put, in their home just over the garden fence, and then Edmund went rather publicly to war with the NTS as they took on the task of further evolving the garden. I think that at last a truce has more or less been declared. Arduaine is one of the most varied of the west coast gardens. In the lower garden around the ponds the primulas are particularly good and there are fine clumps of Chatham Island forget-me-not (*Myosotidium hortensia*). Summer sees the perennial borders reach their peak. The woodland garden lies higher up with a series of meandering paths, lined by *Magnolia* and giant tree rhododendrons such as *R. griffithianum* with large white flowers, the very tender *R. protistum* and the UK's largest specimen of the rare *R. arboreum* ssp. *zeylanicum*, the only species found in Sri Lanka. Arduaine has a national collection of Maddenia hybrid rhododendrons and there is a huge range of scented tender rhododendrons to delight your nose in spring. Don't miss the viewpoint with perhaps the most outstanding panorama of any Scottish garden, a widescreen vista of numerous islands including Mull, Shuna, Luing and Jura. The main woodland garden has become very shaded and over-crowded with larch and endless self-seeding *Griselinia*. The whole site needs thinning, but this can create its own problems in gardens like this, leading to windblow. As the shelter belt has not been that well maintained, the situation is an ongoing dilemma for the Trust. Head gardener Maurice Wilkins is building up collections of ferns, Chilean and New Zealand plants and many rare trees and shrubs. Arduaine has good paths, many suitable for wheelchairs, and has the best such accessibility of any west coast woodland garden.

Benmore (Younger Botanic Garden)

One of the satellite gardens of the Royal Botanic Garden, Edinburgh, Benmore has one of the best collections of rhododendron species in the world, not just in the range of varieties but also in the spacing given to them; most have ample room to grow away for another 50 years. Benmore claims more than 250 species and you should find some in flower from January to August, with a peak in March, April and May. Planted amongst them are magnolias, *Sorbus* and other trees growing under a forest of enormous conifers. The Benmore estate was bought by sugar magnate James Duncan in the 1860s; he planted 6

Benmore (Younger Botanic Garden)
Younger Botanic Garden,
Dunoon, Argyll, PA23 8QU
(*map, pp. 220–21*)

RBGE, Peter Baxter, Curator
Daily: 1 March–31 October,
10am–5pm; April–September,
10am–6pm; ££
On the A815, 7 miles north of
Dunoon on the Cowal peninsula
T: 01369 706261
F: 01369 706369
E: benmore@rbge.org.uk
www.rbge.org.uk
Small café and giftshop

million trees before selling to Edinburgh brewer Henry Younger,
whose son donated it to the nation. On the lawn in front of Scottish
Baronial mansion Benmore House (now an outdoor activity centre),
Rhododendron 'Altaclarense' or 'Cornish Red' has layered itself into
one of Scotland's largest rhododendrons; its flowers are rather hot red-
purple. One of Britain's largest *R. macabeanum* with huge leaves and
enormous trusses of yellow is nearby, surrounded by other giant big-
leaved species. You can't miss the magnificent avenue of 49 giant
redwoods, planted in 1863 by Pearce Patrick now over 40m high,
which runs from the entrance/café towards the main rhododendron
hillside. To the right at the end of the redwood avenue lies the formal
part of Benmore, past a small pond area. This part of the garden is
dominated by dwarf and not-so-dwarf conifers which provide a
warning to gardeners how big they can get. I'm sure it seemed like a
good idea at the time, but now aesthetically, this garden is a bit of a
disaster. The rows of uneven shapes and sizes planted in straight lines
is neither formal nor informal. It is certainly a curiosity worth seeing.
A shelter from the west coast showers, Puck's Hut, was designed by
Sir Robert Lorimer. Beyond this are some herbaceous plantings next
to the walls of the courtyard where a gallery holds a varied selection of
exhibitions in the summer months. Some of Benmore's best plantings
are on the steep hillside, where most of the rhododendrons are.
Beyond these, the Bhutanese hillside, planted by Ian Sinclair, is for
some reason now sadly rather neglected, and was closed when I last
visited. This was one of the best parts of the garden and would benefit
from improved interpretation and further planting as it was an
informative and spectacular feature. Further on still is the Chilean
hillside, dominated at the top by collections of *Drimys andina* with
Nothofagus and myrtles further down, most of which are from wild
seed. This recently planted section needs time to mature. Benmore is
part of the International Conifer Conservation Programme, designed
to provide a living seed bank for threatened and rare conifers, and
Benmore has extensive plantings of less familiar conifers such as
Athrotaxis, Austrocedrus, Fitzroya and Podocarpus. You will find several
UK champion trees around the garden including *Abies densa* and
Nothofagus betuloides. Restoration of Benmore's tall Victorian fernery,
cut into the hillside, is about to commence. This is an enormous
garden (covering 150 acres), much of it on a steep slope, so it is not
one for the infirm or unfit, though there is a reasonable amount to see
on the flat. Those with the stamina to walk up and down many of the
steep paths are rewarded with wonderful views and a memorable and
well-labelled and well-documented collection of plants. Bear in mind
that it rains 200 days of the year, which may please the plants, but
you might find your visit a bit damp and the midges voracious in
summer. Eckford (see p. 240) a short distance away towards Dunoon,
on the other side of road, is also worth a visit if you have stout boots
to struggle through the woodland.

Carradale House

Carradale lies on the east coat of Kintyre between Tarbert and Campbeltown with great views across to the Isle of Arran and south to Ailsa Craig. Carradale House was designed by David Bryce and was the home until her death in 1999 of the writer and political activist Lady Naomi Mitchison. The present owners Colin and Laraine Burgess are currently renovating the estate and gardens and the 4-acre walled garden. The garden is said to have 140 different rhododendron varieties, planted from the Victorian era onwards, some reputedly grown from 1850s Hooker seed from Sikkim.

Cnoc-na-Garrie

This small garden beside the Oban–Lochgilphead road is an inspiring one, built on a sloping, rocky site, it shows what can be done in Argyll using perennials and bulbs to underplant the ubiquitous rhododendrons, which, in this case, are tastefully planted and not over-done. *Trillium, Podophyllum*, huge numbers of *Geranium*, hostas and bulbs are planted in undulating beds, running both above and below the house. This is an intimate garden, well worth a stop. If you are visiting Arduaine and Crarae, you'll pass it en route.

Carradale House
Carradale Estate,
Carradale, Argyll,
PA28 6QQ
(*map, pp. 220–21*)

Colin and Laraine Burgess
By appointment
Off the B842
T: 01583 431234
www.carradale.org.uk

Cnoc-na-Garrie
Ballymeanoch, Lochgilphead,
Argyll, PA31 8QE
(*map, pp. 220–21*)

Mrs Dorothy Thomson
April–October: 10am–6pm,
by arrangement; ££
2 miles south of Kilmartin
on A816. Entrance between
cottages and red brick house
T: 01546 605327
E: tomanddot67@tiscali.co.uk

Colonsay House
Isle of Colonsay, Argyll, PA61 7YU
(*map, pp. 220–21*)

Alexander and Jane Howard,
gardener Katie Joll.
Woodland garden all year round,
private gardens Easter–end
September: Wednesday, Friday
or by arrangement; £
Ferry from Oban 5 days a week
(summer), 3 days a week (winter).
The island and gardens can be
visited on a day trip from
Kennacraig (and from Islay) on
Wednesdays only. Otherwise
you'll need to stay over. Flights
from Oban 2 days per week
T: 01951 200211
F: 01951 200369
E: katiejoll@dial.pipex.com
www.colonsay.org.uk
Café/teas available on
Wednesday and Friday afternoons

Colonsay House

One of Scotland's remotest gardens, the gardens at Colonsay House consist of two parts. Open all year is a 30-acre informal woodland, planted after shelter was established by Lord Strathcona in the 1930s. With lots of sunshine and far less rainfall than mainland Argyll, many tender plants such as mimosa and abutilon thrive here in the free-draining soil. Indeed, it is a constant battle for gardener Katie Joll to remove the jungle of self-sown seedlings of *Rhododendron, Griselinia* and other plants. As well as the large range of rhododendrons in spring, there are fine tree-ferns, *Embothrium,* spectacular giant *Magnolia campbellii* and other species and candelabra primulas in the stream garden. Roses proved unsuccessful and most have gone, but southern hemisphere favourites such as *Olearia, Leptospermum,* myrtles and hebes thrive in the walled garden, giving summer colour, as do the tall spires of blue *Echium.*

The private walled 'lighthouse garden', open on Wednesdays and Fridays only, has the unusual focal point of the lens, formerly from the Islay lighthouse, which gleams in the sunshine. There is an early carved Christian statue from the seventh or eighth century standing next to a well which is dedicated to St Oran. Organic produce from the gardens is available to purchase in season from the reception centre, as is various island produce: oysters, honey, jams, chutneys etc. The only way to visit Colonsay in one day from the mainland is on a round trip on Wednesdays from Kennacraig, leaving very early in the morning. Otherwise you'll need to stay the night in one of the hotels or B&Bs. As there is lots to do on the island, this is not too much of a hardship. Colonsay has an eccentric golf course 'designed by God' and the best antidote to the Augusta National you could find, members only, but anyone can join for a bargain £20. The island also has fine beaches and is a great place for bird and seal watching. So come for a few days.

Corachie Clematis
Taynuilt, Argyll, PA35 1HY
(*map, pp. 220–21*)

Douglas Baird
Daily: 9.30am–6pm (summer),
shorter winter hours
Nursery 1½ miles up the Glen
Lonan road from Taynuilt
(Oban–Tyndrum road). Retail
nursery A85 by Taynuilt
T: 01866 822266 (nursery),
01866 822149 (garden centre)
T: 01866 822570
E: CorachieClematis@aol.com
www.corachie-clematis.co.uk
Children's play area is planned

Corachie Clematis

Corachie Clematis was established by Douglas Baird in 1988 as a wholesale nursery. Corachie has now moved into retails sales too, with mail order, via the website, offering up to 80 varieties of clematis and other climbing plants. A new small garden centre at Taynuilt on the A85 Dalmally–Oban road opened in April 2008 with a coffee machine and picnic tables as well as a good range of Scottish-grown plants.

Crarae

Crarae
Inveraray, Argyll, PA32 8YA
(*map, pp. 220–21*)

NTS
Garden: 9.30-sunset, year round,
visitor centre: 10am–5pm daily,
Easter–end of September; ££*
Between Inveraray and
Lochgilphead on the A85,
well-signposted
T: 0844 4932210
F: 0844 4932210
www.nts.org.uk
Plant sales and shop but no café

Crarae is probably the archetype of the Scottish west coast woodland garden with the steep-sided valley, swift-flowing burn with waterfalls, winding paths and masses of rhododendrons and azaleas forming a 'Himalayan gorge'. The many levels of path allow large plants to be enjoyed from above and below with magnolias and carpets of bulbs and unfurling ferns in March and April and huge rhododendrons such as giant *R. falconeri* with cream flowers and attractive red and pink peeling bark flowering in May. The garden was established in the 1920s by Sir George Campbell and his mother Grace, aunt of plant hunter Reginald Farrer. Crarae's gardens remained in the Campbell family until they were donated to the National Trust for Scotland in 2002. This is a large garden (50 acres) and you need to be fit to see it all. Despite the lack of any formal design plan, the setting and the bridges across the burn do give this garden more drama than most woodland gardens, though I noted that some of the best views are

now becoming obscured by the size of the plants, so a merciless
chainsaw massacre may soon be required. This garden is far more
than a huge collection of rhododendrons, though they have huge
numbers of these, including vast areas of scented yellow azalea *R.
luteum*. The Campbells planted less common conifers and many other
trees and shrubs including an impressive grove of *Eucalyptus*, some
large *Eucryphia*, *Trochodendron*, and a national collection of
Nothofagus from Chile and Tasmania. On a visit in early June, I was
most impressed by a group of three red *Embothrium* next to a bank of
R. luteum right at the roadside entrance to the garden in full exposure.
Experienced head gardener Nigel Price has had to remove a lot of
overgrown and overcrowded plants and has made good progress in
labelling the collection. The garden is well known for its wildlife,
including birds of prey which nest further up the Crarae Glen. The
huge thickets of bamboo used as windbreaks flowered and died in the
1990s and this has given more space to plant summer flowering plants
on the flatter areas of the garden near the entrance. Crarae is also
worth a visit in autumn, when the autumn colour of the azaleas, *Acer,
Disanthus cercidifolius*, beech and other trees and berries from *Sorbus,
Berberis* and *Cotoneaster* give a great show.

Drim na Vullin

You'll seldom find a garden with a more dramatic setting than this one. Drim na Vullin is a handsome converted mill perched at the side of the gorge of the fast-flowing Cuilarstitch Burn. The woodland garden was created in the 1950s by Sybil Campbell, Britain's first woman professional magistrate, who engaged garden designer Percy Cane to help with the layout. Current owners Mr and Mrs Campbell Byatt showed me the original Cane plans. The top of the garden behind the house contains a spectacular waterfall and both sides of the burn are filled with mature but well-spaced species and hybrid rhododendrons, magnolias, azaleas and other shrubs. Recent planting brings the developed area to about 4½ acres, which is an oasis inside the ever-increasing sprawl of Lochgilphead which now surrounds the garden. The steep paths allow a circular route around the garden. Waterproof shoes are recommended. This garden has steep cliffs and paths with long drops into raging water, so children must be well supervised at all times.

Drim na Vullin
Blarbuie Road,
Lochgilphead, PA31 8LE
(map, pp. 220–21)

Mr and Mrs Robin Campbell Byatt
SGS, usually 3 days in May; ££
A83 to Lochgilphead. Top of
main street in front of the parish
church, turn right up Manse Brae.
¼ mile up the hill on the left.
Beyond the houses on the left a
high fence leads to the Drim na
Vullin entrance. Park on the road
T: 01546 602615

[🐾]

Druimneil House

Victorian Druimneil House overlooks the Sound of Shuna and Loch Linnhe. The garden has been considerably renovated in recent years, with overgrown shrubs and trees cut down or cut back, and it will take a few years for new plantings to really fill in. The small walled garden has a new greenhouse and beds are being filled with fruit and vegetables. I was particularly impressed with the bank of deciduous azaleas alongside the house, underplanted with a range of bulbs including an unusual block of *Camassia*. The dinner, bed and breakfast offered here comes highly recommended, and this would be a good base for exploring Argyll's gardens.

Druimneil House
Port Appin,
Agyll and Bute, PA38 4DQ
(map, pp. 220–21)

Mrs J. Glaisher
(gardener Mr Andrew Ritchie)
Daily: 1 April–31 October
9am–6pm; ££
On the outskirts of Port Appin
village 2½ miles off the A828.
Turn in Appin off A828
(Connel–Fort William road).
2 miles, sharp left at Airds Hotel,
second house on right
T: 01631 730228
F: 01631 730668
E: druimneil@aol.com
Teas offered

[B&B]

Eckford
by Dunoon, Argyll,
PA23 8QU
(*map, pp. 220–21*)

David Younger
Daily: early April–early
June 10am–5pm; ££
Next to Benmore, ½ mile
south on A815 Dunoon road
T: 01369 840201

Eckford

This 4-acre garden is a bit of a jungle, but none the worse for that. A series of paths meanders up a steep and sometimes soggy hillside with two burns running through it. There are mature trees, with particularly fine Douglas fir (known as the seven sisters), magnolias and rhododendrons, some labelled with quirky signs telling you what you are looking at. Outstanding plants include *Disanthus, Rhododendron campylocarpum* var. *caloxanthum, R. protistum,* and some giant late scented white *R.* 'Polar Bear'. Eckford is the family home of the Youngers (of the Edinburgh brewery) who earlier donated the next-door estate of Benmore to the nation as an outstation of the Royal Botanic Garden, Edinburgh. The garden is mainly worth visiting in spring for the rhododendrons.

Fairwinds
14 George St, Hunter's Quay,
Dunoon, PA23 8JU
(*map, pp. 220–21*)

Mrs Carol Stewart
SGS 1-2 days and by arrangement
Cowal Peninsula, Hunter's Quay
on A815. Approaching Dunoon on
loch-side road, turn right up
Cammesreinach Brae just before
the Royal Marine Hotel opposite
Western Ferries terminal.
Fairwinds is on left
T: 01369 702666
E: Carol.argyll@talk21.com

Fairwinds

A mature garden first planted in the 1950s on the site of an old orchard, Fairwinds was bought by the Stewarts in 1973 who have gardened it ever since. The garden features daffodils, rhododendrons and azaleas in spring and clematis, passion flower, jasmine and honeysuckle in summer. A range of trees include conifers, acers and *Embothrium.* Carol Stewart explains her gardening philosophy: 'I think love is the most important ingredient; if you love what you're doing then the rest follows. I intend to keep the garden open until I can't!'

Glenarn

When architects Mike and Sue Thornley bought Glenarn in the early 1980s, the gardens were saved from almost certain ruin by developers. A true labour of love, the Thornleys took the overgrown, weed-filled and storm-damaged garden and turned it into what is once again one of the best woodland gardens in Scotland. The garden was originally planted by brothers Archie and Sandy Gibson and filled with rhododendrons and other plants collected by Kingdon-Ward and Ludlow and Sherriff from Tibet and China. The Gibsons kept good records which the Thornleys eventually managed to acquire. The steep slopes and winding paths mean that few areas can be accessed by machinery, so everything has to be done by hand. In spring, some of Scotland's largest magnolias, such as *M. sprengeri* 'Diva' and *M. campbellii* burst into flower overhead, with carpets of bulbs beneath. This is a garden worth visiting in mild spells in late March and early April, as well as in May and early June, when the peak of rhododendron bloom is reached. Don't miss the enormous Rhododendron 'Sir Charles Lemon' with rusty leaf undersides and white flowers on the front lawn, or the lily-like scented trumpets of *R. lindleyi* pouring down the path side banks in May, or the curious orange bells of the rare *R. viscidifolium*. Stout footwear is advised to follow the many paths on either side of the burn which runs through the gorge down to the restored and enlarged ponds at the bottom of the garden. The restoration and replanting of the huge rock garden to the east of the house is an ongoing project.

Glenarn
Glenarn Road, Rhu, near Helensburgh, G84 8LL
(*map, pp. 220–21*)

Mike and Sue Thornley
Daily: late March–late September, dawn till dusk; ££
Off A814 in Rhu, signposted up Pier Road to Glenarn Road.
Helensburgh Station 2 miles
T: 01436 820493
E: masthome@dsl.pipex.com
www.gardens-of-argyll-co.uk
Catering may be available to groups by arrangement.

Hill House
Upper Colquhoun Street,
Helensburgh, Argyll, G84 9AJ
(*map, pp. 220–21*)

NTS
Daily: 1 April–31 October,
1.30pm-5:30pm; £££ (house
and gardens)
1½ miles from Helensburgh
Station, off B832, between
A82 and A814, well signposted
with brown tourist signs
T: 08444 932208
www.nts.org.uk

Hill House

Though it was little appreciated at the time it was built in 1902, Hill House is Scotland's most famous architect Charles Rennie Mackintosh's masterpiece. It is a large family house, commissioned and built for Glasgow publisher Walter Blackie. Indoors, Mackintosh designed everything including the furniture, lampshades, windows, light fittings, carpets and doorknobs. Katie Campbell notes that 'Hill House can be interpreted as an indoor garden' with many floral motifs used in the wallpaper and furniture. The outside of the house is whitewashed (grey washed is more accurate), in some ways plain and traditional, a reaction against the over-embellishment of the Victorians, with the intricate design mainly on the inside. It seems that Blackie, a keen gardener, designed most of the garden himself. The National Trust has attempted to restore the gardens using family recollection and old photographs and has recreated formal features such as the semi-circle of clipped hollies along the edge of the lawn. The garden contains roses, hydrangeas, an orchard and wildflower meadow, and a double herbaceous border along the south side of the house next to Mackintosh's pepperpot tower gardener's hut. A circle of white *Cerastium* was striking when I visited in June. Small garden rooms contain a lily pond, fernery, maples and a rock garden. Katie Campbell calls this garden 'a rare example of modernist landscape garden design'. I struggled to see much significantly 'modernist' about it; I found the garden rather disappointing in its ambition, and I could not really see how it related to the magnificent house. The garden is almost invisible from the windows on the ground floor for example, and two of the lower terraced lawns are virtually empty. It seems ironic that one of the best things in the garden is the modern

kinetic sculpture 'Five Rectangles in Space' by George Ricky, which spins and swivels in the wind at the back of the house. Perhaps this rather bold and self-consciously anachronistic statement points the way to how the rest of the garden might be utilised to better effect as a centre for displaying contemporary sculpture. Hill House perfectly illustrates the compromises that can arise when 'period authenticity' is the priority. By looking at a garden through a sepia lens, it discourages the asking of the question: 'but is it any good?'

Inveraray Castle Gardens

The headquarters of Clan Campbell and the oft notorious dukes of Argyll, the castle is a popular visitor attraction. As a youngster, I recall being impressed with the mass of swords arranged in patterns on the walls of the castle's main staircase. The 16 acres of policies contain fine trees and banks of rhododendrons surrounding lawns used to stage concerts and music festivals. The dukes of Argyll were among the first of the tree-planting Scottish aristocracy during the seventeenth century and the wooded hillsides around Inveraray are the legacy of this. The rival Campbells and the dukes of Atholl even took to uprooting and stealing one another's trees during this period. Inveraray's 'flag borders' alongside the main drive are in the shape of the St Andrews Cross. The private formal gardens are open by appointment only or as part of guided tours (currently on Fridays at 2pm in summer). These contain roses, statues and a large *Magnolia* and good views can be had from the castle. You might be interested to

Inveraray Castle Gardens
Inveraray, Argyll, PA32 8XE
(*map, pp. 220–21*)

Duke of Argyll
Castle: 1 April–31 October,
Monday-Saturday 10am–5.45pm,
Sundays 12-5.45pm; ££-£££,
grounds and woodland free.
Private formal gardens by
appointment only.
Well-signposted from Inveraray.
A83. Approach from Lochgilphead,
Dalmally or Arrochar
T: 01499 302203
F: 01499 302421
E: enquiries@inveraray-castle.com
www.inveraray-castle.com

know that the current duke of Argyll is a member of the Scottish world champion elephant polo team. I hope the elephants are not expected to live at Inveraray.

Jura House Gardens

Jura House Gardens
Ardfin, Isle of Jura,
Argyll, PA60 7XX
(*map, pp. 220–21*)

Riley Smith family,
gardener Peter Cool
Daily: 9am–5pm; ££
Jura can be reached via the short ferry from Islay. You can fly to Islay from Glasgow or take the ferry from Kennacraig on Kintyre. Jura House is c. 5 miles south-east of the Jura ferry terminal. Jura bus company tel 01496 820314. Tayvallich to Jura ferry (www.jurapassengerferry.com; 12 passengers and bikes only) 3 miles to garden, bicycles available to hire
T: 01496 820 315E
E: mirjamcool@aol.com
www.jurahouseandgardens.co.uk
Tea June–August, Monday–Friday 11am–5pm, with fine home baking

Visitors seem to love this garden. It is just as well, as it is somewhat daunting to reach it. The nineteenth-century walled garden has been run organically by gardener Peter Cool for years, long before it became fashionable. It contains a collection of Australian and New Zealand plants which thrive in the mild climate, other tender plants such as *Echium* as well as fruit and vegetables. The garden is full of fine features such as the spectacular moon gate, a sinuous parterre filled with all manner of annuals and perennials and a series of unusual homemade benches. Perennials are allowed to seed informally around the garden and plants are propagated for sale. There are various walks from the car park to the walled garden with most impressive carpets of wild garlic and other bulbs, and you can walk further afield around the estate. One of the best is the route from the

garden all the way down the cliffs to the beach, and there are great views of the Paps of Jura and out towards Islay, Kintyre and Ireland. A guidebook is available at the notice board. Jura House is one of the best of the Scottish island gardens and gives Logan a run for its money as an outstanding walled garden of exotic and tender plants. Don't miss the legendary teas featuring the best of Jura's home baking, offered in the marquee in summer.

Kildalloig

This is the coastal garden of Kildalloig estate which runs an organic beef and lamb farm. The garden surrounds the attractive white house with tall chimneys, and contains an interesting selection of wind and salt-tolerant plants such as cordylines, a woodland walk with mature rhododendrons, a walled garden and a pond area under construction. There are fine beaches nearby and the island of Davaar, with its cave painting and wild goats, can be reached on foot at low tide.

Kildalloig
Campbeltown,
Argyll and Bute, PA28 6RE
(*map, pp. 220–21*)

Mr and Mrs Joe Turner
By appointment (SGS); ££
East coast road south of
Campbeltown to Kildalloig,
3 miles south east of town
past Davaar Island
T: 01586 553192

Kilmory Woodland Park
Kilmory Castle, Lochgilphead,
Argyll, PA31 8RT
(*map, pp. 220–21*)

Argyll and Bute Council
All year round, dawn to dusk; free
On the outskirts of Lochgilphead
on the Inveraray road, turn off and
park in the council car park

Kilmory Woodland Park

These once great gardens laid out by Sir William Hooker (later director of Kew) in the 1830s are now sadly neglected and the wild raspberries and other undergrowth are reclaiming the place. Nature trails and woodland walks seem to be well maintained but the plants and gardens are no longer the focus of attention. The castle itself is now part of the large Argyll and Bute Council building complex. The late Mervyn Kessell was Kilmory's champion and did much to save this important garden and plant collection. His untimely death seems to have left Kilmory without a caretaker and Mervyn would be sad to see the current state of the gardens, which are treated as little more than somewhere for council workers to take cigarette breaks. The walled garden and surrounding parkland are filled with mature trees including *Tsuga, Cryptomeria* and a large number of giant rhododendrons, including *R. thomsonii, R. arboreum* white, *R. falconeri* and *R. niveum,* said to be from Joseph Hooker seed from his 1850s Sikkim expedition. It is not too late to save Kilmory once again, if the council can be persuaded to give it some resources.

Kilmun Arboretum
Kilmun, Dunoon, PA23 8SE
(*map, pp. 220–21*)

Forestry Commission
Daily: dawn–dusk; free
On A880 Midge Lane
between Strone and Benmore
T: 08707 200606
E: cowal.trossachs.fd@
forestry.gsi.gov.uk

Kilmun Arboretum

This is one of Scotland's most important tree collections, situated on the side of the Holy Loch, near Dunoon. The Kilmun Forest extends to around 180 acres and was established in the 1930s to monitor the forestry potential of a variety of exotic tree species in the humid west coast environment. What is special here is that the 162 tree species are planted in groups and groves rather than individually, so it looks like a small forest of each species: redwoods for example. The access road is not called Midge Lane for nothing, as you might imagine. There are great views and it's a good place to spot wildlife.

**Kinlochlaich Gardens
and Plant Centre**
Kinlochlaich House,
Appin, Argyll, PA38 4BD
(*map, pp. 220–21*)

Mr and Mrs D.E. Hutchison
and Miss F.M.M. Hutchison
All year: Monday–Saturday
9.30am–5pm, April–September:
Sunday 10.30am–5.30pm; ££
Midway between Oban and Fort
William on the A828, entrance
beside Appin Police Station
T: 01631 730342
F: 01631 730482
E: hutchison@
kinlochlaich-house.co.uk
www.kinlochlaich-house.co.uk

Kinlochlaich Gardens and Plant Centre

The gardens are set around Kinlochlaich House on south-facing slopes just outside the village of Appin. The original gardens were laid out in about 1790 by John Campbell of Lochend and include an unusual hexagonal walled garden, informal plantings, a spring garden and bluebell woodland walk with rhododendrons, maples, magnolias, *Enkianthus, Embothrium* and other west coast favourites. The walled garden and the area behind it are mainly given over to the garden plant centre, established by Douglas Hutchison in 1976 and now run by his daughter Fiona. Locals come from Oban, Fort William and beyond as Kinlochlaich has long offered the largest range of plants in the area. I was particularly impressed with the range of deciduous azaleas offered, as well as the many perennials, though as they were

laid out in seemingly random order, you'd have to hunt to find what you wanted. The tree house holiday home is rather special (see website for details).

   WC

Kintaline Plant and Poultry Centre

This Argyll farm is not just a nursery: it is well known for its range of 30 breeds of ducks and chickens. The nursery specialises in hardy perennials, herbs, rhododendron hybrids and bulbs. There is also a model railway which runs around the garden; you'll have to go onto the website to see just how far this obsession has gone!

Linn Botanic Gardens

Situated in Cove, on the Rosneath peninsula, 10 miles from Garelochead, this is a garden you would need to make a special journey to visit as it is well off the beaten track, on a peninsula which juts out into the Clyde estuary, opposite Gourock. The garden lies on a steep hillside with a roaring burn running down a gorge to the Clyde estuary. The garden is packed with rare and unusual *Rhododendron* species (some planted up the burnside), interesting trees, shrubs, bamboos, grasses and perennials, many from wild origin seed, assembled by the Taggarts, father and son. A fine bed of *Celmisia* and other tricky subjects lies next to the Victorian house. Over-shaded, and overcrowded, the garden needs a chainsaw and a spade to return it to some sort of order; the whole place, house, gardens, ponds and the small nursery of plants for sale looked as if

Kintaline Plant and Poultry Centre
Benderloch, Oban,
Argyll, PA37 1QS
(*map, pp. 220–21*)

Tim and Jill Bowis
Wildflower Park: Easter–October
daily, 10am–5/6pm; £ for park,
plant centre free
Off the A828 turn off in Benderloch
and follow signs to Tralee, South
Shian (1 mile along this road)
T: 01631 720223
E: home@hardyplantcentre.co.uk
www.hardyplantcentre.co.uk

Linn Botanic Gardens
The Linn, Cove,
Helensburgh, G84 0NR
(*map, pp. 220–21*)

Mr James Taggart
All year round, dawn till dusk.
Organised parties by prior
arrangement; ££
On the Clyde Sea Loch Trail, ¾
mile north of Cove village (B833).
13 miles from Helensburgh, 18
miles from Balloch. Brown signs
T: 01436 842084
E: linnbotanicgardens@
btinternet.com
www.linnbotanicgardens.org.uk

247

they were being reclaimed by nature. Katie Campbell calls the garden 'a densely planted wilderness' which is an apt description, but the term 'Botanic Garden' suggests more than is on offer. Linn could be combined with Geilston and Glenarn for a day's visiting in spring.

Lip na Cloiche
Lip na Cloiche, Ulva Ferry, Mull, Argyll, PA73 6LU
(*map, pp. 220–21*)

Lucy Mackenzie Panizzon
Garden and sales area always open; free
3 miles north of Ulva Ferry on the Calgary road (B8073).
T: 01688 500257
E: info@lipnacloiche.co.uk
www.lipnacloiche.co.uk

Lip na Cloiche

Lucy Mackenzie Panizzon was brought up at Calgary House on Mull's north-west coast and has returned after many years in Italy to live in a renovated cottage not far from her childhood home, on the windswept road between Calgary and Ulva Ferry, only yards from the sea. The garden of a little over an acre is a delightful triumph in an extremely windy site. Shelter is provided by the usual suspects: *Griselinia, Hebe, Fuchsia magellanica*, allowing a large range of tender plants to be grown. I was amazed to see *Agapetes* grown outdoors. The design touches such as labels made from sea shells and driftwood sculpture are beautifully integrated. The roadside wall is lined with carpets of *Inula*, one of the few perennials not munched by rabbits and deer. If you want to know what to grow in Mull, I would suggest coming here for ideas for small gardens, and to Torosay for a larger scale. Lucy is now advising on and gardening several Mull gardens and she sells excess plants at her garden gate: if it grows at Lip Na Cloiche, it should grow almost anywhere on Mull. The garden is now expanding up the burn. You can stay here too, as Lucy offers bed and breakfast.

Lismore

The island of Lismore, 8 miles long and 1 mile wide, can be reached by ferry from Oban or by a much shorter crossing from Port Appin (foot passengers and bicycles only). It is a pleasure to walk over the island's undulating hills and clifftops, with great views of Mull and the other small islands around Oban. There are many seams of limestone on the island, which means that some of its flora differs from that found on Argyll's mostly peaty acidic soils. Almost 300 different types of plant and wild flower have been recorded, including many lime-tolerant species. Wild flowers include helleborine, *Dactylorhiza fuchsii, D. maculata, D. incarnata*, and several species of *Orchis*. There is a post bus and taxi on the island but hiring a bicycle is probably the best way to get around. Ruins include Tirefour Broch and Castle Coeffin. John Raymond is the island's resident expert on the plant life and you'll find pictures and information on the Lismore website.

Lismore
Oban, Argyll
(*map, pp. 220–21*)

Passenger ferry Port Appin every hour, journey 6 minutes. Leave the A828 road between Ballachulish and Connel at Appin. Car ferry from Oban daily Monday–Saturday
www.isleoflismore.com

Minard Castle
Minard, Inveraray,
Argyll, PA32 8YB
(map, pp. 220–21)

Mr and Mrs Reinold Gayre
SGS 1 Sunday in May, open to
B&B and self-catering guests
and by appointment; ££
Just south of Crarae ¾ mile
south-west south of Minard on
the A83 Inveraray–Lochgilphead
road. Signed on roadside
T: 01546 886272
F: 01546 886272
E: reinoldgayre@minardcastle.com
www.minardcastle.com

Minard Castle

This is a mature garden, next door to Crarae, with fine specimen conifers, woodland walks and a large pond, around which are a wide range of rhododendrons, some over 100 years old, others grown from recently collected wild seed. A more formally arranged walled garden has several greenhouses and beds of shrubs and perennials.

Oakbank
Ardrishaig, by Lochgilphead,
Argyll, PA30 8EP
(map, pp. 220–21)

Helga Macfarlane
1 May–31 August: 10am–5pm,
when at home, phone first,
groups by appointment; ££
Tarbert side of Ardrishaig,
just beyond church
T: 01546 603405

Oakbank

There have been several good gardens over the years along this Argyll hillside, near the Crinan Canal. Oakbank has recently been transformed, pretty much single-handedly, by the extraordinary energy of Helga Macfarlane, who has removed lots of overgrown trees and scrub to create a delightful woodland garden of three acres. Paths wind through trees, rhododendrons and other shrubs, bulbs and wild flowers. There are several small ponds, wood carvings are dotted around and your children will enjoy the 'secret garden', tree houses, funky carvings and statues. A viewpoint looks down Loch Fyne to the Isle of Arran. This is a great addition to the range of Argyll gardens and one which stands out from the crowd; you won't forget it once you've been round.

Seafield

This is a hillside site by the sea in Dunoon, gardened by the well-known children's writer and illustrator Scoular Anderson, originally planted by his parents. The upper terrace has heather beds and a circle of standing stones. The garden includes a gravel section, damp area around a rectangular pond, planted with astilbes, *Iris, Primula*, hostas and ferns, a shady area and herbaceous beds.

Stonefield Castle Hotel

I have been coming to this part of Argyll since I was a child and popping in and out of Stonefield every few years ever since. The 1837 Scottish Baronial castle was one of the many Argyll Campbell clan houses and is a now a hotel which always seems to be changing hands, probably accounting for the somewhat shabby look. The rhododendrons get bigger and bigger and the hundreds of self-sown seedlings choke one another out. Many of these have been carted off by locals for years and can be seen in the gardens of cottages around Tarbert. Heroic gardener Peter Robertson has looked after it for years, usually with very little help as he battles to keep on top of things. And the place is still really spectacular in spring; you can't fail to be amazed at the size and number of rhododendrons here, some of which date back to the 1850s from Joseph Hooker's Sikkim

Seafield
173 Marine Parade, Hunter's Quay, Dunoon, Argyll, PA23 7QA
(map, pp. 220–21)

Scoular Anderson
SGS 2 days per year; ££
Situated on the Cowal peninsula at Hunter's Quay on A815 a few hundred yards south (Dunoon side) of the Western Ferries terminal. Parking on promenade.
T: 01369 830227
E: scoulara9@aol.com

Stonefield Castle Hotel
Tarbert, Argyll, PA29 6YJ
(map, pp. 220–21)

Oxford Hotels and Inns
Open to residents, but usually OK to visit
On the A83 Lochgilphead to Campbeltown road, 2 miles north of the village of Tarbert
T: 01880 820836
F: 01880 820929
www.oxfordhotelsandinns.com

expeditions. There are other rare plants such as *Philesia magellanica* creeping over old logs. The views over Loch Fyne are good where you can find holes in the undergrowth. The rhododendrons and trees do keep growing and growing and eventually they'll swallow up the castle completely. And that, as they say, will be that. I asked about visiting arrangements and was assured that the public are welcome to come and wander around anytime.

Strachur House Flower and Woodland Garden
Strachur, Argyll, PA27 8BX
(*map, pp. 220–21*)

Sir Charles and Lady Maclean
4-6 days SGS, 10am–6pm; ££
(honesty box)
Turn off route A83 onto the
A815 down the Cowal peninsula
towards Strachur and Dunoon
The gardens are between
Creggans and Strachur village

Strachur House Flower and Woodland Garden

Strachur was the home of the late Sir Fitzroy Maclean, diplomat, spy, soldier and adventurer, who was one of the models for Ian Fleming's James Bond. A damp May evening and my seventh garden of the day, I was not necessarily in the best frame of mind when I visited, but I really liked this garden. Strachur House is an imposing, stylish white building looking out onto Loch Fyne with semi-formal gardens on the lawns behind the house and woodland gardens around the edges. The woodland walk along the streamside is a mass of deciduous and evergreen azaleas and semi-dwarf *Rhododendron,* backed by very fine mature Japanese maples and carpeted with spring bulbs and bluebells. A left turn leads down an azalea walk with scents and colours set against the greens of the trees. Unusually for Argyll, this garden has a full-scale formal summer perennial display with *Agapanthus,* anemones, dahlias and salvias, not to mention autumn colour from the maples and trees. The central axis is an avenue of pollarded lime trees under which are planted roses, peonies and *Nepeta*. A sunken garden known as 'the bear pit', where Sir Fitzroy used to sit to do his writing, was planted with bold splashes of white and purple tulips when I visited in May. In summer there are roses. The garden looks well tended, with plenty of recent plantings.

Tailored Tours with Lord Grey

Andrew Grey offers escorted tours of the gardens of Argyll in his car, for those who prefer not to drive themselves. He charges approximately £200 per day and the price does not include garden entrance fees. On the website there are three-day tours offered for North, South and Mid Argyll as well as other tours of castles.

Tailored Tours with Lord Grey
Airds Bay House,
Taynuilt, Argyll, PA35 1JR

Andew Grey
T: 01866 822 286
F: 01866 822 286
E: andrew@tailoredtours.
fsworld.co.uk
www.aboutscotland.co.uk/tour/ma
sterofgray/index.html

Torosay

The islands of Iona and Torosay are the two most popular tourist attractions near Mull. The terraced gardens of Torosay Castle (1858) were built in around 1900, and Sir Robert Lorimer may have been involved in their design. The gardens have been well maintained and added to over the last 100 years by three generations of the Guthrie-James family. I visited the gardens first in around 1986 and not again for almost 20 years. Mike Swift, formerly at Lingholm in Cumbria, was head gardener here till 2007 and he made many improvements and extended the cultivated areas. Duncan Travers took over in 2008. Mull's coastal climate is very mild with few frosts, and those that do occur last only a few hours. The main challenge, as in most island gardens, is wind. Relatively sheltered on the east side of Mull, it is nevertheless exposed to easterly winds, protected from the sea by a narrow strip of conifers, *Eucalyptus* and other trees. The gardens consist of a series of terraces, balustrades and garden rooms in Lago Maggiore Italian style, with urns, statues and hedges of *Escallonia*, *Griselinia* and *Fuchsia*. The slightly disquieting rows of eighteenth-century stone figures along the statue walk are by Bonazza, and were brought from a derelict garden near Padua and shipped to Mull, forming the most important collection of such statuary outside Italy. Torosay is well planted for year-round interest, from the rare Chilean *Latua pubiflora* in January and February, through April and May with banks of rhododendrons and azaleas, to early summer in the extensive

Torosay
Craignure, Isle of Mull,
Argyll, PA65 6AY
(*map, pp. 220–21*)

Christopher James
Gardens open all year round; ££
Caledonian MacBrayne Ferries run
a 40-minute service from Oban
to Craignure. Narrow gauge rail
to Torosay. By car: 1½ miles from
Craignure on the A849
T: 01680 812421
E: info@torosay.com
www.torosay.com
Small café with soups and
sandwiches in the castle basement

bog gardens with *Meconopsis* 'Lingholm' (named by Mike Swift at his previous employment), candelabra primulas, *Astilbe* and *Ligularia*. There is a Japanese-influenced section of garden using the imposing Duart Castle as part of the 'borrowed' landscape. For late summer colour, Mike Swift acquired a fine collection of *Hydrangea* from the national collection at Holehird in Cumbria. Most of the hydrangeas here are as blue as you'll see them; only those planted at the foot of the terraces have turned pinkish with the lime mortar seepage. Other memorable plants at Torosay include one of the largest *Cornus capitata* in the UK, the tender *Echium wildprettii* and an enormous *Thuja plicata*, probably an original introduction, which has layered itself forming a cathedral-like framework of branches. One terrace wall is covered with a very fine *Schizophragma hydrangeoides*. A huge collection of Chilean plants, one of the best in the UK, is being assembled at Torosay, including conifers, *Eucryphia*, *Azara*, *Embothrium*, *Crinodendron* and *Myrtus/Ugni*. Torosay is one of the best Scottish island gardens, and well worth a visit at almost any time of year. Do bring an umbrella though, as the 120 inches of rain a year does mean that there's every chance of getting wet. You can always visit the castle, which the family still live in, and enjoy a meal in the café while dodging the showers.

Tree Shop (The)
Cairndow, Argyll, PA26 8BL
(*map, pp. 220–21*)

Ardkinglas Estate
(contact Neil Colburn)
Daily: 9am–5.30pm
A83, at the head of Loch Fyne
between Inveraray (8 miles)
and Cairndow. Local buses
pass through
T: 01499 600263
E: treeshop@scottishtrees.co.uk.
www.scottishtrees.co.uk
Takeaway café serving hot and
cold food and drink

Tree Shop (The)

Part of the Ardkinglas Estate, this small garden centre and nursery at the top of Loch Fyne is an excellent source of trees, rhododendrons and other plants. Many of the trees are grown in the nursery at Ardkinglas and they also offer mail order. There seems to be a good selection of toys, gifts and cards in the small shop every time I call in. The small take-away café is now expanding. The famous Loch Fyne Oyster Bar is next door.

West Central:

Lanarkshire, Ayrshire, Arran and Bute, Glasgow to Stirling and the Trossachs

This area includes some fine coastal and island gardens (on Arran and Bute) as well as some cold inland gardens in Lanarkshire. This is a region with most gardens at their peak in summer with perennials, roses and bedding plants. Glasgow or any of the Ayrshire towns make ideal bases for visiting the region and golf widows will enjoy the houses and gardens on offer up and down the coast.

Other gardens and groups of gardens occasionally open under SGS are the following: **Ayrshire:** *gardens in Bellevale Avenue and Corsehill Place, Ayr; Doonholm, Ayr; Barr village gardens; Dunlop village gardens; West Kilbride gardens; Cumbernauld gardens; Avonhill Cottage, Drumclog; Caprington Castle (snowdrops); Kirkhill Castle, Colmonell.* **Dumbarton, Glasgow and Renfrewshire:** *Ardgowan (snowdrops); Houston gardens; Holmwood; Kilsyth Gardens; Killarden, Rosneath (rhododendrons); Garsube Allotments, Maryhill; Kilmacolm gardens; Lochwinnoch Gardens (now up to 9 opening together every 2nd year); Rhu gardens.* **Lanarkshire:** *Coulter Mains, near Biggar; Lamington village and Overburns; Nemphlar Village Garden Trail; Wyndales Cottage, Symington.* **Stirling, Trossachs and Falkirk:** *The Tors and other Falkirk gardens; Balfunning, Balfron Station; Cambusmore, The Pass House, Kilmahog; Bridge of Allan gardens; Doune Village gardens; Drumbroider Moss, Avonbridge; Blairuskin Lodge, Kinlochard; Broich, Kippen.*

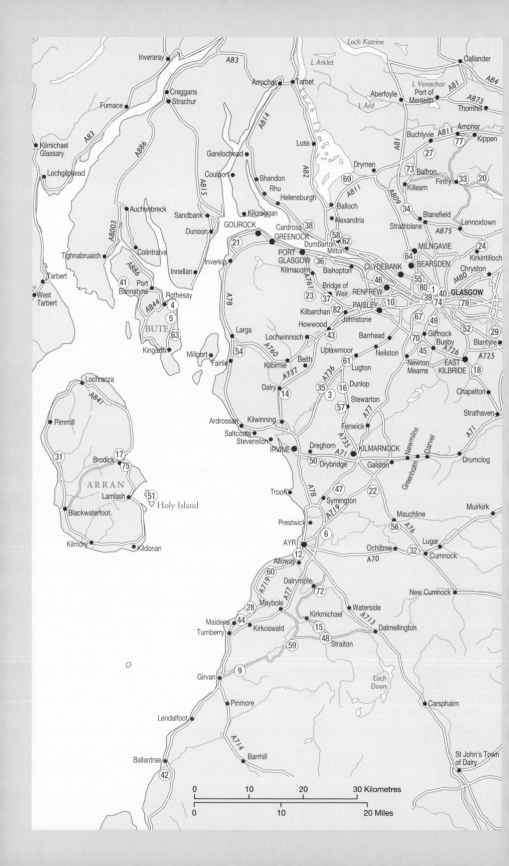

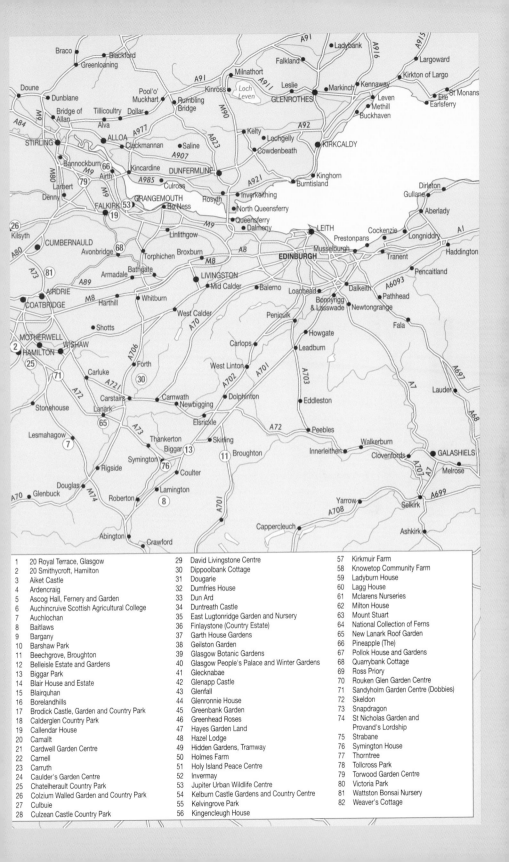

1	20 Royal Terrace, Glasgow	29	David Livingstone Centre	57	Kirkmuir Farm
2	20 Smithycroft, Hamilton	30	Dippoolbank Cottage	58	Knowetop Community Farm
3	Aiket Castle	31	Dougarie	59	Ladyburn House
4	Ardencraig	32	Dumfries House	60	Lagg House
5	Ascog Hall, Fernery and Garden	33	Dun Ard	61	Mclarens Nurseries
6	Auchincruive Scottish Agricultural College	34	Duntreath Castle	62	Milton House
7	Auchlochan	35	East Lugtonridge Garden and Nursery	63	Mount Stuart
8	Baitlaws	36	Finlaystone (Country Estate)	64	National Collection of Ferns
9	Bargany	37	Garth House Gardens	65	New Lanark Roof Garden
10	Barshaw Park	38	Geilston Garden	66	Pineapple (The)
11	Beechgrove, Broughton	39	Glasgow Botanic Gardens	67	Pollok House and Gardens
12	Belleisle Estate and Gardens	40	Glasgow People's Palace and Winter Gardens	68	Quarrybank Cottage
13	Biggar Park	41	Glecknabae	69	Ross Priory
14	Blair House and Estate	42	Glenapp Castle	70	Rouken Glen Garden Centre
15	Blairquhan	43	Glenfall	71	Sandyholm Garden Centre (Dobbies)
16	Borelandhills	44	Glenronnie House	72	Skeldon
17	Brodick Castle, Garden and Country Park	45	Greenbank Garden	73	Snapdragon
18	Calderglen Country Park	46	Greenhead Roses	74	St Nicholas Garden and Provand's Lordship
19	Callendar House	47	Hayes Garden Land	75	Strabane
20	Camallt	48	Hazel Lodge	76	Symington House
21	Cardwell Garden Centre	49	Hidden Gardens, Tramway	77	Thorntree
22	Carnell	50	Holmes Farm	78	Tollcross Park
23	Carruth	51	Holy Island Peace Centre	79	Torwood Garden Centre
24	Caulder's Garden Centre	52	Invermay	80	Victoria Park
25	Chatelherault Country Park	53	Jupiter Urban Wildlife Centre	81	Wattston Bonsai Nursery
26	Colzium Walled Garden and Country Park	54	Kelburn Castle Gardens and Country Centre	82	Weaver's Cottage
27	Culbuie	55	Kelvingrove Park		
28	Culzean Castle Country Park	56	Kingencleugh House		

20 Royal Terrace, Glasgow
20 Royal Terrace,
Glasgow G3 7YN
(*map, pp. 256–57*)

Debbie Hindle and Ken Ross
SGS 1 weekend, ££
Royal Terrace runs along the south
west side of Kelvingrove Park

20 *Royal Terrace, Glasgow*

Shortly after they bought their flat in Glasgow's west end, Debbie Hindle and Ken Ross found out that they had shared ownership of the walled tenement garden which was then buried under weeds and rubbish. The garden they have developed here is a striking contemporary urban space with brick-edged beds, and sections of lawn and decking. The ugly electricity substation has been cleverly hidden and a wooden tree surround is painted a bold shade of purple. Plants are chosen for their year-round contribution to the garden: white-barked birches, *Acer palmatum*, roses and clematis. The garden is shared with and enjoyed by other inhabitants of the tenements which surround the garden.

20 Smithycroft, Hamilton
20 Smithycroft,
Hamilton, ML3 7UL
(*map, pp. 256–57*)

Mr and Mrs R.I. Fionda
SGS 1 Sunday and by
arrangement; ££
Off M74 at Junction 6. 1 mile on
A72. (signs to Lanark) on right-
hand side. Bus/train to Hamilton
T: 01698 281838
E: idafionda@hotmail.com

20 *Smithycroft, Hamilton*

This garden was started in 1998 by a keen plantswoman Ida Fionda and her husband Raphael, and is absolutely stuffed with plants. Some of the plants came from Ida's childhood garden in Italy; a lemon, olive, fig and *Agapanthus* are surviving well despite the Scottish weather. Other tender plants include *Feijoa* and *Hibiscus*. Ida charmingly refers to most of her plants as 'she', reflecting her Italian heritage. We asked if there were any boys? 'Maybe *Gunnera* and *Phormium*', she was prepared to admit. The front garden contains a gravel bed, dominated by Mediterranean plants such as lavender and *Verbena bonariensis*, which seeds freely. The back garden has a mature poplar and structure is provided by a *Eucalyptus*, a red Japanese maple, thick clumps of *Phormium* and *Cordyline*, underplanted with peonies, *Crambe* and other perennials. A damp area is packed with

hostas, *Ligularia* and *Gunnera* while the borders contain a huge variety of shrubs, trees, roses, climbers, perennials, with vegetables in every small space available. The dividing fence has a massive *Clematis montana* 'Marjorie' and a very impressive *Clematis* 'Golden Tiara', while the house is being engulfed by a rampant *Wisteria*. A recently purchased area outside the garden along the roadside has extended the plantings; so far it is mainly an overspill from the old garden. This is a great town garden planted by a real enthusiast.

Aiket Castle

Robert and Katrina Clow rescued Aiket Castle, in the hills south-west of Glasgow, in 1976 and restored its original medieval outline and interior, replacing the remains of the eighteenth-century additions. Diligent research by Robert Clow revealed the castle's fascinating and rather bloody history of sixteenth-century murders and poisonings, its string of alterations and additions and its ownership by the Dunlop family. Two fires on one day in 1957 left the burnt-out ruin as little more than a draughty home for cows and hens. Bureaucrats seemed determined to halt the progress of restoration at every turn, but somehow the Clows prevailed, doing much of the building work themselves. While Robert's prime interest has been the long restoration of the buildings, his wife Katrina has spent 30 years creating the extensive gardens around the castle and her infectious energy was clear in the tour she gave me of both house and garden. In constructing the new garden, Katrina unearthed the remains of a sixteenth-century garden, buried for 500 years. The new garden's exposure to winds was

Aiket Castle
Dunlop, Ayrshire, KA3 4BW
(*map, pp. 256–57*)

Katrina and Robert Clow
By appointment, (groups mainly),
last week April–mid September; ££
Off the A736 at Burnhouse,
(6 miles south of Barrhead) turn
left (signed to Dunlop). First right,
approx ¼ mile onto single lane
road. Aiket is ½ mile on left
T: 01560 484643
F: 01560 484643
E: katrina@kclow.fsnet.co.uk
Tea and coffee can be arranged
for groups

tackled by establishing shelter belts and purchasing some adjacent land to plant woodland. The summer garden, east of the tower, features a herbaceous border running the length of the boundary hedge, with a structure of shrubs and trees, underplanted with tulips and summer bedding in a rainbow of colours. There are two ponds, beds of grasses and *Iris*, and a Christopher Lloyd-inspired 'hot' border. The river Glazert and the mill lade which runs parallel are the dominant landscape features of much of the garden, featuring several bridges and extensive plantings above the gabions which were put there to stop the banks being eroded by floods. Katrina continues to assemble a collection of interesting plants including *Stewartia, Parrotia, Hoheria* and several species of *Nothofagus*. Further from the house is the tranquil, sheltered quarry pond, excavated in the 1990s, and simply planted. The woodland behind this is filled with *Magnolia* and large-leaved rhododendrons, many of which are self-sown seedlings from Brodick. The garden usually has fine autumn colour. The castle tower is the handsome backdrop to most of the garden which is a riot of colour, and the riverside setting is first class. The garden hosts a Shakespeare play once a year, performed by Glasgow Rep. Co.

Amazon Treehouses Ltd
Amazon Treehouses Ltd,
21 Riverside Gardens, Cromberry,
Cumnock, Ayrshire, KA18 3LU

Derek Saunderson
T: 0845 116 1525
www.amazontreehouses.com/

Amazon Treehouses Ltd

This is not your average 'dad knocked up in a weekend' treehouse. Oh no. For a start, prices start at £5,000. This is a room or house in the air. They can be for children, entertaining adults or both. Even if you have not got the means to buy one, I definitely recommend a look at their website; it will awaken the child in you.

Ardencraig

This is as good a display of bedding as you will find in Scotland, not the largest, but probably the best-planted and maintained, even if the sponsor boards do detract from the aesthetic. And I defy even the stoutest bedding-plant snobs not to be impressed if you catch it at its peak in July and August. Apparently, the garden once formed part of a larger layout by Percy Cane. The small walled garden was acquired by Rothesay Town Council (now Argyll and Bute Council). The extensive greenhouses have recently been beautifully restored, and there is a small aviary at the far end. There is a policy of trialling new cultivars annually. Ardencraig is the Joseph's multicoloured coat of gardens, so bring your sunglasses and don't look for any colour matching; everything is just louder and more joyful than everything else; just enjoy it; as we did. This is a perfect first stop before Ascog and Mount Stuart. Keep your eyes peeled for the signs to the garden, as they are somewhat small and easy to miss.

Ardencraig
Ardencraig Lane, High Craigmore, Rothesay, Isle of Bute, PA20 9EZ
(*map, pp. 256–57*)

Rothesay Council
1 May–30 September: Monday–Friday 9am-4.30pm, Saturday–Sunday 1–4.30pm; free
Travel east from Rothesay to Mount Stuart Road, uphill from there to Albany Road, signposted
T: 01700 504644

Ascog Hall, Fernery and Garden
Ascog, Isle of Bute, PA20 9EU
(map, pp. 256–57)

Katherine Fyfe
Easter–end October:
Wednesday–Sunday
10am–5pm; ££
Ferry from Wemyss Bay,
then 3 miles south of Rothesay
ferry terminal on the A844.
Rothesay–Mount Stuart bus.
Or via Colintrave ferry
T: 01700 504555
E: inquiries@ascoghallfernery.
co.uk
www.ascoghallfernery.co.uk

Ascog Hall, Fernery and Garden

This is another heart-warming tale of a derelict and forgotten house and garden being brought back to life. Most significant is the restoration of the architecturally outstanding and historically important sunken Victorian fernery with a glazed roof. It was a crumbling ruin when Wallace and Katherine Fyfe purchased the property in 1986, and has now been beautifully restored with generous support from Historic Scotland and the Royal Botanic Garden, Edinburgh and now contains over 80 sub-tropical fern species from all over the world. *Todea barbara*, the only surviving fern from the original collection, is estimated to be around 1,000 years old. The rest of the garden, with its shrubs and perennials beds, is also well worth a wander, particularly the gravel garden, along the fence nearest the sea. An arch of stones leads to it, and when we saw it in July, the grasses and *Eryngium* were at their peak. Ascog is one of Bute's several excellent garden attractions, conveniently sited on the road to Mount Stuart.

**Auchincruive Scottish
Agricultural College**
Ayrshire, KA6 5HW
(map, pp. 256–57)

SAC
Daylight hours, by appointment
SAC's Ayr Campus is located at
Auchincruive estate. On the B743
Ayr–Mauchline road, 5km (3½
miles) from Ayr centre. Buses
from Ayr
T: 01292 525133 (contact
Mr Davidson or estate staff)

Auchincruive Scottish Agricultural College

The Auchincruive site is important, both historically as a planned landscape, and more recently as a horticultural college where generations of Scottish plantsmen and women received their training. The walled garden with its fine greenhouses and impressive trees is being looked after for the time being, though there are clear signs of neglect on the terraces. More worrying is the state of the important arboretum of tree cultivars planted in the 1990s and covering a huge area. Clearly there is little maintenance going on here and this valuable collection may be lost. Along the river is a steeply terraced slope formerly known as the 'hanging gardens'. Adam's 1778 Tea Pavilion, also known as Oswald's Temple, in the parkland near the west drive is very fine. The future of the whole site is uncertain as the college is planning to move to a new site in Ayr. As this site was donated by its previous owners to be used as an agricultural college, it may be a complex legal matter as to what can happen to the campus. I was assured by the dean of the college that it will be maintained and accessible to the public for the foreseeable future.

Auchlochan

This Victorian parkland outside Lesmahagow has been converted into a large retirement complex which looks a bit like a golf resort. There has been a particularly high standard of landscaping throughout the whole site with mature trees along the river valley, plantings surrounding the housing and two lakes with a large fountain and narrowboat. The walled garden is well-planted and maintained, with a selection of mature trees: cherries, rowans and conifers in several garden rooms with criss-crossing paths and focal points provided by conifer swirls and arches, arbours, greenhouses and sundials. A crowd-pleasing double border of cosmos, backed by trellises of sweet peas reaches a peak in August. Gardener Steve Harrison has filled the gardens with a huge range of plant material. Outside the walls is a further fenced pond and a series of stone-wall terraces which are being planted up. There is excellent wheelchair access over most of the site.

Auchlochan
Trows Road,
Lesmahagow, ML11 0JS
(*map, pp. 256–57*)

The Auchlochan Trust, Steve Harrison (head gardener) SGS 1 day per year. Groups by appointment, guided tours from head gardener. Lesmahagow M74, J9, (from north) J10 (from south). On entering Lesmahagow bear to the right at the main junction (New Trows Road) at The Fountain. Auchlochan House is approx 2 miles along Trows Road
T: 01555 893592
F: 01555 894919
www.auchlochan.com
Courtyard coffee shop

Baitlaws
Lamington, Biggar,
Lanarkshire, ML12 6HR
(*map, pp. 256–57*)

Mr and Mrs Maxwell Stuart
SGS 1 day, June–August
by appointment ££
5 miles south-west of Biggar,
5 miles north-east of Abingdon,
off A702 above Lamington village
T: 01899 850240
F: 01899 850240

Baitlaws

This garden lies in a valley at 900ft with good views of the hills around. The garden consists of four hedged or walled sections, two behind and two in front of the house. Kirsty Maxwell Stuart first took me up to 'the bubble', a conservatory on stilts with a balcony running around the outside, which provides fine vistas of the garden and the countryside. In front of the house is a planting of shrubs selected for their leaf colour, yellow near the house, with green and purple at the far end. A smaller hedged section contains a selection of perennials, many with coloured leaves, part of which is known as the 'Tory border' as it was begun the day Mrs Thatcher resigned: 'blue for the Tories, yellow for Heseltine's locks and white for the fear the Tories felt that they might be out of office any day', Kirsty explained. Behind the house, now 25 years old, is a selection of shrubs round a lawn on the bank, originally designed with help from Iris Strachan. Next to this, a double border, mostly in purple, blue and white shades, leads to a greenhouse. This is a cold garden with late frosts, so foliage and summer flowering is the emphasis.

Bargany

Bargany is a woodland garden and landscaped parkland, surrounding a seventeenth-century house, with many eras of input including that of W.S. Gilpin in the 1820s. Bargany has been planted on a staggering

and frankly almost unmanageable scale along numerous drives and rides. Some of the best features are the giant mature trees under-planted with rhododendrons and maples in the sunken rock garden and on the opposite side of the road a huge lily pond/loch surrounded by deciduous azaleas and hybrid rhododendrons which give way to purple *R. ponticum* into June. I've never seen larger clumps of scented yellow *R. luteum*, and the perfume can be pleas-antly overpowering. Drive along to the second car park by the gigantic several-sectioned walled garden to see the collection of dwarf blue rhododendrons and Kurume azaleas (at both ends of the garden) and some fine shrubs including banks of *Viburnum plicatum* and a flowering cherry walk. The main section of the garden, glimpsed through attractive moon gates, is grassed over and grazed by sheep. Bargany's trees were badly damaged by the Boxing Day storm of 1998 and it has taken a long time to clear all the timber. Many replacement trees have been planted in recent years. The spectacle in mid to late May is outstanding, particularly around the pond. Bargany House is under separate ownership and the area immediately around the house is not open to the public.

Bargany
Girvan, South Ayrshire, KA26 9RF
(*map, pp. 256–57*)

John Dalrymple-Hamilton
May, daily: 10am–5pm; £
Off B741, 4 miles from Girvan
on Girvan–Old Dailly-Dailly road
T: 01465 871249
F: 01465 871282
E: bargany@btinternet.com

Barshaw Park

Paisley's 55-acre park includes plenty of children's activities, a golf course and a walled garden, well known for its impressive displays of bedding plants, backed by herbaceous borders, rose and mixed shrub borders and sensory plantings for the blind.

Barshaw Park
Glasgow Road, Paisley,
PA1 3TJ
(*map, pp. 256–57*)

Renfrew Council
Open year-round, also SGS
open day 1 Sunday in August;
free/donation
Off the A761 Glasgow road, east
side of Paisley. Walled garden car
park is off Oldhall Road
T: 0141 8403106
F: 0141 848 5053
E: am-serv.es@renfrewshire.
gov.uk
www.renfrewshire.gov.uk

Beechgrove, Broughton
Broughton by Biggar,
Peeblesshire, ML12 6DT
(*map, pp. 256–57*)

Tom Shearer
Dawn till dusk in the flowering
season. Donation
On the corner of the A701
and the B7016 in Broughton
T: 01899 220106

Beechgrove, Broughton

Not to be confused with its younger Aberdeenshire namesake, lots of people recommended this garden to me. In the small village of Broughton in the Borders not far from Peebles: 'It's so famous, coaches stop to look over the fence', I was told. Right on the main crossroads of the village, the garden is in two halves, with propagation, composting and vegetable production on the east side of the house. The fame of this garden rests with the displays on the west side and up the bank behind. A figure of eight-shaped lawn with perennials round the edge, two giant beds of scented violas in the middle and large expanses of colour from hundreds of bedding plants. It is a pretty staggering sight from mid to late summer and was still at its peak when I saw it in early September. I stopped to talk to Tom, a former Borders horticultural advisor to the College of Agriculture in Edinburgh. There's not much he doesn't know about growing things, and he has propagated most of the plants in his garden from seed and cuttings, including the violas and a large bank of May–June flowering scented *Azalea luteum*. 'I hope you aren't going to write nonsense like those TV gardeners', he told me. I assured him that I'd try not to. Over the years he has raised lots of money for charity through donations from visitors.

Belleisle Estate and Garden
Doonfoot Road, Ayr,
Ayrshire, KA7 4DU
(*map, pp. 256–57*)

South Ayrshire Council
Dawn till dusk daily; free
Signposted on A719, south of Ayr
Dunoon/Doonfoot road
T: 01292 616255
F: 01292 616284
E: golf@south-ayrshire.gov.uk

Belleisle Estate and Garden

Belleisle estate is now a fine park in the southern outskirts of Ayr with a golf course and lots of room for children to run around on lawns in front of Belleisle House, now a hotel. The walled garden contains heather, *Acer* and rhododendron garden and traditional bedding

schemes as well as a fountain and fishpond. The conservatory had been vandalised when I visited and much of the glass has been replaced with wooden panels. For children there is a play park and pets' corner with a range of birds and animals. This is evidently a popular place; it was packed with people enjoying themselves when I visited in summer.

 [WC]

Biggar Park

This fine and varied garden near Biggar is owned by the former Dobbies garden centre supremo Captain David Barnes and his wife Sue, both passionate about plants and gardening, though not always in quite the same way. Going on a garden tour with them is entertainment in itself as they affectionately josh one another's horticultural passions: she hates the 'flat-leaved lumpen rhododendrons' which he plants outside her kitchen window while he can't stand the metal sculptures she buys from the Edinburgh Art college degree show, particularly if they fall on his foot while he is being forced to put them up. At around 700ft above sea level in central Scotland, the climate is testing and only tough plants will grow well here. David told me that one or two plants such as *Camellia* just don't do well and they have experienced frosts in July and August. But don't worry, there is plenty to see at almost any time of year. There are several sections to the garden: a small water garden on the front lawn with an attractive red bridge, a rectangular sunken Japanese garden with white gravel surrounded by trees, the woodland garden which covers the hillside next to and behind the house, planted with rhododendrons and other shrubs, and a meadow, at its best in early May, with hundreds of *Fritillaria meleagris*. The walled garden features clipped

Biggar Park
Biggar, Lanarkshire, ML12 6JS
(*map, pp. 256–57*)

Captain and Mrs David Barnes
SGS 1 Sunday, or May–July
by appointment; ££
South end of Biggar on A702
near junction with A72
T: 01899 220185

267

yews, long double herbaceous borders, backed by pillars and ropes which hold roses and honeysuckle, and impressive blocks of fruit and vegetables. The two huge clumps of blue poppies just outside the garden are as fine as you will see anywhere in late May and early June. Visitors appreciate the fact that plants are well labelled and the Barnes' sense of humour is evident in the garden's topiary: a cat chasing a hen, and some of the statues (a wooden snake for example) and stonework. I smiled at the poster I saw for their garden openings that 'well-behaved children are welcome'. Do let me know what happens if your children misbehave.

Blair House and Estate
Dalry, Ayrshire, KA24 4ER
(map, pp. 256–57)

Mr and Mrs Luke Borwick,
contact Annemarie Cullinane
Exclusive-use hotel 1 day SGS.
June or by appointment; ££
A737 Dalry follow signs to station,
drive through housing estate,
North Lodge after farm on left.
Use south entrance for coaches
and heavy vehicles
T: 01294 833 100
F: 01294 834 422
E: blairenterprises@btconnect.com
www.blairestate.com

Blair House and Estate

This imposing, handsome building is said to be the longest continually inhabited house in Scotland and part of it dates back to the days of William Wallace and Robert the Bruce. The Blair/Borthwick family have held onto it since it was built. The house, which can be rented as an exclusive-use hotel and for other functions, is magnificent inside and affords fine views of the gardens from many of its windows. The 400 acres of woodland and parkland are very fine, with a double avenue of limes from the North Lodge and several groups of giant redwoods. Impressive snowdrops and daffodils in spring are followed in May by banks of rhododendrons and azaleas with carpets of bluebells. The extensive network of paths around the policies are open at any time. The private gardens around the house are open on SGS open days and by appointment only. These gardens

consist of several formal sections including the azalea and maple-lined Captain's Walk and two rectangles separated by castellated hedges. Beyond this, the river loops round the garden with some fine trees including two noble cedars, a huge cut-leaf beech and a *Davidia* below the battlements as well as vast clumps of *Gunnera*. The backdrop in all directions is provided by banks of scented yellow (*Rhododendron*) *Azalea luteum* and hybrid rhododendrons. The walled garden on the west side is now a forestry plantation. This is a landscape on the grand scale, never cluttered and well maintained by a single gardener, with fine views and vistas to and from the house.

 [H]

Blairquhan

You may recognise Blairquhan as a location for the film *The Queen*, starring Helen Mirren. The castellated regency mansion is the home of the Hunter Blair family and has not been substantially altered since it was built in 1824. Twenty rooms are open to the public with three exhibitions, including one on Robert Burns. There are two ways into the estate, the best is from the B7045 road, which is a delightful 2½-mile drive along the river Girvan. Although the walled garden and pinetum date back to the nineteenth century, the gardens were mainly planted by the late Jamie Hunter Blair, who was a keen plant collector and had a fine eye for design. The grounds boast a fine collection of trees, celebrated in the excellent tree trail leaflet. The charming walled garden has only three walls and unusually has a hollow in the middle, sloping up at both ends, which makes for particularly attractive vistas.

Blairquhan
Maybole, Ayrshire, KA19 7LZ
(*map, pp. 256–57*)

Sir Patrick and Lady Hunter Blair
Castle and grounds open every
Sunday and bank holiday
Mondays, April–end of August.
Special events on some weekends;
££-£££ house and gardens, ££
gardens
B7045 half mile south of
Kirkmichael between Maybole and
Straiton. Also accessible from the
Crosshill–Straiton road
T: 01655 770239
F: 01655 770278
E: enquiries@blairquhan.co.uk
www.blairquhan.co.uk
Teas when house open

Jamie Hunter Blair's walled garden reminds me of a worn velvet smoking jacket, faded and frayed at the edges but well lived-in, from which much pleasure has been derived. Though the garden is partly grassed over for ease of maintenance, the main structure of herbaceous border, rose and fine laburnum arch are still extant, as are the seats and other focal points. The beautiful greenhouses hold figs, lemons, vines and other tender plants. A terrace at the east end is mainly planted with *Buddleja*. Outside the walls at the other end is a long border of *Astilbe* in pinks and whites and a huge cut leaf beech. Along the top end of the walled garden, where the fourth wall would be, is a double border of moisture-loving plants, from where perhaps the best view of the garden can be enjoyed, looking back along the garden's main axis towards the greenhouses. There are rhododendrons here and on the path which leads back to the house, which is carpeted with snowdrops in spring. Don't miss the 'doul' sycamore by the castle, used in former times as a gallows, obviously damaged recently and cut back, but now regenerating. With the combination of garden, house, shop and teas, it makes a fine afternoon out in spring or summer.

   [WC]

Borelandhills
Dunlop, KA3 4BU
(*map, pp. 256–57*)

Prof. and Mrs Michael Moss
SGS 1 Sunday in May; ££
From the centre of Dunlop down Main Street, turn left at the church (right is the B706 to Beith) and the garden is 1 mile on the left on the roadside
M: 07835 924608
E: m.moss@hatii-arts.gla.ac.uk

Borelandhills

This is a hilltop garden created since 1995 with magnificent views of Arran. Garden sections include a bog garden with *Gunnera, Primula* and great clumps of *Iris*, sheltered woodland corners with spring bulbs, rhododendrons, azaleas and *Meconopsis*, roses and clematis on the walls and buildings, large herbaceous borders round a lawn, and vegetable plots in walled sections.

[B&B]   [WC]

Brodick Castle, Garden and Country Park

Arran's Brodick Castle and Country Park lie just north of the ferry terminal and principal town of Brodick. The policies form a large woodland, with over 80 planted acres. There are trails leading up from the garden to Arran's highest point 'Goat Fell' and the whole area has many excellent walking possibilities. The castle was the ancestral home of the dukes of Hamilton. Robert the Bruce is said to have retreated here after defeat in battle and Cromwell attacked and seized it. As with many such castles, it was Victorianised in the 1840s with the usual turrets and crenellations. The castle's contents bear witness to the pastimes of the rich, mainly consisting of trophies of horseracing, shooting, hunting (clearly, they slaughtered a lot of stags) and paintings of the same. The serious interest in gardening started in the 1930s when Molly, the duchess of Montrose's daughter, married John Boscawen, whose uncle owned the well-known garden of Tresco in the Isles of Scilly. Many tender plants were brought up from the south-west and most were found to thrive on Brodick's steep slopes. The duchess and her son-in-law planted huge numbers of rhododendrons and other plants in the valleys of several burns which tumble down through the parkland from the hills above. One of Frank Kingdon Ward's *Rhododendron* discoveries from Tibet was named *R. mollyanum* (later *R. montroseanum*) in the duchess' honour. Early spring, sometimes as early as February, sees the flowering of *R. magnificum* and *R. protistum*; Brodick is one of the few gardens where these species survived cold winters in the post-war period. Enormous *Magnolia campbellii* and yellow *R. macabeanum* flower in March and April. Brodick has three national collections of *Rhododendron*, including the collection of Horlick hybrids, raised at Ascot and on Gigha.

Brodick has suffered from serious setbacks in recent years. A combination of compulsory clearance of diseased plants suffering from *Phythophora kernoviae* and significant storm damage to the very

Brodick Castle, Garden and Country Park
Isle of Arran, North Ayrshire,
KA27 8HY
(map, pp. 256–57)

NTS
Daily: Good Friday–31 October,
10am–4.30pm, 1 November–
21 December Friday–Sunday
10am–3:30pm; ££
From the ferry terminal in Brodick,
take the connecting bus,
approximately 2 miles. You can
walk it in about ½ an hour
T: 01770 502202
E: brodickcastle@nts.org.uk
www.nts.org.uk
Café/restaurant in visitor centre
Good children's play area

mature trees has left areas of the garden seriously depleted, and some
parts are currently out of bounds to visitors. In addition, the garden
was allowed to drift rather aimlessly along for many years, with a
failure to address the replacement of shelter belts, clear over-crowded
plants and self-sown seedlings, and keep records and labeling up to
date, resulting in a diminishing of the value of the collection, as well
as some of the current problems. But despite this, it is well worth a
visit. Brodick Castle boasts a magnificent setting, visible from the
ferry, far out in the bay, particularly fine in spring with snow on the
peaks behind and when the many early rhododendrons are in flower.
Experienced head gardener Colin Tottie has wrestled with all these
problems and has succeeded in making considerable improvements;

misguided projects like the rose garden have gone, the upper walled garden has been redesigned and bedding has been replaced with *Echium,* coppiced *Paulonia* and less common tender flora from the southern hemisphere. Brodick Castle has a good visitor centre and plant sales area, the facilities for children are excellent and the scope for spectacular walks is extensive. It can easily be visited as a day trip from Ardrossan, on a 55-minute ferry journey and a bus which meets the ferry, or you can walk along the bay.

While on the island, tree-lovers might like to search for the rare endemic Arran natives *Sorbus arranensis* and *S. pseudofennica.* Two of Scotland's rarest native trees, there are only a few hundred wild specimens in Glen Catacol and Diomhan, two miles west of Lochranza. Both are natural hybrids of rowan and whitebeam.

Butterworth's Organic Nurseries

John Butterworth is one of Scotland's foremost fruit tree experts and has advised on numerous restorations of old orchards as well as supplying material for new ones. John has trialled over 40 Scottish-raised (and now largely forgotten) varieties of apple and many of these are now being re-established in new and restored orchards and walled gardens throughout Scotland. He runs workshops on aspects of fruit growing, including propagation and pruning and has written a useful booklet *Apples in Scotland,* (Langford Press, 2001, out of print, try second-hand). His was the first commercial organic fruit tree nursery in the UK, all trees having been grown to official organic standards since 1991. The nursery grows apples, pears, cherries and plums. John has concentrated on old and new varieties which are best capable of maturing a crop in the relatively short Scottish season, and which do so without succumbing to disease. The site has poor access and is not available to visit, except by special arrangement.

Butterworth's Organic Nurseries
Garden Cottage,
Auchinleck House Estate,
Cumnock, Ayrshire, KA18 2LR

John Butterworth
By appointment Monday–Saturday
but prefer to do mail order only.
Off the A76 between Mauchline
and Cumnock
T: 01290 551088
www.butterworths
organicnursery.co.uk

Calderglen Country Park

Formerly part of the Calderwood and Torrance Country Estates, this is a wooded glen which follows the Rotten Calder river for approximately 3 miles with some fine waterfalls, woodland flowers and good bird life. Around Torrance House, as well as the visitor centre and gift shop, there is a conservatory, ornamental gardens, children's zoo and play areas for children of all ages. The Langlands Moss local nature reserve is also on-site. The park offers a range of educational activities, guided walks and workshops.

Calderglen Country Park
Strathaven road, East Kilbride,
Lanarkshire, G75 0QZ
(*map, pp. 256–57*)

South Lanarkshire Council
Daily: 10/10.30am–4/5pm or later
in summer for conservatory; free.
From A725 or A726 signed
T: 01355 236644
F: 01355 247618
www.southlanarkshire.gov.uk
Café

Callendar House

Callendar House
Callendar Park, Falkirk, FK1 1YR
(*map, pp. 256–57*)

Monday–Saturday all year: House:
10am–5pm; Sunday 2–5pm;
Grounds: 10am–5pm; House ££,
Parkland free
Just off the Callendar road
on the eastern side of Falkirk
T: 01324 503770
www.falkirk.gov.uk/cultural
Café

French chateau-like Callendar House was built by William Forbes, who also laid out the grounds. This estate was previously the seat of the Livingstone family, who played a fascinating role in Scottish history over hundreds of years. The fifth Lord Livingstone was the guardian of Mary, Queen of Scots, who as a girl lived at Callendar House. James Livingstone fought for and against Charles I and had his house besieged by Cromwell's men. Lady Anne Livingstone gave hospitality to Bonnie Prince Charlie before the Battle of Falkirk and her husband, the earl of Kilmarnock, was beheaded after Cullodon. Callendar House and Park are now run by Falkirk Council. The grounds contain mature trees, large areas of lawns with massed daffodils in spring, woodland walks with rhododendrons and azaleas and you can visit remains of the Roman Antonine Wall close by.

Camallt

Camallt
Camallt Fintry,
Stirlingshire, G63 0XH
(*map, pp. 256–57*)

Rebecca East and Bill Acton
SGS most years in April; ££
2 miles outside Fintry on the
B818 road to Denny from Fintry
village take B822 towards
Lennoxtown, turn left onto B818
T: 01360 860034
E: enquiries@camallt.com

When the Actons bought this large white cottage and 8 acres of land in the valley between the Campsie Fells and the Fintry Hills, they did not realise that under the brambles and other undergrowth there used to be a well-known garden. It was particularly famous for its daffodils planted in the woods and lawns alongside the waterfalls of the burn

which flows into the River Endrick. The bulbs had somehow survived the neglect and once the undergrowth was cleared they began to flower freely. And these were not just your common-or-garden 'King Alfred'. It turned out to be an important collection of rare *Narcissus* cultivars which were planted by Lady Graham, who bought the house in 1944. The woodland also boasts rhododendrons and azaleas and a pond area planted up with irises and reeds, and the terrace has a new planting of roses and perennials.

Cardwell Garden Centre

This long-established garden centre, run by the Gallagher family for over 40 years, is the largest on the west coast of Scotland. It grew out of a nursery operation on 16 acres which is still run as part of the business, and the garden centre has evolved bit by bit up a steep hill, resulting in a rather strange elongated shape with a narrow plant area on several levels. The whole place is a bit chaotic, mainly due to the way it has evolved, and you may have to spend a while finding what you want. They do seem to sell everything: as well as the usual garden centre fare there is a florist, several clothing and building franchises and various interior, food and cookware departments. They are also famous for their ice cream. The new restaurant, in a cavernous building, is impressive and clearly designed to feed a huge number of people. The plant area has an enormous and impressive range of plants, many of them home-grown, but I found the logic of the layout rather hard to fathom. The display gardens are over-grown and need to be replanted, though I liked the red-painted bridges and fences. This is an impressive independent garden centre with plenty of home-grown stock, keen pricing and a huge range of bedding, baskets and pots. Cardwell is worth a detour if you are in the area, perhaps combined with a visit to Findlaystone or some of the gardens and islands further up or down the coast.

Cardwell Garden Centre
Lunderston Bay, by Gourock, Renfrewshire, PA19 1BB
(*map, pp. 256–57*)

Gallagher family
Daily: 8am–6pm
On the A78 between Gourock and Inverkip just off the A770 (signed at the roundabout).
Buses from Gourock, Greenock
T: 01475 521536
F: 01475 521 339
E: info@cardwellnurseries.com
www.cardwellgardencentre.co.uk

Carnell
Hurlford, Kilmarnock,
Ayrshire, KA1 5JS
(*map, pp. 256–57*)

Mr and Mrs John Findlay,
Mr and Mrs Michael Findlay
Groups by appointment, and
SGS 2nd Sunday in July; ££
From A77 (Glasgow/Kilmarnock)
take A76 (Mauchline/Dumfries)
then right onto A719 to Ayr
for 1 mile
T: 01563 884236
T: 01563 884407
E: carnellstates@aol.com
www.carnellestates.com
Morning coffee/afternoon tea
for groups by arrangement

Carnell

Nothing quite prepares you for the pond garden herbaceous planting at Carnell in summer, which is truly one of Scotland's most spectacular and impressive garden sights. Below the walled garden, carved out of a quarry, the high sides and wide borders add to the effect, with water down one side and islands planted with *Filipendula, Darmera, Lythrum* and other thuggish plants which are allowed to spread freely. On the walled garden side the borders are more traditional, with a huge range of vigorous perennials. Carnell is not about colour-coded planting but about maximum impact in rainbow effects. The Findlay family's Asian connections, teak plantations in Burma and trade in Japan, are represented by Japanese stoneware, Burmese dragons and a Chinese pagoda. The walled garden itself is a bit disappointing after the wonders of the water garden outside, consisting of a lawn with borders round the edge, underplanted with begonias and other bedding and a modern house built into the walls. Mr Findlay knows that some are a bit sniffy about his bedding schemes, but as he told me, it is his garden and he plants what he likes. The morning I visited, the Delphinium Society were planting a proposed national collection of *D. elatum* cultivars in part of the garden. Generations of the Findlay family have gardened at Carnell, adding to the landscape. The parkland includes two squares of lime trees, representing the Scottish troop formations at the 1743 Battle of Dettingen, complete with two 'officers' on either side, planted soon after the actual battle. Well, why not? Carnell House has herbaceous plantings on either side of the green walk flanked with castellated yew, which leads to the walled garden and waterside plantings.

Carruth

Carruth was owned by several Glasgow merchants, one of whom founded Burma Oil and once owned the finest collection of French Impressionist paintings in private hands. Charles Maclean, the current owner, showed me the Sothebys catalogue for the sale of the artworks. Charles' father bought Carruth in the 1960s in pretty poor shape and Charles and his wife have turned it into a more attractive and manageable house by demolishing half of it and building two new wings. The house is surrounded by well-landscaped parkland in a natural amphitheatre surrounded by woodland, with bluebells and mature blocks of rhododendron hybrids: lots of bright pink 'Cynthia', huge banks of 'Cunningham's Blush' behind the tennis court and 'Fastuosum Flore Pleno' and 'Gomer Waterer' bringing the season to a close in June. The wide open spaces and sweeping lawns give an open, uncluttered landscape and Charles Maclean is planting more trees, in which he has a particular interest, despite the unwelcome destructive attentions of grey squirrels. The walled garden to the west features *Clematis*, *Ceanothus* and white *Wisteria* on the walls, and a collection of trees and azaleas in the grassed-over paddock. Behind the house is an intimate walled garden within the old house walls. Carruth is a fine landscape and the rhododendrons in late May and early June are quite a spectacle.

Carruth
Bridge of Weir,
Renfrewshire, PA11 3SG
(*map, pp. 256–57*)

Mr and Mrs Charles Maclean
SGS 1 Sunday in May/June,
including plant sale, or
occasionally by appointment; ££
B786 Kilmacolm–Lochwinnoch
road or from Bridge of Weir
via Torr road
T: 01505 872189

Caulder's Garden Centre

At the foot of the Campsie Fells on the A803 between Kirkintilloch and Kilsyth, Caulders Garden Centre was named UK Garden Centre of the Year a few years back. The look of this garden centre is inspired by Australian retail guru John Stanley, who advocates lots of eye-catching and humorous displays and tempting impulse plants. It was well stocked and well looked after when I visited. It also has a small farm shop, a coffee shop and a display village of buildings/sheds. Under the same ownership is Mugdock Plant Area, Mugdock Country Park, 3 miles north of Milngavie. Open daily 9am–5pm, this is a small garden centre, farm shop and restaurant set in a country park. Tel. 0141 955 0011.

Caulder's Garden Centre
63 Kilsyth Road,
Kirkintilloch, Glasgow, G66 1QF
(*map, pp. 256–57*)

Daily: 9am–6pm
A803 between Kilsyth and
Kirkintilloch on outskirts
of Kirkintilloch
T: 0141 776 2001
www.caulders.com
Butterchurn waitress service café

Châtelherault Country Park
Carlisle Road,
Hamilton, ML7 7UE
(*map, pp. 256–57*)

South Lanarkshire Council
House: Monday–Thursday
10am–4pm and Sunday pm;
Grounds: year round; free
Well signed from M74 J6,
or train to Châtelherault station
T: 01698 426213
F: 01698 421532
Café

Châtelherault Country Park

Not a Scottish name, as I'm sure you've noticed, Châtelherault was the name of a French dukedom which was inherited by the dukes of Hamilton, so this part of the Scottish Hamilton estates was named after it. Hamilton Palace, once one of Scotland's finest buildings, was pulled down in the 1920s, leaving the splendid hunting lodge, designed as an 'eyecatcher' or distant focal point from the palace, by William Adam. It is now a visitor centre with exhibitions and a café. The floors are no longer level, due to subsidence from sand quarrying. The gardens around the lodge include a curious sculpture of pillar-like forms, terraced perennial borders at either end of the building and a box parterre of *broderie arabesque*, similar in style to those at Het Loo in Holland. The parterre is best appreciated from the raised bowling green reached via the central steps. The country park covers a large area and there are several good walks through thick woodland and along the sides of the deep ravines of the Avon Gorge, which is crossed by the spectacular towering Duke's Bridge, which is rather hard to get a view of through the undergrowth. Some of the ancient oak trees in the remnants of Hamilton High Parks may be as much as 600 years old. You can also walk up to the ruins of Cadzow Castle. North of the lodge you'll probably see the distinctive 'white park cattle' grazing under the trees. My son Jamie rated the excellent play area 9/10 and there is a garden centre at the entrance.

   [WC]

Clyde Valley, Strathclyde

This section of the Clyde Valley, running from near Hamilton to Lanark, has long been the greatest concentration of horticulture in Scotland and has been known as the 'garden valley'. It was well known for its orchards, strawberry, tomato, vegetable and bedding-plant production, but many businesses have diversified into garden centres, the best known of which is Sandyholm (now owned by Dobbies, see p. 449). Robert Morton and Sons is still a major grower of bedding and houseplants for the trade. Other garden centres include Garrion Bridges Garden Centre, Silverbirch, Andersons, Guyana Garden Centre and Rosebank. You could certainly spend the best part of a day visiting all the plant-related businesses on or near the A72 road. The Clyde Valley misses a trick by not doing better joint marketing to promote itself as a centre for horticulture and garden centres. One reason may be the intense rivalry which some of the businesses feel towards one another, which seems to preclude cooperation.

Colzium Walled Garden and Country Park

The small walled garden at Colzium forms an element in a large country park which was formerly part of Lord Kilsyth's estates. The garden lies behind the house and is not that well signposted (drive

Clyde Valley, Strathclyde
Clyde valley

Various
Along the A72, leave M74 at J7
or drive north from Lanark

**Colzium Walled Garden
and Country Park**
Off Stirling Road, Kilsyth,
Glasgow Strathclyde, G65 0PY
(map, pp. 256–57)

North Lanarkshire Council
Afternoons April–October,
also for snowdrops; free
Off A803, ½ mile (0.8km)
east of Kilsyth
T: 01698 818269
www.kelvinvalley.co.uk/html/
the_colzium.html

past the play park and you'll find another car park). Planted in the 1980s and '90s, it has the best collection of dwarf conifers in Scotland, interplanted with dwarf rhododendrons, with an overstorey of Japanese maples and a huge golden-leaved *Catalpa* which was in flower when I visited in August. The whole garden is dotted with spring bulbs, with an important collection of over 100 varieties of snowdrop. The garden is meticulously maintained and well-labelled (though some of the labels have been mixed up) and overall it has a Japanese feel, only really lacking water to complete the effect. Worth a look at any time of year for foliage effect but the spring bulbs and rhododendrons make March–May the peak season. The parkland contains a good collection of trees and you can also visit the restored seventeenth-century ice house.

Culbuie
Culbuie House, Culbowie Road,
Buchlyvie, Stirling, FK8 3NY
(*map, pp. 256–57*)

Ian and Avril Galloway
SGS by arrangement,
May–October; ££
A811 to Buchlyvie turn south
up Culbowie road and Culbuie
is almost at the top of the hill
on the right
T: 01360 850232

Culbuie

This garden was previously owned by the Drummond family and by Alice Reynard, who planted most of the mature trees and shrubs. The garden commands panoramic views of the Trossachs, Ben Lomond and Ben Vorlich and is worth visiting for the views alone. The garden itself is a mixture of woodland and colour-coordinated perennial beds. Structure is provided by mature trees including *Cornus, Magnolia*, one of my favourites, the weeping *Juniperus recurva* var *coxii*, some fine rhododendrons and some rather large acid-yellow conifers. There is also a wildflower meadow.

Culzean Castle Country Park

Culzean (pronounced 'cull-ain') Castle and estate form one of the National Trust for Scotland's 'flagship' properties. The castle, former home of Ayrshire's Kennedy clan, was rebuilt by Robert Adam from 1777–90 and sits strategically atop cliffs looking out to Arran, set in a 565-acre designed landscape. This became Scotland's first country park in 1969. The castle contains some of Robert Adam's most famous and ostentatious work, including the staircase and the round and blue drawing rooms. The first marquis of Ailsa is said to have authorised the planting of over 5 million trees at Culzean in the early nineteenth century and the woodlands can be enjoyed today via an extensive network of trails. As well as the castle and gardens, the various estate buildings, playpark, beach and walks certainly justify a whole day if you want to see everything. The castle itself is reached by crossing a spectacular, recently restored Adam bridge over a gully. The front of the castle lies on a cliff-edge, while the rear boasts a fine rectangular sunken garden with terracing along one side. If you arrive in July you should be in time for the spectacular red and pink *Astilbe* borders which run the whole length of the terrace. The fountain garden contains a large pool and scalloped central circle topped by dolphins, shells and a nymph, and there is a small orangery in one corner. Back over the bridge the lime avenue leads to the amazing castellated 1818 *Camellia* house, now filled with lemons, passionflowers, plumbago and other conservatory favourites, and on to the enormous double, walled, garden, under the care of Culzean's head gardener Susan Russell. The two halves are divided by the long, recently restored Victorian greenhouses filled with vines. The northern part of the garden contains mature cedars, a *Catalpa*, multi-stemmed *Thujopsis*, hardy banana groves, palm trees and cordylines. The walls are lined with hostas for much of their length, and there is an eccentric bed of ferns, hostas and *Trachycarpus*. The damp garden and grotto arch/rock garden are rather fine. The southern half of the walled garden

Culzean Castle Country Park
Maybole, South
Ayrshire, KA19 8LE
(*map, pp. 256–57*)

NTS
Castle and walled garden:
Daily: 30 March–31 October
10.30am–5pm (last entry 4pm);
£££*
A719 between Dunure and
Turnberry, leave A77 at Maybole.
Stagecoach bus number 60/360
(Ayr to Girvan via Maidens),
1 mile walk
T: 0844 4932149
F : 0844 4932150
E: culzean@nts.org.uk
www.nts.org.uk
Home Farm Restaurant, Stables
Coffee House

contains the greenhouses, a vast central double herbaceous border, areas of flowers, fruit and vegetables at either side, and a wildflower meadow which looked great in its first year. The herb garden outside the garden is too small and would be better brought within the walls. The woodland area beyond needs urgent attention as the once fine rhododendrons are being buried under weed trees. In other parts of the policy grounds you'll find the 13-acre Swan Pond complete with Gothic cottage. And there is also a pagoda, which was restored in 1997. Culzean is a rightly popular attraction, with plenty do for all the family, including a good playpark, and in summer, clubs for 6–12-year-old 'young naturalists' and teenagers.

David Livingstone Centre
165 Station Road,
Blantyre, Ayrshire, G72 9BY
(map, pp. 256–57)

NTS
Late March–20 December:
Monday–Saturday 10am–5pm,
Sunday 12.30am–5pm; ££
Off M74, J5, via A725 and A724.
Bus and train to Blantyre,
5 mins walk
T: 0844 493 2207
E: gardens@nts.org.uk
www.nts.org.uk
Café

David Livingstone Centre

The handsome white buildings of Shuttle Row, a former cotton mill, was the birthplace of Dr David Livingstone. The cottages hold a museum containing a collection of Livingstone's personal belongings, including expedition and navigational equipment, original diaries and notebooks. The gardens and memorial park surroundings have been improved and extended in recent years. Between the visitor centre and the houses are mixed herbaceous/shrub borders surrounding a half-globe water feature 'The World Fountain' by the Scottish-based sculptor Charles D'Orville Pilkington Jackson. The so-called Explorers' Garden is a small woodland garden above the River Clyde with a water cascade flowing into a pond. The potentially good views of the Clyde are obscured by fencing and weed trees and the garden has no labelling and little interpretation. The future of this whole site

hangs in the balance as NTS are reluctant to continue to run it. If it's worth having a garden here, then it should be better than this.

Dippoolbank Cottage

This organically-run cottage garden has been created by its artist owner with raised beds of vegetables, herbs, fruit and flowers and a wooded area with a pond, treehouse and summer house. A fernery was completed in 2007. Much of the garden has been constructed from recycled materials.

Dippoolbank Cottage
Carnwath, Lanarkshire,
ML11 8LP
(*map, pp. 256–57*)

Alan Brash
SGS 2 Sundays in July; ££
Off B7016 between Forth and
Carnwath near the village of
Braehead on the Auchengray road.
Approx 8 miles from Lanark

Dougarie
Dougarie Estate,
Isle of Arran, KA27 8EB
(*map, pp. 256–57*)

Mr and Mrs S.C. Gibbs
SGS 1 day per year, groups
by appointment; ££
A841 between Pirnmill and
Blackwaterfoot. Ferries to
Brodick and Lochranza
T: 01770 840 259/229
F: 01770 840 266
E: bookings@dougarie.com

Dougarie

Dougarie (pronounced 'doogry') estate covers 27,000 acres of the north-western part of Arran. The duke of Hamilton, not content with Brodick Castle, built a summerhouse at Dougarie. The Gibbs family acquired the estate in 1972 and there is considerable new planting taking place. The terraced garden lies in a castellated folly with plantings of shrubs, perennials and a traditional kitchen garden with views out towards Carradale on Kintyre and over the Iorsa Water. Steps and steepness mean this garden is not wheelchair accessible.

Dumfries House
Cumnock, Ayrshire, KA18 2NJ
(*map, pp. 256–57*)

Great Steward's Dumfries
House Trust
House open by appointment
Easter-31 October for pre-booked
tickets only. Grounds open in
daylight hours; free
Parking at main Barony Road
entrance. Just off the A70
between Cumnock and Ochiltree
T: 01290 425959
F: 01290 425464
E: info@dumfries-house.org.uk
www.dumfries-house.org.uk

Dumfries House

Dumfries House, a fine Robert and John Adam 1758 house, extended by Robert Weir Schulz, was recently rescued from being auctioned off by a last-minute rescue led by Prince Charles. The house is a time capsule, little altered since it was built, partly because the fabulously wealthy Bute family had other houses to live in and so Dumfries House remained uninhabited for long periods. Fine though the building is, its contents are the main event, particularly its collection of eighteenth-century furniture pieces, most of which were designed for the house. The policies and gardens are overgrown and will need a considerable period of restoration. The best feature is a group of wellingtonia between the house and the river. The 2,000-acre estate includes features such as Avenue Bridge, a three-arch bridge adorned with obelisks, built at the same time as the house, an older (1671) dovecote, two single-arch bridges, an icehouse, a coach building, a temple, a sundial and the ruins of Terringzean Castle. The parkland is freely accessible to the public, but there is a curtilage around the house which visitors are asked to observe on closed days and after normal visiting hours.

Dun Ard
Main Street, Fintry,
Stirlingshire, G63 0XE
(*map, pp. 256–57*)

Alastair Morton and Niall Manning
By appointment; donations/free
17 miles north of Glasgow
on B822
T: 01360 860369

Dun Ard

Dun Ard has been created from a sloping field in the central Scotland village of Fintry during the last 20 years or so by Alastair Morton and Niall Manning. Hedges create a series of garden rooms, each with its own feel, giving sense of theatre as you walk round: minimalist calm followed by vistas and exuberant planting schemes. At the side of the house is a small vegetable plot which leads into an early summer garden room of blues, purples and yellows: thistles of various kinds, aconites, *Euphorbia, Veronica* and *Clematis* scramble informally but artfully. A path lined with pleached hornbeam leads the eye through a gate, past the orchard to a slate-covered round-roofed summerhouse. Higher still on the hillside is a late summer 'hot' garden of reds and yellows, backed with purple foliage, planted in informal drifts, which

can be looked down on from a small decking viewpoint. A further enclosed space boasts a box parterre which holds roses and vigorous perennials, which in turn leads to a startling Rothko-esque minimalist rectangle with a simple square pond in the centre, all the more effective after all that surrounds it. At the top of the garden is a woodland bog garden, peaking in early summer with hostas, *Rodgersia* and primulas, which is dominated by a beautiful dry stone pyramid bisected by a water channel, probably based on the ones at Wilhelmshöhe in Germany and Desert de Retz in Paris. To the west is a wildflower meadow, left to grow long to encourage wild white orchids, while to the east is another minimalist space, this time circular with a tapering beech hedge, surrounded by a simple reddish dry stone wall. From here the path returns downhill to the back door of the house. Dun Ard is a triumph, with design influences and inspirations from Italy, France, Germany and Ireland, full of breathtaking effects and contrasts, well planted but not over-manicured; it is gardened on organic principles, self-sown seedlings are allowed to thrive and hedges are not clipped every month. A labour of love, full of stimulating ideas and one of the best-designed private gardens in Scotland, the textures and different feels of each area are designed like the multi-course tasting menu at The Fat Duck or El Bulli: a series of morsels, each one starkly different from the next, small explosions of stimuli.

Duntreath Castle

When Julie Edmonstone moved to her husband's family home, it is safe to say that there was not much of a garden. She described it as '20 acres of lawn, wood, tired shrubs and one border, I saw only gloomy conifers which overshadowed the lawn, suffocated the drive and excluded all view of the beautiful landscape'. Her husband's family had been in residence for 575 years. Only Mrs Keppel, mistress to King Edward VII, seems to have had much interest in gardening, but even her water garden had been filled in and covered with conifers. Julie Edmonstone has spent the last 35 years gradually

Duntreath Castle
Blanefield, Glasgow, G63 9AJ
(*map, pp. 256–57*)

Sir Archibald and Lady Edmonstone
By appointment; ££
On A81 between Blanefield and Killearn
T: 01360 770215
F: 01360 770213
E: juliet@edmonstone.com
www.edmonstone.com

building an impressive garden into the castle's overpoweringly large parkland landscape. There is actually a pair of castles, side by side, with a chapel to boot: the fifteenth-century keep and the Victorian house, linked in Edwardian times by a turreted extravagance which was pulled down in 1960. The garden at Duntreath is above all about wide open spaces and huge vistas: no garden rooms here, as the views of the hills around are too good to obscure. Water dominates everything, a fountain trickles away on the small rose and box parterre next to the castle. Alongside the drive is a series of pools, waterfalls and bridges over the burn, planted with all manner of rhododendrons, trees and shrubs. This has now been extended into the wood, ending in a fine small bridge, with plantings dominated by *Magnolia* and *Cercidiphyllum*. The stream then runs into a ha-ha which keeps the vista to the distant Trossachs hills clear. In front of the castle a wide terrace fringed with *Nepeta* 'Six Hills Giant' looks out over a widescreen vista of lawns down to a series of three large oval ponds, linked by rickety wooden bridges with *Gunnera, Iris* and other pond-side favourites, with dwarf rhododendrons on some of the islands. Planting here is bold and works well from a distance as well as close up. This is a garden which is to be strolled around in the eighteenth-century style, enjoying the backdrop of trees, distant hills and handsome castles and terracing. Between the castle and the drive some mature woodland includes a group of wellingtonias, under-planted by bluebells, with a bank of orange azaleas alongside. The old walled garden, just outside the main gates, is now a nursery/garden centre. Julie Edmonstone is a well-known figure in Scottish gardening circles as an author, journalist and television presenter and she has served on committees of the National Trust for Scotland and Scotland's Gardens Scheme. She has lots of further plans for the gardens, which are well worth a visit at any time of year. Dogs encouraged.

East Lugtonridge Garden and Nursery

This is a delightful, little-known gem of a garden and nursery which specialises in unusual herbaceous perennials which are displayed in an immaculately maintained garden which surrounds the farmhouse, probably at its best from June to August. They also sell stone troughs and other useful garden planting materials, and many local gardeners have recommended this nursery both for the plants and for the useful advice on offer. The Goldies are very active 'retired' farmers. Joan showed me some of her treasures such as double *Trillium*, *Rhodohypoxis*, *Lewisia* and *Primula auricula*.

East Lugtonridge Garden and Nursery
Lochlibo Road, Burnhouse,
Beith, Ayrshire, KA15 1LE
(*map, pp. 256–57*)

Jim and Joan Goldie
Easter–October: dawn–dusk; free
On the A736 Irvine–Glasgow road,
¾ mile south of Burnhouse down
a farm drive
T: 01560 484890

Finlaystone Country Estate

Finlaystone House and its estate have a long history, owned by the earls of Glencairn and since the 1890s in the hands of the MacMillan family. The gardens were largely laid out in the 1900s on a slope leading down towards the Clyde, and have been much altered and added to in recent years to provide year-round colour. The season starts in spring with snowdrops on the drive side and along the burn, and waterfalls which lead down towards the Clyde. These are followed in April and May by the rhododendrons and azaleas, with impressive drifts of daffodils giving way to bluebells in the extensive woodlands. Some of the finest large-leaved rhododendrons are being spoiled by the encroaching undergrowth. The walled garden contains a fine small café and the garden walls are furnished with fruit trees. An old greenhouse, with the glass removed, is now covered by a huge *Clematis montana*. The central brick pergola with roses and fountain looks a little out of place here. More effective are the line of flowering cherries and the grove of *Cornus kousa*. On the outside north wall is a

Finlaystone Country Estate
Langbank, Renfrewshire,
PA14 6TJ
(*map, pp. 256–57*)

George and Jane MacMillan
Daily: 10am–5pm; ££
Off A8 Glasgow–Greenock road,
at Langbank, brown signs.
Bus to near gates from Glasgow–
Greenock or a 25-minute walk
from Langbank train station
T: 01475 540505
F: 01475 540285
www.finlaystone.co.uk
Good café in the walled
garden open in summer only
Picnic area in the woodland.

MacMillan family tree/shrine/commemoration and a long planting of ferns of many types. Heading west from the walled garden, is a small 'smelly garden' of scented plants, a greenhouse and a parterre planted with pink and white Astilbes which was impressive at its peak in late July and early August. The creation of a vantage point on the shrub-covered bank behind would allow better views of this. Beyond this, across extensive lawns, are a water garden, island beds of shrubs and deciduous azaleas and one of Scotland's largest clumps of *Kalmia latifolia*, which opens its pink parasols in June. Moving down the slope past a maze laid out on the ground, is a long herbaceous border which leads back to the house. The private gardens are separated from the public area by a castellated yew hedge. There is certainly plenty to see and do at Finlaystone throughout the season with a particularly good children's play area, craft shops (in summer), café and woodland walks (dogs allowed on a lead), as well as the extensive gardens. You may well meet MacMillan family members weeding or digging in some corner of the vast grounds. I can't help thinking that the area under cultivation is so large and spread out that it is more like a park than a private garden, but it is an impressive undertaking.

Garth House

Behind this Victorian house in Bridge of Weir is a fine garden with views over the Clyde, which consists of a series of 'rooms'. The garden has carefully planned structural plantings with hedges, raised beds and trellis which are complemented by a huge range of perennials, roses and climbers. Scent is an important consideration, with more than 120 varieties of shrubs and climbing roses as well as many honey-suckles in the garden. Recent developments include a Victorian greenhouse, a potager and a pond.

Garth House
Garth House, Bankend Road,
Bridge of Weir, PA11 3EU
(*map, pp. 256–57*)

Ann and Craig Campbell
SGS 1 day per year (with other
Bridge of Weir gardens) and
also by appointment; ££
A737 to Irvine, take 2nd exit on
dual carriageway, signposted
Bridge of Weir, left (opposite
Burndale Workshop) up
Locher Road, turn right at top,
immediately right again into
Bankend Road
T: 01505610848
E: ann@garthassociates.com

Garth House

Geilston Garden

Geilston House and Garden, not far from the Clyde in
Dunbartonshire, formed part of a Glasgow merchant's estate
belonging to the Donald family. The gardens were mainly the work of
Elizabeth Hendry and Margaret Bell. The National Trust for Scotland
was bequeathed the 10-acre site and the house is being restored. The
walled garden next to the house is dominated by a rather wind-
pummelled *Sequoiadendron giganteum*. On three sides the walls are
lined with azalea and rhododendron plantings, rather jarringly sited
behind a semi-formal low golden yew hedge. At the side of the house
is an enormous *Cercidiphyllum japonicum*. The east side has herbaceous plantings of *Thalictrum, Filipendula, Eupatorium, Helenium,
Phlox* and *Sidalcea*. To the west of the house, surrounded by sections
of beech hedge, are an orchard, a well laid-out and labelled vegetable
section, some perennial borders, a sunken garden which looks like an
excavated grave and some grassed areas. Produce from the garden is
offered for sale in summer. A series of winding paths forms a

Geilston Garden
Cardross, Dumbarton,
G82 5HD
(*map, pp. 256–57*)

NTS
Daily: 1 April–31 October
9.30am–5pm. House not open;
££*.
On A814 at west end of Cardross,
18 miles north-west of Glasgow.
Local bus from Helensburgh–
Dumbarton. Cardross station
1 mile
T: 01389 849187
F: 01389 849189
E: jgough@nts.org.uk
www.nts.org.uk
Coffee machine

woodland walk filled with rhododendrons and azaleas and carpeted
with bluebells, along the banks of the Geilston Burn. The National
Trust for Scotland claims that this is a 'good landscape design with
the sum of its parts being greater than the individual constituents'.
While the woodland is pleasing but unexceptional and the garden is
well looked after, I could not help asking myself whether Geilston was
exceptional enough for the National Trust for Scotland to have taken
on. The garden needs to find a more ambitious and individual
identity than it has now, perhaps specialising in trialling of fruit and
vegetables. The house is not open to the public. Geilston is worth
combining with a visit to Glenarn or Hill House nearby.

Glasgow Botanic Gardens

The Glasgow Botanic Gardens, founded in 1817 on a site in
Sauchiehall Street, were relocated to Kelvinside in 1842. The gardens
provided facilities for the teaching of botany and medicine for Glasgow
University. Professor William J. Hooker, Regius Professor of Botany at
the University of Glasgow (1820–41) was largely responsible for the
garden's pre-eminence before he took over at Kew. His son was the
plant-hunter Joseph Hooker, later director of Kew. The Glasgow
Corporation took over the gardens in 1891, but maintained links with
the university. It is now a hugely popular park and visitor attraction,
with around 400,000 visits per year. Without doubt, the highlight of

this garden is the Kibble Palace, one of Scotland's engineering and horticultural wonders. Dating from 1873, part of it was originally a conservatory at John Kibble's Coulport mansion before being presented to the City of Glasgow. It was dismantled and shipped up the Clyde. It consists of a large dome and rotunda connected to a smaller dome by a link corridor. The £7 million lottery-funded restoration was completed by Shepley Engineers, who dismantled the whole structure in 2003, took all the metalwork to Yorkshire, where it was repaired and repainted before being returned and reassembled in Glasgow. The restored Kibble Palace is a triumph, re-opening in 2006. The aerodynamic shape is functional in protecting it from wind and also has a magical quality in its curves and sweeps. It contains the national collection of Asian, African and Australasian tree ferns as well as a cactus collection, insectivorous plants and vireya rhododendrons. A curious feature is the reflectors hanging from the ceiling, which are used to light the building from floor-mounted lights. The slightly disconcerting thing about the greenhouse is the way it sits on the lawn. With no terraces, paths or landscaping around it, it looks as if it has just floated down one evening, from outer space perhaps, and is sitting on the lawn, just having a rest before moving on. Nearby is another

Glasgow Botanic Gardens
730 Great Western Road,
Glasgow, G12 0UE
(*map, pp. 256–57*)

Glasgow City Council,
curator Paul Matthews
Daily: 7am–dusk; free
At the corner of Great Western
Road and Queen Margaret
Drive/Byres Road, Glasgow;
Hillhead Underground (5 mins)
T: 0141 334 2422/3354
F: 0141 339 6964
E: gbg@land.glasgow.gov.uk
www.glasgow.gov.uk
Kiosk with refreshments,
Byres Road nearby, many cafés

series of linked glasshouses containing tropical plants from both wet and dry habitats: these include the national collection of *Begonia*, one of the UK's largest orchid collections and houses of desert plants. It is very well planted and maintained. The outdoor collections are rather disappointing compared with those indoors and are better considered a public park than a botanic garden. There are significant plantings of herbs, perennial borders, a rose garden, rhododendrons and azaleas, the arboretum (on the other side of the River Kelvin, separate entrance), and a fine children's garden which is used as part of an ambitious education programme. Children plant seeds, look after the plants and harvest them. The Kelvin river runs through the north of the garden in a wild wooded gorge, a haven for wildlife; it is rare to find such an unmanicured wilderness in the centre of a city.

Glasgow People's Palace and Winter Gardens
Glasgow Green,
Glasgow, G40 1AT
(*map, pp. 256–57*)

Glasgow Museums
All year. Monday–Thursday, Saturday 10am–5pm, Friday, Sunday 11am–5pm; free
Easy access by bus, train to Argyle Street, subway station: St Enoch. M8, J15 head south on A8 or J20 and head east along Clyde. Free parking nearby including disabled parking
T: 0141 271 2962
E: museums@cls.glasgow.gov.uk
www.glasgowmuseums.com
Café

Glasgow People's Palace and Winter Gardens

This place is 'pure dead brilliant' and as a family day out it is 'hard tae beat'. Glasgow's People's Palace opened in 1898, as a popular social museum and celebration of the people and city of Glasgow and it has recently been restored. Outside in the extensive park is one of the best children's play areas in Scotland with death-defying slides. Inside is a spectacular greenhouse with a good value café and displays of cacti, palms and other greenhouse favourites. The compact museum on the two upper floors covers the period from 1750 through the Industrial Revolution to the present. Displays include the 'steamie' (forerunner of the laundrette), Anderson shelters, holidays 'doon the watter', housing, alcohol, shipbuilding and even Billy Connolly's banana boots. If you want to understand what made and makes Glasgow tick, this is certainly the place to come. The kitsch Doulton Fountain, the largest terracotta fountain in the world, was recently restored and

relocated from Kelvingrove Park to the front of the People's Palace. There are some recently planted banks of grasses next to the building and you can't miss the Doge's Palace carpet factory building with its unexpected façade.

Glenapp Castle

This garden's rescue is a heart-warming tale. South-west Scotland hotelier family the MacMillans acquired Glenapp Castle and gardens in derelict state in 1994 and Fay (née MacMillan) and Graham Cowan have transformed both to their former grandeur. The castle was built in the 1870s by James Bryce for James Hunter and the estate was sold in 1917 to James Mackay, later earl of Inchcape, whose family held it until 1982. It is now run as an exclusive, award-winning country house hotel and restaurant, set in 36 acres of woodland. Next to the house there is a terrace and small formal parterre from which there is an impressive vista over a small loch surrounded by azaleas, and out over the trees to the sea, Kintyre and Ailsa Craig. Paths have been opened through the fine mature trees and rhododendron species, including many large-leaved species such as *R. arizelum*. I noticed a particularly fine multi-stemmed *Cercidiphyllum japonicum*. This garden was very well planted in the early twentieth century with the rhododendrons given plenty of room, so that they are now excellent fully clothed specimens. The walled garden is also fine, with a beautifully restored greenhouse and herbaceous borders as well as some more unusual structural planting such as *R. sinogrande*. The garden is open to hotel residents and those eating at the hotel only. You can book for a fine afternoon tea and enjoy the run of the grounds. Or splash out on accommodation or its Michelin-starred restaurant.

Glenapp Castle
Ballantrae, Ayrshire, KA26 0NZ
(*map, pp. 256–57*)

Graham and Fay Cowan
Open to those staying or having meals at hotel, must book in advance; £££+ with afternoon tea
A77 to Ballantrae, south of Ballantrae cross river, first turning on right
T: 01465 831212
F: 01465 831000
E: info@glenappcastle.com
www.glenappcastle.com

Glenfall
Beith Road, Howwood,
Renfrewshire, PA9 1AS
(*map, pp. 256–57*)

Dr and Mrs Chris Woodcock
April–October by arrangement; £
Off the A737 between Paisley
and Beith. Turn off at sign for
Howwood, at 30mph sign turn
right at black and white cottage
before the church. Glenfall in
front of you
T: 01505 705477
E: chris@glenfall.co.uk
www.glenfall.co.uk

Glenfall

This small garden is constructed on the very steep sides of a former quarry surrounded by cliffs and a spectacular 30ft waterfall. The gardens were first created in the 1980s and opened under the Gardens Scheme, but were badly overgrown when the Woodcocks bought the property in 2006. It is gradually being cleared, with improved paths and a range of new plantings of ferns, hellebores and *Meconopsis* and other shade-tolerant plants, many of which are being propagated by the owners. The steep steps and narrow paths require reasonable agility! The website shows pictures of the progress being made.

Glenronnie House
Kirkoswald Road, Maidens,
by Turnberry, Ayrshire, KA26 9NF
(*map, pp. 256–57*)

Mr and Mrs Iain Brown
SGS 1 day per year; ££
A719 to Maidens to top of hill to
parking area at Redgates Chalet
Park (not caravan park). From
Ayr B7024, pass Culzean Castle.
Glenronnie is on Kirkoswald Road
250m on left. On open days
transport provided to garden
T: 01655 760245

Glenronnie House

This young 2-acre garden is well-constructed and packed with plants. The modern house has a long terrace along the front, dominated by a row of pom-pom clipped standard conifers. Below this a cascading burn with a series of ponds is surrounded by a 'jungle' of ferns and other dramatic foliage plants. Behind and beside the house is a woodland/spring interest area with rhododendrons and azaleas. Elsewhere there are borders with perennials, grasses and peonies, as well as a black summerhouse. The hard landscaping is a little stark, with lots of stone walls and paving, and will soften as the planting matures.

Greenbank Garden

This handsome Georgian mansion, woodland and 2½-acre walled garden in Clarkston on Glasgow's south side, was left to the National Trust for Scotland on condition that it was used as a site for horticultural demonstration for small gardens. The garden's central axis leads from the front door of the house across the lawn into a walled garden which is divided into many hedged 'rooms' which feature a large range of plants and planting styles. Recently retired head gardener Jim May was in charge for over 30 years and made Greenbank the fine garden that it is. Jim encouraged Greenbank to become part of the fabric of the local community with a successful Friends' programme and many volunteers who help out with planting and maintenance. At 500ft, Greenbank is a cold site on clay soil and plants need to be tough to survive here. It has a national collection of *Bergenia*, and the magazine *Which* uses this garden for its northern trials of plants which in recent years have included *Achillea, Artemisia, Erigeron* and *Potentilla*. Some of the many garden sections include gravel planting, peony borders, grasses, herbs, a pond and several water features, plants for drying and a rather odd collection of topiary including a giant owl. Outside the walled garden is snowdrop-carpeted woodland which gives over to *Narcissus* in April and May. With more than 450 varieties, Greenbank has one of the best daffodil collections in the UK and the walled garden has varieties planted all round, some in parterres and raised beds. The annual daffodil day in spring sees cut blooms displayed in the house. The good structure and colour in this garden make it worth a visit in winter and early spring with snowdrops, *Viburnum*, witch hazel, *Sarcococca* and trees and shrubs with fine bark: birches, willows, dogwoods and *Prunus serrula*. Dogs are allowed in woodland only.

Greenbank Garden
Flenders Road, Clarkston,
Glasgow, G76 8RB
(*map, pp. 256–57*)

NTS
Garden: all year, daily
9.30am–sunset. Shop and
tearoom: 30 March–31 October,
daily 11am–5pm; ££*
Off M77 follow A727 (formerly
A726), follow signs for East
Kilbride to Clarkston Toll. 6 miles
south of Glasgow city centre. Bus
44A Clarkston station, 1¼ miles
T: 0844 4932201
www.nts.org.uk

Greenhead Roses
Greenhead Nursery,
Old Greenock Road, Inchinnan,
Renfrew, PA4 9PH
(*map, pp. 256–57*)

C.N. Urquhart
Daily: 10am–5pm
Exit junction 29 off the M8.
Follow signs into Inchinnon from
the A8. The nursery is ½ mile
on the left
T: 0141 8120121
F: 0141 8120000
E: sales@rosesscotland.co.uk

Greenhead Roses

This is one of Scotland's few rose specialists and the only one on the west coast. Situated round the back of Glasgow airport, it is a small garden centre which also sells gifts, meat, fruit and vegetables. They grow a wide range of shrubs, perennials and bedding on-site but their main speciality is roses, which are grown in larger pots than most rose growers use which means that (a) the roots need less pruning when dug from the field and (b) the roses have more fertiliser and room to grow so they don't become pot-bound as quickly as those in smaller pots. The Urquharts have a long involvement in judging at the Glasgow Rose Trials and they know their stuff. They also do mail order.

Hayes Garden Land
Tarbolton Road, Symington,
Kilmarnock, Ayrshire, KA1 5PD
(*map, pp. 256–57*)

Michael Hayes
Monday—Saturday
9.30am–5.30pm, Sunday
10am–5.30pm, closed 25
December–2 January
Signed off A77 just north
of Symington
T: 01563 830204,
01563 830204 (café)
F: 01563 830204
E: mail@hayesgardenland.com
www.hayesgardenland.co.uk
Bakery café

Hayes Garden Land

This garden centre was founded by Peter Hayes and his son Michael, whose horticultural roots are in the seven-generation family horticultural business Hayes of Ambleside in Cumbria. This small but well-planned garden centre, very close to the A77 Glasgow–Ayr road, carries a fine range of plants, sundries and furniture. I also liked the range of up-market and unusual Christmas goods offered and the café and small farm shop are clearly popular.

Hazel Lodge

This 1-acre country garden, with fine views to the south, designed by the owners over the last 10 years, is planted to give year-round interest. Features include several stone and water features, ponds, herbaceous borders, rockeries, shrubs, hostas and a vegetable garden. The most unusual feature is a bank of stone cattle troughs filled with hostas.

B&B

Hazel Lodge
Straiton, Ayrshire, KA19 7NJ
(*map, pp. 256–57*)

Irene Munro
SGS most years and groups
by appointment; ££
From A77 take B7045 to Straiton,
then take B741 opposite the Black
Bull Hotel. Hazel Lodge is ½ mile
outside village
T: 01655 770660

Herbscents Cottage Garden Plants

At 700ft up, in cold central Lanarkshire, with fine views over the Forth to Stirling and the Trossachs, this is a garden and nursery where plants need to be tough. The Browns have spent 10 years establishing windbreaks and have planted a 7-acre site with culinary and medicinal herbs, wild flowers, cottage garden plants, grasses, trees and shrubs, many of which have the added bonus of attracting wildlife. The informative website for their mail-order nursery allows plants to be selected under different categories, some you would expect: plants which are bee or bird-friendly, plants for shade; other categories are more unusual: plants for pot pourri, plants for dyeing and drying. You can also search for plants by common name. The nursery is far off the beaten track and is not open to the public, though I'm sure if you made a special appointment, they'd let you come.

**Herbscents Cottage
Garden Plants**
Woodside Cottage, Longriggend,
Airdrie, Lanarkshire, ML6 7RU

Brenda and Mike Brown
Mail order only
Off the A803 between Greengairs
and Slammannan, follow signs
to Longriggend
T: 01236 843826
E: mail@herbscents.co.uk
www.herbscents.co.uk

Hidden Gardens, Tramway
Tramway, 25 Albert Drive,
Glasgow, G41 2PE
(*map, pp. 256–57*)

Monday closed, Tuesday–Saturday
10am–8pm (or dusk if earlier),
Sunday 12–6pm (or dusk if
earlier); free
Off Pollokshaws Road, turn into
Albert Drive at St Ninian's Church.
Pollokshields East Station very
close
T: 0845 330 3501
E: info@thehiddengardens.org.uk
www.thehiddengardens.org.uk
Tramway cafe bar with fine range
of food

Hidden Gardens, Tramway

I have always had a soft spot for the Tramway as it has hosted some of
the best theatre performances I have ever seen. Created out of an old
tram shed, this is one of Scotland's foremost theatre, dance and art
venues/spaces. The Hidden Gardens which lie behind the building are
an exciting piece of contemporary garden design created by NVA and
City Design Cooperative in the industrial heart of Glasgow. The
design is influenced by the contemplative 'paradise' gardens of Japan,
China and the Islamic world and closer to home, meditative monastic
gardens. It is both a community garden, with many volunteer groups
coming to help look after it, and a modern 'sacred' garden, dedicated
to peace. It has several striking design elements including a circular
rill, a raised bed of birch underplanted with anemone, a raised bed of
summer herbs (thyme, fennel, sage, lavender) and a giant old
chimney. A variety of stone, textures and shapes used in the paving,
walls, gabions and beds. The planting includes Scottish natives, fruit
trees and Asian plants such as *Rhododendron thomsonii*, flowering
cherries, *Magnolia* and *Ginkgo*. A small courtyard to the left of the
tower is sometimes open. The garden has been used to host a variety
of festivals and events such as celebrations of Diwali. I'm delighted to
see such a contemporary garden, with some striking repeat planting
and a wide range of hard-landscaping materials. It will require quite a
high level of maintenance to keep it looking sharp.

Holmes Farm
Drybridge, near Irvine,
Ayrshire, KA11 5BS
(*map, pp. 256–57*)

Mr Brian A Young
1 weekend in June SGS or by
appointment, groups welcome; ££
Holmes is the only farm between
Drybridge and Dreghorn on
the B730
T: 01294 311210
F: 01294 311210
E: yungi@fsmail.net

Holmes Farm

This is a wonderful newcomer to Scotland's list of gardens to visit.
Behind this working farm is an amazing collection of plants
assembled by Brian Young, one of the younger SGS garden owners, to
be sure. The garden used to be a formal walled rose garden, then a
conifers and heathers combination and then Brian set to work,
shifting 30–40 tons of soil and gravel. The emphasis here is on herbaceous plants, the highlight of which is the collection of over 300 *Iris*

298

varieties, particularly sibiricas, which should be at their peak in early June on the SGS open days. Recent plantings are more late summer-orientated with *Phlox, Crocosmia*, and late flowerers from the daisy family. Everything looks immaculately maintained: plants, gravel paths and lawns alike. Don't miss the tunnels and greenhouses, raised beds of *Lewisia* and *Rhodohypoxis* and Brian's increasing collection of *Roscoea, Agapanthus* and *Eucomis*. On open days there are plants for sale and an arts and crafts stall. This is a real plantsman's mecca.

Holy Island Peace Centre

After significant fund-raising, Holy Island, off Arran, was purchased as a Buddhist retreat for peace and meditation. Native tree planting was set in motion with help from Scottish Wildlife Trust. The island is also home to Eriskay ponies, Soay sheep and Saanen goats. A garden of Tibetan medicinal herbs is being established and there is an organic vegetable garden.

Holy Island Peace Centre
Holy Isle, Lamlash Bay,
Isle of Arran, KA27 8GB
(*map, pp. 256–57*)

Rokpa Trust
Ferry Ardrossan to Brodick,
bus 323 to Lamlish Pier,
ferry to Holy Isle.
T: 01770 601100
F: 01770 601101
E: reception@holyisland.org

Invermay

This town garden of around a third of an acre in Cambuslaing on the south side of Glasgow has been created over 50 years by keen and knowledgeable plantswoman Margaret Robertson, with help in construction and pruning from her husband Bob, who is keener on conquering Scotland's high ground; he has climbed all the Munros, Corbetts and Donalds. The 1877 Victorian house has a small front garden, packed with plants and a larger, narrow strip of back garden which is equally bursting with all manner of perennials and shrubs, a mixture of old favourites and some very new varieties too: *Geranium, Heuchera, Codonopsis, Thalictrum* and roses, which lead to the vegetable garden with ivy-covered obelisks. When I visited in June, Margaret described the family of foxes which had been playing in the leeks and onions, and bouncing on the fleece which was supposed to

Invermay
48 Wellshot Drive,
Cambuslang, Glasgow, G72 8BN
(*map, pp. 256–57*)

Bob and Margaret Robertson
April–September, groups by
appointment (SGS); ££
Turn off Main Street,
Cambuslang by station
T: 0141 6411632

keep off the carrot fly. Behind this lies the shady lower part of the garden under a giant Norway maple with climbing and rambling roses along the fence. Gates and doors are strikingly painted turquoise, Margaret's favourite colour. This is a great small town garden, proudly maintained by a good gardening team.

Jupiter Urban Wildlife Centre

Jupiter Urban Wildlife Centre
Wood Street,
Grangemouth, FK3 8LH
(*map, pp. 256–57*)

Scottish Wildlife Trust,
KemFine Ltd (owner)
Monday–Friday 10am-5pm; free
North of the M9 between J5 and
J6. From M9 route is shown by
brown tourist signs
T: 01324 486475
E: jupiterranger@swt.org.uk
www.swt.org.uk
Frequent weekend family events
Self-led nature activities always
available

Under the shadow of Scotland's largest industrial complex, the Grangemouth oil refinery, is the Jupiter Urban Wildlife Centre with 10 acres of wildlife gardens and habitats. It was created out of wasteland of an old railway yard and it one of Scotland's best demonstrations of wildlife gardening. The various habitats, wetland, woodland and meadow, contain hundreds of native trees and 300 wildflower species. The wild flowers are at their best from May to July. An educational building was built in 2006 for use with schools/children's groups and frequent weekend activities are also run. There are also native plants offered for sale in the wildflower nursery. The centre's nursery manager Nancy MacIntyre was awarded an MBE in 2007 for services to the environment and conservation.

Kelburn Castle Gardens and Country Centre

**Kelburn Castle Gardens
and Country Centre**
Fairlie, Ayrshire, KA29 0BE
(*map, pp. 256–57*)

Earl of Glasgow
Castle: Easter–end October
10am–6pm; grounds; open all
year; £££ (castle and grounds)
Off A78 coast road 2 miles south
of Largs. Rail (Largs) 2 miles,
buses to entrance on A78
T: 01475 568685
F: 01475 568121
E: admin@kelburncountrycentre.
com
www.kelburncountrycentre.com
Licensed café

Dating back to the thirteenth century but much altered, Kelburn Castle is the family home of the earls of Glasgow. The Kel Burn, which drops 800ft, rushes through the Kelburn Glen from the moors above the castle through a series of waterfalls and there is a network of paths and roads on both sides of the burn with six bridges, eventually leading to the top which allows walks of one to two hours from the castle. Be aware that some of the paths have substantial drops off the sides, so might be dangerous for young children. From the top there are fine views west over the islands of the Firth of Clyde. This is a semi-tamed landscape of snowdrops and bluebells, wild flowers and

ferns, shrubs and trees in a spectacular setting. There are some fine and unusual trees, including Britain's tallest Monterey pine, a pair of 1,000-year-old yews and the enormous weeping larch with fused and rooting branches, considered some of Scotland's important 'heritage' trees. The eighteenth-century walled garden known as 'the pleasaunce' contains mature trees and shrubs. Kelburn has lots of impressive children's activities: pony trekking, the 'Secret Forest' (paths, aerial walkways etc), adventure course, playbarn and outdoor play area, birds of prey centre, pottery workshop. The spectacular graffiti wall on one whole face of the castle was supposed to be painted over in 2008 but was still there when I last enquired.

Kelvingrove Park

Kelvingrove Park, bordered by Glasgow University and Kelvingrove Museum, was created in the centre of Glasgow in the mid nineteenth century. Charles Wilson and Joseph Paxton were among those who contributed to its design. Recent developments include the popular skateboard park, a new heritage centre and the Stewart Fountain restoration. There are great views of the Glasgow skyline and it is a very popular public space with children's play area, long herbaceous borders and a fine collection of trees. The River Kelvin runs through the middle.

Kelvingrove Park
Otago Street, Glasgow, G12 8NR
(*map, pp. 256–57*)

Glasgow City Council
Dawn–dusk; free
Off Woodlands Road and Kelvin Way; Kelvinbridge Underground station
T: 0141 334 6363
0141 357 5973
E: land@glasgow.gov.uk
www.glasgow.gov.uk

Kingencleugh House

Kingencleugh House
Mauchline, Ayrshire, KA5 5JL
(*map, pp. 256–57*)

Etain, Lady Hagart-Alexander
By appointment; ££
A76 road from Kilmarnock to
Dumfries, just south of Mauchline
T: 01290 550217
E: etain.alexander@virgin.net
Tea and coffee can be arranged

This impressive pink seventeenth-century house looks out onto the ruins of Kingencleugh Castle with the rolling hills of Ayrshire beyond. The garden consists of several sections and 'rooms' with plantings of rhododendrons, alpines, trees, and perennials, as well as a woodland walk along the stream bank, which has fine bluebells and daffodils in spring. Lady Hagart-Alexander is a keen plantswoman and supporter of the NCCPG with a national collection of *Trillium*, best seen in April and May.

Kirkmuir Farm

Kirkmuir Farm
Stewarton, Ayrshire, KA3 3DZ
(*map, pp. 256–57*)

Mr and Mrs Brian MacPherson
SGS 1 day per year; ££
Sharon St, west of Stewarton, off
A735 Lugton to Kilmarnock road
T: 01560 485284

This is a garden of c. 2½ acres constructed around a complex of farm buildings. The garden has lots of hidden sections and just when you think you've seem them all, another part of the garden appears. The site is exposed, so conifer hedges have been used to divide the sections and keep out the wind. The section nearest the house contains gravel and rock gardens and a wagon wheel on one of the walls. From here a conifer arch leads to a shadier section with ferns and a sit-ooterie. Other sections include one which features heathers, herbaceous and shrubs, one with a large oval pond and lead herons, another with herbaceous, a curved line of telegraph poles alongside a patio and open-sided summer house and finally along the drive side, a vegetable garden.

Knowetop Community Farm

Started 26 years ago by local people, this is a successful organic, ornamental and productive garden, organised like a series of allotments, managed and worked by volunteers, boasting up to 24,000 visitors annually. The farm is a registered charity, and a member of the Federation of City Farms and Community Gardens. There is a popular community composting site and a wide range of farm and small animals, as well as a garden for the disabled with raised beds. It has provided SVQ training in horticulture and small animal care. On open days there are guided tours of the farm by young volunteers. This is certainly one of the most impressive and active of Scotland's community gardens and contributes enormously to the local community.

Knowetop Community Farm
113 Castlehill Road,
Dumbarton, G82 5AT
(*map, pp. 256–57*)

Knowetop Community Farm
SGS open days, or by appointment; SGS ££, otherwise donations
From Glasgow: A82 to Dumbarton, A814 towards Helensburgh, turn right at flagpole/traffic lights ¼ mile past River Leven crossing, up Castlehill Road. From north on A814, turn left at flagpole/traffic lights. Follow road to top. Buses and trains to Dumbarton
T: 01389 732734/762816
E: eleanor@knowetop communityfarm.co.uk
www.knowetopcommunityfarm.co.uk
Café, using farm produce

Ladyburn House
Ladyburn, by Maybole,
Ayrshire, KA19 7SG
(*map, pp. 256–57*)

Mrs J. Hepburn
May–end September by
appointment; ££
Maybole B7023 to Crosshill. Turn
right at the War Memorial signed
to Girvan – B7023, 2 miles turn
left over the bridge, pass Kilkerran,
Ladyburn on right
T: 01655 740 585
F: 01655 740 206
E: jh@ladyburn.co.uk
www.ladyburn.co.uk
Catering can be arranged
for groups

Ladyburn House

This garden has recently been considerably changed to accommodate the national collections of shrub roses which Mrs Hepburn has been assembling. Beds of these are to be found down the drive, along the fences and boundaries and in various parts of the garden, which is surrounded by mature trees with a small pond in the middle. There is also a box parterre next to the house. This garden is obviously going to mature in the next few years and should be a showcase for relatively disease-resistant roses which should do well in the west, where many hybrid roses suffer disease if they are not continually sprayed. There are fine spring bulbs and rhododendrons for spring colour.

Lagg House

This national collection of *Hydrangea* showcases what outstanding garden plants they are for the west coast of Scotland. The garden is perched inland above cliffs overlooking Arran, blasted by winds,

protected by shelter belts of *Sorbus, Escallonia* and other shrubs. The garden is overflowing with hydrangeas which have to be hard-pruned every few years to keep them in bounds. They are planted in mixed colours and the effect works surprisingly well. They even flower well under trees, as long as they are irrigated. South American evergreen species such as *H. seemannii* grow and flower on the walls of the farm buildings. It's not a mono-culture, there are lots of other plants in the garden, including an overstorey of *Buddleja* and carpets of perennials such as hostas. But there are certainly a lot of hydrangeas which start flowering in June and go on well into the autumn. Even *Hydrangea* snobs who think anything beyond *H. aspera* is vulgar would find varieties to like here. I also admire Anne Greenall's enthusiasm for hydrangeas without taking them too seriously – unlike some national collection-holders who tend towards what might be referred to as 'anoraks'.

Lagg House
Dunure, Ayrshire, KA7 4LE
(*map, pp. 256–57*)

Mrs A. Greenall
By appointment; ££
North of Dunure on A719
Ayr–Girvan road, coming from
Ayr look out for the farm buildings
on left, shortly after Heads of
Ayr farm park and caravan site
T: 01292 500286
E: mag31@ukonline.co.uk

McLarens Nurseries

Easily Scotland's largest nursery and one of the UK's largest, this is a real treasure-trove of plants long established as a wholesale supplier but now also offering plants, composts and pots to the retail market. I was particularly impressed by the Italian-grown box balls and trained spirals and the large range of ferns, grasses and related plants, but they really do have a good range of almost everything at pretty keen prices. The place needs to be better marketed, few non-locals seem to know that the place exists.

McLarens Nurseries
Lochlibo Road, Uplawmoor,
Barrhead, Glasgow, G78 4DN
(*map, pp. 256–57*)

Monday–Friday 8am–4.30pm,
Saturday–Sunday 9am–4.pm
On the A 736 south of Glasgow
between Uplawmoor and Lugton
T: 01505 850666
F: 01505 850698
E: adam@mclarensnurseries.co.uk
www.mclarensnurseries.co.uk

WC

Milton House
Milton, Dunbartonshire, G82 2TU
(*map, pp. 256–57*)

Mr and Mrs Charles Villiers
SGS 1 day and groups by
appointment; ££
On the north side of the Clyde,
off the A82 at Milton. Entrance
is on left up Milton Brae
T: 01389 732568
E: emma.villiers@hotmail.com

Milton House

This garden used to be owned by Sir Peter Hutchison, of Cox and Hutchison plant-hunting renown. It is good news that the Villiers have continued improving the garden and that Milton is open under the Gardens Scheme once again. There are fine mature rhododendron species and hybrids, and some interesting trees, underplanted with spring bulbs and perennials. The hillside garden has impressive views over the Clyde. Unsuitable for wheelchair access, owing to gravel and steep paths.

Mount Stuart
Isle of Bute, PA20 9LR
(*map, pp. 256–57*)

Marquis of Bute
Sunday–Friday 11am–5pm,
10am–2.30pm Saturday; ££
About 5 miles south of Rothesay,
shuttle bus service from Rothesay.
At Mt Stuart, transport runs
between ticket office and
main house
T: 01700 503877
F: 01700 505313
E: contactus@mountstuart.com
www.mountstuart.com
Excellent restaurant in visitor
centre

Mount Stuart

Mount Stuart is one of Scotland's finest tourist attractions and is a must-visit. The house is one of the world's most extraordinary follies, a sumptuous Victorian pile, way beyond extravagance and into the realms of fantasy, the bastard child of a Gothic cathedral, a mosque, a pre-Raphaelite painting and a marble Hollywood stage set. It is not really a house in the sense of somewhere to live but more a theatre set for the playboy rich. Having already transformed Cardiff Castle and restored much of Falkland Palace, the staggeringly wealthy third marquis of Bute used his coal-mining money to build Mount Stuart in the 1880s, dying before it could be completed; it was the first fully centrally-heated and electric house. His heir tried to sell it in the 1920s, with the precondition that it was taken down and rebuilt elsewhere. Thankfully, there were no takers. It was not till 1995 that the doors were opened to the public and with the 200-acre gardens, it can take a full day out to see everything. The visitor centre is a striking modern building, designed by Alfred Munkenbeck, essentially a glass and metal box, but better than this sounds, with an art gallery space downstairs and a fine restaurant/café upstairs with a terrace for warm weather which is within supervising distance of the extensive play area. Mount Stuart's grounds are huge and you have to walk considerable distances to see it all, though there is a tractor and trailer (with seats) to take those unwilling or unable to walk the whole way. The first part of the garden reached is the vast walled kitchen garden, which to my mind has so far defeated the talents of several garden designers: the main borders were originally designed by Rosemary Verey at the instigation of John and Jennifer Bute. Some of the borders were remodelled by James Alexander-Sinclair and these are striking and unusual for Scotland, some of them consist simply of grasses and *Crocosmia* and other prairie planting combinations. There are also large areas devoted to growing fruit and vegetables used in the café. The problem is that the plantings are still dwarfed by the space they are in, they just don't create the magic atmosphere that they might on a more intimate stage. The central glasshouse pavilion, purchased from the Glasgow Garden Festival, is rather shabby and looks out of place in Mount Stuart's sumptuousness. It does have a

good collection of tender plants inside and 2008 saw the addition of a
glass labyrinth in one corner. The walled garden could be improved
with more height from the plantings, garden rooms to humanise the
scale and a vantage point to look down on it all.

Alongside the road which runs to the main house are avenues of
stunning trees and one of the UK's finest pinetums, first planted with
the seedlings raised from seed collections from David Douglas and
other plant hunters in the early Victorian era, and now being
augmented as part of a worldwide conifer conservation programme.
Bute's mild climate is ideal for many conifer species from relatively
low altitudes which are threatened by logging and population
expansion in several parts of the world. Mount Stuart's woodlands are
part of a planned landscape begun in 1718 by the second earl of Bute,
added to and maintained by his successors, most of whom seem to
have made significant additions. The third earl was one of the
founders of Kew Gardens and the first Scottish British prime
minister. The mature lime avenue leads to the shore and was planted
in the eighteenth century. The 200-year-old beech avenue has recently
been replaced with young trees, continuing the 300-year horticultural
tradition of this estate. There are substantial rhododendron plantings
along the edge of the woodland, including many 150-year old
'Altaclarense' (*R. arboreum x ponticum*) which are now towering
specimens. The Butes also planted dozens of large-leaved rhododendron species including many *R. falconeri*, first introduced by
Joseph Hooker in the 1850s. Around Mount Stuart house are many
other fine trees and a well-landscaped rock garden, now full of
Japanese maples and other trees and shrubs. One highlight in July was
the *Hoheria* 'Glory of Amwych', which is the largest I have ever seen,
well over 30ft high, covered in clouds of white flowers like cherry
blossom. Walk further along the main axis past the house and you
come to the 5-acre 'wee garden' (you have to be very posh to make
jokes like that), this time planted with a heavy emphasis on southern

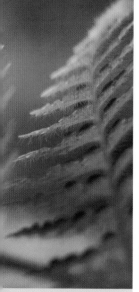

hemisphere plants such as *Drimys, Eucryphia, Olearia* and *Phormium*, as well as *Rhododendron* species. This again is well-landscaped and well maintained. Mount Stuart is not resting on its heritage and the recent patronage of contemporary art, design and architecture is only to be applauded, though some of the guides in the house clearly disapproved of the paintings on temporary show when I visited. Mount Stuart thoroughly deserves all its accolades and should help to restore the Isle of Bute to its former position as Scotland's favourite tourist destination. Bute has a number of impressive gardens with several more, currently not open to the public, which could be. The climate is so benign, as long as you can filter out the wind, and almost anything seems to grow here. It really is Scotland's 'garden island'. And don't miss Ascog Fernery or the famous Victorian gentleman's toilet on the pier. Ladies can ask to see it, as theirs is nothing special.

    WC

National Collection of Ferns
92 Drymen Road, Bearsden,
Glasgow, G61 2SY
(*map, pp. 256–57*)

Alastair and Jacqueline Wardlaw
By appointment
Side lane off east side Drymen
Road; 100 yards north of
Bearsden Station. Park at station
T: 0141 942 2461
E: a.wardlaw@tiscali.co.uk

National Collection of Ferns

This is a 'his' and 'hers' garden which the Wardlaws have been cultivating for the past 37 years. Alastair, a retired microbiologist, gardens the shady side with ferns, while Jacqueline has the sunny side for more decorative gardening with roses and herbaceous and which features some of her own sculptures. In addition to the NCCPG national collection of British ferns, there are also many from other parts of the world. The more tender ones are kept in pots so they can be over-wintered inside. Alastair Wardlaw is testing temperate species of fern for hardiness in Scotland and several other plants too: palms, *Dacrydium, Pseudopanax, Phyllocladus, Clianthus, Sarracenia*, etc.

New Lanark Roof Garden
New Lanark Visitor Centre,
New Lanark Mills,
Lanark, ML11 9DB
(*map, pp. 256–57*)

New Lanark Conservation Trust
Daily: September–May 11am–
5pm, June–August 10.30am–5pm,
closed 25 December, 1 January;
££–£££ for whole site
Signposted from M74 and other
major routes. New Lanark
station 1½ miles
T: 01555 661345
E: visit@newlanark.org
www.newlanark.org

New Lanark Roof Garden

This roof garden and viewing platform were opened in 2008 at World Heritage Site New Lanark. The extensive mill village complex on the banks of the Clyde was transformed by Robert Owen, mill manager from 1800–25, who was ahead of his time with his concern for the welfare of his workers. The roof garden is on the roof of Mill no. 2, one of the A-listed structures on the site, which means that planning regulations for the garden were very strict. The garden was designed by Douglas Coltart, taking his inspiration from the waterwheels of the mills, in a pattern of curves, using decking and paving. Structure is provided by yew and hornbeam hedging and box balls, and planting includes herbs, *Philadelphus, Hydrangea serrata*, grasses, anemones, thistles and poppies. The views of the whole New Lanark site and the River Clyde are impressive from up here.

New Lanark Roof Garden

Pineapple (The)

Known as the Dunmore Pineapple, this is one of Scotland's most extraordinary garden buildings. Built in 1761, it is a two-storey banqueting house, with a circular chamber facing into a walled garden, capped by a pineapple, shaped in stonework. Pineapples were

Pineapple (The)
Dunmore, Falkirk, FK2 8LU
(*map, pp. 256–57*)

NTS/Landmark Trust
Daily: 9.30am–sunset
A905 near Airth, between
Kincardine Bridge and Stirling.
J3 on A876
T: 0844 4932132
www.nts.org.uk

introduced to Britain in Charles II's reign and many gardens attempted to produce some of history's most expensively produced fruit using stove houses, heated walls and other techniques. Dunmore's wall chimneys are disguised by ornamental vases. The walled garden is planted with a collection of *Malus* (crab apples) and there is rather an apologetic narrow border around the edge. The Pineapple was restored in 1974 and you can rent it to stay in from the Landmark Trust. A second curved walled garden is as yet unrestored and there are walks through the surrounding woodland, which is home to large numbers of noisy rooks or crows. The Pineapple really deserves to be in a better context than this; few people visit and there is little to see apart from the building itself. Once there were intricate gardens here with greenhouses, parterres, ponds and canals. Applications to build new housing have been submitted for part of the planned landscape, opposed by conservation bodies, though this might provide funding for a more extensive and better garden. The present situation is not satisfactory.

Pollok House and Garden
2060 Pollokshaws Road,
Glasgow, G43 1AT
(*map, pp. 256–57*)

Glasgow City Council and NTS. Gardens: all year; house: April–October 10am–4pm, November–March 11am–4pm; gardens free, house £££* A736 signposted, 3½ miles from city centre. Buses run through the park but note that it is a long walk from the entrance on the east side of the park to the gardens
www.nts.org.uk
Pollok House restaurant

Pollok House and Garden

This huge park on the south side of Glasgow, with fine mature trees and the White Cart Water running through it, could be considered Glasgow's Hampstead Heath both for its vast size and its wildness, despite being surrounded by the city. Pollok Estate was formerly owned by the Stirling Maxwell family and was donated to the city of Glasgow in 1966. Pollok House, which contains a fine collection of paintings, is now owned by the National Trust for Scotland. The

Burrell Collection museum, housing the pick-and mix art collection of a nineteenth-century Glasgow industrialist, is also sited in the park. The old rhododendron collection to the east of the house is now overshaded and overgrown, and is due for major renovation. You'll probably spot the famous Pollok beech with a squat fat gnarled trunk and a mass of stems protruding in all directions. Below this is the rather odd walled garden configuration containing several elements, divided by large yew hedges and a moat at one end. Features include a new boulder, gravel, a vegetable garden, bold blocks and borders of perennials, roses and sections of traditional bedding. Formal terraces along the front of Pollok House are planted with begonias, pelargoniums and other bedding. Pollok was voted the best park in Britain 2007 and Europe's best park 2008, though from a horticultural point of view there is work to do to bring some of it up to standard.

Quarrybank Cottage

Quarrybank Cottage
Falkirk Road, Avonbridge,
Falkirk, FK1 2NA
(*map, pp. 256–57*)

Malvina Dwyer
SGS some years, by appointment
July and August; ££
Situated on B8028 next to Church
of Scotland, corner of B825
and B8028 at west (Falkirk)
end of village
T: 01324 861337

Quarrybank has won the Falkirk and District garden competition three times. It contains some interesting specimen trees and is a mix of woodland/wild with some formal sections with terracing, several water features and hidden places with statues and figures. Visitors are encouraged to walk a route up the steps past the greenhouse along the top of the garden and down the other side. The garage has a terrace roof garden with bedding spilling over. Not suitable for wheelchairs due to steep slopes and steps.

Ross Priory
Gartocharn,
by Alexandria, G83 8NL
(*map, pp. 256–57*)

University of Strathclyde,
head gardener Tony Farrell
1 day in May SGS, groups by
appointment to head gardener; ££
Turn off A811in Gartocharn,
1½ miles north towards Loch
Lomond
T: 01389 830719 07815 759181
E: ross.priory@strath.ac.uk
E: tony.farrell@strath.ac.uk

Ross Priory

Ross Priory, which lies at the south end of Loch Lomond with fine views of the loch, Ben Lomond and the surrounding hills, was a Gothic remodelling of an existing house by James Gillespie Graham in 1812 for the Buchanan family. The house and estate were purchased in 1971 by the University of Strathclyde, who undertook extensive restoration. The house is used for conferences and other functions and a golf course has been built to the east of the house. To the west are 13 acres of gardens. Part of the woodland was once a formal garden with yew-lined paths, now overgrown and shaded, it blocks the garden's greatest asset, its fantastic views of Loch Lomond and its tree-clad islands, sadly now only visible from the shore. I'd get a chainsaw out and open up vistas to the house and loch, which would completely transform the garden. The woodland contains a significant collection of species rhododendrons such as *R. praestans, R. ririei, R. falconeri*, as well as some gigantic hybrids and plenty of deciduous azaleas and some fine magnolias including large-leaved *M. rostrata* and cucumber tree *M. acuminata*. Both rhododendrons and magnolias were well-spaced when planted, mainly in the 1920s, and without too much tree cover, so most have grown into free-flowering giants. In his time here Maurice Wilkins, now at Arduaine, planted trees and shrubs such as a variegated *Liriodendron, Embothrium, Cornus kousa* and *Cornus controversa*. His successor, Tony Farrell, has particularly concentrated on replanting the walled garden, which is approached along an autumn heather walk. It contains a large pergola draped with white *Wisteria*, a glasshouse and restored cold frames, a yew-backed double allée of white-barked birch underplanted with hardy *Fuchsia*, several beds of perennials, some rockery/scree beds and a double border of Rose 'Cornelia' which leads to a moon gate.

Rouken Glen Garden Centre

This Glasgow garden centre was opened in 1985 at the edge of Eastwood in a leafy part of south Glasgow. It is popular and still very much has the feel of a garden centre rather than a department store. The plant area is extensive, as is the pet centre. There is also a branch at 18 Cauldcoats, Philpstoun, near Linlithgow, EH49 7LY.

Rouken Glen Garden Centre
Rouken Glen Road,
Giffnock, Glasgow, G46 7JL
(*map, pp. 256–57*)

Daily: 9.30am–6pm
In Rouken Glen Park near the
intersection of the A77 and A727
T: 0141 620 0566
F: 0141 620 0275
E: glasgow@roukenglen.com
www.roukenglen.co.uk
Large coffee shop open
9.30am–5pm

Sandyholm Garden Centre (Dobbies)

The A72 Clyde Valley road from Châtelheraut to Lanark has long been the centre of Scottish horticulture with tomato producers, bedding plants and more recently a string of garden centres. Some of the nurseries and garden centres have closed down and been sold for housing, though many of the older nurseries such as Mortons are still going strong. One of Sandyholm's innovations was to cover their whole plant area over to make it rain proof. Not all plants liked this and some have now been moved outside. The under-cover area gave them a vast arena in which to create their famous Christmas displays, which were amongst the best in Scotland. Both it and its popular café won several awards. Sadly, Scotland's finest larger independent garden centre was sold to Dobbies/Tesco in 2008.

Sandyholm Garden Centre
Crossford, by Carluke,
Lanarkshire, ML8 5QF
(*map, pp. 256–57*)

Dobbies/Tesco
Daily: 9am–6pm
On the A72 north of Crossford.
From north leave A74 at J7 and
follow signs for Clyde Valley
T: 01555 860205
F: 01555 860725
www.dobbies.com
Popular café

Skeldon

Skeldon house is a handsome Georgian mansion on the banks of the River Doon. The gardens are surrounded and sheltered by woodland, with some fine specimen trees and interesting walks through 4 acres of informal woodland. There are lots of mature rhododendrons and azaleas in spring and the formal garden, in a curve of the river, consists of lawns surrounded by herbaceous borders, rose beds, annuals and climbing roses on arbours and pergolas. A giant *Cornus kousa* was dripping with white bracts in early summer. The fine Victorian greenhouse has been renovated and is filled with pelargoniums, vines and plumbago and has a noble monkey puzzle next to it. Skeldon was on the market at time of writing so opening arrangements may change.

Skeldon
Dalrymple, Ayrshire, KA6 6AT
(*map, pp. 256–57*)

Ian Brodie QC
SGS 1 Sunday; ££
B7034 Dalrymple–Hollybush road,
entrance just before sharp bend
T: 01292 560656
F: 01292 560656
E: info@skeldonestate.com
www.skeldonestate.com

Snapdragon
Snapdragon, Sunnyside,
Gartacharn Road, Balfron Station,
Stirlingshire, G63 0NH
(*map, pp. 256–57*)

Jane Lindsey
By appointment
T: 01360 660 903
E: snapdragonjane@yahoo.co.uk
www.snapdragongarden.co.uk

Snapdragon

The cutting garden for Jane Lindsey's flower business Snapdragon takes up about three quarters of an acre in what used to be a pony paddock, arranged in raised beds, and is managed according to organic principles. Jane supplies cut flowers and herbs from April to the end of September. A van sells the flowers in Balfron on Fridays. The blog on the website has pictures of the fine work Jane does.

**St Nicholas Garden
and Provand's Lordship**
3 Castle Street, Glasgow, G4 0RH
(*map, pp. 256–57*)

Glasgow Museums
Monday–Thursday and Saturday
10am–5pm, Friday and Sunday
11am–5pm; free
Close to Glasgow Cathedral,
near City Bus Station
T: 0141 552 8819
E: museums@cls.glasgow.gov.uk
www.glasgowmuseums.com

St Nicholas Garden and Provand's Lordship

Provand's Lordship is Glasgow's only surviving medieval house, built in 1471 as part of St Nicholas Hospital. It contains a collection of seventeenth-century Scottish furniture donated by Sir William Burrell. Behind the house is the St Nicholas Garden, built in 1997 as a re-creation of a fifteenth-century medical herb garden. The Tontine Faces are a collection of strange stone masks displayed in the cloistered walkways. Don't miss the excellent St Mungo Museum of Religious Life opposite, which has a small Zen garden outside (rocks and raked gravel) and a popular café. The nearby cathedral and necropolis (housing the remains of the great and the not-so-good alike) are also well worth popping into.

Symington House

Symington House
By Biggar, Lanarkshire, ML12 6LW
(*map, pp. 256–57*)

James and Sarah Dawnay
SGS; ££
East of Symington Village on A72
between Biggar and Symington
T: 01899 308211
E: sd@dawnays.com

When James and Sarah Dawnay bought Symington House in 1993, the walled garden had been abandoned for 20 years and had become buried under 10ft willowherb and self-seeded birches. All that remained was a ruined greenhouse with some struggling vines. With a design by Wiltshire-based Michael Balston (a relative of the family), this is a young but fast-maturing and well looked-after garden with a restored greenhouse. Sections are laid out within yew hedges and buttresses with accents of blue *Chamaecyparis*, some of which have suffered breakages in recent storms.

Thorntree

Thorntree
Arnprior, Stirling, FK8 3EY
(*map, pp. 256–57*)

Mark and Carol Seymour
SGS and by appointment; ££
Off A811, in Arnprior take
Fintry Road, Thorntree is
second on right
T: 01786 870710
E: info@thorntreebarn.co.uk
www.thorntreebarn.co.uk

This garden is constructed around the courtyard home of florist Carol Seymour and her husband Mark. It lies on a windswept hillside with outstanding views to the dramatic cone of Ben Lomond and to Ben Ledi. The attractive white converted farm buildings shelter a series of beds and containers in the courtyard itself, while to the east are several sections of garden. Features include a dense planting of *Primula x bulleesiana* in every shade of pink and orange, a collection of ferns and an espaliered apple walk with late summer flowering *Clematis*. On the east side, the Saltire Garden, designed with the help of Gavin Dallmeyer, is filled with roses and shrubs. The use of containers in many materials including lead, terracotta, wood and stone is well done here.

Tollcross Park

Tollcross Park
254B Wellshot Road,
Glasgow, G32 7AX
(*map, pp. 256–57*)

Glasgow City Council
Daylight hours; free
3 miles east of the city centre.
Wellshot Road, Tollcross Road
and Muiryfauld Drive surround
the park, and it's quite close to
the north end of the M74.
Shettleston Station 10 mins
walk, many buses
www.glasgow.gov.uk
(follow links to parks)
Café in the winter gardens

'Twas with a slightly sore head the morning after a fine dinner for the International Rose Trials that I wandered through Tollcross Park in eastern Glasgow, founded in 1897, looking for the roses I was to judge, dodging a few drug-addled youths looking for change, who looked worse than I felt. And there, laid out down a gently sloping hill, were more roses in more colours than I could ever have imagined. Each year more varieties are added to the collection and judges come from far and wide to assess the latest roses. Two of the stars the year I was on the judging panel were 'The Attenborough Rose' and Cocker's 'Ballindalloch Castle', bred in Aberdeen, named after the castle in Banffshire. Tollcross rose trials are quite a spectacle, carefully pruned, fed and watered to reach a crescendo in late August when the judges come to town. Even if you don't much care for roses, you can hardly fail to be impressed by this. My only misgiving is that all the roses are sprayed with fungicide weekly through the season, which seems to me to partly defeat the point of having trials in the first place. Disease resistance in roses is a prime consideration for many Scottish gardeners, particularly in western Scotland where the rainfall is high, encouraging blackspot, mildew and rust. The trials don't seem to take disease resistance into consideration. Tollcross has plenty of other activities on offer: a leisure centre with swimming pools, a city farm, an indoor and outdoor play area and winter garden greenhouses. Apparently there is also a secret garden in the park, not signposted; you have to find it yourself. It is a sensory garden also used for poetry and drama groups. I failed to find it, but I did not look as hard as I might have.

Torwood Garden Centre

This garden centre lies in the triangle of land between the central Scotland motorways M9, M80, M876 and is approached through Larbert under the M876; finding it is quite a challenge, though there are now brown tourist signs on the approach. This is one of the larger Scottish independent garden centres, with a substantial plant area and a fine range of water gardening and pet supplies. A new bistro/café is due to be redeveloped in a new building beyond the shop. A wide range of plants is on offer, including some rarities you are unlikely to see elsewhere. I was particularly impressed with the range of Japanese maples and a good selection of David Austin roses.

Victoria Park

This Victorian park in the western end of Glasgow is principally known for its 'Fossil Grove' of trees, the remains of an ancient forest, around 330 million years old. The 11 fossilised tree stumps and a long fallen trunk were discovered in 1887 when an old quarry was being landscaped, and a shelter was erected to protect the remains. The park is also known for its rock garden, pond, displays of carpet bedding and putting and bowling lawns.

Torwood Garden Centre
Bellsdyke Road, Larbert,
Stirlingshire, FK5 4EG
(*map, pp. 256–57*)

Stevenson family
Monday, Saturday 9am–5.30pm,
Tuesday–Friday 9-8pm,
Sunday 10am–5.30pm,
seasonal late openings
Approached off the A88 Bellsdyke
road (brown tourist signs) which
you can get to from M9 exit 8
via Larbert
T: 01324 553152
E: mike@torwoodgardencentre.
co.uk
www.torwoodgardencentre.co.uk
Popular café in the shop.
Plans for a new bistro

Victoria Park
12 Victoria Park Drive North,
Glasgow, G14 9NN
(*map, pp. 256–57*)

Park: 7am–dusk, fossil displays:
Easter–late September Monday,
Thursday–Sunday 10am–4pm;
free
In Scotstoun, West End of
Glasgow. Entrances from
Westland Drive, Victoria Park
Drive North and Balshagray
Avenue. Several bus routes, train
to Hyndland and Jordanhill
(15 min walk)

Wattston Bonsai Nursery
Mosside cottage, 104 Greengairs
Road, Wattston, Airdrie, ML6 7SY
(*map, pp. 256–57*)

Douglas and Lil Smith
Mail order, visits by appointment.
M80 to A73, then B8305
T: 01236 830233
E: macbonsai@yahoo.co.uk
www.wattstonbonsai.com
Tea and coffee

Wattston Bonsai Nursery

Scotland's only Bonsai nursery, offering mail-order service via its online shop. They show at Dundee, Gardening Scotland and Ayr flower shows. As well as finished bonsai ranging in price from around £30 to £2,000 or more for the oldest ones, they supply pots, tools, bespoke bonsai display tables, composts and books and run workshop days with leading bonsai practitioners. Dougie and Lil Smith can host open days at their nursery and will make club visits.

Weaver's Cottage
The Cross, Kilbarchan,
Greater Glasgow and
Clyde Valley, PA10 2JG
(*map, pp. 256–57*)

NTS
21 March–30 September:
Friday–Tuesday (closed
Wednesday, Thursday)
1–5pm; ££*
www.nts.org.uk

Weaver's Cottage

This 1723 cottage is typical of those lived in by the weavers in and around Paisley. The village of Kilbarchan had over 800 handlooms in the 1830s. The small garden contains plants used for clothes-dying including woad and madder, the garden wall contains holes for bee-keeping and there is an old cheese press. A recent archaeological dig revealed human remains in the garden. The shop sells hand-woven material.

South-West:
Dumfries and Galloway

Dumfries, Galloway and the southern part of Ayrshire and Lanarkshire offer a huge range of gardens and nurseries for visiting at almost any time of year. This is an ideal area for a weekend break from Glasgow, Edinburgh or northern England if you fancy an alternative to Lake District traffic jams. This corner of Scotland is off the mass-tourism track and is wonderfully peaceful, easy to drive around, with a mild climate, fine stately homes, ruined castles and ancient abbeys to visit as well as all the gardens. Rhododendron lovers will enjoy the acres of Drumlanrig, Castle Kennedy and Corsock, while perennial fans can head for Cally, Elizabeth MacGregor's nursery (Ellenbank) and the walled garden at Threave while Logan has a tropical look and is the most visited garden in the area. There are literally dozens of SGS gardens open for a day or two a year, with Portrack's Garden of Cosmic Speculation the highlight. The A75 route from Dumfries to Stranraer and the A76 from Dumfries north towards Kilmarnock provide access to most of the gardens.

Gardens open from time to time (not listed individually) include Drumclyer, Irongay; Berscar House, Closeburn; The Garth, near Penpont; Crossmichael Gardens (Waterside and 19 Rhonepark Crescent); Crofts, Castle Douglas; the Mill House, Gelston; Skairfield, Hightae; Townhead of Glencain, Moniave; Westerhall and Millhouse, Rhonehouse.

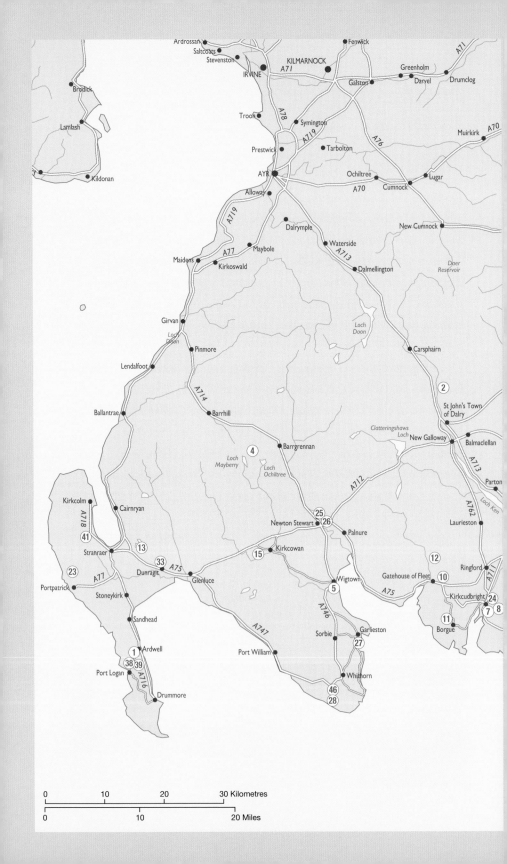

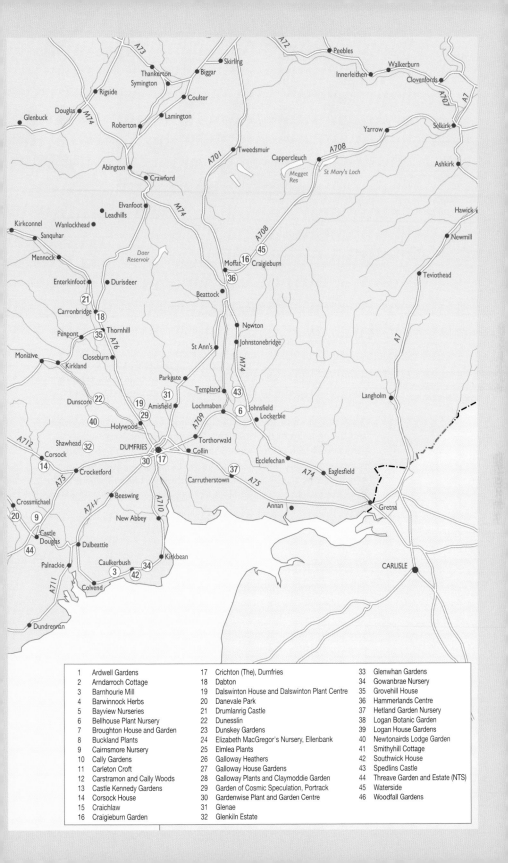

1	Ardwell Gardens	17	Crichton (The), Dumfries	33	Glenwhan Gardens
2	Arndarroch Cottage	18	Dabton	34	Gowanbrae Nursery
3	Barnhourie Mill	19	Dalswinton House and Dalswinton Plant Centre	35	Grovehill House
4	Barwinnock Herbs	20	Danevale Park	36	Hammerlands Centre
5	Bayview Nurseries	21	Drumlanrig Castle	37	Hetland Garden Nursery
6	Bellhouse Plant Nursery	22	Dunesslin	38	Logan Botanic Garden
7	Broughton House and Garden	23	Dunskey Gardens	39	Logan House Gardens
8	Buckland Plants	24	Elizabeth MacGregor's Nursery, Ellenbank	40	Newtonairds Lodge Garden
9	Cairnsmore Nursery	25	Elmlea Plants	41	Smithyhill Cottage
10	Cally Gardens	26	Galloway Heathers	42	Southwick House
11	Carleton Croft	27	Galloway House Gardens	43	Spedlins Castle
12	Carstramon and Cally Woods	28	Galloway Plants and Claymoddie Garden	44	Threave Garden and Estate (NTS)
13	Castle Kennedy Gardens	29	Garden of Cosmic Speculation, Portrack	45	Waterside
14	Corsock House	30	Gardenwise Plant and Garden Centre	46	Woodfall Gardens
15	Craichlaw	31	Glenae		
16	Craigieburn Garden	32	Glenkiln Estate		

Ardwell Gardens
Ardwell, near Stranraer,
Dumfries and Galloway, DG9 9LY
(*map, pp. 320–21*)

Mr and Mrs Francis Brewis
1 April–30 September, daily
10am–5pm; ££
10 miles south of Stranraer off the
A716, turn off in village of Arwell
and the gardens are on the left

Ardwell Gardens

This garden lies just north of Logan Botanic Garden and benefits from a very mild climate. The handsome white eighteenth-century house is surrounded by rhododendrons, azaleas, clipped yew and cabbage trees, with a terrace of alpines to one side. There are *Magnolia*, rhododendrons, camellias, *Embothrium, Eucryphia, Drimys* and spring bulbs in the woodland. Beyond this, the large walled garden with fruit on the walls is used as a nursery, raising bedding plants and shrubs. There are various walks of half an hour or more which start by the small pond and lead through bluebell woods to the large pond/loch.

Arndarroch Cottage
St John's Town of Dalry,
Castle Douglas, Dumfriesshire,
DG7 3UD
(*map, pp. 320–21*)

Annikki and Matt Lindsay
SGS (several days per year)
and June–September by
appointment; ££
About 5 miles from St John's
Town of Dalry or Carsphairn
on the B7000. Follow signs
to the youth hostel
T: 01644 460640
E: alindsay@aquarians.co.uk

Arndarroch Cottage

This 2¼-acre garden was begun in 1991 on a windswept hillside overlooking Kendoon Loch, sheltered by dry stone walls. A wide selection of trees, shrubs and species roses are underplanted with perennials. There is a small vegetable and fruit garden, a range of medicinal plants, and over 20 different bamboos. A small woodland was planted in 2000. The aim has been to create a semi-natural, wildlife-friendly environment. The small decking 'sit-ooterie' has great views.

   WC

Arndarroch Cottage

Barnhourie Mill

This garden and its collection of rhododendrons were built up over many years by Dr Mavis Paton and the late Esther King, who purchased the overgrown woodland and seventeenth-century mill in 1959. This is a fine garden of shrubs and trees, dwarf conifers and an important collection of smaller *Rhododendron* species. The owners were great friends of the Edinburgh rhododendron guru Mr H.H. Davidian and they propagated many plants from the RBGE collections. The garden lies to the north of the mill house, along the burnside and is dominated by a large specimen of *Abies koreana*. The dwarf rhododendrons are planted on a series of rocky outcrops. Bridges have been replaced, the millpond cleared and a new area of garden is being developed. Dr Paton plans to leave this garden to a trust under the care of Jim Sorbie to ensure that it is maintained.

Barnhourie Mill
Colvend, by Dalbeattie,
Dumfries and Galloway, DG5 4PU
(*map, pp. 320–21*)

Dr Mavis Paton
May–October by appointment; ££
On A 710 between Kirkbean and
Colvend, opposite Sandyhills
beach car park
T: 01387 780269

Barwinnock Herbs
Barrhill, by Girvan,
Ayrshire, KA26 0RB
(*map, pp. 320–21*)

Monday and Dave Holtom
Mid April–end September:
10am–5pm (closed Wednesday);
free
12 miles to north-west of
Newton Stewart, turning right
off B7027 near Loch Maberry
T: 01465 821338
E: herbs@barwinnock.com
www.barwinnock.com
Enjoy a picnic out in the fields
or in the garden

Barwinnock Herbs

This is a garden and mail order nursery specialising in organically grown culinary, medicinal and aromatic herbs. The nursery lies in an old farmstead courtyard on windswept moorland, in the Southern Uplands, and the drive up is spectacular, particularly the lochs at the nursery turn-off. Herbs grown here should be hardy and well acclimatised and there are some useful demonstration raised beds with gravel mulch which demonstrate how to grow herbs in heavy soils and high rainfall. One of the sheds contains a rural life exhibition with tools and farm machinery as well as information on using herbs in cooking and for medicine. The range of herbs in their catalogue is pretty staggering. I counted 16 kinds of *Artemisia*, 20 varieties of mint, almost 50 different lavender, 52 varieties of thyme. Mail order to UK and Europe.

Bayview Nurseries
19 Bank Street, Wigtown,
Galloway, DG8 9HR
(*map, pp. 320–21*)

Daily: 9am–5pm
Take A714 to Wigtown from
A7 roundabout south of
Newton Stewart
T: 01988 402040
E:
bayviewnursery@btconnect.com
www.bayviewnursery.co.uk

Bayview Nurseries

Sited in the old walled garden of the rather scruffy looking Wigtown House Hotel, overlooking Wigtown Bay, this is a packed treasure trove of good value plants. Much of what they sell is grown on-site in the tunnels which visitors are welcome to walk through. Specialities include grasses, phormiums, cordylines, tree ferns, *Eucalyptus* and other plants suitable for the mild seaside climates of south-west Scotland. Some of the many bookshops in Wigtown have good selections of gardening books.

Bellhouse Plant Nursery

This expanding nursery in the Annandale valley is run by Doreen Scott. She propagates a range of herbaceous perennials and shrubs for sale and there is also a 3-acre garden where customers can see the plants growing. Doreen sells plants at farmers' markets around Dumfries and Lockerbie.

Broughton House and Garden

Created by painter E.A. Hornel, one of the 'Glasgow Boys', who lived here from 1901 to 1933, Broughton House and its narrow 'long rig' walled garden lies next to the River Dee in the attractive town of Kirkcudbright. The house contains Hornel's studio and a gallery of his later work, which is almost as chocolate-boxy as Renoir's, and rather camp; you'll probably either love it or loathe it. The garden is excellent, one of the best NTS gardens, well restored and cleverly planted, under the skilful care of Nick Hoskins, who took over from long-serving gardener David Russell in 2000. Hornel was clearly inspired by his two trips to Japan, evident in many of the garden features. The garden is constructed with a series of rooms mostly bordered by lines and curves of low box edging. Height is provided by mature trees including *Magnolia wilsonii*, maples, flowering cherries

Bellhouse Plant Nursery
Double D, Johnsfield,
near Lockerbie, Dumfriesshire,
DG11 1SS
(*map, pp. 320–21*)

Doreen Scott
March–October:
by appointment only
1 mile west of Lockerbie, off
B7076. Leave A74M at J17 or
18 and follow signs to Johnsfield
T: 01576 204323
E: doreen.scott@care4free.net
www.scotlands-garden.org.uk

Broughton House and Garden
12 High Street, Kirkcudbright,
DG6 4JX
(*map, pp. 320–21*)

NTS
April–October: house and
garden Thursday–Monday (closed
Tuesday and Wednesday)
12–5pm. Open daily June–August,
11am–5pm. Gardens only
February and March; £££*
Signposted in Kirkcudbright
T: 01557 330437
F: 01557 330437
E: broughtonhouse@nts.org.uk
www.nts.org.uk

over the sunken courtyard and two tall thin cypress. The sunken first section leads through to the restored lily pond with stepping stones, due to be replanted in 2009. The garden features Hornel's collection of stone objects including seven sundials, several sculptures and architectural fragments and some well-planted troughs. The summer house, which once revolved to follow the sun, has also been restored and there is a vegetable and fruit-growing border. The garden is mature, charming, peaceful and intimate. Kirkcudbright is clearly a good place for gardening and I noticed that the gardens next door were as fine as the grounds of MacLellan's Castle nearby. Other Scottish colourist paintings are displayed at the Tolbooth Art Centre nearby and there are usually good exhibitions at other galleries in the town.

  WC

Buckland Plants
Whinnieliggate, Kirkcudbright,
DG6 4XP
(map, pp. 320–21)

Robert and Dina Asbridge
March–end November:
Thursday–Sunday and bank
holidays 10am–5pm
3 miles from Kirkcudbright on
B727 (past the Wildlife Park).
Right at sign for Whinnieliggate,
100m on the left
T: 01557 331323
F: 01557 331323
E: enquiries@bucklandplants.co.uk
www.bucklandplants.co.uk

Buckland Plants

This is a small family-run nursery specialising in perennials, woodland bulbs and alpines. Some of the more unusual plants listed include *Arisaema*, a good range of *Corydalis, Erythronium, Roscoea, Ipheion, Lilium* and woodland bulbs such as *Trillium*. Many local gardeners in Dumfries and Galloway were full of praise for the quality and range of plants. Combine a visit to this nursery with Elizabeth MacGregor's nursery and Broughton House in Kirkcudbright.

Cairnsmore Nursery

Bob and Val Smith started off growing auriculas but it is North American woodland perennials that are their speciality these days, particularly *Heuchera, Heucherella* and *Tiarella*, most of which are imported as tiny plugs from Oregon breeders Terra Nova nurseries. They showed me some of the better, newer varieties when I visited their nursery. They offer mail order and also attend many of the shows, such as Gardening Scotland. They also offer auriculas and other primulas. The catalogue can be downloaded from their website. The nursery is open by appointment only.

Cairnsmore Nursery
Chapmanton Road,
Castle Douglas, DG7 2NU
(map, pp. 320–21)

Bob and Val Smith
By arrangement
On north side of Castle Douglas.
From the A75 follow the sign for
the A713 to Ayr, but at the junction
of the A75 slip road and the A713
turn right towards Castle Douglas,
and then turn immediately left into
Chapmanton Road. The nursery is
150m along on the left
T: 01556 504 819
E: cairnsmorenursery@
hotmail.com
www.cairnsmorenursery.co.uk

Cally Gardens

Cally Gardens is both a fine plant collection/garden and an excellent nursery specialising in unusual perennials. Roy Lancaster describes Cally as full of 'unusual gems about which true plantsmen dream'. The eighteenth-century walled garden was constructed for Cally House, with walls up to 15ft in height. Of the original buildings, the gardener's cottage and a large lean-to vinery remain, backing onto potting sheds, fruit store, mushroom house and boiler house. Michael Wickenden bought the walled garden in 1987, and gradually restored the walls and structures. Visitors can wander amongst established plantings of several thousand varieties of perennials and alpines spilling out of the raised beds and rectangular borders onto the paths. Michael and his partner Sally somehow manage to keep on top of it all. Visitors can choose from a selection of several hundred varieties in the sales area, or plants can be purchased through the mail-order catalogue. Michael is a formidable plantsman with forthright opinions on such things as the morality of plant breeders' rights, and is also an intrepid plant hunter who has made expeditions to Chile, New Zealand, China, India and elsewhere in pursuit of new plants. Nursery specialities include: *Agapanthus, Crocosmia, Eryngium, Euphorbia*, hardy *Geranium*, grasses and unusual climbers and conservatory plants.

Cally Gardens
Gatehouse of Fleet,
Castle Douglas, DG7 2DJ
(*map, pp. 320–21*)

Michael Wickenden
Easter Saturday to last Sunday in September: Saturday and Sunday 10am–5.30pm, Tuesday–Friday, 2–5.30pm, closed Monday; £
Take the eastern Gatehouse road off the A75, through gates for Cally Palace Hotel and follow signs to Cally Gardens
T: 01557 815029
E: enquiries@callygardens.co.uk
www.callygardens.co.uk

Carleton Croft

The Hartleys moved to Borgue in Galloway, with views towards Wigtown and the Machairs, when they sold their farm near Skipton. Mrs Hartley set about transforming this ¼-acre site into a cottage garden which is absolutely stuffed with plants; every possible inch is taken up and then when the soil runs out, the plants are potted up. There must be hundreds of plants in containers and hanging baskets.

Carleton Croft
Borgue, Galloway, DG6 4JT
(*map, pp. 320–21*)

Mr and Mrs D.J. Hartley
July and August by appointment; donation
1 mile north of Borgue on the B272 to Gatehouse of Fleet
T: 01557 870447
E: dave@davehartley.wanadoo.co.uk

There are over 50 clematis on walls, trellis and clambering in conifers, 30 roses, hundreds of perennials, two small ponds and a tree full of bird feeders. Mrs Hartley loves her garden and never stops moving and dividing things. It is a riot of colour all summer. There isn't room here to park cars for a full open day, so just phone up if you want to come, and make an appointment.

Carstramon and Cally Woods

Carstramon and Cally Woods
Galloway Forest Park,
Gatehouse of Fleet, Galloway
(*map, pp. 320–21*)

Free
Carstramon is 2 miles north of Gatehouse of Fleet, turn right onto minor road branching off the B796 and cross the bridge. Cally woods are 1 mile off the A75 on the left (surrounding Cally Palace Hotel)

Part of Galloway Forest Park, the 200-acre Carstramon Wood boasts one of Scotland's best bluebell displays in mid May under ancient broad-leaved trees, mainly oaks. There seem to be no signs to it, so you have to know where to look. Cally Woods, just outside Gatehouse of Fleet, also has good bluebells as well as one of the best snowdrop displays in the south-west.

Castle Kennedy Gardens

This has to be one of the best sited gardens in the country, 75 acres of planned landscape on a jaw-dropping scale and with considerable style. The gardens lie on a narrow strip of land with lochs on both sides and castles at either end, Castle Kennedy, ruined, near the garden entrance, and Lochinch at the far end, completed in 1864 and home of the Dalrymples/earls of Stair. The long drive gives stunning vistas of the distant castles across the water, and of the canal which

joins up Loch Crindl with Loch Inch, lined with cordylines with *Embothrium* behind. The old walls of Castle Kennedy overlook the atmospheric walled garden full of shrubs, herbaceous and bedding. Surrounding this and extending north, the policies and woodland garden are designed around a series of vistas, between avenues of trees and rhododendrons to castles, hills, lochs, over the famously huge lily pond. The rhododendrons and magnolias are now enormous and provide an impressive display in spring. The huge-leaved *Magnolia rostrata* by the lily pond was particularly good when we visited in May. The second earl of Stair had been ambassador at Versailles in the early eighteenth century and developed a taste for the grand scale. This led him to use a garrison of troops stationed locally to build a series of terraced earthworks which are in some ways surprisingly contemporary, even if some sections look in search of a golf course. The *Araucaria* (monkey puzzle) avenue is still impressive but some of the conifer avenues are over-mature and much-needed thinning and tree surgery is taking place. You can walk all the way to Lochinch Castle, where there is a sunken garden surrounded by some gigantic rhododendrons, but the best things to see are at the Castle Kennedy end. Davina, Countess of Stair, has been responsible for most of the garden's development in the last 30 years, in partnership with John McArthur the head gardener for 20 years. The responsibility for this amazing place now rests with the next generation, Jamie, the twelfth earl of Stair, and his wife Emily. Bold decisions need to be made to thin, cut back and replace many of the very mature trees and shrubs and open up overgrown vistas, but at the same time maintain the

Castle Kennedy Gardens
Rephad, Stranraer, DG9 8BX
(*map, pp. 320–21*)

Earl and Countess of Stair
April–September 10am–5pm; ££
3 miles east of Stranraer on the A75, clearly signposted with brown signs at the village of Castle Kennedy
T: 01776 702024
F: 01776 706 248
E: info@castlekennedygardens.
co.uk
www.castlekennedygardens.co.uk
Small café serves homemade light lunches and cream teas

329

garden's integrity. This is a garden well worth visiting at any time: in spring for the rhododendrons, in summer for the walled garden and the enormous *Eucryphia* and at any time just to enjoy the scale of the landscape, the setting and the fine trees. You can easily wear out your children running around it all, though you may take a while to find them again in the undergrowth. It will surprise you to know that it is all looked after by only two super-human gardeners.

  WC

Corsock House

Corsock House
Corsock, Castle Douglas,
Dumfries and Galloway, DG7 3DJ
(*map, pp. 320–21*)

Mr and Mrs M.L. Ingall
SGS May, and April–June and
autumn by arrangement; ££
Off A712, ½ mile south-east of
Corsock village ,10 miles north
of Castle Douglas
T: 01644 440250
E: mickyingall@tiscali.co.uk

This is perhaps my favourite of Scotland's many woodland gardens for its setting, planting and design. The 20-acre garden contains a collection of fine mature trees and rhododendrons which have been planted by three families: the Dunlops in the nineteenth century, the McEwans in the early twentieth century and the Ingalls since 1951. The handsome house was altered by Robert Lorimer and has views to the countryside to the south. The woodland garden begins on the slopes behind the house and the paths meander under and between giant rhododendrons. The handsome water garden consists of several ponds and a fountain, azaleas and Japanese maples as well as a trellis pagoda focal point. The garden rises gradually following the curves of the burn, with new vistas round every corner and focal points of ponds, statues and temples. At the top of the garden the view is of a 40-acre loch, a calm meditative spot after the exuberance of the garden. The fact that the plants are not allowed to obscure Corsock's design is a key element of its success; so many gardens of this type are so overcrowded with trees and giant rhododendrons you just can't see anything any more. My brother Ray Cox, who took most of the photographs for this book, considers Corsock the most photogenic

woodland garden in Scotland. The landscape and buildings are clearly owner Micky Ingall's passion; the use of water and classical buildings has echoes of Stourhead in Wiltshire, and includes an unusual *trompe l'oeil* bridge (disguising the retaining wall of a dam). As well as the fantastic displays of spring flowering, there is particularly good autumn colour. The outstanding rhododendron at Corsock is yellow-flowered *R. lacteum*, which most gardeners struggle to keep alive. Corsock has many thriving examples, grown from George Forrest seed planted by Douglas McEwan, who subscribed to one of Forrest's expeditions. The walled garden contains a rectangular reflecting pool with classical columns behind which can be glimpsed through a small side gate with interesting floral metalwork, or from the main garden gate. The remainder of the walled garden is less successful with two rather jarring curved silver sculptures on mounds and plantings of shrubs within the rather unhappy yew hedging. But overall Corsock is a triumph; anyone looking for woodland garden ideas should come here for inspiration. Every time I show pictures of it in lectures, it seems to stir something in the audience. I can't recommend it highly enough. Owner Micky Ingall was sadly killed in an accident as we went to press, which may mean changes for this superb garden.

Craichlaw

Former landscape architect Mary Gladstone and her husband have completely transformed this garden in the last 15 years and it is now one of the finest private gardens in the south-west. Out went the tired roses and in their place a carefully designed and manageable space has been created around the south side of the large fifteenth-century tower house with tasteful Victorian additions. The terraces around the house have been turned into a gravel garden allowing heat- and sharp drainage-loving Mediterranean plants to be grown which would

Craichlaw
Kirkcowan, Newton Stewart, Wigtownshire, DG8 0DQ
(*map, pp. 320–21*)

Andrew and Mary Gladstone
SGS by appointment; ££
Off A75 8 miles west of Newton Stewart and B733, one mile west of Kirkcowan
T: 01671 830 208
E: craichlaw@aol.com

otherwise suffer in the high rainfall. The granite chips help keep foliage dry in winter and out of contact with the soil and plants include *Stipa gigantea, Verbena bonariensis, Salvia* and *Santolina*. Below this a square enclosed space, surrounded on three sides by yew hedging, is divided into four with bold blocks of perennials, repeating from section to section. A pair of yew pillars leads the eye from the house and terrace across the fields to the loch beyond. To the right of the yew square is an excellent cool and minimalist contemporary formal garden. White gravel chips show off the box balls and parterre enclosures, each one centred with a fastigiate hornbeam. Off-centre is a circle of rough-hewn pale granite stones. The stones and ball shapes are echoed on a smaller scale next door around the perennial blocks. The old walled garden, some distance away, contains soft fruit and a collection of old Scottish apples, many of which were propagated specially from the national collection at Brogdale. In complete contrast is the larger of the lochs which runs alongside the drive. From the lodge the eye is drawn to the far end of the loch to a group of *Sequoiadendron giganteum*. A path runs around the loch leading to an extensive water garden planted around a series of ponds fed from the loch water. This rather shady area is lushly planted with a huge range of perennials such as *Iris, Gunnera* and candelabra primulas. An island is covered with giant reddish-purple *Rhododendron* 'Altaclarense'. This is an outstanding and imaginative garden in a fine mature setting.

WC

Craigieburn Garden

This garden is well worth a short detour off the A74. In a sheltered undulating site above the fast-flowing Craigie Burn, this 5-acre woodland and semi-formal garden is divided into several themed 'rooms', packed with woodland plants, planned and created by the formidable Janet Wheatcroft now with help from her Nepalese gardener Dawa Sherpa, whom she met when trekking in Nepal. The rainfall, soil and shelter seem particularly well suited to Himalayan plants. A small stupa lies next to the car park and the whole garden is garlanded with prayer flags. You might well meet some Nepalese children running round the garden: our kids were taken in tow and shown an excellent tree for climbing. Spring brings displays of rhododendrons, primulas and woodland bulbs followed by damp area favourites such as *Rodgersia* and *Aruncus*. A large collection of *Meconopsis* reaches its peak in June, followed by herbaceous borders, roses and clematis. A pergola tunnel is covered with *Vitis* which makes a fiery display in autumn. Four narrow topiary pyramids and eccentric hedge projections add to the effect, as do a spectacular waterfall, several statues and the various Himalayan artefacts. The range of plants for sale includes *Meconopsis cheldonifolia* and other varieties, lots of *Primula* and *Celmisia*. If you are lucky enough to meet Janet in her garden she really knows her plants and can offer sound advice. This is a major plant collection and an excellent display of what does well in the Scottish climate.

Craigieburn Garden
Craigieburn House,
by Moffat, DG10 9LF
(*map, pp. 320–21*)

Janet Wheatcroft
10.30am–6.30pm, closed on
Mondays, except Scottish and
English public holidays; £
Exit 15, M74, 2 miles from Moffat
on A708 just after the traffic lights
on the narrow bridge
T: 01683 221250
E: ajmw1@aol.com
www.craigieburngarden.com

Crichton (The), Dumfries

Crichton (The), Dumfries
Grierson House, The Crichton,
Bankend Road, Dumfries,
DG1 4ZE
(map, pp. 320–21)

Crichton University Campus
Bankend Road, 1 mile south of
Dumfries town centre, follow
signs for Crichton; free
T: 01387 247 544
F: 01387 257616
E: admin@crichton.co.uk
www.crichton.co.uk
Restaurant at Ashton Hotel

The Crichton, formerly one of the more highly regarded Victorian mental hospitals, is now a university campus on the outskirts of Dumfries, in a 100-acre estate of fine parkland and gardens with mature rhododendrons, azaleas and many specimen trees. The most intensively planted area is a well-maintained extensive rock garden with waterfall and ornamental pond, with shrubs and perennials, surrounded by a large collection of conifers. A statue commemorates Mary Crichton, who in the nineteenth century always desired that her property be used as a university – which eventually it was, 100 years later. The Victorian and Edwardian greenhouse complex is sadly going to have to be demolished due to decay and vandalism. There is also a rose garden at the Annandale Centre.

Dabton

Dabton
Thornhill, Dumfries, DG3 5AR
(map, pp. 320–21)

Buccleuch estates
SGS some years; ££
Entrance off A76 between
Thornhill and Carronbridge
T: 01848 330467

Forming part of the huge Drumlanrig estate, and traditionally the home of the duke's oldest son, Dabton is a nineteenth-century house built of pink stone. The large walled garden is famed for its very long herbaceous border as well as roses, island beds and shrubs, greenhouses and vegetables. A pond is crossed by a striking deep red bridge and is surrounded with hostas, astilbe, azaleas and primulas. Further afield is a woodland walk.

Dalswinton House and Dalswinton Plant Centre

Dalswinton House and Dalswinton Plant Centre
Auldgirth, Dumfries, DG2 0XZ
(*map, pp. 320–21*)

Mr and Mrs Peter Landale
SGS in May and by appointment;
££
Turn off A76 at Auldgirth, 7 miles
north of Dumfries, signed
Dalswinton, pass through village,
gates on the right
T: 01387 740220
E: sarahlandale@hotmail.com
www.dalswintonestate.co.uk

Merchant Patrick Miller built the late eighteenth-century dark reddish Georgian house and related buildings, which sit on a wooded hill opposite Portrack (with Charles Jencks' red-painted railway bridge clearly visible), on the east side of the Nith Valley with the Dalswinton wind farm in the hills behind. Miller also constructed the attractive village of Dalswinton with its two lines of cottages. Around the house are herbaceous beds and well-established shrubs, rhododendrons and azaleas, as well as a maturing laburnum arch. The outstanding feature of this garden is the large loch, also created by Patrick Miller, now surrounded by dense, mature woodland, providing an imposing Capability Brown-style planned landscape. The loch was the site of the maiden voyage of the first steamboat in Britain in 1788 and there is a life-size model under a curved roof beside the water to commemorate this. There are attractive walks through woods and around the loch, drifts of daffodils in spring with a backdrop in early June of *Rhododendron ponticum* and *R.* 'Pink Pearl' on one of the islands, which features a round tower which is the focal point of the vista from the house. The odd-looking semi-circles of hedging are butts for duck shooters to hide behind. The Landales have plans to extend the planting around the loch and the potential is there to make this a truly exceptional garden, Scotland's answer to Stourhead perhaps.

Dalswinton Plant Centre is situated in the walled garden of the house and is run by Sandy Hutchison, for 30 years gardener at Dalswinton. The nursery sells a wide range of plants including wallflowers and polyanthus grown on-site. Sandy is a keen *Fuchsia* shower and these are also featured. T: 01387 740257. E: sandy@dalswintonplants.com.

Danevale Park
Crossmichael, Castle Douglas,
Dumfries and Galloway, DG7 2LP
(*map, pp. 320–21*)

Mrs M.R.C. Gillespie
SGS 1 day in February and May:
2–5pm and by appointment; £
A713, Crossmichael 1 mile,
Castle Douglas 2 miles
T: 01556 670223
E: danevale@tiscali.co.uk

Danevale Park

This is a mature garden with woodland walks alongside the River
Dee, with particularly fine thick carpets of snowdrops amongst the
trees made especially attractive by the backdrop of water. The May
opening usually coincides with the extensive carpets of bluebells.

Drumlanrig Castle

Drumlanrig is one of the homes of Scotland's largest landowners, the
dukes of Buccleuch. A long drive through a fine parkland of mature
trees leads to the magnificent and palatial seventeenth-century house
built by William Douglas, with a set of skull cap-like cupolas on the
turrets, which sits on top of a hill. There is a long history of formal
gardening on a grand scale here and some of the older parts have
recently been restored or recreated. The scale is so large, and the
rabbits and deer so voracious, that attempts to re-impose order on the
landscape have been only partly successful. The formal areas, below
the terrace at the front, include a bedding planting square (the shawl

parterre), with a series of mown patterns on the lawns behind, and to one side, a formal square with hostas, *Aquilegia*, rhododendrons and azaleas, surrounded with rabbit netting. Below the long terrace covered with climbing roses is a well-labelled long narrow herbaceous border. Beyond this is a line of fastigiate beech, alternating copper and green, and the tallest weeping beech in the British Isles. At one side of the castle is a rose and catmint formal garden, while at the opposite end is a curious box and conifer formal square which looks a bit small for the space. Beyond the lawns is an extensive woodland garden with significant recent plantings of rhododendron species, trees and shrubs, many from recent wild collections, as well as a heather-roofed pavilion. The children's play area and picnic area between the woodland garden and the plant nursery is one of the best in Scotland: under a dense, dark canopy of beech trees is a series of aerial walkways, slides and obstacle/assault course equipment. Watch out if your kids are under five as some of the slides and rides are very high up or long. The small walled nursery sells a range of plants and spare bedding plants from the garden. There is a good-value day out for the family in the house and grounds here. Drumlanrig Castle is full of fine paintings including Leonardo da Vinci Madonna which was stolen in 2003 and returned in 2007. There is a popular café and bicycle museum and outdoors there are miles of woodland walks and mountain bike and cycle paths, with a ranger service organising children's outdoor activities. You can also tear up the countryside in a Landrover safari, if that is what turns you on. Consult the website for details.

Drumlanrig Castle
Thornhill, Dumfries and Galloway,
DG3 4AQ
(*map, pp. 320–21*)

Duke of Buccleuch VRD,
contact Robbie Black
Gardens and grounds: Good
Friday–30 September inclusive:
daily, 10am–5pm; ££ (grounds),
£££ (castle and grounds)
16 miles south-west of M74 J14,
18 miles north-west of Dumfries,
3 miles north of Thornhill on A76,
well-signposted
T: 01848 331 555
E: rblack@buccleuch.com
www.drumlanrig.com
Café, picnic area

Dunesslin
Dunscore,
Dumfries, DG2 0UR
(*map, pp. 320–21*)

Iain and Zara Milligan
SGS 1 day June and by
appointment; ££
Take Corsock road from Dunscore.
After 1½ miles turn right at
telephone box to Corsock. Turn
left at first crossroads.
T: 01387 820345
E: zaramilligan@gmail.com

Dunesslin

This garden has fine views of the Dumfries countryside and there are three cairns on nearby land by sculptor Andy Goldsworthy, who lives not far away. The walled garden is a series of connected hedged 'rooms', some of the yew hedges have castellations cut it them. The box-edged rose garden in a cruciform design is punctuated by narrow upright juniper, while the largest section contains shrub roses, honeysuckle and *Nepeta*-edged paths, backed with trees and shrubs. The woodland garden is being restored.

Dunskey Gardens
Portpatrick, Stranraer, Galloway,
DG9 8TJ
(*map, pp. 320–21*)

Mrs Orr Ewing
February: snowdrop weekends;
March–October: daily 10am–5pm,
other times by appointment; ££
One mile from Portpatrick on the
B738
T: 01776 810211
F: 01776 810581
E: garden@dunskey.com
www.dunskey.com
'Seasons' Tea Room 10am–5pm,
T: 01776 810905/211

Dunskey Gardens

Dunskey has opened for many years for its snowdrops in the extensive woodland in spring. More recently the eighteenth-century walled garden has been restored and replanted. The fine greenhouses, originally built by Mackenzie & Moncur, were being re-roofed with considerable skill when I visited. The layout and planting of the garden is refreshingly unconventional, with garden rooms and a dead-end at the top, and a long thyme border almost the width of the garden. This leads, via a conifer arch, down a narrow set of pools and falls to a large pond at the bottom with a huge clump of *Zantedeschia*. The paths are quirkily edged with an uncommon selection of plants: mixed varieties of lavender, *Santolina* and *Geranium*. The garden boasts two hares by Dumfriesshire sculptress Elizabeth Waugh and tender plants such as *Polylepis australis*. There are woodland walks of various lengths around the estate. Next to the walled garden is the popular 'Seasons' tea room, the walls of which have specially commissioned murals depicting the four seasons. The ruins of Dunskey Castle can be visited via a path from the lighthouse along

the clifftops from the attractive village of Portpatrick 1½ miles away. We recorded an impressive list of wild flowers on this walk as well as thickets of invading *Crocosmia* which is spectacular in August.

    [WC]

Elizabeth MacGregor's Nursery, Ellenbank

Elizabeth and Alasdair MacGregor's ½-acre walled garden sanctuary must be many people's idea of the perfect garden, manageable in scale, beautifully planted and what's more, you can buy many of the plants from the nursery outside. A semi-circular parterre follows the curved walls, with a wisteria pergola in the centre leading onwards to a series of perennial beds, some in pink and purple shades, some with mostly white colourings and at the far end, a hot border of yellows and oranges. Amongst other things, Elizabeth MacGregor is Scotland's *Viola* queen and has a particularly good range of these easy,

Elizabeth MacGregor's Nursery, Ellenbank
Ellenbank, Tongland Road, Kirkcudbright, DG6 4UU
(*map, pp. 320–21*)

Elizabeth and Alasdair MacGregor
Late April–end September: Friday, Saturday, Monday 10am–5pm
A711 1 mile north of town centre, opposite council 'Kirkcudbright' sign
T: 01557 330620
F: 01557 330620
E: elizabeth@violas.abel.co.uk
www.elizabethmacgregor nursery.co.uk

long-flowering summer favourites. Other specialities include hardy geraniums, penstemons, campanulas, *Eryngium*, primulas and *Iris* all of which are offered mail order and at numerous shows around the country. The trial beds which are below the car park contain new selections under test. Ellenbank is a special place well worth going out of your way for. You can also visit Broughton House, nearby in Kirkcudbright. It is probably worth phoning to make sure that MacGregors are open as they do attend many shows through the season.

Elmlea Plants
Old Minnigaff, Newton Stewart,
Wigtownshire, DG8 6PX
(*map, pp. 320–21*)

Giles and Moira Davies
March–October: 10am–5pm
Closed Mondays
Turn off A75 at junction for
Minnigaff. 1½ miles, turn right
(signposted RSPB Bird Reserve)
immediately before the Cree
bridge, 200 yards past youth
hostel
T: 01671 402514
E: elmleaplants@yahoo.co.uk
www.elmleaplants.co.uk

Elmlea Plants

This is a delightful, small, family-run nursery specialising in herbaceous perennials and grasses. Specialities include *Campanula, Achillea, Geranium* and late summer border plants such as *Helenium* and *Rudbeckia*. The range of grasses is selected for the local climate and includes large and small growers and several varieties you are unlikely to find elsewhere. The Davies offer personal service and sound gardening advice.

Right. Elmlea Plants

Galloway Heathers
Retail Plant Centre: Holmpark
Industrial Estate, Minnigaff,
Newton Stewart, DG8 6AW
Mail Order Nursery: Carthy Port,
Newton Stewart, Dumfries and
Galloway, DG8 6AY
(*map, pp. 320–21*)

Noel and Marcus Allen
Garden centre off A714, north
from Newton Stewart (follow signs
for Girvan), turn off onto B7079.
T: 01671 402360 (nursery),
01671 401367 (garden centre)
F: 01671 402360
E: enquiries@galloway
heathers.com
www.gallowayheathers.com

Galloway Heathers

This specialist heather nursery runs a mail order business listing up to 120 different varieties. The nursery also runs a small garden centre in Minnigaff, just across the river from Newton Stewart. I was disappointed with the small range of heathers on display when I visited.

340

Galloway House Gardens

The gardens at Galloway House were first created in 1740 by Lord
Garlies, elder son of the fifth earl of Galloway. The garden was later
bought by Sir Malcolm McEacharn, whose son, Captain Neil
McEacharn, was responsible for much of the present-day layout and
planting. Captain McEacharn went on to create gardens at Villa
Taranto on Lake Maggiore in Italy. Lady Forteviot of Dupplin Castle,
Perthshire, bought Galloway House in 1930 and much of the species
Rhododendron collection was planted by her stepson Edward Strutt.
The year starts with drifts of snowdrops and daffodils, with mature
rhododendrons and azaleas, early June sees the fine *Davidia involucrata* (handkerchief tree) flower most years. There is a fine weeping
beech. The secluded and sandy Rigg Bay beach, half a mile walk from
the car park, has pools and rocky outcrops, with picnic tables next to
the wooded shoreline, and is popular with locals and tourists alike.
Eddie Strutt and his wife are buried in the gardens they loved, and
the enormous and rather sinister house was sold off, with the gardens
left in trust to be looked after. The walled garden is dilapidated and
when I visited was unsafe to enter. Apart from mowing, it is hard to
discern what the trustees are up to in the way of upkeep.
Arrangements like this, to maintain gardens in trust, seldom work
unless there is real enthusiasm for gardening. This one seems to be
terminally ill and though a pleasant enough place to walk around,
with an outstanding beach, I can't see much hope for the garden's
future.

Galloway House Gardens
Garlieston, Newton Stewart,
Wigtownshire, DG8 8HF
(*map, pp. 320–21*)

Galloway House Gardens Trust
1 March–31 October: 9am–5pm;
£ (per car) + donations
Off the B7063 south of Garlieston,
c. 8 miles south of Wigtown
T: 01988 600680
www.gallowayhousegardens.co.uk
Tea tent on summer weekends

Galloway Plants and Claymoddie Garden

Claymoddie, Whithorn, Newton Stewart, Dumfries and Galloway, DG8 8LX
(*map, pp. 320–21*)

Robin and Mary Nicholson
Early March–September:
Friday–Sunday 2–5pm and
by appointment; ££
A746 through Whithorn to
Glasserton crossroads, turn left
at war memorial and first right
T: 01988 500422
F: 01988 500422
E: NicM567@aol.com
www.gallowayplants.co.uk

Galloway Plants and Claymoddie Garden

The Nicholsons started this garden in the 1970s, situated at the southern end of the Whithorn peninsula, first establishing shelter from the strong salt-laden winds. The garden now extends to some 3 acres and includes woodland, a stream and pond and several sections of perennials, and a good range of shrubs and trees including a thicket of *Schisandra* and a large *Styrax japonica*. 'It's a bit of a jungle', Robin told me as he showed me round; it is better than this and is packed with plants: *Magnolia sprengeri* 'Diva', rhododendrons and bulbs in spring, *Echium*, day lilies, *Knifophia* and hydrangeas in summer. The small mail-order/retail nursery business started in 2006–07, once the Nicholsons' son took over the farming duties. The nursery specialises in southern hemisphere plants such as *Watsonia, Olearia, Pittosporum, Drimys* and over 20 varieties of *Hydrangea*. The nursery is gaining a good local following as the Nicholsons are keen plants-people and are happy to share their expertise with customers. Another fine garden, Woodfall, is a mile away and St Ninian's Cave is on the beach nearby.

Garden of Cosmic Speculation, Portrack

This is without doubt one of the world's most significant contemporary gardens. American architect Charles Jencks and his wife Maggie Keswick, influenced by 1960s and 1970s land art, began sculpting the landscape of their Dumfries garden in the 1980s. They transformed a Victorian landscape, woodland, walled and vegetable gardens, which had been gardened by Maggie's parents, Sir John and Lady Keswick, in a fairly traditional manner, into a series of theatrical tableaux inspired by cutting-edge science including DNA, fractal geometry, wave forms and quantum theory. This style of didactic gardening harks back to the paradise gardens of Persia and European Renaissance gardens, both of which feature allegorical/religious story-telling. The Keswick family were one of several Dumfries families to run Hong Kong's Jardine Matheson and Maggie's formative years in Hong Kong inspired a lifelong interest and expertise in Chinese gardens and gardening. Maggie died in 1995 but her name lives on in the Maggie's Centres for cancer care, of which the best known of the five in Scotland are the one in Dundee, designed by Frank Gehry, and the one in Kirkcaldy, designed by Zaha Hadid. Charles Jencks has continued to develop the Portrack gardens, with new sections added almost every year. It is up to the individual visitor whether to attempt to explore the often challenging and arcane inspirations for different parts of the garden; the vistas are so unusual and spectacular, you may well consider them stimuli enough. Charles Jencks' book *The Garden of Cosmic Speculation*, published in 2003, spells out in detail the inspiration behind the garden and its components. 'To put it paradoxically, science is clearly providing a brand new iconography for art but one without clear icons . . . The icons have not found their Michelangelo or even their Henry Moore, perhaps because contemporary science is so complex and inchoate.' He then goes on to explain what exactly he is creating: 'An art fitting to the cosmos, what I would call 'cosmogenic art' does not always take nature as beneficent or beyond improvement. The laws of nature may be omnipotent, but they can be challenged. The garden is the perfect place to try out these speculations and celebrations, because it is a bit of man-made nature.' So,

Garden of Cosmic Speculation, Portrack
Portrack House, Holywood, Dumfries, DG2 0RW
(*map, pp. 320–21*)

Charles Jencks
SGS 1 open day in May, or by appointment; ££, entry fee in aid of Maggie's Centres. To make an appointment see the contents page in *The Garden of Cosmic Speculation* published by Frances Lincoln
Off the A76 south of Auldgirth, north of Holywood, c. 4 miles north of Dumfries
www.charlesjencks.com

having given themselves the task of explaining the universe in a garden, which some might term hubris of the first order, we can certainly admire the Jencks' *Fountainhead*-like ambition. It is possible both to admire it and to stick deflationary pins in it for its pretentiousness. Clearly a man as intelligent as Charles Jencks knows that he is attempting something which has its absurd side. As he says himself: 'recounting the story of the cosmos with rocks and objects is like writing poetry with semaphore flags' and there are playful elements: the tennis court is christened 'the garden of fair play' for example. It is also illuminating that Jencks admits his inability to retain Latin plant names, suggesting that plants are clearly secondary (and often irrelevant) to the architecture in this garden. The ambition displayed at Portrack inevitably has its critics. Designer and writer Tim Richardson calls recent developments 'hectoring' and 'a monologue on the universe', but I think we should be more generous: it is the fact that this project is a boundless claim for all that a garden can be that makes it so exciting. I hope that the visitor feels empowered by the experience of Portrack to look at all gardens anew. As a collection of design elements alone, it is an extraordinary achievement which a very substantial amount of money has been spent realising.

Head gardener Alistair Clark, serving over 40 years for two generations of the family, has been charged with putting some of the world's most outlandish gardening ideas into practice. He deserves much of the credit for what the garden has become, as do the craftsmen who have interpreted Jencks' ideas and designs, principally metal-worker John Gibson and carpenter Bobby Dickson. Alistair Clark recommends that the garden is walked through in a roughly clockwise manner, starting with the woodland/rhododendron walk and flower garden, planted by the previous Keswick generation. This leads to the new Time Garden, conceived by Charles' and Maggie's daughter Lily, now herself a landscape architect, which consists of black and white poles arranged in a triangular shape and some landforms which snake around the base of trees. From here, a long ha-ha sweeps along the front of Portrack House, via the 'Black Hole' checkerboard, the geometry break terrace and across the striking new bridge to the nonsense pavilion. Portrack's most celebrated feature, the sensually curved snail lakes and mound, can be appreciated from various angles, with the best views from the top of the highest point of the snail mound. Recent developments include the painting of the new bridge in a dark red, the short section of the old rail bridge next door, and along the railway line, the metal plates with the sometimes rather odd quotations from the 'Scottish Worthies'. Between this and the lakes is a dense planting of white-barked Himalayan birch in the garden of life and death, which will be stunning in years to come. From here the route leads back to the most densely planted and detailed area of the garden, the herb and parterre garden of the six senses (Jencks includes 'intuition' as number six) and the unforgettable jagged white staircases of the Universe Cascade, planted with two varieties of Hebe up either side. The attention to detail at

Portrack is as important as the bigger picture: the series of beautiful arched red wooden bridges, numerous John Gibson metal gates of wave-form designs, the carved and cut-out lettering on the greenhouse, panels, rocks, stones and blocks around the garden, the armillaries and the Chinese-influenced moon windows and adaptations of them in various shapes. And the hedges: I'm sure they are a curse to cut, but I love the effects of the layering and scalloping.

Many consider Portrack to be the world's most extraordinary contemporary garden and Scotland should certainly be proud to play host to such an iconic place. And yet this is a garden that I found easy to admire and respect but harder to love and quite a challenge to enjoy. I missed a core central design. It is more like a series of tangentially related show (or show-off) gardens, or theatre sets; apart from the sensual curved lakes, it seemed very masculine. Some of the time, I felt like shouting 'it's the plants, stupid!' and then wondering if I was being too conservative. Many of the older planted areas are excellent, the walled gardens for example, but in newer sections the plants have taken more of a back seat. The massed plantings of white-barked birches are the exception which proves the rule. The irony is that Portrack's plants may prove more durable than the architectural features. This landscape is so modern as to be almost disposable: parts are decaying, metal bending and splitting, wood rotting, buildings collapsing; Scotland's weather is confronting Jencks' hubristic claims to be able to challenge the laws of nature, taking its gradual revenge on such an 'unnatural' extravaganza. It is hard to put Portrack into context. What are its references? Land art of course, of which this is a great example. Time and time again I could not help but compare it with Little Sparta, and at Portrack I missed the relationship with nature which Ian Hamilton Finlay's equally ambitious garden has; above all I missed Finlay's poetry. Little Sparta engages the heart and mind, Portrack gives the mind a workout but almost bypasses the heart. Portrack is a vast, almost incomprehensible landscape, wildly ambitious, imaginative, bordering on madness, and an extraordinary achievement. You simply must visit it, and make up your own mind. You will never see the like again. It is open once a year under SGS (crazily popular) and by appointment (in writing). There are further Charles Jencks projects being completed or in the pipeline. These include 'Dividing Cells' at Maggie's Centre, Inverness, 'Cells of Life' at Bonnington, near Edinburgh, and two involving sculpting the spoil from open-cast coal mines in Scotland and north-east England (see the Jencks website for details).

**Gardenwise Plant
and Garden Centre**
Castle Douglas Road,
Dumfries, DG2 8PP
(*map, pp. 320–21*)

Alistair Bertram
9am–5.30pm (Sunday from 10am)
A780, off western end of Dumfries
bypass
T: 01387 262654
F: 01387 263 663
E: info@gardenwise-dumfries.co.uk
www.gardenwise-dumfries.co.uk
Food hall with speciality foods.
Coffee shop with home baking
9.30am–4.40pm
(Sunday from 10.30am).

Gardenwise Plant and Garden Centre

This is a popular Dumfries garden centre, recently expanded. Many of the perennials and bedding plants they sell are grown in their own nursery next door. Much of the plant area is under cover. There is a bookshop, popular café and small food hall.

Glenae

I can't resist pointing out that 'Ae', just up the valley from this garden, has the shortest place name in Britain. Glenae, reached by a beech-lined drive, is a garden in two parts, a woodland garden with rhodo-dendrons and azaleas around the house and a couple of ponds, at its best in May and June, and a peaceful walled garden divided into four small lawns surrounded by colourful herbaceous borders, peonies, old apples, cherries and a large ginkgo, punctuated with spiky cordylines, with a restored Victorian glass-house along the top. In June, drifts of mostly pink oriental poppies in one corner were outstanding.

Glenae
Amisfield, Dumfriesshire,
DG1 3NZ
(*map, pp. 320–21*)

Mr and Mrs Sebastian Morley
SGS most years and by
appointment; ££
1½ miles north of Amisfield on
A701. Turn left to Duncow and
Auldgirth and 1 mile on right
T: 01387 710236
E: tottsmorley@btinternet.com

Glenkiln Estate

This important collection of sculpture in a wild setting was collected and laid out by Sir William Keswick between 1951 and 1976 and includes work by Moore, Epstein and Rodin. Henry Moore was delighted to have his work displayed in such a wild setting. You have to know where to look for Glenkiln as it is not well signposted. If you want to see all the pieces, you'll have to walk up to 4 miles (allow 2 hours) and keep your eyes peeled: some are partly hidden in trees while others are on the horizon. Be prepared for rain and wind. From the carpark turn right along the lane towards the bridge to see a Henry Moore, then back to the car park and along the side of the reservoir along a rough path past three further Moores including the Glenkiln Cross (halfway along the west side). The bronze statue of Mary called 'The Visitation' by Sir Jacob Epstein suddenly appears amongst some pines. It is a moving piece with a fragility brought home in the wild setting. Eventually you reach a tarmac path again. Turn right here (east) back towards the reservoir. At the next junction turn left and keep left to return to the car park via the edge of the reservoir. There is nothing quite like this in Scotland and the effect can be magical. At least one of the sculptures was vandalised recently, but thankfully has been repaired.

Glenkiln Estate
Shawhead,
Dumfries and Galloway, DG2 9UE
(*map, pp. 320–21*)

Glenkiln Estate
Free, no formal entry
arrangements
A75 5 miles west of Dumfries,
turn off to Shawhead, at Shawhead
turn right following the sign for
Dunscore, then immediately left.
After c. 100 yards turn left again,
signs to Glenkiln. Pass the
reservoir and turn right into a car
park just by statue of John the
Baptist (Rodin)

Glenwhan Gardens

Carved out of a bleak chunk of moorland in the far south-west of Scotland this 12-acre garden is a fine achievement on an impressive scale. The house was a pigeon-occupied ruin which had to be completely rebuilt when the Knotts bought it in the 1980s. Tessa and Bill began planting shelter belts using the existing gorse as wind protection for young plants, and dug out two impressive lochans, now enjoyed by assorted wildfowl. The highest point of the garden features

Glenwhan Gardens
Dunragit by Stranraer,
Galloway, DG9 8PH
(*map, pp. 320–21*)

Bill and Tessa Knott
Daily: March–October
10am–5.30pm. Guided tours for
groups by prior arrangement; ££
1 mile above the small village of
Dunragit, about 6 miles south
of Stranraer on the A75
Brown signs on A75
T: 01581 400222
F 01581 400222
E: tess@glenwhan.freeserve.co.uk
www.glenwhangardens.co.uk
Tearoom, hot and cold meals,
snacks, drinks (closes 30th
September)

an iconic column of spherical stones by sculptor Joe Smith, clearly influenced by the work of his mentor Andy Goldsworthy. From up here are fine views over the garden and in the opposite direction over the bare moorland. A stream and bog garden run through the ravine from here down to the lochans, lined by a huge range of candelabra primulas, hostas, *Darmera peltata, Rodgersia* and later in the summer, rampant *Mimulus.* The Knotts have amassed an astonishing collection of plants, creating a garden with a very long season from magnolias, bulbs and rhododendrons in spring, through roses and herbaceous to hydrangeas and myrtles in summer and autumn. Patrick Taylor describes the plant collection as 'an idiosyncratic zoo' which I think deserves to be taken as a compliment. Tessa propagated many of the plants herself, from cuttings or seed and has also obtained recent wild-collected rhododendrons and other plants. Habitats range from rocky and exposed to woodland and wet and the variety of plants grown reflect this. Paths meander through the sloping garden (little is suitable for wheelchairs due to the terrain). There is a small plant sales area and café. Some notable plants pointed out to me in an extensive tour from Tessa were a Montezuma pine, a multi-stemmed Ron McBeath-collected *Betula utilis*, a Glendoick *Rhododendron roxieanum*, the rare conifer *Athrotaxus latifolia* and an arch covered in *Schisandra.*

 WC

Gowanbrae Nursery
Mainsriddle,
by Dumfries, DG2 8AG
(*map, pp. 320–21*)

Robert Lyle
Tuesday–Sunday 10.30am–5pm,
closed Monday
7 miles south of New Abbey on
A710 coast road. Bus 373
T: 01387 780273

Gowanbrae Nursery

A traditional small family nursery, with display beds. They sell a good range of alpines, perennials, shrubs, conifers and rhododendrons. It had some unusual plants on sale when I visited.

348

Grovehill House

This 2-acre hilltop garden is surrounded by fine views into the Dumfriesshire countryside. Allen Paterson has a long professional horticultural pedigree, having been curator of the Chelsea Physic Garden and director of the Royal Botanic Garden, Ontario. He served as chair of the National Trust for Scotland garden advisory committee and has written several books on shrubs and trees as well as his latest, a lavishly illustrated history of Kew Gardens. The garden is just the combination of design and interesting planting which I admire. A series of garden rooms and sections around the house are divided by hedges, trees and shrubs, with some striking clipped conifers. Vistas and allées draw the eye around the garden and I enjoyed the carefully placed features such as urns, a stone inscribed *Vivendo Discimus* (by living we learn), favourite motto of Patrick Geddes, and a column topped with a pile of glass balls. A woodland path follows the contour of the burn which runs in a deep gorge round the edge of much of the garden. Vegetables, fruit, perennials and some relatively tender bulbous plants are grown on terraces on the south and south-west sides of the house. Some less common plants I noted on a visit in September included *Heptacodium miconiodes* with its tiny white flowers, *Hedychium* and a double-flowered *Hydrangea quercifolia*. There is plenty of interest here from spring with the rhododendrons and bulbs to good autumn colour at the tail end of the year.

Grovehill House
Burnhead, Thornhill, Dumfries
DG3 4AD
(*map, pp. 320–21*)

Mr and Mrs Allen Paterson
SGS and by appointment
1 mile west of Thornhill on the
A702, the drive is on a corner,
opposite a red phone box

Hammerlands Centre
Moffat, Dumfries, DG10 9QL
(map, pp. 320–21)

Daily: April–August: 8am–6pm;
September–March: 9am–4pm
Off the A708/Holm St in Moffat
(follow signs to Selkirk from south
centre of Moffat)
T: 01683 221220
E: enquiries@hammerlands
centre.co.uk
www.hammerlandscentre.co.uk
Café/restaurant

Hammerlands Centre

Hammerlands in Moffat has several strings to its bow. It is a small garden centre, offers angling at Moffat fishery, events through the summer ranging from sheepdog auctions to farmers' markets, car boot sales and car and caravan rallies, and for children, 'animals to pet', an activity playground and crazy golf.

Hetland Garden Nursery
Carrutherstown,
Dumfries, DG1 4JX
(map, pp. 320–21)

David Wilson
April–June: Monday–Friday 9am–
8pm, Saturday–Sunday 9am–6pm,
July–March: daily 9am–6pm
Off A75 at Carrutherstown,
9 miles east of Dumfries. Bus 389
T: 01387 840632
E: david@hetlandnursery.co.uk
www.hetlandnursery.co.uk
Tearoom

Hetland Garden Nursery

This is an impressive medium-sized garden centre just off the A75 between Dumfries and the M74. The main innovation here is the display garden which is in an old orchard, reached along a section of wooden decking. Each bed has a theme, 'plants which can be grown by the sea' for example, and plants for sale sit alongside. The rhododendrons are planted in such deep shade I doubt they'll flower well. Much of the plant area is under cover and a new café was opened in 2008.

Logan Botanic Garden

There is nothing in Scotland quite like the 'tropical' view from the terrace over the walled garden at Logan, situated on the Rhinns of Galloway in Scotland's far south-west corner. This outstation of the Royal Botanic Garden, Edinburgh has an extremely mild climate and effective wind shelter, allowing a range of plants to be grown which very few other UK gardens could dream of: only the most favourable Cornish and Scottish island gardens have a climate this benign. Barry Unwin, the recently retired director of the gardens, (who worked at Logan for 30 years) showed me pictures of the March 2006 snowfalls which blanketed the gardens, for the first time in all his many years at Logan. It did mainly cosmetic damage. More damaging were the two hard winters of 1979 and 1986, which killed many plants. The magnificent walled garden is filled with an overstorey of tree ferns and cabbage trees, underplanted with exotic and tender plants: South African bulbs such as *Watsonia*, Chilean plants such as *Philesia* and *Lapageria,* and Chatham Island forget-me-nots from New Zealand. I really enjoyed the use of ferns here; the climate allows many handsome, less hardy ones to flourish, including tree ferns, *Woodwardia radicans,* and my favourite *Blechnum tabulare*. In mid summer, you can't miss the *Echium*, with its tall stems of rich blue flowers and southern hemisphere favourites such as *Callistemon* (bottle brush), *Dierama,* massive *Leptospermum,* and New Zealand's clawlike *Clianthus puniceus*. Along the north wall don't miss *Polylepis australis* with its layers of soft bark like puff pastry. Nerines put on a massed show in some of the beds in late summer and into November. An important collection of tender, mostly scented, Maddenia rhododen-drons are found both inside and just outside the walled garden. There is a somewhat municipal parks feel to some of the bedding plants, put

Logan Botanic Garden
Port Logan, Galloway, DG9 9ND
(*map, pp. 320–21*)

Trustees of the Royal Botanic Garden, Edinburgh
1 March–31 October: 10am–6pm (5pm in March); ££
12 miles south of Stranraer
well-signposted off the A716
T: 01776 860231
T: 01776 860333
E: logan@rbge.org.uk
www.rbge.org.uk
Café

in to please summer visitors. Outside the walled garden in the woodland are further plantings of *Eucalyptus*, tree ferns, *Metrosideros* (Rata) from New Zealand, and the tunnel of *Gunnera* which will appeal to adults and children alike. A huge *Magnolia campbellii* 'Charles Raffill' was brought from Windsor Great Park by its director Hope Findlay, who was born nearby. Recently appointed curator Richard Baines is renovating many areas and planting lots more palms and other plants which will make this excellent garden even more exotic looking. Logan attracts 25,000 or more visitors a year and is well worth making a special effort to reach at almost any time of year. There are so many other great gardens and nurseries nearby and en route, whether from Dumfries to the east or down the Ayrshire coast from the north. Logan has a good café and discovery centre upstairs with children's activities. You can also visit Logan House next door (separate ticket and entrance). Port Logan Inn nearby is a good place to stay or eat.

Logan House Gardens
Port Logan, near Stranraer,
Dumfries and Galloway, DG9 9ND
(*map, pp. 320–21*)

Mr and Mrs Andrew Roberts
1 February–1 April: 10am–4pm;
2 April–14 August: 9am–6pm or
by arrangement; ££
Next to Logan (RBG). Entrance to
the gardens is signposted from
the A716. A ticket machine, which
only accepts coins, is at the notice
board to the left of the house
T: 07900 223037
E: vickyr@hotmail.com

Logan House Gardens

'Garden brought back to life'. This is probably the appropriate headline for this garden, which is not to be confused with Logan, its former walled garden next door which is now run as an outstation of the Royal Botanic Garden, Edinburgh. Logan House was built in 1702 and despite the attentions of Victorian architect David Bryce, it is still a handsome early Georgian structure, painted pale pink. The reclaiming of the overgrown wilderness filled with fine plants began in 1995 when Mr and Mrs Michael Coburn bought the estate. Head gardener Jimmy Reid got to work with a chainsaw and 'lost' areas were reclaimed. The 1998 storms which felled a large number of mature trees were a setback but it proved to be an opportunity for new planting. The garden changed hands again in 2001 and new

owners Mr and Mrs Andrew Roberts opened the garden to the public in 2002. Recent plantings have included Maddenia rhododendrons, a rock garden known as Coburn's Rocks, in memory of the late Michael Coburn, and a heather/scree garden next door. The woodland below the house is a veritable jungle under some spectacular conifers such as *Thuja plicata* and *Thujopsis dolobrata*. Here are a range of huge old rhododendrons as well as a view of the smaller of the two Logan lochs. Behind the house in the woodland there is a somewhat wind-battered monkey-puzzle avenue, underplanted with cordylines and beyond this, a row of shrub roses. In one part of the wood are extensive plantings of *R. macabeanum* and *R. sinogrande* which would benefit from a lot more light to encourage flowering and good habit. There are also recent plantings of azaleas. Two UK champion trees are *Eucryphia cordifolia* and *Leptospermum lanigerum*, both of which flower in late summer, as does the huge clump of *Eucryphia ×nymanensis*. The maturity and informal/wild layout of the garden are a fine contrast to the more mannered plantings at Logan next door and visits to the two can easily be combined with Ardwell a couple of miles away.

WC

Newtonairds Lodge Garden

This is an interesting, densely planted 1.2-acre plantsman's garden punctuated with shrubs and spiralled topiary trees, surrounding a nineteenth-century listed baronial lodge. The National Collection of *Hosta plantaginea* hybrids and cultivars is integrated with a further 150+ other hosta varieties, climbing roses on posts and ropes, perennials and grasses on a natural terraced wooded bank with grassy paths. Some heritage vegetables are also grown.

    WC

Newtonairds Lodge Garden
Newtonairds, Dumfries, DG2 0JL
(*map, pp. 320–21*)

James and Carol Coutts
By appointment May–September inclusive. NCCPG open 1 day a year; £
From Dumfries A76 north. Holywood B729 to Dunscore, Moniave, 1 mile left towards Newtonairds, after 3 miles, red sandstone lodge on right black iron railings
T: 01387 820 203
E: jcoutts@toucansurf.com
newtonairdshostas.website. orange.co.uk
Refreshments and homebaking on request

**Riverside Trees,
Dildawn and Forestmoor**
Garden Cottage, Walled Garden,
Dildawn Estate, Bridge of Dee,
Kelton, Castle Douglas, DG7 1SE
Forestmoor, Kirkinner, Newton
Stewart, Dumfriesshire, DG8 9DF

Tim and Katy Ewing
Garden and nursery: 15 March–
31 October, Thursday–Saturday
10am–6pm and by appointment.
Off A75 at Bridge of Dee, 2 miles
south of Castle Douglas
T: 01556 680357
E: ewing468@btinternet.com

Riverside Trees, Dildawn and Forestmoor

The Ewings have run a tree and rhododendron nursery near Bridge of Dee in a walled garden for several years. Rhododendrons have been propagated from Barnhourie Mill, Mavis Paton's Dumfries garden. Trees and shrubs include species conifers, *Embothrium*, *Halesia*, willows, *Sorbus* and lots more. The Ewings also run Forest Moor near Newton Stewart which has national collections of *Schizostylus* and *Liriodendron* and are likely to be moving their operations from Dildawn shortly. Forestmoor is a 2-acre garden which can be visited by appointment (donation £1 to NCCPG). Directions: A714 from Newton Stewart; A746 to Whithorn; Forestmoor is half a mile after Kirkinner on right.

Southwick House
Southwick, Dumfries and
Galloway, DG2 8AH
(*map, pp. 320–21*)

Mr and Mrs R.H.L. Thomas
SGS 2 Sundays in July; ££
On A710 near Caulkerbush,
Dalbeattie 7 miles, Dumfries
17 miles
Teas and foodstall on open days

Southwick House

This large garden, not far from the Solway Firth near Dumfries, lies in mature woodland. The Southwick Burn which runs through the property is being used to develop a water garden with a series of ponds. The traditional walled garden is divided into several sections, the largest of which has a greenhouse complex, cutting borders, fruit and vegetables. A smaller part has a raised rectangular lily pond and some surrounding rosebeds, while a further section, leading to a white gate, is mainly planted with roses.

Spedlins Castle

Spedlins Castle is a fifteenth-century tower house restored and added to by architect Nick Gray and his wife Amanda, a designer. A new yew-hedged enclosed formal garden has been created over the last 15 years. Designed by Ann Nevett to be looked down on from the castle, it consists of a parterre with white and pink gravel, with a doocot and small banqueting pavilion in the corners, designed by Nick Grey. The parterre's box hedging was replaced with *Ilex crenata* a few years back. A walk of holm oaks planted into a high box hedge leads from the doocot to the castle. The entrance court is another small enclosure with follies in each corner and roses, honeysuckle, perennials and box balls along the edges. The whole is an interesting and well-conceived design which manages to be both traditional and contemporary. There is also a large pond which provides a fine foreground for a vista to the castle.

Spedlins Castle
Templand, Lockerbie,
Dumfriesshire, DG11 1EW
(*map, pp. 320–21*)

Nick and Amanda Gray
By appointment in late June/July;
££
A74(M) exit 17. Go to Templand.
Take B7020 (direction Moffat).
½ mile first right. ½ mile left at
T-junction. 250 yards first track
on right. Leads to castle
E: graydsgn@aol.com

Threave Garden and Estate

This large and varied garden has long been used by the National Trust for Scotland for training its garden staff, though this role has been somewhat reduced in recent years. Former curators Bill Hean and Magnus Ramsey are responsible for much of the garden's layout, planting designs and impressive range of plants. A long drive through the 1,500-acre estate leads to a fine visitor centre, small plant centre and café which are at the edge of the 64-acre garden. The first section reached is the rose garden, informally planted with mainly shrub and

Threave Garden and Estate
Castle Douglas, Dumfries
and Galloway, DG7 1RX
(*map, pp. 320–21*)

NTS
Gardens: all year, daily
9.30am–5pm (closes 4.30pm
Friday). House: 21 March–31
October, Wednesday–Friday and
Sunday, 11am–3.30pm; ££–£££*
Off A75, 1 mile west of Castle
Douglas, well-signed
www.nts.org.uk
Café in visitor centre. Visitor
centre and gift shop closed in
January.

species roses. Below this is the walled garden which is Threave's best feature: I love the vista through the stone arch between the great herbaceous borders to the lovely old glasshouses on the back wall. With trained fruit and a fine selection of vegetables, this is a traditional walled garden. Particularly interesting are the interpretive signs on each wall demonstrating how aspect (north, west etc) affects sunlight, temperature and rainfall, and therefore which plants do best planted where. A fine long border runs along the outside of the walled garden too, which contains *Trillium* and *Euphorbia* amongst others. Opposite this are the fine peat beds with primulas, rhododendrons and other acid-loving plants. In contrast, the species rhododendrons behind are in too much shade under beech trees and are suffering dieback as a result. The rock garden is not yet mature but is well made and well labelled. The secret garden, with an emphasis on plants with interesting foliage, has some striking planting, including the use of hardy fuchsias as bedding/ground cover. The conifer area is suffering; the old ones are overcrowded and most look sick with dieback and signs of spruce aphid damage. The heather garden is also rather disappointing, over-mature and poorly labelled. Heading back towards the visitor centre through parkland and fine trees, there are extensive azaleas beds. Overall Threave is an interesting and informative garden, with room for improvement in several areas, worth visiting at any time of year. There are over 200 varieties of *Narcissus* in spring and dahlia beds and autumn colour in October. We visited on the first Sunday of July, school holidays in Scotland had started and it should have been busy, but it wasn't. Perhaps Threave is just too far off the beaten track? I can't help but think that this garden is a missed opportunity as a Rosemoor or Harlow Carr of Scotland with plant trials, demonstration gardens and education. In some ways this is a ready-made 'National Garden for Scotland', unlike the one proposed in Perth. Threave is already mature and there is almost infinite space for expansion. New training courses in conservation and heritage horticulture are being instigated at Threave in the next few years which should give the garden a much needed boost. My children also recommend a visit to Threave Castle nearby on an island in the River Dee, which can only be reached by a 10–15 minute walk and a short boat ride.

Waterside

This is a new garden, not yet fully planted, let alone open to the public. I have included it as I'm sure it's going to be good in the future. Ronnie Cann and Robert Bradford gardened at the well-designed and planted Holestone Lodge (now Hollytree Lodge) at Yetts O' Muckhart and have now moved on to a larger garden outside Moffat. They told me they spent the first year 'slashing and burning' (the place was awash with overgrown *Rhododendron ponticum*, self-seeded geans, birches and *Cotoneaster*). They will be featuring grasses once again, as they did in their previous garden, and making use of the water meadows and mature woodland around the house to plant rhododendrons and other suitable plants. The main perennial planting area, the 'amphitheatre', leads to a centrepiece of a birch circle surrounding a statue by Estonian ceramicist Tonis Kriisa. This is a garden to watch out for in years to come.

Waterside
Moffat, Dumfriesshire, DG10 9LF
(*map, pp. 320–21*)

Ronnie Cann and Robert Bradford
From 2010/2011 by appointment
for individuals and small groups.
Limited parking.
Off the A708 just further up the
glen from Craigieburn on the right
E: garden@holestone.net
www.holestone.net

Woodfall Gardens

This garden near the southern tip of the Machairs in Galloway, once belonged to the Glasserton estate. The 'big house' was torn down in the 1940s, leaving the eighteenth-century triple-walled garden with a backdrop of the spire of Glasserton Church, surrounded by sheltering sycamore woods. Now named Woodfall, it has been given a new lease of life by the current owners, who live in the extended gardener's cottage. The small, arched doorway is the only entrance into the garden, which consists of three roughly equal sections, divided by internal walls and filled with lots of mature trees and shrubs, making it far from conventional in the way it feels and is planted. The reclaiming of the derelict gardens was begun by David and Jenny Eckford and continued under current owners Lesley and David Roberts, who are carrying on an ambitious programme of restoration and planting. A commercial box (*Buxus*) nursery was run here for a time, which is reflected in the numerous box plants and the extensive parterre, inter-planted with two geraniums suggested and supplied by Michael Wickenden at Cally Gardens, Gatehouse of Fleet. The bed of

Woodfall Gardens
Glasserton, Whithorn,
Dumfries and Galloway, DG8 8LY
(*map, pp. 320–21*)

Lesley and David Roberts
SGS days and by arrangement
May–August; ££
2 miles south of Whithorn
by junction of A746/747
T: 01988 500 692
E: enquiries@woodfall-gardens.co.uk
www.woodfall-gardens.co.uk

English shrub roses and the perennial borders are planted around the foundations of some old pit houses. The garden also has many rambling roses on the walls and up the old apple trees. The middle section has two fine grass borders with *Eremuris* and other complementary plants, as well as extensive borders of fruit and vegetables, raspberries and asparagus being particularly impressive. Other features include a box-edged herb garden, a winter garden, a small fernery in the remains of the former summer house and a woodland garden. The Roberts are building up a national collection of *Parthenocissus* (Virginia Creeper) on their high walls. As well as some outstanding *Paulonia* which flower well, two other plants which grabbed my attention were a large clump of the yellow daisy *Telekia speciosa* (*Buphthalmum salicifolium*) and two staggering drifts of white-flowered *Rodgersia* hybrids from Cally Gardens. As most of my readers must know by now, I get very enthusiastic about rescued walled gardens and this one is a great example, full of interesting plants and planting. You can combine it with a visit to Galloway Plants/Claymodie next door.

South-East:

Lothians and Borders west to M74

Edinburgh and its environs offer a range of gardens, with the Royal Botanic Garden in Edinburgh one of Scotland's top horticultural attractions. South towards the Borders, the Tweed Valley and surrounds offer a huge range of fine castles, country houses and gardens which could easily absorb several days of visiting, particularly in summer. There is a fine circuit of Border towns taking in Kelso, Jedburgh, Hawick, Galashiels and Melrose or alternatively a more linear route from Dawyck and Stobo in the west to Paxton House not far from the mouth of the Tweed at Berwick. Both routes offer a range of gardens and great houses, most of which are open for long periods, with several more gardens opening under SGS for one or more days a year. Floors Castle walled garden, Monteviot, Manderston and Dawyck open regularly. Some of the best private walled/rose/perennial gardens, open on SGS days or by appointment include Carolside, Portmore and Newhall. East Lothian is full of attractive towns and villages, many of which have gardens open under SGS. Some of the most attractive include Haddington, Gifford and Dirleton.

Gardens which open some years under SGS, but are not included in the main entries include: **East Lothian:** Johnstounburn House, village gardens in Gifford, Stenton and Dirleton; **Midlothian, Edinburgh, West Lothian:** Morningside Park, EH10; Merchiston Cottage, 16 Colinton Road, Edinburgh; Midmar Allotments, EH10 (140 allotments); Lymphoy House, Currie; Penicuik House; The Old Manse, Crichton; village gardens include: Inveresk, Pomathorn, Silverburn, St James's Gardens, Penicuik; Temple village. **Borders:** Yetholm village gardens (up to nine gardens opening together); Gattonside village gardens; Melrose gardens; Torquhan, Stow; Liddesdale Road Gardens, Hawick; West Linton gardens; Meldonfoot, Lyne; St Boswells gardens; Glenmayne, Galashiels.

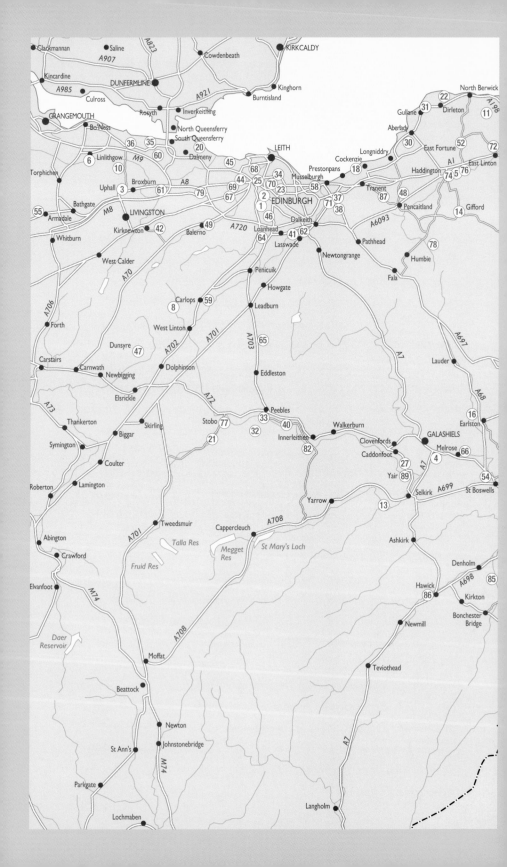

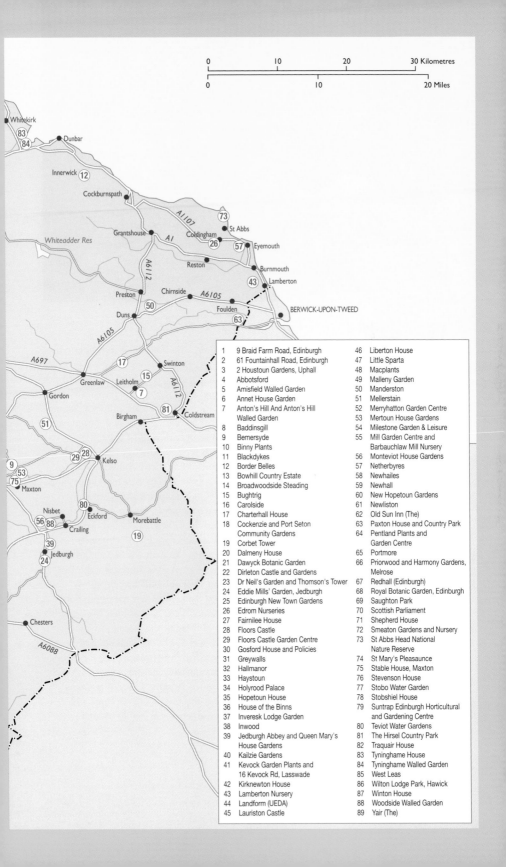

1	9 Braid Farm Road, Edinburgh	46	Liberton House
2	61 Fountainhall Road, Edinburgh	47	Little Sparta
3	2 Houstoun Gardens, Uphall	48	Macplants
4	Abbotsford	49	Malleny Garden
5	Amisfield Walled Garden	50	Manderston
6	Annet House Garden	51	Mellerstain
7	Anton's Hill And Anton's Hill	52	Merryhatton Garden Centre
	Walled Garden	53	Mertoun House Gardens
8	Baddinsgill	54	Milestone Garden & Leisure
9	Bemersyde	55	Mill Garden Centre and
10	Binny Plants		Barbauchlaw Mill Nursery
11	Blackdykes	56	Monteviot House Gardens
12	Border Belles	57	Netherbyres
13	Bowhill Country Estate	58	Newhailes
14	Broadwoodside Steading	59	Newhall
15	Bughtrig	60	New Hopetoun Gardens
16	Carolside	61	Newliston
17	Charterhall House	62	Old Sun Inn (The)
18	Cockenzie and Port Seton	63	Paxton House and Country Park
	Community Gardens	64	Pentland Plants and
19	Corbet Tower		Garden Centre
20	Dalmeny House	65	Portmore
21	Dawyck Botanic Garden	66	Priorwood and Harmony Gardens,
22	Dirleton Castle and Gardens		Melrose
23	Dr Neil's Garden and Thomson's Tower	67	Redhall (Edinburgh)
24	Eddie Mills' Garden, Jedburgh	68	Royal Botanic Garden, Edinburgh
25	Edinburgh New Town Gardens	69	Saughton Park
26	Edrom Nurseries	70	Scottish Parliament
27	Fairnilee House	71	Shepherd House
28	Floors Castle	72	Smeaton Gardens and Nursery
29	Floors Castle Garden Centre	73	St Abbs Head National
30	Gosford House and Policies		Nature Reserve
31	Greywalls	74	St Mary's Pleasaunce
32	Hallmanor	75	Stable House, Maxton
33	Haystoun	76	Stevenson House
34	Holyrood Palace	77	Stobo Water Garden
35	Hopetoun House	78	Stobshiel House
36	House of the Binns	79	Suntrap Edinburgh Horticultural
37	Inveresk Lodge Garden		and Gardening Centre
38	Inwood	80	Teviot Water Gardens
39	Jedburgh Abbey and Queen Mary's	81	The Hirsel Country Park
	House Gardens	82	Traquair House
40	Kailzie Gardens	83	Tyninghame House
41	Kevock Garden Plants and	84	Tyninghame Walled Garden
	16 Kevock Rd, Lasswade	85	West Leas
42	Kirknewton House	86	Wilton Lodge Park, Hawick
43	Lamberton Nursery	87	Winton House
44	Landform (UEDA)	88	Woodside Walled Garden
45	Lauriston Castle	89	Yair (The)

9 Braid Farm Road
Morningside,
Edinburgh, EH10 6LG
(*map, pp. 360–61*)

Mr and Mrs R. Paul
SGS 1 weekend, summer and
by arrangement on request; ££
From central Edinburgh, up
Morningside Road, near Braid Hills
Hotel, 11 and 15 bus routes
T: 0131 447 3482

9 Braid Farm Road, Edinburgh

This small town garden, surrounding a modest house in Edinburgh's fashionable Morningside district has one of the best-designed town gardens I have seen in Scotland. The garden is divided into several compartments all around the house. Even the narrow carparking strip is fenced in by an intertwining combination of late summer *Clematis*, honeysuckle and Paddy's Pride ivy. The main garden at the front of the house is constructed around a lawn with beds of grasses, perennials and shrubs behind, entered via arches and wicker gates. At the back there is a secluded compartment with a trellis bower and a selection of seats and table. The Pauls have been here for 36 years and the garden is a masterclass of hard landscaping effects in wood, concrete, stone and particularly mosaics, which are set into the stone paths and circles and also inset into raised beds, walls and mirrors all round the garden. Add to this the imaginative use of containers planted with box, grasses, hostas, tender annuals and perennials and the use of walls, trellis and climbers to make maximum use of the space and you can't fail to be inspired by the brilliance on show. Anyone with a small garden should rush along here for inspiration; take your camera. On my exploration of the garden I left the best till last; checking another door, I found it led through a narrow passage into a tropical and Mediterranean courtyard of exuberance and humour. Moroccan blue trellis, pots, window frames, pebble-planting alcoves and different levels, cannas and other exotics, and paving with multicoloured checkerboard and starry mosaics. This is a garden so full of detail you can wander round and round and see more and more every time you look: I can't really praise it highly enough.

61 Fountainhall Road, Edinburgh

Few Scottish gardens have more plants crammed into a small space than this gem of a small town garden in the leafy streets of south Edinburgh. Retired music teacher Annemarie Hammond explained to me that she took up gardening seriously when she gave up teaching and playing the flute. This well-laid out cornucopia of carefully selected plants includes shade lovers under the sycamore in the back garden by the street and a range of trees, shrubs, perennials and alpines in the main garden. Some of the more unusual plants include *Caragana, Drimys andina, Rhododendron* 'Everred', numerous helle-bores, *Trillium*, hostas and tiny alpines in troughs and pots, as well as small rockery sections which line the front of many beds. There are lots of fine design features: grasses in upturned pipes, narrow paved paths and quirky planting combinations. With her serious sideline in the ecology of amphibians, several small ponds have been constructed to encourage frogs and their relatives into the garden. Proceeds from garden visits are donated to the Froglife charity.

   [WC]

61 Fountainhall Road
Edinburgh, EH9 2LH
(*map, pp. 360–61*)

John and Annemarie Hammond
3 weekends SGS and
February–October by appointment;
££
Off St Thomas Road, off Grange
Loan, between Morningside Road
A702 and the A701 Minto Street
(see map on website)
T: 0131 667 6146
E: froglady@blueyonder.co.uk
www.froglady.pwp.blueyonder.
co.uk
Teas available for groups

2 Houstoun Gardens, Uphall

I visited this small garden, planted around a detached 1980s bungalow, in Uphall, not far from Edinburgh, on a wet day in August and despite the weather this was a garden in perfect condition, famed for miles around, which has won best West Lothian garden three times. This is as good an example of what can be achieved in a modest space as you will find anywhere. The garden is famed for its bedding displays, particularly the hanging baskets at the front of the house. The back garden is constructed around a small lawn with apples, soft fruit, sweet pea trellis and vegetables along the back fence,

2 Houstoun Gardens, Uphall
Uphall, West Lothian, EH52 5PX
(*map, pp. 360–61*)

John and Isabel McDonald
SGS 1 weekend in August every
2nd year; ££, includes tea
Leave A89 at the B8046 junction
towards Uphall, 100m turn right
into Stankards Road, take 2nd left
into Houstoun Gardens. From
Uphall village travel west along
Main St, turn left at mini-
roundabout onto B8046, travel
150 yards then turn left into
Stankards Road and then onto
Houstoun Gardens
T: 01506 857066
E: mcdonald33@btinternet.com

363

a rockery, a fine collection of grasses planted with Japanese ornaments and a pond/stream crossed by two wooden bridges. There are pots of bedding and fuchsias everywhere. At the side of the house a shadier area contains another small pond with ferns and other green plants. The McDonalds clearly love showing off their excellent garden and it provides inspiration for many of their visitors.

Abbotsford
Abbotsford, Melrose,
Roxburghshire, TD6 9BQ
(*map, pp. 360–61*)

Abbotsford Trust
17 March–31 October:
Monday–Friday 9.30am–5pm,
Sunday (March–May, October)
10am–4pm; November–March:
Monday–Friday, group bookings
only, by appointment; ££
On the A68, take the A6091
Melrose Bypass, heading north
towards Galashiels. Turn left at
the second roundabout onto the
B6360
T: 01896 752043
F: 01896 752916
E: enquiries@scottsabbotsford.
co.uk
www.scottsabbotsford.co.uk
Tearoom in the house

Abbotsford

Overlooking the Tweed outside Melrose, Sir Walter Scott's home Abbotsford, designed by William Atkinson, was completed in 1821 and Scott spent much of his life writing frantically to pay for it. Unusually for the laird, Scott was very much hands-on in establishing his gardens and woodlands; he is said to have planted all the trees himself and documented them in his book *Sylva Abbotsfordiensis*. His strongly held theories of garden design are reflected in the garden structure: the main feature is the three-part walled garden right next to the house: Scott did not approve of the prevailing fashion of building walled gardens far from the house, which he describes as 'a strange and sweeping sentence of exile'. Abbotsford's gardens were partly re-designed by Susan Luczyc-Wyhowska, to make them easier to look after. When I visited in June 2007, much of the property, including parts of the gardens, was covered in scaffolding due to much-needed restoration work on the walls. The formal section of the garden nearest the house, with a yew hedge with holes cut in it to reveal alcoves, looks rather comic, and was put in by one of Scott's descendents. This section looks at its best from the windows of the house, where the box balls stand out against the gravel. A series of arches forms the dividing wall between this section of garden from the middle section. They look as if they might carry a small Roman

aqueduct. Here there are a fountain, pergola, statues and plantings of roses and other plants. There is an impressive double herbaceous border in the furthest 'kitchen garden' section with an orangery at one end and a handsome arch leading to the walled garden's middle section at the other. Outside are woodland walks and rhododendrons and azaleas in the spring. The house is of course of great interest to Scott fans and is full of fascinating historical memorabilia. The trust that runs Abbotsford is in a somewhat precarious financial state, due to the cost of the major repairs under way to the house and gardens. What's more, the expanding towns of Melrose and Galashiels seem hellbent on engulfing the estate. Abbotsford is one of Scotland's most important cultural sites and it is imperative that it, and the landscape which surrounds it, are put on a sound financial footing via the National Trust for Scotland or a similar body. This house virtually invented the idea of public visiting of stately homes, as it first opened its doors in 1833. There is nowhere else in Scotland which combines architecture, literature and landscape theory and practice in the way Abbotsford does.

Amisfield Walled Garden

This 7½-acre 1783 walled garden with 3m-high walls was once part of the Wemyss estates. Amisfield House was demolished in 1928, and the walled garden was used as a council plant nursery, abandoned due to competitive tendering, leaving large numbers of unwanted trees, many of which still need to be removed. The Amisfield Preservation Trust was formed to look for a future use for the garden. Lottery and Scottish Enterprise funding have saved the summer house from

Amisfield Walled Garden
Haddington, East Lothian,
EH41 4PT
(*map, pp. 360–61*)

Amisfield Preservation Trust
Work parties in the garden every
Wednesday 10am–12pm,
1st Saturday of each month,
10am–2pm; free
Access from the east is via the
Stevenson/Hailes junction on the
A199; or from Haddington go past
the Amisfield Park Golf Course,
then turn left at the Stevenson
junction
T: 01368 864953 (Colin Will)
E: colin.will@zen.co.uk
www.amisfield.org.uk

collapse and allowed a historical survey to be made. Volunteers, including some from Port Seton Resource Centre (a community group of adults with learning difficulties), have cleared scrub and begun replanting. The focus is on fruit and vegetable production, using 'heritage' varieties of potatoes, globe artichokes, cardoons, figs and old apple varieties, some of which are being specially grafted, to bring back some East Lothian specialities. There are plans for cherries, plums, pears, peaches, grapes and other fruit bushes and trees, trained as fans, cordons or espaliers, to make maximum use of the warmth and shelter of the walls. Laudable though all this is, to really make this into a viable and sustainable place will require a huge dose of imagination, hard work and funding as simply making a fruit and vegetable garden here will not be enough. Ideas mooted include a community garden and/or a market garden with coffee shop and retail outlet, a specialist tree nursery, a play area and an educational garden.

Annet House Garden

The gardens at Annet House are a restoration of a medieval garden known as a rig or rigg or burgage plot, with the house fronting onto the main street and the back garden used for cultivating herbs, fruit and vegetables for food and medicines. The house is now a fine small local museum detailing the history and industry of this part of West Lothian. The narrow garden is on a steeply sloping site, and is divided into four terraces. The lowest is a paved seating area with troughs of herbs, the next would once have been a formal garden, where flowers

for cutting and decoration would have been grown. Borders now run round the grassed area, contained within a low box hedge, in-filled with marsh mallow, *Astrantia major, Centaurea* and *Anaphalis margaritacea.* The third level contains potager beds of vegetables, herbs and flowers. The walls on this and the upper levels are lined with apples, pears, currants, and most interestingly two fruiting medlar trees, a quince and a fig. The garden grows an impressive range of vegetables including some less well-known ones such as strawberry spinach, rare Scottish leeks, kale and varieties of oats and barley. The top terrace contains a small group of alpines, planted between paving slabs. My children enjoyed the stocks (pity I could not lock them in) and other ancient implements which are laid around the garden. All in all this is worth a visit in tandem with the much larger Linlithgow Palace, not far away.

Annet House Garden
Linlithgow Museum,
143 High Street, Linlithgow,
West Lothian, EH49 7EJ
(*map, pp. 360–61*)

Linlithgow Heritage Trust
Easter–October: Monday–Saturday
10am–5pm, Sunday 1–4pm; £
On Linlithgow High Street. Exit
M9 J3 or 4 and follow signs
to centre of Linlithgow
T: 01506 670677

[🖾] [WC]

Anton's Hill and Walled Garden

Anton's Hill estate was broken up and sold off in several lots, but happily the purchasers of both of the two main sections, the house/policies and the walled garden, turned out to be keen gardeners. They have restored their respective gardens and open together under SGS so you get two gardens for one. The house at Anton's Hill sits amongst mature trees and the garden slopes gently down to the new pond, surrounded by well-planted shrub borders, with many plants chosen for their yellow and purple foliage as well as their flowers. In a

Anton's Hill and Walled Garden
Leitholm, Coldstream, TD12 4JD
(*map, pp. 360–61*)

Mr and Mrs Wills, Alec West
and Pat Watson
SGS 1 Sunday 2–6pm and
by arrangement; ££
Signed off B6461 west of
Leitholm, after hump-back bridge,
left up lane, few 100 yards on
right, lodge and gates
T: 01890 840203

clearing in the trees on the left-hand side is a stumpery, inspired by the one at Highgrove, where Mrs Wills used to guide visitors. There are impressive massed displays of daffodils around this area in spring. Beyond this a work in progress is a family of topiary elephants, and further yet, an area of trees and another pond are ripe for development as a woodland garden. The whole feel is of a southern English idyll, sheltered, well planted and well maintained.

The walled garden alongside was bought by Alec West, a retired RAF engineer and clearly a man of immense practical ability when it comes to restoring buildings, garden walls and greenhouses, not to mention maintaining his garden model railway, which sometimes runs on open days. Alec West and Pat Watson have transformed this double walled garden and former orchard into one of the most important fruit collections in Scotland. With help from Scotland's fruit guru John Butterworth, old apples were identified and budded by Alec and replanted in the garden. There are over 230 varieties of apples and pears, most trained as cordons and other shapes, immaculately maintained. Alec is also interested in all sorts of other plants including cacti and the garden has lavender borders, bedding plants and a very fine *Cercis* 'Forest Pansy'.

Baddinsgill
West Linton,
Peebleshire, EH46 7HL
(*map, pp. 360–61*)

Gavin and Elaine Marshall
SGS (1 Sunday in May); ££
A702 to West Linton. turn north at sign marked Baddinsgill, Golf Course. After 2½ miles you come to the end of the public road. Continue and fork right, and we are the house at the end of that drive
T: 01968 660698
E: elaine@baddinsgill.com

Baddinsgill

This secluded woodland garden lies amongst bleak moorland 1,000 feet up in the Pentland Hills above West Linton with great views south down the valley. There are riverside walks along the Baddinsgill Burn, through the woodland with mature azaleas and rhododendrons planted in the 1940s and 1950s underplanted with bluebells. The Marshalls have recently uncovered and replanted a rock garden above the pond which features *Gunnera* and *Iris*. Various paths and tracks run up into the Pentland Hills from Baddinsgill.

Baddinsgill

Bemersyde

The Haig family have been at Bemersyde since 1162. The sixteenth-century peel tower was reconstructed in the seventeenth century and converted into a mansion. The garden was laid out by Field Marshal Earl Haig in the 1920s after his time as commander of the British Army in the First World War, where he took much of the blame for the fruitless carnage of the trenches of the Western Front. Bemersyde was one of Walter Scott's favourite spots with views of the Eildon Hills, woodland garden and river walks. A sweet chestnut on the lawn has layered itself round the edge with the centre dying out. The garden has fine mature trees, drifts of daffodils (for which it is usually open under SGS), with cherries overhead, rhododendrons and a long herbaceous border. The curiously shaped (half octagonal) walled garden is used for fruit and vegetables.

Bemersyde
Melrose, Roxburghshire,
TD6 9DP
(*map, pp. 360–61*)

Earl and Lady Haig
SGS 1 day, April. Mid May–mid October 10am–4pm;
££ honesty box
B6356 Between St Boswells and Redpath. St Boswells via Clintmains or Melrose via Leaderfoot bridge. ½ mile from Scot's View.
T: 01835 822762
F: 01835 824104

Binny Plants

Binny Plants
Binny Estate, Ecclesmachan,
West Lothian, EH52 6NL
(*map, pp. 360–61*)

Billy Carruthers
Daily all year round; free
Signed Binny Plants/Huntercombe
Hospital on the B8046, north of
Uphall. Follow the road past front
of the big house.
T: 01506 858931
F: 01506 858155
E: info@binnyplants.co.uk
www.binnyplants.co.uk

The first time I visited Binny Plants in West Lothian, I bumped into one of their customers in one of the tunnel houses. 'Visiting this nursery is like being a child in a sweetshop' he told me with a wide-eyed grin. And certainly if perennials or peonies are your thing, this is probably the best place in Scotland to come. Better still, if you can't visit in person they offer mail order with an excellent website. Billy Carruthers once ran record shops but his first love has always been plants and he found the site he'd long been looking for to establish his nursery in the overgrown walled garden on the Binny estate, west of Edinburgh. The catalogue lists almost 2,500 plant varieties and there are particularly fine selections of *Hemerocallis, Iris, Astilbe*, ferns, grasses and over 200 varieties of peony. Billy is particularly excited about the new intersectional peony hybrids which are a cross between tree and herbaceous varieties. The nursery is crammed with plants and you may need some time to ferret out what you are looking for. Plantings are starting to creep down the road by the carpark, with *Astilbe,* ferns and other goodies. Binny is not the easiest place to find, perhaps, but definitely worth the effort. The nursery has put on great displays at Gardening Scotland in recent years. Billy's latest project is to set up several national collections in the walled garden at House of the Binns.

Blackdykes

This East Lothian garden constructed around a beautifully restored old farmhouse, with striking grey-green window frames and doors, is a fine mixture of traditional and contemporary design. The compact hedged garden was constructed to filter the winds which can blow up the Forth. A box-edged parterre is next to the house, with a pebble mosaic of the Bass Rock, while another narrow parterre of triangular sections along the front of the house is in-filled with herbs. From the front door, a central path is bordered by narrow upright yew and *Alchemilla*, with a rectangle of lawn on each side, backed by perennials, on one side red, pink and blue, on the other side blues and yellows. The path leads down some steps through a scalloped-topped yew hedge, onto a lawn of formally clipped hawthorn balls with a skirt of geranium under each one and a pair of parterres with roses and an urn in the centre. The central path has a pergola covered with climbing roses, underplanted with *Allium* in early summer giving way to *Nepeta*. To one side, a grass spiral mound allows a fine view over the garden including the potager containing soft fruit and salad crops. Now that the trees are maturing around the edge of the garden, vistas to the borrowed landscape are being created with yew and hornbeam allées, one of which focuses on the striking form of volcanic plug North Berwick Law. I admired the Dalrymples' many deft design touches here, and there are plans for further extensions and improvements in the coming years.

Blackdykes
North Berwick, East Lothian,
EH39 5PQ
(*map, pp. 360–61*)

Hugh and Janie Dalrymple
SGS some years and by appointment
Off the A198 North Berwick to Dunbar Road, 2 miles from North Berwick south of Tantallon Castle.
T. 01620 894 019

Border Belles
Old Branxton Cottages,
Innerwick, near Dunbar,
East Lothian, EH42 1QT
(*map, pp. 360–61*)

Gillian Moynihan
March–September:
Thursday–Saturday 10am–5pm,
or by appointment
Turn off the A1 south of Dunbar
at Innerwick junction and follow
signs for 2 miles
T: 01368 840325
E: mail@borderbelles.com
www.borderbelles.com

Border Belles

Recently celebrating 10 years in business, this is a small retail and wholesale perennial nursery near Dunbar run by Gillian Moynihan, with a good range of plants. Specialities include *Actaea, Anemone, Allium, Campanula, Diplarrhena,* hardy geraniums, *Hosta, Trillium* and *Tricyrtis.*

Borders Organic Gardeners
Bowhill North Lodge,
Selkirk, TD7 5LZ

Maggie Warner
(membership secretary)
www.bordersorganic
gardeners.org.uk

Borders Organic Gardeners

This society (which is a charity) was founded in 1989 in the Galashiels area and now has over 400 members in the Borders (on both sides), making it one of the largest and most active organic gardening groups in the UK. Some of the popular society-run events run include the seed potato day at the Border Union Agricultural Society Showground in Kelso, now christened 'Potato Plus'. Another popular event is the Apple Day at Harestanes Visitor Centre, near Jedburgh. BOG (not the nicest acronym) produces a newsletter of organic gardening advice and other topical articles. The best way to contact the society is via its website. The society has recently formed eastern and western groups which cover the width of the Borders.

Bowhill Country Estate

The 60,000-acre estate at Bowhill is one of four owned by the dukes of Buccleuch, whose lands extend to 280,000 acres. The enormous house, extended and remodelled by generations of Scottish architects, squats on the banks of a loch, near the confluence of the Ettrick and Yarrow rivers. The house is open in July only. The policy woods, designed by John Gilpin, have extensive conifer plantings, carpeted with snowdrops and planted with drifts of rhododendrons and azaleas. The Victorian kitchen garden has been recently restored. There are river walks and a network of paths; mountain bikes are available for rent.

   [WC]

Bowhill Country Estate
Bowhill, Selkirk,
Scottish Borders, TD7 5ET
(*map, pp. 360–61*)

Buccleuch Heritage Trust
Daily: April, July and August;
May–June weekends and bank
holidays; all 10am–5pm.
House open in July only. ££
3 miles west of Selkirk on the
A708 Moffat/St Mary's Loch road
T: 01750 22204
F: 01750 23893
E: bht@buccleuch.com
www.bowhill.org
Tearoom

Broadwoodside Steading

This is one of Scotland's most exciting contemporary garden projects. The long narrow garden is constructed around a restored steading complex just outside the attractive East Lothian village of Gifford. The derelict farm buildings were converted and extended in the 1990s with a two-part enclosed courtyard inside and a series of garden rooms outside. The building conversion was designed by Nicholas Groves-Raines, whose offices and home at Liberton House, Edinburgh, have a fine garden (see p. 402). Fine features of the Broadwoodside buildings include the corner tower, gatehouse and the trademark ochre render. The gardens have been a long-term project since 1999, driven by the team of owners Rob and Anna Dalrymple and imaginative and highly motivated gardener Guy Donaldson. Guy showed me round the various sections, pointing out the many successes and few failures which have demanded a re-think due to issues of drainage or climate. The west end of the garden consists of

Broadwoodside Steading
Gifford, East Lothian, EH41 4JE
(*map, pp. 360–61*)

Robert and Anna Dalrymple
1 day SGS most years
and by appointment; ££
On the B6355 on the western
outskirts of Gifford, towards
Saltoun and Pencaitland. Turning
by the deer signpost and golf
course
E: mail@broadwoodside.com

373

an apple orchard, with each variety planted in a square of grass which is filled with naturalised spring bulbs, a series of *Narcissus* cultivars, followed by the blue of *Camassia*. In late summer the reds and greens of the fruit contrast beautifully with squares of grasses with billowing bronze and yellow seed heads. Next to the orchard, the narrow paddock has a long, narrow 'canal' of blue *Iris sibirica* with red poppies sown through it. From here you'll catch sight of what looks like part of a Greek temple in the distant corner of the field next door, which is in fact the Victorian portico of Strathleven House in Dunbartonshire, rescued by the Dalrymples and adding a neoclassical feel to the hinterland of an otherwise very contemporary garden. Ian Hamilton Finlay's influence can be seen in the statuary and stonework in the garden, such as the stone carving on a slate cube which is actually a 'Latin joke' ('twould be a shame to say more). The western boundary of mature lime trees was once part of the famous lime avenue leading to the gates of Yester House. A pair of beech hedges runs towards the 'dogs' tomb' with the centrepiece of a finial rescued from the Holyrood brewery, demolished to make way for the new Scottish Parliament. Along the north side of the steading a short row of 'knuckled' or pollarded limes are underplanted with snowdrops, 'West Point' tulips and a fringe of *Muscari*, provide a stunning spring display, followed by geranium, *Nepeta* and *Phlomis* in summer. Rows of hornbeams lead down the drive, meeting at the point at the bottom, at a beech pyramid. The enclosed kitchen and cutting garden at the south end of the building complex features a rectangular pond surrounded by arched willows which are cut back to a framework in winter and become wildly lush by later summer. I'm not sure that this shows off the pond to its best advantage, but it is a bold planting

statement. The narrow section of walled garden on the west side of
the house has a fantastic combination of white *Pulmonaria* along the
fieldside wall and opposite along the house, *Euphorbia* and purple
Cotinus. Further on, the boundary wall is lined with a bog garden,
kept moist by field-water run-off, contrasting with the Mediterranean
plants such as lavender and *Santolina* along the side of the house. The
top end has an elm monument carved by Ralph Curry and the small
formal garden here features squares of box topiary and grasses, once
again underplanted with spring bulbs. The climax of any visit to
Broadwoodside is the two-part inner courtyard, entered via pillarbox-
red doors. The upper courtyard consists of a pattern of squares of
lawn, cobbles or planting. Some sections contain a central standard
tree, underplanted with box balls, grasses, *Pachysandra* or box, and the
central square contains an aviary. The planted squares contain a single
spring bulb variety: snowdrops, tulips or *Allium* and the effect in
April is magical. The lower courtyard is a lawn with a cruciform
paved path, with trained fruit and roses around the perimeter as well
as a cloud-pruned *Ceanothus*. This is one of Scotland's finest contemporary private gardens, with excellent structure, imaginative use of
objects, and some of the most eye-catching planting in Scotland. It is
a masterclass in 'less is more' patterned plantings, showing how a
limited palette in each area creates some unforgettable combinations.
I can't think of anywhere which uses spring bulbs better and the
garden has a very long period of interest, probably at its best from
April to July. This is cutting-edge garden design combined with
imaginative planting; who could ask for more?

Bughtrig

Bughtrig
Coldstream, Borders, TD12 4JP
(map, pp. 360–61)

Major General and Hon. Mrs
Charles Ramsay
Daily: 1 June–1 September
11am–5pm by appointment. The
house is also available for visits
from groups by appointment; ££
¼ mile east of Leitholme on
B6461. 5 miles north-west
of Coldstream
T: 01890 840678
E: ramsay@bughtrig.co.uk

Bughtrig is a Georgian house surrounded by mature trees and banks of rhododendrons, as well as the main attraction, an enclosed garden, hedged rather than walled, with a combination of herbaceous plants, roses and peonies, shrubs, annuals and fruit in box-edged beds, looked after by the Ramsays and their gardener Mark Gardner. A pair of long, narrow early summer borders is planted with peonies and lupins. Late summer brings to the fore blocks of red *Lobelia*, and bold plantings of dahlias. Espaliered fruit and beech hedges create rooms. A memorial garden to soldiers killed in the Second World War in France was created in memory of the present owner's father, Admiral Sir Bertram Ramsay, who bought the property in 1928, commanded the evacuation from Dunkirk in the Second World War and was killed in active service in 1945.

Carolside

Carolside
Earlston, Berwickshire, TD4 6AL
(map, pp. 360–61)

Anthony and Rose Foyle
SGS some years and by
appointment; ££
Turn off A68 at sign 1 mile
north of Earlston, 6 miles
south of Lauder
T: 01896 849 272
(Mrs Wilkie, housekeeper)
E: a.foyle@virgin.net

Carolside would probably match many people's vision of the perfect English garden, though Rose Foyle says that it is more inspired by gardens familiar from her childhood in Northern Ireland. The old drive to the house crosses a handsome arched stone bridge over the Leader Water which can be appreciated from the newly planted riverside walk where you might meet the collection of black and white ducks. The main plantings are in and outside the walled garden and around the house. The oval-shaped garden appears to have a skirt of *Nepeta* which spills out from under the shrub roses and *Philadelphus* on either side of the main door. Inside it has the traditional cruciform layout, dividing it into quadrants, and the curved walls create an intimate space. The deep main herbaceous borders up the middle are backed with climbing roses on a series of poles linked with chains. The perennials include *Delphinium*, *Campanula* and lupins at the back with *Salvia*, peonies, *Viola*, *Alchemilla* and *Nepeta* spilling out onto the path. The centrepiece pergola is covered with *Wisteria* and two vigorous rambling roses. There are 200 varieties of old roses planted around the perimeter walls and these are Rose Foyle's particular passion; she reels off the names of each one as we walk round and she has assembled what is clearly a collection of historical importance. Next to the greenhouses at the far end a parterre is filled with a David Austin rose 'Eglinton' which produces its double pink flowers from midsummer to autumn. East of the main walled garden are two further enclosed sections, the first is a small oval walled 'secret garden' which features an urn, surrounded by pink roses and a pool of tumbling blue-purple *Nepeta*. Next to this is a further walled area with a set of four triangular box beds filled with herbs, with muscular sprawling tufts of comfrey and spikes of angelica around the outside. Again the walls are covered with roses, including the flamboyant *Rosa gallica* 'Versicolor'. Carolside is one of Scotland's finest walled gardens and one of the best collections of roses; the garden's reputation in the Borders is exceptional; other garden owners were high in their praises and for good reason. Carolside is a brilliantly planned and executed garden by a passionate gardener; Rose has a clear vision of exactly what she wants to achieve: she delights in the 'calm oasis and beautiful serene place' she has created, full of memorable colour combinations, vistas and bold contrasts from one 'room' to another. I particularly liked the sudden change from the luxuriant colours of the walled garden, through the door to the cool, simple colours of the *Hosta* border, minimalist green hedged square and pillar with a surround of white *Iris sibirica*. Carolside is at its best from late June to early August and is one of Scotland's finest private gardens.

Charterhall House
Charterhall, Duns,
Berwickshire, TD11 3RE
(map, pp. 360–61)

Major and Mrs Alexander Trotter
SGS 1 day, usually late May; ££
6 miles south-west of Duns, 3
miles east of Greenlaw on B6460.
T: 01890 840210
E: info@charterhall.net
www.charterhall.net

Charterhall House

A Victorian house overlooking the Teviot Hills, Charterhall's mature woodland garden of rhododendrons and azaleas has been much augmented in recent years, replacing large clumps of *R. ponticum*. The lawn is terraced, leading to beds of deciduous azaleas. A walled garden contains vegetables and a greenhouse. Best visited in late May.

Cockenzie and Port Seton Community Gardens

Cockenzie and Port Seton Community Gardens
Cockenzie Primary School,
Cockenzie, EH32 0AR
(map, pp. 360–61)

Marlene Love
1 day SGS some years, and you can enjoy most of the gardens by wandering around the town.
Bus: First Bus No. 129 (66 on Sunday); Car: east along B1348; right immediately before Chalmers Church (middle of village with spire) into Osborne Terrace. Nursery Garden in grounds of Cockenzie Primary School
T: 01875 811788
E: marlenelove@fsmail.net
www.cockenzieandportsetonin
bloom.co.uk

The Cockenzie and Port Seton in Bloom Project was established in 1998 and is clearly something which has galvanised this community and demonstrates what can be achieved with good organisation and, I dare say, huge amounts of hard work. The town has won many awards for its gardens and plantings, which includes a series of community gardens created by local people. There is a 'secret' walled garden, a woodland garden, two herbaceous plots and some seaside gardens with planting appropriate for their exposed sites. The walled garden's raised beds were created with the help of the Beechgrove Garden. All of the gardens are maintained by the local 'In Bloom' group (recognised by their bright orange jackets) and are within walking distance of each other. The ones I looked at were well maintained and the beds around the war memorial had great displays of grasses. A descriptive leaflet and map is available at the Nursery Garden on open days. The Nursery Garden is situated in the grounds of Cockenzie Primary School, and is the meeting-place for the 'In Bloom' group. The polytunnels are used to produce bedding plants for the community gardens and for sale. Marlene Love, the prime mover in this organisation, was honoured at the Scottish Parliament in 2005.

Corbet Tower

The Frasers bought this house and garden in the scenic Cheviot Hills
to the south of the Tweed in 2004. The garden was already well established, planted by Katherine Waddle. The Corbet Tower, which
stands in the garden, was built to allow the local inhabitants to retreat
inside during the frequent cross-border warfare of the Middle Ages. It
was restored in Victorian times and is still in good condition. The
gardens falls into four sections: parkland, woodland, rose garden and
walled gardens. The parkland contains a mixture of fine mature and
recently planted trees. From here a path leads across the drive to the
woodland gardens, full of snowdrops in early spring, followed by
Trillium, Hosta and *Ligularia* along the paths, pond and stream side.
Above this, to the east of the house the rose garden is a box parterre
with 32 beds of pink and white shrub roses. Higher still is the sloping
walled garden, the four main squares are bordered with *Nepeta* and
packed with fruit and vegetables, including 12 varieties of rhubarb. A
bed running along the outside wall contains large drifts of *Rodgersia*.
The Frasers bought this property almost unseen and most people
would have been daunted by the scale of the garden which came with
it. But Simon has excellent gardening genes: his mother and father
garden at the wonderful Shepherd House, Inveresk, and he and his
wife are clearly evolving the garden with enthusiasm in combination
with gardener Barney Madox. Simon was planting in the walled
garden in the rain when I visited. The valley is stunningly wild and
beautiful and I particularly recommend the steep single-track road
from Hownam to Oxnam if you are heading for Jedburgh and the
A68 to or from the garden.

Corbet Tower
Morebattle, Kelso,
Roxburghshire, TD5 8AW
(*map, pp. 360–61*)

Simon and Bridget Fraser
SGS every 2nd year; ££
A 698 Kelso–Jedburgh road,
B6041 Eckford to Morebattle,
then road marked Hownam
T: 01573 440203

Dalmeny House
Rosebery Estates, South
Queensferry, Lothian, EH30 9TQ
(*map, pp. 360–61*)

Earls of Rosebery
Closed 2008, re-opening 2009,
snowdrops. ££
Signposted off the A90 at
roundabout south side of
Forth Road Bridge to B924
T: 0131 331 1888
F: 0131 331 1788
E: events@dalmeny.co.uk
www.dalmeny.co.uk

Dalmeny House

Nineteenth-century Dalmeny House, with fine views down to the
nearby Forth Estuary, is filled with Rothschild and Rosebery treasures:
paintings and furniture. The house was closed for restoration in 2008
re-opening in 2009. The gardens have not received much attention in
recent years and are mainly used for corporate events. The grounds
contain extensive woodlands with ponds, mature conifers and lots of
rhododendrons and there is a walk along the shoreline. The Mons
Hill (or snowdrop hill) snowdrops are staggering, some of the best
displays in Scotland, very thickly planted around some ruined
cottages, well worth seeking out in February–March; there is
sometimes an official open day under the Snowdrop Festival. The
steep paths can be muddy so wear sensible footwear.

  WC

Dawyck Botanic Garden

One of the outstations of the Royal Botanic Garden, this is an
outstanding collection of plants in a magnificent setting in one of the
side valleys south of the Tweed. You need to be fit to walk round it
all, as it is carved out of a beech wood on a steep hillside; the highest
point of the garden is at 250m (850ft) above sea level. Of the four
gardens of the RBGE, this is the coldest; indeed this part of the
Borders in an inland valley far from the sea is one of harshest climates
in Scotland. The Dawyck estate passed through various families
during its history including the Veitches (till 1691) and the Naesmiths,

famous for their plantings of European larches in the Borders and who later financed several plant hunters. The subsequent owners, the Balfours, continued tree planting before donating Dawyck to the nation in 1978. This garden is particularly suited to plants from the cold northern Chinese province of Sichuan and to North American conifers. Significant collections in the garden include *Rhododendron, Abies, Juniperus, Picea, Pinus, Berberis, Betula, Prunus, Sorbus* and *Spiraea* and a collection of Scottish rare plants. Dawyck was looked after for many years by one of Scotland's friendliest and most knowledgeable plantsmen, David Knott. Spring begins with extensive carpets of snowdrops, followed by daffodils in April when the many wild-origin rhododendrons start showing colour if there are no night frosts, which can ruin the flowers. Into May and June the azaleas join in, underplanted with carpets of *Meconopsis*. One of the features of the garden is the 'rides' which run along and up and down the hillsides, with Italian statuary and urns providing ornament. Some of the best are the steep 'long ride' down to the still privately owned Dawyck House, the line of beech across the hill, and the viewpoint from the top of the garden with a vista to the chapel below, surrounded by plantings of birch, alder and *Sorbus*. The Scrape Burn rushes through the ravine which bisects the garden, bridged in several places. Near the burn you'll find several of Dawyck's famous trees, including the UK champion Austrian Pine, Britain's oldest *Picea breweriana* and original Dawyck beech, whose offspring are grown all over the globe. There is a leaflet available listing 25 of the most significant trees to look out for. Don't expect formality or manicure here, it's a vast expanse of informal woodland planting with great labelling, so you always know what you are looking at. There is also a

Dawyck Botanic Garden
Dawyck Botanic Garden, Stobo, Peeblesshire, EH45 9JU
(*map, pp. 360–61*)

Trustees of the Royal Botanic Garden, Edinburgh
Open February–November from 10am, closing at 4pm in February and November, 5pm in March and October and 6pm April–September; ££
28 miles south of Edinburgh on the B712, 8 miles south-west of Peebles
T: 01721 760254
F: 01721 760214
E: dawyck@rbge.org.uk
www.rbge.org.uk
New café with window overlooking garden, and terrace

cryptogamic sanctuary for mosses and other simple plants. This is one of Scotland's best gardens to visit in autumn with lots of turning leaves (*Cercidiphyllum* is particularly good), *Sorbus* berries and a backdrop of distant hills, often accompanied by cool but sunny weather ideal for clambering around hillsides. The much-improved new visitor centre opened in 2008. Pick a weekend when Stobo is open next door and you can do both together.

Dirleton Castle and Gardens

Dirleton Castle and Gardens
Dirleton, East Lothian, EH39 5ER
(*map, pp. 360–61*)

Historic Scotland
1 April–30 September:
Monday–Sunday, 9.30am–
5.30pm; 1 October–31 March:
Monday–Sunday 9.30am–4.30
pm; ££*
Dirleton village 3 miles west
of North Berwick on the A198
T: 01620 850 330
www.historic-scotland.gov.uk

Dirleton Castle's heyday was from the 1200s to the 1500s, when it was in the hands of three families: the de Vauxs, Halyburtons and Ruthvens. It's certainly a fine castle which I remember visiting when I was about 10 years old; my children loved the drawbridge. The main garden next to the entrance gate consists of four spectacular parallel herbaceous beds with an emphasis on asters and daisies. The main borders are said to be of world record length at 215m. Being so near the sea, this would be a great site for some more unusual and tender material and while the borders are colourful, the plant selection is rather mundane; I gather that 10 years ago the selection was more choice but has not been maintained. Elsewhere in the grounds there are old yews and a formal bedding display surrounded by cedars and other conifers. Up to 12 gardens in attractive Dirleton village open under SGS every second year or so, and are well worth a visit.

Dr Neil's Garden and Thomson's Tower

This is one of Edinburgh's best-kept secrets, and is an idyllic spot which mainly the locals seem to know about. The garden is situated in the attractive Edinburgh village of Duddingston, on the edge of Holyrood Park with Arthur's Seat and Duddingston Loch forming the 'borrowed landscape'. Apart from occasional traffic noise, this is as peaceful a setting as you can find in a big city, with the sound of wind in the rushes at the lochside and what looks like wild countryside all around. The 2-acre site was established by doctors Andrew and Nancy Neil from 1965 on a piece of waste ground, part of the 'glebe' of Duddingston Church. The Neils gardened it for many years and it is now run by a trust, maintained largely by volunteers with one full-time gardener, the welcoming Claudia Pottier. This is a landscape of mature trees including a fine monkey puzzle, underplanted with spring bulbs, alpines, heathers, azaleas and smaller conifers. The garden is dotted with stone and wooden benches and sculpture and a small pond is crossed by a curved metal bridge. In the bottom left-hand corner is the William Playfair-designed Thomson's Tower, which was named after Duddingston Kirk's most famous minister, John Thomson, who used the upper floor as an artist's studio. The tower was built by the Duddingston Curling Society who drew up the rules of curling in 1804. The tower has been a near ruin for many years but

Dr Neil's Garden and Thomson's Tower
Duddingston Village,
Edinburgh, EH15 7DG
(*map, pp. 360–61*)

Dr Neil's Garden Trust
Daily: 10–4pm, 1 day SGS some years and annual May open day in aid of MS; donations; ££ (SGS days, for charities)
At the corner of Duddingston Road and Old Church Lane on the south side of Holyrood Park, Edinburgh, enter via the manse gate, turn immediately right and the gate is at the far end
E: claudiapottier@gmail.com

is now being restored with the aid of a lottery grant. The upper part of the tower will be used for exhibitions and private functions, while the lower part will be devoted to exhibitions on curling. I popped into this garden one warm late afternoon in May, had the place to myself and thought that this was just about the closest thing to heaven. Please don't tell anyone. A few plants are offered for sale.

Eddie Mills' Garden, Jedburgh
Along A68, Jedburgh
(*map, pp. 360–61*)

Eddie Mills
Not officially open, but can
be seen from road.
A68 through Jedburgh

Eddie Mills' Garden, Jedburgh

Though this garden is not open to the public, it is well-known to locals and those who drive down the A68, for the amazing bedding-plants displays in raised beds surrounded by gravel paths. This is a year-round project as Eddie grows his own plants from seed and overwinters begonias and other tender plants in his greenhouses. He explained to Antoinette Galbraith in 2003 that he put in at least 4,500 plants each year. And everything is meticulously deadheaded and weeded. You can see it all from the street and you probably won't be the only one admiring the incredible display. Apparently tour buses now stop to enjoy the show. It looks as if Eddie's neighbours are now joining in, with bedding spreading like a rash down the front gardens along the street.

Queen Street Gardens, Edinburgh

Edinburgh New Town Gardens

Edinburgh New Town boasts some fine public spaces and a whole series of private gardens, many of which were laid out in the eighteenth and early nineteenth centuries. The private gardens are maintained for the residents of the surrounding streets who pay an annual fee for a key. Those in the know seem to have keys for several of them. I have managed to get into most of them over the last few years. The triangular-shaped Regent Gardens on Calton Hill, designed by William Playfair, are particularly fine, partly because of the views, which can also be enjoyed from the public park on top of the hill. Queen Street Gardens divide into three sections, all of which have giant mature trees, underplanted with thickets of shrubs. Robert Louis Stevenson played here as a child. There are plans for rejuvenating them but the budget is small and the bureaucracy required to remove some of the trees is probably insurmountable. The middle section is probably the most interesting with a Doric pavilion. The largest of the public New Town gardens are the two sections of Princes Street Gardens, which are hugely popular and host a fair and ice rink at Christmas. The 13½-acre Dean Gardens run along the north side of the Water of Leith. St Bernard's Well is an attractive 1789 building here. On the opposite side of the Water of Leith are Bank Gardens, almost 6 acres of wild gardens with lawns, trees and shrubs and banks of bulbs leading down to the river, with good views over south Edinburgh to the Forth and Fife. There are also gardens in Randolph Crescent, Ainslie Place, Royal Circus and Drummond Place. Moray Place's 3½ acres have had a recent makeover. All these gardens have been opened under a Parks and Gardens Open Day organised by the Cockburn Association (see website listed above) and Edinburgh World Heritage every year or two. Some open under SGS from time to time. Otherwise you'll need to befriend a resident with a key. A book, *The Edinburgh New Town Gardens, Blessings as well as Beauties* by Connie Byrom, was published recently.

Edinburgh New Town Gardens
New town Edinburgh,
various locations
(*map, pp. 360–61*)

Edinburgh City Council and
Residents Associations
Some open under SGS
some years
Various sites in New Town
Edinburgh
www.cockburnassociation.org.uk

Edrom Nurseries
Coldingham, Eyemouth,
Berwickshire, TD14 5TZ
(map, pp. 360–61)

Terry Hunt and Cath Davis
Daily: 9am–5pm. Owners are
often away at shows; free
c. 12 miles north of Berwick-
upon-Tweed on A1107. Brown
tourist signs on A1 and also in
Coldingham village
T: 018907 71386
F: 018907 71387
E: info@edromnurseries.co.uk
www.edromnurseries.co.uk

Edrom Nurseries

This famous nursery was founded by Edith and Molly Logan Hume
in 1925, was passed on to Alex Duguid and was more recently owned
by Jim Jermyn, who now runs the show Gardening Scotland at
Ingliston and writes books on alpines. Edrom Nursery moved long
ago from Edrom to the site outside Coldingham. The nursery is now
owned by Terry Hunt and Cath Davis, who worked as gardeners at
Hartlepool Council before moving north. They specialise in
woodland bulbs and alpines including *Primula, Arisaema, Fritillaria,*
Trillium, Gentiana, Dierama, Meconopsis, Hepatica and *Rhodohypoxis.*
As well as operating their mail order nursery, there is a newly planted
garden of terraced raised beds and the woodland garden is planned to
be extended to 4 acres. The website is excellent and Edrom probably
has Scotland's finest selection of woodland perennials and bulbous
plants; I was very impressed with the range and quality of material
offered. They have won gold medals at shows, including Chelsea.

Fairnilee House
Fairnilee House, Selkirk, TD1 3PR
(map, pp. 360–61)

Mr and Mrs Mason
SGS some years, and by
appointment; ££
A708 between Caddonfoot and
Yair, turn off A7 at Yair between
Galashiels and Selkirk
E: traceymason@mac.com

Fairnilee House

After 40 years of neglect, Fairnilee has found its saviour in the shape
of transplanted Americans the Masons, who arrived here from Texas
and Arizona, fell in love with the place and have gradually adapted to
growing plants in Scottish conditions as they restored the gardens.
The ruin of an older house lies in the garden next to some imposing
green metal gates which divide the drive from the garden. Striking
white Fairnilee House, built by John Burnet in 1904 for mill owner
A.F. Roberts, contains some fine detailing in the carvings and
metalwork and is one of the finest Scottish houses of this period,
though sadly it has remained largely unlived-in until recently. The tall
windows on the upper floors frame the formal gardens which the
Masons began planting in 2003. The section next to the house is a

yew parterre filled with roses which adjoins the next section, a privet parterre, filled with herbs, not all of which can tolerate the cold and wet of a Tweed Valley winter. A rose arch path leads past the formal sections into a large and impressive vegetable and fruit garden with currants, strawberries, asparagus and a huge range of other edibles. The greenhouse complex beyond this is being restored, with peaches, vines and figs filling the houses. Along the long back wall at the top of the garden is a perennial and shrub border, backed with pears and apples. The lawn which runs along the side of the garden has four formally cut-out beds of annuals, an orchard and a collection of young trees backed by a mixture of mature deciduous trees and conifers. Fairnilee lies in a peaceful, idyllic and hidden Borders valley off the main routes and the Masons seem to have found their own piece of paradise here.

Floors Castle

Floors Castle is said to be the largest house in the UK and it certainly looks a bit like Scotland's answer to Versailles. Despite its size, tours of the house only allow access to a rather miserly 10 rooms and a basement, though there are fine paintings by Matisse, Redon and Augustus John amongst others on display. *Scotland the Best* describes Floors as 'spectacularly impractical' and I can't argue with that. The walls of the estate lie along much of the edge of Kelso, where the main entrance is. To visit the gardens alone it is better to enter via the walled garden/garden centre, which is approached from the north. The main walled garden is one of the best nursery/garden combinations in Scotland, with the small plant centre/garden centre taking up a section of the vast space, surrounded by fine planting. The walls of the garden have a different set of climbing plants for each aspect: on the south wall at the entrance are more tender plants and exotics such as *Carpenteria* and jasmine. On the west-facing wall is a series of

Floors Castle
Kelso, Scottish Borders, TD5 7SF
(*map, pp. 360–61*)

Duke and Duchess of Roxburgh
Walled garden open all year;
grounds and castle Easter and
May–September; also snowdrop
days in February-March; garden
free, grounds and castle ££
On the west edge of Kelso,
signposted from the town. Garden
centre and walled garden, entrance
off the A6397. Bus to Kelso
T: 01573 223333
F: 01573 226056
E: marketing@floorscastle.com
www.floorscastle.com
Terrace Café at walled garden
Restaurant at castle

white rambling rose 'Sander's White', on another yellow *Lonicera* and *Clematis orientalis,* on another, *Garrya elliptica* and *Hydrangea petio-laris.* There are several substantial perennial plantings: the longest are a June–July border featuring *Aruncus* and *Campanula* and an August border of yellow daisies, late summer bedding and other late summer favourites. What make these particularly effective are the Victorian iron poles along which are trained climbing roses such as 'American Pillar'. At the end is a *Phlox paniculata* border; such displays are less common these days due to eelworm and mildew. Along the wall nearest the entrance is the blue border with a long *Agapanthus* strip running parallel. There are also extensive fruit and vegetable plantings and a whole series of perfectly restored greenhouses. I spoke to one of the gardeners, who turned out to be the owner of an extensive collection of *Streptocarpus* which I saw in full flower in a greenhouse in the walled garden. There is a popular and attractive small café in the extensive buildings which line the wall at the entrance and a large children's play area. The fine walled garden is in stark contrast to the millennium parterre next door. The parterre represents the family crest and some other designs cut into the lawn, with white gravel paths. As you cannot look down on it there is no way whatsoever of seeing the design, and the whole project and its conception can only really be described, at best, as daft. The series of French-style trained Scottish apples is eventually supposed to cover their pergolas. Like the parterre, this requires endless labour for minimal return. I'd remove both elements and think again. The best feature of this section is a fine lavender border and a wall covered in *Vitis coignetiae* which colours to dark red in autumn. Beyond this is extensive parkland with considerable recent tree-planting in the Star Plantation with old and newer clumps of rhododendrons and azaleas. There are huge drifts of snowdrops in spring. Head gardener Andrew Simmons is back in the Borders again, this time at Floors, after a stint up north at Balmoral.

Floors Castle Garden Centre

I can't think of many garden centres with a finer setting than this, in the large walled garden at Floors Castle. The small garden centre offers a good range of plants, HSP garden buildings and landscaping services. See under previous entry for Floors Castle for details of plantings in the walled garden. There is a large children's play area at the bottom of the garden and a café in the buildings along the garden wall.

Floors Castle Garden Centre
Near Kelso (B6397 road),
Borders, TD5 7SF
(map, pp. 360–61)

In the walled garden at Floors Castle off the B6397. Don't come in the main Floors Castle entrance from Kelso
T: 01573 224 530
F: 01573 225 004
E: info@floorscastlegarden centre.co.uk
www.floorscastlegarden centre.co.uk

Gosford House and Policies

The great thing about Gosford, home of the earls of Wemyss, is that much of the parkland/pleasure grounds have been left more or less intact as it was designed in the eighteenth century and is now at full maturity, dominated by the palatial Robert Adam-designed Gosford House, completed in 1800. A Victorian architect knocked down the fine Adam wings for one of the earls and stuck on 'improvements'. The house suffered for much of the twentieth century, taken over by the military in the Second World War, set on fire, and beset by dry rot. Somehow the house still stands like a noble, if sozzled, old trooper. The central portion was re-roofed in 1987 and Gosford houses an extraordinary art collection. There are several interesting buildings in the grounds, including a pyramid-shaped mausoleum, an ice house and curling house which looks like it ought to have goblins living in it, and a series of restored, substantial ponds. Lord and Lady Wemyss have been replanting trees and daffodils. I have always admired the amazing wind-blown trees along the seaside walls of Gosford on the road to Gullane.

Gosford House and Policies
Longniddry, East Lothian,
EH32 0PX
(map, pp. 360–61)

Wemyss estates
Grounds: season tickets available.
House: mid June–early August, Saturday–Sunday 2–5pm; ££
2 miles north-east of Longniddry
T: 01875 870201

Greywalls
Muirfield, Gullane, EH31 2EG
(*map, pp. 360–61*)

Ros Weaver
SGS or by appointment; £
5 miles west of North Berwick on
A198, eastern outskirts of Gullane.
Nearest station North Berwick or
Drem
T: 01620 842144
F: 01620 842241
E: enquiries@greywalls.co.uk
www.greywalls.co.uk

Greywalls

Greywalls was Lutyens' only Scottish commission and he described it as his favourite house. It is built of a warm yellowish stone, rather than the grey you might expect from the name. Greywalls was turned into one of the first upmarket country house hotels in the 1950s, catering mainly for golfers as it lies at the edge of the exclusive Muirfield Golf Club. The fine gardens, surrounded by low walls, were laid out by the architect, possibly with some input and certainly some influence from his regular collaborator, Gertrude Jekyll. These consist of a series of rooms divided by hedges of holly. The central deep double borders on either side of a wide path are very fine, filled with undulating mats of repeat-planted perennials. Off this is a series of paths and garden rooms including a *Zelkova* walk and orchard. On a visit in late October I was impressed with the long double border of box, santolina and bright pink nerines providing striking late colour. The attractively pointed walls bear pineapple broom and fruit trees. The south wall contains a raised *claire voie* to frame the hills beyond, which can be seen from inside the house. The curved walls of the southern entrance to the house are flanked by the grassed turning circle; this is certainly an elegant place to be dropped off for dinner. Sadly in 2008 the hotel became one of the many exclusive-use venues for corporate events, weddings and house parties so you can't just book for dinner anymore but Ros Weaver assured me that you can still visit the gardens.

Hallmanor
Kirkton Manor,
Peebles, EH45 9JN
(*map, pp. 360–61*)

Mr and Mrs K. St C. Cunningham
SGS (early June); ££
Peebles 6 miles. Off A72
Peebles–Glasgow road –
follow SGS signs on open days
T: 01721 740207

Hallmanor

The setting of this garden is outstanding, in Manor Valley, one of the most attractive in the Borders, in wooded grounds surrounded by Hallmanor Forest. Spring sees displays of rhododendrons and azaleas around the loch. Perennials round the attractive white farmhouse include bold plantings of lupins and iris.

Hallmanor

Harmony Garden, see p. 422

see p. 422

Haystoun

This handsome cream-coloured house, dating back to the fifteenth century, is bordered on one side by lawns surrounded by well-planted perennial borders. The walled garden has extensive herbaceous beds, fruit and vegetables and outside there is a wild burnside garden with rhododendrons and azaleas, created since 1980, leading to an ornamental loch. There are fine views further up the Glensax burn. Several Borders gardeners particularly recommended this garden to me.

Haystoun
Peebles, EH45 9JG
(*map, pp. 360–61*)

Mr and Mrs Coltman
SGS alternate years; ££
Take A703 Edinburgh–Peebles
road to Peebles, over Tweed
Bridge, 1½ miles south of
Peebles via Springhill Road/
Glen Road

The Hirsel Country Park, see p. 438

The Hirsel Country Park, see p. 438

Holyrood Palace
Canongate, Royal Mile,
Edinburgh, EH8 8DX
(*map, pp. 360–61*)

The Royal Palaces
Daily: 9.30am–2pm in winter,
9.30am–4.30/6pm in spring
and summer; £££ (palace and
grounds)
Bus 35 and 36. East/bottom
end of Royal Mile by Scottish
Parliament
T: 0131 556 5100
E: bookinginfo@royal
collection.org.uk
www.royalcollection.org.uk

Hopetoun House
South Queensferry, near
Edinburgh, West Lothian,
EH30 9SL
(*map, pp. 360–61*)

Hopetoun House
Preservation Trust
Daily: Easter–September
10.30am–5pm (last entry 4pm);
£££ house and grounds
Turn off the A90 at the exit south
of the Forth Road Bridge and head
west along the A904; ½ mile
along this road turn right into
South Queensferry. Directly under
the Road Bridge there is a sign
to Hopetoun House
T: 0131 331 2451
F: 0131 319 1885
E: enquiries@hopetounhouse.com
www.hopetounhouse.com
Stables tearoom

Holyrood Palace

Situated at the bottom end of Edinburgh's ancient street Royal Mile, with Edinburgh Castle at the top end, Holyrood was founded as a monastery in 1128 and the Palace of Holyroodhouse is the monarch's official residence in Scotland. Holyrood once had extensive formal gardens in what is now Holyrood Park, the evidence for which can be seen in the 1646 engraving 'Birds'-Eye View of Edinburgh' by Gordon of Rothiemay. Many Scottish and English monarchs including James IV, James V, Charles I, Charles II and George IV have left their mark on the buildings here, adding to or altering the complex. The gardens are attractive as far as they go, but play second fiddle to the large expanses of lawn used for holding garden parties. There are some substantial shrub beds in the northern part. The setting is very fine however, with the ruined abbey within the grounds, Arthur's Seat and Holyrood Park on the south side and the Scottish Parliament building next door.

Hopetoun House

This is one of Scotland's largest, finest and most sumptuous stately homes. Built by Bruce and remodelled by William Adam and his sons, it is home to the Marquis of Linlithgow. The policies and parkland, with much of the Adam design still visible, lie around an impressive axis which runs in front of and behind the house and includes a large fountain in the Round Pond, which lies on the far side of extensive lawns. Between the wars the 25-acre walled garden was a popular tourist attraction and one of Scotland's most famous gardens. Part of it was used as a garden centre in the 1980s, while much had become derelict. It is now gradually being restored on an

392

impressive scale. With a long rill running along the lowest point, it has several compartments and is being re-planted with the intention of opening it to the public in years to come. Outside in the policies there are several good walks: the Sea Walk, which also overlooks the deer park, the Spring Walk with carpets of bulbs and Hope's Walk with mature rhododendrons and azaleas and views of Abercorn Church.

House of the Binns

This is the home of former maverick labour MP Tam Dalyell, thorn in the side of many a government. Some of his forbears are an equally colourful lot; seventeenth-century General Tom Dalyell, nicknamed 'The Muscovy Brute', escaped the Tower of London and fled to Russia, returning to Scotland to fight covenanters, which earned him the further nickname of 'Bloody Tam'. The seventeenth-century house contains a fine collection of porcelain, paintings and furniture.

House of the Binns
Linlithgow, West Lothian,
EH49 7NA
(*map, pp. 360–61*)

NTS,
Tam and Kathleen Dalyell
Grounds: all year, daily; house:
1 June–end September,
Saturday–Wednesday 2–5pm;
house ££*, grounds free
Near Old Philipstoun on the
A904 road from Forth Road
Bridge to Linlithgow
T: 0844 4932127,
Ranger: 0131 665 1546
E: houseofthebinns@nts.org.uk
www.nts.org.uk

There are no formal gardens here, but rather a fine designed landscape and parkland with 27 peacocks and outstanding drifts of snowdrops in February–March, followed by daffodils and bluebells. Walk up to the tower at the top of the hill for great views over the Forth and across West Lothian (Tam's searching question). The walled garden and ponds have lain abandoned for years but plans are afoot. Billy Carruthers from Binny Plants is planning to use part of the House of the Binns walled garden to display the national collections of peonies including Saunders peonies, *P. lactiflora* hybrids, intersectionals and gold medal varieties as well as the national collection of *Leucanthemum*. This will be accessible on special open days only.

Inveresk Lodge Garden
Inveresk Lodge Garden,
24 Inveresk Village,
Musselburgh, EH21 7TE
(*map, pp. 360–61*)

NTS
Daily 10am–6 pm; ££
A6124 south of Musselburgh,
6 miles east of Edinburgh
T: 0844 4932126
www.nts.org.uk

Inveresk Lodge Garden

The house at Inveresk Lodge, which is not open to the public, was built by James Wedderburn with profits from the slave trade. Ironically, his son by a black Jamaican mother, disowned by his father, went on to become a leading Scots abolitionist and lived to see the slave trade outlawed in the Caribbean. The garden, built on the side of a hillside, was originally planned by Mrs Helen Brunto who owned Inveresk from 1910 and it was re-designed by Eric Robson after the National Trust for Scotland took over in 1959. It consists of several terraces leading down to a wooded wilderness area at the bottom of the hill around the meadow pond, with the River Esk meandering round a deep bend beyond. By the entrance is a pair of greenhouses, with an aviary in one. The terrace walls are used to grow choice and tender shrubs such as *Rosa banksiae, Indigofera, Clerodendron* and *Piptanthus*. The garden also boasts a national collection of *Tropaeolum*, perhaps an odd choice as only two are hardy enough to grow outdoors, and one of them is so common most of us want to get rid of it. Other features include a *Nepeta* border and long herbaceous plantings on the lower terrace. The rose border designed by

Graham Stuart Thomas has been replaced. This garden has considerable unrealised potential, with focus, better maintenance and more imaginative planting, but it looks likely that NTS will not invest further and the garden may close. The woodland and wetland area in the lower part of the garden seems to have been largely ignored and could be incorporated. Inveresk is a good place for bird watching with chiff chaffs, warblers and siskins being recorded. If you are lucky enough to be visiting when Shepherd House across the road is open, don't miss it. Other gardens in the village of Inveresk open some years under SGS.

Inwood

Inwood
Carberry, Musselburgh,
Lothian, EH21 8PZ
(*map, pp. 360–61*)

Mr and Mrs Irvine Morrison
April–September: Tuesday,
Thursday, Saturday 2–5pm,
other times by appointment; ££
(free to RHS members)
Off A1 A6094 to Dalkeith, at next
roundabout (before the village of
Whitecraig), turn left heading
south up the hill on the A6124
1½ miles
T: 0131 665 4550
E: lindsay@inwoodgarden.com
www.inwoodgarden.com

This relatively small (1 acre) garden, started in 1984, is a labour of love for Irvine and Lindsay Morrison. Lindsay told me that Christopher Lloyd was her gardening guru and this is manifest in the tropical plantings: cannas, dahlias, *Echium* and other tender plants, as well as the love of self-sown seedlings and bold planting combinations. The garden is carved out of a wood, and consists of a series of irregular beds some under trees, others in the open, crammed full of a huge collection of plants: rhododendrons, bulbs, perennials and shrubs. On the boundary fence are rose-clematis combinations for summer. Feature plants include a fine *Cornus controversa* 'Variegata' and a handsome *Pinus wallichiana* with long needles. Plants which do well, such as *Matteuccia struthiopteris* and white and purple thalictrums, are allowed to spread and sow themselves around, forming dramatic clumps. This is an enthusiast's garden, full of interesting plants, fine combinations and on a domestic scale, which will inspire many gardeners. Worth a visit at any time with a fine collection of hydrangeas, *Colchicum* and *Tricyrtis*, for late summer colour.

**Jedburgh Abbey and
Queen Mary's House Gardens**
Jedburgh, Borders, TD8 6JQ
(*map, pp. 360–61*)

Historic Scotland
Daily: 9.30am–5.30pm summer
(closes 4.30pm winter);
££ (abbey and gardens)
T: 01835 863925

Jedburgh Abbey and Queen Mary's House Gardens

One of Scotland's most impressive medieval abbeys, it was frequently attacked by the English during border warring. The Abbey garden is historically important as a demonstration of a Scottish monastic garden of around 1500; it was restored and planted in 1986. A juniper centrepiece is surrounded by plants which were cultivated in the Middle Ages including culinary and medicinal herbs. Next door is Mary, Queen of Scots house with an excellent museum visitor centre on Mary's life and a garden which contains some old pear trees and bedding plant sections cut into the lawns.

Kailzie Gardens
Kailzie Gardens, Kailzie,
Peebles, EH45 9HT
(*map, pp. 360–61*)

Lady Angela Buchan-Hepburn
April–October: 11am–5.30pm;
November–March: daylight hours,
woodland and wild garden only; £
(winter), ££ (spring–autumn)
2½ miles from Peebles town
centre on the B7062
T: 01721 720007
E: info@kailziegardens.com
www.kailziegardens.com
Family-run restaurant in old stable
square, 70-seater

Kailzie Gardens

Kailzie (pronounced 'kailie') estate lies on the banks of the Tweed, and consists of 18 acres of woodland gardens including Scotland's largest larch tree, and an extensive walled garden. Like Dawyck, not far away, this is a cold garden, far inland, in a river valley, which can experience frosts as late as June. Kailzie House was torn down in the 1960s with a new house built at one end of the walled garden. Lady Buchan Hepburn re-designed most of the gardens in the 1960s when she took over the property and she looks after everything with gardener Guy Crowhurst. The walled garden contains a number of features, including a set of well-maintained greenhouses, packed with pelargoniums and an indoor *Wisteria*. The central axis of the garden runs between two gates, and the eye is led out of the garden to fountain and pond. Accent planting is created with now large *Chamaecyparis*. The small laburnum arch at one end of the copper

beech-backed hedges frames the view to the hills beyond. A rose garden forms a separate 'room' containing a significant collection of shrub roses including albas and gallicas. A potager is planted in raised beds. Outside the walled garden is a stream-side path surrounded by rhododendrons and azaleas, the stream itself is lined with giant *Gunnera, Primula, Meconopsis* and skunk cabbage. Visitors early in the year can enjoy the huge drifts of snowdrops through the mature parkland and along the burnside, which are followed by fine daffodils and bluebells. The garden is only part of the Kailzie offering. In the old stable block are a small shop and café/restaurant and some plants for sale. By the carpark is a children's play area and several fishing ponds and a putting green. There are ospreys breeding nearby which can be seen by camera link. The excellent Kailzie website provides extensive information about what is on offer.

Kevock Garden Plants and 16 Kevock Road, Lasswade

'It's like walking into another dimension' exclaimed my friend Steve Hootman, director of the Rhododendron Species Foundation, as we had our first glimpse of this garden. Nothing prepares you for the *coup de théâtre* as you pass onto the terrace. One minute you are in suburbia, one step through a white door and the world is transformed to a breathtaking view of the tree-lined valley beyond the garden which tumbles down the steep slope below the house. Stella and David Rankin bought 16 Kevock Road in 1983 for its gardening potential. But what they also acquired was an amazing steel and glass

Kevock Garden Plants and 16 Kevock Road, Lasswade
16 Kevock Road, Lasswade, Midlothian, EH18 1HT
(*map, pp. 360–61*)

Stella and David Rankin
SGS 2 days per year, or for groups only, by appointment; ££
Kevock Road is south side of A768, between Lasswade and Loanhead, Wadingburn Road, sign to Drummond Grange Nursing Home. Kevock Road bends immediately to the right
T: 0131 454 0660
F: 0131 454 0660
E: info@kevockgarden.co.uk
www.kevockgarden.co.uk

home designed by James Morris and Robert Steedman previously owned by radar and magnetron pioneer Sir John Randall. Stella Rankin retired from teaching and started the nursery Kevock Garden Plants in 1998, since when the Rankins have dazzled visitors to Gardening Scotland with their 'best in show' gold medal gardens. The 1-acre garden, which feels much larger, on an extremely steep slope, overlooks the North Esk Valley and the ruins of Mavisbank House. The advantage of the steep terrain can be seen when the flowers and autumn colours of the trees can be enjoyed at eye level from the terrace and from the huge picture windows which run the length of the house. Under the mature trees are rhododendrons, azaleas and shrubs, including *Daphne walongense*, which the Rankins discovered on one of several expeditions they have made to China, underplanted with a wide range of woodland plants such as *Trillium, Meconopsis* and *Arisaema*, and a pond surrounded by *Iris* and other waterside plants with a particularly fine range of candelabra primulas. Higher up the south-facing slope there are terraces with rockeries and the famous 'stone' troughs, which are actually made with peat, sand and cement and aged with manure and soot. The nursery (nearby but not on-site), which can only be visited by appointment, sells a huge range of perennials, bulbs and alpines mail order and at shows. Kevock Plants specialises in plants collected by Scots plant hunter George Forrest who lived for a time at a house visible from Kevock. Stella Rankin designs and plants gardens for people who want something out-of-the-ordinary. As a house and garden combination, with its huge collection of plants and views to die for, this is an exceptional garden.

Kirknewton House

This is a fine mature garden in a landscape of trees, including a giant cedar, dating back to the 1800s or earlier, though there has been a garden here since the mid seventeenth century. The Welwood family have been gardening here for generations and this is a fine mix of formal elements and woodland garden. Situated at 650ft, this is a cold and late garden where the daffodils come out in late April and the extensive plantings of rhododendrons and azaleas flower in late May and early June. The formal elements by the house include clipped conifers and well-placed urns leading to vistas in several directions. Some fine gates are the focal point for a long perennial and shrub border which forms the boundary of a semi-walled garden, now mainly down to grass. One wall of a Playfair extension to the house, which was demolished due to dry rot, now sustains a fine range of wall shrubs, including a large white *Abutilon*. The recently restored stables are used as a venue for corporate events and weddings.

Kirknewton House
Kirknewton, West Lothian,
EH27 8DA
(*map, pp. 360–61*)

Mrs and Mrs Charles Welwood
Monday–Friday by arrangement;
££
From either A70 or A71 take
B7031. ¼ mile from Kirknewton
going south, drive on left
opposite small cottage
T: 01506 881235
F: 01506 882237
E: cwelwood@kirknewton
estate.co.uk
www.kirknewtonestate.co.uk

Lamberton Nursery

Ron McBeath is one of Scotland's best-known plantsmen through his many years in charge of the herbaceous department at RBGE, his nursery and his many plant-hunting expeditions to Nepal and China. You may well grow the *Potentilla* named after him. Ron and his wife Sue set up Lamberton nursery, just north of the English border, on a windswept hillside next to the A1, looking out into the Forth estuary and North Sea. The nursery specialises in alpines and bulbs: *Liliaceae, Arisaema, Roscoea, Primula, Meconopsis* and other perennials. The peat garden which adjoins the nursery was constructed with help from

Lamberton Nursery
No. 3 Lamberton,
Berwickshire, TD15 1XB
(*map, pp. 360–61*)

Ron and Sue McBeath
1 April–30 September,
Sunday–Tuesday only.
Parties by arrangement.
A1 southbound, 2nd exit for
Lamberton, cross the road bridge.
A1 northbound follow signs for
Lamberton immediately after
entering Scotland
T: 01289 308515
F: 01289 308515
E: Ron@LambertonNursery.co.uk
www.lambertonnursery.co.uk/

Peter Korn using large Swedish peat blocks. Ron also had help from his friends Zdenek Zvolanek, Joyce Carruthers, Josef Halda and Jarmila Haldova in constructing the Czech-style crevice garden. Two further borders, next to an aviary, contain woodland and sun-loving plants. Ron is cutting back a little on production and plans to augment his plantings of alpines to extend what is already a treasure trove of material to something even more spectacular. Alpine enthusiasts are certain to find plants to interest them here: I counted at least four *Cyananthus* varieties in flower on offer when I visited in August. It is a perfect stop-off if heading up or down the A1, as is Edrom Nurseries, not far away.

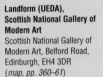

Landform (UEDA), Scottish National Gallery of Modern Art
Scottish National Gallery of Modern Art, Belford Road, Edinburgh, EH4 3DR
(*map, pp. 360–61*)

Free
www.nationalgalleries.org

Landform (UEDA), Scottish National Gallery of Modern Art

Charles Jencks' landform at the front of the Scottish Gallery of Modern Art in Edinburgh has become one of the best-known

artworks in Scotland since it was constructed in 1999–2002. It is the cousin of the larger mounds and lakes at Portrack in Dumfries (see p. 342). The work consists of curved terrace mounds and crescent-shaped shallow pools of water. The website says: 'A combination of artwork, garden and social space, the landform was inspired by chaos theory and shapes found in nature.' Most of the time people are free to walk on the artwork, but some damage occurs in wet weather so access is sometimes restricted. It seems to inspire people of all ages and children love running along the terrace paths.

Lauriston Castle

This sixteenth-century castle was given a makeover by Victorian architect William Burn and was donated to the city of Edinburgh in the 1920s. It can be visited on guided tours, and contains a collection of paintings, tapestries, textiles, porcelain and British and Continental furniture. There are fine views from the front of the house over the popular croquet lawns (run by Edinburgh Croquet Club), to Cramond Island and over the Forth to Fife. The Kyoto Friendship Japanese garden, opened in 2002, was designed by Takashi Sawano who continues to be involved in its maintenance. It contains many traditional Japanese elements: the dry garden, the series of pools flanked by Japanese maples and cloud trees and extensive plantings of flowering cherries. The Central Doric pillar which was already on-site is incorporated into the garden. Some of the plants, particularly rhododendrons, do not look very happy and there is rather a lot of bare earth, which is apparently part of the design. Though Scotland has several Japanese-influenced gardens such as Stobo, this is one of the few authentic ones.

Lauriston Castle
2A Cramond Road South,
Davidsons Mains, Edinburgh,
Lothian, EH4 5QD
(*map, pp. 360–61*)

Edinburgh City Council
Daily: 8am–dusk; free
3 miles from Edinburgh city centre
take Queensferry Road (A90) to
Davidsons Mains
T: 0131 336 2060
www.edinburgh.gov.uk

Liberton House
73 Liberton Drive,
Edinburgh, EH16 6NP
(*map, pp. 360–61*)

Groves-Raines Architects Ltd
Parts of the house and the garden
are open to the public by prior
appointment only, during the
summer
Off the A701 road into Edinburgh.
Turn off into Liberton. Limited
parking and for cars only
T: 0131 467 7777
F: 0131 467 7774
E: practice@grovesraines.com
www.grovesraines.com

Liberton House

Liberton House on the south side of Edinburgh was rescued from oblivion by architects Nicholas Groves-Raines and Kristin Hannesdottir, who use it as their home and office. It is the third Scottish tower house they have restored and when they bought Liberton it was a burnt-out ruin, riddled with dry rot. Now one of Edinburgh's most handsome buildings, the three-storey tower house, where country meets town, is rendered in a striking ochre (see also Culross Palace and Bankton House, by the A1). This singular colour provides a vertical backdrop against which most of the garden's colours stand out, rather like Scotland's response to the orange walls of Mexican architect Luis Barragan. I particularly liked the contrast with the cool greens of the small formal garden on the south-east side, the ferns around the walls and the formal potted trees. The rectangular walled garden's main structure is a box parterre, filled with perennials, herbs and vegetables, and a central path rose arch, around which runs a wide gravel path. Nearest to the house is a double border of lavender and white standard roses, again set off by the coloured walls behind. Along the west wall is a deep perennial border, on the north side a blue-green summer house and on the east side of the garden is a raised bank with trees and fruit. To the south of the house is a vegetable and compost area, a grove of silver birch and a series of paths cut into the long grass. Along the drive side, a fine restored doocot is also rendered in ochre. Liberton was the site of one of the few ghosts to have been successfully photographed – the picture appeared in the *Scotsman* in 1936. The Liberton website indicates that the ghost has not been seen since a fire in 1991, however its voice is still heard and it causes electrical equipment to malfunction.

Little Sparta

'All the Noble sentiments of my heart, all its praiseworthy impulses, I could give them free rein, in the midst of this wood.' So says a plaque on a tree in the midst of Little Sparta. Wander a little further and you'll find three white beehives with inscriptions, a curved currant walk, a snake of raised grass though birch trees, several ponds, lochans and lochs and a series of striking rills. Then there are metal kalashnikovs, submarines, Roman columns, a giant gold head of Apollo and rocks carved with poems about plants: 'Periwinkle became Restless, Calendula became Ready, Begonia became Impulse . . .' At the top of the garden a fence is crossed by a wooden stile which carries an inscription 'a style *n.* an escalation of the footpath'. Set in the windswept Pentland Hills, south-west of Edinburgh, Little Sparta is the creation of poet and artist Ian Hamilton Finlay and is a fusion of poetry, sculpture and natural landscape. There are over 275 artworks in the garden, many of which are inscriptions carved in stone by Finlay's many collaborators. It is clear that Finlay had moral, philosophical, political and more anarchic and mischievous intentions as he created his garden over a 35-year period. Little Sparta is an 'evolved

Little Sparta
Dunsyre, near Biggar,
Lanarkshire, ML11 8NG
(*map, pp. 360–61*)

Little Sparta Trust
15 June–end September:
Wednesday, Friday, Sunday
2:30–5pm weather permitting; £££
From Edinburgh A702 to
Dolphinton, right turn to Dunsyre.
Continue through village for
c. 1 mile and Little Sparta is
signed on the right. Car parking
is about ½ mile from the
garden and strong footwear
is recommended
T: 07826 495677
E: info@littlesparta.co.uk
www.littlesparta.co.uk

landscape' rather than a planned one, with echoes down the ages and across continents, from classical times (Apollo looms large) via eighteenth-century emblematic gardening (Alexander Pope), the French Revolution (St Just and Robespierre), Zen Japanese gardens of contemplation to modern-day found object creations. When Finlay moved here, Stonypath Farm was surrounded by little more than open moorland and the garden grew somewhat organically as shelter was established and sites for artworks were required and filled. The resulting layout is very effective; meandering paths give constant changes of mood, open and empty to claustrophobic and shady, from one magical vista to another. Prudence Carlson remarks that the artworks often 'ambush' the visitor and Ambra Edwards praises the 'juxtapositions between fury and gentleness'. The name 'Little Sparta' refers to Finlay's earlier declaration of war against the rates demands from his local council for his art gallery.

A great deal of learned but sometimes distracting art criticism has been written about the garden, glossing the many references. By all means read these accounts, but I think it is more rewarding just to allow the various metaphors, allusions and aphorisms to percolate and diffuse through your senses as you wander round. Leave the 'explanations' till you get home. As the *Good Gardens Guide* says: 'this is a garden, not a crossword puzzle'. Little Sparta is very much a collaborative work, with over 30 craftsmen and stone carvers responsible for work on the site. On the landscape and plants side, Sue Swan, Pia Simig and more recently Ralph Irving all worked closely with Finlay creating the various parts of the garden. Ralph continues to look after the garden with great skill and sensitivity and worked closely with

Finlay in his later years. He explained to me that: 'Ian wanted people to react personally to the garden: there was no route to take, no instructions and no interpretation'. Ralph explained to me that native plants provide most of the garden structure as most exotics had struggled for survival, particularly when the garden was young. Now the micro-climates which the shelter has provided allow a larger range of plants to be grown. Native willows, dogwood, hazel, rowans and birch are underplanted with species roses, honeysuckle, foxgloves, ferns and meadowsweet along the watercourses. I found the Little Sparta experience moving, poetic, sometimes baffling, joyous and melancholic but above all thought-provoking in a way that no other garden has matched. It is 'poetry' to other gardens' 'prose' and it demands and inspires a different way of looking and thinking. Those who come in search of a traditional garden can be disappointed. The garden looks and feels like the ruins of a Greek or Roman village, building remains lying in the undergrowth, being reclaimed by the wilderness. The complexity of man's relationship with nature seems to be invoked round every corner. At the loch at the top of the garden there are two stubborn trees and beyond them, just empty moorland: this really is the edge of possibility; beyond this man can tame no more. The garden refers constantly to the landscape around it: sheep pens with carved inscriptions inside echo to the bleating of sheep just outside the fence. Trees trunks are wrapped and framed by wood and stone inscriptions. The recently completed small enclosed garden (the *Hortus conclusus*), behind the house, seems the most traditional and in some ways artificial part of the site. This was the only part of the garden which failed to inspire me; perhaps this is apposite, showing the one dimensionality of traditional gardening, behind walls, cut off from nature.

Little Sparta can't fail to suggest the potential for gardens to provide more than simple aesthetic pleasure and plant collections. On the page it may sound pretentious; nothing could be further from the truth; the garden is beautiful, provocative and amusing. Finlay's somewhat black sense of humour is a common theme: grenades instead of urns on top of a pair of columns, aircraft carrier birdbaths, stone tortoises with 'panzer leader' carved onto their shells and Greek classical figures armed with machine guns. Following Finlay's death in 2006 the garden was taken over by the Little Sparta Trust. The impressive list of trustees includes Magnus Linklater, Victoria Miro, Sir Nicholas Serota and owner of Edinburgh's finest commercial contemporary art gallery Richard Ingleby, but I don't envy them their task of ensuring that this amazing but fragile place survives. Bold decisions will have to be made on how to keep the undergrowth under control and to keep the spirit of the place intact. I urge you to visit, and more importantly to join the garden's Friends. This fragile space is both one of Scotland's most important works of art and one of its most inspiring gardens. I cannot praise it highly enough. There is a fine eponymous book on the garden published by Frances Lincoln, written by one of Finlay's collaborators, Jessie Sheeler.

Macplants
Berrybank,
5 Boggs Holdings, Pencaitland,
East Lothian EH34 5BA
(*map, pp. 360–61*)

Beryl and Gavin McNaughton
Mid March–September:
10.30am–5pm or by appointment.
From the A1, B6363 towards
Pencaitland, 2½ miles, right-hand
side
T: 01875 341179
F: 01875 340842
E: sales@macplants.co.uk
www.macplants.co.uk

Macplants

Beryl McNaughton founded Macplants in 1978, moving to its third and largest site at Berrybank in 1996. Supplying both retail and wholesale customers, the nursery grows one of Scotland's widest ranges of perennials and alpines. Specialities include *Meconopsis, Epimedium, Geranium, Heuchera, Hosta, Iris, Primula,* ferns and grasses. Beryl's husband Dr Ian McNaughton breeds gentians, the most significant of which is a range of new autumn flowering varieties with upward-pointing flowers which are due to be launched on the market in 2009–10, look out for 'Braemar', 'Balmoral' and 'Iona'. The retail plant centre carries a good range of the nursery's plants and there is a small well-planted garden next to the car park, with winding paths and fine displays of perennials in summer. All four members of the family Ian, Beryl, Gavin and Claire McNaughton are well respected plantsmen and women.

Malleny Garden
Balerno, Edinburgh,
Midlothian, EH14 7AF
(*map, pp. 360–61*)

NTS
Daily: 10am–6pm or dusk,
if earlier; ££*
In Balerno village, brown signs
off A70 Edinburgh–Lanark road.
T: 0844 4932123
E: pdeacon@nts.org.uk
www.nts.org.uk
Villages of Currie and
Balerno nearby

Malleny Garden

This garden in the village of Balerno, on the outskirts of Edinburgh, lies at 500ft at the foot of the Pentland Hills. Next to the car park is a group of species rhododendrons including *R. sutchuenense* and *R. thomsonii.* The semi-formal walled garden is reached through a small gate with an honesty box. There are two greenhouses on the right-hand walls, while in front loom the four 'disciples', the famous clipped yews, in the shape of pointed toadstools. There were once 12 disciples, but 8 were cut down in 1961. These magnificent trees dominate the garden and take a week to prune each year. The two halves of the garden are divided by a fine yew hedge. Unusually, the four-section parterre is hedged with dwarf red foliage *Berberis* and the bedding (white daisies) in the middle was still looking fresh in September. This garden is a fine balance of formal lines and informal

combinations: roses are dominant and the gardens hold a national collection of nineteenth-century shrub roses which could be better labelled. *Philadelphus, Kolkwitzia*, geraniums, clematis and peonies dominate the borders in the centre of the garden, while the far end contains an impressive potager with squares, rectangles and triangles forming beds planted with nasturtium in terracotta pots and sweet peas as well as a wide selection of vegetables. Next to the seventeenth-century house (not open) is a fountain pool surrounded by lush, green-leaved hostas and royal ferns. This is a small, secluded and charming garden, looked after for many years by gardener Philip Deacon; I have visited often and like it very much. It is peaceful apart from the noise of school children at playtime at the school next door. It is in many ways a perfect 'English' garden with a long season of interest, reaching a peak from June to August. No café here, but Al Borgo on the Lanark Road in Juniper Green has good coffee.

Manderston

This colossal Edwardian house with 109 rooms was greatly re-modelled from an eighteenth-century Adam-style house in 1900–05 by John Kinross for James Miller. There was no expense spared in house or garden, using a fortune made by James' father William Miller trading hemp and herrings with the Russians, creating the decadent, sumptuous staterooms and what is said to be the world's only silver staircase. Just as interesting is the warren of domestic quarters; 'upstairs and downstairs', the house was used to film the television series *The Edwardian Country House*. The 56 acres of gardens include spacious lawns and parkland to the north of the house with impressive daffodil drifts in spring which give way to bluebells in May. The formal garden on the south and east sides consists of four terraces with fine balustrading, urns and pineapples echoing the ornamentation on the roof line of the house behind. I like Patrick Taylor's description of the

Manderston
Duns, Berwickshire, TD11 3PP
(*map, pp. 360–61*)

Lord Palmer
Mid May–end September,
Thursday and Sunday;
££ (garden, house extra)
Signposted from A1: take the
A6105 (signposted Foulden,
Duns). 2 miles east of Duns
T: 01361 882636
F: 01361 882010
E: palmer@manderston.co.uk
www.manderston.co.uk
Café in courtyard

main steps down to the lawns below as 'swashbuckling'; they do look perfect for an Errol Flynn sword fight. The terraces are planted with roses, silver and red-foliaged plants with a collection of mostly flat-topped topiary of yew and variegated holly. Below the terracing the lawns gently sweep downhill to the lake and woodland garden. A spectacular display of daffodils covers the lawns above the lake while on the other side a dense *Rhododendron ponticum* bank creates sheets of mauve-purple in June. The wooden *chinoiserie* dam/bridge leads up a steep path into the rhododendron and azalea-filled woodland planted in the 1950s, which has had some thinning and transplanting in recent years. The collection of hybrids and species is impressive and boasts some rarities such as *R. anthopogon, R. cowanianum,* a very fine *R. cinnabarinum* Blandfordiiflorum and two giant domed *R. williamsianum* as well as a curved arch of yew. Far away on the north side of the house is the walled garden, which was laid out by James Kinross and is entered by a pair of extravagant gates. This formal garden contains box- and yew-edged beds with peonies, roses and *Galtonia* with two sunken gardens, one of which is surrounded by low walls, with May-flowering *Aubrietia* and yellow *Alyssum* tumbling down the sides. Beyond this are the glasshouses, with grotto-like lumps of tufa. Manderston was once one of Scotland's most extravagant gardens; up to 100 gardeners were said to look after it. It is still pretty impressive, with the two gardeners to look after it now. Because of Lord Palmer's connections with Huntley and Palmers biscuits, Manderston also boasts a biscuit tin museum. You can stay in the house by arrangement.

🏛

Mellerstain

One of the many opulent houses and estates in the environs of Kelso, this one was built in two stages in the eighteenth century by William and Robert Adam, and very fine it is too. At the front of the house is a formal nineteenth-century Italian garden, an impressive series of terraces and balustrades designed by that lover of the straight line Sir Reginald Blomfield, who frequently locked horns with woodland garden champion William Robinson. The terrace lawns are filled with parterres planted with roses, *Nepeta* and perennials. From here there are formidable views of the landscaped park, laid out by the Adams, a grand sweep down to a lake which is actually the end of a canal, with views of the Cheviot Hills behind. The Hundy Mundy folly, which looks like a piece of crude theatre scenery in the shape of a church façade, is the focal point of the view from the house but it is becoming obscured by the surrounding trees. The woods around the folly have recently been established as a non-religious or humanist burial ground. There is a rhododendron walk on the west side, now mostly *R. ponticum*, while behind the house in the parkland is a small garden surrounding a folly, a thatched cottage *orné* surrounded by parterres planted with perennials. Considering it is looked after by one gardener with some help from the forestry staff, Mellerstain is surprisingly good and the setting and parkland woods are very fine. The visiting arrangements are rather over-complicated, even the staff admitted that they have trouble working out when it is open, so it might be best to phone or check the website to make sure before you go.

      WC

Mellerstain
Gordon, near Kelso,
Borders, TD3 6LG
(*map, pp. 360–61*)

Mellerstain Trust,
Earl of Haddington
April–September: Sunday and
Wednesday, with extra days in
summer. Best to consult website;
££
Off the A6089 Kelso to Gordon
road, signposted from Earlston
(7½ miles) and Kelso (5 miles)
T: 01573 410225
E: enquiries@mellerstain.com
www.mellerstain.com
Tearoom

Merryhatton Garden Centre
Merryhatton, East Fortune,
near North Berwick, EH39 5JS
(*map, pp. 360–61*)

Helen MacDonald
Daily: 9am–6pm.
Café closes at 5pm.
On the west side of East
Fortune village
T: 01620 880 278
F: 01620 880 278
E: info@merryhatton.co.uk
www.merryhatton.co.uk
Café

Merryhatton Garden Centre

Very near the Museum of Flight, home to Concorde, this small garden centre, now established for more than 30 years, is well known for its range of herbs and other plants and locals value it for good gardening advice offered. I was impressed with the standard of displays inside and out and the café was good.

Mertoun House Gardens

Mertoun House Gardens
St Boswells, Roxburgh, TD6 0EA
(*map, pp. 360–61*)

Mertoun Gardens Trust, contact
Mertoun Estate Office
April–September: Friday–Monday
2–6pm, last entry 5.30pm; ££
On the A6404 road just east of
St Boswells
T: 01835 823 236
F: 01835 822 474
E: mertounestatefarms@
farming.co.uk

Family home of the dukes of Sutherland, Mertoun is one of the oldest Borders gardens, with a walled garden built in 1567. Fishing on the Tweed is big business here so the gardens are geared to produce maximum displays in spring and late summer/autumn. The house, designed by William Bruce in 1703, defiled by Victorian embellishments which were removed in the 1950s, has outstanding views across the lawns and over the bends of the River Tweed. A public footpath leads along the river to a suspension bridge to the west of the house. To the east are some imposing herbaceous borders with a fountain and pond in front, designed to be viewed from the house across the lawns and pond. In September, the pampas, hydrangeas and *Persicaria* were very striking. Beyond this lies an extensive wild woodland garden with fine trees, such as a weeping elm, and bold plantings of azaleas. In the spring there are extensive displays of snowdrops, providing one of the best displays in the Borders, followed by daffodils. The jewel of Mertoun is the walled garden, which is

probably the nearest to a full production Victorian or Edwardian garden still in existence in Scotland. Every fruit and vegetable that you can think of is produced on an impressive scale. Two vast asparagus beds, rows and rows of leeks and onions, peaches and figs in greenhouses, melons in frames, not to mention blocks of lilies, dahlias and other flowers for cutting. Food from the garden is taken to the house each day, some of which is eaten by the hungry guests fishing the Tweed. The head gardener lives in the attractively gabled, pink-rendered Old Mertoun House in the walled garden, which was formerly the estate's main residence. Outside the walls is a well-preserved rounded sixteenth-century doocot, said to be the UK's oldest, which had birds in residence until recently.

Milestone Garden Leisure

This recently built (2006) small garden centre on the outskirts of Newtown St Boswells has a good café and a fast-serve take-away coffee shop. Future plans include display gardens and a landscaping service.

Milestone Garden Leisure
Newtown St Boswells,
Roxburghshire, TD6 0PL
(*map, pp. 360–61*)

Daily: 9am–5.30pm
Junction of A68 and B6398
on south side of Newtown
St Boswells
T: 01835 825959
F: 01835 825960
E: info@milestonegarden
andleisure.com
www.milestonegarden
andleisure.com

Mill Garden Centre and Barbauchlaw Mill Nursery

This is a small family-owned nursery and garden centre in a cold part of central Scotland. Many plants are grown on-site and there are extensive display gardens with conifers, grasses and other plants. The

**Mill Garden Centre
and Barbauchlaw Mill Nursery**
Barbauchlaw Mill, Armadale,
West Lothian, EH48 3AP
(*map, pp. 360–61*)

Summer: Monday–Friday
9am–8pm, Saturday 9am–5pm,
Sunday 10am–6pm;
winter: Monday–Friday 9am–5pm,
Saturday 9am–5pm, Sunday
10am–5pm
On Mill Road off the A89, Just
outside the town of Armadale,
about four miles north of
J4 off the M8
T: 01501 732 347
F: 01501 730 578
www.millgardencentre.co.uk

garden centre shop is part of an old mill building dating back to the fifteenth century. The nursery specialises in dwarf conifers and a good range is offered for sale in the garden centre. There were so many plants packed in here I could hardly get down the paths. I liked the boards detailing plants of seasonal interest, and the range of plants was impressive. This is an old style nursery: plants, chemicals, pots and that's about it. And all the better for that. It was the first time I had seen *Hydrangea paniculata* 'Pinky Winky'; nice plant, shame about the name.

Monteviot House Gardens

Home of the Marquis of Lothian, better known as Michael Ancram MP, Monteviot is an evolving garden around an eighteenth-century villa, built on a more modest scale then many of the Versailles-like Scottish Borders stately piles. The older parts of the gardens are built on the terraces overlooking the Tweed in front of the house, and the garden has long been famous for its densely planted daffodils above the river. The house's wings enclose a three-sided courtyard containing a handsome parterre and herb garden with climbing roses behind. In front of this lies a short *Sorbus* and daffodil walk and a rose and box parterre, with *Lobelia* spilling over the walls. To the west of the house,

below a fine curved high terrace wall, is an extensive mixed planting of perennials and shrubs known as the river garden, originally a Percy Cane design, which still contains some of Cane's shrubs but has otherwise been completely replanted. Above this is a curious planting of named *Acer palmatum* cultivars which are almost buried under the candelabra primulas planted beneath. As the maples get bigger the effect will improve. There are further areas under development to the west, via a *Laburnum* arch planted in 2000. The Japanese-style water garden, created from the old curling pond, with four red bridges linking a series of islands, is planted with all manner of waterside plants with particularly fine candelabra primulas. Feeding into this is a further series of ponds and walls under construction, known as the 'Dene' project. Behind this is an impressive arboretum, on the site of one planted in the 1840s, with only a few trees such as Douglas firs remaining from this time. A curiosity is a large beech which is 50 per cent variegated and 50 per cent green. I also noticed a *Pterocarya* and some rather over-optimistic *Olea* (olives). Along the wooded paths are plantings of camellias and azaleas. The labelling is good, this is a plantsman's garden with impressive collections of many genera looked after by head gardener Ian Stevenson, who designed many of the planting schemes. The various elements of the garden don't yet link up, but addressing this seems to be part of ongoing projects. You will certainly find plants here which are probably not in other Borders gardens. Monteviot is definitely a garden to watch for the future as there are still further plans for expansion and improvement. Monteviot House itself is also open on several days in June and/or July (check the website for details) and there is lots of information on the website about house and garden. Don't miss Woodside Walled Garden across the road, which was formerly the walled garden for Monteviot but is now a nursery and fine café.

Monteviot House Garden
Monteviot House Garden,
Jedburgh, Roxburghshire,
TD8 6UQ
(*map, pp. 360–61*)

Marquis and Marchioness of Lothian, Michael Ancram MP
1 April–31 October: 12–5pm; ££
On B6400, turn off A68 south of St Boswells, 3 miles north of Jedburgh, signed to Nisbet
T: 01835 830704/830380
F: 01835 830626
E: enquiries@monteviot.com
www.monteviot.com
Self-service coffee and tea from a machine in a summerhouse.

Netherbyres

Apparently Netherbyres is the only walled garden ever built in the shape of a perfect ellipse. The 1½-acre garden, near the sea just outside Eyemouth, was built in 1740 by mathematician and philosopher William Crow, to prove to doubters that he could build an effective garden in this shape. Simon Furness grew up here and always felt that Netherbyres House was too far from the garden, so it became a home for the Gardeners' Royal Benevolent Society (now renamed Perennial) and he has built a new house in the walls of the garden, harled in white Barra seashells. Simon has gardened here since the age of four, when he recalls weeding the gaps in the slabs with his mother. He served for many years as chairman of the National Trust gardens advisory committee as well as running Scotland's Gardens Scheme in Berwickshire. He tends Netherbyres with the help of his

Netherbyres
Garden House, Netherbyres, Eyemouth, TD14 5SE
(*map, pp. 360–61*)

Lt Col. S.J. Furness
April–September: by appointment,, groups preferred; ££
500m from Eyemouth on the A1107.
T: 01890 750337
F: 01890 750337

excellent and hard-working gardener Ian Jeffry, which is a high-
maintenance job with bedding out, dahlia borders, parterres and
substantial fruit and vegetables to look after. An elliptical path follows
the walls, a bed's width away, round the whole garden and this shape
with the curved beds and parterre edges gives the garden a certain
magic. The garden is divided into two sections by a yew hedge. The
smaller western section, containing an orchard, soft fruit and
vegetables, is reached via a purple and silver border. The larger section
in front of the house is a semi-formal arrangement of lawn and island
beds, herbaceous and rose beds, a box knot garden/parterre and a rose
'Bonica' and *Echium* border radiating out from the centrepiece
circular lawn and urn. To the east of the centre is a bold turquoise
pergola based on the one in Lady Haddington's garden at
Tyninghame. The greenhouse contains plumbago, vines and
Brugmannia. The parterres are filled with tulips, annuals and lavender.
This garden has a long season but Simon considers June–July to be
the peak.

Newhailes

Newhailes House and policies in Musselburgh, were acquired by the
National Trust for Scotland in 1997, which almost certainly saved the
extensive grounds from housing development. Long owned by the
Dalrymple family, the late seventeenth-century 'villa' by James Smith,
with very well–preserved rococo interiors, contains a significant
collection of eighteenth-century furniture and paintings. It is
surrounded by the remains of an eighteenth-century designed

landscape, the structure of which has changed little in 300 years, making it of great interest to garden historians and archaeologists though you'd be hard pressed to see anything significant to look at now. The framework of the landscape and some of its elements remain: the burn, shell grotto, summerhouse, raised 'lady's walk' and part of the walled garden, but most has been filled in, removed or left derelict. The locals have used these woodlands for dog-walking and some less desirable activities for years and the wildness of the place has made it an important refuge for wildlife. The views from the front steps over the Forth are still intact. The challenge for the NTS is to know how to restore the garden; to do it fully will be extremely costly and the project appears to be on hold for the time being, due to budget constraints. Perhaps some of the land may need to be sold off to finance the next stage, lest it remain a white elephant. The house is fine; the gardens could be too, as long as they are not treated with too much insipid historical reverence.

Newhailes
Newhailes Road, Musselburgh,
East Lothian, EH21 6RY
(*map, pp. 360–61*)

NTS
Good Friday–Easter Monday,
1 May–30 September Thursday–
Monday 12–5pm. House open
for tours. Grounds free, £ parking
A1 exit at Newcraighall
roundabout, head towards
Musselburgh, ½ mile left at
roundabout. Newcraighall station
20-minute walk through village
of Newcraighall
T: 0131 653 5599 (for tours)
www.nts.org.uk
Newhailes Coffee House, serving
tea, coffee and locally produced
bakery products

Newhall

The eighteenth-century house at Newhall, on the lower southern slopes of the Pentland Hills, used to play host to the two Allan Ramsays, father and son, poet and painter respectively. John and Trish Kennedy bought Newhall in the late 1990s. Tricia is chair of Scotland's Gardens Scheme and sits on the National Trust for Scotland's gardens advisory panel. The house is approached by a long drive, which passes a substantial pond and some recently planted

Newhall
Carlops, Midlothian, EH26 9LY
(*map, pp. 360–61*)

John and Tricia Kennedy
SGS open days May–early
August by appointment; ££
Turn south off the A702,
1 mile east of Carlops just
west of Ninemileburn
T: 01968 660206
E: pak@kenmore.co.uk

hardy hybrid rhododendrons which flower in late May and early June. Jasmine Cann helped redesign the now impressive walled garden, originally laid out in the traditional cruciform by Robert Brown in the late eighteenth century with attractive cobbled paths. The greenhouses have been restored and extended and there is also an old melon pit house, now used for tomatoes. The central axis passes through a pair of yews along a cobbled pathway, flanked by deep perennial borders to a pair of giant *Sequoiadendron giganteum*. Whether whoever planted them knew what time bombs they were unleashing no one knows, but they certainly create a memorable feature. A double section of silver pear archway leads off the central long double herbaceous border to a statue focal point. When I visited in June the bold plantings of *Meconopsis* 'Lingholm' were at their peak on a raised bed next to a lawn with a pool cut into it. The vegetable garden is extensive and is bordered by a long hedge/border of Jerusalem artichoke. Other vistas and paths lead to a blue-green door, statues and a sundial which predates the garden itself. Outside the garden is a wooded glen where Trish's husband John Kennedy has been tidying the mature trees, planting new ones and opening up vistas with help and advice from David Binns, formerly of RBG Dawyck. Tricia took me on her golf buggy at full speed down the steep winding slopes to 'The Glen' on the valley floor. The Kennedys call this the 'Cresta Run' for good reason, though she promised me that she had never tipped up the golf cart. This looks like a fine site for a woodland garden around the old ruined washing house.

New Hopetoun Gardens
New Hopetoun Gardens,
Newton, West Lothian, EH52 6QZ
(*map, pp. 360–61*)

Dougal Philip
Daily: 10am–5.30pm
A904 road between
South Queensferry and
Linlithgow/Bo'ness; 3 miles west
of the roundabout on the south
side of the Forth Road Bridge
T: 01506 834433
F: 01506 834444
www.newhopetoungardens.co.uk
Orangery tearoom

New Hopetoun Gardens

This popular garden centre started life in the walled garden at Hopetoun House and moved here in 1998. One of the most popular independent garden centres in central Scotland, it carries a wide range of plants; it can be over-stocked, and a bit of a tangle. There is a series of themed display gardens around the perimeter fence, Japanese, formal, shady and so on, to provide planting ideas and these are described in useful leaflets which list the plants which the garden contains, as well as planting plans. A recent campaign called 'From the Potager to the Plate' encouraging the use of fruit and vegetables is for the ornamental garden rather than the dedicated vegetable plot. Hopetoun is also a place to come for garden fashion: you'll find quirky stoneware, pots and metalwork on their patio and the recently instigated 'Avant-Gardens' which they describe as the 'catwalk of garden design'. This is a series of small contemporary gardens built anew each year after a design competition. The small shop is paired with another building which contains the popular café and gift area, and there is also a third 'lifestyle building' with classic and designer furniture.

Newliston

Newliston has an interesting history. Soldier and Member of
Parliament the second earl of Stair, who also laid out parts of Castle
Kennedy gardens in Galloway, set to work on improving the
landscape here after he lost his parliamentary seat. The woods are said
to have been laid out in the formation of the British Army at the
Battle of Dettingen (1743), where the earl had been in command. The
wood to the east of the house is in the pattern of the Union Jack, best
appreciated by standing in the centre where all the radiating paths
meet. Caroline Maclachlan showed me the original plans for the
garden which were only partly implemented. The handsome Robert
Adam house is open in tandem with the gardens in May. This is a
parkland/designed landscape rather than a garden as such, full of
mature rhododendrons and azaleas, fine vistas and allées of trees. The
3-acre walled garden is now mainly down to grass. The circular walk
south around the policy woods and canal/lake is a carpet of wild
garlic and bluebells in spring with fine vistas back to the house. The
roar of traffic from the motorway and the aircraft landing nearby
mean that this is one of Scotland's noisier gardens, but for anyone
interested in a well-preserved eighteenth-century planned landscape, it
is well worth a visit. The doocot converted into a house by the drive
is unusual and Newliston Coach House, home of the Edinburgh
School of Food and Wine, offers food on SGS Sunday open days.

Newliston
Kirkliston, West Lothian,
EH29 9EB
(*map, pp. 360–61*)

Mr and Mrs R.C. Maclachlan
Early May–early June:
Wednesday–Sunday 2–6pm; ££
Entrance off B800 which
runs from A89 to Kirkliston,
west of Edinburgh airport
T: 0131 333 3231
E: mac@newliston.fsnet.co.uk

Old Sun Inn (The)

Keen gardeners both, the Lochheads have lived for over 40 years at
the attractive former coaching inn dating back to 1690, which they
bought as a virtual ruin. They pointed out to me the now enormous
birch, walnut and oaks which they planted for shelter at the
beginning. There was no garden here in those days, just a pile of
builders' rubble which was used as hard standing for cattle. It's very
different now, a veritable plantsman's paradise, packed with rarely seen
plants; examples include a pure white *Codonopsis* 'Himal Snow',

Old Sun Inn (The)
Newbattle Road,
Dalkeith, EH22 3LH
(*map, pp. 360–61*)

Mr and Mrs J. Lochhead
May–July by appointment; ££
From Eskbank take B703 south
(Newtongrange); garden is
immediately opposite entrance
to Newbattle Abbey College
(park here)
T: 0131 6632648
E: randjlochhead@uwclub.net
Teas can be arranged for parties

Deinanthe bifida, *Weldenia candida*, *Tulbaghia* from South Africa and a *Roscoea* with large red flowers 'Red Ghurkha'. A raised gravel bed is filled with a collection of *Daphne* obtained from Robin White's nursery. Behind this is a collection of no-longer-so-dwarf rhododendrons from Glendoick which are underplanted with quantities of spring bulbs, *Meconopsis*, lilies, *Fritillaria*, gentians and other treasures. The two linked ponds are surrounded by drifts of *Primula florindae* in yellow and orange forms as well as waterside favourites such as *Ligularia* and *Iris*, while structure is provided by rounded dwarf conifers. Every nook and cranny is filled, with climbers such as *Clematis* and *Codonopsis* clambering on and through larger shrubs and trees. The centrepiece of the lawn is a weeping blue cedar backed by pots of lilies and a plunge bed for tender vireya and Maddenia rhododendrons, which come into the conservatory in winter. How they squeeze indoors all the tender material I saw is anyone's guess; there was a pretty large *Luculia* for example. This is a fine town garden, and the owners' enthusiasm and knowledge make a tour a great pleasure.

Palace of Holyroodhouse, see p. 392

Palace of Holyroodhouse, see p. 392

Paxton House and Country Park

This garden and Palladian mansion, designed by John and James Adam in 1758, overlooks a stretch of the River Tweed, not far from its mouth at Berwick. Paxton is a well-planned visitor attraction with lots to do for adults and children and is an outstation of the National Galleries of Scotland. As well as an impressive range of paintings on display it also boasts a large collection of Chippendale furniture. The eighteenth-century parkland was designed by Robert Robinson, with Victorian additions such as the croquet lawn. The grounds extend to

80 acres in all, with woodland walks along the Tweed, fine trees underplanted with rhododendrons and azaleas and on the terrace in front of the house an L-shaped herbaceous border and a fountain/lily pond. Paxton boasts fishing exhibitions, hides for spotting wildlife, a teddy trail, adventure playground, Highland cattle and ponies, and in summer a whole raft of children's activities. You can play golf or try putting on the lawns. There are often contemporary art and sculpture exhibitions in the gardens. You might be advised to avoid summer Saturdays as weddings tend to restrict access to parts of the house and gardens. At present Paxton is probably not worth a visit for the gardens alone but as a visitor attraction there is plenty to do. There is considerable potential here for improving the gardens, particularly if the woodland between the terrace and the river were cleared of scrub and replanted. The rhododendrons on the bank are currently in too much shade and would appreciate much more light. There is also a large abandoned walled garden alongside the drive.

 [WC]

Pentland Plants and Garden Centre

Scotland's largest bedding plant producer, established at Loanhead for more than 40 years, Pentland Plants grow 40 million bedding-plant plugs each year for professional growers and parks departments, using state-of-the-art techniques. They have recently installed a biomass boiler to heat their greenhouses. They run trials of new varieties each year and have also hosted the ScotGrow showcase for Scottish horticulture in late summer. Each year, they run a five-day open-day period, with three days for the trade and then, usually the following weekend, open to the public under SGS. As well as the outdoor garden of bedding plants, visitors can enjoy the demonstrations in the

Paxton House and Country Park
Berwick-upon-Tweed,
Borders, TD15 1SZ
(*map, pp. 360–61*)

The Paxton Trust
Easter–31 October: grounds
11am–sunset, house 11am–5pm;
££ grounds and gardens, £££
house and grounds
Off the B6461 road to Swinton
and Kelso, 3–4 miles off the
A1 north of Berwick-upon-Tweed,
signposted. 1 bus daily from
Berwick
T: 01289 386291
F: 01289 386660
E: info@paxtonhouse.com
www.paxtonhouse.com
Stables Tea Room

**Pentland Plants
and Garden Centre**
Loanhead, Midlothian, EH20 9QG
(*map, pp. 360–61*)

David, Hilda, Carolyn and
Richard Spray
Garden centre open daily. Bedding
displays open under SGS most
years 1st weekend in August.
On the A701, south of the
Edinburgh bypass. Leave the
bypass at the Straiton junction.
400 metres past Ikea on the
right, brown signs
T: 0131 440 0895
F: 01314 482108
E: info@pentlandplants.co.uk
www.pentlandplants.co.uk

large greenhouses. I visited as Carolyn Spray, familiar as a presenter of *The Beechgrove Garden*, and her team were putting the finishing touches to the displays which were frankly amazing, with over 1,000 varieties of bedding and basket plants. The garden centre, which is open all year, stocks a good selection of plants, many brought in from Holland, sundries and gifts, and as you might expect, a good range of bedding.

Portmore
Eddleston, Peebles, EH45 8QU
(*map, pp. 360–61*)

Mr and Mrs David Reid
SGS some years + June–August
by appointment; ££
½ mile north of Eddleston
on A703 Edinburgh–Peebles
road turn off on east side.
Edinburgh–Peebles bus 62
T: 01721 730383
F: 01721 730291

Portmore

This fine garden has gained lots of plaudits in recent years, with good reason. The David Bryce mansion and the surrounding gardens have been brought back to life over the last 20 years by the Reids. The policies around the house are full of fine mature trees, rhododendron and azalea-lined woodland walks and fine vistas to the south and east. A stark rectangular pool surrounded by Italianate statues and yew hedging lies behind the house. Portmore's star turn is undoubtedly its walled garden, walled on three sides, roughly square in shape, which is divided into a series of garden rooms. The entrance at the low end faces the main path running up the gentle slope to a handsome restored greenhouse, flanked on either side by artful pink-purple-dominated borders of *Salvia, Lythrum, Hemerocallis* and *Astilbe,* at their peak in early August when I visited. Along the fence-ine at the bottom of the garden yellow and white borders are fringed with *Alchemilla mollis,* backed with *Thalictrum,* lilies and *Crocosmia.* The east–west central axis, with urns at either end, is an allée of pleached limes, a stilt hedge of vertical trunks militarily standing to attention, contrasting with the circle of apples, centred on a sculptured figure. This is an outstanding garden, classical in structure; each garden room

is both traditional and contemporary with deft individual touches: the rose and herb potager with mint squares, the two turquoise pergolas with clematis scrambling up them, the box parterre along one wall, complete with box spirals, planted with violas, and the minimalist sections with dalek-like yew pyramids with heads. Each room is a bold contract to the next, and all are memorable. The latest development is a water garden outside the walled garden wall on the east side, with ponds and lush clumps of hostas, *Ligularia*, primulas, iris, grasses and reeds and much more. This garden is not often open, so take any chance you get to see it. It is undoubtedly one of Scotland's best.

**Priorwood and
Harmony Gardens, Melrose**
Abbey Street, Melrose, TD6 9PX
(*map, pp. 360–61*)

NTS
5 January–31 March:
Monday–Saturday 12–4pm;
1 Apr–24 December:
Monday–Saturday 10–5pm
and Sunday 1–5pm; ££*
In Melrose, next to the abbey
T: 01896 822493
E: priorwooddriedflowers@
nts.org.uk
www.nts.org.uk

Priorwood

Priorwood and Harmony Gardens, Melrose

These are two small walled gardens with a combined entry ticket, both of which formed part of the lands and gardens of Melrose Abbey. Priorwood is a garden of under 2 acres specialising in the production of dried flowers which can be purchased in the shop. The peonies in June are pretty spectacular. It also has a collection of interesting historical apple varieties which include 'Court Pendu Plat' which dates back to Roman times and locally raised 'White Melrose'. You can have a picnic on the orchard tables. The site next to the abbey is fine, but is spoiled by a hideous grey concrete box building in one corner of the garden, which is apparently the council-built toilet block. It should either be blown up (with the councillors who gave permission for its construction inside) or at the very least, covered with climbers. The small shop and flower-drying displays are worth a look and the garden offers courses in drying flowers for various uses. Harmony Gardens are across the road oposite the abbey. The house was built by James Waugh and donated to the National Trust for Scotland in 1996. The garden itself consists of a number of herbaceous borders, an extensive organic vegetable garden, the produce from which is on sale in the Priorwood shop, and a spring bulb meadow. The lawns have been used to host the excellent annual Borders Book Festival. There is also a small council rose and bedding garden next door to Harmony, opposite the entrance to Priorwood. Pleasant through these various gardens are, they don't amount to all that much individually. What would make a far better attraction would be to treat them as a single entity as Melrose Abbey and gardens. The whole thing should be integrated into a single ticket operation with one shop/entrance/café/gift shop. Currently run by NTS and Historic Scotland, with separate entry fees and separate

Harmony Gardens

shops, I can't believe it makes sense financially. I have it on good authority that this idea has been talked about, but the wheels move ever so slowly. They'll probably get round to it eventually.

Redhall (Edinburgh)

Redhall is an inspiring place, managed by the Scottish Association For Mental Health. It consists of an eighteenth-century walled garden run on organic principles and a wild woodland (known as 'walk on the wild side'), situated in Edinburgh's Colinton Dell, by the Water of Leith. Horticulture, IT and art are used as part of a programme of recovery for people suffering from mental health problems. The far-reaching ambitions of this project are clear from its mission statement: 'We have to create conditions for growth and positive mental wellbeing: to create a safe place for people to be and to unfold, often at a time in their life when they are experiencing great distress. The environment has to be safe enough to allow that person to take the risks involved in learning to trust again, to survive making mistakes and to take responsibility and control back into their life.' (*Redhall: The Inside Story*, SAMH). The walled garden contains a number of designed small gardens: Woodhenge (a wooden version of Stonehenge), a Zen garden, grass-roofed mud hut, grass garden, vegetable and fruit production (mostly eaten by the people who work there) and a nursery producing plants for sale. Outside the walls is a large composting area and the end product is available to buy in bags. When I visited, Redhall was a buzz of activity and it is surely a beacon of its kind; the centre is so successful and popular that the waiting list has had to be closed. It seems to be the sort of place that Scots anti-

Redhall (Edinburgh)
97 Lanark Road,
Edinburgh, EH14 2LZ
(*map, pp. 360–61*)

Scottish Association
for Mental Health
Monday–Friday 9am–4pm;
donations welcome
The Lanark road runs from
near the city centre out to Currie
and Balerno. You can reach it
from the bypass, 44 bus from
Princes Street or the Water
of Leith path
T: 0131 443 0946
F: 0131 455 7561
E: redhall@samhservices.org.uk
www.samh.org.uk

psychiatrist and writer R.D. Laing would have been proud of, as the ethos seems close to his ideas. Those who have benefited from Redhall are encouraged in turn to teach and support others and guide visitors round. Ask to see some of the inspiring booklets which explain what horticultural therapy means to those who are benefiting from it. For some reason, open days are described as 'infamous' on the Redhall website. I can't think why. Jean Bareham offers tours here as part of a day called 'Herbs and Healing' (*www.greenyondertours.com*, telephone 0131 444 1725).

Royal Botanic Garden, Edinburgh

Royal Botanic Garden, Edinburgh
Inverleith Row,
Edinburgh, EH3 5LR
(*map, pp. 360–61*)

Spring–autumn: 10am–5 or 6pm,
closing 4pm in winter; free,
glasshouses ££
On the north side of the Edinburgh
New Town, easily reached by
bus from the centre, from North
Bridge or Hanover Street to
Inverleith Row
T: 0131 552 7171
F: 0131 248 2901
E: info@rbge.org.uk
www.rbge.org.uk
Popular Café in Inverleith House

The Royal Botanic Garden, Edinburgh (known as 'the Botanics' to locals and 'RBGE' to scientists) is one of the world's foremost botanical and horticultural institutions and is usually at the top of the list for any garden visitor to Scotland. I've been coming here since I was a wee boy. The RBGE has the world's second richest collection of living plants (after Kew), and a long history of plant taxonomy and other research. Regius Keeper from 1887 to 1921 Isaac Bayley Balfour was one of the key figures in the evolution of the RBGE into a world-class botanical institution, but the garden's origins go back much further. It was founded in the seventeenth century as a 'Physic Garden', growing medicinal plants used to teach doctors how to recognise plants used in remedies. Several doctors trained here went on to become important plant hunters on long sea voyages as ship's surgeons. The garden was originally sited in the grounds of Holyrood Palace and after moving to Leith Walk, it was relocated to its current 75-acre site in Inverleith in the 1820s. The donation of the land came with the condition that it should always be free to access for the citizens of Edinburgh, for which Scots can be thankful that they avoid

the charges now levied at Kew Gardens, which rose over a 20-year period from 50p to £12.75. At Edinburgh only the glasshouses and exhibitions levy a charge. The gardens are a great vantage point from which to enjoy Edinburgh's skyline with excellent views of the castle, the many church steeples and the backdrop of Arthur's Seat. Indeed, many people come here to sunbathe, relax, feed the squirrels and on Sunday mornings it is full of dads and kids giving mothers a lie-in. But of course, the Botanic Garden is first and foremost a scientific institution, dedicated to the study of plants and their relationships, evolution and conservation. As well as the living plant collection, the herbarium contains over 2 million pressed specimens. There is also a large specialist library which can be visited by appointment.

The fine set of glasshouses is a must for most visitors. The most striking part of the complex is Britain's tallest palm house, built in the 1850s, recently replanted and now the entry point to the glasshouse complex. The other more modern houses, built in the 1960s, house collections of plants in different climate zones, ranging from arid to rain forest. The heat and humidity of each house is carefully controlled to suit the plants inside. Don't miss the peat house, which is behind the main complex at the east end and contains a small selection of the gardens' vast collection of tropical rhododendrons. As Vireyas flower all year round, it is worth looking in here even in the depths of winter. There are plans to allow more of the huge collection to be displayed. Currently most of it is out of sight.

The garden in Inverleith is only part of the picture. The RBGE also has outstations at Dawyck in the Borders, Benmore in Argyll and Logan in Galloway (all have their own entries in this book) which allows the staggering collection of plants to be grown in a variety of climates. The current database lists 34,000 plants, representing nearly 17,000 species. The world's largest collection of rhododendron species is spread through all four gardens. Plant hunters such as George

Forrest were trained at Edinburgh and much of the complex taxonomy of rhododendrons has taken place here. The hardy outdoor rhododendrons at Edinburgh have been suffering from poor drainage and disease in recent years and are not looking as good as they did, but they are still very impressive from early spring to midsummer. You'll find rhododendrons in almost every corner of the garden, from the rock garden and peat garden (near the east gate) down the slopes and back up again to Inverleith House and from here north towards the long herbaceous borders. Edinburgh's tree collection is outstanding, both conifers and broadleaves. The Tree Register lists over 25 UK champion trees here. RBGE has the world's richest culti-vated collection of Chinese plants, however the Chinese hillside planted in 1993 is a disappointment. This was an example of the cart driving the horse; or in this case a sponsor driving the garden's planting policy. At the time, the garden's trustees opposed the management decision to proceed with this project, and with good reason; the resulting 'Chinese hillside' is a mess: a jungle of plants, shoved in too close together for instant rather than long-term impact. The few token interpretation boards do not really add much. The money would perhaps have been better spent looking after and inter-preting the extant Chinese plant collections in the four gardens.

The Queen Mother's Memorial Garden which opened in 2006 was designed by Lachlan and Annie Stewart, who garden at Ballone Castle near Tain. The Queen Mother, a keen gardener, let it be known that she had no time for commemorative statues and it was decided that a memorial garden should be set up in her name. The semi-enclosed space lies behind low hedges with a central maze of bog myrtle 60cm high, and the layout is formed around a Celtic cross, around which are plants from all over the globe arranged in conti-nents. The plants, mostly sourced from Scottish nurseries, have, in a childlike manner, been selected by their 'royal names', so you'll find *Anemone* 'Queen Charlotte', *Rhododendron* 'Princess Anne' and so on. But the Queen Mother would surely not have approved at the choice of some mawkish, sentimental names such as *Tradescantia* 'Innocence' and *Agapanthus* 'Blue Heaven'. Whether RBG Edinburgh is really an appropriate place for this garden at all is open to question.

There are so many outstanding plants and plantings in this garden, it is only possible to mention a few highlights. In spring the large-leaved species rhododendrons are worth a detour to the garden's south-east corner, where there are also the most extensive beds of *Trillium* I have seen in the UK, which have most gardeners green with envy. Nearby, the rock garden, built in 1875, has plants in flower all year round with numerous paths leading over and through the boulder-strewn mounds. I'm rather fond of the little patch of Cairngorm forest which runs round the edge of the rock garden: here it is easy to forget you are in Edinburgh. In late May the azalea lawn near the glasshouses is a blaze of colour in almost every shade while the long herbaceous borders, backed by a beech hedge are a patchwork of colour from June to September. The garden boasts collections of Scottish native plants, and more unusually of a cryptogamic garden, containing plantings of somewhat unglamorous fungi, mosses and lichens. Inverleith House often houses fine and sometimes challenging exhibitions of twentieth-century art and the café there is good. There are extensive education programmes for adults and children, guided walks, lectures and exhibitions running year-round in the Exhibition Hall. The Friends of the RBGE have their own programme of activities and a popular annual plant sale. Due to open in 2009 is the new John Hope Gateway visitor centre at the old West Gate, named after the founder of the garden, which will have a combination of roles to play: educational, retailing and café. No matter what time of year you come to Edinburgh, there is always plenty to see at RBGE; this is truly a national treasure, and you could easily spend several days here.

Saughton Park

This once-famous Edinburgh park, bordered by the Water of Leith, is little heralded these days but was the site of the 1908 Scottish National Exhibition which ran for 6 months and attracted almost 3½ million visitors. It is still gardened in the traditional park style with 26,000 bedding plants planted in island beds in the lawns and sunken gardens. The rose garden, enclosed by hedging, is extensive, again planted in formal beds with 4,000 hybrid teas and floribundas. The modest glasshouse/winter garden has recently been renovated and contains tender plants and a fishpond. The staff do their best to keep such a large area in good order but it is probably too much to manage. Time will tell whether the planting is scaled down or not. Enjoy it while you can. The Royal Caledonian Horticultural Society 'The Caley' holds plant sales at the Winter Gardens on some May weekends.

WC

Saughton Park
Gorgie, Edinburgh, EH11
(*map, pp. 360–61*)

Edinburgh City
Daily: dawn–dusk
Between Stevenson Drive
and Balgreen Road at the
western end of the city,
near Murrayfield stadium

Scottish Parliament
Edinburgh, EH99 1SP
(*map, pp. 360–61*)

Guided tours of the building,
which include the courtyard
garden when parliament is
not sitting: Friday–Monday
10am–4pm and holidays/recess,
may need to book; ££–£££.
Grounds can be seen at any time.
Between the Canongate (Royal
Mile) and Holyrood Road, by
Holyrood Palace. Buses 35
and 36 run closest
T: 0131 348 5200
F: 0131 348 5601
E: sp.bookings@scottish.
parliament.uk
www.scottish.parliament.uk
Café in the parliament building

Scottish Parliament

I hardly need to remind anyone of the troublesome birth of the
Scottish Parliament building. The Royal High School, long destined
to house the new parliament,was turned down as the site by
government minister Donald Dewar, who had more grandiose plans.
A new site and new building were selected instead. And then almost
everything that could go wrong, did go wrong: the Catalan architect
Enric Miralles died mid-project, the MSPs squabbled away, evidently
way out of their depth, continually tinkering with the design while
the budget leapt ever upwards, costing 10 times the estimate.
Everyone blamed everyone else. The private sector would never have
run a construction project with this level of naivety.

What is not in doubt is that the building and its grounds are a
stunning example of contemporary architecture and design and the
landscaping is an integral part of this. The building materials: wood,
granite, slate, steel, concrete, are used in striking combinations,
though every time I look at it, I wonder how long any of it is likely to
last, as it all looks rather fragile. Miralles' vision was for a building
'growing out of the land' so the hard and soft landscaping has been
designed to relate to the surroundings: to Holyrood Palace and the
Salisbury Crags, using native plants such as pines, rowans, gorse and
Scottish wild flowers. The problem is that it is rather hard to actually
get a good look at it all. The courtyard garden can be seen from the
hour-long guided tour of the building, but however hard you try you

can't get a good view of the fine grass and wildflower-planted sails or tails which radiate out towards Holyrood Park, from where the only views can be enjoyed. The great disappointment is the Scottish Parliament courtyard garden which is overlooked by MSPs' offices and the garden lobby of the building; it could hardly be in a more prominent position. Here was an opportunity to create something magical, worthy of the exuberance and vision of the building. Instead it is one of the most banal and inappropriate bits of landscaping I have seen. A scraggy triangular box parterre is already burnt and dying back. A row of apples and pears, planted far too close together, under which are planted a row of sad and sickly dwarf rhododendrons, behind which are some lavender and rosemary and grasses, mulched with slate chips. The garden has little discernible relevance to Scotland and it's what you might expect to find in the middle of a roundabout. I'd rip it all out and do it again properly; I can think of dozens of Scottish landscape architects and garden designers who could bring this space to life for a fraction of the budget squandered on it last time. Why not have a competition? Many of the trees planted around the Parliament were too big, did not establish and have been replaced; again questions of competence should be asked of those who planned and implemented it. I don't wish to be too negative about this place. It is well worth a visit and the building is memorable and iconic; book yourself on a guided tour inside and take the time to walk all the way round the outside and better still climb Arthur's Seat or Salisbury Crags for a great view of the whole complex.

It is also worth popping into the intimate Dunbar's Close garden down a narrow close off the Canongate opposite the Parliament. A tiny garden recreated in seventeenth-century style which was donated to the City of Edinburgh by the Mushroom Trust in 1978, it consists of a box parterre filled with herbs and fruit and there are benches to sit on. 2008 saw the launch of walking tours of some of the Royal Mile's small and hidden gardens, led by Jean Bareham (*www.greenyondertours.com*, telephone: 0131 444 1725).

Shepherd House

The small walled garden at Shepherd House in the attractive village of Inveresk is the creation of Sir Charles and Lady Ann Fraser. The melding of structure and plants, all in the space of less than 1 acre, can be explained by the Frasers' respective roles in the project: his love of ordered design and her emphasis (as a painter) on colour and plant combinations, has clearly been a winning formula. The main axis of the walled garden is a most attractive shallow stone rill, lined with borders of *Nepeta* and *Allium,* arched with roses and wisteria, joining two ponds, complete with fountains and statues. The gardens on either side consist of a series of hedged 'rooms'. On either side are two potagers, inspired by Rosemary Verey, an alcove of potted azaleas at

Shepherd House
Inveresk, Musselburgh, EH21 7TH
(*map, pp. 360–61*)

Sir Charles and Lady Fraser
1 Sunday in February
(snowdrops), April–June: Tuesday and Thursday 2–4pm, 1 Sunday in May SGS. Groups by appointment; ££
From A1 take the A6094 exit signed to Wallyford and Dalkeith and then follow signs to Inveresk. Junction of Carberry and Crookston roads
T: 0131 665 2570
E: annfraser@talktalk.net
www.shepherdhousegarden.co.uk

the back and a bulb meadow along the west wall. Along the east wall of the potting sheds are iris beds and *Wisteria*. Every nook and cranny is used, with walls covered with trained fruit and paths lined with clipped hollies and other plants. Next to the house the millennium parterre is planted with lavender, irises, oriental poppies, salvias and other goodies. The garden even spills out onto the street outside the walls, with a lavender border and perennials. This garden is an exquisite gem. See the website for up-to-date opening information. There are plant sales on some open days.

Smeaton Gardens and Nursery

Smeaton Gardens and Nursery
Preston, East Linton, EH40 3DT
(*map, pp. 360–61*)

Monday–Saturday: 9.30am–4.30pm; Sunday: 10am–4.30pm, closed Monday and Tuesday in January and February
Take the B1407 out of East Linton towards Tyninghame. Turn left, signed, along 1½ mile drive
T: 01620 860501
Popular café/tearoom in conservatory

Friends in the Dunbar area told me about this place so I popped in to have a look. Down a long driveway, this nineteenth-century walled garden is an old-style nursery/garden centre, ideal if you've had enough of Dobbies. There was a good selection of plants and a delightful tiny tea shop tucked into the greenhouses and sheds. *Scotland the Best* features it too and Peter Irvine has discovered a 'lake walk' through a small gate halfway down the drive 'a 1-km walk around a finger lake in mature woodland'. Sounds fun. This forms part of the arboretum owned by Mr and Mrs George Gray which is being renovated and is now open under the SGS one day per year.

St Abbs Head National Nature Reserve
Northfield, St Abbs, Eyemouth, Borders, TD14 5QF
(map, pp. 360–61)

NTS
Nature Reserve: daily, all year;
Visitor Centre: 31 March–31 October, daily 10am–5pm; £
(parking)
On the Berwickshire coast, 5 miles north of Eyemouth. From the A1 follow the A1107, signposted as the Berwickshire Coastal Trail
T: 0844 4932256
www.nts.org.uk
Coffee shop, art gallery, textiles shop, exhibition

St Abbs Head National Nature Reserve

St Abbs Head is a 200-acre national nature reserve, the high cliffs are a noisy nesting place for seabirds such as guillemots, razorbills, puffins, fulmars and gulls. Wild flowers include rock-rose, wild thyme, *Silene* and purple milk-vetch which attract small copper and common blue butterflies on sunny days. Meadow pipits, linnets and wheatears hunt for food, especially at Kirk Hill, sometimes nesting in empty rabbit burrows there. The sea off St Abbs is Scotland's only marine reserve. There are several looped walks which run from the visitor centre along the cliffs leading to Stevenson's Lighthouse. The gorse was spectacular when I visited in May.

  WC

St Mary's Pleasaunce
Sidegate, Haddington,
East Lothian, EH41 4BU
(map, pp. 360–61)

Haddington Gardens Trust
Daily; free
In central Haddington, behind Haddington House. Turn off A1 Edinburgh–Berwick road

St Mary's Pleasaunce

Haddington's St Mary's Church was restored in the 1970s. The garden site next door dates from the seventeenth or early eighteenth century and was the orchard associated with Haddington House. By 1972 it was in a derelict state and the late duke of Hamilton donated the ground to the Haddington Garden Trust, established to preserve the garden. Sir George Taylor, former director of Kew who retired to Dunbar, took charge of the planting of the garden. The orchard is filled with apples, pears, medlars and a mulberry, spring bulbs carpet the ground, and there is a spiral mound viewpoint. The major feature is a cloister-like formal laburnum arch which turns 90 degrees and becomes a pleached hornbeam allée. This leads into a courtyard surrounded by attractive white buildings and shrub roses with a seventeenth-century style formal box parterre sunken garden planted with herbs, labelled with their uses in old remedies. Nearby is the Tynepark Garden Project which, like Redhall in Edinburgh, is a centre for people with mental illness, set up in 1992. It features extensive gardens with greenhouses, lawns, vegetable and fruit areas. The garden hosts frequent plant sales.

St Mary's Pleasaunce

Stable House, Maxton

This is a fine ½-acre garden around a converted stables and courtyard, planted by Patsy Blacklock from 1982 onwards with carefully chosen plants from many sources. I was particularly impressed by two rarely seen ground covers *Fragaria chiloense*, which is a non-flowering Chilean strawberry, and the dry- and shade-loving *Asarum europaeum* with shiny rounded leaves. This is a garden with excellent planting combinations: inspiring pairings and groupings of trees, shrubs, perennials in both the sunny borders and the cool shady areas along the southern fence line, as well as good use of metalwork, statues and other focal points. Two combinations which grabbed my attention were the pale green variegation of *Syringa emodii* 'Variegata' with ferns and *Pulmonaria* in the shade border and hostas and bronze grasses in the sunny beds.

Stable House, Maxton
St Boswells, Roxburghshire,
TD6 OEA
(*map, pp. 360–61*)

Colonel and Mrs Blacklock
SGS 1 day and by appointment; ££
Off A68 on A699 to Kelso, second
road on left after turn off, signed
Benrig cemetery, second white
gate
T: 01835 823024
E: p4p@btinternet.com

Stevenson House
Haddington, East Lothian,
EH41 4PU
(*map, pp. 360–61*)

Mr and Mrs R. Green
SGS some years; ££
Two miles east of Haddington
on the road to Hailes Castle

Stevenson House

This handsome East Lothian house and grounds have had a considerable makeover in recent years. The long drive through horse paddocks leads to the front of the house, next to a huge old oak said to date to 1560. The back of the garden to the east of the house consists of a curved lime walk, underplanted with lavender, leading to a wildflower meadow, mature trees surrounded by striking stone and wooden seats, a summer house and a small formal garden, enclosed with a beech hedge. The main herbaceous border runs towards the house backed by espaliered apples. Around the house itself is a terrace, a statue of a seated figure on a swing, a box parterre surrounded by white climbing roses and further herbaceous beds. The constituent parts, though quite striking in themselves, look rather detached from one another and the garden lacks a sense of unified design, though it is young and should improve as it matures. The walled garden which runs along the back of the property is owned separately and in the past has been opened with Stevenson House under SGS.

Stobo Water Garden

The vogue for Japanese-style gardening began in the late Victorian era when Japan opened up to foreign visitors for the first time. At one time, Scotland had several important Japanese-influenced gardens which date from this era, but only Kildrummy, Stobo and the smaller gardens at Broughton House remain. Gardens at Shah-rak-uen, Cowden by Dollar (the largest in Scotland), Taymouth Castle and

Stobo Water Garden
Stobo, Peebles, EH45 8NX
(*map, pp. 360–61*)

Hugh and Georgina Seymour
SGS (spring and autumn) and
by appointment; ££
Follow signs to Dawyck on B712,
off the A72 west of Peebles. Stobo
is just before Dawyck, between
A72 and A701. Turn right ½ mile
south of Stobo village marked
Stobo Castle, then 1st right to
Stobo home farm, then bear left
T: 01721 760245
E: hugh.seymour@btinternet.com
Catering can be arranged for
groups

Kinfauns Castle (Perthshire) have all but disappeared. The Stobo estate was owned by sportsman Hylton Philipson, who had visited Japan on his way back from playing cricket with W.G. Grace in Australia. An amateur landscape gardener, he decided to create a woodland water garden with Japanese influence in the valley of the Weston Burn, which runs into the Tweed. He first dammed the burn to make a sizeable loch for hydroelectric power, the outlet from which created an impressive waterfall that forms the garden's upper boundary. From the bridge across the dam there are fine views both over the loch and down the burn into the gardens, through a series of pools to the humped bridge at the bottom end. Only a handful of Scottish gardens are at their best in autumn and Stobo is certainly one of the finest, with the maples, *Cercidiphyllum, Enkianthus* and other trees and shrubs, including the rarely seen *Disanthus cercidifolius* providing a backdrop to the running water, tea house, stepping stones and Japanese statues. The Stobo estate was bought by Leo Seymour in 1971 and the nineteenth-century Stobo Castle, built by the Montgomery family from Kinross House, was sold and is now a health spa. Stobo garden's current owners, Hugh and Georgina Seymour, live in the farmhouse nearby. They have embarked on a gradual restoration of the garden, removing overgrown trees and cutting back the undergrowth to reveal once again the fabric of paths, ponds and stone objects. Stobo is in no way a traditional Japanese design, but rather a woodland garden with Japanese plants and ornamentation. Coupled with Dawyck a mile or two further up the valley, this is one of the best gardens to visit in late October, when it is usually open under SGS.

435

Stobshiel House
Humbie, East Lothian, EH36 5PD
(*map, pp. 360–61*)

Mr Maxwell and Lady Sarah Ward
SGS some years, and by
appointment; ££
B6368 Haddington–Humbie road,
turn off opposite turning to
Gilchristen. B6368 to Stobshiel
1 mile
T: 01875 833646
E: wardhersey@aol.com

Stobshiel House

Max and Sarah Ward's garden at Stobshiel in East Lothian lies in the foothills of the Lammermuirs at 700ft. The castellated house has a water garden on the south side, bordered by a lawn with some formal statuary. Beyond this lies a small woodland garden, full of rhododendrons and azaleas and a tree house which my children admired. The jewel of this garden though is the narrow two-section garden to the west of the house. This consists of a series of box-lined paths with beautifully planted beds of roses and other shrubs and a huge range of perennials. The Wards happily sing the praises of gardener Pat Robertson their 'right-hand woman'. This lovely space inspired my wife Jane to raptures of delight, despite the rain. In one corner is a fairytale rustic summerhouse, in the centre a small parterre, at the far end, fizzing white stars of *Crambe*. Paths lead through the yew hedge to the second half of this garden, with a different feel: oriental poppies, lavender, framed by an Edwardian greenhouse, behind which lay a potting shed with tools lined up lovingly, as if from another era. Everywhere were quirky touches: a rose bed with a border of white saxifrage, a path leading to a blue Lorimer-style bench; this is a garden with precise, clever design elements and we loved it. Humbie House nearby sometimes opens in tandem.

Suntrap Edinburgh Horticultural and Gardening Centre

I called in here one Saturday morning in October. There wasn't a soul about, so I popped my money in the honesty box and wandered around. The garden consists of a series of demonstration 'rooms' on a slope: a rock garden, woodland plantings, peat beds, mixed shrub borders, a vegetable potager, herbaceous borders and the national bonsai collection. Suntrap is not as peaceful as it once was owing to the construction of the M8 motorway extension next door, whose roar is a constant presence. George Boyd Anderson, philanthropist, innovator and gardener, started the garden in 1957. He was a pioneer of the use of solar energy, and insulation and energy-saving was incorporated in some of the charming and quirky garden buildings and is the origin of the name 'Suntrap'. The garden was bequeathed to the National Trust for Scotland and Lothian Regional Council to provide a centre for amateur gardening and advice and to encourage horticultural education. Activities offered include evening classes through Oakridge College, workshops, a schools education inclusion project and monthly meetings of the Suntrap garden club. Finances are tight and Suntrap seems to be rather under-appreciated; its future is uncertain and I think a radical rethink may be required to find a new, extended role for it. A centre for renewable energy and energy efficiency would be an obvious direction, given its history.

Suntrap Edinburgh Horticultural and Gardening Centre
43 Gogarbank, Edinburgh, EH12 9BY
(*map, pp. 360–61*)

NTS, Oakridge College
October–April: 10am–4pm;
May–September: 10am–6pm; ££
Between Mid Calder and Edinburgh airport accessible from A8 and A71
T: 0131 339 7283
E: suntrap@btopenworld.com
www.suntrap-garden.org.uk

Teviot Water Gardens
Kirkbank House, Kelso,
Roxburghshire, TD5 8LE
(*map, pp. 360–61*)

Wilson family
Daily: 9am–5pm; free
A698 Kelso–Jedburgh road, just
north of Eckford
T: 01835 850253
F: 01835 850293
E: teviot.gamefare@btconnect.com
www.teviotwatergardens.co.uk
Popular café, deli, smokehouse

Teviot Water Gardens

This is a garden centre, restaurant, smokery and food shop perched
on the south bank of the Teviot. A garden has been cut out along the
steep hillside with a series of terraces and linked ponds. The garden
centre has a wooden terrace on stilts out front which unfortunately
does not really overlook the gardens. The gardens, a bit overgrown
when I visited, are a scramble down the hillside and filled with *Astilbe*,
candelabra primulas, *Rodgersia* and other waterside plants, with
wooden bridges over the ponds and streams. The garden centre sells
pond and water gardening equipment, the restaurant/café is popular
and it looks as if the smokehouse and deli are receiving more
emphasis these days than the gardens. There is a circular walk above
and along the Teviot, and a bird hide.

    [WC]

The Hirsel Country Park
Coldstream, Scottish Borders,
TD12 4LP
(*map, pp. 360–61*)

The Home family
Daily: dawn–sunset; £–££
Off the A697 on the western
edge of Coldstream
T: 01573 224144
F: 01573 226313
E: info@hirselcountrypark.co.uk
www.hirselcountrypark.co.uk
Tearoom

The Hirsel Country Park

The Hirsel (meaning sheepfold) has been in the Home family since
the early seventeenth century and was the home of 1960s British
prime minister, Alec Douglas Home. The estate lies near the English
border on the River Leet, which runs into the Tweed. The man-made
Hirsel lake contains a fine collection of wildfowl and a huge range of
birds including kingfishers, flycatchers and marsh tits are regularly
recorded here. Dundock Wood, half a mile's walk away on the far side
of the lake, contains a high canopy of oak and Scots pine under
which are an extensive collection of mature but well-spaced blocks of
hybrid rhododendrons and azaleas which are underplanted with
aconites, snowdrops and daffodils. Apparently when this was planted
a huge quantity of peat was brought on a long journey by cart, as the
local soil was said to be alkaline. The time to see this display is from
mid May to early June as the collection contains very few early
flowering varieties. There is no sign of any recent planting and as the
clumps get ever larger, what few vistas exist are being obscured. A
little more active management of the collection would certainly

improve the displays. The woods also provide good autumn colour. Next to the car park is the visitor centre at the Homestead, which includes a small tearoom, craft shop, museum of country life, a children's play area and picnic site. The estate also has a herd of Douglas pedigree highland cattle.

Traquair House

Said to be the oldest inhabited house in Scotland, Traquair was once owned by the kings of Scotland, was later home of the earls of Traquair and is now home to the Maxwell Stuart family. The famous Bear Gates, built in 1738, according to legend were closed following a visit of Bonnie Prince Charlie and the then earl of Traquair vowed they would never be opened again until a Stuart king was crowned once more in London. Unsurprisingly, they remain closed. There is not much in the way of formal garden as such, but the fine parkland

Traquair House
Innerleithen, Borders, EH44 6PW
(*map, pp. 360–61*)

Traquair Charitable Trust
Open daily from 10 April–
31 October; weekends only
in November
April, May and September
12pm–5pm
June, July and August
10.30am–5pm
October 11am–4pm
November 11am–3pm
Corporate or Group events can
be accommodated outwith the
stated opening dates/times
Please contact Traquair House
for more details. Signposted
off the A72 at Innerleithen
T: 01896 830323
F: 01896 830639
E: enquiries@traquair.co.uk
www.traquair.co.uk
Restaurant in walled garden
Shop, brewery

contains mature trees including some of Scotland's oldest yews, and there are walks down to the River Tweed. The fine ½-acre maze was planted in 1981 using leylandii and beech and is used for a popular Easter-egg hunt each spring. There are some new perennial plantings in the walled garden with fruit trees and a metal horse sculpture in the centre and some grey and white borders in Cupid's garden next to the house. The grounds are used for activities through the year, including plays and music.

B&B   WC

Tyninghame House

Tyninghame House
Dunbar, East Lothian,
EH42 1XW
(*map, pp. 360–61*)

Tyninghame House Company
SGS open days; ££
Take A198 to North Berwick from
A1, leave onto A199 via East
Linton (from north) or West Barns
(from south)

Tyninghame House and its gardens are a good example of how a change of use for a stately home can save both the home and significant gardens for the future. When the twelfth earl of Haddington died in 1986, the enormous house was divided into 14 properties, the new owners of which share the cost of maintaining the gardens. These are looked after by two gardeners, who are not always able to please all of their 14 bosses, but somehow manage to maintain the extensive parkland and gardens to a high standard. Surrounding the house are woodlands and a wild garden with azaleas, under-planted with spring bulbs and primroses. There is a mature long lime avenue to the north of the house beyond the parkland and wide shrub and perennial borders surround the east side of the house. A huge jasmine and an arch of honeysuckle drew my attention. At the front of the house looking south is an avenue of trees leading to a

ruined church. The front lawn is planted with bold blocks of deep purple *Cotinus*. To the west of the house are the finest parts of this garden, built on terraces. The rose garden is a parterre of triangular box beds planted with white and yellow roses. Further west lies Lady Haddington's 'secret garden', created on the site of a former tennis count, which is a densely planted, more informal and intimate space, with winding paths and scented soft-coloured roses, peonies and other favourites. One of the Tyninghame owners, Jane Clifford, has had a strong input into this part of the garden. The central feature is a gazebo, replaced in 2007 after the old one collapsed. The gardens are usually open in tandem with the separately owned and outstanding Tyninghame Walled Garden.

Tyninghame Walled Garden

The vast 1760 walled garden at Tyninghame was sold separately from the house and is now owned by Mrs Gwyn, originally from southern Ireland, who lives in the house, converted from a former apple store, in the garden walls. Mrs Gwyn has restored the walled garden, which is now one of the finest in Scotland, both in its architecture and planting. Four acres in size, it is rectangular with an additional

Tyninghame Walled Garden
Dunbar, East Lothian,
EH42 1XW
(*map, pp. 360–61*)

Charnisay Gwyn
SGS open days, or by appointment; ££
Take A198 to North Berwick from A1, leave onto A199 via East Linton (from north) or West Barns (from south)
T: 01620 860559

semicircle at the top. The rectangle is divided into four quadrants, with box-lined paths and a theatrical main axis flanked by clipped yew hedging with statues in the alcoves, much in the northern Italian style. The layout of the garden was redesigned in the 1960s by Jim Russell. The west side is a dense, perhaps now over-shaded woodland area with carpets of hostas, *Bergenia*, honesty and other plants under mature trees. The far west walk is flanked by a long border of *Euphorbia griffithii* and *Hosta sieboldii*, unusual but effective, and a dense planting of shrub roses which probably need more light. At the south end, through a door in the wall, is an unusual apple walk, with apples and crab apples trained over a series of archways creating a tunnel 90m long, of pink and white at blossom time. Towards the top end of the walled garden, from one side to the other, across the yew walk, is a fine *coup de théâtre*. The *Nepeta* walk cuts through the garden like a double jet of purple-blue, looking as fine from the side as it does from each end. It is usually at its peak for the late June SGS open day at the gardens. Over it is a series of rose arches with 'Seagull' and other favourites. The effect is magical. Next to the tennis court is a peony border, all the more impressive for the fact that when I visited in June 2006, there had been torrential rain all week, and the pink and red peonies were still upright and looking fine. Other parts of the garden are filled with fruit trees, a parterre filled with lavender, summer plantings of *Agapanthus* and *Kniphofia* and some well-kept greenhouses, some once used for pineapples, now with vines in them. This is a fine garden, with plenty to see at almost any time of year, the late June–July periods would see the peak of colour from the roses and perennials. There are also some good gardens in Tyninghame village which you can see spilling out onto the roadside.

West Leas

This is a new garden in the making, on a considerable scale in several sections around a house and farmyard. The garden was carved out of a field and rough woodland and included many plants brought from the Laidlaws' previous garden. New developments include a terraced waterfall down the burn, a bog garden, an orchard and extensive new shrub and perennial planting along the Rule Water. The candelabra primulas were outstanding in June.

  WC

West Leas
Bonchester Bridge,
Jedburgh, TD9 8TD
(*map, pp. 360–61*)

Mr and Mrs Robert Laidlaw
SGS 1 day, and sometimes
by appointment; ££
Jedburgh/Bonchester Bridge
Road on the minor road
between Hellrule and Bedrule
T: 01835 862524 (office)
F: 01835 864358
E: ann.laidlaw@btconnect.com

Wilton Lodge Park, Hawick

This 107-acre park in Hawick on the banks of the River Teviot has tree-lined walks along the river, a fine waterfall, glass houses, formal gardens, a museum and walled garden which, at least until recently, contained impressive traditional bedding schemes. There are extensive spring bulb displays and good autumn colour on the trees. Recreational facilities include bowling lawns, tennis, putting, crazy golf. A heritage lottery application may be going in for further park developments.

 WC

Wilton Lodge Park, Hawick
Wilton Dean, Hawick,
TD9 7JL
(*map, pp. 360–61*)

Scottish Borders Council
Open daily
Signposted in Hawick
T: 01896 662734
Café

Winton House
Pencaitland, East Lothian,
EH34 5AT
(*map, pp. 360–61*)

Sir Francis Ogilvy Winton Trust,
contact events office
SGS 1 Sunday in March/April for
snowdrops, or by appointment; ££
Entrance off B6355 Tranent–
Pencaitland road
T: 01875 340 222
F: 01875 342 042
E: enquiries@wintonhouse.co.uk
www.wintonhouse.co.uk
Winton café on open days

Winton House

Winton Gardens has been opened for the Scotland's Garden Scheme for over 50 years. The handsome white house with tall Gaudiesque chimneys and fine outbuildings, was the seat of important Lothian family the Seatons from 1150, but they backed the losing side in the 1715 rebellion and the earl of Winton was sent to the Tower of London. Winton also hosted Bonnie Prince Charlie in 1745. The Hamilton-Nisbets bought the estate, which at one time included Muirfield and Gullane golf courses. Winton is now the home of Sir Francis and Lady Ogilvy and is also used as a venue for weddings and corporate events. There are three terraces on the south side of the house decorated with busts on pedestals, and planted with perennials and box. These look down on Sir David's Loch below. The Peacock Terrace lies on the house's east side. The Winton Walks consist of four routes, from 1½ miles to 6.6 miles with points of interest along the way including giant carved totem poles, a pirate ship and the 'Ormiston Express' train as well as some weather shelters. The parkland is particularly famous for its daffodil displays and cherry blossom for which the gardens open under SGS in spring and it is also worth going round the terraces, which have lots of early colour. The website is excellent, particularly on the complex history of the estate and its owners. Head gardener Toby Subiotto is renovating the terraces and other parts of the gardens and has plans for the large walled garden, to the north of the house, currently largely down to grass. Winton is a great landscape and could be a magnificent garden. Time will tell how much is to be invested in it.

Woodside Walled Garden

This is the old walled garden of Monteviot House (see p. 412), which lies across the road, and is now run as a delightful nursery, café and demonstration garden. It was previously run by Jane and David Allen as Borders Organic Garden but is now run as a nursery by Annie Neath and Jane Vickers. The nursery/garden centre has a good range of plants, sourced in Scotland where possible, and informative display gardens with perennials and other plants. The garden adheres as far as practical to organic principles and actively promotes gardening to encourage wildlife. The café, where you can sit inside or out, is excellent and serves food made from the garden's produce. Some useful organic trials have taken place here including slug deterrents and the eradication or control of marestail without using chemicals. There is also extensive advice on composting, wildflower and native plant gardening and creating potagers. Plans for 2009 include a new shop building (no gnomes, they promise!) and local art and crafts for sale. Long a place of pilgrimage for Scotland's organic gardeners and now an excellent nursery, this is a wonderful new use for an old walled garden, no longer required by the house which it was attached to. Highly recommended by myself and many locals who give it glowing reports.

   [WC]

Woodside Walled Garden
Woodside Nurseries,
Harestanes, Jedburgh,
Roxburghshire, TD8 6PU
(*map, pp. 360–61*)

Annie Neath and Jane Vickers
Daily: 10am–5pm; free
3 miles north of Jedburgh off
the A68. Follow the B6400
towards Nisbet 500m on left
T: 01450 860291
E: woodside.garden@virgin.net
Excellent café serving freshly
made local and seasonal food
and drink

445

Yair (The)
Galashiels, Borders, TD1 3PW
(*map, pp. 360–61*)

Mr and Mrs W. Thyne
1 Sunday SGS most years, and
by appointment; ££
On A707 between Caddonfoot and
Selkirk. Drive runs from Selkirk
side of the river at traffic lights
E: didi@theyair.co.uk

Yair (The)

Yair House was built for Alexander Pringle in 1788 and is a handsome Georgian mansion on the banks of the Tweed. The Thyne family bought the Yair in 1944. The Thynes have gradually moved the focus of the garden nearer to the house, and the lawns are now planted with a fine mixture of shrubs and perennials, looked after by gardener Helen Taggart. The section at the far end, around the stone bench, is a colourful memorial to the Thynes' son William. A New Zealand bed of hebes and grasses has been planted along the path up to the tennis court. The woodland walk passes by a handsome old cedar, banks of snowdrops and bluebells in spring, via mature rhododendrons to the unusual steeply sloping wide walled garden, terraced in the middle to provide an extra wall for fruit growing. The walled garden is gradually being restored and simplified. A screen of *Schizandra* on the bridge which crosses the back drive, caught my attention.

Stop Press

Glecknabae

Ian and Margaret Gimblett had already created several gardens in other parts of the UK when they bought this derelict farm and turned it into this beautifully designed garden on the little-visited north-west coast of Bute. This windswept site proved to be good for growing most plants once the shelter belts were established using both trees and shrubs and a series of courtyards and garden rooms. All are designed with year-round interest in mind and using stone and wood, mostly recycled from the farm buildings, to create contrasting textures to show off the enormous numbers of plants they have assembled. The stone cattle-troughs have all been filled with alpines and bulbs. There are many upended rocks, resonant of Japanese gardens and of prehistoric standing stones. Round every corner is another compartment, each one a vignette of planting and landscaping styles: a bog garden, screes, a formal garden with blue containers, fruit, a wildflower meadow, spring bulbs, trees with fine bark; there is a bit of everything here. The Gimbletts moved on in 2008 but happily the new owners are continuing to maintain and open this excellent garden.

Glecknabae
North Bute, Isle of Bute,
PA20 0QX
(*map, pp. 256–57*)

John and Marianne McGhee
SGS 1 day, and by appointment.
A844 to Ettrick Bay signposted off
the coast rd between Rhubodach
and Rothesay, continue past the
beach at Ettrick, to end of made up
road, approx 5 miles
T: 01700 504742
E: john.a.mcghee@btopenworld.
com

Dunans Castle Woodland Gardens

This is an ambitious project to restore Dunans Castle and its woodland garden and spectacular 1815 Telford bridge. The Victorian castle was remodelled from the existing Dunans House in the 1860s. The castle was ruined in a fire in 2001, and the present owners began restoration in 2003. The woodland is a spectacular landscape, featuring the ravine walk and a landscape of some of Britain's tallest trees, underplanted with rhododendrons.

**Dunans Castle Woodland
Gardens**
Glendaruel, Argyll, PA22 3AD
(*map, pp. 220–21*)

Mr and Mrs Charles Dixon-Spain
SGS several days per year.
Guided tours by arrangement. £
T: 01369 820115
E: info@dunans.org
www.dunans.org

Pennyfields

Jim Davidson is a well-known exhibitor and breeder of *Narcissus* and has planted an orchard with hundreds of varieties of daffodils including trials of many new varieties.

Pennyfields
Howe of Gellymill,
Banff, AB45 3QL
(*map, pp. 54–55*)

Mr J. Davidson
By arrangement during April,
groups welcome. ££
Off main A947 Turriff–Banff road,
½ mile from Banff, signposted
Gellymill Road
T: 01261 812836
E: jim@daffodils.ndo.co.uk

Smithyhill Cottage
Leswalt, by Stranraer,
DG9 0LS
(*map, pp. 320–21*)

Mr and Mrs Humphreys
SGS weekends and by
appointment. £
A 718 from Stranraer towards
Leswalt. Take 2nd left after
leaving Stranraer, ¼ mile on left
01776 870662

Smithyhill Cottage

The Humphreys recently relocated their extensive collection of alpine plants from Yorkshire to Galloway. The collection is planted in 8 themed raised beds and a small alpine house.

Strabane
Brodick, Arran, KA27 8DP
(*map, pp. 256–57*)

Lady Jean Fforde
SGS 1 day ££
On east side of Brodick, Arran

Strabane

Woodland garden with rhododendrons and azaleas. Walled garden with herbaceous borders. Lying below and south of Brodick Castle, the two could easily be combined in a day trip.

Goat Fell, Strabane and Brodick
Castle from the Arran Ferry

448

Scotland's Garden Centre Chains

Space does not permit or justify individual entries for members of Scotland's two garden centre chains listed below. Both have some excellent centres and some rather average ones. I have not included any of the DIY sheds or supermarkets which have garden centres, as I assume the fact that you are reading this book means that you are more discerning.

Dobbies Garden Centres

Dobbies Garden Centres
Various sites all over Scotland (see below)
Tesco
Daily, late closing on certain days
T: 0131 663 6778 (head office)
www.dobbies.com

I remember when Dobbies was nothing more than a single nursery and garden centre in Dalkeith. David Barnes, his son James and their team turned it into Britain's second largest garden centre chain with new stores opening all the time. Then in 2007 they sold out to Tesco after a battle with owner of rival Wyvale Garden Centres, Scottish entrepreneur Tom Hunter. The Dobbies centres are variable in size and quality, some have extensive ranges of plants and some don't. All have cafés and many of the newer and larger ones have food halls. Their stated aim a few years ago was to be an 'out-of-town John Lewis', and often they feel more like this and less like garden centres. The best Scottish ones are the very impressive flagship store at Melville and some of the newer stores such as Stirling and Dunfermline. Some of the English ones have theme parks, farms and mazes attached. It remains to be seen how Tesco will change Dobbies.

Dobbies Scottish Store locations

Aberdeen Dobbies Garden Centre, Hazeldene Road, Aberdeen, AB15 8QU. Telephone: 01224 318658

Ayr Dobbies Garden World, Old Toll, Holmston, Ayr, KA6 5JJ. Telephone: 01292 294750

Dalgety Bay Dobbies Garden Centre, Western Approach Road, Dalgety Bay, Fife, KY11 5XP. Telephone: 01383 823841

Dundee Dobbies Garden World, Ethiebeaton Park, Monifieth Dundee, DD5 4HB. Telephone: 01382 530333

Dunfermline Dobbies Garden World, Whimbrell Place, Fife Leisure Park, Dunfermline, KY11 8EX. Telephone: 01383 842757

Kinross Dobbies Garden Centre, Turfhills, Kinross, KY13 7NQ. Telephone: 01577 863327

Melville Dobbies Garden Centre, Melville Nursery, Lasswade, Midlothian, EH18 1AZ. Telephone: 0131 6631941

Milngavie Dobbies Garden World, Boclair Road, Milngavie, Glasgow, G62 6EP. Telephone: 01360 620721

Paisley Dobbies Garden Centre, Hawkhead Road, Paisley, PA2 7AD.
Tel: 0141 8875422
Perth Dobbies Garden World, Huntingtower Park, Crieff Road,
Perth, PHI 3JJ. Tel: 01738 638555
Sandyholm Garden Centre, Crossford, by Carluke, Lanarkshire,
Clyde Valley, ML8 5QF. Tel: 01555 860205
Stirling Dobbies Garden World, Drip Road, Craigforth, Stirling,
FK9 4UF. Tel: 01786 458860

Klondyke Garden Centres
Head Office: Klondyke Garden
Centres, Beancross Road,
Polmont, Falkirk, FK2 0XS
Bob Gault
T: 0800 20 40 80
E: info@klondyke.co.uk

Klondyke Garden Centres

The Klondyke garden centre chain, now merged with the English
Strikes Group, is the second largest Scottish garden centre group after
Dobbies. It was founded by Bob Gault. Klondyke still run their own
nursery, supplying bedding plants to all their centres. The group was
formed by buying up independent garden centres such as Howdens in
Inverness. They are variable in size and quality and are generally not
as impressive as centres owned by rivals Dobbies. Topiary cafés are
run at each branch.

Howdens Garden Centre, Stoneyfield, Inverness, IV2 7PA.
Telephone: 01463 711134
Klondyke Garden Centre, Campus Roundabout, Kirkton Campus,
Livingston, EH54 7AW. Telephone: 01506 410053
Mayfield Garden Centre, Glebe Lane, Kelso, Roxburghshire, TD5 7AU.
Telephone: 01573 224124
Mortonhall Garden Centre, Frogston Road East, Edinburgh,
EH16 6TK. Telephone: 0131 6648698
Klondyke Garden Centre, Beancross Road, Polmont, Falkirk,
FK2 0XS. Telephone: 01324 717035
Klondyke Garden Centre, Stirling, Glasgow Road, Whins Of Milton,
Stirling, FK7 8ER. Telephone: 01786 816167

Horticultural Societies and Organisations; Tourism and Environmental Bodies

Scotland has many specialist horticultural societies, many of which are affiliated to national and international organisations. These tend to have similar benefits for members: shows, meetings and lectures, seed and plant exchanges and garden visits.

BRITISH CACTUS AND SUCCULENT SOCIETY

www.bcss.org.uk. Scottish branches in Ayr, Fife, Glasgow, Grampian and Highlands and Islands.

COTTAGE GARDEN SOCIETY

c/o Clive Lane, 'Brandon', Ravenshall, Betley, Cheshire, cw3 9bh
T: 01270 820940
E: clive_lane_cgs@hotmail.com
www.thecgs.org.uk
Formed in 1982, there is a Scottish branch based in Edinburgh.

DELPHINIUM SOCIETY IN SCOTLAND

c/o James McMaster, Pinaulton Cottage, 21 Coal Hall Road, Drongan, Ayr, ka6 6ng
T: 01292 590757
E: pinaulton@tiscali.co.uk www.delphinium-society.co.uk

FEDERATION OF SCOTTISH FUCHSIA SOCIETIES

A loose association of the many local Fuchsia groups in Aberdeen, Ayrshire, Bute, Central Scotland, Dumfries and Galloway, Dundee, Dunfermline, Fife, Glasgow, Perth, East Scotland and West Lothian.

HARDY PLANT SOCIETY

E: Scottishgroup@hardy-plant.org.uk
www.hardy-plant.org.uk
Specialising in hardy perennials/herbaceous plants.

HEART OF SCOTLAND HERB SOCIETY

Secretary: Mrs Patty Hope, The Old Manse, Ardeonaig, by Killin, ph9 0lw
www.hshs.org.uk. Based in Aberfeldy.

NATIONAL VEGETABLE SOCIETY

Scottish Branch, membership secretary: Mr J.G. Grant Cathro, Bracklinn, 14 Dronley Road, Birkhill, Dundee, DD2 5QD
E: jgrant.cathro@btinternet.com
www.nvsuk.org.uk
Several regional branches; shows in late summer in Dundee and Ayr.

ROYAL HORTICULTURAL SOCIETY OF ABERDEEN

Chair: Hazel Main, Treorchy, Hillside, Portlethen, AB12 4RB
E: gardening@rhsofaberdeen.co.uk
www.rhsofaberdeen.co.uk

SCOTTISH ASSOCIATION OF FLOWER ARRANGEMENT SOCIETIES

E: flowers@nafas.co.uk
www.nafas.org.uk
Scotland has 93 affiliated clubs.

SCOTTISH BEGONIA SOCIETY

Cathy and Allan Walkinshaw (Secretaries)
T: 01236 754012 (president), E: allanwalki@supanet.com
www.scottishbegoniasociety.co.uk.

SCOTTISH BONSAI ASSOCIATION

Deganwy, 22 Gartcows Road, Falkirk, FK1 5QT
T: 01324 625145, F: 01324 625145, E: info@scottishbonsai.org,
www.scottishbonsai.org. Regional groups in Ayr, Edinburgh, Forth Valley, Lanarkshire, Grampian, Highland, Inverclyde, Penicuik, Perth and West Lothian.

SCOTTISH NATIONAL CHRYSANTHEMUM AND DAHLIA SOCIETY

3 Bearcroft Gardens, Grangemouth FK3 9EJ
Contact Ian Turner
E: ian@turneridmt.freeserve.co.uk

SCOTTISH NATIONAL SWEET PEA, ROSE AND CARNATION SOCIETY

E: society@snsprcs.org.uk, www.snsprcs.org.uk

SCOTTISH RHODODENDRON SOCIETY

Membership Secretary, SRS, Glengilp Farm, Ardrishaig, Argyll, PA30 8HT
E: membership@scottishrhodos.co.uk
www.scottishrhodos.co.uk

SCOTTISH ROCK GARDEN CLUB

PO Box 14063, Edinburgh, EH10 4YE
E: info@srgc.org.uk, www.srgc.org.uk
One of Scotland's largest and most active plant-related societies,
with over 4,000 members in 38 countries. Good shows.

Beautiful Scotland in Bloom

Running for over 40 years, Scotland's version of *Britain in Bloom*
helps communities to improve and enhance their local area. A
series of awards is given out in autumn for towns, villages and
communities. Some of Scotland's repeat champions include
Aberdeen, Perth, Falkland, Pitlochry, Comrie, Alness, North
Berwick and Forres.

Beautiful Scotland in Bloom
Islay House, Livilands Lane,
Stirling, FK8 2BG1
T: 01786 471333
F: 01786 464611
www.beautifulscotland.org

Brightwater Holidays

Brightwater is the UK's leading specialist garden tour operator,
visiting large, small, public and private gardens, as well as specialist
nurseries. Bear in mind that most of the best Scottish gardens are
hard to reach by public transport so if you don't wish to drive, a
garden tour might be the best way to see the more out-of-the-way
gardens and countryside. As well as brochure tours, they can offer
tailor-made tours for groups and societies.

Brightwater Holidays
Eden Park House, Cupar,
Fife, KY15 4HS
Graeme and Kay Mitchell
T: 01334 657155
E: info@brightwaterholidays.com
www.brightwaterholidays.com

Garden Designers and Landscapers in Scotland

Garden design and landscaping can be a bit of a minefield. The
industry is not regulated and anyone can claim to be a designer or
stick the word 'landscaper' on the side of a van and off they go. On
the other hand, there are lots of excellent and knowledgeable
garden designers and first-class landscapers. Most of these have
websites which showcase their work. All I can do is mention some
individuals and companies whose work I have seen and admired,
those who have been in business for many years and those whose
reputation and experience bears scrutiny. Many of these have been
involved in designing gardens in this book, so that is a good place
to start if you wish to see their work. Best garden design practice is
a collaboration between owner and designer. After all, the owner
has to live with the results and be prepared to look after the
garden. Dutch designer Piet Oudolf says that the first question he
asks a potential client is: 'How many hours a week do you intend
to devote to looking after it?' I think this is a very sound strategy.
Some of the best garden designers are members of the Society of
Garden Designers, which should vouch for their reliability. Scottish
members include Michael Ballam, Douglas Coltart, Gordon T.
Gray, Sam McGowan, Marion Parker and Judy Riley. All can be

contacted via the SGD website *www.sgd.org.uk*, and at Katepwa House, Ashfield Park Avenue, Ross-on-Wye, Herefordshire, HR9 5AX. Not all the best designers are members however. Some of these whose work I have seen and admired include: Michael Innes, Landmarkers (Jasmin and Doug Cann), Twigg Garden Design, Plant It Landscaping, Diane Pyper, Carole Bainbridge (Greenscene design), Stella Rankin (Kevock) (Further details on the website *scotlandforgardeners.com*)

Garden History Society of Scotland

Garden History Society of Scotland
The Glasite Meeting House, 33 Barony St, Edinburgh, EH3 6NX
T: 0131 557 5717
E: scotland@gardenhistory society.org
www.thegardenhistorysociety.org

The Garden History Society was founded in 1965 and is widely recognised for its expertise and advice in horticultural history and conservation of gardens and landscapes. It publishes a scholarly journal. Its professionally qualified conservation officers are consulted by government agencies, local authorities and others on a wide range of issues affecting historic parks and gardens. The Scottish branch has regular meetings and lectures in Edinburgh.

Guerrilla Gardening

Guerrilla Gardening
No fixed abode
www.guerrillagardening.org
www.glasgowguerrilla
gardening.org.uk

Guerrilla gardening is a movement which supports and encourages unofficial gardening on land you don't own. The movement is alive and well in Scotland. (see the website link). Richard Reynolds' book *Guerrilla Gardening* came free with a packet of sunflower seeds designed to be planted on some wasteland or a roadside verge. The book states 'Guerrilla gardeners themselves variously describe their approach as communist, egalitarian, situationist, liberterian, spiritual, therapeutic and even fascist. I describe it as common sense.' Whether you agree with any of this is up to you. It seems to be a colourful, anarchic movement which may well encourage people who would not otherwise consider gardening to get involved. See the website for all you might ever need to know, or buy the book.

Royal Caledonian Horticultural Society

Royal Caledonian Horticultural Society
Mrs Alison Murison, secretary: The Royal Caledonian Horticultural Society, 17 Jordan Lane, Edinburgh, EH10 4RA
T: 0131 4782141
www.rchs.co.uk

The Royal Caledonian Horticultural Society, usually known as 'The Caley', is Scotland's national gardening society. Founded in 1809, it is based in Edinburgh but with members Scotland-wide. Membership benefits include talks at the Royal Botanic Garden, Edinburgh, garden tours and visits, plant sales, expert advice on gardening problems, and books and videos on loan. Publications include an annual journal, *The Caledonian Gardener*, and a newsletter. The Society awards medals to people who have made major contributions to Scottish horticulture.

Scotland's Garden Scheme (SGS)

Formed in 1931, SGS opens private gardens to raise money for charity. In 2007 some £260,000 was raised by the scheme. Sixty per cent of funds raised goes to the main beneficiaries: the Queen's Nursing Institute Scotland, the National Trust for Scotland, Perennial, the Royal Fund for Gardeners' Children and most recently Maggie's Centres. The garden owners can choose their own charities for the remaining money raised. The salaried director has the onerous task of trying to organise some of Scotland's most formidable ladies (and they are mostly ladies) who make up the regional organisers and volunteers. Most attempts to modernise are generally fiercely resisted; for example it is only in the last few years that postcodes have been included in the annual *Gardens of Scotland*, widely known as the 'Yellow Book'. Another eccentricity is the way the book is divided up by the old Scottish counties. Am I the only one who has no idea where exactly Inverclyde, Tweeddale or Ettrick and Lauderdale might be? It is encouraging that smaller gardens, allotments and community gardens are now opening in greater numbers, as well as groups of village gardens open together. Why is SGS so successful? The gardens are wonderful, of course, but for many people the big attraction, apart from the great opportunity to be nosy, are the teas, which are usually delicious and extremely good value.

Scotland's Garden Scheme (SGS)
42a Castle Street,
Edinburgh, EH2 3BN
T: 0131 2263714
E: info@sgsgardens.co.uk
www.gardensofscotland.org

Scottish Allotments and Gardens Society

SAGS (an unfortunate acronym) represents allotment sites and plot holders throughout Scotland and promotes the value of allotments for healthy activity and good food. Pressure by developers who eye up council-owned allotment sites for house-building has led to much friction in recent years. Three Scottish sites were lost to development in 2007. The website details the issues that allotment holders face in considerable detail. In 2007 Scotland had 211 active allotment sites containing at least 6,300 individual plots. Sixty-nine per cent of sites are local authority owned. At least 3,000 people are on waiting lists, but it is apparent that some waiting lists are so long that they have been closed, so the demand is clearly even higher. COSLA (Convention of Scottish Local Authorities) recently published recommended good practice for Scottish councils regarding allotments. Councils have a statutory duty to respond to demand for the provision of allotments. It only needs 6+ residents on the electoral roll to make representation in writing. This information is not well known; funny, that. So I thought I'd broadcast it and help unleash the power of local democracy.

Scottish Allotments and Gardens Society
E: secretary@sags.org.uk
www.sags.org.uk

Scottish Gardeners' Forum
E: arutherford@perennial.org.uk
www.scottishgardeners
forum.org.uk

Scottish Gardeners' Forum

This umbrella organisation, formed in 1999, provides a register of horticultural societies, horticultural speakers, register of show judges, and provides information and assistance to anyone seeking a local gardening club/specialist society. It also runs the very popular 1m × 1m pallet garden competition for schools and garden clubs at Gardening Scotland, a highlight of the show for many.

Scottish Snowdrop Festival
VisitScotland
T: 0845 22 55 121
E: info@visitscotland.com
gardens.visitscotland.com

Scottish Snowdrop Festival

The Scottish Snowdrop Festival, featuring some of the very best snowdrop gardens, woodlands and estates across Scotland, was started in 2007, coordinated by VisitScotland, and will hopefully be an annual event in February and March with many gardens all over the country opening, with events, tours, sales and just great walks, at a time of year when almost all Scotland's attractions are closed to visitors. See the leaflets and website for details. Cambo in Fife is the model for snowdrop opening with a whole range of activities, gift shop and plant sales. I have listed some of the best snowdrop displays on p. 458.

Trellis
40 St John Street, Perth, PH1 5SP
T: 01738 624348
E: info@trellisscotland.org.uk
www.trellisscotland.org.uk

Trellis

Based in Perth, Trellis is the national Scottish charity that supports, promotes and develops the use of horticulture to improve health, wellbeing and life opportunities, otherwise known as 'therapeutic horticulture'. This includes training as well as clinical or medical benefits. Projects take place in hospital units and prisons, nursing homes, schools, allotments and community gardens. Gardens are designed which enable people who have physical disabilities or limited mobility or sensory impairments to garden independently. Trellis' literature details over 130 projects all over Scotland. Jim McColl is one of their patrons.

Woodland Trust Scotland
Woodland Trust Scotland,
South Inch Business Centre,
Shore Road, Perth, PH2 8BW
T: 01738 635829
F: 01764 662553
E: publicaffairs@woodland-
trust.org.uk
www.woodland-trust.org.uk/policy

Woodland Trust Scotland

This is the Scottish branch of the UK-wide charity the Woodland Trust and exists to protect woodland heritage and expand native woodland, to promote sustainable use of woods, to examine and respond to issues of climate change and its effect on the environment and to educate adults and children on all aspects of woodlands including urban projects, community participation and tourism. Nationally, the trust has over 180,000 members and it protects and manages over 1,000 woods across the UK. It has planted over 8 million trees in creating new native woodlands.

The Best of Scotland Lists

GARDENS WITH OUTSTANDING VIEWS

16 Kevock Road, Lasswade
Arduaine
Ardmaddy Castle Gardens
Abriachan Garden Nursery
Bolfracks
Castle Kennedy Gardens
Crarae
Crathes Castle
Culbie, Buchlyvie
Culzean
Earlshall Castle
Drummond Castle Gardens
Inverewe Gardens
Kerracher
Kiln Den
Lip na Cloiche
Leith Hall
Royal Botanic Garden, Edinburgh
Teasses House, Fife
Tillypronie

GARDENS WITH GREAT CHILDRENS' ATTRACTIONS AND ACTIVITIES

Brodick Castle Gardens
Châtelherault: play area
Culzean Castle Country Park: adventure playground
Drumlanrig Castle: adventure playground
Floors Castle walled garden: playground
Gardens with mazes: Hazlehead Park, Aberdeen; Cawdor Castle, Nairn; Scone Palace, Perth; Traquair, Peebles
Glasgow Botanic Gardens
Kelburn Castle
Logan House Gardens
Oakbank: Argyll
Paxton House, Berwick
People's Palace, Glasgow
Threave

SOME GREAT SMALLER AND TOWN GARDENS

Hollytree Lodge, Pool O' Muckhart
5 Rubislaw Den North, Aberdeen
63 Fountainhall Road, Edinburgh
9 Braid Farm Road, Edinburgh
16 Kevock Road, Lasswade
23 Don Street, Aberdeen
East Lugtonbridge Nursery, N. Ayrshire
Kirkside of Lochty, Menmuir, by Brechin
Shepherd House, Inveresk
The Cottage, Longforgan

AVENUES OF TREES

Blair Castle: lime avenue
Benmore Botanic Gardens: *Sequoiadendron giganteum* avenue
Castle Kennedy Gardens: *Araucaria*
Drummond Castle Gardens: beech-lined drive
Dunecht House: copper beech avenue
Meikleour Beech Hedge
Murthly Castle: drive (conifers and limes)
Scone Palace: Copper beech avenue, by racecourse
Yester Lime Avenue, Gifford: 59 trees, 400m

SOME OF SCOTLAND'S MOST REMARKABLE TREES

Ardkinglas: *Abies noblis* and other giants
Benmore Botanic Gardens: conifers and wellingtonia avenue
Cluny House: champion *Sequoiadendron giganteum*
Cortachy Castle Gardens: arboretum
Dawyck Botanic Gardens: champion trees
Glendoick Gardens: *Euodia hupehensis (Tetradium daniellii)*
Kilmun, Argyll: arboretum
Murthly Castle: avenues and champion trees
Mount Stuart, Bute: pinetum and gardens

Perthshire Big Tree Country
Pitmuies
Royal Botanic Garden, Edinburgh:
    champion trees
Yews at Ormiston, Dundonnell,
    Fortingall, Kelburn

FORMAL GARDENS, PARTERRES, ETC.

Carestown Steading courtyard
Châtelherault
Craichlaw
Drumlanrig Castle
Drummond Castle
Dunrobin Castle
Kinross House
Pitmedden
Wormistoune House

HOUSE AND GARDEN COMBINATIONS

An Cala
Broughton House
Crathes Castle
Earlshall Castle
Greywalls
House of Pitmuies
Kinross House
Kellie Castle
Manderston
The Murrel
Wormistoune House

ORGANICS, SUSTAINABLE
AND ECO GARDENING

Findhorn Community Garden, Forres
Jura House
Kellie Castle, Fife
Pillars of Hercules Farm, Falkland
Redhall, Edinburgh
Rubha Phoil Forest Garden, Skye
Seer Centre, near Pitlochry
Woodside Nursery, near Jedburgh

HERBS

Barwinnoch Herbs, Ayrshire
Poyntzfield Herb Nursery
Culross Palace
Cromarty Old Orchard

BEDDING PLANTS

Ardencraig, Bute
Barshaw Park, Paisley
Beechgrove, Broughton
Eddie Mills' Garden, Jedburgh
Pitmedden

PRIMULAS

Cluny House
Cortachy Castle
Dowhill
House of Gruinard
Rossie House
Threave

SNOWDROPS

Brechin Castle woods
Cambo House
Dalmeny House (Mons Wood)
Danevale Park
Floors Castle and Springwood
House of the Binns
Mertoun House
Kailzie

DAFFODILS

Angus Growers bulb fields
Ballindalloch Castle
Braco Castle
Brodie Castle
Cammalt
Crathes Castle
Castle Fraser
Dundee Riverside Drive
Greenbank
House of the Binns
Manderston

WOODLAND GARDENS AND /
OR RHODODENDRONS

Arduaine
Ardkinglas
Benmore
Blackhills
Brechin Castle
Castle Kennedy
Corsock House
Crarae

Dawyck
Glendoick
Glenarn
Hazlehead Park, Aberdeen
Royal Botanic Garden, Edinburgh
Stonefield Castle

MAGNOLIAS

Arduaine
Benmore: *Magnolia campbellii*
Birkhill
Brodick Castle: *Magnolia campbellii*
Castle Kennedy
Glenarn: *Magnolia rostrata* and others
Glendoick
Logan: *Magnolia campbellii* 'Charles
   Raffill'

AUTUMN COLOUR

Biggar Park
Branklyn
Crarae
Corsock
Dawyck
Kildrummy Castle
Stobo water gardens
The Hermitage

GREAT WALLED GARDENS

Cambo House
Carolside
Crathes Castle
Drum Castle
Dunbeath
Ellenbank, Elizabeth McGregor
Floors Castle
Hercules Garden, Blair Castle
Jura House
Logan
Netherbyres
Pitmuies
Portmore
Stobshiel
Threave
Tyninghame walled garden
Wormistoune

FINE HERBACEOUS BORDERS AND DISPLAYS

Balcarres
Cambo House
Carnell quarry gardens
Carolside
Craichlaw
Crathes Castle
Cally Gardens
Culzean walled garden
Dun Ard
Floors Castle walled garden
Hercules Garden, Blair Castle
Kinross House
Langwell Lodge
Leith Hall
Pitmedden
Pitmuies (House of)
Portmore

ROCK AND SCREE GARDENS

16 Kevock Road, Lasswade
Askog Hall, Bute
Branklyn
Royal Botanic Garden, Edinburgh
Threave
The Steading, Hillhead
Tillypronie

FRUIT: APPLES, PEARS, PLUMS ETC

Anton's Hill walled garden
Hercules Garden, Blair Castle
Pitmedden
Kellie Castle
Old Orchard, Cromarty
Strathmore Cottage (Willie Duncan)
Teasses House, fan-trained fruit
Tyninghame walled garden

VEGETABLES, SOFT FRUIT

Culross Palace
Floors Castle walled garden
Mertoun House
Hatton Castle
Kellie Castle
SCRI Invergowrie

GRASSES

Cambo House
Castle Fraser
Fordmouth Grass Nursery
Myres Castle
Hollytree Lodge
Mount Stuart, Bute
Parleyhill Garden, Culross
Woodfall

ROSES

Aberdeen roundabouts and roadsides
Carolside, Borders
Cockers trial grounds, Aberdeen
Drum Castle
Duthie Park, Aberdeen
Hazlehead Park, Aberdeen
Ladyburn Ayrshire (NCCPG collections)
Tollcross Park, Glasgow rose trials
Tyninghame House and walled garden
Wemyss Castle, the finest climbing roses

WATER: LOCHS, PONDS, WATER FEATURES AND BURNS WITH WATERFALLS

Bargany lily pond
Castle Kennedy lily pond, lochs and canal
Corsock Loch, burn and ponds
Crarae burn
Dawyck burn and bridges
Doulton Fountain, Glasgow Green
Dowhill ponds
Dunvegan Castle, Skye, water gardens
Duntreath Castle water gardens, ponds
Glenwhan's lochans
Kelburn Castle glen and waterfalls
Kerrachar boat trip
Kildrummy Castle bridge
Monteviot House water gardens and
    bridges
Novar
Portrack landforms and lakes
Stobo waterfalls and ponds
The Hermitage thundering waterfalls

CONTEMPORARY GARDENS / CONTEMPORARY DESIGN

5 Rubislaw Den North, Aberdeen
    (Tom Smith)
Broadwoodside Steading
Carestown Steading
Craichlaw parterre
Dun Ard
Garden of Cosmic Speculation, Portrack
Hidden Garden, Tramway, Glasgow
Landform at Scottish National Gallery of
    Modern Art, Edinburgh
Little Sparta
Maggie's Centre, Dundee
Wormistoune parterre

GARDENS WHERE YOU CAN STAY

B&B

Ard Daraich Hill Garden
Balmeamach House, Skye
Cambo House
Ethie Castle
Inwood
Kirklands
Ladyburn House
Lip na Cloiche, Mull
Kirknewton House
Newtonmill House
Rossie House

Hotels

Ardenasaig Hotel, Argyll
Glenapp Castle, Ayrshire
Myres Castle, Fife
Stonefield Castle, Argyll

GARDENS AND GARDEN CENTRES WITH PARTICULARLY GOOD CAFÉS / RESTAURANTS

Bonhard Nursery
Culross Palace, by Dunfermline
Dunskey, Galloway
Gallery of Modern Art, Edinburgh
Glendoick Garden Centre, Perth
Hidden Gardens, Tramway, Glasgow
Royal Botanic Garden, Edinburgh
Mount Stuart, Bute
People's Palace, Glasgow
Woodside Nursery, Borders

BEST TOPIARY

Crathes Castle
Drummond Castle
Earlshall Castle
Fingask Castle
Tormore Distillery

ISLAND AND REMOTE GARDENS

Achamore, Gigha
Colonsay House, Colonsay
Jura House, Jura
Kerrachar, Sutherland
Lea Gardens, Tresta, Shetland
Mount Stuart and Ascog Fernery, Bute
Lip na Cloiche, Mull

GREAT GREENHOUSES, GARDEN BUILDINGS AND ARCHITECTURE

46 South St, St Andrews: the doocot
Ascog Hall Fernery, Bute
Châtelherault, Hamilton
Craigtoun, St Andrews: the boating pond
Duthie Park, Aberdeen: David Welsh gardens
Glenbervie, Stonehaven: greenhouses
Glasgow Botanic Garden: Kibble Place
Pitmedden: gazebos
Kinross House: the Fish Gates
Little Sparta, Dunsyre
Pineapple, Dunmore
Portrack House, Dumfries
Royal Botanic Garden, Edinburgh
St Andrews Botanic Garden
Winter Gardens, People's Palace, Glasgow

GREAT GARDEN CENTRES

Bonhard, Perth
Cardwell, Gourock
Dobbies, Dalkeith
Floors Castle, Borders
Glendoick, Perth
Highland Liliums, near Inverness
New Hopetoun, near Edinburgh
Raemoir, Banchory
Rouken Glen, Glasgow
Sandyholm, Clyde Valley

GREAT MAIL ORDER NURSERIES

Abriachan
Argyll Tree Nursery
Cally Gardens
Elizabeth MacGregor's Nursery
Fordmouth Ornamental Grass Nursery
Glendoick Gardens
Kevock Plants
Poyntzfield Herb Nursery
Wattston Bonsai Nursery

MY PERSONAL CHOICE OF THE BEST OF THE BEST IN SCOTTISH GARDENS

If you asked me on another day, I'd probably make an entirely different list.

Carestown Steading, Buckie
The topiary at Earlshall Castle
The walled garden at Logan
Cambo in August and September
The walled garden at Crathes
Drummond Castle parterre
The walled garden at Portmore
The lakes at the Garden of Cosmic Speculation, Portrack
Little Sparta
Carolside walled garden in July
The bluebells at Dunninald
Floors Castle walled garden
The bedding at Ardencraig, Bute
Tom Smith's garden at 5 Rubislaw Den North, Aberdeen
Carnell herbaceous/water garden
Castle Kennedy, the setting
Murthly Castle conifer avenues
Broadwoodside Steading
Kellie Castle walled garden in summer
The bridge at Kildrummy Castle
The Kibble Palace, Glasgow Botanic Gardens
Corsock House in spring and autumn
Kerrachar

Bibliography

The most established guide to Scotland's gardens is *Gardens of Scotland*, published annually by Scotland's Garden Scheme. The famous and invaluable annual 'Yellow Book', it is stubbornly in the dark ages in many ways: its design, gardens listed by counties, incomplete addresses and contact details. They finally discovered post codes in 2005, hooray!

Bown, D., *4 Gardens in One, The Royal Botanic Garden, Edinburgh*. HMSO, 1992

Campbell, K., *Policies and Pleasaunces, A Guide to the Gardens of Scotland*. Barn Elms, 2007. Very good on history and packed with fascinating red herrings which have little to do with the gardens, let down by the lack of pictures and obscure title.

Cox, E.H.M., *A History of Gardening in Scotland*. Chatto and Windus, 1935

Cox K. and Curtis-Machin, Raoul, *Garden Plants for Scotland*. Frances Lincoln, 2008

Dingwall, C., *Landscaping of Scotland*. Birlinn (to be published in 2009). A very readable historical survey by Scotland's foremost garden historian.

Galbraith, A., articles in *Scotsman, Scotland on Sunday* and *Scottish Field*.

Greenoak, F., *The Gardens of the National Trust for Scotland*. Aurum, 2005

Hobhouse, P., *The Story of Gardening*. Dorling Kindersley, 2002

House, S. and Dingwall, C., 'Introducing the new trees 1650–1900' in Smout, C.T., *People and Woods in Scotland: A History*. Edinburgh University Press, 2002

Jencks, C., *The Garden of Cosmic Speculation*. Frances Lincoln, 2003

Lindsay, J. and M., *Good Scottish Gardens Guide*. Chambers, 1995

Lusby P. and Wright, J., *Scottish Wild Plants*. Mercat Press, 1997

King, P. et al (eds), *The Good Gardens Guide*. Frances Lincoln, 2007. An institution this one, with Julie Edmonstone and Ann Fraser writing the Scotland entries. Unfortunately the garden entries are being shortened, which loses both the charm and the detail. I would suggest ignoring the star rating system.

Little, A. (ed), *Scotland's Gardens*. Spur Books, 1981. A fascinating snapshot of Scotland's gardens open to the public in 1981.

McKelvie, A. and Roberston, F. (eds), *Scottish Rock Gardening in the Twentieth Century*. SRGC, 2000

Mabey, R., *Flora Britannica*. Chatto and Windus, 1998

Maxwell, Sir Herbert, *Scottish Gardens*. Arnold, 1911

Quest-Ritson, C. (ed), *The RHS Garden Finder 2007–2008*. Think Books, 2007

Rodger, D., Stokes, J and Ogilvie, J., *Heritage Trees of Scotland*. Forestry Commission Scotland, 2006. Full of pictures and the stories of some of Scotland's finest trees.

Scott, A., *A Pleasure in Scottish Trees*. Mainstream, 2002. A wonderful book full of personal anecdote as well as useful first-hand knowledge of Scotland's trees.

Sheeler, J., *Little Sparta,* Frances Lincoln, 2003

Spenser Jones (ed.), *1001 Gardens You Must See Before You Die*. Quintessence, 2007

Stuart Thomas, Graham, *Gardens of the National Trust*. Weidenfeld and Nicholson, 1979

Taylor, Patrick, *The Gardens of Britain and Ireland*. Dorling Kindersley, 2003. Not very comprehensive, but Patrick is one of the more 'writerly' garden surveyors with a fine turn of phrase and he has visited all the gardens he writes about.

Toman, R. (ed), *European Garden Design*. H.F. Ullman, 2003/5

Truscott, J., *Private Gardens of Scotland*. Weidenfield and Nicholson, 1988

Urquhart, S. (photographs by Ray Cox), *The Scottish Gardener*. Birlinn, 2005. A singular look at Scottish gardens, ignoring many of the best known, and including many others, some not open to the public.

Uglow, J., *A Little History of British Gardening*. Chatto and Windus, 2004. Probably the best introduction to this subject.

Wightman, Andy, *Who Owns Scotland*. Canongate, 1996

Woodland Trust. *Scotland (Exploring Woodland)*. Frances Lincoln, 2008

Yellow Book, see *Gardens of Scotland* above

Guidebooks

There are lots of guidebooks to Scotland, many of which are perfectly acceptable. There are three books/online guides which I found to be outstanding, with an honorary mention to the *Cadogan Guide to Scotland*.

Humphreys, R. and Reid, D., *The Rough Guide to Scotland*. Rough Guides Ltd, 2008. Superior to the *Lonely Planet Scotland* guide, the writers have truly got under the skin of the country and are well in touch with what is going on. The detail and up-to-dateness of the sections on Scottish music and books is outstanding.

Irvine, P., *Scotland the Best*. Harper Collins, 2007 This idiosyncratic guidebook is a challenge to navigate around, and the latest edition is peppered with anarchic and sometimes impenetrable asides. However, it is a great book, and one which I would not be without, because Pete says what he thinks and supports all that is best in Scotland. He organises large-scale events such as Edinburgh's Hogmanay celebrations. The book covers hotels, food, drink, castles and houses, sport, walking, shopping, even a few gardens and garden centres.

Websites

Undiscovered Scotland, *www.undiscoveredscotland.co.uk*. This outstanding website is superior to the 'official' *www.visitcotland.com* website in terms of detailed useful information and background on Scotland's attractions and history. There are lots of good pictures and as they are not trying to sell you anything, it is a pleasant and honest look at Scotland's riches.

Rampant Scotland, *www.rampantscotland.com*. Another good site.

Historic Scotland, *www.historic-scotland.gov.uk*. This site contains the the vast and impressive inventory of gardens and planned landscapes. Masses of historical information gleaned from a 20+-year survey.

Acknowledgments

Books such as this cannot be written without the help of many people. I would like to thank all the garden owners and gardeners who have shown me round, given me lots of information and the odd cup of coffee, as well as returning garden information which they have checked before publication.

I am extremely fortunate that my wife, Jane Bradish-Ellames, formerly a literary agent at Curtis Brown, is my agent and in-house editor. She also let me off the leash to visit the huge number of gardens and nurseries covered. My sons Jamie and Finn have had to visit endless properties with only a few cries of 'Not another garden, Dad!' And they have test-driven a great number of children's play areas. Ray's wife, Penny, has worked very hard for both Ray and myself, contacting gardens and arranging visits. I managed to visit about 90 per cent of the entries in this book. For those I could not visit, I managed to delegate to a number of family members to whom I'm very grateful for their comments and photos. Together, we managed to visit all but a handful of the entries. Ray visited and reported on several gardens which I could not manage to reach, my parents Peter and Patricia Cox inspected the gardens of Shetland, Jura, Caithness and Sutherland and did some invaluable proofreading, while my cousin Peter Milne and Caroline Beaton covered gardens in Orkney. Jamie MacKenzie (my wife's cousin) and his wife Rosa Steppanova provided invaluable information and photographs of gardens on Shetland. Our office accountant Stella Bowers posted out check sheets to all the gardens and nurseries who don't do email.

My brother Ray took thousands of great photographs; you should see the ones we did not manage to fit in the book!

I wish especially to thank Anna Buxton, who very generously volunteered to check the historical details in this book. Her invaluable input included pointing out a number of howlers as well as setting me straight on pertinent aspects of historical detail and inconsistency. Raoul Curtis-Machin provided lots of useful leads as we toured Scotland for our previous book and while he was researching information for the Historic Scotland Inventory of Planned Landscapes. Garden historian Christopher Dingwall kindly let me read part of the manuscript of his book *The Landscaping of Scotland* before it was published and provided other useful historical information. Thanks too to Julie Edmonstone, long-time gardens inspector for the *Good Gardens Guide*, for her generous sharing of her assessment of gardens all over Scotland. Jenny Taylor first gave me details on Orkney gardens which I have used in this book and the previous one. Catherine Erskine, from Cambo, accompanied me on our 'snowdrop' dash and provided information on snowdrops in many other gardens. Catherine also shows the rest of Scotland how gardens should be properly marketed. I would like to thank Jan Haenrats, Veronica Barrington, Benedict Lyte and other staff at NTS as well as the many NTS head gardeners past and present who have shown me round.

I'm grateful to the following people for giving me invaluable information on gardens all over Scotland, while often kindly providing food and/or drink or accommodation. These include: Trish Kennedy, Patsy Blacklock, Lt Col. Simon Furness, Kirsty Maxwell Stewart, Carole Baxter, Peter and Sarah Landale, Minette Struthers, Mrs C. Welwood, Catherine Erskine, The Hon. Mrs R. Noel Paton, Paddy Scott, Hazel Reid, Dr Tom Smith, Anne Greenall, Willie Duncan, John Butterworth, Jim

McColl, David Knott, Calum Pirnie, Mr and Mrs David Barnes, Stella and David Rankin, John Hooper, Gavin and Araminta Dallmeyer, Syd House, Katrina Clow, Michael and Charlotte Wemyss, Laura Donkers, Alan and Ruby Inkster, Lucy Mackenzie, Mike Swift, Alan Romans, Sandy Masson, John Hammond, Jenny Taylor, Jasmine Cann, Geoff Stephenson, Donald Lamb, Rora Paglieri, Anthony and Rose Foyle, Mr and Mrs M.L. Ingall, Steve Hootman, Tam Dalyell, Billy Carruthers, Michael Wickenden, Carol Seymour.

Thanks also to those who supplied pictures: David Knott, Peter and Patricia Cox, Jamie Mackenzie, Hartweg Schepker, Alan and Brenda Clouston, Rowena and Stewart Oakley, Alan and Ruby Inkster and Julia Corden.

At publishers Birlinn, I would like to thank Hugh Andrew for taking on this book in the first place, Andrew Simmons (editorial), Liz Short and Peter Burns, (production), Mark Blackadder and Jim Hutcheson (design), Kenny Redpath and Jan Rutherford (marketing and publicity) and particular thanks to Helen Bleck for such diligent copyediting and fact checking, including spotting those gardens which had floated off into the wrong geographical section. Thanks also to Maggie McKernan for expert editorial/marketing advice and Nancy Norman for proof-reading.

Ray Cox

The people behind Scotland's gardens are almost without exception welcoming, friendly and good company, and their talent and enthusiasm for all things gardening is infectious. A huge thanks to all the garden owners and gardeners I've met while photographing for this book, especially to those who have kindly fed and watered me or put me up for the night, sparing me from another night in my tent! Special thanks go to Katrina Clow, Minette and Charles Struthers, Ken and Kristina Dupar, Lady Ruth Crawford, Donald Lamb, Victoria Morley, Tessa and John Knott, Peter and Mirjam Cool, Peter and Tricia Kohn, Christine and Livingston Russell, Graham Cowan, Lizzie and Jamie Montgomery, Anne Greenall, Trish Kennedy, James and Gemma McCallum, Caroline Beaton, Lorne Herriot-Maitland. And to my wife Penny for her support, for holding the fort in my absence and helping coordinate what has been a somewhat challenging logistical exercise.

Photographic Acknowledgements

All photographs are copyright © Ray Cox, except the following: © Julia Cordon (p. 127, lower); © Kenneth Cox (pp. 7, 36, 38, 50, 79, 80, 84, 90, 94, 98 (lower), 100, 103 (upper), 109, 113 (upper), 120, 122, 133 (upper), 143, 153, 156, 179, 203 (upper), 206, 215 (upper), 217, 223, 235 (lower), 247, 248, 254, 261 (upper), 264 (lower), 266, 267, 274 (upper), 275, 278, 287, 288, 292, 301 (lower), 305, 316, 317, 322, 324, 326, 329, 339 (lower), 340, 342, 349, 350, 358, 362, 363, 372, 378, 400 (upper), 411, 412, 414, 418, 420, 423, 424, 431, 432, 440, 446, 448; © Patricia Cox (p. 13); © Jamie McKenzie (pp. 29, 30); © New Lanark Trust (p. 309, upper); © Rowena and Stewart Oakley (p. 48); © Hartwig Schepker (p. 49).

Index